SOCIAL CHANGE
The Colonial Situation

SOCIAL CHANGE
The Colonial Situation

Immanuel Wallerstein

JOHN WILEY & SONS, INC.
New York · London · Sydney

Library of Congress Catalog Card Number: 66–14144
Printed in the United States of America

To Robert S. Lynd,
because he is committed

CONTENTS

SOCIAL CHANGE
The Colonial Situation

INTRODUCTION

This is a set of readings whose choice was dictated by a point of view. The subject matter is the process of change in colonial societies within a world context of modernization. That is to say, we shall be looking at a colony as a set of interrelated institutions, all of which are changing, first because of the impact of the imposition and stabilization of colonial rule, and later because of the rise of nationalist movements and the process of decolonization.

Historically there has been disagreement about how such social change is studied. It has revolved about the unit whose change we study. Many persons, especially administrators and a school of anthropologists most prominently represented by Malinowski (see pp. 11–24), have argued that the logical unit of study was the tribe, or the traditional unit of political authority, whatever it was called. They argued that the traditional authority remained, even under colonial rule, the basic moral authority for the individual, hence was the unit within which significant social action took place. Colonial rule was interpreted as one more of a series of outside forces with which the traditional unit was in culture contact, more or less extensive according to the case, more or less profound in its impact.

For administrators it was in many ways a comforting view to hold. It allowed them to contrast two social orders, a traditional and a European, and to conclude that by comparison, indeed by the very fact of conquest, the European social order was more powerful, more technologically advanced, hence more progressive; thus providing in a somewhat circular way a justification for colonial rule. Such a conception of the social situation in a colony meant that a colonial administrator could debate how appropriate it was to exercise direct or indirect (i.e., via the traditional authority) controls on the population. It meant that he had a rural bias, deploring the rise of modern urban centers or seeing them as an unhappy necessity. It meant that he would reject the early nationalist arguments of urban intellectuals as sociological nonsense.

What attracted the anthropologist to this view of the social situation was his own intellectual tradition which made the existence of a common culture the defining feature of a social group. If one asked how one knew a tribe or a traditional unit when one saw one, since some had elaborate and complex political hierarchies and some were "stateless" or "anarchic," the answer was couched in terms of the language, the customs, and the cosmology they shared. If a society is defined as a group which shares a common culture, then it does indeed follow that in a colonial situation, certainly at the outset and probably throughout the colonial era, the traditional units come closest to meeting this definition. The colony itself, then, is nothing but a helter-skelter collection of such units without a significant set of common values and hence not a significant social reality. If the traditional unit were the social unit worthy of study, it might then seem reasonable to try to uncover its nature in its pure form, that is, before colonial rule, in order to analyze in what (limited) ways colonial rule had altered the social order.

If, however, a society is defined not as a unit which shares a common culture but one which shares at the very minimum a common authority capable of maintaining itself and propagating its values and whose legitimacy is recognized by peer authorities elsewhere, then it is the colony and not the traditional unit that is the unit worthy of study. The colony is the ultimate legal authority, commands the monopoly of legitimate force (as it itself defines legitimacy), and enacts the minimum set of common values which it proceeds to enforce. The common values may at first be few and their acceptability to the majority of the population limited, but they have more force at their disposal and more coherence in their application than any counter-set. It is within the framework of such a common authority, as we shall see, that the participants will begin to identify more and more with the nation-in-creation, first by the medium of the nationalist movement and even more, after independence, in many different ways.

As colonial administrators were comforted by the first view of the social situation, nationalist leaders in colonies staunchly upheld the latter conception. For once the colony is seen to be the basic unit of social action, the question of the basis of legitimacy of the current governing authorities can be raised. The thesis of self-determination can be safely applied, because it has previously been determined what area it was that would have self-determination.

Gluckman in his famous critique of Malinowski (pp. 25–33) and Balandier in his parallel analysis of the colonial situation (pp. 34–61) lay out the basic sociological outlook as it applies to colonial territories. They see the colony as a single power structure within which two (or more) strata existed. These strata were often caste-like and were almost always distinguished on racial grounds. The dominant group were the whites (or Europeans), most but not all of whom were citizens of the metropolitan power, or, if it was a self-governing settler colony like the Republic of South Africa, were descendants of such citizens who at an earlier point of history had conquered the territory. This color stratification is not theoretically essential to the description of a colonial situation, but it is historically crucial. This can be most clearly seen in the reactions of sophisticated nationalists like Nehru, Mboya, and Fanon (pp. 62, 69, 75). It is striking that the three, coming respectively from India, Kenya, and Martinique—thus three different continents—and having lived under two different colonial regimes (Britain and France), identified the core of their frustrations in terms of racial limitation. Indeed, even in areas of the colonial world, such as North Africa, where color distinctions were hard to draw, a "racial" distinction was created nonetheless. Balandier argues the usefulness to the colonial system of such racial distinctions, and the anger they have produced is clearly reflected in the writings of the three nationalist intellectuals included here.

The structure of this book grows out of this conception of the colonial situation set forth by Gluckman and Balandier. European contact with the rest of the world took various forms. They came first as traders, as missionaries, as settlers, in limited contact with the indigenous population. However they came, they felt in time the need for a surer context within which to live and to work. This led to the demand by these people for the establishment of a colonial administration, which would make possible the various kinds of economic exploitation and cultural aggrandizement they deemed necessary. Thus was born the modern colony, a political unit under the sovereignty of a European power which assured law and order within its bounds.

One of the basic problems of the colony was to see that labor was available in the right places with the right skills. Labor migration was a far more rational procedure, on all sides, than early commentators tended to give it credit for being. Colonial powers tended to use an admixture of force, pressure via taxation, and high-powered persuasion to obtain the labor they needed—within the boundaries of the colony and quite often overflowing them. Harris (pp. 91–106) analyzes the many factors that induced Mozambique Thonga to go to South Africa, including their desire to avoid the worse alternative of Portuguese forced labor. Colson (pp. 107–113) indicates how the ideal of temporary migration which was hoped for by many administrators was undone by other considerations which tended to make some migration permanent. Berg (pp. 114–136) debunks the so-called backward-sloping labor supply function, whose origin is ideological presumption rather than empirical fact. Skinner (pp. 137–157) analyzes the ways in which the returned migrant caused social change in his home community. Van Velsen (pp. 158–167) further specifies this by demonstrating that such change did not necessarily lead to the disintegration of a traditional unit. Under certain circumstances, the traditional society could be restructured so as to meet some modern demands while maintaining a certain cohesion.

All the essays on labor migration illustrate the central point that measures undertaken by the colonial administration in its own interest (in this case, furnishing an adequate labor supply for export industries) created in their train a series of consequences that went far beyond the desires of the administration. In the end, as we shall see, this led to the creation of forces hostile to the administration and capable of destroying it.

The impact was first felt in the rural areas. The emigration, especially of young men, not only changed the social structure of the village; it affected the mechanisms of social control for those who remained. For now one weapon that a villager was able to use to sanction his traditional rulers was the threat to migrate. This was one of the first manifestations that the colony, and not the traditional unit, was becoming the central arena within which and with regard to which social action took place. In addition, as we have mentioned, the returning migrants brought with them new habits, new attitudes and new perspectives. Thus increased migration alone would be enough to cause a change in the role of traditional authorities.

But colonial rule also meant colonial administration. Hence, the traditional ruler was no longer the ultimate authority. And however indirect the rule—indirectness merely meaning that there remained a hierarchy of traditional officials between the village ruler and the colonial administrator—the total power of the set of traditional rulers could not but decline over the long run, although individual functionaries may have increased their power.

Dorjahn (pp. 171–209) and Chilver and Kaberry (pp. 210–213) detail the changing functions of the traditional ruler, as he became more enmeshed in the system of colonial bureaucracy. Barnes (pp. 214–231) notes the effect of colonial rule on stateless societies and Fallers (pp. 232–248) on a highly structured traditional society. Fallers analyzes the multiple roles the traditional ruler was required to undertake and how the conflicting demands led to a high casualty rate among such rulers.

If the authority of traditional rulers declined, or in some cases rose for a while to decline later, this did not mean that the solidarity of the traditional unit disappeared. In the urban areas, it reappeared most spectacularly in the emergence and flourishing of ethnic associations. Gluckman (pp. 251–264) develops how tribalism persisted in the towns of Central Africa, but it was now a different tribalism. This urban tribalism, or ethnicity as we prefer to call it, differed in membership and functions from the rural solidarity. It was a step towards modernism, not a relic of the past. Skinner (pp. 265–277) points out that these urban ethnic loyalties, reshaping the Indonesian countryside, were not necessarily in conflict with the emergent nationalist sentiments. Freedman (pp. 278–289) treats the difficult case called pluralism (or miscalled, for all colonial societies are essentially plural societies), where there were two or three major quite distinct ethnic groups, which called for very special and conscious kinds of political compromise. Sklar (pp. 290–300), pursuing a similar theme, goes further, arguing that ethnicity had an actually positive impact on the development of national sentiment.

Change is a very slippery word and often is used to blur the exact direction of the change. But most societies are stratified, and changes do not affect everyone identically. New strata or classes sometimes emerge to take the place of the old. In the colonial situation, money and education have been the major leverage of such shifts. But, once this is noted, it becomes relevant to inquire if there have not been patterns of access to money and education. Cohn (pp. 303–320) analyzes how colonial rule in India led to the creation not merely of an urban bureaucracy as is evident and common knowledge, but of a new landed class. What may have seemed traditional from the perspective of the late colonial era was in fact in part an innovation of the early colonial era. Southall (pp. 321–339) gives a detailed description of how functional stratification often took on the face of racial stratification, which as we noted above is perhaps not theoretically essential but is historically crucial. Mercier (pp. 340–358) raises the important question of whether the emerging strata should be called classes or, as he believes, merely socio-professional strata. By implication, Hodgkin (pp. 359–362) and Wertheim and Giap (pp. 363–380) answer Mercier by describing respectively the nature of the African middle class, and the new class structure which developed in Java in this century and which was greatly affected by the educational system.

One of the key institutions that grew up in the urban areas to enable individuals to cope with the new national society, its norms and its demands, was the network of voluntary associations. Some of them developed out of traditional structures, as Lloyd (pp. 383–401) illustrates. Many more were created afresh, permitting the members to respond more rationally to their conditions. Banton (pp. 402–419) describes how the Temne in Freetown used voluntary associations to enable them to cope with their new urban environment. Geertz (pp. 420–446) spells out the function in Java of one special kind of voluntary association, the rotating credit association, and indicates that similar groups were created for similar reasons throughout Asia and Africa. The Rudolphs (pp. 447–464) discuss how these new associations began to play a directly political role in India (and indeed elsewhere).

A different kind of voluntary activity was to be seen in the various kinds of religious movements which emerged in the colonial situation, and whose significance is partially in their links to the creation of national sentiment. Bastide (pp. 467–477) sees messianism as a way of acculturation. Shepperson (pp. 478–488) traces the pattern of two very different styles of religious movements of reaction to Christianity in Africa, breakaway churches and prophetic sects, and points out how their initial political role changed and diminished as other, more directly political movements came into being. Abu-Nasr (pp. 489–502) relates how a religious reform movement paved the way for Moroccan nationalism.

It is, in fact, out of such a network of voluntary associations and religious movements that proper nationalist movements developed, as indicated in the historical account of Rotberg (pp. 505–519) for East and Central Africa. Emerson (pp. 520–532) spells out some of the structural and ideological ambivalences of the emerging nationalist movement, which was at once unifying and divisive, at once Westernizing and anti-Western. Kilson (pp. 533–550), using data from West Africa, shows the role of the new urban middle class in the rise of the nationalist movement. Hourani (pp. 551–558) describes Arab nationalism, especially in Syria and Lebanon, whose etiology was very similar. Potekhin (pp. 559–571) expounds the applicability of Stalin's definition of a nation to colonial nationalism, arguing that modern nationalism can be viewed in part as a modified continuation of an interrupted process—the aspiration of various *narodnosti* (traditional, hierarchical political structures) to nationhood. This hypothesis is probably the most significant Soviet contribution to the discussion of the colonial situation. Eisenstadt (pp. 572–582) treats the phenomenon of uneven social and economic change, and the ways in which this unevenness affected the politics of anticolonial nationalism.

A nationalist movement may start as an expression of the needs and dissatisfactions of the urban, educated middle class. To succeed, it must obtain mass support of a population taught by the colonial power to consider itself inferior, one unsure of itself and its values as a consequence of the changes which are constantly occurring in the social structure, and yet one which had experience in the possibilities of organizing itself in new organizations with new and old values to achieve their needs. The paradoxes which Emerson discussed led to rational action on the part of nationalist leaders. Fernandez (pp. 585–591) analyzes how a Fang origin legend was made to serve the interests of Gabonese nationalism. A central effort in the attempt to furnish a viable ideology for nationalism has been in the rewriting of history. Monteil (pp. 592–605) describes on a global basis what he has aptly called the decolonization of the writing of history. Ajayi (pp. 606–616), Majumdar (pp. 617–630), Oetomo (pp. 631–642), and West (pp. 643–657) relate the details of the relationship of such rewriting to the rise of nationalism in four disparate colonial areas—Africa south of the Sahara, the Indian subcontinent, Indonesia, and the South Pacific (especially Tahiti). We end with an essay by Von Grunebaum (pp. 658–674) who explores the problems which the double commitment of nationalists of the Muslim world—to modernization, and to their dignity and hence originality and worth—created for them and for their movements. What he says is applicable to the colonial world as a whole.

As we have said, these readings have been selected because, collectively, they argue a point. It is that the imposition of colonial administration created new social structures which took on with time increasing importance in the lives of all those living in them. The rulers of the colonial system, as those of all social systems, engaged in various practices for their own survival and fulfillment which simultaneously resulted in creating movements which in the long run undermined the system. In the case of the colonial situation, what emerged as a consequence of the social change wrought by the administration was a nationalist movement which eventually led a revolution and obtained independence.

The headings under which this process is explained in this book have been chosen heuristically because they seemed to advance clarity. But obviously, other categories could have been chosen with perhaps almost equal validity. The articles, of course, were not written with this reader in mind, and some of them may wander off on what, for our purposes, are irrelevant considerations. We have tried to minimize this factor by occasional judicious cuts.

The ideal set of articles for this book might have been a series of analytic, theoretical articles based on wide comparative data, each article arguing a single point, such as those, for example, by Berg, Geertz, and Eisenstadt. But such an ideal set does not exist because all the necessary articles have not yet been written. Even if they had been, we might not have used such a set exclusively, for psychological if not for intellectual reasons. Case studies allow the reader some air. Coming closer to empirical reality, he can begin to reflect himself on the generalizations that seem so plausible, yet do not englobe all the reality. And, when the generalization seems to be confirmed, it then has an inner veracity to the reader it might not otherwise achieve. Thus there are many such case studies in this book. We have occasionally reduced the descriptive data that illustrated or demonstrated the hypothesis, for the reader may not be always concerned with the particular history of a particular small unit.

In any case, we have tried to choose the case studies on a basis of geographical spread throughout the colonial world. This presented a problem. Most of the articles of the type that would fit this book have been written about black Africa, India, and Indonesia. Discovering why other colonial areas are neglected in terms of this kind of sociological analysis would be an interesting exercise for someone interested in the sociology of knowledge. We make no speculations here and only bring to the attention of the reader this geographical disproportion and state that we have no reason to believe that the process of social change was significantly different elsewhere.

One last caveat. Many of the articles speak in the present tense. The situation in a given country may, however, have changed somewhat since the article was written and some archaisms may result. We have noted next to the title the date of original publication of the article and the reader may then take this into account.

I

The Colonial Situation:
Definitions

B. Malinowski

DYNAMICS OF CULTURE CHANGE (1945) *

THEORIES OF CULTURE CHANGE
The Contact Situation as an Integral Whole

As regards the nature of culture change, one simple solution occurs immediately. A contact situation is at any moment a cultural reality. Why should we not regard it as an "integral whole," since in any particular case we have Africans and Englishmen, Indians and Mediterranean immigrants working together within the same habitat on joint cultural tasks? Once we make this assumption the problem of empirical field work solves itself. We should have to use the same methods and devices which the old anthropologist used in the study of his primitive, relatively unaffected, single culture.

It is now generally agreed upon that Europeans form an integral part of any contact situation. Some time ago I somewhat flippantly urged that "an enlightened anthropologist has to take account of European stupidity and prejudice" quite as fully as of African superstition and backwardness.[1] I would now reframe it more soberly in claiming that the whole range of European influences, interests, good intentions, and predatory drives must become an essential part of the study of African culture change. This point of view, indeed, has now become almost a commonplace of field work and theory. But I think it is pushing a legitimate commonplace too far when it is suggested that "the missionary, administrator, trader and labour recruiter must be regarded as factors in the tribal life in the same way as are the chief and the magician."[2] And as regards field work,

* The book was edited posthumously by P. Kaberry and much of the material included here had been previously published in 1938 and 1940.

SOURCE. B. Malinowski, *Dynamics of Culture Change,* New Haven: Yale University Press, 1945, pp. 14–18, 64–72.

11

we are advised that "there is no special technique required for investigations of this kind. . . ." Yet another writer has claimed: "Contact agents
can be treated as integrally part of the community." [3] This sounds plausible and would certainly make matters very simple. We should have only
a slight numerical addition to our informants and perhaps an improvement
in their quality. We could regard local Europeans as expert sources of
information and employ them for this purpose in the same way as one
would use Native informants. [4]

Unfortunately, this type of simplification is not advisable. The treatment of the complex situations of change as one "well integrated whole,"
the "one-entry" approach as we might call it, ignores the whole dynamism
of the process. It takes no account of the main fact in culture change,
that is, that European residents, the missionaries and the administrators,
the settlers and the entrepreneurs, are indeed the main agents of change.
The concept of a well-integrated community would, indeed, ignore such
facts as the color bar, the permanent rift which divides the two partners
in change and keeps them apart in church and factory, in matters of mine
labor and political influence.

Above all, it obscures and distorts the only correct conception of
culture change in such areas: the fact that it is the result of an impact
of a higher, active culture upon a simpler, more passive one. The typical
phenomena of change, the adoption or rejection, the transformation of
certain institutions and the growth of new ones, are ruled out by the
concept of a well-integrated community or culture.

This concept, however, expresses the partial and minor truth: a small
community, stationary or stagnant, or one which has been hardly affected
as yet by the full impact of westernization, can be regarded as being in a
state of temporary adjustment. The missionary has converted part of the
tribe while the rest remain heathen. The administrator may not have
opportunities or motives for encroaching on the old tribal life. The trader
established some time ago may be furnishing the goods which have
already become indispensable, and receives in return money or Native
produce. This group of people who coöperate, who live side by side for
the time being in relations which have little of the "dynamic" in them;
who are temporarily adjusted to each other—this can be studied as an
integral whole.

What assumption, however, were we compelled to make in order to
achieve this temporarily useful simplification? We agreed for the moment
to forget the fact of change. This obviously is illegitimate when change
is the main subject of our study. Just when we are trying to organize our
work and interests round the *concept of change* and methods of field work
for the study of culture contact, it is not admissible to forget that European agents constitute everywhere the main drive in change; that they
are the determining factors as regards the initiative of change; that it is

they who plan, take measures, and import things into Africa; that they withhold; that they take away land, labor, and political independence; and that they themselves are in most of their actions determined by instructions, ideas, and forces which have their origin outside Africa.

Take the missionary.[5] He cannot "be regarded in the same way as the magician. . . ." The missionary is the initiator and center of the religious revolution now taking place in Africa. He would not be true to his vocation if he ever agreed to act on the principle that Christianity is as "any other form of cult." As a matter of fact, his brief is to regard all the other forms of religion as misguided, fit only for destruction, and to regard Christianity as entirely different, the only true religion to be implanted. Far from leaving other cults side by side in juxtaposition with the message of the Gospels, the missionary is actively engaged in superseding them.

The administrator, again, far from ever becoming an equivalent of the old chief, far from representing tribal authority in any sense of being an integral part of it, must always remain over and above the tribe, and must control from without. He is not regarded as the chief, because he does not act as such. The average British official tries to administer justice and to be a father of his wards. But is he from his point of view an integral part of the tribe? No. He was neither born nor bred to it, nor is he very conversant with any of its ideas; he is, in fact, a servant of the British Empire, temporarily working in such and such a colony, a public school boy, an Englishman, or a Scotsman. He has to safeguard the interests of the empire first and foremost. He has to watch over European interests in the colony, as well as to maintain the balance of these interests as against native claims. To conceive of the part played by European political agents in Africa in terms of a fictitious "well-integrated" community would blind us to the very definition of the tasks, nature, and implications of colonial administration.

Nor can industrial enterprise be regarded as part of a tribal unit. It would be a strange African tribe which would embrace the gold mines of the Rand, with their gigantic plant; the stock exchange of Johannesburg, and the banking system stretching from Cape to Cairo. The communication systems, railroads, and planes of the Imperial Airways, the system of motor roads with the cars and lorries which run on them—all this is part of culture contact. But the concept of an extended African tribe, into which this could be squeezed in order to produce a unified tribal horizon, falls to the ground as soon as it is stated.[6]

It would be equally difficult to regard the settler and his African neighbor as brethren of a large family; quite as difficult as to apply this concept to some of the Afrikaans-speaking groups and to the Kaffirs, the integration with whom runs against the fundamental principles of the Grondwet, or constitution of the Boer Republics.

As regards the possibility of practical applications, the conception of culture change as the impact of Western civilization and the reaction thereto of indigenous cultures is the only fruitful approach. We must treat the plans, intentions, and interests of White contact agents as something which can only be realized through coöperation with the African; or which fails because of real conflict of interests, faulty planning, misunderstanding, or lack of a common ground for effective joint work. Here the anthropologist can act as adviser only if he realizes clearly that at times there is a possibility of effective coöperation; that there are definite conditions under which this is possible, while in certain cases an inevitable clash must result.[7]

The subject matter of culture change differs then from that of stationary cultures, studied by ordinary anthropological field work, in several respects. There are the impinging culture and the one which receives. There are, therefore, two cultures to deal with instead of one; the modifications wrought on the recipients by the aggressors, and also *vice versa*. Not only that. There is always the formation of an aggressive or conquering community *in situ* (i.e., White settlers). This community is by no means a direct replica of its mother community at home. The interaction between Native and European communities offers opportunities for the introduction of third parties, such as Indians, Syrians, and Arabs in Africa; at times, the growth of a mixed population, such as Cape Colored in South Africa. All this complicates the problem immensely, or rather, multiplies the constituent parts of the subject matter.

The anthropologist here cannot study any more a well-defined, circumscribed entity like an Oceanic island. He deals with a segment of a vast continent,[8] with a community surrounded by an enormous hinterland. In reality, he has two such hinterlands to deal with in an ethnological sense: one of them the hinterland of European culture with which the White community are in contact, by which they are directed, from which they constantly import goods and receive ideas, and into which in one way or another they will ultimately return. The African has also his hinterland, his old culture, now a thing of the past; and in another sense, his own community to which he has to return after his short excursions into White contact; and more than that, the hinterland of other tribes with whom he will have to coöperate.

If the ordinary anthropology is therefore a matter of one-column entries, that of culture change will have at least three: White hinterland, Black hinterland, and the column of culture contact. No phenomenon in the middle column of contacts can be studied without constant reference to both White and Native sides. . . .

THE PRINCIPLE OF THE COMMON FACTOR
IN CULTURE CHANGE

It is possible now to frame the positive and constructive results emerging from our critical discussions and our survey of evidence.

The African world of contact and change consists of three distinct orders of cultural reality: the African, the Western, and that of transition. Each of these orders is subject to a specific determinism of its own which will be elaborated presently. At the same time, all three orders or phases are related to or dependent on each other. The impact and initiative come from the organized forces of Western civilization. They are directed onto the largely passive tribal resources which respond to contact with adaptation or conflict. This process of reaction, positive or negative—the interaction between Black and White, between Western culture and tribalism —covers the field of contact and change. Between the two boundaries of color bar on the one side and the dead weight of tribal conservatism on the other there lies the no-man's-land of change. This is not a narrow strip but really embraces most of what is going on in Africa. As yet it is but partly accomplished; adaptation is imperfect and piecemeal; conflict is open or concealed; and at times also there is fruitful coöperation or else disorganization and decay.

In this wide area, which is our specific subject of study, European interests and intentions do not act as a united influence. They are largely at war with each other: the genuine tendency to raise the African, and the tendency to keep him back; the gospel of brotherhood and that of the color bar; the discriminative give and the invidious take. The Europeans contribute the initiative and driving force, capital, organization, and technique. They largely determine the form of the new cultural realities, and to a certain extent they still control the process of change. In all this they have to coöperate with and work upon the indigenous humanity who have their own racial characteristics; their institutions of age-long historical growth; their customs, ideas, and beliefs. Once change is set going, it acquires a momentum of its own; becomes a process and a reality *sui generis*, and possesses a cultural determinism which is neither African nor European.

Change cannot be studied by either of the two determinants, African or European, or yet by any device of combining the two. The phenomenon of change is not a mixture; nor even simple acculturation. Change under conditions of the color bar, that is, under conditions where the Black section of the community is not completely, wholeheartedly accepted but on the contrary kept at arm's length—such change becomes a cultural *tertium quid*. Typical facts of change such as Indirect Rule, mining and plantation enterprise, schooling, and so on, obey laws which cannot be deduced from either culture or from both. The working of such contact phenomena, of the coöperation, the conflict, and the reaction, has to be studied in its own right.

Another theoretical by-product of our discussions is that all sociologically relevant impact and interaction is organized, that is, it occurs as between institutions. The real agencies of contact are organized bodies of human beings working for a definite purpose; handling appropriate apparatus of material culture; and subject to a charter of laws, rules, and principles. The chartered company of early days, the European colonial government, the missionary body or the industrial enterprise, a community of planters or settlers—these have been and are the effective influences of the Western world, and each has to direct its impact primarily upon its indigenous counterpart: chieftainship, African religion, African systems of agriculture, hunting, fishing, or industry. The missionary has to supplant the Native forms of belief and worship, to supplement them or to develop an organized system of African dogma and ritual. The entrepreneur or settler has to appropriate a portion of the natural resources of Africa, exploit them by means of European capital, and use African labor in conjunction with Western techniques and methods of working. In Indirect Rule, European administration with its established force and treasury, with its European-bred tradition of Civil Service, with its bases in the European home country, has to coöperate with an equally strongly welded and traditionally founded Native chieftainship.

Whenever effective coöperation occurs, a new form of social organization is engendered: a Native Christian congregation under the supervision and guidance of a White clergy; a mine or a factory where African labor works under the direction of a White staff; a bush school where African children are taught by European teachers; an organized system of Native administration under European control. Thus what results from impact is not a higgledy-piggledy assortment of traits, but new institutions, organized on a definite charter, run by a mixed personnel, related to European plans, ideas, and needs, and at times satisfying certain African interests. We find, therefore, that to marshal evidence in any other form than by stating the interaction of two institutions, and the resulting creation of a third composite one, leads theoretically to confusion, and practically to blundering.

The real problems of compatibility, adaptability, and conflict center around the main function and the subsidiary influences of an institution and its constituent factors. And here we come to the concept of the *Common Measure* or the *Common Factor* of interests and intentions. Indeed, this concept seems to me to furnish the clue to all the discussions of change and contact.[9]

The common factor exists wherever there is a long-run identity of interests between Europeans and Africans, as well as competence and knowledge on the part of the Whites in carrying out a well-planned policy. Under such conditions there will be a basis for collaboration and agreement in ideas, sentiments, and general outlook between the two races. Policies of Indirect Rule, of indigenous economic development, of the incorporation of certain African rites into Christian worship, of gradual education with full opportunities for educated Africans, are examples to be found in many parts of the continent, where the existence of the common factor of good-will and converging interests has led to a harmonious process of development. Any analysis of culture change must therefore collate the European intentions or policy with the corresponding African institutions, and assess whether in the process of change the interests of the two sides clash or dovetail.

Difficulties arising out of African land shortage, including overstocking and erosion, the handling of the labor problem, the color-bar principle, are cases of what might be called the "negative common factor," to introduce an arithmetical figment. To destroy something in African life simply because it displeases the Europeans is a classic case of an absence of any common factor, a deficiency which must lead to conflict. Again the African sense of order and respect for law is not fostered but thwarted when the Whites impose burdensome regulations such as pass laws, restrictions on freedom of movement, or deprivation of ordinary privileges in transport, public parks, and other places of amenity. Or to take another example: let us imagine contingents of Natives transported from the reserves into urban locations or made to "squat" on farms, where they have to live under a strictly monetary economy, depending on a wage system. If a study of their budgets shows that their necessary expenditure exceeds their regular wages, this is a definite state of maladjustment, an objective symptom of a negative common factor.[10]

The treatment of witchcraft, where the ultimate aim, viz., the abolition of its menace is identical, but the legal methods are based on European ignorance of African mentality and institutions, is another instance of how the common factor in ultimate ends may be vitiated by the absence of the common factor in methods. In the educational system we have another mixed and complicated problem. In so far as the acquisition of European knowledge is advantageous, education has been one of the great forces of uplift. But education may be given merely to make the African a better subject for evangelization; it may be concerned too much with theoretical knowledge, which on the one hand he cannot use to any practical purpose and which on the other hand kindles in him ambitions and just claims, never to be satisfied owing to the European policy of segregation. It may develop technical skills which he will never be able to utilize because of the color-bar discrimination, legal or customary. The educated African convert is then individually and collectively made to suffer for the fact that, owing to his religion and education, he is the equal of his White neighbor. But owing to the color of his skin, he is deprived of political rights, economic opportunities, and the social privileges of equality. Since education is one of the crucial processes in culture change, let us consider it in greater detail from the functional point of view.[11]

Education is a process which starts at birth; it is the social and cultural heritage of the individual. An African is born to a definite tribal status; whether this be of a chief, magician, commoner, warrior, or medicine man matters not. Now, in order to occupy that final position, he has to pass through a Native training.

If you give him a European education, you deprive him of the possibility of a Native training. Here the very common measure of the two determines that you cannot achieve the one without destroying the other. Yet the compatibility and interchangeability of the two phases are demonstrated by the facts. You *can* train Natives to be parsons, teachers, lawyers, and journalists; engineers, skilled workers, and farmers of the European type. Yet the full training of that type requires, above all, opportunities. And here the real difficulty comes in. Full opportunities for professional men, skilled artisans, and workmen, to say nothing of statesmen, financiers, businessmen, require as wide a background of civilization as we have in Europe, and this does not exist in Africa. Nor can it be conjured up as rapidly as the educational processes can produce the unadapted individuals or groups.

Again, the lower ranks of the educational system, which are molded on European patterns, are slavishly given a type of instruction which is useful as a foundation for higher training but mostly a waste of time for an African who needs a minimum of skills and abilities, taught from a very special point of view, if he is to qualify for a position as a servant, an unskilled laborer, a lower government official, or as a member of the police force.

The Europeans, instead of regarding all education or any education as an asset, might consider here that what the African takes from the European culture may be a handicap and a malediction, a blight or an injury, if it opens horizons, develops ambitions, raises him up to a standard of living which cannot be achieved.

The common measure of interest would first of all require a careful consideration of what role the skilled African and the educated African will have to play; what European types of book learning, skill, and ability he will need within the limitations imposed on him by segregation, differential policy, professional disabilities. The principle of common measure declares that only what is effectively useful, both to him and to the European community, should be administered to him educationally, and that in a form directly compatible with his future functions. That such an education should never completely destroy his tribal bonds; estrange him from family and clan; above all, should not make him despise things African, is implied in all the arguments.[12]

Let us glance at the contact problems involved in missionary work. The missionary is the master educator; the master builder of the new African morality; the leader in the appreciation by the African of all that is finest in Western culture. He is often the first to come, and quite as often the last to abandon the ideal attitude in the treatment of African problems. But the missionary is also handicapped by insidious difficulties, incongruities inherent in his work, and obstructive associations. To start with the last named: he has to preach the Gospel of Universal Brotherhood in an atmosphere where this gospel is not always practiced. Indeed, whenever and wherever the principle of the color bar is officially (or unofficially) the law of the land, the whole work of the mission is doubly hampered. This negative common factor is expressed in the conflict and incompatibility within the European camp.

Ancestor worship seems to me in many ways the crucial problem and the touchstone of missionary work. It is with regard to this aspect of African culture that the repressive tendency of the mission has hindered the process of evangelization. One of the wrong attitudes to adopt toward ancestor worship is to regard it as entirely reprehensible, simply because it is the core of African paganism and because it involves sacrifice, divination, and communion with ancestors, which seem essentially un-Christian. This is the position which has usually been taken. But a fuller knowledge of ancestor worship in Africa and of religious principles would dictate a different course, one not too late to be adopted in some parts at least. For the principle of ancestor worship itself is as sound a theoretical principle as the Fourth Commandment. To work it gradually into a subordinate position, to make it an outcome of monotheism—in short, to harmonize it completely with the Christian attitude of filial piety and reverence to ancestors—would achieve the same end in a slow and much more effective way. In such a compromise may be found the common factor between Christianity and ancestor worship.

As it is, ancestor worship driven underground survives often in forms of fear and dread, reverted to even by ministers of the Christian religion and always there as a stepping stone to religious separation. In general, the principle of an open and honest expression of mental attitudes is preferable to their violent puritanical suppression. But the most important point about ancestor worship is the fact that it is connected with a type of social organization—the family and the clan; the whole legal system is intimately bound up with it. The complete destruction of the dogma is thus sociologically deleterious. The relegation of the dogma to its proper place, while retaining its social, economic, and legal influences, would produce the same dogmatic results and satisfy the puritanism of the missionary without producing the nefarious results.[13]

To sum up the preceding arguments and examples, we can say that wherever there is a common measure between the intentions of European impact and the existing needs of the African society, change can lead to new thriving forms of cultural coöperation. When on the contrary it is, or seems, necessary for the Europeans to take away from the African his territory; to curtail his opportunities; to use his labor to the detriment of Native enterprise without satisfactory remuneration, then the absence of a common factor leads to conflict.

The concept of common measure or common factor is the direct corollary of our principle that human institutions are commensurable across the dividing line of culture; but that in each of these they fulfill the same function under a different type of determinism. The African family and type of marriage are equivalents of European marriage and family. But the legal conception, the safeguards, the type of kinship, differ substantially. In Africa, as in Europe, central authority, education, economic wealth, and value do exist. Each fulfills the same function, and therefore it is possible to implant gradually and constructively European administration, money economy, or book learning in Africa. At the same time, we know that an institution has its legal and religious charter; that it must dispose of a material apparatus; and that it organizes a group of people, united to perform a definite task. Now, if the same group of people has to be reorganized into satisfying some definite need by entirely different means, the process is by no means simple or easy.

Imagine an African agricultural community, and look at them as a food-producing team, that is, an economic institution. There is no reason whatever why we should not in future envisage them as tilling the soil by highly developed methods, using all the modern appliances, with enormously increased output. But in order to achieve this transformation, first and foremost an enormous capital outlay would be necessary; secondly, the legal relation of man to environment would have to be profoundly changed: not only the improvement in land but also new systems of land tenure would have to be introduced. Thirdly, if a surplus of cash crops is produced, opportunities for marketing would have to be created or safeguarded.[14]

There is one more factor which must not be forgotten. The transformation from African tribal agriculture to a highly Western system cannot take place overnight. The introduction of the new methods disorganizes the old ones. In order to progress, the African often has to pass through a stage of chaos and disorientation, and he would have to be tided over this stage. In the past such help has usually not been forthcoming. Exactly the same analysis could be made in the matter of administrative change;

transition in the organization of family and household; and even more cogently in matters of education, morals, and religion.

The ultimate reality in culture change thus hinges on the fact that corresponding institutions in two cultures satisfy analogous needs in different ways and with different techniques; but in the process they have to use the same human and natural resources: land, capital, labor, politically organized force, the impulses of human reproduction, and also the standardized emotions, values, and loyalties specific to each culture. This means that institutions cannot be replaced rapidly, piecemeal, and without considerable sacrifice on the part of the community which has engendered the change and is carrying it on. On either side of the bar we have the same demand for the limited material resources and limited human energies. It is impossible either to develop the African on his own lines or to change him into a colored Westerner, without leaving him a substantial margin of material prosperity, of political autonomy, and of civic rights. Full development in an economic and spiritual way is also difficult, even perhaps impossible, while we make him feel constantly inferior as regards his racial position and his cultural heritage. Even the maximum of autonomy, economic opportunities, and civic freedom granted to the African would still imply a considerable amount of European control. But all this need not blind us to the fact that if we are to lead the African in the common enterprise of a satisfactory and harmonious transformation; if the African is to coöperate with the European under the terms of the Dual Mandate in exploiting the continent for the world, it is not enough if we supply the spiritual substance and expect the African to give the Marxian quota.

It is in this clash of interests and greeds, as well as in the intrinsic difficulty of piecemeal and institutional change, that the real dynamic issues of contact and change reside. Here, as elsewhere, the only way out of such a difficulty, out of this conflict between the two sets of vested interests, to a certain extent irreconcilable, lies in a compromise. Scientific analysis teaches that the compromise must be real as well as intelligently engineered. The knowledge of facts and an adequately informed framing of policies are indispensable; but let us remember that cold scientific analysis teaches also that the stronger partner cannot rely only on his own intelligence and on feeding the weaker one with fine phrases and good intentions. He must also honestly, albeit with a heavy heart, give up some of his material advantages, some of his privileges, and learn how to share his political influence with the indigenous population. For you cannot develop a strong and healthy culture on anything else but the material basis necessary for it. Nor can you establish a politically sound community if you degrade some of its members into the semblance, at times even the substance, of slaves. Nor yet can you inculcate moral responsibility if you make them feel that no moral justice is exercised toward them.

But although it is the legitimate task of science clearly and forcibly to point out truths, even if these happen to be moral truths, its main business lies on the intellectual side. We have found that the crucial concept of our analysis is that of the common measure. By this we mean the existence of certain elements of common interest, of tasks in which Africans and Europeans can coöperate in their joint interest. The absence of a common factor, or the common factor in its negative form, appears whenever the European in pursuing his own aims has to take away some elements essential to the African's progress; whether this element be land or labor, self-confidence or his own personal dignity; a cherished belief or a type of customary law indispensable to the sound working of marriage, family, or tribal life.

Since this central concept obviously can be defined only as a result of the direct correlation of European and African interests and institutions, the best way of obtaining it is by collating the two cultural realities. Here, as in every scientific work, it is profitable to develop a tangible formal instrument for the handling of evidence. We have already tentatively outlined such a device when discussing the concepts of "mechanical mixture of cultural elements" and "the zero point of tribal culture." We shall see that it will at the same time be useful as a chart for field work, as a method of presenting evidence theoretically, and as a simple and concise way of bringing out practical conclusions.

NOTES

1. Malinowski, "Practical Anthropology," *Africa*, Vol. VII (1929).

2. I. Schapera, "Contract between European and Native in South Africa—2: in Bethuanaland," *Methods of Study of Culture Contact in Africa*, p. 27.

3. *Vide* M. Fortes, "Culture Contact as a Dynamic Process," *Methods of Study of Culture Contact in Africa*, p. 62.

Malinowski's criticism of this position would also apply to that adopted by Dr. Gluckman in an article entitled "Analysis of a Social Situation in Modern Zululand," in *Bantu Studies*, Vol. XIV (1940). Dr. Gluckman there states: "We see that the dominant form of the structure is the existence *within a single community* [my italics] of two co-operating colour groups which are differentiated by a large number of criteria so as to stand opposed and even hostile to one another" (p. 28). Dr. Gluckman admits the existence of a color bar; unfortunately, he does not define the term community. If, however, we take it to mean a territorial group which participates in a common culture, it is difficult to see how it can be applied to the African contact situation, in view of the profound differences of language and culture between the two groups involved. Ed.

4. *Vide* Schapera, *op. cit.*, p. 28, for this suggestion.

5. The following discussion of European agents considered as part of an African tribe is taken from Malinowski's "The Anthropology of Changing African Cultures," *Methods of Study of Culture Contact in Africa,* pp. xv–xvii; but I have also inserted sections from his other manuscripts. Ed.

6. End of quotation from Malinowski's "The Anthropology of Changing African Cultures." Ed.

7. I should like to add that Professor Schapera in his article puts on the map of ethnographic work the study of "the various motives and interests which have driven each of these agencies to encroach upon the natives" (*vide op. cit.,* p. 33). But the manner in which he would like to lay the foundations for field work, as stated in his essay under the subheading "Basic Investigations" (pp. 27 ff.) is not quite compatible with his more correct subsequent statement of the problem.

There is one more argument from the contribution of Professor Schapera I would like to challenge. His insistence on "personalities" as opposed to "institutions" is puzzling. It leads him to the assertion: "to the native . . . there is no such thing as Western civilization in general" (*op. cit.,* p. 34). But is not the essence of tribal reaction to White contact, of Bantu nationalism, and of the various Pan-African movements, a public opinion in which the Western world as a whole is made the object of violent views and strong sentiments?

8. Dr. Audrey I. Richards in "The Village Census in the Study of Culture Contact," *Methods of Study of Culture Contact in Africa,* p. 46, also makes a similar point, and suggests that this will modify the guiding principles of field work from the start.

9. The following discussion of the *Common Factor* incorporates material from a lecture given by Malinowski on "Culture Change in Theory and Practice," to the Oxford University Summer School on Colonial Administration, July 5, 1938. Ed.

10. See the following articles for a detailed discussion of such conditions in rural and urban areas: Ellen Hellman, "Native Life in a Johannesburg Slum," *Africa* (1935); F. W. Fox, "Nutritional Problems amongst the Rural Bantu," *Race Relations,* Vol. VI, No. 1; Hellman, "The Diet of Africans in Johannesburg," *Race Relations,* Vol. VI, No. 1; see also Hunter, *Reaction to Conquest,* pp. 140–141, 450–454, and 516–517, for some specimen budgets and discussion of earnings.

11. See "Native Education and Culture Contact," *International Review of Missions,* Vol. XXV (October, 1936), for a more detailed exposition of Malinowski's views on education. Ed.

12. See p. 58, n. 2, where there is a reference to the committees which have been appointed recently (1943) to study these problems. Ed.

13. One of the greatest difficulties in missionary work is sex. An objective and scientific definition of sex morals must be sought, i.e., the type of conduct within the context of a given culture which is in harmony with the institutions of marriage and the family found there. If prenuptial intercourse is allowed as a form of trial marriage, then to abolish it without changing the context is dangerous. It may lead to developments of unnatural vice, of clandestine instead of open fornication. Here it is clear again that parts of an institution ought to be transformed gradually and in harmony with one another.

14. While nothing on this large scale may be said to have occurred in African communities, it should be noted that commercial crops for export have been grown in certain areas—thus cotton in Uganda, coffee in Tanganyika, and cacao on the West Coast. In view of the points made above, it is significant that on the West Coast the new system of agriculture has resulted in new conceptions of land tenure. *Vide* Lord Hailey, *An African Survey,* p. 884. Ed.

M. Gluckman

MALINOWSKI'S "FUNCTIONAL" ANALYSIS OF SOCIAL CHANGE

MALINOWSKI'S CONCEPTION OF THE FIELD OF STUDY

Malinowski introduces his conception of the field of study by attacking the view which regards the Africans of to-day as an integral part of the modern world. To do this, he distorts the arguments supporting this view. Then, with the inconsistency which we found in his use of history, he adopts it in many of his own analyses. I shall briefly demonstrate this and indicate that his concepts make it inevitable.

The view that Malinowski attacks is assumed in the studies of historians (e.g. Macmillan), economists (e.g. Frankel), and psychologists (e.g. Macrone). He attacks it as put forward by Fortes and Schapera. I have already exposed his distortions [1] but have here to repeat the argument, because Kaberry, in editing this book, similarly distorts what I wrote.

Malinowski writes: "It is now generally agreed upon that Europeans form an integral part of any contact situation. . . . But I think it is pushing a legitimate commonplace too far when it is suggested [by Schapera] that 'the missionary, administrator, trader and labour recruiter must be regarded as factors in the tribal life in the same way as are the chief and the magician' . . . Yet another writer [Fortes] has claimed: 'contact agents can be treated as integrally part of the community.'" Malinowski attacks: "Unfortunately, this type of simplification is not advisable. The treatment of the complex situations of change as one 'well-integrated whole,' the 'one-entry' approach as we might call it, ignores the whole dynamism of the process. . . . The concept of a well-

SOURCE. M. Gluckman, "Malinowski's 'Functional' Analysis of Social Change," reprinted from *Africa*, XVII, 2, 1947, pp. 106–109, 118–121, by permission of the International African Institute, Cohen & West for the British rights, The Free Press of Glencoe for the United States rights, and M. Gluckman.

integrated community would, indeed, ignore such facts as the colour bar, the permanent rift which divides the two partners in change and keeps them apart in church and factory, in matters of mine labour and political influence" (pp. 14 ff.).

I need not quote more extensively. "Integral" becomes "well-integrated whole," and then a "well-integrated community" meaning "harmonious." Similarly, Schapera's statement that White personalities have to be studied *in the same way* as Black, is perverted by reading the words *in the same way* as if they referred to the social position of the personalities, and not to a field-technique. Then obviously the missionary is not socially equivalent to the magician. Again, where Schapera speaks of using White informants on matters which they know about, Malinowski says "we should [then] have only a slight numerical addition to our informants": as if an administrator cannot give valuable data on the matters which Africans bring to his office.

Kaberry uses the same technique to dismiss my argument. "Dr. Gluckman . . . states: 'We see that the dominant form of the structure is the existence *within a single community* [Kaberry's italics] of two cooperating colour groups which are differentiated by a large number of criteria so as to stand opposed and even hostile to one another.' Dr. Gluckman admits the existence of a colour bar; unfortunately, he does not define the term community. If, however, we take it to mean a territorial group which participates in a common culture, it is difficult to see how it can be applied to the African contact situation, in view of the profound differences of language and culture between the groups involved" (p. 14, n. 3). If, indeed, one defines *community* as an ethnic group recognizing common values—or as a group of people who believe the earth is flat—or as anything I clearly did not imply it to mean, then I wrote nonsense. It is unfortunate, perhaps, that I used the word *community:* it was the best term I could find to express the fact that there is a large field of interdependence in which individuals of the two colour groups have standardized norms of behaviour to each other. But it is dishonest to give to a word a meaning other than the one I intended, and then to make it the basis for a rejection of my whole analysis. The dishonesty is made manifest in the words: "Dr. Gluckman *admits* [my italics] the existence of a colour bar"; whereas in fact my analysis of the situation deals wholly with the colour bar, the opposition of colour groups, and the differences in culture.

We can thus reject Malinowski's initial denial of the existence of a single social body, to use a neutral word, of Whites and Blacks. Neverthe-less, Malinowski might still be justified in rejecting the concept as a tool of analysis. Let us examine his own position. He says that the missionary "cannot 'be regarded in the same way as the magician.' . . . He would not be true to his vocation if he ever agreed to act on the principle that Christianity is as 'any other form of cult' [Schapera said Christianity has to be studied in the same way as any other form of cult] . . . his brief is to regard all other forms of religion as misguided. . . . Far from leaving other cults side by side in juxtaposition with the message of the Gospels, the missionary is actively engaged in superseding them." He contrasts similarly administrator and chief. He states that it would be difficult to regard the "settler and his African neighbor as brethren of a large family" (p. 17)—and who has said they are?

"Nor can industrial enterprise be regarded as part of a tribal unit. It would be a strange African tribe which would embrace the gold mines of the Rand with their gigantic plant; the stock exchange of Johannesburg, and the banking system stretching from Cape to Cairo. The communication systems, railroads and planes . . . all this is part of culture contact. But the concept of an extended African tribe, into which this could be squeezed in order to produce a unified tribal horizon, falls to the ground as soon as it is stated" (pp. 16–17).

No one has said that the Rand mines, etc., were within the embrace of an African tribe or could be "squeezed" into "a unified tribal horizon." We state that the Rand mines and the African tribe which supplies their labour are both parts of a single social field; that the administrator who represents a government in London ruling over settlers and Africans, and the chief who rules over only a tribe whose members are in constant relationships with settlers and with Government, are both parts of a single political body. For example, the son of a Zulu councillor was selected by the Zulu paramount to work for him, a signal honour for the father. The youth ran away home. His father upbraided the youth for spoiling his name with the paramount. The youth retorted that the chief paid him nothing—look at his clothes; the Native Commissioner was better than the chief, since he paid those he employed. Afraid of his father's wrath and desirous of money, the youth ran away to a sugar-cane plantation—it might well have been the Rand mines. He could only flee from the paramount because the latter's writ of compulsion was limited by government. Here we have a right of the chief to call for labour which honours a father, the son desiring money and asserting a "preference" for the administrator because he pays, the development of a family conflict, and the solution of the conflict by flight to an enterprise of European capital. I quote this simple example to make explicit our conception of tribal group and Rand mines, of administrator and chief, as parts of a single social field. Indeed, Malinowski himself constantly has to use the conception, though he explicitly denies it. "Divination and witchcraft found in a town yard are not mere replicas of the genuine African institution. The performance I saw in Johannesburg was African divination, but it was applied to a case of witchcraft turning around the competitions and jealousies of mine employment; the fee was paid in English money, and the verdict was given in terms which no tribesman would understand" (p. 22).

But his denial of the existence of this single social body involves him in difficulties of which he is not aware. This emerges, for example, when he discusses "the problems of native diet in their economic setting." He states (p. 102) that "the method of study here, of course, would be based on field work among the Whites who control Native nutrition, including the research workers in biology, medicine and social conditions." He goes on (p. 109) to point out that though mine-labourers are well fed, the diet of their women and children at home suffers because the men are away and are not producing food. Cash wages "on broad and sociological lines" should compensate for this. Presumably, the diet of the women and children in the reserves has to be studied by the biochemist, who is himself studied by the sociologist. The biochemist thus becomes a factor in the tribal horizon though the administrator is not. The facts force Malinowski to analyse in terms of a social frame in which all personalities and groups, Black and White, are in theory mutually interdependent.

Malinowski's inconsistency is not chance: it arises from the weakness of his theoretical framework. Briefly, in general wherever Blacks and Whites co-operate he classifies the phenomena as "processes of social contact and change"; wherever they conflict he regards them as distinct and "not integrated." I am aware that examples from his writings can be cited against this statement, but these are the fruits of his inconsistency. Thus at p. 65 he says: "whenever effective cooperation occurs, a new form of social organization is engendered: a Native Christian congregation under the supervision and guidance of a White clergy; a mine or a factory where African labor works under the direction of a White staff; a bush school where African children are taught by European teachers; an organized system of Native administration under European control. Thus, what results from impact is not a higgledy-piggledy assortment of traits, but new institutions, organized on a definite charter, run by a mixed personnel, related to European plans, ideas, and needs, and at times satisfying certain African interests." But he cannot admit "conflict" into his frame of integrated institutions; that is, conflict as an inherent attribute of social organization, though in practice he uses it. He cannot see that the Rand mines are a field of conflict as well as a field of co-operation in which Africans, for the money they desire, assist the

Europeans to mine gold. Nor can he see that the separatist sects, which significantly he pigeon-holes not as "processes of social contact and change" but in a special column, as "new forces of spontaneous African reintegration or reaction," are an aspect of the colour bar plus "the Native Christian congregation under . . . White clergy." Theoretically, he regards the parties to conflicts as not "integral" factors in the same field and excludes them from the region of culture contact. . . .

MALINOWSKI'S CHARTING OF THE "THREE CULTURAL REALITIES"

Malinowski produces charts to enable us to study changing Africa. He projects "the three cultural realities each with its own determinism"— a concept which he does not clarify—on to three columns. He allows another column for the "reconstructed past," another for "new forces of spontaneous African reintegration or reaction," and later suggests a sixth to cover European culture outside Africa. This multiplication of columns is significant.

Specimen Chart to Be Used for the Analysis of Culture Contact and Change

	A	B	C	D	E
Europe	White influences, interests and intentions	Processes of culture contact and change	Surviving forms of tradition	Reconstructed past	New forces of spontaneous African reintegration or reaction

What is the value of the scheme? Malinowski gives the chart an almost autonomous methodological merit in the posing and solving of problems. This it has not. For in practice what he does is to examine the reality of modern Africa, and fit what he observes into the various columns. There is no indication that an entry under "A" automatically poses problems under "B" and "C." In my opinion, the chart might serve at best as a check on the comprehensiveness of field-work, but not as a tool of analysis.

I take an example covered to some extent by his notes on African warfare.

A	B	C
1. European con-quest and po-litical control.	1. The new political sys-tem as affected by loss of military sovereignty of the African tribe or monarchy, and result-ant changes in African organization.	1. African resistance and political submission in tribal memory and re-action.

That is only one of his horizontal columns but it illustrates the type of entry he makes. The chart, if it has universal effectiveness, should cover all problems. I pose one from Zulu history.

In the 1830's Boer trekkers under Retief came to Dingane, King of the Zulu, to ask for land. They did not then wish to wrest land from the Zulu by force, but to get Dingane's permission for them to take up land in the parts of Natal which Shaka's wars had depopulated. Dingane agreed to allow this if Retief's party attacked and recovered for him cattle he claimed from another chief. Retief did this, but Dingane mur-dered the Boer party and killed many of the Boers in Natal. Another group of Boers two years later attacked and defeated the Zulu, and confined them north of the Tugela River. Meanwhile, Dingane was ruling tyrannously, and his brother Mpande was able to lead his own following over to the Boers, who assisted him to defeat Dingane and installed Mpande as king. Let us fit these events, or the institutions behind them, into the columns:

A	B	C
1. Boer desire for land, temporary wish to come to peaceful terms with the Zulu. 2. Boer military power, and readiness to use enemy fifth column, Mpande v. Dingane.	1. Dingane uses Boers against enemy chief and they agree to be used to gain favour. Dingane murders Boers, and other Boers avenge. 2. Mpande gets Boer power to support him and rebellion against Dingane is successful.	1. Zulu independence and mili-tary power, hostility to neighbouring chiefs. 2. Zululand divided into seg-ments under king and brothers. People use seg-mentation in rebellions against bad king: support Mpande against Dingane. Mpande ready to use out-side power to help him.

Has the sorting-out added to our knowledge and understanding? To some extent it has, for we have simplified the set of historical events which we are attempting to analyse, and they do stand out more clearly. But the sorting-out itself does not give us the interpretation of data, which has been made prior to the sorting: nor, when put together, does column "B" alone give an analysis of the dynamics of the whole situation. In horizontal column 2, all personalities, Boers, Dingane, and Mpande, appear in every vertical column. There is no major distortion, but I consider that the all-important interconnexions of the columns, which are relationships between social groups and social personalities as operated on by social forces, are better covered by the concept of the social field. Here we have a numerically powerful Zulu military state in hostile relations with another less-powerful native state (the enemy chief). The Boers, numerically less powerful than the Zulu but technically better-armed (400 of them defeated the Zulu army because of mounted mobility and guns), cross the Drakensberg. A social field is established which consists of unlike territorial states—though the Boers, having as yet no territory, are only the outliers of an incipient state. Dingane uses the unlike Boer state as a weapon to defeat his like enemy, Sekunyane, just as Shaka employed the stabbing-spear to overcome the javelin. Then he wipes out the Boers, thus attempting to restore the previous balance. Other Boers (and English) react to avenge: Dingane is defeated and the Boer power establishes in Natal a system of unlike territorial states, Boer and Zulu, opposed to each other. A cleavage in Zululand enables one of the parties, Mpande, to find Boer support, as he might have found support from another chief. So the deposed Lozi king, Mwanawina, came with a party of *Mazungu* (it is not even known if they were Portuguese, Arabs, or half-castes) to regain his throne from Lewanika. The Boers use the Zulu cleavage to weaken the Zulu state further and install a friendly rather than a hostile king. It is forty years before the Whites are powerful enough to subjugate the whole Zulu state.

It seems manifest to me that it is most profitable to treat the situation in Natal in 1836–40 as a single social field in which there is mutual interaction throughout, e.g. in Dingane's use of the Boers against his external enemy Sekunyane; in Mpande's use of the Boers in his internal revolution, based on a cleavage in Zulu social organization; and in the advantage taken by the Boers of that cleavage.

I have temporarily isolated Natal at 1836–40. Clearly, a full analysis requires consideration of the drives which brought the Boers to Natal: so that the field of reality in which these events occurred is extended in space-time to the Cape with its own conflicts which produced the Great Trek. Similarly, a full analysis would refer in greater detail to the history which produced the war between Dingane and Sekunyane and the cleavage of Zulu in attachment to Dingane and Mpande: so that the field of reality in which these events occurred is extended in space-time to the whole creation of the Zulu nation under Shaka. Thus in reality, events in the Cape are brought into interaction with events in Zululand and with its history: for the legislative measures which precipitated the Great

Trek enabled Mpande to get Boer help to rebel successfully against Dingane. But though these legislative enactments helped to give victory to Mpande rather than to Dingane, they are sociologically irrelevant to the cleavage of Zulu society into potentially hostile segments attached to brothers of the royal family, and to the process by which Zulu used this segmentation to get rid of a tyrant king and install a brother in his place: i.e. the process by which they defended the values of kingship in rebellion against a bad king. For in this analysis it is partly irrelevant who won the battle. To that extent, Malinowski would be justified in classifying the cleavage under "C" rather than "B," though in practice I am certain he would have put these events under "B."

I hope I have indicated how much more fruitful it is to conceive this set of events as a single field, rather than as "three cultural realities." We have seen that this also applies to the establishing of industrial enterprise in Africa. The three columns have as little value as the extra flanking ones he adds. It is significant that not one of his pupils has published an analysis in these terms.

One advantage of the concept of the single field is that it does away with sterile disputes about whether or not an administrator is an integral part of modern political organization. We have seen that Malinowski rejects the concept in a distorted form and then frequently uses it himself, as when he discusses divination in an urban slum-yard. I have analysed the political structure of modern Zululand [2] to show that though chief and administrator co-operate in routine administration, and under the pressure of the force of government, in many ways they are opposed. The administrator stands for one set of values, some of which are desired by many Zulu, the chief for another set. The chief represents tribal history and values; he is related by kinship to many of his people; he lives his social life with them. Above all, he leads their opposition to European innovations and rule. Under Malinowski's scheme, the routine co-operation is classified under "Contact," and the kinship-links and opposition under "tribal reaction." But all form a coherent complex about the chief. The Zulu express this by the antithesis: "the administrator has only the prestige of his office; the chief has the prestige of blood." The value of the chief's position in the kinship system comes also from the fact that the administrator has not got any position in the system and lives across the colour bar. But many individual Zulu turn to the administrator to gain personal advantages, and, as we have seen with the runaway youth, by some values prefer him to the chief. From the point of view of the individual Zulu the administrator has no place in the kinship system and little in social life, though he enters these in, e.g. law cases. The chief has a place in both.

I break off the analysis abruptly, for I cannot here elaborate other theoretical frameworks. I have tried to indicate that whatever our ultimate abstractions may be, we may best conceive the situation to be studied as a field of interdependent events, on the lines set out in African sociology by Fortes, Schapera, and others. We may isolate zones of the field for analysis, but we have to allow for the operation in one zone, of events emerging from all others.

NOTES

1. In my "Analysis of a Social Situation in Modern Zululand," *Bantu Studies,* June 1940, pp. 168 ff.

2. See my essay in *African Political Systems,* edited Fortes and Evans-Pritchard, Oxford, 1940.

G. Balandier

THE COLONIAL SITUATION:
A THEORETICAL APPROACH (1951)

One of the most striking events in the recent history of mankind is the expansion throughout the entire world of most European peoples. It has brought about the subjugation and, in some instances, the disappearance of virtually every people regarded as backward, archaic, or primitive. The colonial movement of the nineteenth century was the most important in magnitude, the most fraught with consequences, resulting from this European expansion. It overturned in a brutal manner the history of the peoples it subjugated. Colonialism, in establishing itself, imposed on subject peoples a very special type of situation. We cannot ignore this fact. It not only conditioned the reactions of "dependent" peoples, but is still responsible for certain reactions of peoples recently emancipated. The *colonial situation* poses problems for a conquered people—who respond to these problems to the degree that a certain latitude is granted to them—problems for the administration representing the so-called protective power (which also defends that power's local interests), problems for the newly created state on which still rests the burden of colonial liabilities. Whether currently present or in process of liquidation, this *situation* involves specific problems which must arrest the attention of a sociologist. The postwar period has clearly indicated the urgency and importance of the colonial problem in its totality. It has been characterized by difficult attempts at reconquest, by the granting of independence to some, and by more or less conditional concessions to others. It has announced a technical phase in colonialism in the wake of a political-administrative phase.

It was only a few years ago that a rough but significant estimate

SOURCE. G. Balandier, "La Situation Coloniale: Approche Théorique," reprinted from *Cahiers internationaux de sociologie*, XI, 1951, pp. 44–79, by permission of the Presses Universitaires de France.

noted the fact that colonial territories covered at that time one-third of the world's surface and that seven hundred million individuals out of a total population of some two billion were subject peoples.[1] Until very recently the greater part of the world's population, not belonging to the white race (if we exclude China and Japan), knew only a status of dependency on one or another of the European colonial powers. These subject peoples, distributed throughout Asia, Africa, and Oceania, all belonged to cultures designated "backward" or "pre-industrial." They constituted the field of research within which anthropologists or ethnologists carried on—and still carry on—their investigations. And the scientific knowledge that we have of colonial peoples is due in large part to the efforts of these scholarly investigators. Such studies, in principle, could not (or should not) ignore such an important fact as colonialism, a phenomenon which has imposed, for a century or more, a certain type of evolution on subjugated populations. It seemed impossible not to take into account certain concrete situations in which the recent history of these peoples evolved. And yet it is only now and then that anthropologists have taken into consideration this specific context inherent in the *colonial situation*. (We have substantiating evidence to present in a study presently in preparation.) On the one hand, we find researchers obsessed with the pursuit of the ethnologically pure, with the unaltered fact miraculously preserved in its primitive state, or else investigators entirely absorbed with theoretical speculations regarding the destiny of civilizations or the origins of society. And on the other hand, we find researchers engaged in numerous practical investigations of very limited scope, satisfied with a comfortable empiricism scarcely surpassing the level of using a technique. Between the two extremes the distance is great—it leads from the confines of a so-called "cultural" anthropology to the confines of one described as "applied" anthropology. In one case, the colonial situation is rejected as being a disturbing factor or is seen as only one of the causes of cultural change. In the other case, the colonial situation is viewed only in certain aspects—those immediately and obviously relating to the problem under investigation—and never appears as a force acting in terms of its own totality. Yet any *present-day* study of colonial societies striving for an understanding of current realities and not a reconstitution of a purely historical nature, a study aiming at a comprehension of conditions as they are, not sacrificing facts for the convenience of some dogmatic schematization, can only be accomplished by taking into account this complex we have called the *colonial situation*. It is precisely this situation that we wish to describe. But first it is necessary to sketch the essential outlines of this system of reference that we have invoked.

Among recent studies undertaken in France, only those of O. Mannoni assign an important role to the notion of *colonial situation*.[2] But as

Mannoni was intent on treating the subject from a purely psychological or psychoanalytical point of view, he offers only an imprecise definition of the phenomenon we refer to. He presents it as "a situation of incomprehension," as "a misunderstanding," and, accordingly, he analyzes the psychological attitudes that characterize the "colonizer" and the "colonized," attitudes that permit an understanding of the relationship maintained on both sides.[3] This is not enough, and O. Mannoni seems to recognize the fact when he cautions against "under-estimating the (capital) importance of economic relationships." Moreover, he concedes having selected a rather ill-defined aspect of the colonial situation. We, for our part, assume an opposite position from his. We are biased in favor of dealing with the question as a whole, believing there is something deceitful in examining only one of the many facts implied in this situation.

Such a situation as that created by the colonial expansion of European states during the last century can be examined from different points of view. Each one constitutes an individual approach to the subject, a separate analysis with a different orientation depending on whether the point of view is that of a colonial historian, an economist, a politician and administrator, a sociologist preoccupied with the relationships of foreign cultures, a psychologist concerned with a study of race relations, etc. And if one is to hazard an over-all view of the problem, it seems indispensable to discover what can be gleaned from each of these individual specialties.

The historian examines the various periods of colonization with respect to the colonial power. He enables us to grasp the changes that occur in the existing relationships between that power and its territorial dependencies. He shows us how the isolation of colonial peoples was shattered by a caprice of history over which these peoples had had no control. He evokes the ideologies which, at different times, have been used to justify colonialism and have created the "role" adopted by the colonial power, and he reveals the discrepancies separating facts from theories. He analyzes the administrative and economic systems which have guaranteed "colonial peace" and permitted an economic profit (for the metropole) from the colonial enterprise. In short, the historian makes us understand how, in the course of time, the colonial power implanted itself in the heart of its colonial societies. Acting in this manner he furnishes the sociologist with his first and indispensable frame of reference. He reminds the sociologist that the history of a colonial people has developed as a result of a foreign presence while at the same time he elucidates the different aspects of the latter's role and influence.

Most historians have insisted on the fact that the pacification, the organization, and the development of colonial territories were carried out "with respect to the interests of the western powers and not with local interests in mind . . . by assigning (the needs) of native producers to

a position of secondary importance." [4] They have shown how, in less than
a century, the European absorption of Asia, Africa, and Oceania "transformed the shape of human society through force and the imposition of
reforms, often bold reforms." They have shown how such upheavals were
made necessary by "colonial imperialism (which) is merely one manifestation of economic imperialism." [5] They have reminded us that economic
exploitation is based on the seizure of political power—the two characteristic features of colonialism.[6] Thus historians enable us to see to what
extent a colonial society is an instrumentality of the colonial power. We
can observe this instrumental function in the politics practiced by the
European power, which consists in compromising the native aristocracy
by tempting it with inducements calculated to appeal to its self-interest:
"Enlist the ruling class in our cause," said Lyautey; [7] reduce the native
chiefs to the role of "mere creatures," said R. Kennedy; and the evidence
is even more obvious in the policies pursued in transplanting populations
and in the recruitment of workers, all based exclusively on the economic
interests of the colonial power.[8] By reminding us of certain "bold" measures—population transfers and the policy of "reserves," the transformation of traditional laws, and questioning the ownership of resources,
policies requiring a certain level of productivity, etc.—the historian draws
our attention to the fact that "colonialism was literally at times an act of
social surgery." [9] And this observation, more or less valid, according to
the peoples and areas under consideration, is of great interest to a sociologist studying colonial societies. It indicates to him that these societies
are, in varying degrees, in a state of latent crisis, that they are involved
to some extent in a kind of social pathology. It is valuable evidence of
the special features of the sociology of colonial peoples and suggests the
practical and theoretical results one may expect from such a discipline.
We shall have occasion to note its importance elsewhere in our analysis.

But after having noted this external pressure applied to colonial societies, the historian points out the various kinds of reactions that have
resulted. The reactions of Far Eastern peoples, the Arab world, and
Black Africa have often been the subject of comparative studies. In general terms we learn of the opposition of "closed societies" in the Far East
despite outward appearances of westernization; the tense relations with
Islamic society which refuses to abandon a notion of superiority and
maintains "a competitive spirit that can be veiled and silent but nevertheless remains at the heart of the problem"; the "openness" of the black
world which is explained by "the African readiness to imitate," by a lack
of "confidence in the depths and resources of its own past." [10] And in a
rather special case, the history of Africa, the colonial continent *par excellence,* reveals important differences in ways of resisting the ascendancy
of European nations within the very heart of Black Africa. After having
exposed the importance of "the external factor" with respect to transfor-

mations affecting colonial societies, the history of colonialism confronts
us with an "internal factor" inherent in social structures and subjugated
societies. At this point the history of colonialism touches on territory
familiar to the anthropologist. But in offering a picture of the varied responses to the colonial situation, history shows us how much that situation can reveal to us. Colonialism appears as a trial, a kind of test imposed on certain societies or, if we may call it such, as a crude sociological experiment. An analysis of colonial societies cannot overlook these
specific conditions. As certain anthropologists have perceived,[11] they reveal not only the processes of adaptation or rejection, the new guideposts
set up for a society whose traditional models have been destroyed (the
"patterns" of Anglo-American authors), but they also disclose "the points
of resistance" among colonial peoples, the fundamental structure and
behavior of such a people. They touch society's bedrock. Such information offers unmistakable theoretical interest (if we consider the colonial
situation as a fact calling for scientific observation, independent of any
moral judgments it may provoke), and it has a truly practical importance:
it shows the fundamental premises in terms of which each problem must
be conceived.

The historian reveals the way in which the colonial system was
established and transformed. He describes, according to differing circumstances, the various political, juridical, and administrative aspects of
the system. He also enables us to take due note of the ideologies used
to justify colonialism.[12] Numerous studies emphasize the gap that has
existed between announced principles and actual practices, between "the
civilizing mission" (*la mission civilisatrice*—a phrase used with particular
emphasis under Napoleon III)—and the desired "utility" that Eugène
Etienne, the "colonialist of Oran" defined in 1894 as "the sum total of
profits and advantages accruing to the metropole" from any colonial
enterprise.[13] H. Brunschwig calls attention, in his history of French
colonization, to the long series of misunderstandings (nay, outright lies)
that stand out so conspicuously. L. Joubert reminds us of "the gulf that
separated facts from theories following the formal declarations of responsibility for civilizing the subject peoples; the rupture between these
alleged objectives and their application, if not the blatant hypocrisy
which, in the name of humanitarian principles, condoned exploitation
pure and simple. . . ."[14] The colonial situation thus appears to have
assumed an essentially spurious character. It sought continually to justify
itself by means of pseudo-reasons. In his study entitled "The Colonial
Crisis and the Future," R. Kennedy shows how each characteristic of
"colonialism"—the *color line*, political dependency, economic dependency,
virtually non-existent "social" benefits, the lack of contact between natives and "the dominant caste"—is predicated on "a series of rationalizations"; for example: the superiority of the white race; the inability of the

native population to govern itself correctly; the despotism of traditional chiefs; the temptation for present leaders to form "a dictatorial clique"; native inability to develop their own natural resources; the feeble financial resources of colonial peoples; the need to maintain national prestige, etc.[15] In the light of such evidence, the sociologist understands the extent to which a European colonial power, motivated by a dubious doctrine whose historical development can be traced, condemned to resort to deceit and hypocrisy, and wedded to a fixed image of the native population, acted upon colonial societies in terms of these concepts. We have called attention elsewhere to the importance of this fact.[16] No valid sociological study of colonial peoples is possible which ignores this attention given to ideologies and to the more or less stereotyped behavior they produced.

The historian reminds us that contemporary colonial societies are the product of a dual history. Thus in the case of Africa, the one history is entirely African: "these societies, so stable, so seemingly immobile, all resulted, or almost all, from the variable combinations of diverse peoples who were thrown together, clashed with one another, or were superimposed on each other by historical events" [17]—a history that "brought together (in a relationship of domination or assimilation) homogeneous social forms"; [18] while on the other hand, the other history, largely conditioned by European domination, "brought into contact social forms that were radically heterogeneous" and presented a picture of "disintegration." "Three forces," says Ch.-A. Julien, "have disintegrated Africa: governmental administration, missionaries, and the new economy." [19] Any current study of these societies can be made only by viewing them in terms of this dual history.

It is customary to recall that colonialism, broadly speaking, has involved the interplay of three closely inter-related forces—an historical association, as R. Montagne has pointed out by observing that "the effort to spread the Christian gospel has been tied historically to European expansion in the commercial, political, or military spheres." [20] The economic, governmental, and missionary objectives have been experienced by subject peoples as closely associated activities,[21] and it is in terms of these factors that anthropologists have usually analyzed "social changes." But in an effort to describe modern European colonialism and to explain its appearance, certain historians have been inclined to place the greatest emphasis on one of these aspects—the economic factor. "Colonial imperialism is but one form of economic imperialism," Ch.-A. Julien has written in an article on this subject.[22] At this point history impinges on another point of view that is indispensable for understanding the colonial situation.

The propaganda for political expansion based its arguments, in part, on economic arguments. In 1874 P. Leroy Beaulieu argued France's need to become a colonial power. J. Ferry wrote in 1890: "Colonial policy is the child of industrial policy . . . colonialism is an international manifestation of the eternal laws of competition. . . ." [23] It was economic reasons that colonial powers invoked to justify their presence—the resources that were developed and the equipment built were regarded as property as of right—and economic advantages were the last to be surrendered even after more or less genuine agreements for political independence had been arrived at. Even before the studies of Marxist writers appeared, certain analyses devoted to "imperialism" revealed its economic characteristics. [24] Lenin was the first Marxist to offer a systematic theory in his famous work: *Imperialism: the Highest Stage of Capitalism.* Ch.-A. Julien stressed its central thesis by recalling that "colonial policies are the offspring of monopoly, of the exportation of capital and the quest for spheres of economic influence." [25] Whether it involve colonization or an economic protectorate, a Marxist discovers one and the same reality, one that is linked to capitalism and must disappear with it. The close ties that exist between capitalism and colonial expansion have prompted certain non-Marxist authors to compare the "colonial question" with the "social question" and to observe, like J. Guitton, "that they are not fundamentally different because the *metropole-colony* relationship is in no sense different from the *capital-labor* relationship, or the relationship Hegel has termed *master-servant.*[26] Note the possible identification of "colonial peoples" with the "proletariat." "In both cases," P. Reuter writes, "we are dealing with a population that produces all the wealth but does not share in its political or economic advantages and constitutes an oppressed 'class.'" [27]

For a Marxist there is no doubt whatsoever about this common identity. Politically, it justifies the combined action of the proletariat and the colonial peoples. Stalin devoted a number of studies to the colonial question and, after having showed that "Leninism . . . destroyed the wall separating Whites from Blacks, Europeans from Asiatics, the 'civilized' from the 'non-civilized' slaves of imperialism," he recalled that "the October Revolution *inaugurated* a new era, the era of *colonial revolutions in the oppressed countries* of the world, in *alliance* with the proletariat and *under the direction* of the proletariat." [28] The colonial peoples themselves stress the economic aspect of their condition more than its political aspect. An African journalist from the Gold Coast writes on this subject: "Nations whose economic power is preponderant are precisely those whose political influence predominates. . . . As of now the authorities have made no effort at all to encourage native populations in their colonies to reach an economic level commensurate with their political advancement." [29]

Without envisaging the colonial situation exclusively in terms of its economic manifestations, a sociologist who tries to understand and interpret colonial societies must recognize the importance of such demonstrable facts. They will remind him that the structures of these societies are not explained simply in terms of contacts between a technically advanced civilization and a primitive, nontechnical society. They will indicate that between the colonial power and the colonized population certain relationships exist which connote tension and conflict. (We have already referred to the instrumental nature of relationships in the colonial society.) This observation would have proved useful to the theoretical views of Malinowski. When the famed anthropologist established the doctrine of "a practical anthropology," he declared that a "wise" control of the forces for change "can guarantee a normal and stable development," [30] and this misunderstanding of the extremely antagonistic nature of the situation led him, according to one commentator, to pose the problems "in the most naïve terms." [31]

The economic aspect of the colonial situation has been expressed in general terms by certain anthropologists or geographers who have specialized in tropical countries. R. Kennedy (in a previously mentioned study) has indicated its principal characteristics: [32] the quest for raw materials by colonial powers for utilization in the metropolitan industrial complex—a fact that explains the inferior (if not in fact nonexistent) [33] industrial equipment in colonial territories; large-scale exploitation and import-export trade are entirely within the hands of "societies" which reap all the profits for themselves; [34] the "distance" separating the Europeans from the colonial peoples (the latter essentially reduced to the role of peasants, laborers, and domestics), explaining the native's difficulty "in raising himself economically"; and finally, the economic stagnation of the indigenous masses.

Among French-language studies, those dealing with Indo-China are particularly valuable (indeed, they are the only ones which have real depth). That they are the work of geographers like Charles Robequain and P. Gourou [35] is quite indicative of the current disregard for the present that has characterized French ethnology. "Peasants" represent 90 to 95% of the Indo-Chinese population, and these studies are essentially concerned with the peasantry. Aside from the importance attached first of all to available technical means (which were not improved, or only slightly improved, by the colonial power) emphasis is placed on the loss of property holdings,[36] on "property dispossession" producing an uprooted and proletarian population. And we find, as a concomitant trend, the establishment of a bourgeoisie (essentially agrarian in origin) born "like the proletariat, from contact with western civilization and from a weakening of traditional values." The growth of this class results almost always "from exploitation of the rice fields and the system of moneylending associated therewith." [37] The observations dealing with business (native businesses are broken up into many small and unimportant enter-

prises while big businesses and export trade are in the hands of Europeans or foreigners—Chinese and Indians) and the observations concerning industry (a stagnation of local industry, a lack of any industrial
processing, and a negligible growth of the work force—since 1890 the
average annual increase in the work force was only 2,500 according to
Charles Robequain—and the low level of skilled workmen) all substantiate the general picture presented by R. Kennedy. It is on the basis of
such facts that P. Naville could give a precise and strictly Marxist interpretation of the economic and political conditions of the Vietnamese
revolution.[38]

Studies relating to Africa, especially Central and South Africa, disclose the same kinds of facts. These studies are primarily by Anglo-
American anthropologists rightly concerned with "practical anthropology." The situation created in South Africa by a European minority is
well known: territorial segregation imposed by the *Native Land Act* of
1913 (*native areas* comprise only 12% of the entire territory of the Union
of South Africa); social segregation legalized by the *Colour Bar Act* of
1926 which restricts black workers to jobs requiring manual labor only;
the disproportionately small share of national income enjoyed by the
Negroes (representing 69% of the population, they receive only 20% of
the national income, whereas the Whites, who make up 21% of the population, receive 74% of the income); the racial bases and racist premises of
economic and political structures; the profound contradictions in a policy
that establishes segregation (the Whites fearing to be overrun by the
Blacks) while at the same time it must "sound the call for native workers," [39] thus provoking a rural exodus resulting in "proletarization" and
"de-tribalization" of the indigenous population. The special situation in
South Africa, in some ways almost a caricature of these conditions, shows
the extent to which economic, political, and racial questions are closely
interrelated.[40] And it shows, too, how these questions cannot be ignored
by anyone undertaking a study of present-day conditions in the Union
of South Africa. It is in the light of these facts that we reaffirm the com-
pelling need to consider the *colonial situation* as a single complex, as a
totality.

Anglo-American anthropologists have assigned an important role to
economic facts considered as one of the principal "forces" responsible for
"culture-change." In her celebrated work, *Reaction to Conquest*, Monica
Hunter examines the transformations that occurred in Pondo society (in
South Africa) in terms first of the economic factor and then of the political factor ("which, historically speaking, has an economic origin, whatever non-Marxists may say about it"). But these studies, already quite
numerous on the question of Africa alone,[41] are conducted solely along
economic lines, analyzing the "primitive" social organization and economy
with regard to the dislocations brought about by a "modern" economy

and the problems created by the latter. They fail to relate these to the colonial economy, the colonial situation. They fail to convey the notion of reciprocity of outlooks existing between the colonial population, on the one hand, and the colonial power, on the other. The studies inspired by Malinowski are conspicuous for these shortcomings since they reveal only the results of "contact" between "institutions" of the same nature, and scarcely go beyond a simple description of certain transformations and the enumeration of certain problems. This explains why they are concerned primarily with rural questions, with changes affecting the village and "the family," with rural depopulation. In this field, they have outlined significant patterns of "culture-change": destruction of the extended family, predominance of economic values, the emancipation of the younger generation, the establishment of a monetary economy which upsets personal relationships, the threat to traditional hierarchies (wealth and rank no longer always being closely associated), etc. Certain special research fields—such as that relating to living standards [42]—have been developed, but important facts—such as the new social groupings resulting from the dislocation of traditional groupings, the appearance of social classes, the nature and role of the proletariat, etc.—are touched on only in very general terms, and the conflicts they imply are rarely analyzed.[43]

Yet it is precisely these aspects of the problem that are given highest priority in studies inspired by the condition of crisis that exists in colonial societies and by the political and administrative implications deriving from this crisis. In this area of study, the declarations made by a Marxist observer find common ground with those of the highly placed colonial administrator. Each, for different reasons, draws attention to the degradation of the peasantry, to the constant increase of a colonial proletariat, and to the antagonisms arising therefrom. With respect to French North Africa and French Black Africa, we call the reader's attention to two general studies that complement or reinforce each other, one by geographer J. Dresch and the other by High Commissioner R. Delavignette.[44] The movement of dispossession on the one hand ("730,000 rural families are totally deprived of land and must be regarded as indigent," J. Dresch writes), of "uprooting" the peasantry, and the correlative increase in the proletarian population, measured by the accelerated growth of urban centers, are analyzed within the framework of local conditions. Elsewhere the accent is on those characteristics peculiar to the colonial proletariat. "The natives of North Africa are becoming proletarians, but unskilled proletarians, colonial proletarians, judged equally good and equally unfit for any kind of employment, servants of an elementary and speculative economy, threatened by crises alternately produced by droughts and the uncertainty of sources of raw materials" (J. Dresch). The proletariat "is the vehicle for racism, imbuing the class struggle with a fierce degree of violence by linking it with a racial struggle," and, in the face of this threat there is a mounting temptation on the part of "certain Europeans" to keep the peasantry as long as possible in a primitive state (which they think) is one of tranquility" (R. Delavignette). Such observations indicate to what extent the colonial population, in its urban as well as its rural aspects, together with the colonial power, form a system, a whole. There is a need for any study dealing with one of these elements to take cognizance of the whole. Such observations also draw attention to the antagonisms existing in the very heart of this situation as a result of a stratification by classes that is achieved at the expense of traditional social structures, and to the conflicts that can be explained only within the framework of the colonial situation. In other portions of these studies we find that the concept of "crisis" is at the very root of these preoccupations ("a crisis that strikes a dislocated society and, little by little, destroys it," to quote J. Dresch). These observations enable us to discover—by singling out and even perhaps exaggerating the situation—this pathological aspect of colonial societies to which we have called attention.

Elsewhere in these same studies considerable attention is given to the role of the judicial and administrative apparatus charged with maintaining this domination. One critic, after having denounced its "arbitrariness," talks of the actions of an organization "that has separated peoples of the same ethnic origin and the same social structure and has thrown together dissimilar ethnic groups of different social structures. . . ." The arbitrary nature of the colonial boundaries and administrative divisions, between and within colonies, results in—or aims at—fragmenting important ethnic groups, breaking up political units of any significance, and artificially juxtaposing incompatible or antagonistic ethnic groups.[45] Certain recent actions on the part of colonial peoples can be explained as a reaction to such conditions as, for instance, the manifestation of a desire to restore former social groupings. In the case of Black West Africa alone, we can point out: the demands for unification among the Ewe (divided between French and British Togoland); the attempts to establish tribal federalism in the South Camerouns; the more or less explicit desire for regrouping evidenced by the African churches—known by the name of Kimbangism—occurring in the Ba-Kongo country (in the Belgian Congo and in the French Congo).

The maintenance or creation of this type of "balkanization" with its attendant rivalries or hostilities among ethnic groups, treated as pawns of administrative policies, have imposed on these groups, within the framework of the colonial situation, a particular history which no sociological analysis can afford to ignore. And a recent study dealing with the Malagasies indicates how this desire to weaken an ethnic group (for fear of encountering a national consciousness) is often accompanied by the desire to destroy the group's historical record (for fear of providing a

basis for "pride in being a malagasy and thus justifying a sense of nationalism," as the author puts it.[46] We again come upon the already mentioned question of ideologies. The effort to pervert a people's history
affects their collective memory, provoking an inevitable backlash, and
thus we see the possible importance of such facts in any effort to understand colonial peoples. . . .

In the light of these basic facts, it is easier to establish and evaluate
the contributions of sociology and social psychology as applied to colonial
society. In a recent work devoted to "colonies," E. A. Walcker calls our
attention to the fact that the former are made up of "plural societies." [47]
He demonstrates that the "colony" (as a global society) "is composed in
general of a number of groups more or less conscious of their existence,
often opposed to one another on the basis of color, and who seek to lead
different kinds of lives within the limits of a single political framework."
And Walcker adds: these "groups, who speak different languages, eat
different kinds of food, are often engaged in quite different occupations
in keeping with their laws or customs, wear different types of clothing . . . , live in different kinds of dwellings, cherish different traditions,
adore different gods, and maintain different ideas about good and evil.
Such societies are not communities." To these observations he adds a
useful element for our analysis when he writes, with regard to the *color
bar*, that it "reflects the world-wide problem of minorities in tropical
terms, with this difference that, almost everywhere in the colonies, the
lower class constitutes a majority."

These observations offer a point of departure. The interesting fact is
not the existence of pluralism (a characteristic of any global society),
but the indication of its specific features: the racial basis of "groups,"
their extreme dissimilarity, the antagonistic relationships this entails, and
the necessity imposed on them to co-exist "within the limits of a single
political framework." Also important is the attention given to the colonial
power as the dominant minority (minority in the numerical sense). In
a study that is primarily of political interest, H. Laurentie, for his part,
has defined the "colony" as a country in which a European minority has
imposed itself on an indigenous majority whose civilization and behavior
are different from the European; this European minority exercises its
influence over the native population with a force disproportionate to its
numbers. This force, if you will, is extremely contagious and, by its nature, causes social distortions." [48] This active "minority," with its distort-
ing influence, predicates its domination on the basis of an incontestable
material superiority (it imposes itself on nonindustrial societies), on a
legal status established in its own favor, and on a rationale with a more
or less racial foundation (for certain authors, like R. Maunier, the colonial phenomenon is primarily a "contact" between races). The European
minority reacts all the more aggressively as it becomes more firmly in-

trenched, and all the more hostile to racial intermingling as it feels itself threatened by demographic pressures from colored peoples. Thus in South Africa the white population "is beginning to view its situation as a minority problem whereas the Blacks view theirs as a colonial problem and one of trusteeship." [49] The same holds true in North Africa. This fact of "beginning to view its situation as a minority problem" is interesting. It reminds us clearly that this numerical minority is not a sociological minority, and risks becoming such only by an upheaval in the colonial situation.

Certain sociologists have already made this observation. L. Wirth, in defining a minority and establishing a typology of minorities, has insisted on this point: "the concept is not a matter of statistics," and he cites the example of Negroes living in the southern states of the United States who, in several states, are a numerical majority but nevertheless constitute a minority "by being socially, politically, and economically suppressed." He notes the situation created by the colonial expansion of European nations, establishing the Whites as "dominant groups" and colored peoples as "minorities." [50] The quantity of a group is not enough to make it a minority even though "it may have some effect on the laws and on its relations with the dominant group." The characteristic feature of a minority is a certain way of life in the larger society. Fundamentally, it implies the relationship of the dominated to the dominant. We have constantly encountered this kind of relationship in our previous analysis in depicting the colonial society as an "instrument" in the hands of the colonial power (the historical perspective), the relations between the exploiter and the exploited, the close parallel between "the metropole-colony and the capital-labor relationship" (the economic perspective), the "relations of domination and subjection" (political perspective). This description of a minority (in the sociological sense of the word), as applied to colonial populations, indicates rather clearly to what extent the latter must be considered in terms of the other groups comprising the colony—a necessity we have underscored on several occasions by pointing out the importance of examining the colonized population and the colonial power from reciprocal perspectives. But that does not indicate wherein a colonial population is distinguishable from other minorities (the American Negroes, for instance) who are placed in a different situation. The first step to be undertaken is to clarify the precise position of the "colony" in the larger society.

If we set forth in a very schematic fashion the various social groupings brought together by the colonial situation, classifying them, starting with the colonial power (the dominant group) and ending with the colonial population (the subject group), we find: (a) the colonial power, not including foreigners of the white race; (b) white "foreigners"; (c) the "coloured"—to use the English expression which is defined broadly;

(d) the colonized population, namely, all those whom the British call "the natives." We find a distinction and a hierarchy based, first of all, on criteria of race and nationality, implying as a sort of postulate the excellence of the white race, and more especially, of that fraction which is the colonial power (its supremacy is given as a fact of history, established by nature).

Of course this is only a rough outline which needs to be filled in. R. Delavignette has devoted a chapter of his book to a study of colonial society [51] (that is, its European component). He recalls certain general characteristics that define it: a society "of European origins, oriented to the homeland," constituting a numerical minority, middle class in character, given to the "notion of heroic superiority" (a doctrine partially explained by the greater percentage of males—and, for the most part, young men especially numerous during the early stages of colonization). Above all we are dealing with a society whose function it is to achieve political, economic, and spiritual domination. In the words of R. Delavignette, this society tends to instill in its members "the feudal spirit." The important fact is that this dominant group constitutes a numerical minority to a very large degree. There is a great imbalance between the mass of the "colonizers" and the mass of those "colonized." And there is a more or less persistent fear of seeing the hierarchy re-established on the sole basis of the size of the masses. This fear is revived in times of crisis and explains seemingly inexplicable reactions such as the "events" in Madagascar. And L. Wirth offers an oversimplified judgment when he declares, with respect to colonial situations, that "the dominant group can maintain its superior situation simply by utilizing its military and administrative machinery." So great is the disproportion between civilizations! [52] He underestimates thus a number of important aspects—the means by which the European population renders itself untouchable: (a) keeping contacts at a bare minimum (segregation); (b) offering the European as the model for emulation, while effectively blocking any means to that end (assimilation is held out as the basis for equality—because it is known full well that assimilation is either impossible of attainment or is restricted to a very limited few); (c) maintaining ideologies justifying the position of the dominant group; (d) employing political tactics designed to preserve the imbalance in favor of the colonial power (and its European homeland); (d) more or less deliberately transferring to certain groups the attitudes and feelings provoked by political and economic domination: thus, for example, to the Lebanese-Syrians in French West Africa (where they represent about one-fourth of the population designated administratively as "European and assimilated") or regularly to the Indians and "Coloured" in the Union of South Africa (at the time of the troubles in 1947, 1948, and 1949, the Africans attacked only Asians). To the extent that the distance between cultures is less, the relative size of the groups plays a greater role. Force alone no longer suffices to maintain control, and more indirect methods are resorted to—the element of "misunderstanding" comes into play (a fact that struck H. Brunschwig in his historical analysis and O. Mannoni in his psychoanalytical one). These indirect methods use most frequently, depending on individual circumstances, racial or religious differences of an antagonistic nature (as in India during the heyday of British colonialism). It must be remembered that the European colonial society is not perfectly homogeneous. It has its "factions," its "clans" (the "administrators," the "private sector," the "military," and the "missionaries," according to the terminology used in French territories). These groups are more or less self-contained, more or less competitive (antagonism between the administration and the missions, or between the administration and the commercial sector occurs frequently). Each group practices its own native policies (indeed, to such an extent, that certain English anthropologists have regarded each one of them as "an agent" provoking "cultural change"). They cause widely varied reactions. In other respects the European colonial society is essentially a closed one, more or less remote from the colonized population. But a policy of domination and prestige demands that it be closed and aloof, a situation that does not facilitate mutual understanding and appreciation, a situation that allows (or encourages) the easy recourse to "stereotypes." Isolated in the "colony," this society has also partially severed its connections with the homeland. R. Delavignette has made due note of this fact in writing about "the colonials": "Europeans in the colony, they become colonials at home . . . ," "they seek to channel their energies into a jealous sort of particularism. . . ."[53]

This particularism is seen first in relations with "foreigners" of the white race. The latter constitute a minority in the full sense of the word, numerically and sociologically. They may hold an important economic post, but they are nonetheless subject to administrative controls. They are suspect by virtue of their nationality. A distrust of foreign religious missions, for example, is common in colonial states. They are often cut off from the real colonial society. In French West Africa, for instance, the Lebanese-Syrians are not accepted in "good society" except for a very few who happen to be quite wealthy. To the extent that they are rejected, they regroup into ethnic minorities and enjoy closer relationships with the indigenous population. This greater degree of "familiarity" and their minority status explain the ambivalent reactions towards them on the part of the indigenous population (a certain intimacy tinged with scorn) —reactions to be noted with regard to the Lebanese-Syrians, the Greeks, and the Portuguese in French West Africa.[54] The resentments of colonial peoples can be directed against them with a certain impunity. They offer outlets for hostilities at minimal cost or risk. At the time of the troubles in certain French West African cities after 1945, it was only the Lebanese-Syrian minority that was affected. They are one of the most constantly threatened groups in this fragile edifice that is the colonial social structure.

Among the groups discriminated against by those in control, colored people (mixed breeds and colored foreigners) are held in the lowest esteem. For what amounts to an essentially racial reason, the colored man is rejected both by the colonial power and by the colonial peoples themselves. He has few contacts with either. His isolation becomes even greater (by means of discriminatory measures) reducing him to the role of an "exotic" community, as he achieves greater economic importance. The Indian problem in South Africa is thus explained by the fact that certain Indians "have become too rich and are surreptitiously acquiring positions held by the Whites." [55] Here we see clearly an overlapping of facts of a racial nature and facts of an economic nature. In the case of half-breeds (*métis*), the isolation is even more absolute because of their racial impurity—"a racial compromise." Only in rare instances do they succeed in regrouping and forming a viable society. The case of the "Bastards of Rehoboth" in former German Southwest Africa is especially famous. And a very strict isolation was imposed on this group. As A. Siegfried has noted with regard to the "Cape coloured," these half-breeds are forced "into the hands of a black race with which they do not want to be identified." They aim at becoming assimilated by the colonial society which remains closed to them (more or less, according to local circumstances), or which grants them a special status [56] conferring a legal recognition of their particular position. If they are "a racial compromise," they are in no sense "a social compromise." One can scarcely regard them as being a liaison between the colonial power and the colonized population. Their political alliance with the élite of a colonial society was never durable. Thus, for example, the *Conference of Non-Europeans,* created in 1927 in South Africa, which tried to unite in a common endeavor Coloureds, Indians, and Bantus, produced no effective results and was short-lived. The "Coloureds" are more in conflict than in agreement with the colonized population, because of their improved economic and social condition and because of the racial factor. They cannot pretend thus to leadership of the colonial peoples.

The colonial population presents two salient characteristics: its overwhelming numerical superiority [57] and the rigid control to which it is subjected. While a numerical majority, it is nevertheless a sociological minority. In the words of R. Maunier, "colonialism is a fact of power": it involves the loss of autonomy and "a legal or *de facto* trusteeship." [58] Each sector of the controlling society has as its function to maintain the domination of the colonial power in some specific domain (political, economic, and, almost always, spiritual). This domination by the European power is an absolute one owing to the absence of any advanced technology or material power other than sheer numbers. It finds its *de facto* expression in practices which, while not codified into laws, incur sharp and immediate disapproval if they are not respected, whereas other practices are given legal sanction. As we have already mentioned several times, colonial domination is based on an idealogy, on a system of pseudo-justifications and rationalizations. It has a racist foundation, more or less acknowledged, more or less obvious. A colonial people is subjected to the pressures of every group comprising the colony. All exert their pre-eminence in some area with the result that a colonial people is made to feel all the more keenly its subordinate status. The agencies of the colonial power regard the colony itself as essentially a productive source of wealth (whereas the colonial people keep only a very small part of that wealth despite their greater numbers). This fact conditions in part the relations it maintains with the other groups (who derive from the colony their economic advantages). These relations, however, are not simple. They are not merely the relationship of the exploiter to the exploited, of the dominant to the dominated. They are not that simple because of the lack of unity among colonial peoples themselves and, above all, because of the extremely heterogeneous character of the culture (or rather, the cultures) which are to be found in the society.

The colonial population is divided ethnically. The divisions are rooted in the society's own history but are utilized by the colonial power (we recall the utility of that old principle: "Divide and rule"), and these divisions are complicated by the arbitrary colonial "divisions" and by administrative "splitting up" of tribes within the colony. These ethnic divisions not only orient the relations of each ethnic group with the colonial power [for example, the peoples who acted as "intermediaries" during the period of African slave trade and the establishment of trading settlements (*comptoirs*) tried to transfer their role from the economic to the political plane and became "militant" minorities], but these divisions likewise orient their attitude with respect to the culture introduced by the colonial power (some ethnic groups are more "assimilationist" or more "traditionalist" than certain neighboring groups, a reaction, in part at least, to the attitudes adopted by the latter). The colonial population is spiritually divided. Spiritual divisions may have preceded European colonization and be associated notably with the waves of Islamic conquest. But we are familiar with the tactics adopted by European colonial powers. The strategy of English domination in India is well known. In many places colonialism brought about religious confusion by opposing Christianity to traditional religions, while Christian churches presented differences among themselves. We mention in this connection an African of Brazzaville who recalled "this state of affairs whose only effect is to create a lamentable confusion in the individual's moral and psychological development" and who added: "The Black African, whoever he is, has the rudiments of a religion. To deprive him of them by introducing atheism or a confusion of religious doctrines can only result in completely unhinging him." [59] The author almost went so far as to ask the "colonizer" to impose unity! This serves to illustrate the extent to which these new divisions, added to the old ones, have had the most painful effects on certain groups. But colonization has brought other divisions we may designate as social in nature, products of administrative and economic action and of educational policies: the separation of city dwellers from rural groups,[60] the separation of proletariat from bourgeoisie, of the "élites" (or "évolués"—groups who have evolved, according to the usual expression) from the masses of the population,[61] and that between generations. We have touched on all these factors and indicated their importance in various parts of our analysis. Each of these fragmented groups participates differently in the world society. The contact between races and civilizations, which colonization has brought about, has neither the same meaning nor the same consequences for any one of them. The contact must be studied in the light of this diversity (for which it is partly responsible in the first place, but which is now in turn partly influenced by the very conditions it helped bring about).

Conditions among the colonial population differ greatly from those prevailing in the European colonial society. In race and culture, the differences are unmistakable. They are reflected in a language that opposes "the primitive man" to the civilized man, the pagan to the Christian, a technically-advanced society to a backward society. More than the colonial situation, it is this fact that stands out clearly—it is the contact between heterogeneous civilizations that has attracted the attention of anthropologists in recent decades, and, above all, the shock that it has produced, "the clash of cultures" noted by English authors. We have shown elsewhere how, starting with this observation, new studies have developed called *acculturation* in the United States and *culture contact* in England, with the aim of determining the most dynamic aspects of cultures placed in confrontation and of discovering, if possible, the essential features of the whole of cultural reality. The stages of the "contact" have been set forth in a more or less simplistic and arbitrary manner: the phases of conflict, adjustment, syncretism, assimilation (or a counter-acculturation reaction) to be found in the writings of North American anthropologists; phases of opposition, of imitation (from "top to bottom" and from "bottom to top") and of aggregation as analyzed by R. Maunier in his *Sociologie Coloniale;* the appearance of a new culture ("the *tertium quid* of contact"), different from those placed in confrontation, according to B. Malinowski and others. We will not dwell at this point on all the criticisms such writings and doctrines call for. We call attention to these works only to illustrate, on the one hand, that the

relations between colonial peoples and colonial powers cannot be envisaged solely in the economic and political terms emphasized by these
authors who are *engagés*. And we do so, on the other hand, to remind the
reader that the contact between civilizations takes place at the moment
of a very special situation, the colonial situation, which becomes transformed historically—that the contact is made by means of social groups
(and not among cultures existing in the form of independent realities)
whose reactions are conditioned internally (according to the type of
group affected) and also externally. In this respect, a precise typology
of the groupings comprising this global society, the colony, is at the basis
of any accurate and fairly comprehensive investigation. We have frequently insisted on the necessity for such by pointing out how the sociologist was obliged to view the colonial population and the European
population in reciprocal fashions. Similarly, we have suggested in an
earlier study the special kind of evolution that the colonial situation imposes on sociocultural facts. And we have shown notably how the "crises"
created by colonialism have in part oriented this evolution.

Most studies dealing with present-day colonial societies stress the
state of crisis affecting them and "the arduous and complex problems"
they pose. To a greater or lesser degree, they are regarded as sick societies,[62] which is true to the extent that the colonial power opposes any
genuine solutions. For it is an apparent fact that, among colonial peoples,
the quest for norms coincides with the quest for autonomy. And this
fact imposes on the sociologist an analytical method that is in some
measure clinical. We have indicated, in the previously mentioned study,
how an approach to the question of colonial societies, concentrating on
their specific crises, constitutes "an unexcelled standpoint for analysis,"
"the only point at which one can grasp *the evolution of indigenous social
structures placed in the colonial situation.*"[63] Such crises force reexami-
nation of the society as a whole, its institutions as well as its component
groups and symbols; the social dislocations provide opportunities for the
analyst to penetrate and explore from within, and not merely arrive at
some abstract notions of the phenomena arising from the contact between
a colonial power and a colonial people. The analyst will be better able
to understand the latter in its traditional forms by discovering certain
systems and weaknesses (as we shall indicate in the case of the Fang of
Gabon, a people among whom the colonial situation encouraged certain
ruptures already inherent in its previous social structure), or certain un-
shakeable structures and collective representations (thus, for example, a
study of the religious crisis and of "Negro churches" characteristic of
Bantu Africa would reveal what remains of traditional religions despite
all the other pressures brought to bear—the irreducible element). Each
crisis, affecting the global society as a whole, constitutes a point of insight
into that society and the relationships it implies.[64] Looking at such crises

permits of that concrete and comprehensive approach already recommended by Marcel Mauss. And to complete the illustration just given, we recall a recent thesis devoted to "the Negro churches" and the activities of Bantu prophets (in South Africa) in which the author, B. G. M. Sundkler shows that the problems posed are not only of a religious nature, but raise the question of Bantu reactions as a whole to White domination, and that the study of these "churches" leads to a study of all the social problems characterizing the Union of South Africa.[65]

At first glance these crises are noteworthy for the radical changes in, or the outright disappearance of, certain institutions and certain groups. But a sociological analysis cannot limit itself to these aspects of the social picture—its institutional or structural forms—and merely note the changes and disappearances, locating new social structures and describing them. It is indispensable to go beyond these considerations and to reach for "the forms of sociability," to borrow the expression of Georges Gurvitch.[66] For it seems quite apparent that certain "ways of forming links," certain social ties persist, even when the structures within which they operate are radically altered or destroyed, while at the same time new ties appear as a result of the colonial situation and the social conjunctures it creates. These social ties can co-exist and impart to the innovations conceived by the colonial society those characteristics that are both traditionalist and modernist, that peculiar state of ambiguity noted by several observers.

We have frequently alluded to the importance of race relations, the racial basis for social groupings, to the racial coloration of political and economic facts (current literature confuses or associates racism and colonialism) in the framework of the colonial situation. And various authors insist on the interracial nature of "human relationships in overseas territories," on the fact that, beneath "the political or economic causes still dividing the white race and the colored peoples, there is almost always a racial motive." These authors insist that the society remains "interracial" even when national independence is acquired.[67] We have several times indicated that colonial anthropologists have paid little attention to these racial facts and problems and given little room to them in their research projects. This is explained by the greater attention given to cultures rather than to societies and can be attributed to the more or less conscious desire on the part of these anthropologists to avoid questioning the very foundations (and ideology) of the society to which they belong, the society of the colonial power.[68]

We find just the reverse situation among anthropological studies carried out in the U.S.A. and in Brazil. These are largely devoted to the subject of race relations and racial prejudices, especially to the relations between Whites and Negroes. These facts cannot be brushed aside because the vast differences in civilization, language, religion, and customs (so conspicuous in the colonial situation) do not exist to any comparable degree in America (or Brazil) and cannot therefore serve to mask or complicate the true facts of the matter. The Negro's inferior status and a justification for racial prejudice cannot be made to appear rooted in nature, precisely because cultural differences are virtually imperceptible and a common identity of rights has been affirmed (which explains, among other reasons, why American society appears "confused, contradictory, and paradoxical," to quote Gunnar Myrdal [69] . . .), because these facts represent what remains to be liquidated from a colonial past. And it was precisely at the moment of liquidation that they gave rise to violent conflicts (in the United States, it was during the period called the Reconstruction). At times such studies emphasize the economic implications and, at other times, the sexual implications of various forms of racial behavior. They show the connection between racial reactions and cultural reactions, as R. Bastide [70] has clearly indicated. We refer in particular to his analysis of Negro messianism in the United States, which shows how closely messianism is linked to racial conflicts and to a "psychology of resentment." These find their expression in a variety of behavior patterns corresponding to the circumstances producing them.

We have risked offering this hasty reminder since it reveals ties and relationships that cannot be disregarded, and it illustrates the utter impossibility of separating the study of cultural contacts from that of racial contacts, and the impossibility of contemplating such studies, in the case of colonial peoples, without referring to the colonial situations themselves. . . .

We have just considered certain facts which Anglo-American writers place under the headings of "the clash of civilizations" or "the clash of races," but we have shown that, in the case of colonial peoples, these "clashes" (or "contacts") occur under very special circumstances. To these collective circumstances we have given the name *colonial situation*. The latter may be defined by singling out and retaining the most general and most obvious of these conditions: (1) the domination imposed by a foreign minority, racially (or ethnically) and culturally different, acting in the name of a racial (or ethnic) and cultural superiority dogmatically affirmed, and imposing itself on an indigenous population constituting a numerical majority but inferior to the dominant group from a material point of view; (2) this domination linking radically different civilizations into some form of relationship; (3) a mechanized, industrialized society with a powerful economy, a fast tempo of life, and a Christian background, imposing itself on a nonindustrialized, "backward" society in which the pace of living is much slower and religious institutions are most definitely "non-Christian"; (4) the fundamentally antagonistic character of the relationship between these two societies resulting from the subservient role to which the colonial people are subjected as "instruments" of the colonial power; (5) the need, in maintaining this domination, not only to resort to "force," but also to a system of pseudo-justifications and stereotyped behaviors, etc. But this enumeration by itself is inadequate. With the help of the particular "views" offered by each discipline, we have preferred to grasp the colonial situation as a whole, and as a system. We have set forth the elements in terms of which any specific situation can be described and understood and have shown how these elements are interrelated, with the result that any analysis of a part is necessarily distorted. This oneness raises doubts about the reality of the "groups" comprising "the global society" (the colony) as collective representations peculiar to each of these groups. This sense of totality is felt at all levels of social reality. But owing to the heterogeneous character of the groups, of the cultural "models," of the various representations confronting each other, and owing to the changes that occur in the system responsible for maintaining artificially the conditions of domination and subordination, the colonial situation becomes greatly modified, and at a rapid pace. This fact requires that the situation be studied in an historical manner, that the dates be specified.

The colonial population, as it interests the anthropologist (who calls it "primitive" or "backward," etc.), participates in the colonial situation to a greater or lesser degree, depending on its size, its economic potential, its cultural conservatism, etc. It is one of the groupings that make up "the colony." And he is misguided who thinks that a present-day study of this society can be made without taking into account this dual reality, "the colony," a global society within which the study must situate itself, and the colonial situation created by "the colony." This is especially true of any study whose avowed purpose is to set forth the facts resulting from "the contact" and the phenomena or processes of evolution. Whenever a study proceeds in a unilateral fashion and reveals these facts only in terms of a traditional premise (or a "primitive" concept), it can do little more than enumerate and classify them. And the same is true of investigations that limit themselves to examining "the contact" between "institutions" of the same nature (as B. Malinowski has recommended). The fact is that "modernist" aspects (once they are located) become intelligible only with respect to the colonial situation. Certain English anthropologists (Fortes, Gluckman) are moving in the direction of recognizing this fact by taking the view that, in the case of colonial black Africa, both the white and black societies participate integrally in a single whole and by thereby moving toward the concept of "situation." [71] Similarly, R. Bastide has noted the importance of "the situation in which the process occurs" in his studies concerned with the inter-penetration of cultures. We have tried to go beyond the framework of these simple indications by showing how a colonial situation can be "approached" and what the situation implies. We have tried to make clear that any current sociological problem regarding colonial peoples can only be studied in the light of this totality. The notion of "situation" is not the exclusive property of existentialist philosophers. It has forced itself on various specialists in the social sciences, whether they use it under the name of "social situation," as H. Wallon does, or in the expression "particular social conjuncture," as G. Gurvitch has done. The idea of "a total social phenomenon," as elaborated by Mauss, laid the basis for thinking in such terms.[72]

It is rather significant that many anthropologists, operating within the structure of a colonial society and preoccupied with its current aspects and problems, have avoided (unconsciously, in most cases) describing the concrete situation applicable to such a society. Out of a more or less conscious fear of having to take into consideration a specific kind of "system" and society: the society of the colonial power to which they themselves belong. They have dealt with less compromising systems—"western civilization" and "primitive cultures," or else have confined themselves to limited problems for which they have proposed solutions of a limited nature. And it is because of a refusal to accept this attitude, which they regard as inevitable and profitable only to the colonial power, that certain anthropologists decline to treat their discipline as "an applied" science.[73] We are confronted here with a fact that belongs in the framework of critical judgment in the domain of human sciences and one which suggests the extensive critical preparation incumbent upon anyone who contemplates offering an analysis of colonial societies.

We have frequently noted the somewhat pathological character of colonial societies, the crises marking the stages of the so-called process of "evolution"—crises that do not correspond to necessary phases of this process, yet which have nevertheless specific characteristics in relation to the type of colonial society under consideration and the nature of the colonial society (the Islamized Africans do not react like "animist" Africans or pseudo-Christians; African societies of the same type do not react in the same manner to "the French presence" and "the British presence," etc.) By focusing clearly on those facts that characterize a society subjected to colonial domination, and on those facts that characterize the colonial situation in its particular aspects, these "crises" enable a sociologist to achieve a comprehensive analysis since they constitute the only points of reference from which one can grasp, in a global sense, the transformations occurring among a colonial people under the influence and actions of the colonial power. They are conducive to reaching over-all views, an awareness of essential ties and relationships. They allow one to avoid fragmentary analyses (changes in the economic life, in the political life, etc.) which are both incomplete and artificial and can only lead to an academic sort of description and classification. We have already indicated that these "crises" constitute so many vantage points from which to view not only the phenomena of contact, but also the colonized society in all its traditional aspects. We must add that they also permit in this manner an analysis which takes into account, simultaneously, "the external milieu" and "the internal milieu"—and takes them into account in terms of existing conditions and relationships, in terms of actual life experiences.

We may be criticized for having resorted, in a more or less explicit manner, to the dangerous notion of the pathological and be asked to define the criteria characteristic of colonial crises. Our answer is to refer the critic to all the passages in this study which set forth the antagonistic aspects of relations between a colonial people and a colonial power, between a native culture and an imported culture—aspects tied to the relationships between domination and subjection, to the heterogeneous nature of societies and cultures in contact with each other—and in which the critic will find a suggestion as to the way in which these conflicts are felt by the individuals involved. The history of colonial societies reveals periods during which conflicts are merely latent, when a temporary equilibrium or adjustment has been achieved, and periods during which conflicts rise to the surface and are apparent on one level or the other, according to circumstances (religious, political, and economic). But conflicts expose at the same time the totality of relationships between colonial peoples and colonial powers and between the cultures of each of them (as we have reminded the reader in the case of Negro churches in Bantu Africa), moments when the antagonism and the gulf between a colonial people and a colonial power are at their maximum and are experienced by the colonial rulers as a challenge to established order, but by the colonial peoples as an effort to regain their autonomy. At each of these moments, which can be clearly delineated throughout the history of a colonial people, the latter present an unmistakable state of crisis, and it is precisely at such moments we can study the colonial society in terms of the concrete colonial situation. Paris.

(Translated from the French by Robert A. Wagoner, State University of New York Maritime College.)

NOTES

1. R. Kennedy, "The Colonial Crisis and the Future," in R. Linton, ed., *The Science of Man in the World Crisis*, 1945, p. 307.

2. O. Mannoni, *Psychologie de la Colonisation*, Editions du Seuil, 1950. This author did not however originate the expression which is found with different connotations in previous works, notably, in studies by the American sociologist, L. Wirth, devoted to the "typology of minorities." (This book is translated in English as *Prospero and Caliban*—Ed. note.)

3. We refer the reader to our summary of O. Mannoni's work published in the *Cahiers Internationaux de Sociologie*, vol. IX, 1950, p. 183 to 186.

4. L. Joubert, "Le Fait colonial et ses prolongements," *Le Monde non-chrétien*, 15, 1950.

5. Ch.-A. Julien, "Impéralisme économique et impéralisme colonial," in *Fin de l'ère coloniale*, Paris, 1948.

6. Cf. R. Kennedy, *op. cit.*, pp. 308–309, and R. Grousset, "Colonisations," in *Fin de l'ère coloniale*.

7. Quotation appears in the excellent book by H. Brunschwig, *La Colonisation française*, Calman-Lévy, 1949.

8. For example, the displacements carried out on behalf of the *Office du Niger* which gave rise to the most heated controversy; see P. Herrart's pamphlet, *Le Chancre du Niger*, with a preface by André Gide, Gallimard, 1939.

9. E. Chancelé, "La Question coloniale," *Critique*, no. 35, 1949.

10. Cf. L. Joubert, *op. cit.*, part II.

11. Cf. L. P. Mair, "The Study of Culture Contact as a Practical Problem," *Africa*, VII, 4, 1934.

12. Cf. J. Harmand, *Domination et Colonisation*, Flammarion, 1910, as a "classic" example of a juridical type of justification.

13. Quoted from H. Brunschwig, *op. cit.*, p. 64.

14. *Ibid.*, p. 265.

15. R. Kennedy, *op. cit.*, pp. 312–318.

16. G. Balandier, "Aspects de l'évolution sociale chez les Fang du Gabon," *Cahiers Internationaux de Sociologie*, vol. IX, 1950, p. 82.

17. R. Montagne, "Le Bilan de l'oeuvre européenne au-delà des mers," in *Peuples d'Outre-Mer et Civilisation Occidentale*, Semaines Sociales de France, 1948.

18. G. Balandier, *op. cit.*, p. 78.

19. Ch.-A. Julien, *Histoire de l'Afrique*, Collection *Que sais-je?*, Presses Universitaires de France, 1944, p. 123.

20. R. Montagne, *op. cit.*, p. 49.

21. Cf. especially Pham Nhuam, "Appel," in *Que pensent les étudiants coloniaux*, Le Semeur, Dec. 1947, Jan. 1948.

22. Ch.-A. Julien, "Impérialisme économique et impérialisme colonial," *op. cit.*, p. 25.

23. P. Leroy-Beaulieu, *De la colonisation chez les peuples modernes*, 1874, 1st edition; J. Ferry, preface to *Le Tonkin et la Mère-Patrie*, 1890.

24. Cf. A. Conant, *The Economic Basis of Imperialism*, 1898, and J. A. Hobson, *Imperialism, A Study*, 1902 (whose worth was recognized by Lenin), both works quoted by Ch.-A. Julien, *op. cit.*

25. Ch.-A. Julien, *op. cit.*, p. 29. Cf. on the subject of Africa, S. H. Frankel, *Capital Investments in Africa*, 1936.

26. J. Guitton, "Crises et valeurs permanentes de la Civilisation occidentales," in *Peuples d'Outre-Mer et Civilisation Occidentale*, p. 61.

27. P. Reuter, "Deux formes actuelles de l'Impérialisme colonial: protectorat économique et pénétration communiste," in *Peuples d'Outre-Mer . . . .*, p. 142.

28. J. Stalin, *Le Marxisme et la question nationale et coloniale,* éd. française, Editions Sociales, 1949, p. 179 and 247.

29. *The African Morning Post,* June 2, 1945, quoted in *Univers,* "L'Avenir de la colonisation," October 1945.

30. B. Malinowski, *The Dynamics of Culture Change,* Yale University Press, 1945.

31. Cf. the excellent analysis of M. Gluckman, "Malinowski's 'Functional' Analysis of Social Change," *Africa,* XVII, April 2, 1947.

32. R. Kennedy, *op. cit.,* pp. 309–311.

33. Cf. L. Durand-Reville, "Le Problème de l'industrialisation des territoires d'Outre-Mer," *Le Monde non-chrétien,* 13, Jan.–Mar. 1959, where this aspect is suggested and in which the author, a member of the French parliament from Gabon, sets forth the changes made necessary by the last war as well as present-day needs.

34. For facts concerning French Africa we refer the reader to the excellent studies of the geographer, Jean Dresch.

35. Cf. especially Ch. Robequain, *L'Evolution économique de l'Indo-chine française,* Paris, 1940, and P. Gourou, *L'Utilisation du sol en Indochine française* and *Les Pays Tropicaux,* Paris, 1948.

36. For a comprehensive study of this phenomenon see *Land Tenure in the Colonies,* V. Liversage, 1945; quoted by P. Naville, *La Guerre du Viet-Nam,* Paris, 1949.

37. Cf. Ch. Robequain, *op. cit.*

38. P. Naville, *op. cit.,* Paris, 1949; cf. especially, "La Politique française en Cochinchine," "La Bourgeoisie cochinchinoise," "Les Paysans annamites et la Révolution," "Le Développement de la classe ouvrière et de l'industrie."

39. J. Borde, "Le Problème ethnique dans l'Union Sud-Africaine," *Cahiers d'Outre-Mer,* no. 12, 1950; an excellent over-all view and bibliography.

40. Cf. W. G. Ballinger, *Race and Economics in South Africa,* 1934.

41. For South Africa we mention I. Schapera, M. Hunter; for East Africa, L. P. Mair, Audrey Richards, M. Read, M. Gluckman; for West Africa, M. Fortes, D. Forde, K. L. Little. We regard their works as the most important.

42. Cf. M. Read, *Native Standards of Living and African Culture-Change,* London, 1938.

43. K. L. Little, "Social Change and Social Class in the Sierra-Leone Protectorate," *American Journal of Sociology,* 54, July 1948. An important study.

44. J. Dresch, "La Prolétarisation des masses indigènes en Afrique du Nord," in *Fin de l'ère coloniale, op. cit.,* p. 57–69, and R. Delavignette, "Les Problèmes du travail: Paysannerie et Prolétariat," in *Peuples d'Outre-Mer et Civilisation Occidentale,* p. 273–291.

45. G. D'Arboussier, "Les Problèmes de la culture," *Afrique Noire,* special edition of *Europe,* May–June 1949.

46. O. Hatzfeld, "Les Peuples heureux ont une histoire. Etude malgache," *Cahiers du monde non-chrétien,* 16, 1950.

47. *Les Colonies, passé et avenir,* chapter entitled: "Colonies tropicales et sociétés plurales."

48. H. Laurentie, "Notes sur une philosophie de la politique coloniale française," in a special issue of *Renaissances*, Oct. 1944.

49. J. Borde, "Le Problème ethnique dans l'Union Sud-Africaine," *op. cit.*, p. 320.

50. L. Wirth, "The Problem of Minority Groups," in *The Science of Man in the World Crisis*, pp. 347–372. By the same author on this subject: *The Present Position of Minorities in the United States.*

51. *Les Vrais chefs de l'Empire*, a new edition under the title *Service Africain*, 1946; chapt. II, "La Société coloniale." [Translated as *Freedom and Authority in French West Africa*, 1950]

52. *Op. cit.*, p. 353.

53. *Op. cit.*, p. 41.

54. There is a significant proverb: "God created the White Man, then the Black Man, and finally the Portuguese." And also: "There are three kinds of men: Whites, Blacks, and Portuguese" (a proverb in the Belgian Congo).

55. Cf. A. Siegfried, *Afrique du Sud*, Armand Colin, 1949, p. 75. Also, *Handbook on Race Relations in South Africa*, E. Hellmann, 1949, and J. Borde, *op. cit.*, p. 339–340.

56. As was attempted before 1939 in territories under French control: in French West Africa (1930), in Madagascar (1934), in French Equatorial Africa (1936), and in Indo-China (1938).

57. For Black Africa alone, R. Delavignette gave, in 1939, the following proportions in respect to the population designated as European: the Union of South Africa (25.0%, former German Southwest Africa, 10.0%), Rhodesia (4.5%), Angola (1.0%), Kenya (0.5%), Belgian Congo (0.2%), French West Africa and French Equatorial Africa (0.1%); *op. cit.*, p. 36. Concerning the latter territories, since 1945 the increase in European population has been important.

58. Cf. R. Maunier, *Sociologie Coloniale*, p. 19, 30, 33.

59. J.-R. Ayouné, "Occidentalisme et Africanisme," in *Renaissances*, special edition, October 1944, p. 204.

60. We call attention to Brazzaville where the African population rose from 3,800 inhabitants in 1912 to 75,000 in 1950; that is more than one-tenth of the population of the Central Congo.

61. Cf. Dr. L. Aujoulat, "Elites et masses en pays d'Outre-Mer" in *Peuples d'Outre-Mer et Civilisation Occidentale*, *op. cit.*, p. 233–272.

62. Cf. L. Achille, "Rapports humains en Pays d'Outre-Mer" in *Peuples d'Outre-Mer et Civilisation Occidentale*, *op. cit.*

63. G. Balandier, "Aspects de l'Evolution sociale chez les Fang du Gabon; I. Les implications de la situation coloniale," *op. cit.*

64. Monica Hunter had come close to making this observation. She wrote: "The study of culture contact makes very clear that society is a unity, and when one aspect is modified, the whole is affected."; *Reaction to Conquest*, p. 552. She was content simply to make this observation and did not seek to explore its implications or discover its consequences in a methodical manner.

65. B. G. M. Sundkler, *Bantu Prophets in South Africa*, London, 1948.

66. Cf. *La Vocation Actuelle de la Sociologie*, in particular, pp. 98–108.

The definition of sociology and its essential distinctions are set forth. Chapters III and IV are devoted to microsociology, whose true founder is Georges Gurvitch.

67. Cf. L. Achille, *op. cit.*, pp. 211–215.

68. A carefully reasoned and concise critical analysis was given by M. Leiris in a lecture entitled "l'Ethnographe devant le colonialisme" in 1950, later published in *Les Temps Modernes*.

69. Gunnar Myrdal, *An American Dilemma*, New York, 1944.

70. Cf. especially R. Bastide, *Sociologie et Psychanalyse*, Chapt. XI: "Le Heurt des Races, des Civilisations et la Psychanalyse," Paris, P.U.F., 1950.

71. Cf. M. Gluckman, "Analysis of a Social Situation in Modern Zululand," in *Bantu Studies*, vol. XIV, 1940; and Malinowski's controversy on this subject in *The Dynamics of Culture Change*, p. 14 ff.

72. G. Gurvitch, moreover, associates the three terms in his "Prefatory Remarks" written for the section entitled "Psychologie Collective" for *L'Année Sociologique*, 3rd series, 1948–1949. Likewise, a psychiatrist like Karen Horney emphasizes the fact that all neuroses, individual or collective, can be explained by a process involving *all* personal and socio-cultural factors; cf. Dr. Karen Horney, *The Neurotic Personality of Our Time*, New York, 1937.

73. Cf. F. M. Keesing, "Applied Anthropology in Colonial Administration," in R. Linton, ed., *op. cit.*

Jawaharlal Nehru

THE DISCOVERY OF INDIA (1946)

THE IDEOLOGY OF EMPIRE

The New Caste

"Our writing of India's history is perhaps resented more than any-thing else we have done"—so writes an Englishman well acquainted with India and her history. It is difficult to say what Indians have resented most in the record of British rule in India; the list is long and varied. But it is true that British accounts of India's history, more especially of what is called the British period, are bitterly resented. History is almost always written by the victors and conquerors and gives their view. Or, at any rate, the victors' version is given prominence and holds the field. Very probably all the early records we have of the Aryans in India, their epics and traditions, glorify the Aryans and are unfair to the people of the country whom they subdued. No individual can wholly rid himself of his racial outlook and cultural limitations, and when there is conflict between races and countries even an attempt at impartiality is considered a betrayal of one's own people. War, which is an extreme example of this conflict, results in a deliberate throwing overboard of all fairness and impartiality so far as the enemy nation is concerned; the mind coarsens and becomes closed to almost all avenues of approach except one. The overpowering need of the moment is to justify one's own actions and condemn and blacken those of the enemy. Truth hides somewhere at the bottom of the deepest well, and falsehood, naked and unashamed, reigns almost supreme.

Even when actual war is not being waged there are often potential

SOURCE. Jawaharlal Nehru, *The Discovery of India*, New York: The John Day Company, 1946, from Chapter VII, Part I. Copyright © 1946 by The John Day Company. Reprinted by permission of The John Day Company, Inc., publisher.

war and conflicts between rival countries and interests. In a country dominated by an alien power, that conflict is inherent and continuous and affects and perverts people's thoughts and actions; the war mentality is never wholly absent. In the old days when war and its consequences, brutality and conquest and enslavement of a people, were accepted as belonging to the natural order of events, there was no particular need to cover them or justify them from some other point of view. With the growth of higher standards the need for justification has arisen, and this leads to a perversion of facts, sometimes deliberate, often unconscious. Thus hypocrisy pays its tribute to virtue and a false and sickening piety allies itself to evil deeds.

In any country, and especially in a huge country like India with its complicated history and mixed culture, it is always possible to find facts and trends to justify a particular thesis, and then this becomes the accepted basis for a new argument. America, it is said, is a land of contradictions, in spite of its standardization and uniformity. How much more then must India be full of contradictions and incongruities. We shall find there, as elsewhere, what we seek, and on this preconceived basis we can build up a structure of belief and opinion. And yet that structure will have untrue foundations and will give a false picture of reality.

Recent Indian history—that is, the history of the British period—is so connected with present-day happenings that the passions and prejudices of today powerfully influence our interpretation of it. Englishmen and Indians are both likely to err, though their errors will lie in opposite directions. Far the greater part of the records and papers out of which history takes shape and is written come from British sources and inevitably represents the British point of view. The very circumstances of defeat and disruption prevented the Indian side of the story from being properly recorded, and many of the records that existed suffered destruction during the great revolt of 1857. The papers that survived were hidden away in family archives and could not be published for fear of consequences. They remained dispersed, little known, and many perished in the manuscript stage from the incursions of termites and other insects which abound in this country. At a later stage when some of these papers were discovered, they threw a new light on many historical incidents. Even British-written Indian history had to be somewhat modified, and the Indian conception, often very different from the British, took shape. Behind this conception lay also a mass of tradition and memories, not of the remote past but of a period when our grandfathers and great-grandfathers were the living witnesses, and often the victims, of events. As history this tradition may have little value, but it is important as it enables us to understand the background of the Indian mind today. The villain of the British in India is often a hero to Indians, and those whom the British have delighted to honor and reward are often traitors and Quislings in the eyes of the great majority of the Indian people. That taint clings to their descendants.

The history of the American revolution has been differently written by Englishmen and Americans, and even today when old passions have subsided and there is friendship between the two peoples, each version is resented by the other party. In our own day Lenin was a monster and a brigand to many English statesmen of high repute; yet millions have considered him as a savior and the greatest man of the age. These comparisons will give us some faint idea of the resentment felt by Indians at being forced to study in their schools and colleges so-called histories which disparage India's past in every way, vilify those whose memory they cherish and honor, and glorify the achievements of British rule in India.

Gopal Krishna Gokhale once wrote in his gently ironical way of the inscrutable wisdom of Providence which had ordained the British connection for India. Whether it was due to this inscrutable wisdom or some process of historic destiny or just chance, the coming of the British to India brought two very different races together. Or at any rate, it should have brought them together, but as it happened they seldom approached each other and their contacts were indirect. English literature and English political thought influenced a tiny fringe of those who had learned English. But this political thought, though dynamic in its context, had no reality in India then. The British who came to India were not political or social revolutionaries; they were conservatives representing the most reactionary social class in England, and England was in some ways one of the most conservative countries of Europe.

The impact of Western culture on India was the impact of a dynamic society, of a "modern" consciousness, on a static society wedded to medieval habits of thought, which, however sophisticated and advanced in its own way, could not progress because of its inherent limitations. And yet, curiously enough, the agents of this historic process were not only wholly unconscious of their mission in India but, as a class, actually represented no such process. In England their class fought this historic process, but the forces opposed to them were too strong for them and could not be held back. In India they had a free field and were successful in applying the brakes to that very change and progress which, in the larger context, they represented. They encouraged and consolidated the position of the socially reactionary groups in India, and opposed all those who worked for political and social change. If change came, it was in spite of them or as an incidental and unexpected consequence of their other activities. The introduction of the steam engine and the railway was a big step toward a change of the medieval structure, but it was intended to consolidate their rule and facilitate the exploitation, for their own benefit, of the interior of the country. This contradiction between the deliberate policy of the British authorities in India and some of its unintended consequences produces a certain confusion and masks that policy itself. Change came to India because of this impact of the West, but it came almost in spite of the British in India. They succeeded in slowing down the pace of that change to such an extent that even today the transition is very far from complete.

The feudal landlords and their kind who came from England to rule over India had the landlord's view of the world. To them India was a vast estate belonging to the East India Company, and the landlord was the best and the natural representative of his estate and his tenants. That view continued even after the East India Company handed over its estate of India to the British crown, being paid very handsome compensation at India's cost. (Thus began the public debt of India. It was India's purchase money, paid by India.) The British government of India then became the landlords (or landlords' agents). For all practical purposes they considered themselves "India," just as the Duke of Devonshire might be considered "Devonshire" by his peers. The millions of people who lived and functioned in India were just some kind of landlord's tenants who had to pay their rents and cesses and to keep their place in the natural feudal order. For them a challenge to that order was an offense against the very moral basis of the universe and a denial of a divine dispensation.

This somewhat metaphysical conception of British rule in India has not changed fundamentally, though it is expressed differently now. The old method of obvious rack-renting gave place to more subtle and devious devices. It was admitted that the landlord should be benevolent toward his tenantry and should seek to advance their interests. It was even agreed that some of the more loyal and faithful among the tenants should be promoted to the estate office and share in a subordinate way in the administration. But no challenge to the system of landlordism could be tolerated. The estate must continue to function as it used to, even when it changed hands. When pressure of events made some change inevitable, it was stipulated that all the faithful employees in the estate office should continue, all the old and new friends, followers, and dependents of the landlord should be provided for, the old pensioners should continue to draw their pensions, the old landlord himself should now function as a benevolent patron and adviser of the estate, and thus all attempts to bring about essential changes should be frustrated.

This sense of identifying India with their own interests was strongest in the higher administrative services, which were entirely British. In later years these developed in that close and well-knit corporation called the Indian Civil Service, "the world's most tenacious trade union," as it has been called by an English writer. They ran India, they were India, and anything that was harmful to their interests must of necessity be injurious to India. From the Indian Civil Service and the kind of history and record of current events that was placed before them, this conception spread in varying degrees to the different strata of the British people. The ruling class naturally shared it in full measure, but even the worker and the farmer were influenced by it to some slight extent and felt, in spite of their own subordinate position in their own country, the pride of possession and empire. That same worker or farmer if he came to India inevitably belonged to the ruling class here. He was totally ignorant of India's history and culture and he accepted the prevailing ideology of the British in India for he had no other standards to judge by or apply. At the most a vague benevolence filled him, but that was strictly conditioned within that framework. For a hundred years this ideology permeated all sections of the British people and became, as it were, a national heritage, a fixed and almost unalterable notion which governed their outlook on India and imperceptibly affected even their domestic outlook. In our own day that curious group which has no fixed standards or principles or much knowledge of the outside world, the leaders of the British Labour party, have usually been the staunchest supporters of the existing order in India. Sometimes a vague sense of uneasiness fills them at a seeming contradiction between their domestic and colonial policies, between their professions and practice; but regarding themselves above all as practical men of common sense, they sternly repress all these stirrings of conscience. Practical men must necessarily base themselves on established and known practice, on existing conditions, and not take a leap into the dark unknown merely because of some principle or untested theory.

Viceroys who come to India direct from England have to fit in with and rely upon the Indian Civil Service structure. Belonging to the possessing and ruling class in England, they have no difficulty whatever in accepting the prevailing I.C.S. outlook, and their unique position of absolute authority, unparalleled elsewhere, leads to subtle changes in their ways and methods of expression. Authority corrupts and absolute authority corrupts absolutely, and no man in the wide world today has had or has such absolute authority over such large numbers of people as the British viceroy of India. The viceroy speaks in a manner such as no prime minister of England or president of the United States can adopt. The only possible parallel would be that of Hitler. And not the viceroy only but the British members of his council, the governors, and even the smaller fry who function as secretaries of departments or magistrates. They speak from a noble and unattainable height, secure not only in the conviction that what they say and do is right but that it will have to be accepted as right, whatever lesser mortals may imagine, for theirs is the power and glory.

Some members of the Viceroy's Council are appointed direct from

England and do not belong to the Indian Civil Service. There is usually a marked difference in their ways and utterances from those of the civil service. They function easily enough in that framework, but they cannot quite develop that superior and self-satisfied air of assured authority. Much less can the Indian members of the council (a fairly recent addition), who are obvious supers, whatever their numbers or intelligence. Indians belonging to the civil service, whatever their rank in the official hierarchy, do not belong to the charmed circle. A few of them try to ape the manners of their colleagues without much success; they become rather pompous and ridiculous.

The new generation of British members of the Indian Civil Service are, I believe, somewhat different in mind and texture from their predecessors. They do not easily fit into the old framework; but all authority and policy flow from the senior members, and the newcomers make no difference. They have either to accept the established church or, as has sometimes happened, resign and return to their homeland.

I remember that when I was a boy the British-owned newspapers in India were full of official news and utterances; of service news, transfers, and promotions; of the doings of English society, of polo, races, dances, and amateur theatricals. There was hardly a word about the people of India, about their political, cultural, social, or economic life. Reading them, one would hardly suspect that they existed.

In Bombay there used to be quadrangular cricket matches between four elevens made up respectively of Hindus, Moslems, Parsis, and Europeans. The European eleven was called "Bombay Presidency"; the others were just Hindus, Moslems, Parsis. Bombay was thus essentially represented by the Europeans; the others, one would imagine, were foreign elements who were recognized for this purpose. These quadrangular matches still take place, though there is much argument about them and a demand that elevens should not be chosen on religious lines. I believe that the "Bombay Presidency" team is now called "European."

English clubs in India usually have territorial names—the Bengal Club, the Allahabad Club, etc. They are confined to Britishers, or rather to Europeans. There need be no objection to territorial designation or even to a group of persons having a club for themselves and not approving of outsiders' joining it. But this designation is derived from the old British habit of considering that they are the real India that counts, the real Bengal, the real Allahabad. Others are just excrescences, useful in their own way, if they know their place, but otherwise a nuisance. The exclusion of non-Europeans is far more a racial affair than a thoroughly justifiable way for people having cultural affinities meeting together in their leisure moments for play and social intercourse, and disliking the intrusion of other elements. For my part I have no objection to exclusive English or European clubs, and very few Indians would care to join them.

But when this social exclusiveness is clearly based on racialism and on a ruling class always exhibiting its superiority and unapproachability, it bears another aspect. In Bombay there is a well-known club which did not allow, and so far as I know, does not allow, an Indian (except as a servant) even in its visitors' room, even though he might be a ruling prince or a captain of industry.

Racialism in India is not so much English versus Indian. It is European as opposed to Asiatic. In India every European, be he German or Pole or Rumanian, is automatically a member of the ruling race. Railway carriages, station retiring rooms, benches in parks, are marked "For Europeans Only." This is bad enough in South Africa or elsewhere, but to have to put up with it in one's own country is a humiliating and exasperating reminder of our enslaved condition.

It is true that a gradual change has been taking place in these external manifestations of racial superiority and imperial arrogance. But the process is slow, and frequent instances occur to show how superficial it is. Political pressure and the rise of a militant nationalism enforce change and lead to a deliberate attempt to tone down the former racialism and aggressiveness; and yet that very political movement, when it reaches a stage of crisis and is sought to be crushed, leads to a resurgence of all the old imperialist and racial arrogance in its extremest form.

The English are a sensitive people, and yet when they go to foreign countries, there is a strange lack of awareness about them. In India, where the relation of ruler and ruled makes mutual understanding difficult, this lack of awareness is peculiarly evident. Almost, one would think, it is deliberate, so that they may see only what they want to see and be blind to all else. But facts do not vanish because they are ignored, and when they compel attention, there is a feeling of displeasure and resentment at the unexpected happening, as of some trick having been played.

In this land of caste the British, and more especially the Indian Civil Service, have built up a caste which is rigid and exclusive. Even the Indian members of the service do not really belong to that caste, though they wear its insignia and conform to its rules. That caste has developed something in the nature of a religious faith in its own paramount importance, and round that faith has grown an appropriate mythology which helps to maintain it. A combination of faith and vested interests is a powerful one, and any challenge to it arouses the deepest passions and fierce indignation.

T. Mboya

FREEDOM AND AFTER (1963)

TRADE UNIONS AND THE EMERGENCY

Working as a sanitary inspector for the Nairobi City Council brought me face to face with racial prejudice in a way I had not known before.

One day in 1951, when one of my European colleagues was away on leave, I was working alone in the food section of the Health Department, testing milk samples. European dairy farmers had to come to us for licenses to bring their milk into Nairobi for sale, and our job was to see that the milk was free of disease and conformed to certain standards. I was in the laboratory busy with some tests when a European woman came in with a sample bottle of milk. She looked around for a few moments and did not say anything.

"Good morning, madam," I said.

When I spoke, she turned round and asked, "Is there anybody here?"

I was a bit shocked and angry, but decided her question was amusing. So I asked, "Is there something wrong with your eyes?"

She was furious and rushed away to find the mayor and the chief sanitary inspector. I had been cheeky and disrespectful, she complained, and the next day she brought a petition she had persuaded other farmers to sign saying they did not want to deal with an African and wanted a European inspector instead. The chief sanitary inspector told the woman she would have to deal with an African if she wanted her license, and the mayor took no action on the petition. He came to me later and said I should not mind these reactions, which were to be expected.

But there were a good many other racial incidents. I was put under a European inspector to gain experience, and the two of us went around Nairobi together several times in the course of our work. I was surprised to find that from time to time he expected me to sit in the car when he went to inspect premises. I refused to do this and we had some heated words. He drove back to City Hall and said we could never work together again.

A number of times I was thrown out of premises I had gone to inspect by Europeans who insisted they wanted a European, not an African, to do the job. The City Council had to prosecute some of them for obstructing African inspectors in the course of their duties. But even inside the department there was discrimination. African inspectors were paid only one-fifth of the salary which a European inspector received for doing the same job. African inspectors were told to do their work in khaki uniforms, while the Europeans wore lounge suits. I objected and said either we should all wear uniforms or should all be free to wear what we liked.

I found there were many grievances of this sort among the lower-paid workers in the City Council, the sweepers and the workers in the cleansing section in particular. Most of the members of the Staff Association belonged to this group. When I joined the City Council, the secretary of the Staff Association was just about to resign and I was immediately asked to take his place. From that point I began to interest myself in the problems of the workers and my years as a trade union leader started.

There were only 450 members of the Staff Association when I took over the secretaryship, and in eight months we were able to raise the membership to more than 1,300. We spent a lot of time dealing with heads of departments over the grievances of the workers. People complained that they had not received their correct wages, or they had not been paid when they were sick, or their house allowance was wrongly calculated, or they had not got a house yet although they had worked for the Council for many years. Many grievances grew out of the bad relationships between workers and supervisors, who were all European and who expected everyone to accept their every word as law.

No machinery existed for negotiation or consultation between the City Council and the workers, so from time to time it was necessary to take matters to the government's Labor Department. In this way I got to know James Patrick and to learn from him about trade unionism. As part of the policy of the British Labour Party government to encourage trade unions in the colonies, James Patrick had been sent out as trade union adviser to the Kenya government. He was a very liberal Scotsman who was keen to see trade unionism develop in Kenya, but at the same time often puzzled about how this aim could be achieved. Soon after his arrival, he spoke to a meeting of Europeans in Thika about his job. Almost unanimously his audience told him the time had not yet arrived for the establishment of trade unions in Kenya, and he should come back in twenty years or so. When he reported this to the Labor Commissioner, to his surprise the commissioner agreed with the resolution passed at

Thika. Patrick wondered why he had ever been sent to Kenya in the first place, if that was the attitude of the Kenya government. However, he decided he was going to do his best to help in advising trade unionists how to organize, employers how to deal with trade unions, and the government how to create machinery to recognize trade unions.

Through meetings with him, I became more and more interested in the trade union movement, and also in the labor laws of Kenya. I borrowed books and had long discussions on our problems. These talks resulted in my resolve to organize a more effective movement than the Staff Association to help the City Council workers.

Government hostility to trade unions was based on the belief that they meant riots and communism. The first real trade union movement in Kenya had started in Mombasa when Chege Kebacha tried to organize a union of general workers. It had by 1947 become strong in numbers, but it was an omnibus union without real sense of direction in terms of collective bargaining and joint consultation. Matters came to a head that year when the workers demanded increased wages and better conditions. The demands could not be put to any particular employer, and so they were presented as though they were political demands to the government. There were riots and looting throughout Mombasa in the general strike which followed, and Kebacha was deported to Baringo in the Northern Province.

There followed a commission of inquiry under the chairmanship of Judge R. S. Thacker, who six years later became a controversial figure at the Kapenguria trial of Jomo Kenyatta. He found that living costs around the port had risen sharply without a corresponding rise in wages, and that there was no machinery for consultation or negotiation. He recommended increases in wages and said immediate steps should be taken to create the necessary industrial relations machinery. This was the beginning of what became the formal trade union machinery in Kenya. But because of the riots and because the only person who had been able to end the rioting had been an African—Eliud Mathu, then a nominated member of the Legislative Council—many Europeans were angry. There were riots also in Nairobi in 1950 when the Transport and Allied Workers Union called a strike. Again, there was no machinery for negotiation and consultation, and the demands were couched as though directed to the government. Makhan Singh, who had been connected with the Nairobi strike as a trade unionist, told a meeting at Kaloleni about this time that he was a communist. So trade unionism was connected in the minds of many people either with riots or communism.

As a result of this background and attitude, government officers advised us to form staff associations rather than trade unions. It was easier, they knew, to deal with staff associations, which had no legal backing and virtually no right to strike. But we could not accept this negative attitude to trade unionism. We traveled around Kenya's main towns—Mombasa, Nakuru, Kisumu, Eldoret—to solicit support of other staff associations for a country-wide Kenya Local Government Workers Union. It was interesting to find that most of the men playing a leading role in the formation of local government staff associations were sanitary inspectors who had been at Jeanes School with me. This made it easy to establish close relations between our different associations.

Our big difficulty in forming the KLGWU was restriction of movement, which began when the Emergency was declared in October 1952. Like most unions at that time, we had women collectors who went round collecting members' dues, but with decrees restricting movement—particularly of Kikuyu—we could get money only from workers who came directly to the office headquarters. This in turn was very difficult because of the security forces who used to raid the union offices, arrest many of the union officers, and search people on the roadside or raid their houses in the African locations in the middle of the night. Normally they took away for questioning and maybe detention anyone who was found with a union card in his pocket. Such a person was regarded as part of the hard core of the subversive element among the Africans. Many union members sent back their cards to the office to be kept there rather than run the risk of being caught with them in their pockets.

Nevertheless, the KLGWU soon became the strongest union in Kenya. In those days unions were very poorly administered: office routine never existed; there was virtually no filing system or any system at all. Within a year we had created proper office routine and administration, an efficient filing system and a large bank balance, with proper financial administration. My experience at Jeanes School, presiding over the Student Council and helping to administer the finances of all the college clubs, had given me some idea about office routine and management. My colleagues Ben Gituiku and James Karebe could not tour the country because of movement restrictions imposed on members of the Kikuyu, Embu and Meru tribes, but I was able to visit our branches regularly, while they built the office system.

It is, perhaps, not surprising that the Medical Officer of Health was annoyed about my activities. I had by then entered active politics. I was not a member of the Kenya African Union before Jomo Kenyatta and the other leaders were arrested, although I had heard him speak at several meetings. But I became a member just after the arrests in October 1952, because I was incensed at the manner in which this was done and, like many young people, I felt excited at the thought that this was an opportunity for us to play some part in ensuring that the nationalist movement did not collapse. Quite a few of my friends thought I was mad when I came out at that time to take part, and especially when I accepted first the role of director of information and later on the office of acting treasurer of KAU. It was difficult to organize the party or raise funds in those days. We were always being followed by police, and expected that KAU might be banned any time. As a precaution against the party's funds being seized by the police when banning KAU, the officials sometimes carried them round in a large wicker basket and at night slept with the basket in a hut guarding it.

The Medical Officer of Health told me the City Council was concerned about my political and trade union activities, and since I knew it would not be long before I got a notice of dismissal, I handed in my resignation. Even before I had served my three months' notice, the City Council asked me to leave. For in the meantime the KLGWU had been registered as a trade union and at its first conference I had been elected National General Secretary. So I became a full-time—but unpaid—trade union official. Until the union finances increased after months of hard work, I lived on donations from some executive members and branch officials.

Our union immediately affiliated with the Kenya Federation of Registered Trade Unions. The KFRTU had been formed only in 1950 with five main unions—the Transport and Allied Workers Union, the Domestic and Hotel Workers Union, the Tailors Union, the Building Workers Union, and the Night Watchmen and Clerical Workers Union. The same week we affiliated, the secretary, Aggrey Minya, was suspended. There was a misunderstanding about his activities after he had returned from a world congress of the International Confederation of Free Trade Unions in Stockholm. So I was asked to act as temporary secretary. This dispute ended in Mr. Minya's being dismissed from his post, and in September 1953 I was elected General Secretary of the KFRTU, which was later renamed the Kenya Federation of Labor.

My interest in labor problems had led to my being appointed a member of the Labor Advisory Board in 1952 and the Wages Advisory Board in 1953. But after the banning of KAU, the work of the KFL, and of me as its Secretary-General, was as much political as trade unionist. For the KFL became the voice of the African people, in the absence of any other African organization remaining to speak for them.

There were plenty of occasions when we had to speak out. There was the mass eviction from the Rift Valley Province of farm workers of the Kikuyu, Embu and Meru tribes. An army of fifteen hundred white settlers descended on Government House one morning and demanded tougher measures against these tribes, which they suspected of being oathed by Mau Mau. The result was the eviction of thousands of farm workers from the only livelihood and home they knew. At the same time the government ignored our warnings that these evictions could only create more frustration and bitterness. There was also one November morning in 1953 when seven hundred families were thrown out of their homes into the streets in the Eastleigh suburb of Nairobi. There were many children who were left without any care when their parents were taken away to detention camps during the night. There were wives whose husbands disappeared during the course of the day, having been arrested on their way to work. There were collective punishments, with confiscation of cattle and other property. There were the "green books" which Kikuyu had to carry about Nairobi—later followed by the famous "pass books." We condemned these pass books strongly, and suggested we might have positive action in the form of civil disobedience in protest against them. We were threatened with detention if we persisted. When a boycott of buses, beer and cigarettes began, the District Commissioner of Nairobi, Arthur Small, summoned me to his office and asked me to condemn the boycott. I told him I would not do so: I had not called the boycott and I was not responsible for the conditions which created the boycott.

The only encouragement we had in our battles at that time came from the International Confederation of Free Trade Unions. They sent David Newman as their first representative in 1953 and the following year a Canadian called Jim Bury, and together we worked day and night on many of these cases. The ICFTU sent money to help feed evicted families, they pleaded our case with the International Labor Organization, they made strong representations at the Colonial Office, and briefed MPs in Britain. I wrote several articles in their publication *Free Labor World* and in other papers to help get our case to the world—the side of the unhappy story which was not receiving any publicity otherwise. At that time the only publicity from Kenya was of Mau Mau oaths and terrorist activities. Nothing was written of how some members of the security forces were given a present of money if they "shot straight and shot an African," until the ICFTU and affiliates like the American Federation of Labor gave us the use of their publications. A Nairobi lawyer, Peter Evans, who had asked for an inquiry into the behavior of the security forces, was promptly deported. Jim Bury himself was several times threatened with expulsion, and the KFL too was several times threatened with being banned. In 1956 it needed a visit by Sir Vincent Tewson of the British Trades Union Congress to prevent the Kenya government's taking that step.

F. Fanon

THE ORDEAL OF THE BLACK MAN (1952)

"Dirty nigger!" or simply, "Look, a nigger!" I had arrived in the world, anxious to discover a meaning for things, my soul filled with the desire to be part of the world from its very beginning when I found that I was but one object among other objects.

Imprisoned in this crushing objectivity, I turned imploringly to the Other. His liberating gaze took in my entire body which had suddenly lost all physical solidity through his rudeness. It gave me a lightness I thought I had lost and, by taking me out of the world, placed me in the world. But over there, right there on the counter-slope, I stumbled, and the Other, through gestures, attitudes, and glances, transfixed me as one fixes a color by infusing a dye into a solution. I was indignant. I demanded an explanation. It was to no avail. I exploded. Here are the bits and pieces gathered up and assembled by another "me."

As long as the Black Man is among his own people, except on the occasion of minor internal struggles, he will have no need to put his own being to the test for someone else's benefit. There is indeed the Hegelian moment of "being for the Other," but any ontology is made unrealizable in a society that has been colonized and civilized. This fact does not seem to have been sufficiently kept in mind by those who have written on the subject. In the *Weltanschauung* of a colonial people, there is a taint, an impurity that precludes any ontological explanation. The objection may be raised that this is true of every individual, but this objection only obscures a fundamental problem. Ontology—when one concedes once and for all that it sets aside the question of existence—does not enable us to

SOURCE. Frantz Fanon, "The Ordeal of the Black Man," from *Peau Noire, Masques Blanc*, Paris: Editions du Seuil, 1952, pp. 113–125, 129–131, 133–135. Copyright Editions du Seuil, 1952. This book will be published in an English translation by Grove Press in 1966.

understand the Black Man's being, *l'être du Noir*. For the Black Man
has no further occasion to be black, but is only such when confronted
by the White Man. It will occur to some to remind us that the situation
works both ways. We reply that that is not so. The Black Man cannot
withstand the White Man's gaze. Overnight, as it were, Negroes had two
frames of reference in terms of which they had to adjust themselves.
Their metaphysics or, less pretentiously, their customs and the procedures
relating thereto, were abolished because they were found to be in contradiction with a civilization of which Negroes had no knowledge and which
imposed itself upon them.

The Black Man among his own race in the twentieth century is
unaware at just what moment he came to be regarded as inferior. . . .
Undoubtedly, we have discussed the color problem with our friends or,
less frequently, with American Negroes. Together we protested and
affirmed the equality of all members of the human race. In the West
Indies there was also the little bar separating *la békaille* (the whites),
la mulâtraille (the mulattos), and *la négraille* (the blacks). But we
contented ourselves with an intellectual awareness of these divergences.
Indeed, there was nothing dramatic about it. And then . . .

And then we were confronted with the white man's gaze. An unfamiliar and oppressive weight settled down upon us. The real world
was challenging our rightful share in it. In the white world the colored
man encounters difficulties in establishing the schematic elements of his
physical existence. Taking cognizance of one's body is a purely negative
activity. It is knowledge in the third person. The body is surrounded by
an atmosphere of acute uncertainty. I know that if I wish to smoke a
cigarette, I must extend my right arm and seize the pack located at the
other end of the table. As for the matches, they are in the left drawer.
I will have to move back slightly. And all these movements I make, not
out of habit, but out of an implicit kind of knowledge. A slow and
gradual construction of my ego, insofar as I am a body within a spatial
and temporal world, such appears to be the schema of my physical being.
It does not force itself upon me. Rather it is a definitive structuring of
the self and the world—definitive, because an effective dialectic is established between my body and the world around it.

For some years now laboratories have undertaken to discover a
serum to eliminate black pigmentation. With utter seriousness, laboratory
workers have rinsed their test tubes, adjusted their scales, and initiated
researches intended to permit unfortunate blacks to bleach themselves
and thereby cast off the burden of their corporeal curse. I had created
an historico-racial rationale underlying the physical one. The elements
I had used were not provided by "residual sensations and perceptions
of an essentially tactile, aural, kinesthetic, and visual order"[1] but were
furnished me by the Other, the White, who had woven me from a tissue

of countless details, anecdotes, and stories. I felt I had to construct a physiological self, to establish a spatial equilibrium, to localize my sensations, whereupon I found they were demanding even more of me.

"Look! A nigger!" It was an external stimulus that pricked me as it passed. I broke into a smile.

"Look! A nigger" It was true. I was amused.

"Look! A nigger!" Little by little, the circle contracted. I did not conceal my amusement.

"Mama, look at the nigger. I'm afraid!" Afraid! Afraid! Now they were beginning to fear me. I wanted to laugh until I choked. But that had become impossible for me. I could not do so any longer, for I knew already that there existed legends, stories, history, and especially *historicity* which Jaspers had taught me. Then my corporeal schema, assailed at several points, collapsed and gave way to a racial and epidermic schema. In the wake of this experience there was no longer a question of knowing my body in the third person, but rather as three persons. In its wake I was left not one, but two, three places to occupy. Already I had ceased to be amused. I could find no living connecting points with the world about me. I existed in triplicate. I occupied one place; I was moving toward the other . . . and the other, evanescent and hostile but not opaque—transparent, absent, was in process of disappearing.

Nausea. . . .

At one and the same time I was responsible for my body, responsible for my race, and responsible for my ancestors. I viewed myself objectively, discovered my blackness, my ethnic characteristics—and my ear drums were shattered by the sounds of *cannibalism, mental retardation, fetishism, racial defects, slave-traders.* . . .

That particular day I was disoriented, incapable of being outside with the Other, with the White, who was mercilessly engaged in locking me within a prison. I betook myself a long way from that particular *self* and became simply an object. What kind of experience did I undergo if it was not that of a violent dislocation, like a wrenching of limbs from their sockets, a stripping away of one's flesh, a hemorrhage causing black blood to congeal all over my body? Yet I did not want this reappraisal, this formulization. I simply wanted to be a man like any other man. I would have preferred to arrive fresh and young in a world of our own where we could work together in a common endeavor.

But I refused to be emotionally inoculated. I wanted to be a man, no more, no less. Some there were who tied me to my ancestors, enslaved and lynched. I decided to assert myself, to make assumptions. It was in an intellectual sense that I understood this internal kinship: I was the grandchild of slaves just as French President Lebrun was the grandson of peasants held in serfdom by their feudal masters. Within the depths of my being the cry of alarm soon subsided.

In North America Negroes are segregated. In South America Negroes who strike are whipped in the streets and gunned down. In West Africa the Negro is an animal. And here, close to me, right at my side, is this school pal, who comes from Algeria, who speaks to me in these words: "As long as they treat the Arabs as though they were like us, there can be no viable solution."

You see, my dear fellow, racial prejudice is unknown to me. . . . Why, of course, come in, sir. There is no color prejudice among us. . . . Quite so, the Negro is a man like ourselves. . . . The fact that he is black does not make him less intelligent than we are. . . . I had a Senegalese buddy in my regiment. He was very cultivated. . . .

Where was I to put myself? Or, if you prefer, where was I to hide myself? A native of Martinique, from one of "our" old colonies, where could I hide?

Look at the nigger! —Mama, a nigger! Hush, child! He's going to get angry. . . . Don't pay any attention to him, sir. He doesn't know you're as civilized as we are. . . .

My body was returning to me, piecemeal, disjointed, re-covered and re-coated, plunged into deep mourning on this white winter's day. The Negro is an animal. The Negro is evil. The Negro is nasty. The Negro is ugly. —Look! a Negro! It's cold. The Negro is shivering. He shivers because he is cold. The little boy shivers because he is afraid of the Negro. The Negro is shivering from cold, a cold that gnaws at your bones. The pretty little boy is trembling because he believes the Negro is trembling with rage. The little white boy rushes to his mother's arms: "Mama, the nigger is going to eat me."

'Round about me is the White Man. Heaven above has wrenched my navel, torn from me my umbilical cord. The earth crunches under my feet and a white song, white, white. All this whiteness is reducing me to white ash. . . . I sit by the fireside and become aware of my livery. I had never really noticed it before. It is indeed ugly. I go no further, for who is to tell me what beauty is?

Where must I take refuge from now on? From the scattered fragments of my being I felt a rush of emotion immediately recognizable. I was about to become angry. The fire had long since gone out, and once more the Negro was shivering.

Look, that Negro is a handsome fellow.
The handsome Negro says, To hell with you, Madam!

Her face registered shame and embarrassment. At last I was freed from my introspection. At the same time I was accomplishing two things: I was identifying my enemies and causing a scandal. I was gratified. From now on I would be able to enjoy myself. Having limited the field of battle, I entered the lists. What? How's that? Here was I ready to forgive and forget and wanted only to be friends, and my intention was thrown back at me like a slap in the face. The white world, the only respectable one, denied me any participation whatsoever. They demanded that a man conduct himself like a man. But I was expected to behave like a black man—or at least like a Negro. I was calling out to the world, eager to make its acquaintance, and the world was rejecting me because of my eagerness. They wanted me to contain myself, to shrink and withdraw.

But they'd find out! I had put them on their guard. Slavery? No one discussed that any longer. It was just an ugly memory. My alleged inferiority? That was a cock and bull story, good for a laugh. I was ready to forget everything, but with the understanding that the world would no longer ignore me. I wanted to test my incisors. I felt that they were strong and sharp. And then . . .

What? How's that? While I was the one with every possible reason to hate and despise, it was I who was being rejected? Whereas I should have been pleaded with and implored, I was refused all recognition? Since it was impossible for me to act from any "innate complex," I decided to assert myself, to affirm my existence on the basis of my color—as a *Black*. Since the Other was reluctant to recognize me, there was only one solution left: to make myself recognized.

Jean-Paul Sartre has written in his *Réflexions sur la question juive:* "They (the Jews) have allowed themselves to be poisoned by a certain image that others have of them, and they live in fear lest their actions may conform to that image. Thus we may say that their modes of behavior are perpetually super-determined from within." (p. 123) Still, it is possible for a Jew to live without others being aware of his Jewishness. He is not inescapably, inexorably committed to being a Jew. He can hope. He can wait. In the last analysis it is his actions and his behavior that are the deciding factors. He is a White Man, and apart from a few debatable characteristics, he can pass unnoticed. He belongs to a race which, from time immemorial, has never known cannibalism. What a bizarre notion to devour one's father! It is as simple as that. You need only not be a Negro. Of course the Jews are bullied and harassed. Nay, they are persecuted, exterminated, and cremated, but those are just little family arguments. The Jew is disliked from the moment he is spotted and tracked down. But with me everything is viewed in a different light. I am given no opportunity at all. I am super-determined from the outside. I am not the slave of an "idea" which others have of me. I am the slave of my appearance.

I make very slow headway in the world. I have become accustomed not to entertain any notions of rapid advancement. I move by crawling. Already the gaze of the White Man—the only gaze that matters—is dissecting me. I am immobilized. Having adjusted their scalpel, they proceed objectively to slice up my reality. I am betrayed. I sense, I see in the white man's looks that he sees me not as a new man who has just appeared. Rather, as a new *kind* of man, a new genre—a Negro, in short. Like an insect, I crawl into corners, touching with my long antennae the scattered truths on the surface of things: a Negro's linen smells of the Negro; a Negro's teeth are white; a Negro's feet are large; his chest is broad. I crawl into corners. I remain silent. I long for anonymity, for oblivion. Look, I accept everything but ask that I be unnoticed.

Here, let me introduce you to my black comrade Aimé Césaire, a black man, a PhD from the University. . . . Marian Anderson, the greatest Negro singer. . . . Here, say hello to my friend from Martinique (Be careful! He's very sensitive). . . .

Shame. Shame and contempt for myself. Nausea. When people like me, they tell me they like me in spite of my color. When they hate me, they hasten to add that it isn't because of my color. . . . Whether here or there, I am a prisoner of this vicious circle.

I turn away from these scrutinizers of an antediluvian era and clutch at my own brothers, Negroes like myself. Horrors! *They* reject me. They are almost white. And then they are going to marry a white woman. They will have children who are slightly brown. . . . Who knows? Little by little, perhaps. . . .

I had been dreaming.

Now look, sir, I am one of the greatest negrophiles in Lyons.

The evidence was there, inescapable and implacable. And my blackness was solid and indisputable. It tormented me, pursued me, perturbed me, and exasperated me. Negroes are savage, bestial, illiterate. But I knew that, as for myself, these accusations were false. There was a myth about the Negro that had to be disproved and demolished regardless of the cost. We were no longer living in a time when people were astonished to discover a Negro priest. We had doctors, professors, statesmen. . . . Yes, but the idea persisted that there was something exceptional about these cases: "We have a Senegalese history professor. He is very intelligent. . . . Our doctor is a Negro. He is very gentle."

It was I, the Negro professor, the Negro doctor, who began to weaken. I trembled at the slightest alarm. I knew, for instance, that if the doctor committed a single mistake, he was finished, as would be all the others who might follow him. After all, what could one expect of a Negro doctor? As long as everything went well, he was praised to the skies. But take care! Don't make a slip under any circumstances whatever. The Negro doctor will never know how perilously close he is to professional disgrace at any moment. I speak from experience. I was hemmed in. Neither my polished manners, nor my knowledge of literature, nor my understanding of the quantum theory found favor or ensured my acceptance.

I demanded, I insisted on explanations. Gently, in the manner one speaks to a child, they revealed to me the existence of a certain opinion held by certain individuals, but, they would add: "One must hope for its early disappearance." What was it? Color prejudice.

"Color prejudice is nothing more than the unreasoning hatred of one race for another, the contempt of the stronger and richer peoples for those whom they consider inferior to themselves, and the bitter resentment of those who are kept in subjection and so frequently insulted. As color is the most obvious manifestation of race, it has been made the criterion by which men are judged, irrespective of their social or educational attainments. The light-skinned races have come to despise all those of a darker color, and the dark-skinned peoples will no longer accept the inferior position to which they have been relegated." [2]

What I had read I had read intelligently. It was hatred; I was hated, detested, scorned, not by my neighbor across the street or my maternal cousin, but by an entire race. I was confronted with something irrational. Psychoanalysts say that there is no more traumatic experience for a child than contact with the rational. I can affirm personally that, for a man who has no weapon except reason, there is nothing more disconcerting than contact with the irrational. I felt myself giving birth to sharp knives. I resolved to defend myself. As a good tactician, I wanted to rationalize the world, to prove to the White Man that he was mistaken.

With the Jew, says Jean-Paul Sartre, there is "a kind of passionate imperialism of reason; for he wants not only to convince others that he is in possession of the truth, his aim is to persuade his listeners that there is an absolute and unconditional value to rationalism. He regards himself as a missionary for the universal. In the face of the universality of the Catholic religion from which he is excluded, he seeks to establish the "catholicity" of the rational, the instrument for attaining truth and the spiritual tie that binds the human race." [3]

And, the author adds, if there have been Jews who make intuition the fundamental basis of their philosophy, their intuition "in no way resembles the *esprit de finesse* of Pascal. And it is this *esprit de finesse*, incontestable and moving, based on a thousand imperceptible perceptions which the Jew regards as his worst enemy. As for Bergson, his philosophy offers the curious spectacle of an anti-intellectualist doctrine entirely constructed by the most rational and critical kind of intelligence. And it is by rational arguments that he establishes the existence of a pure duration, of a philosophical intuition. And this very intuition, which discovers duration or life, is universal in the sense that everyone can practice it. And it is related to the universal since its objects can be named and conceived." [4]

Zealously, I began to take inventory, to probe my environment. In the course of time men had seen the Catholic religion justify and then

condemn slavery and racial discrimination. But in referring everything
to the notion of human dignity, they were ripping prejudice to shreds.
After a good deal of hesitation, scientists had conceded that the Negro
was a human being. *In vivo* and *in vitro* the Negro had shown himself
analogous to the White Man: the same morphology, the same histology.
Reason was ensuring her victory on every plane. I rejoined the assemblies.
But I was soon forced to sing a different tune.

Victory was playing cat and mouse. It was taunting me. As the Other
would say: When I'm there, it's somewhere else, and when it's there,
I'm somewhere else. On the intellectual plane there was agreement: the
Negro is a human being. That is to say (as the least convinced would
add) his heart is on the left side like ours. But on certain questions the
White Man remained intractable. Under no circumstances would he con-
done intimacy between the races, for it is a known fact that "crossing
between widely different races results in lowering the physical and mental
level. . . . Until we have more definite knowledge of the effects of race
crossings, we shall certainly do best to avoid crossings between widely
different races." [5]

As for myself, I would know how to react. In one sense, if I had to
define myself, I would say that I am waiting. I question my surroundings.
I interpret everything in the light of my discoveries. I have become a
sensory individual. At the outset of the history given me by the Other,
they had assigned a conspicuous place to cannibalism just to remind me
of the fact. They described the presence in my chromosomes of certain
genes of varying consistency which represented cannibalism. Alongside
the *sex-linked* genes they had discovered some that were *race-linked*.
This sort of science is disgraceful!

But I understand this "psychological mechanism." For as everyone
knows, it is only psychological, this mechanism. Two centuries ago I was
lost to humanity, a slave forever. And then some men arrived on the
scene, declaring that all of that had lasted too long. My tenacity did the
rest. I was saved from the deluge of civilization. I made headway. . . .

Too late! Everything is foreseen, discovered, proved, and exploited.
My nervous hands can retrieve nothing. The vein has been completely
worked and exhausted. Too late! But once again, I would like an explanation. Ever since the time someone complained of arriving too late and
lamented that there was nothing further to say, there has seemed to exist
a nostalgia for the past. Could it be the lost paradise of one's beginnings
that Otto Rank speaks of? How numerous are they who, apparently tied
to the world's uterus, have spent their lives wrestling with the riddle
of the Delphic Oracle or have struggled to retrace the route traveled by
Ulysses? Pan-spiritualists, wishing to prove the existence of a soul in
animals, use the following argument: a dog lies down on his master's
grave and dies there of hunger. It was Janet's task to have shown that the

aforesaid dog, contrary to man, was simply not capable of liquidating the past. One speaks of the grandeur of Greece, says Artaud, but, he adds, if people today no longer understand the *Choephoroe* of Aeschylus, it is Aeschylus who is found wanting. It is in the name of tradition that anti-Semites justify their "point of view." It is in the name of tradition, of this long historical past, of this blood relationship with Pascal and Descartes, that the Jews are told: you cannot find a place in our community. Recently, one of these good Frenchmen declared on a train in which I happened to be riding: "If only the true French virtues survive, the human race is saved. At this moment it is our duty to achieve National Unity. No more internal struggles! Face up to foreigners (and, turning toward me) whoever they are!"

I must say in extenuation that he smelled of cheap red wine. Had he been able to, he would have said that the blood of a liberated slave was incapable of passionate feelings at the mention of Villon or Taine.

A disgrace!

The Jew and I: not content to racialize myself, by a happy stroke of fortune I was becoming human. I was rejoining the Jew, brothers in misfortune.

A disgrace!

On first thought it may seem surprising that an anti-Semitic attitude can be related to that of a Negro-hater. It was my philosophy professor, a West Indian, who reminded me one day: "When you hear derogatory remarks about the Jews, pay close attention. They are talking about you." And I believed him right, universally speaking, meaning by that that I was responsible in my body and my soul for the fate reserved for my brother. Since then I have come to realize that all he meant to say was: "An anti-Semite is necessarily a Negro-hater."

You have arrived too late, much too late. There will always be a world—a white world—separating you from us. . . . This impossibility for the Other to liquidate the past once and for all. You can understand why, confronted with the emotional ankylosis of the White, I decided to utter my Black cry. Little by little, reaching out here and there with pseudopods, I secreted a race. And this race staggered beneath the weight of a fundamental element. What was it? *Rhythm!* Listen to Senghor, our poet: "It is something extremely sensitive and divorced from the material. It is the vital element par excellence. It is an essential requisite and sign of Art just as respiration is a sign of life. Respiration is fast or slow, regular or spasmodic, according to the individual's degree of tension, the intensity and quality of his emotion. Such is rhythm in its primitive purity. Such is the rhythm encountered in the masterpieces of Negro art, especially in sculpture, an art that consists of one theme—its sculptural form—opposed to a parallel and contrasting theme, just as inhalation is the opposite of exhalation. It is not a static kind of symmetry that engenders monotony. Rhythm is alive and free. . . . It is in this way that rhythm affects the least intellectual part of our being, relentlessly forcing us to penetrate deeply into the spirituality of an object. This attitude of total abandon, which is an intrinsic part of our nature, is in itself rhythmic." [6]

Had I read rightly? I read it again with rapt attention. On the far side of the white world an entrancing Negro culture was beckoning me. Negro sculpture! I began blushing with pride. Would that be my salvation?

I had rationalized the world, and the world had rejected me in the name of color prejudice. Since no agreement was possible on the rational plane, I had withdrawn into the irrational. It was up to the White Man to be more irrational than I. I had adopted the regressive technique to serve my own ends. But the fact remained that it was an unfamiliar weapon. Here I was completely at home. My being was a product of irrationality. I was wallowing in the irrational. Irrational up to my neck!

And now we find the Negro rehabilitated, "standing at the helm," governing the world with his intuition, the Negro rediscovered, salvaged, vindicated, given responsibility. And it is a Negro, no, not *a* Negro, but *the* Negro, sending out signals to the earth's sensitive receivers, standing on the proscenium of the world's stage, sprinkling on one and all the holy water of his inspired poetry, "porous to every breeze that blows." I have espoused the world! I am the world! The White has never comprehended this magic substitution. The White wants control of the world. He wants it for himself alone. He regards himself as the fore-ordained master of the world. He bends it to his will. There is established between him and the world a coercive form of possessiveness. But values exist which elude him, which find their true expression in me, and only in my spiritual make-up. Like a magician, I steal from the White Man "a certain world" that is beyond the grasp of him and his kind. On that day the White Man must have felt a return shock that he could not identify, being so unaccustomed to such reactions. The truth of the matter is that I had carefully and delicately established the *real* world above the objective world of earth and banana trees and rubber plants. The world's essence had become my property. Between the world and me a rapport of co-existence was established. I had rediscovered the primordial One. My "sonorous hands" were devouring the hysterical cries of the world. The White had the painful impression that I was breaking free of him and that I was taking something with me. He frisked me. He searched my pockets. He probed the darkest recesses. Everywhere he found only the familiar and recognizable. Nevertheless, it was obvious that I possessed a secret. . . .

The soul of the White was corrupted and, as a friend of mine who taught in the United States put it to me: "Negroes, vis-à-vis the

Whites, constitute in some manner a degree of human reassurance. When the Whites feel too oppressed by mechanization, they turn to the colored people and ask them for a bit of human nourishment." At last I was recognized. I was no longer a nonentity.

I was soon disillusioned. The White, thrown off guard for a moment, demonstrated to me that genetically speaking, I represented a stage in human evolution: "Your qualities have been absorbed and exhausted by us. We have had earthly mystics such as you will never know. Study our history closely, and you will realize to what extent this fusion has taken place." I was left with the impression of repeating an evolutionary cycle. My originality had been extorted from me. I wept for a long time. And then I began to live again. But I was haunted by a procession of over-powering thoughts: the *peculiar* odor of the Negro . . . the *peculiar* child-like spontaneity of the Negro . . . the *peculiar* naïveté of the Negro. . . .

I had tried to escape from the gang, but the Whites had caught me and amputated my left leg. I surveyed the limits of my personal domain. There was no doubt about it. It was rather meager. It was in this cir-cumscribed area that I made my most extraordinary discovery—a discov-ery that, properly speaking, was a re-discovery. Feverishly, I investigated the history of black antiquity. What I found there left me breathless. In his book on *The Abolition of Slavery*, Schoelcher furnished us with com-pelling arguments. Since his time, Frobenius, Westermann, and Dela-fosse, all white men, joined in the chorus: Ségou, Djenné, cities of over 100,000 inhabitants. They mention Negro doctors (doctors of theology who journeyed to Mecca to discuss the Koran). These exhumations, laid bare with their viscera exposed, enabled me to rediscover a valuable historical category. The White Man was mistaken. I was not a primitive creature, any more than I was a half-man. I belonged to a race which had already worked gold and silver two thousand years ago. . . .

I put the White back in his place. Emboldened, I jostled him and taunted him: "Adjust yourself to me. I don't have to adjust to anyone." I laughed openly and derisively. The White was snarling. The snarl was audible. His reaction time was indefinitely prolonged. . . . I had won. I was exultant.

"Forget your history and your studies of the past. Try to get in step with us. In a society like ours, highly industrialized and scientific, there is no room for your sensibilities. You've got to be tough in order to sur-vive. The time has passed for playing games with the world. Rather we must subject it to mathematical and atomic control. Of course (they would say to me from time to time) when we are weary with life and with our buildings, we shall go to you, as we do to our children, those unspoiled . . . wide-eyed . . . spontaneous creatures. We will turn to you as to the world's childhood. Your lives are so authentic, that is to say, so playful, so uninhibited. Let us forsake our polished and ceremonious civilization for a few moments and look at those adorably expressive faces. In a certain sense you reconcile us with ourselves."

Thus they were opposing a rational view to my irrational one—to my rational view they were opposing "a truly rational view." No matter how I played the game, I couldn't win. I experimented with my heredity. I drew up a complete balance sheet of my afflictions. I wanted to be typically Negro—it wasn't possible. I wanted to be white—the idea was preposterous. And when I attempted a justification of my negritude on the intellectual or ideological plane, they tore it away from me. They showed me that my argument was nothing but a dialectical proposition.

"But there is something more serious. The Negro, as we have said, is fashioning an anti-racist racism. He has no desire to dominate the world. He wants the abolition of ethnic privileges whatever the original justification. He affirms his solidarity with oppressed peoples irrespective of color. Immediately, the subjective, existential, ethnic idea of *negritude* "passes," as Hegel says, into the objective, positive, precise notion of the *proletariat*. "For Césaire, the 'White' symbolizes *capital*," says Senghor, "while the Negro symbolizes *labor*. . . . He sings of the struggle of the world's proletarian through the black-skinned men of his race."

"It is easy to say so, but less easy to think so. And it is doubtless no accident that the most ardent poets of the black race are at the same time militant Marxists.

"But that does not prevent the notion of race from not being linked with the notion of class. The former is concrete and particularized; the latter is universal and abstract. The one can be equated with what Jaspers calls comprehension and the other with intellection. The first is the product of a psycho-biological syncretism, and the other is a method-ical construction predicated on experience. Indeed, negritude appears as the weak step in a dialectical progression. The thesis is the theoretical and practical affirmation of the White Man's superiority; the position of negritude, as antithetical value is the moment of negativity. But this negative moment is not self-sustaining, and the Blacks who make use of it are well aware of its inadequacy. They know that it is aimed at pre-paring the synthesis, the fulfillment of the human potential in a society without racism. Thus, negritude is dedicated to its own destruction. It is transition, not terminus, means and not ultimate end."[7]

When I read this page, I felt as though I was being robbed of my last opportunity. I declared to my friends: "The new generation of black poets has just received an unpardonable blow." They had appealed to a friend of the colored peoples, and this friend had found nothing better to offer than to point out the relativity of their actions. For once in his life this born Hegelian had forgotten that the human conscience has need of losing itself in the dark night of the absolute, the sole condition for achieving self-consciousness. Against rationalism, he was invoking its negative aspects but forgetting that this negativity derives its value from a quasi-substantial absoluteness. Consciousness preoccupied with experience is unaware, and necessarily so, of essences and determinations of one's being.

Black Orpheus is a landmark in the intellectualization of the black man's "being." Sartre's error lay not only in wanting to get to the source of the source, but in some way or other, causing the source itself to dwindle and dry up: "Will the source of Poetry's stream run dry? Or will the great black river, in spite of everything, color the sea into which it flows? No matter. Every era has its poetry. In every era historical circumstances select a nation, a race, a class to grasp the torch and hold it aloft by creating situations which poetry alone can express or transcend. At times the poetic élan coincides with a revolutionary élan. At other times they go their separate ways. Let us today salute the historical opportunity that permits Black Men to utter "the great Negro cry with such intensity as to shake the foundations of the world." (Césaire).[8]

(Translated from the French by Robert A. Wagoner, State University of New York Maritime College.)

NOTES

1. Jean Lhermite, *L'Image de notre corps,* ed. de la Nouvelle Revue Critique, p. 17.
2. Sir Alan Burns, *Le préjugé de race et de couleur,* Payot, p. 14.
3. *Réflexions sur la question juive,* pp. 146–147.
4. *Ibid.,* pp. 149–150.
5. J.-A. Moein, *IIe Congrès international d'eugénisme,* quoted by Sir Alan Burns.
6. Senghor, "Ce que l'homme noir apporte," *L'Homme de couleur,* pp. 309–310.
7. Jean-Paul Sartre, *Orphée Noir,* preface to *l'Anthologie de la poésie negre et malgache,* pp. xi et suiv.
8. J.-P. Sartre, *ibid.,* p. xliv.

II

The Migration of Labor
and Its Social Consequences

M. Harris

LABOUR EMIGRATION
AMONG THE MOÇAMBIQUE THONGA:
CULTURAL AND POLITICAL FACTORS (1959)

I

The emigration of Moçambique labourers to the South African mines has been governed by a series of international agreements beginning in 1897 between Moçambique and the Transvaal Republic, followed by the Modus Vivendi of 1901, the Transvaal–Moçambique Convention of 1909, and the Portuguese–South African Convention of 1928, revised in 1934, 1936, and 1940. The essential point in these agreements is that the interests represented by the Transvaal Chamber of Mines are to be granted large-scale labour-recruiting privileges in the southern portion of Moçambique in return for guarantees that a certain proportion of the seaborne traffic to the so-called "Competitive Zone" of the Transvaal—the industrial heartland around Johannesburg—must pass through the Portuguese port of Lourenço Marques rather than through the rival South African ports of Durban, East London, Port Elizabeth and Cape Town. Direct monetary payments per native recruited, guarantees to repatriate clandestine emigrants, maximum contract time, and permission to establish Portuguese Native Affairs inspection and tax-collecting facilities (*Curadoria*) on Union territory have also figured prominently in the bargaining.

The recruiting of international labourers in Moçambique south of parallel 22° S. has been carried out since 1900 by the Witwatersrand Native Labour Association (WNLA), a company set up by the mines and granted a monopoly by the Portuguese authorities. According to the existing agreements, a minimum of 47.5 per cent. of the seaborne import traffic to the Competitive Zone must pass through the port of Lourenço

SOURCE. M. Harris, "Labour Migration among the Moçambique Thonga: Cultural and Political Factors," reprinted from *Africa*, XXIX, 1, 1959, pp. 50–64, by permission of the International African Institute. Copyright by M. Harris.

Marques. Twelve months is the minimum and eighteen months the maximum contract time. The maximum number of mining recruits per year is 100,000, while the guaranteed minimum is 65,000.

Despite their best efforts, the Portuguese have found it impossible to confine the total labour emigration to the Union within the limits envisaged by the international agreements. Many of the natives employed outside the mines are illegal or "clandestine" migrants who have been brought under the control of the *Curadoria*. In 1954 some 21,596 illegal migrants were identified by the *Curadoria do Transvaal* (*Anuário Est.*, 1955, p. 132). There is every reason to believe, however, that substantial numbers of clandestine migrants remain undetected. The illegal migratory current is largely sustained by the desire of the Portuguese natives to choose the place and conditions of work within the Union. By leaving Moçambique without a contract, the clandestine migrant, unlike the WNLA recruit, is relatively free to search and bargain for better wages, more sympathetic employers, and shorter contract periods.

According to the census of 1950, there were 351,702 males between the ages of 15 and 54 years who were habitual residents of the Districts of Lourenço Marques, Gaza, and Inhambane in which the Thonga are the principal ethnic group. Of these, some 117,213 were reported by the native respondents as being temporarily absent in service outside Moçambique. It is probably due in large measure to the fact that native informants were reluctant to name members of the family who were abroad under illegal circumstances that the number of extra-territorial migrants listed for the three districts in question falls short by 40,489 of the number of Moçambique natives actually identified and registered in the *Curadoria do Transvaal* for the same year. Accepting the figure of the *Curadoria* (157,702) as representing the more accurate total of men abroad, we obtain the estimate that 40 per cent. of active Thonga males are at work in the Union of South Africa. Since these calculations fail to take into account many additional thousands of Thonga men who are away in the Union under illegal circumstances unknown to the *Curadoria,* we may feel confident that the direction of probable error is toward minimizing rather than exaggerating the total movement.

The significance of the extra-territorial migration can scarcely be appreciated without reference to the disposition of the active males who remain within Moçambique. Many additional thousands of Thonga males are away from their homesteads at work on farms and plantations, in factories, on the roads, railways, and in the homes and commercial enterprises of Moçambique's urban centres. In 1950 in the city of Lourenço Marques alone there were some 20,000 porters, servants, washboys, and office boys who were in large proportion rural inhabitants temporarily at work within the city under six-month or one-year contracts. During 1953 an additional monthly average of about 16,000 Thonga were employed on European farms. It seems safe to conclude, therefore, that during any given year well over 50 per cent. of the active male Thonga population is away from home working for wages in the employ of Europeans.

The early date of the large-scale movement to the mines by Thonga workers should be emphasized if we are to interpret correctly the circumstances of the international labour migration. Before the Boer War about 80,000 labourers or three-quarters of the total native labour forces at the mines were from Moçambique [1] (*Transvaal Labour Commission*, 1904, p. 28; cf. Amery, 1909, p. 105).

. . . for the first twenty years of the industry's development the mines were almost entirely dependent upon the East Coast area for their native labor supply. The Mozambique "boy" may, therefore be described as the pioneer coloured labourer of the Witwatersrand. (*The Gold of the Rand*, 1927, p. 58.)

It should be recalled that the earliest phases of the mining operations were precisely the most hazardous and the most disagreeable from the standpoint of living-conditions in the compounds. Although wages were higher during this period than at a later date, the mortality rate among the "East Coast Boys" was very great. Between 1902 and 1914 an official total of 43,484 Moçambique natives died as a result of accident and disease while employed on the Rand (Ribeiro, 1917, p. 160). A proportionately greater number probably died at home as a result of diseases contracted during their underground work. The grand total of Portuguese migrant labourers who have lost their lives in the Rand, not counting those who have died elsewhere, or those who died before 1902, stands officially at 81,166 (*Anuário Moçambique*, 1940; *Anuário Estatistica*, 1940–54). Although mining continues to be a hazardous occupation, much improvement has been made since the days when the underground force consisted almost exclusively of Moçambique migrants. This fact needs to be considered in any comparison between the circumstances surrounding the Thonga migratory current and those currents which have more gradually evolved in other areas of Southern Africa.

Another special characteristic of the Thonga contribution to the mines concerns the length of time which they have remained at work. Since pre-Boer War days, the Portuguese natives have stayed on the Rand for longer consecutive periods before returning home than any other migrant group. When Zulu migrants were reported to resist more than four consecutive months of mine labour and Basutos averaged only three months, the East Coast Boys were spending an average span of three years underground (*Transvaal Labour Commission*, pp. 4, 20, 246). With the Convention of 1909, a maximum period of two years of consecutive service at the mines was established for the Moçambique contingent. Under the Convention of 1929 this was further reduced to eighteen months on the basis of an original twelve-month contract renewable for six months. None the less, the British South African native still averaged about half the length of stay of the Portuguese group. In 1914 the latter were reported as averaging seventeen months while the Union Natives stayed only six or seven months (*Report of the Tuberculosis Commission,* 1914, cited in Saldanha, 1931, pp. 47–51). According to the Report of the Board of Management of the WNLA for 1924, "From the length of service standpoint, the contracted Portuguese native is apparently the equivalent of two contracted Union natives" (p. 23). In 1927 the Thonga miner was staying for nearly two years as compared with the average of about eleven months for the Union natives (*The Gold of the Rand,* p. 58). Since the imposition of the legal maximum of eighteen months in 1928, the gap between the length of stay of the Portuguese and British South African contingents has tended to become narrower. The overall trend since the earliest phases of mining operations has been for the length of stay of the Portuguese natives to decline while that of other contingents has risen. Bechuanaland mine workers in 1947, for example, were said to be staying away from home about twice as long as twenty or thirty years earlier (Schapera, 1947, p. 58). In contrast, the average length of stay of the Portuguese native now falls between twelve and eighteen months [2] or about half of what it was at the beginning of the century. This unique characteristic of the Thonga current suggests the operation of factors not present in other areas.

The fact that the Portuguese migrants have consistently remained at the mines for periods greater than a year is related to another unusual feature of the Thonga migratory movement. Unlike the other ethnic groups in the mining labour force, the East Coast contingent does not appear to be influenced in any way by the labour requirements of the native homesteads during critical phases of the agricultural cycle. Portuguese natives are not permitted to migrate to the mines under the Assisted Voluntary System established in 1928 whereby Union and Protectorate natives may enlist for periods short enough to permit them to do the ploughing or to take part in the harvest of their fields at home. On the contrary, the Moçambique natives seem to be of special importance to the entire system of migrant mine labour because their engagement can be regulated to counteract the seasonal fluctuations in the supply from other sources (Van der Horst 1942, p. 219). The Portuguese supply also appears to be protected against larger cyclical fluctuations such as those produced by droughts or exceptionally abundant harvests (*The Gold of the Rand,* p. 60).

Thus, the Thonga have been migrant wage-earners on a large scale since at least as long ago as the last decade of the nineteenth century. Large-scale Thonga emigration to the mines began at a period corresponding to the most dangerous and disagreeable phases of mining operations. The Thonga migration is also noteworthy for its failure to respond to the seasonal fluctuations to which other sources of mine labour are sensitive, for its protracted length of stay, and for the ease with which it can be manipulated in relation to fluctuations in demand.

II

The conversion of the Thonga into migrant wage-earners is the result of complex pressures applied by the Europeans upon an equally complex matrix of primitive social institutions. During the formative decades of the migratory current only the resistance offered by the native way of life stood out clearly before the European observers. Yet native institutions were not uniformly intractable with respect to the modifications appropriate to the introduction of wage labour. Indeed, in retrospect, it is possible to identify a series of native institutions whose presence greatly facilitated the early work of the recruiters.

Although the traditional Thonga household is accurately described as a self-contained economic unit, such a characterization ought not to be accepted as also meaning that the unit was self-sufficient in the sense of being secure and adequate to all its bio-culturally established needs. The technological inventory of the Thonga in relation to the environment in which it had to operate was an unreliable instrument for satisfying the basic economic requirements of the population. Irregular rainfall, prolonged droughts, and epidemics of cattle diseases led frequently to famine conditions. Each year the storehouses of most households emptied out before the new harvests became available and the unhappy "hungry season" was an annual ordeal. This situation underlies certain features of the traditional social organization, a correct rendering of which is of paramount importance for understanding the acculturative processes leading to participation in the European economy.

Designated a tribe by their famous student, Henri Junod, the Thonga never enjoyed the measure of political or cultural unity implied by that term. Even at the height of the political hegemony established under Gungunhana, the last of the Nguni chiefs, raids and counter-raids were the order of the day. Junod makes this perfectly clear:

There is no feeling of national unity in the tribe as a whole; its unity consists only in a language and in certain customs which are common to all the clans [1927, vol. 1, p. 356].

. . . The regular break-up of the residential unity of the patrilineage appears to be a certain conclusion, yet no proof is thereby furnished that the residentially dispersed agnatic group suffered a concomitant loss of functional significance. Undoubtedly some of the junior segments remained in close proximity to the parent settlement. Today it is still not uncommon to encounter the homesteads of one or two sons a few hun-

dred yards away from the homesteads of their father. These sons, together with others who may have dispersed to greater distances, continue to fulfil the ritual functions associated with common agnatic descent
and sometimes still assemble as a body on the ceremonial occasions provided by fruit harvest, deaths, and marriages. . . .

Thus the agnatic descent group among the Thonga encompassed
both a corporate core of localized kinsmen with a continuity of rights
over women and cattle and a wider aggregate of dispersed agnates whose
theoretical claim to a voice in the disposition of the agnatic estate dwin-
dled rapidly with the passage of time and removal in space. As a result
of the marked differences in wealth occurring among the members of the
agnatic group, and in the absence of compensatory distributive mechanisms, the junior branches tended to fall away from the main body and
to establish both new homesteads and new descent lines. This analysis
of the traditional Thonga social system alone renders intelligible the fact
that within a hundred-mile radius of Lourenço Marques there are several
hundred different patriclans.

In brief, the Thonga social order before European influence exhib-
ited a moderate amount of genuine social stratification (cf. Fried, 1956,
pp. 23–24). Rich and poor households were to be found among the membership of each patrilineage. This feature of Thonga social structure
neatly coincided with the requirements of the European economy, since
it predisposed a numerically preponderant segment of the Thonga population, consisting of underprivileged males, to accept intrusive opportunities for altering their traditionally subordinate position within the socio-
economic hierarchy. Before the European influence began to make itself
felt, the Thonga social system stood poised in precarious balance. The
young men lacked neither precedent, motivation, nor an ideology for
seeking to alter their position in the socio-economic hierarchy. The goal
of the Thonga youth was to become headman of his own village, to be
surrounded by many wives and children, and to have abundant food and
drink. Before the introduction of wage labour, ecological conditions
imposed strict limits upon the number of males who might achieve this
favoured status. Hence it is not surprising that wages were quickly
accepted as a welcome alternative to the struggle to win status through
the traditional mechanisms, and that even before the final pacification
of the Thonga area in 1895 the English pound had already become
the most prevalent form of brideprice (cf. Falcão, 1909, p. 101; Almeida
da Cunha, 1885, p. 114; Nunes, 1936, pp. 89 ff.).

One further aspect of Thonga culture needs to be emphasized in
order to complete the picture of the aboriginal contribution to the development of the migratory currents. This aspect is the aboriginal division
of labour. The delegation of productive tasks among the Thonga followed
closely the general pattern common to most of the Southern Bantu. Most

of the agricultural tasks were regarded as ideally women's work. In the agricultural cycle, only the felling and burning of heavy growth was designated as a proper male activity. This division of labour between the sexes provided the European economy with the basic ingredients for a system of migratory labour which, although characteristic of many African regions, has perhaps nowhere been more systematically exploited than in Moçambique.

While the outlines of the Thonga division of labour can be established with considerable confidence, caution must be exercised in accepting the ideal as an accurate expression of the total male contribution to agriculture. Much of the vigour and excellence of the aboriginal agricultural effort actually depended upon the presence of the men. None the less women were quite capable of carrying on alone, and with the help of good rainfalls could meet the basic food requirements of the household while the men were away working for Europeans. Thus the withdrawal of a high percentage of the men from the Thonga households has never seriously threatened the ability of the population to survive and reproduce. On the other hand, the fact that the migrant wage-earners need not be expected to supply their families with food has constituted a great saving to European industrial and farm interests. Free of the responsibility of buying food for their wives and children, the migratory mass has been able to accept wages below what would be required to maintain a work force patterned after a nineteenth-century European industrial proletariat.

The relative unimportance of male agriculture occupies a position basic to the migratory labour compound system, and hence, historically, to the growth of the entire South African industrial complex. Paradoxically, however, it is also the feature of aboriginal life which has supplied the basic juridico-philosophical rationale for the Portuguese native labour policy. The traditional sexual division of labour has persistently been interpreted by Europeans as *prima facie* evidence that the African male is an incorrigible drone. The remedies chosen for the supposed traditional "idleness" of the Thonga are the various prescriptions for forcing or cajoling them into wage labour for European employers.

Yet strict attention must be paid to the fact that every attempt to cajole or force the men into European employ has as its premiss the continued existence of the sexual division of labour. Whether the destination of the migrant male is a European farm, mine, or industry, he is called upon to leave his home for extended periods while the women continue their traditional agricultural routine. The net result of the European pressures has been to establish the female agricultural specialization with a force and clarity immeasurably heightened by comparison with the aboriginal situation. The most decisive testimony to this effect is the failure of the Thonga migratory current to respond to seasonal or climatic fluctuations associated with the agricultural cycle. Such responsiveness is elsewhere clearly indicative of a larger importance attached to the male role in basic food production. Today in Moçambique the demand of the mining complex for migrant labour has been satisfied to the point where the Thonga homestead is regarded by neither the Europeans nor the Africans as the proper scene of manly effort. For the Thonga male, the homestead today is primarily a place to "rest," to recuperate from the strenuous efforts by which wages are won, and to exhibit purchased goods before returning to the European areas where wages can be earned again.

It is widely believed that "the central problem which faced employers at the beginning of the era of European exploitation was to evolve a means of introducing wages as an incentive to labour" (Noon, 1944, p. 6). This proposition cannot be accepted as an accurate expression of the central problem facing European employers of the Thonga. Wage payments for labour tasks contradicted nothing of significance in the old way of life. On the contrary, the attraction of wages in relation to the Thonga system of social stratification was irresistible.

The central problem faced by the employers of the Thonga was not to get them to work for wages, but to employ masses of unskilled workers under those historically and economically determined conditions peculiar to the South African mining enterprise and the Portuguese colonial venture which alone rendered the payment of wages viable economically and secure politically. These conditions were that the wages paid could not include the cost of sustaining the family of the workers; that the wage-earner and his family be widely separated in space; and that this separation endure for uninterrupted periods of considerable duration, yet not so long as to break the ties binding the worker to his "tribal" domain. The problem, in other words, was the very much more complicated one of converting the male half, and only the male half, of a rural society into a labour force sensitive to the demands of an urban industrial economy.

Obviously, the operation of a free market economy could not alone be depended upon to meet the peculiar set of conditions proposed to the native sellers of labour. It is to be expected of any labour force consisting only of men whose place of employment does not coincide with its habitual residence that there will be a strong tendency to return home frequently. When the basic subsistence of the workers' family does not depend upon remittances from the migrant, this tendency can confidently be expected to result in short and irregular working intervals.

III

The defeat of Gugunhana in 1895 was accompanied by a concerted attempt to make use of the native labour supply in Southern Moçambique, especially for the amplification of the port facilities and the construction of the railroad and other basic installations. From 1895 on, a large part of the region was placed under military government and harsh measures were used to collect taxes and maintain order (cf. Botelho, 1936, pp. 533–47). All these circumstances had the effect of driving thousands of Thonga across the borders of the Province. Without the co-operation of the Transvaal authorities there was no way of stopping this clandestine exodus, some of which took the form of permanent migration. Although the arrangement of 1867 with the South African Republic and the Modus Vivendi of 1901 and subsequent international agreements did not diminish the movement to the Rand, they at least had the virtue from the Portuguese point of view of yielding an income from the labour traffic and of diminishing the rate of permanent emigration, as well as of stimulating the growth of one of Africa's greatest ports.

None the less, the signing of the international agreements formally established the Portuguese authorities in the midst of a dilemma from which they have yet to extricate themselves. The employment of thousands of men on foreign soil vastly complicates the task of meeting Moçambique's own internal labour requirements. To satisfy the local demand, the government in 1899 radically altered the laws regulating the use of native labour, sanctioning for the first time the impressment of workers for both public and private purposes (Silva Cunha, 1955, pp. 147–54). Under the circumstances, the application of this law necessarily had a profound effect upon the recruitment of labour for the mines (cf. Buell, 1928, p. 31). Although the wages paid to native mine-workers were low by comparison with the wages paid to white miners, they have always been far higher than those offered by the provincial government or by private employers within Moçambique.[3] In 1907 an administrator of a district near Lourenço Marques noted:

> I understand and advocate the principle that we ought to pay £2 per month for forced labour because the native is our most important resource and it would be unwise to lose him, which as all can see, may very well happen; but agriculture can neither progress nor develop if such high wages are paid [Roque de Aguiar, Administrator of Maracuene; quoted in Saldanha, 1931, p. 315].

Contract time within Moçambique was considerably less than that offered by the WNLA, but, in both cases, separation from the family was involved, and working conditions left much to be desired in Moçambique as well as in the Transvaal. Moreover, the shorter contracts offered within Moçambique in many cases simply meant that repeated recruitments of the same personnel for different employers would be made during the year (cf. Weise, 1907, p. 383).

Heavily in the balance on the side of the mines was the greater glamour and prestige associated with work in the Transvaal. It would be contrary to the purpose of this paper to support the widely disseminated notion that the migratory current to the mines is motivated largely by the desire of the African male to see the wonders of Johannesburg and to enhance his stature in the eyes of the people at home, especially the women. The belief that enlistment for mine labour is proof of manhood was certainly spread as much by the recruiters as by the recruits. This factor is only significant in so far as it influences the choice made among alternative modes of wage-employment under conditions where such a choice is obligatory. In Moçambique, the preference expressed by the young women derives simply from the fact that the man who has worked at the mines has demonstrated his superiority over those suitors too stupid, frightened, or lazy to avoid government impressment (cf. Schapera, 1947, p. 117). All that can be asserted is that the greater prestige of the mine-worker together with his higher wages made the rigours of the mines preferable to employment within Moçambique (cf. Camacho, 1926, p. 65). Thus the law which empowered the administration to force the Thonga into what was defined as productive labour, had the perhaps not unanticipated effect of greatly facilitating the task of the WNLA.

Although the *Regulamento* of 1897 and subsequent labour legislation all contain provisions for exempting from forced labour natives engaged on their own behalf in agricultural activities, sheer limitations of population size made it impossible from the beginning to extend the exemption with any degree of regularity. If the labour demands of both foreign and domestic employers were to be met, little real encouragement could be offered for native males who wished to become cash crop farmers (cf. Saldanha, 1928, xxi–xxv). The Thonga male had to choose between working for Europeans in Moçambique or working for Europeans in the Transvaal. No third choice existed. Those who remained at home were subject to forced labour and did so usually only as a calculated risk.

The 1897 *Regulamento* had guaranteed that there should be "full liberty for choosing the method of fulfilling the obligation" to work, but, as a result of the Transvaal migratory current, the legal niceties of recruiting procedures for domestic purposes found little opportunity for expression. The procurement of agricultural and other types of domestic labour early assumed the character of a hunt carried out at night in the hope of surprising the males who were at home before they had a chance to flee to the safety of one of the ubiquitous stations of the WNLA. This hunt was conducted by agents of the native chiefs and sub-chiefs acting upon the command of the administrator or chief of post that they recruit a certain number of volunteers. Wherever possible care was taken to exempt close relatives of the chief or those who had been especially liberal in meeting the traditional prestations due to native political leaders. The quarry were assembled at the local administrative centre and arbitrarily assigned to government projects or to various European employers who had submitted requests to the administrator. Native labourers recruited under such circumstances are called *shibalos*.

In 1928 a new labour code applicable to all Portugal's African territories was created. This code continues to be the basic legal instrument governing the employment of native labour in Moçambique (Silva Cunha, 1955, p. 13). It was designed to correct such abuses as those noted by Professor Edward Ross in the much-discussed report submitted to the Temporary Slavery Commission of the League of Nations in 1925. It prohibited the administration from compelling native labour to work for private employers (Article 271), while permitting recourse to forced labour "when for the execution of public projects it is not possible by virtue of the urgency or some other reasonable motive to obtain the necessary number of native volunteers" (Article 272).

Despite this attempt to bring Portuguese native labour policy into line with that of other colonial powers, the fundamentals of the situation in 1897 remain those of the present. The *shibalo* system has never enjoyed legal sanction, having actually been specifically prohibited in Southern Moçambique as early as 1906 by an edict of Governador Geral Freire de Andrade:

> In consideration of the fact that our laws, while imposing the obligation to work, leave all persons free to choose the mode, time and place for the fulfilment of the obligation [*Portaria* 917, B.O. No. 49, 8 December 1906].

Thus the contents of the 1928 Code and subsequent legal documents bearing upon the issue of forced labour—the Colonial Act, 1930; the Organic Charter of the Portuguese Empire, 1933; the Organic Law of Overseas Portugal, 1953; and the Statute of the Natives of Guiné, Angola and Moçambique, 1954—are uniformly irrelevant to the issue of the *shibalo* system as it actually affects native labour. All these documents reiterate the 1897 provisions for guaranteeing full liberty of choice with respect to the place and mode of work (Silva Cunha, 1955, pp. 201–13). But any violations of such liberty since 1897 have been contrary to the existing legislation and have stemmed from administrative irregularities rather than from the execution of the law. Under existing statutes, the administration continues to be assigned a strategic role in the attempt to make maximum use of native manpower for the purposes of both private and public enterprises. This role is played out in a multitude of individual situations whose complexity is entirely unprovided for by the dominant legal formula and there is little doubt that it continues to be abused.

Despite the considerable degree to which native manpower has been made available to foreign and domestic employers since the beginning of the century and earlier, from the point of view of the Europeans in Moçambique there is and always has been a critical manpower shortage:

As we have seen, one of the most characteristic traits of the labour market in Africa is the lack of a spontaneous offering of manpower. While in civilized countries, unemployment is feared and attempts made to avoid it, in Africa, there is the attempt to conquer, by all kinds of means, the manpower shortage [Silva Cunha, 1955, p. 249].

The official Portuguese analysis of this shortage is today identical with the analysis presented by the authors of the 1897 labour code (cf. Enes, 1893, pp. 70–71). The basic premiss of the labour policy, under both the 1897 and 1928 laws, is that the domestic shortage is the result of a deep-seated reluctance upon the part of the African male voluntarily to seek wage-employment. This resistance is officially thought to arise from the low level of material desires characteristic of the native economy and from the perversity of the primitive social organization whereby males exploit female labourers in order that they may enjoy a lifetime of idleness. According to the report for 1940–2 of Governor General José Tristão de Bettencourt:

> The problem of native manpower . . . is probably the most important preoccupation of European agriculture. Generally speaking, throughout the various epochs of the year there is an insufficient number of workers for the accomplishment of the undertakings which have been planned. The recruiters struggle with great difficulties to engage the needed numbers of workers; then a number of those contracted leave the scene of work with or without the slightest pretext, causing great complications and increasing the expense of production. Although Bantu manpower is many times greater than the internal activities of the civilized population require, even after one discounts the 200,000 [*sic*] or so men under contract in the Union of South Africa and the Rhodesias, the large majority of them do no work, neither for themselves nor for others, but simply live from the labour of their wives . . . [Bettencourt, 1945, pp. 75–76].

Relief from this situation had been sought under Governor Bettencourt's aegis through Circular 818/D-7, 7 October 1942, whose introductory remarks are as follows:

> The rendering of work in Africa cannot continue to depend upon the whim [*arbitrário*] of the Negro, who is by temperament and natural circumstances, inclined to expend only that minimum of effort which corresponds to his minimum necessities.

Subsequent paragraphs of this circular define the conditions under which natives are considered to be idle and obliged to seek employment. In Circular 566/D-7, 5 May 1947 these conditions were re-stated together with certain illuminating comments as to how the earlier recommendations had been acted upon at the local administrative level:

> In spite of the clarity of the doctrine and purpose of Circular 818/D-7 of October 7, 1942, it has not always been judiciously interpreted in practice, above all, in reference to the recruitment of native labour for private purposes. . . .
> The recruiters, because of a deficient comprehension of their duties . . .

have limited themselves to appearing at the administrative centres of the Cir-
cumscriptions, where they have contracted workers, idle ones or not, who have
been ordered to appear there by the administrative authorities.

In subsequent paragraphs, Circular 566/D-7 reaffirms the principle
that native males are presumed to be idle unless they can supply proof
to the contrary:

1. All active native males between the ages of 18 and 55 years of
age are obliged to prove that they live from their work.

2. The required proof is satisfied in the following ways:

   (a) Be self-employed in a profession, in commerce or industry
       by which he supports himself.

   (b) Be employed permanently in the service of the State, ad-
       ministrative corps or private persons.

   (c) To have worked for at least six months in each year as a day
       labourer for the State, administrative corps or private per-
       sons.

   (d) To be within the period of six months after having returned
       from the Union of South Africa, or the Rhodesias, from a
       legal contract in conformity with international agreement.

   (e) Be a cattle-raiser, with at least 50 head of cattle.

   (f) Be registered as an *agricultor africano* under the terms of
       the Statute of the African Agriculturalist approved by the
       Diploma Legislativo 919, 5 August 1944.

   (g) To have completed military service and be in the first year
       of reserve status.

The natives who cannot supply proof in any of the above terms are considered to be idle and as such are subject to recruitment by the government for six months of labour in the public interest (Article 6). The intervention of the authorities in the recruitment of workers for private
parties was again specifically prohibited (Article 10).

It is clear from the provisions reproduced above that the perpetuation of the Rand migratory current among the Thonga continues to be
intimately related to the pressures maintained by Portuguese colonial
policy. An analysis of the conditions acceptable as proof of significant
economic activity reveals a deep politico-economic commitment to the
international *status quo* first established in 1897, and thus, in the circular
fashion already defined, to the perpetuation of the migratory currents
to both foreign and domestic destinations at the expense of the development of native agricultural enterprise. Out of the seven acceptable proofs
of significant economic activity, only two refer to activities which can
normally be carried out within the precincts of the native homestead.
Five of the conditions of proof involve the male either in migratory forms
of employment or in activities requiring the removal of his family to an

urban environment. The two exceptions, items (e) and (f), are conditions which can be met only in an insignificant percentage of cases.

According to the instructions supplied with the 1950 Census form, the profession of all active native males who had no specific kind of employment was to be denoted by the term "trabalhador" (worker). In the districts of Lourenço Marques, Gaza, and Inhambane, 183,294 males were so designated. These, together with the 157,000 men registered in the Curadoria do Transvaal, constituted about 85 per cent. of the Thonga active male population. For the same year, the Census lists 1,246 Thonga males as exercising the profession of cattle-raiser, while 23,473 were classified as agriculturalists (agricultores). Of the latter, it is not clear what percentage actually held the certificate of agricultor africano under the terms of the statute mentioned in item (f). Most of the men classified as agriculturalists by the census were probably merely engaged in the production of rice or cotton, upon which special administrative emphasis is placed throughout Moçambique, but especially in the districts to the north of the Thonga area. The point to be made is that in 1950 only some 25,000 or 7 per cent. of the Thonga male working force, at the very most, was in a position to provide proof of not being idle by citing activities which did not involve urban or migratory wage-employment. The remaining 93 per cent. constitute the pool from which foreign and domestic wage-labour requirements are being met.

In view of the demonstrable magnitude of the various migratory currents in which the Thonga are already involved, the statutory neutrality with respect to the various modes of proof of non-idleness actually constitutes a legal bias heavily in favour of migratory forms of employment. This bias is further strengthened and given a special geographical meaning by the continuing disparity between the legally established minimum wages for industry and agriculture within Moçambique in contrast to those available to the international migrant. It is also to be noted that the six-months exemption from the threat of forced labour within Moçambique granted to those returning from the Rand (item (d)) amounts in the context of the law to the underwriting of six months of withdrawal from all activity economically significant by either native or European standards. Over the years, the temporary immunity granted at the completion of a WNLA Contract has actually tended to be used for a vacation, during which the "idleness" so persistently combated by the administration has tended in fact to correspond to a genuine reluctance to perform useful activity within the native homestead. With the traditional male activities in agriculture and in other economic tasks defined officially as "idleness" and subject to the threat of forced labour, there is little incentive for the Thonga male to engage in them. On the other hand, the re-conversion of any substantial portion of Thonga manpower to self-employed agriculturalists and pastoralists to the satisfaction of the European concept of such activities, cannot be achieved without large-scale technical and economic assistance from the administration. Although room for doubt exists, there is little evidence that such assistance is contemplated on a scale large enough to threaten the security of the manpower pool upon which WNLA, the government-owned railroads and ports, and the domestic planters depend.

In the meantime, the net result of the official, legal, and administrative understanding of the economic functions performed by the male within his homestead is to deprive the overwhelming majority of Thonga men of the opportunity of remaining with their families for more than six months in a year. Yet the interminable paradox, as we have seen, is that the expulsion of this formidable labour force from the scene of subsistence agriculture has never eliminated the manpower "shortage" within Moçambique. The pressures responsible for driving the Thonga male from his homestead have helped to fill the WNLA quotas, have helped to satisfy the demand for urban workers within Moçambique who are paid wages comparable to those of the Rand, and have driven uncounted thousands clandestinely across the border into the neighbouring territories, but they have never succeeded in making available a sufficient quantity of unskilled gang labour for employment within Moçambique at the prevailing domestic wage for such workers. Part of the deficit— for stevedoring, public construction, and public sanitation—is supplied by the administration through its legal power (but not necessarily legal procedure) to apprehend "idlers" and force them to sign contracts for work interpreted as being in the public benefit.

Despite the perfect illegality of the alternative, it is difficult to conceive how the rest of the shortage—on the private farms and plantations— can be met by volunteers, when the wages offered are less than half those of the Rand or of household servants in Lourenço Marques and the conditions of work are scarcely more desirable.

NOTES

1. Until 1913, part of the Portuguese contingent was drawn from areas north of Parallel 22° S. and hence included groups other than Thonga.

2. In 1953, 61,078 out of 71,752 Portuguese natives repatriated from the Union were returning after a stay of between one and two years.

3. Wages for ordinary labourers in Southern Moçambique correspond at present to the wage minimums established by the Bureau of Native Affairs in 1950: 150 escudos per month for agriculture, railroads and roads, and 180 escudos for industry ($£1 = 80$ escudos). Wages for mine-workers today average over £5 per month (cf. *Transvaal and Orange Free State Chamber of Mines, Annual Report,* 1955, p. 98).

REFERENCES

Almeida da Cunha, Joaquim. 1885. *Estudo acêrca dos Usos e Costumes, etc.* Moçambique, Imprensa Nacional.

Amery, L. S. 1909. *The Times History of the War in South Africa.* London: Sampson Low, Marston & Co.

Bettencourt, José Tristão de. 1945. *Relatório do Governador Geral.* Lisboa: Agência Geral das Colónias.

Botelho, José J. T. 1936. *História Militar e Politica dos Portugueses em Moçambique.* Lisboa: Centro Tip. Colonial.

Buell, Raymond. 1928. *The Native Problem in Africa.* New York: Macmillan Company.

Comacho, Brito. 1926. *Moçambique.* Lisboa: Livraria Editora Guimarães.

Enes, Antonio. 1945. *Moçambique,* 3rd ed. Lisboa: Agência Geral das Colónias.

Falcão, José Bravo. 1909. "Emigração dos indígenas do sul da província de Moçambique, etc.," *Revista Portuguesa Colonial e Maritima, Lisboa,* vol. xxiv, no. 141, pp. 99–114.

Fried, Morton H. 1957. "The classification of corporate unilineal descent groups," *Journal of the Royal Anthropological Institute,* vol. lxxxvii, part 1, pp. 1–29.

Jeppe, C. Biccard. 1946. *Gold Mining on the Witwatersrand,* 2 vols. Johannesburg: T.C.M.

Junod, Henri A. 1912. *The Life of a South African Tribe,* 2 vols. Neuchâtel.

———— 1927. *The Life of a South African Tribe,* 2nd ed. 2 vols. Neuchâtel.

———— 1914. "The condition of the natives of South-East Africa in the sixteenth century, etc.," *South African Journal of Science,* vol. x, no. 6.

Junod, Henri P. 1939. "Os indígenas de Moçambique," in *Moçambique,* nos. 17, 18, 19. Lourenço Marques: Imprensa Nacional.

Noon, John. 1944. *Labour Problems in Africa.* University of Pennsylvania.

Nunes, Joaquim. 1936. "O lobolo," *Moçambique,* no. 8, pp. 89–117. Lourenço Marques: Imprensa Nacional.

Ribeiro, Sousa. 1902, 1917. *Anuàrio de Moçambique.* Lourenço Marques: Imprensa Nacional.

Ross, Edward. 1925. *Report on Employment of Native Labour in Portuguese Africa.*

Saldanha, Eduardo. 1931. *Moçambique perante Genebra.* Porto: Tipografia Porto Médico.

———— 1928. *O Sul do Save.* Lisboa: Tipografia Formosa.

Sheppard, W. C. A. 1934. "Recruiting in Portuguese East Africa, etc.," *Journal of the African Society,* vol. xxxiii, no. 132, pp. 253–60.

Schapera, I. 1947. *Migrant Labour and Tribal Life.* London: Oxford University Press.

Schapera, I., and Goodwin, A. J. H. 1937. "Work and Wealth," in *The Bantu-speaking Tribes of South Africa,* pp. 131–71. London: Routledge and Kegan Paul.

Silva Cunha, J. M. da. 1955. *O Trabalho Indígena.* Lisboa: Agência Geral do Ultramar.

———— 1953. *O Sistema Português de Politica Indígena.* Coimbra: Coimbra Editora.

Transvaal Chamber of Mines, 1927. *The Gold of the Rand.* Johannesburg: T.C.M.

Transvaal Labour Commission, 1904. *Minutes of Proceedings and Evidence* (Cd. 1897). London: H.M.S.O.

Van der Horst, Sheila. 1942. *Native Labour in South Africa.* London: Oxford University Press.

Weise, Carlos. 1907. "A 'labour question' em nossa casa." *Boletim da Sociedade de Geografia de Lisboa,* no. 6, pp. 381–7.

E. Colson

MIGRATION IN AFRICA:
TRENDS AND POSSIBILITIES (1960)

Large-scale migrations have been a feature of African life for many
centuries, both in the form of conquering hordes acquiring new territories and in the more peaceful form of a slow infiltration of small groups
seeking new land as old land became exhausted. Sometimes the movements were presumably sparked by population pressure. In West Africa
they were also caused by a desire to obtain control of trading routes and
to have a greater share of trade goods, as witness the drive of interior
peoples toward the coastal regions. Such movements have therefore been
guided by considerations other than those of simple subsistence. In West
Africa there has long been a tradition of seasonal or periodic movement
comparable to the modern phenomenon of labor migration in that men,
and sometimes women, left their home communities to engage in prolonged expeditions for economic gain. By the middle of the nineteenth
century various East African peoples, such as the Nyamwezi and the
Yao, were similarly involved in expeditions which withdrew men from
subsistence agriculture for many months and sometimes for several years.
There is no evidence that their home communities considered this a hardship or suffered unduly from the prolonged absence of a number of able-
bodied men, and often of women. We do not, of course, know how many
of the men were away from their home communities in those days. The
point is that many African societies had early developed an adjustment
to a form of labor migration.

Migrations, both temporary and permanent, are therefore old stories
throughout much of Africa. The movements which have taken place in
the twentieth century, great as they have been, are no such breaks with

source. E. Colson, "Migration in Africa: Trends and Possibilities," from F. Lorimer
and M. Karp (editors), *Population in Africa*, 1960, pp. 60–67. Reprinted by permission of Boston University Press.

the past as is sometimes suggested. One might argue that what is new is the attempt to stabilize population; this perhaps explains the general lack of success of such attempts.

The colonial era was marked by an attempt to tie people to given areas of land as their permanent homes and thus to perpetuate the population distribution that existed when the European Powers took over. Permanent migration was discouraged by administrative regulations and by a freezing of the rules under which land was held. At the same time the temporary migration of workers needed by industries and plantations was encouraged and sometimes forced upon a reluctant people. Since then attention to movements within Africa has very largely centered on the phenomenon of labor migration. This has overshadowed interest in the very considerable movements which have continued to take place as people have moved to seek new land either for subsistence purposes or for the planting of cash crops or for the exploitation of other marketable commodities. Only very spectacular migrations, especially if these have crossed international boundaries, have aroused much comment such as the continual eastern and southern drift of the Fulani in West Africa or the migration of the Nguru and the Luvale groups into Nyasaland and Northern Rhodesia from Mozambique and Angola.

It has usually been assumed that labor migration and permanent migration are unrelated phenomena and that they are basically different in their motivations and consequences. The one is held to be motivated by a desire for cash, the other by population pressure. This is probably a carry-over from the early thinking which held that labor migration was alien to Africa and that it served to provide a cash income to be spent on taxes or luxury goods, while land produced the basic subsistence for the family unit. Today labor migration may provide the basic necessities of life, while land may be the source of a cash income. From the point of view of the area which he leaves, a man's ultimate destination makes little difference, though it may of course determine his eventual return, the amount of his remittances, and whether or not he goes accompanied by dependents.

Official policy has long tended to be affected by underlying assumptions, which have led to a general disregard of the importance of permanent migration. Land has been equated with the family unit, and anything that might take a man from his family has been assumed to be wrong and detrimental to the continuation of a rural society. The development of industries and plantations has led to a constant demand for labor, but fluctuations of world prices and other considerations have tended to discourage the building up of a permanent labor force dependent upon wages. A man could be considered eligible for temporary labor only if he had a permanent home in some rural area to which he could be returned and which in the meantime could be expected to support his family. In a sense a situation has been created comparable to the one engendered by the English Poor Law. The African must be tied to a particular home area and independent migration that makes it difficult to assign him to a home community must not be encouraged. Movement between rural areas has therefore been favored only in the form of planned resettlement of a community group. This, however, has usually been considered necessary only if land pressure has been apparent, as in various resettlement schemes in Kenya and Northern Rhodesia, or if the land has been desired for economic development, as in the Kariba resettlement program.

Both the collection of data on population movements and policies for the control of movements have been affected by these assumptions. The bulk of the published information on population movements in rural areas relates to the number of men going out to work for wages, the reason being assumed, while little or no information is available on the transfer of men from one rural area to another or on the movement of women and children. Reports from labor centers usually deal with the number of men available for work; little attention is given to the women and children who tend to accompany them in increasing numbers. This situation may be corrected by the improvement of periodic censuses. Already the best information we have from some areas on the actual flow of migration comes from the general census rather than from the district reports.

In earlier days, it was assumed by many that labor migration was detrimental to tribal life, regardless of the type of family organization, of the form of agriculture, of the relation of population to resources, or of the rate of population increase. I can find no evidence that labor migration has led to a fall in birth rates, though there is some very unsatisfactory evidence that it may have increased mortality rates in a few areas. Recent work, such as Watson's among the Mambwe of Northern Rhodesia, indicates that the effect of labor migration on social life in rural areas may be far from disruptive. Nevertheless official thinking on the subject seems to have been influenced by a report from the Belgian Congo, published in 1925, which argued that the withdrawal of more than 5 to 10 per cent of the able-bodied men from a district disrupts rural life and should therefore be discouraged. It has become established practice in most territories to report annually upon the percentage of able-bodied men absent from a district and assumed to be at work; high rates have been considered cause for alarm, even though those dependent upon the flow of labor might be demanding more manpower. It has, moreover, been felt that a given district or area ought to maintain a constant or increasing population whether or not the area was capable of supporting the existing number. Since it has been assumed that only the urgent need for money could take an African from his beloved tribal community, a solution has been sought in the introduction of cash crops that would obviate the necessity of going out to work. Over the years valiant attempts have been made to find suitable cash crops to this end and thus bring about the desired stabilization of population on the land. Few have been willing to consider that some regions might more reasonably be regarded as temporary way-stations from which the people should be encouraged to move on.

The successful development of cash crops has decreased the flow of population from areas where they have been introduced, but it has often been accompanied by an influx of new settlers into districts which have in the meantime become economically attractive. Many cash-crop areas now appear to have sizable immigrant populations. Immigrants may first come as laborers, in a typical migrant labor pattern, and then establish themselves as independent producers. In 1948, 34.0 per cent of Buganda's total population consisted of immigrants from other parts of Uganda, from Tanganyika or the Sudan, or from Ruanda-Urundi. The majority of these either worked for Baganda cotton or coffee growers, or were themselves growing cash crops. In Kyagwe Saza the percentage was as high as 45.5 per cent.[2] A large number of the immigrants were still seasonal migrants, but in recent years many brought their wives and children with them and planned to settle in Buganda permanently. This was particularly true of immigrants from Ruanda-Urundi who felt that they had little opportunity in their homeland. Busoga, another cotton growing area in Uganda, also had a high proportion of immigrants among its population.

Elsewhere in Africa the same picture obtains. Cash-crop areas tend to attract populations from regions where transportation costs, poverty of soil, or other handicaps diminish the opportunities for the people. Rouch estimates that in 1953–54 some 300,000 to 400,000 immigrants from the northern areas of French West Africa were living in Ghana. Of these, 120,000 were working in agriculture, many of them being employed on African cocoa farms or else working as independent producers.[3] Many are still migrants in the sense that they move regularly between their home villages and centers in Ghana. Others ought to be considered permanent settlers. In addition, Ghana has attracted settlers and migrant workers from its own Northern Territories, Dahomey, Nigeria, and other parts of West Africa. These are to be found both in towns and on mines as well as in rural areas.

In Northern Rhodesia, three rural areas are known to have attracted settlement in recent years. One is the Luapula River region; its rich fisheries supply the markets of Katanga and of the Rhodesian Copper Belt. Cunnison found the region settled by a heterogeneous population, drawn from neighboring regions of the Congo and Northern Rhodesia, many of whom had come in recent years to participate in the fishing industry. Again along the Kafue River, commercial fishing, though on a smaller scale, has brought settlers from various parts of Northern Rhodesia, first Lozi and more recently Ngoni and Bemba. Some of its settlers are from districts 500 miles away from the Kafue. The maize-growing area of the railway belt is the third largest rural focus of immigration. Among the Plateau Tonga of the maize belt I found a heterogeneous group of immigrants living either in Tonga villages or in separate settlements. These included Ndebele and Shona from Southern Rhodesia, Valley Tonga from the Gwembe District, Lozi and various Luvale people from western Rhodesia, Bemba from the Northern Province, Chewa and Ngoni from the Eastern Province, and various tribesmen from Nyasaland. The maize-belt had therefore attracted settlers from an area with a radius of 500 miles or more. Many had originally come to work on European farms and then settled in nearby Tonga reserves to grow maize for the market.

The evidence of far-ranging individual movements for settlement in what are considered economically desirable areas is therefore clear. Unfortunately, we lack good quantitative material in most instances which would allow us to assess the extent of the flow and its permanence. If we are to have some ideas of the growth of African populations, it is vital that censuses report births on a district basis. We also know little about the effect of such immigration upon local societies and the means whereby they are incorporated into the local community.

I have referred to the fact that, temporarily at least, the development of a cash crop inhibits labor emigration. I would argue that this situation is not likely to endure, but here again there is as yet little information against which this hypothesis can be tested. There is some evidence that the migration rate in some areas in which cash crops have been successful is now beginning to rise; men are no longer able to find sufficient land within the favored region to provide the income that they have come to regard as essential to their needs and the proper return for their labor on the land. In these areas they may prefer to turn to wage labor rather than to move to inferior lands away from markets where they would still have to find subsidiary employment to produce a cash income. For them land is now valued for the income which can be derived from it rather than solely for subsistence purposes.

Among the Plateau Tonga there was a drastic fall in the migration rate when cash cropping developed in the late twenties and early thirties. During the thirties and forties land became scarce in some areas, but men could find new fields in the western portions of the country where water resources had been made available. Crops could be transported from the new areas as easily as from the old, and land was eagerly taken up. By 1950 most of the available land was under cultivation, and with a rapidly increasing population fragmentation had begun to appear.

Ambitious men were no longer able to obtain sufficient land locally to increase or even to sustain their incomes. Some moved on to cultivate in reserves near Lusaka, about 120 miles to the north, in a region inhabited by another tribe but close to transport and markets. Few were willing to move to equally fertile land in the Tonga reserves away from roads and transport. Some met the situation by going out to work. Officials have noted that since 1950 there has been a slight but steady increase in the percentage of able-bodied men away at work.

In Buganda fertile land at a distance from transport and markets does not attract Baganda settlers, though it may be taken up by immigrants from elsewhere who are just beginning to shift from labor migration to cash-cropping as a way of life. To the Baganda, the returns from such land do not justify the effort of bringing it into cultivation. In the Nyakyusa region of Tanganyika, although both rice and coffee have been established as cash crops, young men now find it difficult to get land to grow them. They depend on labor migration to maintain their present standard of living, though some of them have begun to settle in the Central Province of Tanganyika where the Administration is sponsoring a peasant farming development near Tabora.

Once cash-cropping has been introduced it becomes a way of life, and the cash may become more important than the cropping. In areas where cash-cropping has not been developed (and these represent a large proportion of the surface of Africa), labor migration of a periodic sort continues as a regular way of life, though even here there is a tendency to settle permanently in towns or in rural areas more favorably endowed. In some of the regions the land is no longer able to provide food for the existing population, and people must either find permanent wage employment or move to new regions. Here the people are prepared to move to new land away from transport routes and markets, since they do not value land in terms of its cash potential. But the opening of new land for settlement will have little effect upon the rate of migration, since the people are still dependent upon outside employment for the cash portions of their incomes. However, the opening of new land for subsistence agriculture will probably encourage the continuation of a pattern of migrant labor for limited periods, especially during youth, rather than a permanent settlement in labor centers.

One may therefore expect that new cash crop areas will show an initial influx of population, often of a settlement type that includes women and children, and then a rising rate of emigrants in search of work. Non-cash-crop areas are likely to show a steady outflow to labor centers and, where land is available, also for settlement purposes. At some point the number of people who remain on the land will tend to remain stationary. This now seems to be happening in parts of Kenya and in the Union of South Africa. Labor migration then becomes a means of coping with a surplus population that cannot be supported within the region rather than a source of cash supplementing subsistence. The Xosa have nearly tripled in the last 50 years, but the population of the Keiskamahoek District has remained nearly stationary between the 1936 and 1946 Union censuses. Monica Wilson says that "a number equivalent to the natural increase emigrated either to towns or to white farms as labourers, indicating that the 'Reserve' had reached a saturation point." [4] At present one-third of the married men are without arable land and no family produces enough food to feed itself. These people are in part supported by remittances from the towns. In such regions only the investment of considerable sums of capital is likely to increase the capacity of the land to feed those who have a claim upon it.

Though the phenomenon of periodic labor migration as it has existed in Africa over the past 50 years may disappear with the development of a permanent force of wage-laborers, the continued movement of people from the country into the towns and to other centers of employment will no doubt continue and prove as enduring a feature of African life as it is of European and American life.

NOTES

1. Before presenting her paper, Miss Colson pointed out that interpretations of conditions in Africa are usually biased by experience in a particular region. Her own work has been in Central Africa and her readings have been in large part focused on studies in Central and East Africa.

2. Audrey I. Richards, ed., *Economic Development and Tribal Change*, Cambridge, n.d., p. 95.

3. Jean Rouch, "Migrations au Ghana," *Journal de la Société des Africanistes*, Vol. 26 (1956), p. 192.

4. *Communal Rituals of the Nyakyusa*, London, 1959, p. 5.

E. J. Berg

BACKWARD-SLOPING
LABOR SUPPLY FUNCTIONS
IN DUAL ECONOMIES—THE AFRICA CASE (1961)

Few discussions of labor supply in underdeveloped countries fail to bring up the backward-sloping labor supply function. Wage-earners in newly-developing countries are alleged to have relatively low want schedules or high preference for leisure as against income, so that they work less at higher wage rates and more at lower ones. In the underdeveloped world, and notably in Africa, this has been the almost universal opinion of foreign employers of native labor, an opinion shared by outside observers.[1] It was no less common a view in eighteenth century England, where a typical complaint was that "If a person can get sufficient in four days to support himself for seven days, he will keep holiday the other three; that is, he will live in riot and debauchery." [2]

From this general observation about the behavior of individual wage earners the conclusion is almost invariably drawn that the supply of labor is inversely related to the rate of wages—that labor supply functions are backward-sloping. Labor-short European plantation owners in the Ivory Coast (ex-French West Africa) resisted, for example, granting increases in African wages in the 1920's on these grounds. One writer described their views as follows:

> The majority [of the planters] . . . rebel against any suggestion that wages be raised, and assert that they have gone the limit in wage sacrifices. They assert that . . . [higher] wages could not be paid to natives without destroying their taste for work. The needs of the native being limited, they say, he who works two days in order to earn 12 francs will work half as much if the rates are increased. . . . So the labor crisis would be intensified.[3]

source. E. J. Berg, "Backward-Sloping Labor Supply Functions in Dual Economies." Reprinted by permission of the publishers from *The Quarterly Journal of Economics,* Vol. LXXV, No. 3, August 1961, Cambridge, Mass.: Harvard University Press, Copyright, 1961, by the President and Fellows of Harvard College.

Everywhere in Africa this argument was common. It found some of its most refined and recurrent expression in the Union of South Africa. In the 1890's, for example, the South African Chamber of Mines argued:

> In support of a general reduction of wages, if possible by a fixed tariff, it is forcibly argued that the high wages now paid are themselves a principal reason of short supply . . . it is found that the average period of service among our Kaffirs is much shorter than in districts in which a lower rate of wages is paid.[4]

The widespread conviction that labor supply functions in countries in early stages of development tend to be backward-sloping is no mere intellectual curiosity. It is one of those ideas in history which has had genuine impact on the practical world of affairs. It has served as a rationale for wage and labor policies which influenced the course of economic and political development not only in Africa but elsewhere as well.[5] It has also been brought into the arena of methodological debate to serve as part of the underpinning of theories which claim that the analytic tools of "Western" economic theory are inapplicable to "dual" societies.[6]

Given its popularity and its influence it is surprising that this hoary concept of the backward-sloping labor supply curve has been exposed to so little systematic analysis, particularly since there runs through most discussions of the matter a considerable confusion over fundamentals.[7] The sources of this confusion are twofold. First, many writers tend to mix the present with the past; they write of contemporary nonindustrial societies as ideal types of pre-industrial societies untouched by contact with the market economy. Most contemporary nonindustrial societies, however, even in Africa's isolated corners, are societies in varying degrees of transition. They have been in contact, however sporadic and tangential, with the goods and ideas of the outside world for two or three generations at least. They have consequently undergone changes which have made them responsive to the money economy outside the villages. Discussions of labor supply which heavily underscore the immobilities of labor in underdeveloped countries, the unwillingness of villagers to enter wage employment, the indifference to monetary incentives are concerned more often with the past than the present.

The second and more important source of confusion derives from a general fuzziness about *which* labor supply functions are at issue. As in the citations noted above, conclusions about aggregate labor supply have been drawn from individual labor market behavior. But this is correct only with the implicit assumption—the classical assumption—that the size of the labor force is some constant proportion of the total population. However useful this assumption is in analysis of the labor supply in industrial countries, it is obviously misleading in countries with large non-market sectors. Aggregate man-hours of labor available for paid employment is a function not only of average time spent in employment by individuals in the labor force; it depends also on the number of people at work (the labor force participation rate) in a given population, a variable which is subject to considerable short-run fluctuation, particularly in dual economies. No a priori statements about aggregate labor supply can, therefore, be derived from observations about the time each worker spends in employment.

In this paper an attempt is made to avoid these common confusions by explicitly recognizing the fact of change over time, and by sorting out several of the various labor supply functions pertinent in the African context. We try to show the sense in which labor supply curves were in the past or are presently backward-sloping. The analysis centers on the factors determining the shape of three labor supply curves—that of the individual, that of the exchange economy as a whole, and that of the country or territory—the standard political unit. While the analysis refers specifically to sub-Saharan Africa, it has applicability to other areas of similar economic structure.

THE DUAL ECONOMY AND THE MIGRANT LABOR SYSTEM

African economies are "dual" in both the structural and the sociological sense. A modern exchange or money sector and a traditional subsistence sector exist side-by-side. Though the extent of the money economy varies widely between the different parts of the continent, in Africa as a whole a relatively large proportion of land and labor resources are devoted to subsistence production.[8] This does not mean that Africans have been untouched by the money economy; in fact, its impact is felt in every village.[9] In all areas African villagers sell some part of their output on local markets. In some areas (notably in West Africa, Uganda, parts of Tanganyika) villagers produce export crops on a substantial scale. Everywhere some Africans are absent from their villages, at work for wages in towns, on mining sites, on European or (in certain cases) African farms. But the limited extent of the exchange economy in the continent generally is suggested by the fact that out of a total African population of perhaps 160–170 million in Africa south of the Sahara only about 8 million work for wages during any part of the year.[10]

Most of the unskilled workers employed in the exchange sector are temporary emigrants from the villages of the subsistence sector; the characteristic feature of the labor market in most of Africa has always been the massive circulation of Africans between their villages and paid employment outside. In some places villagers engage in wage-earning seasonally. More commonly today they work for continuous though short-term periods of roughly one to three years, after which they return to the villages. Tendencies toward more or less permanent stabilization in wage-earning are increasingly emerging, especially in southern Africa, the ex-Belgian Congo and some of the West African towns. But even today the majority of wage-earners in most African countries are not permanently fixed in towns or wage employment.[11] It is with these migrant workers that we are concerned.

THE INDIVIDUAL'S OFFER OF LABOR

What are the factors that determine whether and for how long an individual African villager will offer his labor for paid employment in the exchange sector? In general terms, they are the same factors that determine how much labor an individual in any market economy will offer for hire: the nature of the individual's preference between income and leisure, the level of his non-wage income, the rate of wages. The potential migrant laborer balances the benefits to be obtained from income-earning outside against the inconveniences of a given spell in wage employment. He decides to migrate when, given the rate of wages and his "leisure"-income preference function, the anticipated satisfactions from his net expected income exceed the costs to him of migrating, "costs" being defined as sacrificed "leisure."[12] Since the villager usually has non-wage sources of money income (i.e., marketed portions of village output) his decision to migrate and the length of time he will stay in employment depends also on the level of his village income and the effort-price of income in wage employment as compared with the effort-price of income in alternative income-earning pursuits. The major factors determining the individual's decisions therefore are: (1) the intensity of his preference for money income as against "leisure" in the village; (2) the level of his income from village production; (3) the effort-price of income earnable in the village; (4) the effort-price of income earnable outside the village.[13]

Some writers have attacked this kind of approach on the grounds that implicit in it are unrealistic assumptions about the character of labor markets and the economic behavior of individuals in non-Western societies.[14] These writers emphasize the complexity and diversity of value systems in different societies. They point out that in tradition-oriented societies there is little room for notions of individual "utility"-maximization, that economic behavior is guided by traditional factors and community norms. Individual reactions to changes in wage rates, prices and other market variables are thus said to be shaped by factors unamenable to the economist's ordinary tools.[15] More extreme writers of this general persuasion see "perverse" economic reactions everywhere in these sociologically dual societies, from which they conclude that conventional economic theory is a "tender hot-house plant" which withers in the unfamiliar cultural environment of the non-Western world.[16]

    The essence of this criticism is that economic analysis assumes in-
dividual utility-maximization, and that this implies a specific kind of
economic behavior which is rarely found in traditional or transitional
societies. But this is not correct. Conventional economic reasoning can
proceed from any of an extensive range of behavioral assumptions. All
that is demanded if the analysis is to be meaningful and useful is the
setting down of behavioral postulates which approximate individual
behavior in the real world and are general enough to be interesting but
not so general as to be capable of "explaining" everything.

    To illustrate this, and because it is revealing in its own right, we
will analyze the individual African's offer of labor under a highly
restrictive set of behavioral assumptions. First, let us assume that the
African villager, the potential migrant into paid employment, has a relatively low, clearly-defined and rigid income goal; he wants money to
pay head and hut taxes, to make the marriage payments required of
prospective bridegrooms, or to purchase some specific consumer durable
(a bicycle, a rifle, a sewing machine, a given quantity of clothing or
textiles, etc.). Second, we will assume that the ordinary African has a
strong preference to remain in the village and only goes out to work
when he cannot earn in the village sufficient income, or can earn it only
with very much greater effort, to meet his money income target. It is on
the basis of these two assumptions that we will analyze the individual
African's offer of labor.

    For the reluctant villager with a fixed income goal the key elements
determining the decision to migrate and the amount of time to stay in
employment are the level of his demand for money income (the size of
his income goal), the level of his income from village sources, and the
rate of wages in the exchange sector. The size of his income goal depends
mainly on tax rates and the accumulated level of his wants; it can be
taken in the short run as given. It is therefore the level of the individual's
village income and the rate of wages which are the decisive short-run
factors in determining the quantity of labor which he will offer in the
exchange economy. Given his income goal, and supposing all other
factors unchanged, the function relating the time he is prepared to spend
in employment with the rate of wages in the exchange sector is a curve
of unit negative elasticity—a rectangular hyperbola; if wage rates rise
(fall) the migrant spends proportionally less (more) time in paid employment. Similarly, given his income goal and the rate of wages outside, his
"time spent in employment" function varies inversely and proportionally
with respect to changes in village income; if harvests are good and his
village income rises, he spends correspondingly less time in paid employment. If village income is sufficient to allow him to attain his income
goal he will not go out to work regardless (within realistic limits) of the
rate of wages.

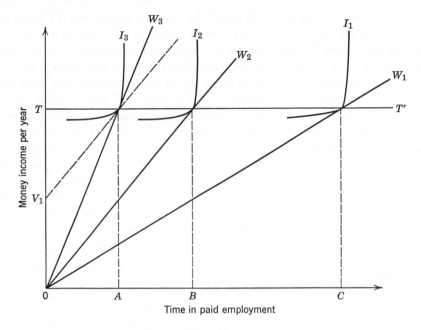

Figure 1

The nature of the preference function implied by the reluctance and target income assumptions is shown in Figure 1. The indifference lines (I_1, I_2, I_3) show combinations of money income and "leisure" (time not in paid employment outside the village) that the villager finds equally preferable. The individual's labor offer curve (TT') is derived in the familiar way, by joining points of tangency between wage lines (W_1, W_2, W_3) and indifference lines.

The elbow shape of the indifference curves indicates that the target income (OT) is an inflexible goal. The individual will spend in paid employment whatever time is required to reach that goal, given his village income and the rate of wages. Once he has attained it he will refuse to make further sacrifices of "leisure" whatever (within realistic ranges) the rate of wages; at OT income his income-elasticity of demand approaches zero for everything except "leisure." When wages double, therefore, from OW_1 to OW_2 he spends half as much time in wage employment (OB months instead of OC). Similarly, when income from village production rises from O to OV_1 ($OV_1 = \frac{1}{2} OT$), the wage in the exchange sector remaining OW_2, he will work half as long as before (OA months instead of OB).

The shape of the indifference curves below OT depends on the urgency of the individual's demand for the target income. If OT represents an income needed for subsistence (village output not meeting subsistence needs) then the demand for money income would be very urgent and the indifference lines would approach the horizontal below *OT*, as in Figure 1. If, on the other hand, the individual already has sufficient income to meet tax payments for the year and other minimal needs, but has a mild hankering after a new bicycle or some new clothing —things which might be regarded as "discretionary" consumption—then his indifference lines below *OT* would have a more conventional shape; he would not be willing to give up very great amounts of "leisure" to attain the money income target. Between these two extremes there is a wide middle ground into which most African migrant workers probably fall; they are modified target workers. And for these individuals the slope of the indifference lines above *OT* is flatter; their elasticity of demand for income above *OT* is positive, though it may remain relatively low.

It should be clear that this analysis rests on extreme assumptions about African economic behavior—that the villager finds strongly repugnant the idea of leaving the village for even temporary work outside, that he migrates into paid employment only when his village income is inadequate to meet his low and rigid income target, that he stays in employment only long enough to earn the difference between his village income and his target income. Even in the earliest days of European penetration not all Africans were in fact reluctant to work outside.[17] And in contemporary Africa the reluctance concept has much less general validity. Patterns and customs of migration have become established, risks and costs of outward journeys have diminished, and demands for money income have grown while in many areas the income-generating capacity of the subsistence sector has declined because of population growth or soil erosion. For many Africans today, periodic emigration is necessary regardless of variations in their village incomes.[18]

Equally serious reservations exist regarding the general applicability of the target income assumption. The wants of many Africans were never so sharply defined as has been postulated. Most Africans, moreover, do not now and did not in the past change their stay in paid employment in proportion to changes in wage rates or village incomes. Many are contract laborers signed on for a stated period; others fix their length of stay in employment with reference to the needs of village agriculture rather than to wage rate changes. Analysis in terms of a target income is, moreover, short-term; over longer periods rising wages open up new consumption possibilities and so increase the propensity to work outside by raising income goals. Even within the short-run context the target income assumption implies that the income goal is fixed independently of income-earning possibilities. While this is not unrealistic for middle ranges of wage rates, at relatively low and high rates different forces come into play; low rates lead many individuals to abandon their demands for "discretionary" consumer goods (lowering their income goals) whereas unusually high rates lead to upward adjustments in the target income. Finally, the analysis does not apply to that growing proportion of the African wage labor force which consists of fully committed workers, men who can no longer be regarded as "migrants."

Despite these reservations, the analysis in terms of a "leisure"-income preference function characterized by extreme reluctance to leave the village and by a rigid target income goal is useful for a number of reasons. It provides, first, a limiting case, permitting analysis of labor supply reactions under the most restrictive possible assumptions about African willingness to work for money. It would apply, for example, to the villager who had absolutely no demands for money income beside tax money. Second, it is in fact an approximation to the actual preferences of many Africans, particularly in the early decades of European contact. In the early years most villagers had only sporadic contact with the exchange economy. Wants were few and land relatively abundant. Knowledge of the outside was sparse and transport difficult. The choice between emigrating and staying at home involved much more than simply exchanging some "leisure" for some income at the margin. It involved abandoning (temporarily) the security of a traditional way of life for the risks and discomforts involved in a venture into a radically different social environment. Most Africans in the past (and many today) could therefore be regarded as reluctant—indifferent to the appeals of money income attainable outside the village; the fact that higher incomes were available outside was not sufficient to induce them to emigrate. Like most men in pre-industrial societies or those in early stages of transition, African villagers had great attachment to their traditional social system and generally preferred, in the absence of strong "push" factors, to remain within it; it is no surprise that until about 1930 in most of the continent the securing of a labor force in the exchange sector depended largely on the exercise of direct or indirect coercion.[19] And since force or some special need for money drove them out of the village they would work only long enough to meet this need; they could be regarded as target-workers.

Finally, this analysis provides a convenient framework for summarizing the effects of change over time on economic behavior. The process of economic and social change, as it affected the villager and his willingness to work for money, can be characterized as changing both the target goal of income and the elasticity of the individual's labor supply curve. In the period of early contact the target income of most villagers was low and inflexible; the amount of labor offered by the individual varied inversely with the rate of wages or village income. In later years increasing contact with the outside and a consequent expansion of wants and needs for money income increases the target income and blurs it at the edges, so to speak. The income level at which the villager refrains from entering paid employment undergoes continuous increase, and the growing flexibility of wants erodes the rigidity of the relationship between the level of wage rates and time spent in employment, reducing its negative elasticity. In contemporary Africa the average target income, to the extent that targets can be said to persist, is not only much higher than earlier; it is much more plastic, less well-defined.[20]

THE SUPPLY OF LABOR TO THE EXCHANGE ECONOMY AS A WHOLE

A great many factors influence the rate of emigration in any given area and hence determine the size of the aggregate labor supply available for employment in the exchange sector. The most significant of these are the level of village income, wage rates, the size of the African population in the area concerned, the extent and intensity of the need for money income (which in turn depends on the degree of penetration of new wants, tax levels, the size of the bride price, etc.), the degree of compulsory recruiting (which is of minor importance today outside of Portuguese Africa), the scarcity or abundance of jobs and the "agreeableness" of these jobs, the nearness of employment centers to population concentrations and transport costs and difficulties, the intensity of contact between the villages and the exchange sector, the habits and customs of the particular ethnic groups in the area, the degree of knowledge about conditions existing outside the village. We will look at two of these factors: the level of money income from village sources and the rate of remuneration in the exchange sector. Changes in these two variables are most important in explaining short-run changes in the aggregate labor supply available outside the villages.

The Level of Village Income and the Supply of Labor

The level of income derived from village sources, and changes in the level of this income are major influences on the supply of labor presenting itself for employment in the exchange sector. The influences operate both "cross-sectionally" and in a time-series sense. First, at any moment of time, differences in the average per capita village income between areas are closely associated with differences in the rate of emigration. Within a given country or region, those areas where village incomes are relatively high tend to have relatively low emigration rates. Evidence of this tendency is plentiful, and can be found in all parts of Africa.[21]

This then is the first sense in which the supply of labor in the exchange sector depends on the level of village income: areas with relatively high village incomes tend to send out relatively few men. In addition, in any given area the rate of outmigration varies over time with fluctuations in the level of village income. These fluctuations arise, in the short run, from variations in the size of village harvests or changes in the prices of the crops grown. We will consider each in turn.

Fluctuations in the size of village harvests. When village harvests are bad the number of migrants increases. In places where income-earning outside is required to provide foodstuffs for the subsistence sector (as in much of southern Africa) a bad harvest means more men must go out to fill the subsistence gap. In places where Africans live in the neighborhood of famine much of the time (Ruanda-Urundi, Northern Nigeria, parts of East Africa) increased emigration when harvests are abnormally low is a necessary alternative to hunger.[22] More commonly, a bad harvest means difficulties in meeting the customary money needs of the villagers, for taxes and commodities regarded as essential. If these needs cannot be satisfied by selling local crops, then they can only be met by increasing the export of labor.

If the effect of a bad harvest (low village income) is to stimulate more villagers to migrate, the effect of a good one is to keep more men at home. Enough food or cash crop production can be sold to meet subsistence needs, to buy necessities not produced in the village, and to pay taxes. Because under these conditions many villagers would be able to make ends meet, some men who might otherwise have migrated prefer "leisure" in the village to the gains available outside.

This inverse relationship between the number of men leaving the villages in any given year (the rate of outmigration) and the size of village harvests has long been recognized everywhere in Africa. It is most dramatically manifested at times of crop failures.[23] But less extreme fluctuations in harvests also have clearly observable effects on labor supply. The following description, referring to the Union of South Africa, is widely applicable:

. . . the African came out [of his village] to supplement the income from his land, and the number that came out for this reason varied with the seasons and the richness of the harvests. It was a minimum during and immediately after the harvest; then increasing until it checked when the rains came and ploughing became necessary and possible, and rising again to its peak just before the next harvest. A bad harvest stimulated a greater movement from the reserves, while a year of "full belly" tended to inhibit it. . . .[24]

Although for many Africans in various parts of the continent migration is no longer simply a way to pick up "pocket money," but has become an absolute necessity, the effect of village harvests remains significant. The Annual Report of the Labour Department of Tanganyika for the year 1953 notes: "The most outstanding feature of labour supply during the year was the fact that owing to the failure of the rains in many areas and consequential restricted harvests of staple foodstuffs, most districts had no lack of manpower." And the *Economic Survey of the Colonial Territories* (1951) stated, with reference to Kenya: "Labor supply is held generally to be dependent on harvests of various crops. Years of large crops will be years of labour shortage, which will be seen in urban as well as rural areas."

Agricultural prices fluctuations and the supply of labor. Fluctuations in village incomes depend, of course, on prices obtainable for marketed crops as well as on the size of the harvests. Price fluctuations thus entered from the beginning as a factor determining the size of the labor force in the exchange sector. A decline in the price of cash crops tends to increase the rate of outmigration in two ways. First, it results in lower village incomes (other things equal) and brings the income of some villagers below their minimum income goal. Second, it raises the effort-price of income earned in the village. This is a particularly important consideration in the case of annual cash crops—cotton, peanuts, tobacco, maize, rice, etc., for the villager has each year the option between growing such a cash crop or emigrating. A fall in cash crop prices leads some villagers to migrate, since the effort-price of income from growing cash crops (given expected yields, marketing facilities and transport costs), increases relative to the effort-price of income from paid employment outside (given the rate of remuneration, the cost of transport and subsistence while away).

During the early years the second effect—balancing of effort-prices of income earnable in the village and outside—did not come into play to any great extent. Since departure from the village was generally repugnant to most men, it was only when cash crop prices fell to the point where income goals were unattainable in the village that the rate of outmigration was significantly affected. For in the early period of African development it did not matter to many Africans that income could be earned more easily on the outside. So long as they could earn with reasonable effort what they needed at home they would stay at home.

With time, increasing knowledge of the outside world and the establishment of patterns of migration, the trip to work outside for wages became less forbidding, less risky, less distasteful. More Africans came to consider a spell in wage earning outside as a possible alternative to income earning in the village, even when income needs could be met by expanding or diversifying village production. At this stage the relative effort-prices of income in cash crop production and in paid employment outside became an important factor determining the size of the migrant labor force. The supply of migrant labor became much more sensitive to small changes in the prices of cash crops. When there is a fall in peanut prices in Senegal or Nigeria, cotton prices in Uganda, French-speaking Equatorial Africa, or parts of the Congo, tobacco and maize prices in East and Central Africa, the supply of migrant labor available to employers outside the villages increases. The Lacey Commission in Nyasaland (1935) described the nice balance involved in the migratory mechanism:

. . . We have found that among people who have become accustomed to emigration the balance between the advantage of staying at home and growing a cash crop for sale, on the one hand, and the lure of employment for wages out of the Protectorate, on the other, is a very delicate one. If, for example, the tobacco crop is good, the price satisfactory and market facilities available, there is practically no emigration from the producing districts; if the crop fails, or the price drops or market facilities are lessened, emigration commences almost immediately.[25]

It should be noted that the cash crop price effect on nonvillage labor supply involves, in most cases, only a redistribution of the total labor devoted to market-oriented activity, not an increase in its total supply; the nonvillage labor supply increases while labor devoted to income earning in the villages declines. A decline in cash crop prices can lead to an expansion in the total quantity of effort expended in production for sale if villagers maintain their village cash crop production in the face of a decline in crop prices, and undertake wage employment *in addition*. This is likely to occur where two conditions exist: first, where there are opportunities for seasonal or short-term employment, so that villagers can utilize slack time not required for tending to their cash crops, or where there exist in the village social arrangements whereby wives and kinsmen left in the village can tend to cash crops in the absence of migrant husbands; second, where the group in question has attained a high level of habitual consumption. When, among such people, a decline in crop prices brings income below the level deemed acceptable, the level of cash crop production is maintained (the villagers' total stock of "leisure" is drawn upon) and the rate of outmigration increases. The total sum of village "leisure" is diminished as men struggle to maintain a standard of living they have come to regard as essential. Adapting some of the terminology of recent theory of international trade, we can say that in this case a drop in cash crop prices has a "labor-creating" effect, whereas if village income-earning activity is reduced following a decline in cash crop prices, the effect is "labor-diverting." [26]

The Rate of Wages and the Supply of Labor in the Exchange Sector

In considering the relationship between changes in wage rates and changes in labor supply to the exchange economy as a whole let us simplify the analysis by assuming that: (1) the unskilled labor supply of the exchange economy consists only of migrants from the subsistence sector; (2) all these migrants are what we earlier called "modified" target workers; (3) the total labor supply in the exchange economy has only two dimensions: the number of men in paid work and the amount of time they work. The aggregate labor supply, that is, consists of the number of men at work for wages multiplied by the average amount of time each spends in wage employment.

Now suppose all other determinants of the supply of labor are constant. How do changes in the level of wages offered in the exchange sector affect the aggregate labor supply in that sector? Given the stated conditions, any change in wage levels will influence the supply of labor in each of its dimensions. It will change the number of men presenting themselves for hire, and it will change the amount of time the men in employment are prepared to remain in employment. The two dimensions of labor supply, however, react in opposite directions. An increase in wage rates will tend to draw more men out of the subsistence sector; but the increase of wage rates also means that those who are in wage employment will work shorter periods of time since they can attain their targets more quickly at the higher rates. Whether an increase in wages increases or diminishes the total supply of labor depends, therefore, on whether the fall in average time worked has greater or less impact than the increase in the number of men working.

The effect of any wage change on the aggregate supply of labor in the exchange sector is therefore ambiguous. Even under the most restrictive assumptions about the individual African's economic behavior once he is in wage employment—that he is a target worker—it is not possible to conclude anything a priori about the shape of the aggregate labor supply curve to the exchange economy.

We can, however, speculate about the likely magnitude of the diverse effects of wage changes. To do so meaningfully it is essential to recognize that the behavior of the two dimensions of labor supply varies according to the historical period being considered.

Even during the early years of African development a wage increase tended to increase the number of men seeking work outside the villages. The higher rate reduced the effort-price of income; given consumption goals could be reached with smaller expenditure of time and effort in paid employment. This lower effort-price was just enough to convince some men in each village that it was now worthwhile to emigrate temporarily; it also made migration a more attractive way of earning income than production in the village. Further, with given transport costs, every wage increase widened the geographical extent of the labor market; at the higher wage it paid men from more distant villages to migrate.

In these early years, however, the positive elasticity of labor supply with respect to wage increases tended to be slight. Because of sociological factors and because the level of wants and hence the need for money income was restricted, the subsistence sector responded sluggishly to wage rises in the exchange sector. Most villagers were deaf to the appeal of wages. They went out of the village to earn money when necessary. Most of them were unconcerned with marginal differences in income-earning possibilities; they were simply out of the labor market. Furthermore, the geographical impact of wage changes tended to be limited because of lack of transport and communication facilities.

In the early years, therefore, changes in wage levels had limited effects in augmenting the number of migrants into paid employment. At the same time, a wage increase was likely to result in a decided shortening of the length of time most migrants stayed in employment. When opportunities to earn money income first appeared, those who left the villages voluntarily were mainly target workers with rigidly fixed goals. The goals were so clearly defined that the possibility of earning a little more for the same time spent in employment did not appeal to many migrants. So when the early wage earners were granted higher wage rates they tended to return earlier to their villages or stay longer at home between trips. In the early period of contact, then, the net result of a wage increase was not likely to be a substantial increase in aggregate labor supply, and was quite possibly a reduction. The aggregate supply function of labor to the exchange economy as a whole was either highly inelastic or negatively elastic through most of its range. For while the "men in employment" function (relating numbers of migrants to rates of wages) was positively sloped, the "average time in employment" function (relating average time spent in paid employment to wage rates) was sharply backward-bending, and the effect of the latter probably outweighed the effect of the former.

In the later period and in contemporary Africa more villagers have moved to the margin of possible inducement; they can be drawn into wage employment by relatively small changes in wages. Transport and communication facilities have been improved. Knowledge of the outside is widespread in the villages. The geographical extent of the labor market has widened. Men move many hundreds of miles from village to workplace. When wages rise the number of men in paid employment thus increases much more substantially than formerly.

At the same time, African wants have become greater and less definitely structured. Many men no longer quit their jobs sooner when wages rise; they stay as long as they had planned to, and are happy to bring back to the villages a richer collection of goods. Many are even induced to stay longer, and to come out to work again sooner, since with every rise in the level of wages a new and different variety of goods falls within the range of achievable consumption. Many wage earners are disposed to semipermanent settlement in the exchange sector, and the higher wage fortifies this disposition. Though many others remain target workers in a vague sense, their target goals have become hazier. The sharply backward-bending "time in employment" function of the early years has become a more gently backward-turning curve.

In most parts of Africa today, then, the aggregate supply curve of labor to the exchange economy as a whole (the relation between the general level of wages and the total quantity of labor available in the exchange sector) is positively sloped throughout most of its length. The positive "men in employment" reaction to wage changes now swamps the negative "average time in employment" reaction. Except at relatively high and low wages it tends to be inelastic; the target tendencies of the labor force brake the increase in aggregate labor supply when wages rise. Moreover, at each wage rate much more labor is available now than formerly; the curve has shifted outward. This is due to population increase, faster, better and cheaper transport and communication, and the continuing expansion of wants and hence of income needs.

The analysis has thus far been framed in terms of wage *increases*. Few amendments are needed when wage *decreases* are considered. The net effect on aggregate labor supply of a cut in the general level of wages is ambiguous. It tends to increase the average time spent by emigrants in employment, but also tends to reduce the number of emigrants in employment. Which effect prevails depends on the relative elasticities of the "men in employment" and the "time in employment" functions.

Under certain conditions wage cuts could lead to substantial increases in aggregate labor supply. Where there were incompressible needs for money income and restricted income-earning alternatives the number of men leaving the villages would not decline following a general wage reduction, but would increase, since income was needed for food and other essentials. Since the average time in employment would also increase, the total labor supply would unambiguously expand following a reduction of wages.

These conditions were, however, rarely present, though they did exist by the 1930's in southern Africa where the Africans in the reserves imported much of their food and where there were few alternative income-earning possibilities. In most parts of the continent, however, demands for nonvillage goods could be contracted easily; except for tax money and a few basic commodities there were in most instances few demands for money income that could not be abandoned or postponed. When wage rates fell, therefore, some men would be led to do without cash income and the number of men available for paid employment in the exchange sector would drop.[27]

The fact that the conditions for increasing the supply of labor by wage cutting were rarely present did not prevent numerous employer attempts to reduce wages. Several particularly revealing examples occurred around the turn of the century, one in South Africa, the other in the Gold Coast (now Ghana). In 1902 and 1903 the South African gold mining industry put into effect a substantial wage reduction, for which much of the economic rationale was that the supply curve of labor was backward-sloping. In the Gold Coast in 1903 a general wage cut was introduced by the government in co-operation with the mining companies. The notion of the backward-sloping labor supply curve again appeared, in target-worker form. ("It is not anticipated," wrote a government official in 1903, "that a reduction in the rate of wages will tend to reduce the supply of labour. A native usually goes on working until he has obtained a definite sum of money with which to return to his country.") [28]

In both instances employers were deceived. The aggregate supply of labor showed itself not only positively related to the rate of wages, but quite elastic in response to wage cuts. After the 1902 wage reductions the South African gold mines found themselves in the midst of the most severe labor shortage in the history of the industry, a shortage which was surely not unrelated to the companies' wage policy. [29] In the Gold Coast the aim of the wage reduction of 1903 was thwarted by the existence of labor-hiring African cocoa farmers who were in competition with European employers and the government for the available labor supply. Because the wage cut was not general, labor ebbed away from the wage-cutting European employers to the African farmers. In a few years labor shortage pushed wages back to their former levels. [30]

THE SUPPLY OF LABOR TO THE TERRITORY

In the above discussion we centered on the exchange economy as a whole. This permitted a simplified analysis of the effects of changes in the general level of wages on aggregate labor supply. In reality, of course, the exchange sector consists of firms and industries grouped in inter-related sub-markets. There is no room here to consider in detail all the complications this introduces into the analysis of labor supply. We will instead focus on one sub-market within the exchange economy as a whole —the country within an international labor market.

Labor markets for unskilled labor in Africa in most instances cut across political boundaries. Thus the Union of South Africa has since the beginning of this century imported hundreds of thousands of laborers from Mozambique, the High Commission Territories (Bechuanaland, Basutoland, Swaziland), the Rhodesias and Nyasaland. For many decades about half of Southern Rhodesia's work force (African) has come from Northern Rhodesia, Nyasaland and Mozambique. Ruanda-Urundi provides Uganda with a significant portion of its African labor force. Ghana has always relied on labor from outside the country—from Upper Volta, Niger, Togo and Nigeria. [31]

In various regions of Africa, therefore, individual countries form parts of what can be regarded as "regional" labor markets for unskilled labor. Most of southern and central Africa form one such regional labor market. Uganda, Ruanda-Urundi and the Eastern Congo form another. In West Africa the Ivory Coast, Ghana and the Upper Volta make up a closely connected labor market area with ramifications in the Soudan (now Mali), Niger, Dahomey, Togo and Nigeria.

It is not easy to define in a precise way the geographical extent of the regional labor markets since countries within the region are connected like links in a chain. The effect of a change in wages or working conditions or job opportunities in any country is felt in varying degrees by the countries around it. Even where there are no direct relationships between two countries in a given regional labor market area, the two can be held together through a third country.

Any wage increase in a country forming part of a regional labor market will cause a two-way increase in the number of men in paid employment in that country: more villagers will be attracted into paid employment, and migrants, both "domestic" and "foreign," who might have gone elsewhere will work in the wage-increasing country instead. Each wage change has, in other words, a volume (labor-creating or -reducing) effect and a geographical redistribution (labor-diverting) effect. If wage rates rise in the Ivory Coast more villagers are drawn into paid employment, and some migrants from Mali (who might otherwise have gone to Senegal) and from the Upper Volta (who might otherwise have gone to Ghana) come to seek employment in the Ivory Coast. A French student of these matters in West Africa writes:

> Investigations going back many years have shown that the seasonal workers are perfectly informed on hiring opportunities, conditions of work, of salary and of accessory benefits in the different regions. There is an unquestionable correlation between a rising or falling price of peanuts in Senegal and of cocoa in the Gold Coast or the Ivory Coast and the flow of seasonal workers or their abstention.[32]

Our earlier analysis, then, which related to the supply of labor available to the exchange economy as a whole, has to be amended to take account of the international character of labor markets for African labor. The aggregate labor supply function to any given country (say the Union of South Africa, or the Ivory Coast or Uganda) may have been backward-sloping in the early years of African development, but when these countries are placed in their regional context this becomes unlikely. Where the connections with other countries were strong, as in the Ivory Coast and South Africa, there is in fact good reason to suppose that almost from the beginning the aggregate labor supply function of labor within these countries was positively-sloped in its relevant portions. That it is so shaped in most African countries today is certain.

SUMMARY AND CONCLUSIONS

By distinguishing various types of labor supply functions, and by attempting to take account of changes over time, we have tried to see in what sense and during what historical period it is legitimate to speak of backward-sloping labor supply curves in Africa.

First, the quantity of wage labor offered by the individual African tends to be inversely related to changes in village income and changes in wage rates in the exchange sector. This relationship was pronounced in the early years, when migrants tended to be reluctant target workers whose elasticity of demand for income, once their target income was achieved, approached zero for everything except "leisure." In contemporary Africa the target income concept is losing its applicability as wants increase in size and flexibility. It does not apply at all to "committed" workers who no longer shuttle between village and outside employment.

Second, the *number* of individuals in wage employment varies with the level of village income and changes in the level of village income; the income-elasticity of labor supply is negative, "income" referring to village income. This was markedly true in the early period of contact and remains a strong tendency today.

The shape of the aggregate labor supply function—the "ordinary" function relating aggregate quantity of labor to wage rates—cannot be predicted a priori, since it depends on the net outcome of two contrary changes that follow a wage change: changes in the number of villagers in wage employment and changes in the average time each man spends at work. In the early years the aggregate supply of labor to the exchange economy as a whole probably tended to be backward-sloping in relevant ranges; a rise in wages induced few new men into employment while it encouraged many of those in paid employment to cut short their stay. In contemporary Africa this is no longer true; a wage rise stimulates relatively many more men to emigrate into paid jobs and leads far fewer to reduce their time in paid employment. And when account is taken of the international character of African labor markets it is most unlikely that for any given country (*a fortiori* for any given industry or firm) the aggregate supply of labor was ever negatively elastic with respect to wage rates.

NOTES

1. Cf. Wilbert E. Moore, *Industrialization and Labor* (Ithaca: Cornell University Press, 1951), pp. 35–37 and the references cited therein.

2. Powell, *View of Real Grievances* (1772), cited in E. S. Furniss, *The Position of the Laborer in a System of Nationalism* (Boston and New York:

Houghton Mifflin, 1920), p. 143. Chapter VI of this book contains a classic collection of such statements.

3. Henri Labouret, "La main-d'oeuvre dans l'ouest-africain," in *Afrique Française*, Bulletin du Comité de l'Afrique Française, May 1930, p. 248.

4. *Annual Report of the Chamber of Mines, 1891*, cited in Sheila T. Van der Horst, *Native Labour in South Africa* (London: Oxford University Press, 1942), p. 129, n. 2. See also, Union of South Africa, *Report of the Economic and Wage Commission (1925)*, (Pretoria: Government Printer, 1926), p. 38.

5. See H. Myint, "The Gains from International Trade and the Backward Countries" in *Review of Economic Studies*, XXII (1954–55), 129–42.

6. Cf. Moore, *op. cit.*, Chap. VI, and J. H. Boeke, *Economics and Economic Policy of Dual Societies, as Exemplified by Indonesia* (New York: Institute of Pacific Relations, 1953), esp. pp. 143 ff.

7. See, however, the discussion in P. T. Bauer and B. S. Yamey, *The Economics of Under-developed Countries* (Cambridge: Cambridge University Press, 1957), pp. 82–89; and in Van der Horst, *op. cit.*, esp. pp. 197–205 and pp. 298–302.

8. Actually, no clear-cut separation between subsistence and exchange sectors is possible in anything except an analytic sense. Some part of village production is marketed in almost all African countries, so some part of village resources is included in the exchange economy.

For a bold attempt to classify areas under African cultivation according to whether crops are grown mainly for sale, partly for sale or wholly for subsistence consumption, see United Nations, *Enlargement of the Exchange Economy in Tropical Africa* (New York, 1954), p. 11. In this study, which uses data from nine countries covering two-thirds of Africa's population, it is estimated that between two-thirds and three-quarters of the total land area cultivated by Africans in the period 1947–50 was devoted to subsistence production. A more recent U.N. study states, with reference to labor resources, that except in the Union of South Africa the majority of economically active Africans are engaged fully or partly in traditional agriculture. [United Nations, *Economic Survey of Africa since 1950* (New York, 1960), p. 49.]

9. "Village" is used throughout this paper in a generic sense. In parts of Africa the traditional residence unit is the household, grouping the extended family.

10. This is a very rough estimate, which includes not only Africans at work in modern-type enterprises, but also those employed by African farmers for wages. (See E. Berg, "Recruitment of a Labor Force in Sub-Saharan Africa," unpublished Ph.D. thesis, Harvard University, 1960, Appendix II. See also, International Labour Office, *African Labour Survey* (Geneva, 1958), Table II, pp. 666–67; and United Nations, *Economic Survey of Africa since 1950*, pp. 41 ff.).

Africans at work for wages in European enterprises (including government) form less than 5 per cent of the total population in West Africa, between 5 and 10 per cent in most of the rest of the continent, and over 25 per cent only in Southern Rhodesia and the Union of South Africa.

11. The extent to which African labor forces remain migratory varies widely from country to country, and—within countries—from industry to indus-

try. In the Union of South Africa about 27 per cent of the African population (excluding Coloureds), or some 2.3 million people, live in urban areas. [Union of South Africa, *State of the Union; Economic, Financial and Statistical Year-book for the Union of South Africa, 1958* (Cape Town, 1958), p. 80.] According to a recent government report about 1.5 million of these town-dwelling Africans can be regarded as committed more or less permanently to wage-earning and the urban life. [Union of South Africa, *Summary of the Report of the Commission for the Socio-Economic Development of the Bantu Areas Within the Union of South Africa* (Pretoria: Government Printer, 1956), p. 28.] In the Congo almost 40 per cent of the adult male Africans live outside the traditional villages. Some indication of the extent of permanency in paid employment of these men is given by figures of length of residence in main towns; in Leopoldville, some 40 per cent of the population in 1955 had been in town ten years or more, and another 26 per cent had been born in Leopoldville. In Elisabethville more than 40 per cent of the 1955 African population had been there for ten years or more, and 70 per cent for five years or more. [See J. Denis, *Le Phénomène urbain en Afrique Centrale* (Bruxelles, 1958), pp. 614 ff.] In West Africa, between half and three-quarters of those in paid employment can be regarded as migratory workers. [Cf. E. Berg, "French West Africa," in W. Galenson (ed.), *Labor and Economic Development* (New York: Wiley, 1959), pp. 199 ff., and J. B. Heigham, "Notes on Labour in the Gold Coast" (Accra, 1952, mimeographed), III.] A recent report in Southern Rhodesia claims that in that country "90 per cent of the indigenous labour force . . . still has one foot in the Reserves" (Southern Rhodesia, "Report of the Southern Rhodesia Department of Labour for the Calendar Year 1957" (Salisbury, 1959, mimeographed), p. 24). An investigatory commission in Kenya estimated that in 1953 half the paid workers in that country were "migrants," and that 80–90 per cent of the workers in the two main towns had been employed there for less than two years [Kenya Colony, *Report of the Committee on African Wages* (Nairobi, 1954), p. 13].

There are, it should be noted, difficult problems involved in defining a "migrant worker." See J. C. Mitchell, "Urbanization, Detribalization and Stabilization in Southern Africa: A Problem of Definition and Measurement," in UNESCO, *Social Implications of Industrialization and Urbanization in Africa South of the Sahara* (Paris, 1956), pp. 693–710.

12. There is some conceptual difficulty connected with the notion of "leisure" in transitional societies. In that part of the total society already wholly integrated into the modern market economy it does not involve too great a distortion of reality to regard "leisure" as simply time not spent at "work." In the traditionally oriented sector, however, which is to say in most villages, "leisure" is the sum of village activities not immediately or directly concerned with production. Within village society it is by no means easy to distinguish between "economic" and "noneconomic" activity, between "work" and "leisure." Because of these considerations "leisure" is placed within quotation marks throughout the discussion in this paper.

13. These are not the only factors determining whether and for how long the villager will enter paid employment. Also important are the following, which we take as given throughout the analysis in the text: habits and customs in the

village; whether the individual is married or single, accompanied or unaccompanied by his wife; whether he can count on friends and family in the village to carry out the planting and harvesting of crops while he is gone; the "agreeableness" of the employment available outside and the ease of securing such employment; the nearness of places of employment to the home village, and the ease and costs of transport; whether he hires out on a contract for a specific period of time.

14. Cf. Moore, op. cit., Chap. VII.

15. W. E. Moore, "Labor Attitudes toward Industrialization in Underdeveloped Countries," in American Economic Review, XLV (May 1955), 156 ff.

16. Boeke, op. cit., p. 143.

17. Some anthropologists have suggested that emigration into paid work replaced valor in warfare as a test of manhood, so that men who worked in strange and distant places enjoyed a prestige denied to those who never did. (Cf. I. Schapera, Migrant Labour and Tribal Life, London and New York, Oxford University Press, 1947). To the extent that this is so, many men would prefer at least one trip outside to never going out at all. Also, a taste for travel and adventure, a desire to "see the world" stimulated some men to emigrate even when there was no clear deficit between their demand for money and their village income. See, for discussions of noneconomic factors in the migration phenomenon, A. W. Southall, "Alur Migrants," in A. I. Richards (ed.), Economic Development and Tribal Change (Cambridge, England: Heffer, 1954), pp. 141–46; E. H. Winter, Bwamba Economy (Kampala, Uganda: East African Institute of Social Research, 1955); and J. Maquet, "Motivations culturelles des migrations vers les villes d'Afrique Centrale," in Folia Scientifica Africae Centralis (Bukavu, 1956), pp. 6–8.

18. This is so in areas where subsistence production has ceased to be sufficient to satisfy the food requirements of the village, as in much of southern Africa. It is also so in places where surplus crops cannot be produced, or where local markets are inexistent or too small to allow villagers to sell surplus crops in order to earn tax money and other income. Finally, young unmarried men in all but the most prosperous villages must do at least some wage-earning in order to accumulate enough income for bridal payments and the capital goods or consumer durables needed by young men.

19. See Berg, "Recruitment of a Labor Force in Sub-Saharan Africa, op. cit., Chap. V. See also, discussion of the labor problem in the various chapters of R. L. Buell, The Native Problem in Africa (New York: Macmillan, 1928), International Labour Office, Forced Labour Report, International Labour Conference, Twelfth Session (Geneva, 1929), and The Recruiting of Labour in Colonies and in Other Territories with Analogous Labour Conditions, International Labour Conference, Nineteenth Session, Report IV (Geneva, 1935).

20. One increasingly important decision has not been discussed—the decision of the migrant laborer as to whether to commit himself permanently to wage employment. If the migrant is to choose permanent commitment one necessary economic condition must be met: total family income must be greater for the permanently committed worker than for the migrant worker. This condition is by no means always met. Given the division of agricultural labor in the villages (women doing much of the cultivation and harvesting) and the

fact that most migrants leave their families behind in the village, per capita agricultural output is frequently maintained at or near a constant level despite the temporary absence of substantial proportions of adult males. This means that periodic emigration (without his family) is frequently the most rational economic choice open to the villager, allowing him a greater family income than if he migrated permanently with his family. The differential between the family income of the permanent wage-earner and the migrant must moreover be substantial, in order to compensate for the psychological costs of changing styles of life and for the harassments (common until recently in much of Africa) of town life—racial discrimination, restrictions on freedom of movement, etc. (See W. J. Barber, "Economic Rationality and Behavior Patterns in an Under-developed Area: A Case Study of African Economic Behavior in the Rhodesias," in *Economic Development and Cultural Change*, VIII (Apr. 1960), 237–51; W. Elkan, "Migrant Labor in Africa, An Economist's Approach," in *American Economic Review*, XLIX (May 1959), 188–97; and W. Watson, *Tribal Cohesion in a Money Economy* (Manchester University Press, 1958).

21. Cf. Nyasaland Protectorate, *Report of the Committee Appointed by His Excellency the Governor to Enquire into Emigrant Labour* (Zomba, 1935), p. 22; M. Read, "Migrant Labour in Africa and its Effects on Tribal Life," in *International Labour Review*, XIV (1942), 617; W. Southall, *op. cit.*, p. 160; P. Gulliver, "Nyakusa Labour Migration," in *Human Problems in British Central Africa*, XXI (1957), 18, 25–26; F. Bezy, *Problèmes Structurelles de l'Economie Congolaise* (Louvain, 1957), pp. 109 ff.

Cases of relatively high emigration rates in areas with relatively high per capita cash income from village agriculture have been found in several studies. (W. Elkan, "Labour Problems in the Industrialisation of an African Society; A study of Urban Industrial Employment in Uganda" (unpublished Ph.D. thesis, University of London, 1956), pp. 92, 98; P. Gulliver, *Labour Migration in a Rural Economy* (Kampala, Uganda: East African Institute of Social Research, 1955), p. 27; Barber, *op. cit.*, pp. 247 ff. The reasons for these variations from the general pattern vary. The Ganda of Uganda have high wage-labor participation rates despite high average village incomes because they have greater opportunities for employment, are closer to employment centers and have a more insistent set of wants than most other groups. Among the Ngoni of Tanganyika and the Shona of Southern Rhodesia population pressures seem to be the major factor.

22. Cf. R. M. Prothero, "Migratory Labour from North-western Nigeria," in *Africa*, XXVII (1957), 251–61.

23. Cf. Gold Coast Colony, *Annual Report on the Gold Coast for the Year 1914*, pp. 12–13; J. Rouch, "Migrations on Ghana," *Journal de la Société des Africanistes*, XXVI (1956), 39–57; Richards, *op. cit.*, p. 38; Van der Horst, *op. cit.*, p. 28; G. Deherme, *L'Afrique Occidentale Française* (Paris: Bloud, 1908), p. 516.

24. G. E. Stent, "Migrancy and Urbanization in the Union of South Africa," *Africa*, XVIII (July 1948), 169. The records of the labor recruiting organizations in South Africa leave little doubt as to the importance of village harvests on the supply of migrant labor; years of good harvests in the villages have always been years of difficult recruiting, while after bad harvests the

recruiters sit back and relax. Cf. Van der Horst, *op. cit.*, p. 301; Schapera, *op. cit.*, p. 144; Union of South Africa, *Report of the Native Economic Commission, 1930–1932* (Pretoria: Government Printer, 1932), p. 118; D. H. Houghton and E. M. Walton, *The Economy of a Native Reserve*, Vol. 2 of *Keishammahoek Rural Survey* (Pietermaritzburg, South Africa: Shuter and Shooter, 1952), p. 87.

25. Nyasaland Protectorate, *Report of the Committee on Emigrant Labor* (Zomba, 1935), p. 22.

26. The economic history of the Ganda of Uganda offers examples of both effects. The post-World War I depression brought cotton prices in Uganda to new lows in 1921. The reaction of many Ganda was to abandon cotton and seek wage employment; in 1921 cotton acreage fell to 30,000 acres as compared with 55,000 in 1920, and during the year the supply of labor in towns and elsewhere was plentiful. The fall in cotton prices had thus led many Ganda villagers to substitute wage-earning for cotton-growing; the "labor-diverting" effect was predominant. In 1928, when cotton prices again fell sharply the response of the Ganda was different. Cotton acreage remained unchanged while the rate of out-migration increased. During 1928 ". . . it was noted with surprise that the Ganda, who were supposed to be averse to this sort of work, were supplying 40% of the Public Works Department's unskilled labour supply in Mengo. . . ." (Richards, *op. cit.*, p. 236.) Audrey Richards, who has studied the Ganda closely, explains it thus: "Despite the Ganda's traditional regard for status and contempt for unskilled labour, his taste for certain goods and services which only money can buy has become so ingrained that if forced by adverse circumstances, he will descend to such work rather than give up his accustomed standard of living. . . ." (*Ibid.*)

27. This explains why the sharp drop in wage rates after the 1930 depression led to complaints in some countries of labor shortage. See, for example, the 1933 *Report on Labour in the Tanganyika Territory*, which comments on the "apparent paradox" of depression causing a "shortage of labour, especially in the completely unskilled type which draws the lowest scale of wages."

28. Gold Coast Colony, *Annual Report on the Gold Coast for the Year 1903*, p. 50.

29. Van der Horst, *op. cit.*, pp. 165 ff.

30. Cf. *Annual Report on Ashanti, 1910*, p. 40; *Report on the Ashanti and Northern Territories Roads Department for the Year 1910*, p. 1.

31. Cf. "Inter-Territorial Migrations of Africans South of the Sahara," in *International Labour Review*, LXXVI (Sept. 1957), 292–310; United Nations, *Economic Survey of Africa Since 1950* (New York, 1960), p. 49.

32. H. Labouret, "La main-d'oeuvre autochtone," in *Le Travail en Afrique Noire* (Paris: Editions du Seuil, 1952), p. 128. Similar international relationships exist in southern Africa and East Africa. Migrations from Ruanda-Urundi to Uganda, for example, are influenced by variations in the rate of exchange between the Congolese franc and the East African pound. (See P. G. Powesland, "History of the Migration in Uganda" in Richards, *op. cit.*, p. 49. See also Powesland, *Economic Policy and Labour* (Kampala, Uganda: East African Institute of Social Research, 1957), pp. 77 ff.)

E. P. Skinner

LABOUR MIGRATION AND ITS RELATIONSHIP TO SOCIO-CULTURAL CHANGE IN MOSSI SOCIETY (1960)

I

Labour migration is an outstanding feature in most contemporary African societies. It not only touches on nearly all aspects of the lives of the peoples involved, but is often the cause as well as the result of important social and cultural changes. It therefore holds a special interest for students of such changes. Here they can observe the movements of vast numbers of people, and the concomitant problems which arise with the exposure of these people to new social, political, and economic conditions. Furthermore, working with data from migrants and their home and host communities, social scientists are able to test many theoretical assumptions which are held about the nature of socio-cultural change.

The relationship between labour migration and socio-cultural change has been well documented for South and Central African societies by Richards, Schapera, and the Wilsons.[1] Less work has been done in West Africa, although this area is also characterized by such labour migrations as the *navetanes,* in Sudan and Senegal, the migrations of thousands of Guineans who go annually to Liberia and Sierra Leone, and by a like number of Nigerians who go to work in the Cameroons. For example, it is only recently that Davidson and Rouch [2] have given us any substantial data on the 320,000 or more migrants from the Togolands, Nigeria, and the former French West African dependencies who flock annually to Ghana—that Mecca for migrants with its mining, plantation, and urban complexes. Thanks to these scholars we now know something about the number of migrants in Ghana, their countries of origin, their working and

SOURCE. E. P. Skinner, "Labour Migration and Its Relationship to Socio-Cultural Change in Mossi Society," reprinted from *Africa*, XXX, 4, 1960, pp. 375–377, 379–388, 393–397, 399, by permission of the International African Institute. Copyright by E. P. Skinner.

living conditions in the country, and their contribution to Ghana's econ-omy. On the other hand, except for two short statements by Mercier and Prothero,[3] there is little information on the effects of this migration on the migrants' home communities. The need for this information is obvious; and it is especially pressing for students and officials interested in Mossi society, which furnishes the greatest number of migrants to Ghana.

Most authorities believe that more than 50,000 Mossi workers migrate annually to Ghana, and some officials would increase this figure to 100,000.[4] Mossi also form the majority of the 50,000 workers officially recruited every year to work in the coffee and cocoa plantations of the Ivory Coast. Additional thousands of Mossi labourers migrate to the farms and cities of the Ivory Coast of their own accord. The reasons given for this migration tend to conform to a familiar pattern. Sister Marie-André du Sacré-Coeur records that the Mossi migrate "to earn money, often to pay their taxes. Most of them, return [annually], but several thousands stay behind each year, attracted by the lure of the towns, or simply because they have not enough money to return home and do not want to work on the land any more."[5] Similarly, Church reports that many thousands of migrants, "especially from the poor and densely peopled Mossi country of the Upper Volta and other poor areas," seek work in Ghana and the Ivory Coast because they are "attracted by wages to provide bride money, by lower prices, simpler administration, the love of adventure and the mark of distinction which travel confers."[6] These statements are too general to give us a true picture of the nature of the Mossi migration, its causes, and its effects on Mossi society. From data collected in two Mossi communities with heavy migration to Ghana, I will now attempt to delineate the reasons for this migration, show its relation to the other changes taking place in Mossi society, and make some comments about the general nature of socio-cultural change.

Socio-cultural change is fairly rapid in present-day Africa, and be-cause of this, many anthropologists have a tendency to regard African societies as in various states of "disequilibrium." The Wilsons, among others, believe that this is due mainly to "the failure to adjust novelty with tradition—a change in one respect without changes in other re-spects."[7] The belief is that only gradual changes can prevent disequi-librium. The major shortcoming of this concept as an analytical tool for studying socio-cultural change is that it cannot deal with situations of constant and accelerating changes. The belief that social systems return to equilibrium tends to obscure the analysis of the new emergent institu-tions and practices which are of vital concern to those interested in studying and understanding the processes of transformation in modern Africa. Given the context of change today, where the institutions of African societies are still changing with no end in sight, the most profit-able concern is not with disequilibrium or equilibrium, with all the problems of valuation or value positions that such concern implies, but with the direction and processes of change.

A point which will be emphasized throughout this paper, and one first stressed by Malinowski, is that socio-cultural change in Africa cannot be understood without taking the presence and the activities of Europeans into consideration.[8] Indeed, labour migration in Africa is most properly seen as a post-European phenomenon, even though one scholar has seen it as a continuation of the ancient displacements of populations occasioned by the slave trade.[9] In most cases the first labour migrations were involuntary, either because Africans were forcibly displaced to work on European projects, or because they went to work centres in response to the introduction of taxes which had to be paid in European currencies. Those African societies with traditions of compulsory or tributary labour for the chiefs or specific types of social institutions often accepted forced labour and labour migration quite easily.[10] Similarly, those colonial nations which had traditions of the *corvée* or slavery experienced little difficulty, from a moral point of view, in using Africans as forced labourers in areas where they were needed. But when both the Africans and the Europeans lacked traditions of compulsory labour, the Africans often fled in order to escape the recruiters. The European administrations, with very few exceptions, put aside any scruples they might have had and resorted to "forced labour," "compulsory service," "the *corvée*," or "prestations," in order to obtain the necessary workers.[11] After a lapse of some decades a complex of factors permitted the abolition of forced labour in most African areas, but by this time many African workers, who formerly had to be forced to do extra-tribal labour, began to migrate voluntarily to centres of European employment.

II

The Mossi live in the Volta Republic (the former French colony called Upper Volta), a relatively poor and infertile tract of territory, which covers an area of 105,791 square miles and extends from the boundaries of northern Ghana to Bandiagara in the western Sudan. Today they number over 1½ million, and represent the largest group in the country. Traditions record that ancient Dagomba warriors left Gambaga in northern Ghana, fought their way northwards, assimilated the weaker populations, and gave rise to the dominant Mossi kingdoms. The Mossi continued to expand northwards but their raids on Timbuktu and other towns in the Niger Bend were stopped when this area was conquered by the Moroccans in 1594. After that period the Mossi remained quiescent and retained their autonomy until they were conquered by the French in September 1896.

The four principal Mossi kingdoms and lesser principalities had similar political systems, and were united by kinship, ritual, and military bonds. The principal kingdom was and still is Ouagadougou, and its ruler, the Moro Naba, has long been recognized as the senior Mossi potentate. He, like the other rulers, was head of an administrative apparatus which included provincial ministers, district chiefs, and village chiefs. This structure extended the Moro Naba's rule into the smallest village, and funnelled goods and services back to him. When the French conquered the Mossi they first tried to modify this political organization, but, faced with local opposition, the efficiency of the system itself, and their own lack of administrative personnel, they allowed it to persist. The result was that until about two decades ago one European official, working through the traditional chiefs, was able to administer and supervise 60,000 Mossi. At the same time this permitted the chiefs to retain effective control of their subjects. French rule modified the political organization of the Mossi without changing it substantially. . . .

By 1914 the Mossi had developed a pattern of seasonal migration which harmonized with their agricultural cycle and were able to cultivate their fields as well as obtain money for taxes.

As soon as the crops were harvested in November and December, the young men went off to work and did not return until the planting period early in May. This migration was directed towards the southern Gold Coast for many reasons. First, the Mossi had ancestral links with Gambaga, and most of their traditional trade was with such market towns as Salaga in Ghana. More important, however, was the fact that although both the British and the French were building roads at the time and developing plantations, the British paid their workers adequate salaries, whereas the French did not. Moreover, very often the French did not even try to attract labourers with wages, but resorted to the *corvée* or forced labour.

The Mossi were especially vulnerable to forced labour because they were very numerous and their country was poor and lacking in natural wealth. As a matter of record, in 1919 M. de Beauminy, an administrator of the new territory of Upper Volta, declared that "the principal riches that one can presently utilize in Mossi country are its numerous labourers." [12] These labourers were employed both in the public works and in private commercial enterprises of the Sudan and the Ivory Coast. In 1922 the Upper Volta officially furnished "6,000 workers for the Thies-Kayes railway, replaceable every six months, and under the same conditions furnished 2,000 labourers to build railroads in the Ivory Coast. Similarly, with the consent of the chief administrator of the colony, it was possible to recruit a thousand workers in the regions of Ouagadougou and Bobo Dioulasso for private business in the Ivory Coast." [13] Albert Londres visited the Upper Volta in the late twenties and reported that Mossi country was then known under the name of " 'reservoir' of manpower: three million Negroes. Everyone comes here to get them as one would go to wells for water. For the building of the Thies-Kayes and Kayes-Niger railroads the Mossi were tapped. For the railroads of the Ivory Coast, Mossi country is tapped. The woodcutters leave their lagoons and tap the Mossi. And then it is found astonishing that the Sudan and the Upper Volta no longer produce cotton." [14] So important was Mossi labour to the Ivory Coast that when the Upper Volta was abolished as a separate territory in 1932, on account of its insolvency, Mossi country was attached to the northern Ivory Coast. Only in 1937, after the economic depression had lifted, was there some official recognition that "a grave injustice had been done to the Mossi people simply to further the interests of a small and selfish group of coastal planters and foresters." [15] The impressment of Mossi labourers for private persons was thereafter prohibited, but recruitment for public works and military service was continued. The Mossi, on their part, also continued to migrate seasonally to Ghana whenever they could, and often fled to that country when threatened with forced labour or military service. There, at least, they were free to negotiate for wages and leave unsatisfactory employment. The decrees of the Brazzaville Conference in 1944 abolished all forms of forced labour in French Africa, and in 1946 these decrees were promulgated in Mossi country. But the end of forced labour was not the end of labour migrations. By this time the traditional economy of the Mossi had been so transformed by the activities of the Europeans that migration for work, with all its implications, was, and still is, an integral part of the Mossi's economic system.

Except for the Gounga Naba (a traditional provincial minister) and a few perceptive men, most of the Mossi elders were disappointed when the young men continued to migrate for work. This minister, in a speech he made in a district announcing the end of forced labour, remarked: "You have cursed us, and have said that we were the ones who had 'sold' you to the Europeans [referring to forced labour], but today you will see that you will sell yourselves." The minister's words were later substantiated when a great number of young men who had been returned to Ouagadougou from those areas where they were engaged in public works did not even return home, but left immediately for either Ghana or the Ivory Coast. A large number of those who returned home soon left to join their fellows in "the search for money."

The majority of the Mossi who migrate to Ghana are men in the 16–30 age group. Men over 40 and boys as young as 14 are occasionally seen among the migrants. Also in the minority are men fleeing their homes and families for crimes or torts against both foreign and traditional authorities. The overwhelming majority of these migrants, however, leave to earn money. When one asks either the migrants or their relatives why the young men leave home, the answers are similar and almost stereotypic: "I am poor, I need money to pay taxes and to buy clothes," or "I want a bicycle, clothes for myself, and clothes for my wife and relatives." Or again, "Men go off to find money," and "He went to get money to pay taxes." The investigator patiently waits for some response which would indicate to him that at least some migrants go to Kumasi for pleasure and adventure. He is disappointed, because present-day Mossi migrants appear to be as determined to ignore pleasure for the sake of money as were those dedicated Mossi traders, described by Dubois, who ignored the fair ladies of Timbuktu. When one calls the attention of respondents to the possibility that those Mossi who remain in Ghana for several years may be attracted by the pleasures of the cities, the immediate response is: "Perhaps, but the hearts of such men have changed" (meaning that they have lost their heads). The consensus is that no clear-thinking Mossi can live outside Mossi country if he has a sound mind. So strong is this feeling that children born to Mossi parents living outside their homeland are not considered real Mossi but Tarboussi— i.e. people born "in the bush."

The Mossi have now built up an ideal pattern of the way in which migration must take place if it is not to upset their socio-cultural system. Of course, not all the migrants accept this pattern, and many of the elders accept it only because their opposition to migration is fruitless. Ideally, the migrants should not leave for work in the cities, mines, vegetable and cocoa farms of Ghana until the end of November, when most of the crops have been harvested. They should remain in Ghana for about five months, during which period they should hoard all their money and ignore women "because a man does not go away to work for women." When the flowering of certain trees (shea butter, etc.) and the orientation of the Pleiades in April show that the rains are approaching, the migrants should collect their seasonal wages. The next step is to visit the markets of Kumasi in order to buy goods, including presents for wife or wives and parents. And without dallying along the road the migrants are expected to hurry home in time for the planting. Unless this goal is accomplished, most Mossi families feel that their cultivation will suffer. The migrants endeavour to follow this schedule because they look forward to a few weeks for the display of their new clothes before settling down to serious cultivation.

The Mossi are always anxious for the timely return of migrants, because their agricultural cycle is short and exacting. Those households which plan new bush farms in addition to village farms start work in February, but most households start clearing the fields in April to be ready for the first rains in late May or early June. The Mossi sow most of their major crops, such as millet, maize, sorghum, and rice, during the first rainy month. They leave the cotton for August. Those families whose migrants do not return in time (for any one of such various reasons as misdating, delay by employers, or desire to compensate for initial un-employment) must cut back on the sowing. They cannot sow as usual in the hope that the migrants will return; for if these men stay away, the family will not have enough labour to prevent the rapidly growing weeds from choking the crops. And once the first rainy month has passed, none of the early crops can be profitably sown, for although the rains continue until September late-sown crops make small harvests. In former days, if a household was faced with labour shortage, it could and did receive help from relatives and marriage partners. This form of communal help is now almost unobtainable because most families have to compen-sate for absent men.

One of the major characteristics of migration on Mossi agriculture is the failure of about 20 per cent of the migrants to return home in any one year. Mossi migrants, more so than men of other groups, tend to remain in Ghana from two to three years before returning home. But, on the other hand, they tend to make fewer trips per total migratory period than other migrants.[16] The reasons for this unusual migratory behaviour may be summarized as follows. First, there is the unwillingness of the Mossi to leave his country: when he leaves he attempts to make as much money as possible so that he will be able to remain at home for longer periods.[17] Secondly, there is the important fact that customs tolls which the returning migrant must pay on the goods he brings back are so high that he must work extra months in order to pay for them. Rouch, complaining that the exorbitant tolls contribute to "the too extended absence of the Mossi migrants which is prejudicial to efficient agriculture in the Upper Volta," suggests that one of the possible remedies ought to be "a flexibility of the customs which should cease to be an obstacle to the return of Mossi labourers." [18]

The returning migrant, whether returning after one season or after two or three years, attempts to make his homecoming as unobtrusive as possible by arriving at his home during the night. As a matter of fact, one can tell which migrants live in a certain district because they will dally until sundown under the roadside trees long after their comrades, who had stopped for the midday rest, have resumed their homeward march. There are several reasons for returning home at night: first of all, this practice is a cultural survival from the time when a migrant seen returning would be seized and robbed by the local labour recruiters and sent away with the next batch of forced labourers; secondly, the migrant attempts to evade the watchful eyes of the chiefs' people, whose reports may well bring unreasonable requests for gifts; and thirdly, the migrant, like most Mossi, tends to avoid or to play down the emotion-provoking scene which would take place if he suddenly arrived in the middle of the day. The migrant likes nothing better than to get up in the morning after his return and greet his family as though he had never been away.

And they, with the possible exception of his mother, also feign apparent unconcern at seeing him, and greet him as though they had seen him the night before. The subdued excitement of this homecoming is only revealed by "accidental" visits which the migrant's many friends and relatives make to his household. It is only after several days have gone by that the migrant begins to distribute the gifts he has brought back, and to talk about his experiences. But even then he seldom leaves his neighbourhood. He waits patiently until the day of the "great" market, which is held every third Friday in the month, before showing himself publicly.

The only occasion when the migrant is the centre of attraction is the day of his grand tour (*mané do*) in the main market-place of the district. Early that morning he dresses in his best clothes, lends the remainder of his wardrobe to relatives, and together they go and pay homage to the local chief during his morning ceremony (*Wend pous yan*). The migrant gives the chief a small amount of money, an article of clothing, or kola nuts, and replies to his questions about the health and welfare of all the Mossi in Ghana, the whereabouts of absent migrants, the news of Mossi chiefs in Ghana, the nature of the work the migrants are now doing, and the state of the "fight" between the Asantehene and Nkrumah. The chief and his entourage treasure every bit of news received from a migrant; for it is only the exceptional man who can provide much information. As soon as the chief gives him permission to leave, the migrant goes to the market, where he is quickly surrounded by *griots* (minstrels) who accompany him in his periodic circumambulations of the market-place, drumming and singing praises to his ancestors. The migrant greets his friends with presents of money, beer, and kola nuts, takes pride in seeing his female relatives dressed in the cloths and clothes he brought them, arranges rendezvous with former or potential paramours, and towards evening amply rewards the *griots* with money and beer. Then the migrant wends his way homeward, often quite satisfied that his grand tour was a success. Many a migrant attempts to prolong this feeling of grandeur by visiting other markets and by dressing up on subsequent grand market days, but by this time the rains have soiled his fine clothes, much of his money is spent, and the spotlight shifts to new arrivals.

Migration itself brings little lasting prestige. It is not seen as a *rite de passage* or even an unusual feat. The men who go away are not considered brave but poor: "Only poor people go away. People go away because they want things. Those men who have money do not need to migrate for work; they can go to Ouagadougou or even to Kumasi to buy things." The man who returns is fêted because he has been away, and his friends and relatives are happy to have him back. Once the celebrations are over the migrant is quickly absorbed into his local community. This happens very rapidly, especially if he returns just before the rains. This process is clearly apparent as the planting season proceeds. Other villagers are seen wearing his clothes, and investigation reveals that they have bought them from him. His brand-new bicycle has also been exchanged for an old one plus a head of livestock; and eventually this old bicycle is sold for money to meet other obligations. In the end, the migrant becomes indistinguishable from other Mossi youths who at some time in the past have migrated to Ghana, and like them dreams of going back as and when circumstances permit. When that time comes, the migrant slips off one morning, with or without the consent of his relatives, just as the cock's crow announces the end of the darkness.

It is difficult for the short-term observer to verify the reports of agricultural officers that excessive migration has curtailed food production. However, he can check and observe for himself the reports that the traditional allocation of agricultural labour has shifted. Under ideal conditions during the planting season—that is, with the full complement of the household available—all members of the family work collectively under the supervision of the household head for about seven hours a day. After this period the individual members are free to cultivate for themselves such lesser crops as rice and peanuts. The household head uses the food grown by collective labour to feed his charges during the year, and takes some of it to fulfil his political (and now fiscal), social, and religious obligations. Each man or husband sells a part of his own crops in the markets to buy presents for himself, his sweethearts, or his family. The women use their own produce to supplement their daily rations, to cook extra meals for their children, or sell some of it to buy condiments for their sauces. Now that a shortage of labour is created by the absence of men, this whole pattern shifts. No longer can the household head allow his people enough time to grow crops for their personal use. Every hand is needed to grow the millet used to make *saghabo*, the staple food. The result is that women and young men of the household are unable to satisfy all but their alimentary needs in the traditional way, and must look elsewhere for the money to buy the clothes and goods that they desire. The men follow in the steps of their absent relatives and migrate to Ghana; many women take to selling cooked food to the migrants who pass through their village on the way to work. The household heads complain bitterly about the departing men, and object most strongly to the women selling food at the roadside. They fear, and with good reason, that many of the women who must sleep away from home in order to catch the early rising migrants establish sexual liaisons with other men. Moreover, they fear that disgruntled wives and daughters may run off with migrants or other passers-by.

Mossi elders state almost unanimously that migration, whether seasonal or extended, causes hardships for the sedentary population and does little for the household economy. They discount any suggestion that the goods brought back by the migrants can compensate for their absences. Furthermore, they point out that families who must cultivate without the help of absent men must often sell part of their crops to pay taxes for the absentees. Many local European administrators admit that their tax policy imposes a hardship on those families whose men have been away for years, but at the same time they declare that once a man's name has been taken off the tax records, his relatives will not restore it when he returns. The interesting fact is that the administrative policy of holding a family responsible for the taxes of all its members provides one of the mechanisms which continue to link the absent migrant with his relatives at home, and serves to prevent the growth of that "individuality" which uninformed people see as the natural reason for the origin and growth of migration.

Surprisingly enough, although the elders complain about paying the taxes of absentees and "the search for money to pay taxes" is given as one of the main reasons for migration, not many migrants contribute to imposts of their household, nor do many elders ask for this help. When quizzed about taxation, the young men insist that their elders are responsible for all taxes. They point out that they worked for their fathers before they started to migrate for work, and will continue to help the old people when they have ceased to migrate. Some of the young married men do give the elders money for taxes, but others (and most of the single men), even when they give money to the elders, insist that it is not for taxes. Of course, the old men take this money and pay taxes with it, but the young men choose to ignore this fact for fear of changing the traditional relationship with their elders. Some young men add that they should not be asked about taxes since for many years they do not "profit" from the agricultural work done at home. These are the men who return just in time for the rains, work very hard on a meagre diet because of the "hungry period," and leave just before or soon after the harvest. Some men consciously follow this schedule in order to leave as much food as possible for their relatives.[19]

Almost all the migrants defend their desire to seek work outside the country. Many admit that the old people suffer when men remain away too long, but declare that their country is poor, that local Europeans have no work for them; therefore, they must migrate whether they wish it or not. Some men in their zeal to defend themselves paint a rather unglamorous picture of Ghana. They talk of catching colds and pneumonia in the dank cacao fields; of being bitten by snakes and insects; of dying away from home; and, worst of all, of coming home to find a loved parent or relative dead and buried. They called the attention of the investigator to a fact, which he verified, that during those dry seasons when the administration builds or repairs the local roads, very few men migrate to find work. Most men prefer to work near home, even though by so doing they are unable to accumulate much money. This is compensated for by their being able to see their relatives every day, and being able, therefore, to aid them during non-working hours. Moreover, they are close enough to home to keep on working until the cessation of work, the coming of the rains, the pressure of relatives, or any combination of these factors forces them to devote all their time to cultivation.

Most of the rural Mossi, including those who have worked outside the country, still regard agriculture purely as a means of subsistence. Men might accept wages from Europeans or from other Mossi to cultivate "European" crops such as tomatoes and table vegetables, but they find it shameful to accept pay for cultivating the traditional crops. Despite the persistence of this ideal, many men who have worked for wages in the cacao and vegetable farms of Ghana are beginning to regard agriculture in a new light: it must not only produce a mere subsistence, it must be profitable or it is useless. One very articulate young man complained: "When I was born, I was told that to hoe [agriculture] was the occupation of the Mossi. But today the hoe is nothing! You work on cacao under shade trees in Ashanti; you find yams for food; and the *Asanteneba* [Ashanti people] give you money. Here, you work in hard soil in the hot sun, and then you have to sell your millet to pay taxes. You have nothing!" The speaker complained, but he continued to cultivate his crops. Other young men have not expressed their grievances in such articulate terms, but they all indicate that agriculture is not meeting their needs. There are several young men in the two districts where I studied who have never cultivated a stalk of millet since they returned from Ghana. A few of them used their meagre capital to buy small stocks of merchandise which they hawk in the markets; and others make short and frequent trips to northern Ghana with livestock and other commodities. Those men who did not like trading or who failed in their efforts, went off to Ouagadougou to join an ever-increasing urban Mossi population. There, at least, some of them can use skills such as road-building, truck-loading, and sanitation control, which they may have acquired while in Ghana but which are useless, with few exceptions, in their home communities.[20]

So far this paper has emphasized the effects of seasonal migration upon Mossi agriculture in the rainy season, but the absence of men during the non-agricultural dry season also has serious economic implications for Mossi society. It is during the dry season that the men must clear new bush farms, dig new wells and clean old ones, build new huts, and repair those huts and compound walls which are inevitably ruined by the rains. The dry season also used to be, and still is to some extent, the period during which the Mossi weave cloth for internal use and export. Today the growing use of plaited grass for both hut and compound walls and the serious shortage of huts are attributed to the absence of men who traditionally used to prepare sun-dried bricks for these purposes. This

TABLE 1. *Results of investigation made among 9,518 Mossi migrants who crossed the Yeji Ferry in March 1954, in an attempt to discover their occupations while in Ghana* [21]

Occupation	Number	Percentage
Vegetable farms	6,356	66.7
Cacao farms	1,437	15.9
Timber	431	4.5
Gold mines	345	4.4
Other mines	84	
Public Works Dept.:		
Roads and other	209	2.1
Building and construction	100	1.8
Railroad and transport	83	
Work for municipalities	95	.9
Commerce	87	.8
Other	285	2.9
Unknown	6	

problem sometimes becomes so acute that elders who have reconciled themselves to the seasonal migration of their men plead with them to remain at home at least every other season to take care of these necessary household tasks.

The relationship between the decline of cotton-cloth production and the seasonal migration of men for work is much more complex. Almost immediately after the conquest the Mossi were required to provide cotton for export, since it was one of the few "exportable commodities" which they possessed. Cotton cultivation was encouraged, and the local chiefs acted as collecting agents for the administration. At the same time there was also a demand for labourers on the coffee plantations of the Ivory Coast and on railroads in the Sudan; and thousands of Mossi labourers were exported to meet these demands. Unfortunately, cotton turned out to be the Mossi crop most easily affected by a forced labour régime. When households ran short of labour, cotton was among the first crops neglected because it was not a food crop; it was sown quite late in the agricultural cycle, it required a great deal of cultivation and fencing to protect it from weeds and livestock, and, finally, it was the last crop harvested. Those men who feared recruitment for forced labour, or who planned to migrate for work after the main harvest in order to get the then mandatory five-francs piece, did not plant cotton because they were uncertain of harvesting it. The administration attempted to maintain cotton production and even instituted rather harsh measures for this purpose. All these efforts failed and the officials could not understand why cotton production fell off. But Albert Londres, whose visit to the Mossi has already been referred to, saw the relationship between the official forced labour policy and cotton cultivation, and he could not believe that the administrators were "astonished that the Sudan and the Upper Volta no longer produce cotton." [22]

Another factor in the decline of cloth-making among the Mossi was the administration's drive to export cotton, which reduced the amount available for local cloth manufacture. Fortunately for the Mossi, however, the migrants were by this time bringing back the more colourful European cloth, which until that time had been a luxury item sold by the Hausa caravan traders. And as cotton production declined and more European cloth came in, more and more Mossi men lost interest in producing local cloth. Ironical as it may seem, the French helped to realize their own fear that the British would inundate the country with their cottons. Today there are old men who regret the loss of this traditional skill and fear that the time may come when Mossi cloth will be unavailable for use in ceremonials and to make burial clothes. A few old men in the two districts have refused to wear European cloth, and vow never to wear it during their lives. Needless to say, these men are confident that they will not wear machine-made cloth to their graves. Yet it is often the desire to promenade at funeral ceremonies in smart cotton and serge robes "from Kumasi" that inspires the sons of these old men to migrate for work. When youths migrate at a very early age they never learn to weave; moreover, they often regard clothmaking as an outmoded economic activity of dubious utility.

It is fairly easy to delineate the gross changes in the economic activities of Mossi society which have accompanied labour migrations, but it is difficult to assess whether Mossi society is much better off economically than it was before. Migrants do bring back a great amount and variety of goods. A trunk containing the purchases of two typical migrants contained the following items:

> Two kerosene lamps, two bottles of kerosene, two black serge robes trimmed with pink silk, one white cotton robe, two blue shirts, two pairs of khaki shorts, two tubes of a medicated rub called Thermogene, eight women's headscarves, two Moslem fezes, two mirrors, two jars of Vaseline petroleum jelly, two pairs of sandals, one black scarf, two packs of camphor balls, and one bottle of perfume.

Some migrants bring back mosquito nets, wooden bedsteads, chairs, eating utensils, and, most important of all, bicycles. The migrants pay a heavy toll on all these articles. In 1953 alone the migrants paid $1,027,100 into the treasury of the Upper Volta as customs duties—a toll which Jean

TABLE 2. *Average wages, mean budgets, and savings of individual migrants in Ghana during 1954* [24]

Occupations	Wages			Expenditures—monthly				Savings	
	Per day	Per mo.	Per yr.	Food	Lodg-ing	Divers	Total	Per mo.	Per yr.
Salaried	4s. 6d.	£6	£72	£3. 10s.	4s.	£3. 10s.	£5. 4s.	£1	£12
Agriculture	4s. 0d.	£5	£42	—	—	£2. 10s.	£2. 10s.	£2. 10s.	£21
Merchants-traders	11s. 0d.	£14	£140	£4. 10s.	10s.	£3	£8	£6	£60

Rouch considers as intolerably high and as one of the factors keeping many of the migrants away until they amass a sufficiently large amount of money.[23] Dufour, a French economist who studied the economy of the Upper Volta in 1956, declared that the migrants played an important role in the economy of the territory, but that they would play an even larger role if they brought back money instead of the lower-priced British products from Ghana. He calculated that the importation of these goods represented "a traffic of more than a billion francs, which is undoubtedly a loss for the economy of the territory and of the French Union, but also a rise in the standard of living of the population." [25] In the face of these statistics, the anthropologist can do little more than call attention to the conviction of agricultural officers that food production has declined, and to the complaint of the older people that they would rather have *saghabo*, the staple food, than all the goods in Kumasi. A comprehensive study of Mossi food production remains to be done, and it is only when such data become available that it will be possible to ascertain whether, in the absence of new crops and new agricultural techniques, the possession of manufactured goods, which is said to represent a higher standard of living, is not really at the expense of overall food production. . . .[26]

The socio-political hierarchical system of the Mossi is being modified, but this change is not so much the effect of migration as it is the result of European rule. But here, as in the other aspects of socio-cultural change in the society, these two factors are closely linked. There is no difference in the rates of migration of any Mossi classes except for the very near relatives of the district chiefs. The men of this select group have always occupied favoured positions. In pre-European times they more than the other nobles were the official messengers and used their position to extract goods and services from the commoners. During the early period of European occupation and the time of forced labour, they were the official labour recruiters and often received presents from men not wanting to be sent away. In addition to these bribes, they themselves were often exempted from forced labour and therefore never left their districts. Today these men still play their traditional roles as official messengers, but in addition they act as paid foremen when the administration has any public work to be done in the districts. However, it appears that now it is only a matter of time before these men lose their favoured status, because the administration has appointed personnel as secretaries to important district chiefs, and the senior public works officials are recruiting foremen on the basis of qualification. The very first voluntary migration of a son of the Nobéré district chief to Ghana in November 1956 may well presage the coming of a new era.

The way in which European rule has affected the traditional sociopolitical structure can best be seen in the reaction of those lesser nobles who had fled to Ghana and have returned after several years of migratory labour there, to find the prestige of their class diminished. The longer the man has been away, the more difficult it is for him to adjust to the changes in Mossi society; and instead of being a force for change in view of his long stay in a more dynamic society, he often remains conservative by local standards. For example: a member of a lesser noble lineage fled to Ghana for about twenty years to escape forced labour, and returned as a poor and wifeless old man in 1953. He had no "friend" from whom he could receive a wife, and while waiting until his lineage or the chief could find him one, he discovered that the widow of a lineage brother had refused to accept a husband from her deceased husband's lineage and was living with a commoner. When the returnee found this out he abused the chief and his lineage members for not having killed the couple and for allowing the French "to spoil" the lineage. He vowed that he would take the woman back. The chief and the nobles, in turn, chided him for his shameful desire to possess a woman who had violated tradition by living with a commoner. They argued that for a noble to take back a woman who would have been killed for her action before the coming of the Europeans, was tantamount to accepting the destruction of all differences among social classes. The returnee could not be persuaded to leave the woman alone, however, and one day he seized her in the market place, dragged her to his house, and placed the "bracelets of Ngado" on her wrists. His use of these bracelets, which at one time were luxury items reserved to noblemen's wives who were interdicted to commoners, shows that he was clinging to the past, since most noblemen's wives now wear and prefer costume jewellery to these bracelets. The chief and the other nobles could not debase their status any further by deserting their impudent relative, and persuaded the woman and her relatives to accept the abduction. Interestingly enough, this returnee is now considered somewhat mentally disturbed, and is pointed out as an example of what can happen to a Mossi who spends most of his life in Ghana.

There is no way for a migrant of commoner, serf, or slave origin, who has been to Ghana, to raise his status as a result of his trip. Some of these men attempt to assert themselves by stealing other men's wives, and especially the wives of nobles, secure in the knowledge that they cannot be fined for taking the former or killed for taking the latter. However, if these men continue to violate the traditional social and political norms they soon discover that customary sanctions can still be imposed upon them. Many a man has discovered that he cannot seize a nobleman's wife with impunity, because there has been so much intermarriage between noble and commoner lineages that the nobles can always recall one of their daughters married to the abductor's own relatives. And if the culprit does not relent and return the woman, he is ostracized both by his own relatives who lost the wife and by the other nobles within the district. Men who are especially recalcitrant may be ambushed and beaten, unless they flee to Ghana or to another district beyond the control and sanction of the local people. But even in these places they are not completely safe, because Mossi chiefs both in Ghana and at home apprehend and return evildoers to their districts.

The presence of about 42 Mossi chiefs (*serkin*) in Ghana has an important influence on the way migrants have been treated there, and on the way in which migration has affected Mossi society. These chiefs are most often nobles or descendants of nobles, who fled their homeland in order to avoid military conscription, forced labour, penalties for non-payment of taxes, or some criminal or civil offence. Once in Ghana these noble exiles settled among fellow exiles or migrants and created models of the traditional chiefdoms, complete with courts and officials. These chiefs in exile have no territory of their own; nor do they need any, because Mossi chiefs never control land; they always control people. Moreover, many of these self-appointed chiefs have succeeded in obtaining the *nam* (that symbol of Mossi sovereignty) from the Moro Naba in Ouagadougou, and this enables them to rule over those Mossi who come into their area.[27] Apparently the indigenous chiefs in Ghana also welcomed the establishment of Mossi chiefdoms; for these institutions take care of strangers, a task for which many of the indigenous chiefdoms were not qualified.

The Mossi chiefs in Ghana also perform many important functions for their fellow chiefs in the homeland. They trace lost migrants, apprehend stolen women, take care of sick and dead migrants, and dispose of surplus merchandise that chiefs may send to them from Mossi country. In return for such services, the chiefs of the Volta Republic send grain to their comrades in Ghana, and, most important of all, send them *pogsioure* as wives. The recipient of a *pogsioure* does not send back his daughter to Mossi country, however, but is instructed by the donor to give the girl to another Mossi in Ghana, thus widening the nexus of reciprocal relations and gift-giving between the two countries.

When a migrant arrives in Ghana he is not compelled to attach himself to a Mossi chief, but most do so, since these men give them shelter, sometimes find work for them, and, most important of all, protect them from the strangers among whom they must work. So important is this last function, that even if migrants have work and shelter, they pay allegiance to the Mossi chiefs, give them small gifts of money, and place themselves under their protection. Thereafter, if the migrants have any difficulties with their fellow migrants, townspeople, or employers, they appeal to their chiefs for help. Under such conditions the migrants, especially those who stay in the country for a short time, feel no necessity to pay any attention to the political changes taking place in their surroundings. Even when the loud-speaker trucks of the various Ghanaian political parties visit the farm areas where most of the migrants work, the Mossi seldom understand the language being used, and even when they do, go about their own affairs and do not interfere with what they regard as local matters. In this way they never learn about the issues involved, and are therefore not able to introduce new political concepts into their country when they return.

Those migrants who remain in Ghana for long periods, and who live in the larger cities, do take part in Ghanaian politics and create many problems for the local authorities. One of the main problems is that some of the local politicians do not want the Mossi to vote because they do not consider them permanent residents of Ghana—and in fact many of them plan eventually to return to their homeland. The second problem is that the many Mossi residents in Ghana are encouraged by their chiefs to support the Moslem Association Party and the Northern People's Party which stand for strong traditional chieftainships, rather than the Convention People's Party which favours representative government. The political behaviour of these Mossi chiefs explains why many of them were among those persons deported from Ghana for subversive activities after the 1956 election. Mossi chiefs were certainly among those "French subjects" deported from Ghana as recently as 17 February 1959, "on the grounds that their presence is not conducive to the public good." The deportees were accused of "covertly participating in partisan politics," and it was the hope of Ghana's government that by taking this drastic action "non-Ghanaians residing in this country may realize that their participation in political activities is unacceptable to the Government." [28]

The paradox here is that while the influence of the Mossi chiefs on the minority of migrants with political views has created unpleasantness in Ghana, their traditional control over the majority of migrants has served to insulate their men from new ideological forces and has effectively limited the flow of nationalistic ideas to Mossi country. The European administrators in Mossi country have always been fearful lest the migrants should become a source of anti-colonial feeling.[29] For example, in 1956, during the Franco-British and Israeli attack on Egypt, the French administration placed a close watch on Nobéré, a strongly Moslem community on the Ghana-Ouagadougou road, to make sure that any migrants returning at that time brought back no pro-Nasser propaganda from the Moslem political parties in northern Ghana. French fears were unfounded, since during that period most of the migrant traffic was bound towards Ghana, and those few persons who were coming back knew only that something had affected the price of cacao. Jean Rouch feels that France's "fear of the propagation of politically subversive ideas" by migrants appeared to him "at present unjustifiable," especially when it led to action on their part to try to prevent it.[30]

Actually, most migrants I interviewed had only vague ideas of the vast political changes then taking place in Ghana. Many of them told the district chiefs that Nkrumah, a commoner, was a man of unusual qualities. The fact that he had no wife (at that time) was evidence to the migrants that he was "a devil and did not need to eat," and therefore, would be more than a match for the Asantehene. Several migrants stated that they voted for the M.A.P. on the advice of their chiefs, but I met only one young man who had voted for the C.P.P. and one old man who was sympathetic to that organization. The old man claimed to have taken part in some of the early strikes in the gold mines of Ghana, and feels that Nkrumah is good for Ghana. On the other hand, being a noble, he did not like the loss in prestige of the chiefs and nobles and would have liked to see the end both of European dominance and of the importance of mission-educated commoners. But although he visited the district chiefs, he did not take part in the political affairs of his district because he wished to remain anonymous to the Europeans and keep his name off the tax rolls. The young man who voted for the C.P.P. while in Ghana actually fled Mossi country several years ago in order to escape military conscription (taking another man's wife with him) and would not have returned if his elder brother had not been seriously ill. He openly criticized the traditional chiefs, the modern Mossi politicians, and the European district officials. When the people of the district were summoned to hear a political speech by a neighbouring traditional chief, this young man was the only person to stand and make a reply. The visitor was both pleased and surprised by this action, and had a long discussion with him afterwards, since this behaviour harmonized with the new political activities of this traditional chief. However, other people were angry with the young nobleman because they felt that he was disrespectful to a man who, although a modern politician, was still a traditional chief.

Since the migrants are not the main carriers of new political ideas, they are not the main catalysts for the growth of nationalism in the Volta

Republic. Yet the mission-trained young men, who have never migrated to Ghana for work but who formed the incipient political parties in Mossi country, were undoubtedly stimulated by the events in Ghana, a country of which they were highly aware, since a large number of their relatives and countrymen work and have found asylum there. . . .

SUMMARY AND CONCLUSION

The socio-cultural change which has taken and is still taking place in Mossi society came not only as a result of seasonal migration of labourers, but also because of European social and economic requirements and legislation. The first changes introduced were economic ones, and migration was the result. However, as time passed, changes in the economic institutions of the Mossi engendered changes in their social institutions, and when these changes were supported by French precept and law, further changes took place in turn. The characteristics of these changes are very different from those which the Wilsons believed would have restored equilibrium to Mossi society. One set of changes brought forth others, but instead of the subsequent changes countervailing the first set of changes, they supported them, and moved the society towards greater change. Given the multifarious complexities of the multi-dimensional changes which are operating in Mossi society it seems to me that the processes of socio-cultural transformation would tend to be cumulative, and accelerative rather than equilibratory. Moreover, since these changes can be expected to accelerate as Mossi society increases in scale, I question the validity and usefulness of the disequilibrium concept which expects and hopes for some point of equilibrium in the foreseeable future.

NOTES

1. See Audrey Richards, *Economic Development and Tribal Change* (Cambridge, 1955); I. Schapera, *Migrant Labour and Tribal Life* (London, 1947); and Godfrey Wilson, "The Economics of Detribalization in Northern Rhodesia," Part I, The Rhodes-Livingstone Papers, No. 5, published by Rhodes-Livingstone Institute, Livingstone (Northern Rhodesia, 1941).

2. R. B. Davidson, *Migrant Labour in the Gold Coast* (Achimota, 1954); Jean Rouch, "Migrations au Ghana," *Journal de la Société des Africanistes*, tome xxvi, 9, fasc., i–ii (Musée de l'Homme, Paris, 1956).

3. P. Mercier, "L'Affaiblissement des processus d'integration dans des sociétés en changement," *Bull. d'IFAN*, ser. B, vol. 16, 1954, Dakar; R. M. Prothero, "Migratory Labour from North-Western Nigeria," *Africa*, vol. xxvii, No. 3, July 1957, pp. 251–61.

4. "La Haute Volta," *Magazine A.O.F.*, vol. 17, ser. II, No. 2, Nov. 1955, p. 9; H. Labouret, *Paysans d'Afrique occidentale* (Paris, 1941), pp. 222 ff.

5. Sister Marie-André du Sacré-Coeur, "Tribal Labour and Social Legislation in French Tropical Africa," *Inter. Labour Review*, vol. 68, July–Dec. 1953, p. 506.

6. Harrison Church, *West Africa* (London, 1957), pp. 168–9.

7. P. Mercier, *op. cit.;* E. B. Ward, "Some Observations on Religious Cults in Ashanti," *Africa*, vol. xxvi, No. 1, Jan. 1956, pp. 47–61; G. and M. Wilson, *The Analysis of Social Change Based on Observations in Central Africa* (Cambridge, 1945), p. 132, to cite a few examples.

8. B. Malinowski, Introductory Essay on "The Anthropology of Changing African Cultures," *Methods of Study of Culture Contact in Africa*, International Institute of African Languages and Cultures, Memo. XV reprinted from *Africa*, 1938, vols. vii, viii, and ix, pp. vii–xxxv. See also Schapera, *op. cit.*, p. 191.

9. Lewis Gann, "The End of the Slave Trade in British Central Africa: 1889–1912," *The Rhodes-Livingstone Journal*, No. 16, pp. 49–51.

10. Marvin Harris, "Labour Migration among the Moçambique Thonga: Cultural and Political Factors," *Africa*, vol. xxix, No. 1, Jan. 1959, p. 53.

11. Lord Hailey, *An African Survey*, Oxford University Press (London, 1938), p. 603.

12. A. deBeauminy, "Le Pays de la boucle du Niger, étude économique," *Revue géographique et commerciale de Bordeaux*, vol. 6, pp. 71–78, 1919.

13. Paul-Louis Ledange, "Une Colonie nouvelle, La Haute Volta," *La Revue indigène*, Nos. 157–9 (Paris, 1922), pp. 133–6.

14. Albert Londres, *Terre d'Ebène* (La traite des Noirs) (Albin Michel, Paris, 1929), pp. 126 ff.

15. V. Thompson and R. Adloff, *French West Africa* (New York, 1958), p. 174.

16. Rouch, *op. cit.*, pp. 80, 196.

17. Church believes that a combination of factors such as healthy climate and the strength of political, social, and economic systems have all made for attachment to the soil even when nearby areas could be inhabited with profit. *Op. cit.*, pp. 163–8.

18. Rouch, *op. cit.*, p. 196.

19. Interestingly enough, Prothero reports that the large number of migrants who leave Northern Nigeria "must help considerably to conserve the food supplies in the home areas." *Op. cit.*, p. 256.

20. In 1956, for the first time in many years, the local Public Works Department in Nobéré district was able to retain enough workers to continue road-building during the planting period. Those men who stayed on did not work the whole week, but allowed their relatives and friends to substitute for them on those days when they had to help in the fields. The foreman often noticed the substitutions, but pretended not to notice as long as the work was accomplished.

21. This table was prepared from data published in Davidson, *op. cit.*, pp. 31–37, and Rouch, *op. cit.*, pp. 93 ff.

22. Albert Londres, *op. cit.*, p. 126.

23. Rouch, *op. cit.*, p. 139.

24. Table compiled with data taken from Rouch, *op. cit.*, p. 135.

25. Pierre Dufour, "L'Economie de la Haute Volta," *Paris-Dakar,* no. 6, 151, lundi, 9 avril 1956, p. 3. Dakar, Senegal, West Africa.

26. Godfrey Wilson, "An Essay on the Economies of Detribalization in Northern Rhodesia," *The Rhodes-Livingstone Papers,* No. 5, 1941.

27. Cf. Rouch, *op. cit.,* p. 156.

28. *The New York Times,* vol. cviii, no. 36,915, Wed. 18 Feb. 1959, p. 4.

29. The irony here is that it was the French themselves who first tried to use returning migrants as subversive agents. During the Second World War the Free French Forces in Ghana gave returning migrants anti-Petain leaflets to distribute in Mossi country. The migrants made poor couriers, however, because they burned the leaflets just after they crossed the border to avoid trouble with the pro-Petain Europeans who were then in control of the colony.

30. Rouch, *op. cit.,* p. 196.

J. Van Velsen

LABOUR MIGRATION AS A POSITIVE
FACTOR IN THE CONTINUITY OF
TONGA TRIBAL SOCIETY (1961)

The Tonga [1] live on the western shores of the northern half of Lake Nyasa, at a distance of about 1,000 miles from the main employment centres in the Rhodesias and of about 1,500 to 2,000 miles from those in the Union of South Africa. They live in small scattered homesteads which I have called "hamlets." The overwhelming majority of Tonga wage-earners find work in those three countries; very few are employed in Nyasaland. Tongaland is still undeveloped and very little cash is generated locally. Compared with other tribal areas the Tonga are relatively prosperous; this prosperity is largely due to their export of labour. Their staple diet is cassava whose cultivation does not require much labour. Subsistence cultivation is almost entirely in the hands of the women and does not seem to be adversely affected by the exodus of male labour. There is no shortage of land.

Formally Tonga society is matrilineal: descent and office follow the matriline and ideally a person should reside matrilocally but wives live virilocally. In fact, however, there are many deviations from these rules and patrilateral kin play an important role in a person's life. Indeed, there are no clear foci of social and political relationships and there is ample scope for political manipulation and usurpation of offices and titles.

Absent labour migrants are an important category of Tonga; at any one time between 60 and 75% of the adult males are absent whilst working abroad (viz. outside Tongaland), the majority of them leaving their families behind. Indeed, even the most casual visitor to Tongaland cannot fail to notice the marked preponderance of women. In this paper I will

SOURCE. J. Van Velsen, "Labour Migration as a Positive Factor in the Continuity of Tonga Tribal Society," reprinted from *Economic Development and Cultural Change* as reprinted in A. Southall (editor), *Social Change in Modern Africa*, 1961, pp. 230–241, by permission of The University of Chicago Press. Copyright 1961 by The University of Chicago Press.

show that these absent villagers generally maintain a stake in the social and political structure of Tongaland; that they have a vested interest in its continued functioning and try to play their social and political role despite their absence. Tonga working abroad thus belong to two contrasted and distinguishable (but not rigidly separated) economic and social environments. On the one hand there is their tribal area with the villages where they come from, where they are likely to retire and where their status is largely determined by birth. On the other hand there are the urban areas where they work (often for the best part of their adult lives) and where their status does not depend on their birth (apart from the fact that they are black).

Tonga who seek employment abroad are quite explicit about their objections to taking their families with them. These objections may refer to urban life in general (as it is experienced by Africans in Rhodesian and South African towns) or to life in particular urban areas. The reasons they give for their objections are corroborated by the literature on urban conditions for Africans. As I will describe later, it is largely for the same reasons that Tonga want to retire in the village after a lifetime in the towns. I will therefore continue to use the term "labour migrants" because, through necessity, and hence by intention, most Tonga who go abroad retire to their villages in Tongaland. My view is that those who manage to settle in the towns permanently and have given up the intention to return to the village, are the exception rather than the rule. This view cannot easily be supported by figures from either the rural or the urban end. One would need life histories of men who have reached such a stage in their lives (or who are now dead) that one can assume that they are not likely to move from the urban to the rural area or vice versa, depending on where they are found. Considering the number of men who are away at any one time and the long average duration of a man's absence abroad, in the relatively short time that I lived with the Tonga I could not gather sufficient systematic numerical data.

The urban data in particular would be very difficult to collect because they could be reliably obtained only through the usual anthropological method of intensive study rather than through surveys which tend to lay too much emphasis on such quantitative data as the number of years spent by Africans in towns, or, alternatively, their attitudes towards urbanization. From my experience with Tonga labour migrants, it seems to me that the number of years spent in the towns by a person is not a reliable index of that person's "urbanization." I understand by this term a condition in which the African has given up his loyalty to his tribe and his continued dependence on the economic and social system of his tribe, and has become, as an individual and no longer through membership of his tribe, a citizen of the larger state which now contains his tribe. It is relatively unimportant whether an African has lived for one, ten, or twenty years, with or without intervals in his tribal area, in the specialized and industrialized economy of the towns if he relies for his ultimate security on his tribal society, after his limited security of urban employment has come to an end.

In the light of my Tonga evidence it might perhaps be more fruitful if in urban surveys one tried to discover a correlation between length of residence on the one hand and distance from tribal area and the nature of a man's employment (whether skilled or not or whether well paid) on the other hand. For I found a definite reluctance among the Tonga to come home frequently because their journey to their place of employment is generally long and expensive; moreover Tonga tend to have the rather better paid jobs and they are afraid that if they go on holiday too often or too long at a time they may lose their jobs.

I remarked before that the Tonga retire to the village from necessity rather than from choice. The Tonga living in the towns are all "urbanized" in the sense that they come under the urban authorities and live in an industrial, urban, cash economy and so forth.[2] But their integration into the industrial, urban economy, particularly as regards social security, is only partial for reasons which are beyond their control. It seems to me that this is or should be the crucial element in any discussion of "urbanization." Since the majority of the Tonga working abroad maintain social and economic links with their village, they remain "migrants" and do not become "urbanized." Consequently when Tonga migrants eventually retire to their village, they do not fall back upon the security of a tribal social system which *happens* to have continued during their absence; the migrants themselves, during their absence, have been contributing actively and consciously to its continuance because they know that they may have to rely on it when they are no longer usefully employed in their urban habitat. In other words, the decision of Tonga urban workers to maintain a position in their tribal society is therefore not so much a matter of choice but rather it is inherent in the social and economic system of the urban areas in which they live and work. And such variations between individual Tonga as the length of their stay abroad, the amount of money sent home, and, in general, the frequency and intensity of their contacts with the rural area,[3] are differences of degree and do not alter the fundamental fact that the majority of the Tonga working abroad look to the economic and social system of their tribal area for their ultimate security.

Tonga men who go abroad for the first time or go to a place where they have not lived before, frequently say that they do not want to take their families because the journey is difficult and they want to explore the place first. Large numbers of Tonga (perhaps half or more) go to work in South Africa where they are legally prohibited immigrants unless they sign a contract for work in the mines. But in contrast to the neighbouring Tumbuka who sign on for the mines in large numbers, Tonga never sign on as contract labourers for the mines (although many work on the mines on a monthly basis); they often enter the Union of South Africa by various illegal means. They obviously do not want to be burdened with a family; an illegal immigrant when caught may find himself working as a prisoner on a farm instead of in a relatively well-paid and certainly much preferred job in a town, as was his intention. After they have explored the new conditions, some Tonga may then fetch or write for their wives who frequently also enter the Union illegally.

Another factor which tends to discourage a Tonga from settling in the towns with his family is the fact that the minimum wage is adjusted to the requirements of quasi-bachelors without family commitments, and that in general the wages structure is based upon the assumption that families are left behind in the rural areas where they support themselves.[4] But even when wages are adequate for the maintenance of a family in the towns, the acute shortage of housing for Africans is still a deterrent to urban family life.[5]

Housing provided by employers has the great disadvantage that it offers little security—"no job, no house" is the Tonga comment on this kind of housing. Housing provided by municipalities in "locations" or elsewhere is for various reasons also virtually "tied housing." In addition there is the inadequacy of social services (educational, medical, recreational, etc.) for Africans in the urban areas. Even if these services are no more inadequate than in the tribal area, the Tonga at home have at least the compensation that they live among their own kin on whose support they can rely.

RECIPROCAL SERVICES BETWEEN TOWN AND VILLAGE

The families who stay in the village have no difficulty in maintaining themselves, even if only on a subsistence level. This means that those who stay behind can feed themselves and that the money which is sent in from abroad is net income and not needed to make up for the absence of male labour (as for instance among the Bemba). This income is largely available for the purchase of goods other than the basic subsistence requirements. In the rising standard of living of the Tonga minimum requirements tend to include more and more manufactured goods and other items which can only be purchased with money. There are few opportunities for earning cash locally.

The Tonga who goes abroad without his family leaves them behind in the care of his own kinsmen or of his in-laws. Wherever the wife lives during her husband's absence, her relatives will see to it that she receives the treatment due to her as a wife: for instance her husband must send her money with which to buy salt, cloth, and the other necessities which a husband is expected to provide. Conversely the husband's kin take care that his marital rights are not abused.

Wives who have accompanied their husbands to the urban areas often come back to Tongaland, alone, to be confined, or to bring home their children because "the town is a bad place for small children." Children may also be sent home with some other returning migrant.

Money is sent from abroad for a great variety of other purposes. Relatives at home may appeal to kinsmen working abroad for clothes or for financial help (and often receive it) to pay a fine, damages, or bridewealth, to buy clothes, or to pay for the fare to go abroad. Others may help a kinsman in the country by sending him money for a gun with which he can shoot meat for his own pot and for sale to others.

The total amount of cash which is sent to the District from abroad is quite considerable and is, incidentally, larger in proportion to the population than for the other Districts of the Northern Province and perhaps of the whole of Nyasaland.[6]

Finally, labour migrants help their kinsmen at home also with other services. I mentioned already the opportunities for education which they sometimes offer. Intending labour migrants generally depend for their contacts, introduction to employment, etc., on Tonga kinsmen, and others, who are settled in the towns already. The latter will help the intending migrants with papers (genuine or forged) to facilitate their entry into the Union of South Africa.

I have not tried to give an exhaustive description of the manifold reciprocal services which are expressions of the continual contact between Tongaland and the labour migrants. I merely wanted to indicate the range of these reciprocal contacts and to show that they are the result of normal kinship relationships (such as exist between persons who are still in personal touch in Tongaland), and partly the result of the special circumstance of the considerable separation, in terms of geographical distance and social and economic environment, between the two places where Tonga earn a living. Thus in spite of this separation there is still a great deal of interdependence between what one might call the rural and the urban Tonga. Rural Tonga society is geared to a permanent situation in which only a minority of its menfolk in the prime of life is available in Tongaland. The Tonga do not consider this situation as exceptional: migration to the urban centres has become part of Tonga culture. The Tonga accept it as part of life that every normal man should spend at least some years away from Tongaland. They see Tongaland as a training ground for the young and a place of retirement for the old. Young men consider their stay in the village, before they can go off to the towns, as a period of marking time.

Women on the whole do not expect to go abroad and few have ever gone. The result is that the knowledge, the experience and, one might almost say, the culture of the two sexes differ considerably. Whilst many men are literate in or can at any rate speak at least one if not several other languages (often including one or two European languages) besides Tonga, women on the whole do not have these accomplishments. Men have seen and know about the ways of Europeans and other peoples from first-hand experience, but the knowledge of the women in this respect is mostly second-hand or restricted to what they have seen in the District. On the other hand, since the women have been able to follow the developments at home during the absence of their sons, brothers, or husbands, it is the women who are more fully *au fait* in that respect. Village and town have come to represent, for the men at least, different phases of life. The same people move from one environment to another and have interests in both.

MIGRANTS' CONTINUED RELIANCE ON THE VILLAGE

I have given a short description of the links between town and village, and some of the interests they serve. We saw that the Tonga migrants leave certain interests behind which they expect their kinsmen at home to protect. It is not only a certain number of specific interests which a labour migrant expects his kinsfolk to protect, but also his total legal personality—his membership of, and his place in, Tonga society. As I mentioned before, the Tonga leave their villages for the towns with the intention of returning and they want, therefore, a niche to return to. For they know that a time comes when they will no longer be employable in the urban economy and will therefore ". . . relinquish their rights to be housed (in the urban areas)." [7] Thus the same factors which make it difficult for a Tonga to take his family to the towns, also make it difficult for him to stay in the towns when he is no longer employed. Therefore, they expect their rural kinsmen to continue to consider them as members of the village and the kin-group who are only temporarily absent. And both groups of Tonga see their respective services on a reciprocal basis. The labour migrant sees his contributions of cash and goods to the rural economy as a kind of insurance premium: "How can we expect our *abali* (kin, friends) to help us later when we are old, if we do not help them now?"

To keep the place of labour migrants means, amongst other things, that their kinsmen in the rural area must make sure that there will always be enough land for them. This is one reason why those who have, in one capacity or another, control over land, are chary of indiscriminate settlement even though there is enough land.

But a person's relationship to land, his claim for a garden, is only one aspect of his membership of Tonga society. Status in the social and political structure within the village and outside it is closely connected with access to land, and a person's rights to land cannot be isolated from his relationships involving other rights and obligations in the community. It is therefore his status as a Tonga in its entirety which a labour migrant wants to be preserved during his absence. Although the Tonga have been drawn into the orbit of a cash economy, those who live in Tongaland still need land as the principal source of their living. It provides them with food, fire, and building materials for their houses. As regards most basic requirements of life such as food and housing, though not clothing, the economy of Tongaland is still essentially the traditional subsistence economy. It is within this framework of basically traditional values that a Tonga occupies a position into which he is born and by virtue of which he is a member of Tonga society. And it is within this framework, too, that Tonga hold gardens, marry, have children, occupy political office, seek for protection of their rights—in brief, expect security in life. This means that a member of this society who wants to maintain his status cannot do so only in relation to one aspect of life—he is inevitably drawn into the maelstrom of the total life of the community.

MIGRANTS AND TRIBAL POLITICS

Thus Tonga, whether at home or abroad, who are interested in the preservation of rights in land, are inevitably involved in tribal politics. This explains why labour migrants continue to compete for political office at home as well as they can in spite of their absence, and notwithstanding the fact that the monetary rewards of the office, if any, are likely to be very small in comparison with their earnings abroad.

It is a common practice for labour migrants to write to the District Commissioner or the Protectorate Secretariat in Zomba asking for clarification of or protesting against political events in Tongaland.

I have seen many similar cases: sophisticated men with (as far as I could judge) quite good positions and cash incomes who come back for a few months' holiday in the village and get involved in competition for headmanships or other minor political honours or make every effort in trying to rectify what they consider is a usurpation of office.

MIGRANTS' SUPPORT OF TRADITIONAL VALUES

We have seen that the rights associated with a person's social and political status (including claims to office) require continuous vigilance against encroachment. A labour migrant expects his kinsmen at home to protect his status, though those kinsmen may be in a weak position through the very absence of male relatives. In the flexible political system of the Tonga, struggles for political power are won and lost, and titles appear and disappear. The Tonga political system shows relatively little continuity of titles of office and produces great numbers of rival claimants for political titles. And when a labour migrant's claim has gone by default (which can easily happen since many Tonga stay abroad for long periods) he loses no time to put in his claim on his return.

Whatever other effects labour migration may have upon Tongaland, it is clear that most Tonga do not cut their ties with the rural area. When they return from an urban life abroad they settle again in the pattern of Tonga life which is still dominated by traditional values. There are no obvious signs of social disorganization and the Tonga still hold together as a tribal unit, distinct from other such units surrounding them. There are indeed various factors and pressures which work towards the continuance, if not reinforcement, of tribal integration rather than towards tribal disorganization. Firstly there is the basic assumption, explicit or implicit, of the industrial economy that the average African "is not in any real sense a wage-earner," [8] but is a labour migrant who has his tribal village to fall back upon. Secondly, the Tonga abroad have therefore a vital interest in maintaining their position in the community and the economy of Tongaland. I mentioned several factors prevailing in Tongaland which encourage the Tonga, including the migrants, to conceive of their social and economic security in the rural area in terms of traditional Tonga values.

A third important factor is the Administration of the territory which is based upon "tribal integrity." [9] Consequently the Administration of the District makes extensive use of Tonga tribal agencies. This means in practice that some village headmen [10] receive recognition from the Administration and are appointed Administrative Headmen or Native Authorities, the latter with their own court warrants. Such Administrative appointments are on the whole made upon the assumption that the appointees hold office in the Tonga political structure. Thus Administrative recognition not only puts a premium on political leadership in the Tonga political structure, but the competition for this recognition is also largely in terms of traditional values. Consequently the tribal political structure receives powerful support from the Administration. The idea of tribal integrity is also implicit in the tax census in respect of which a Tonga who is *de facto* resident abroad, is *de jure* still a resident in his village.

I suggest that all three categories of persons—industrial employers, Administration, and the Tonga themselves—have under present conditions, an interest in maintaining the cohesion of the Tonga as a tribal community: and that there is a connexion between this interest and the fact that the social and economic systems (including the land-holding system) are still largely dominated by traditional norms.

In this paper I have tried to explain an apparent contradiction. On the one hand we have the continued predominance of traditional values; on the other hand the exodus of large numbers of men who return to the village with a great deal of sophistication and education in the ways of the Europeans, who have become in many ways a reference group for the Tonga. And I have tried to show that in general these returning labour migrants are actively stimulating the traditional values of their rural society, and the reasons why they do so.

I would like to add one "practical" conclusion. If my analysis is correct, that would mean that as long as Tonga (or for that matter, members of other tribal societies) in the urban areas are not given an opportunity to make their living entirely in the towns, in other words to urbanize themselves, so long will they have to rely on making their living partly in the rural area. And this pull of the rural area (and the economic and social system found there) will continue to exert its influence on the stabilization of the urban population, the labour turnover, the efficiency of labour, etc. The apparent failure of the majority of Africans to settle down as a fully urbanized labour force is too often ascribed to inherent personal "failings" of the African employees; too rarely the cause is sought for in the peculiar and ambivalent lives which so many urban Africans are forced to live.

NOTES

1. I lived among the Tonga for thirty months from 1952 to 1955 as a Research Officer of the Rhodes-Livingstone Institute, Lusaka.

2. Cf. also Gluckman, 1945.

3. These are the criteria which Wilson uses to distinguish between "labour migration" and "temporary urbanization": Wilson, 1942, p. 46.

4. Bachelor-based wages are an obstacle to urban family life, particularly at the lower levels of income: cf. Thompson and Woodruff, 1954, p. 75. For African wages and family standard of living, see, for instance, Dalgleish, 1948, pp. 30, 35; Hellmann, 1949, p. 270; Thompson, 1954, pp. 25 et passim.

5. Cf. Dalgleish, op. cit., p. 36; Hellmann, op. cit., pp. 246, 268 et passim.

6. See, for instance, the Annual Report of the Provincial Commissioners, 1946, pp. 38, 45.

7. Noble, 1951, p. 128.

8. Nyasaland, Colonial Reports, 1954, p. 22.

9. Lacey, 1935, pp. 36, 40, 63.

10. I emphasize "some" headmen and by no means all of those who claim to have a title and to be headmen.

REFERENCES

Annual Report of the Provincial Commissioners, 1946. Zomba: Government Printer.
Dalgleish, A. (Chairman), 1948. Report of the Commission Appointed to Enquire into the Advancement of Africans in Industry. Lusaka: Government Printer.

Gluckman, M., 1945. "Seven-Year Research Plan of the Rhodes-Livingstone Institute." *Rhodes-Livingstone Journal,* No. 4, pp. 1–32.

Hellmann, Ellen, 1949. "Urban Areas." *Handbook on Race Relations in South Africa.* Cape Town: Oxford University Press.

Lacey, T. (Chairman), 1935. *Report of the Commission to Enquire into Migrant Labour.* Zomba: Government Printer.

Noble, G. W., 1951. "African Housing in the Urban Areas of Southern Rhodesia." *Journal of African Administration,* Vol. III, No. 3.

Nyasalands, 1954. *Colonial Reports.* London: H.M.S.O.

Thompson, B. P., 1954. *Two Studies in African Nutrition.* Rhodes-Livingstone Paper, No. 24.

Thompson, C. H., and Woodruff, H. W., 1954. *Economic Development in Rhodesia and Nyasaland.* London: Dennis Dobson.

Wilson, G., 1952. *An Essay on the Economics of Detribalization in Northern Rhodesia.* Rhodes-Livingstone Paper, No. 6.

III

The Decline
and Changing Role
of Traditional Authorities

V. R. Dorjahn

THE CHANGING POLITICAL
SYSTEM OF THE TEMNE [1] (1960)

I

The purpose of this study is to consider some of the changes that have taken place in the positions of political officials and in the administrative hierarchy of the Temne of Sierra Leone, British West Africa. The time period under concern extends from approximately 1880, towards the end of the "tribal wars," as they are called by the Temne, through the establishment of the Protectorate and the later introduction of the Native Administration system, to the "disturbances in the Provinces," November 1955 to March 1956.

The data used, except where indicated to the contrary, refer specifically to Kolifa Mayoso chiefdom,[2] and generally to what has come to be known as the "Kolifa area" of Temne country. The delimitation of this area varied from one informant to another, but always included the chiefdoms Kolifa Rowala, Kolifa Mamunta, Kolifa Mayoso, Kolifa Mabang, and usually Yoni Mamela. These chiefdoms, the "Kolifa area" broadly defined, lie within the south-eastern portion of Temne country where the Paramount Chiefs are installed by members of a secret society, be it *Pɔro, Ramɛna,* or most commonly *Ragbenle,* as opposed to the north-western portion where chiefs are installed in largely Muslim ceremonies. This bifurcation is important in terms of the political system.[3]

Before the establishment of the Protectorate, Temne chiefs and their subjects had struck a balance between the prerogatives of the former and the expectations of the latter. The people did not question that they should be ruled by chiefs, nor the manner of selecting or rewarding a chief. They did not object to a particular chief so long as he conformed

SOURCE. V. R. Dorjahn, "The Changing Political System of Temne," reprinted from *Africa,* XXX, 2, 1960, pp. 110–139, by permission of the International African Institute. Copyright V. R. Dorjahn.

to their conception of what a chief should be and performed chiefly duties in an approved and generally accepted manner. When a chief became oppressive there were socially approved ways to deal with him. The administrative hierarchy that developed to aid a Paramount in carrying out his obligations to his people contained a system of checks and balances that curbed, even if it did not preclude, excesses of various sorts.

The feelings of subjects towards their chief—and this may characterize most authority systems, not merely the political system of the Temne—were ambivalent. On the one hand the chief was regarded as a benign individual, one who was powerful, owing to the sanctions of armed force and the supernatural, who looked after his people, and to whom one could turn in times of difficulty. The Paramount, and to a lesser degree his subchiefs, settled disputes and protected those over whom they had jurisdiction in times of strife ranging from famine to invasion. The Temne saying "The chief is our father" was not without substance. Truly, the chief was regarded as the father of his chiefdom. Yet, like other "father-figures," the chief was at the same time seen as something of an ogre, for the Temne also speak of a chief "eating his chiefdom." The conception of a chief as benign father or despot depended largely on whether or not the chief lived up to the expectations of the majority of his subjects in a given situation.

Almost from the founding of the Protectorate, the position of Temne chiefs began to change rapidly and profoundly. As Colson [4] has phrased it, such changes were "in the direction of bureaucratic government." In addition to being a figurehead, locus of unity, and representative of his subjects, the Paramount also became an agent of Government.[5] This was a difficult, if not impossible, dual role for even the most talented, diplomatic, and best-intentioned Paramount, and it is not surprising that many Temne chiefs were unable to serve two masters to their complete satisfaction. As Mair [6] has pointed out, the European representatives of Government "also had a dual role, as the supporters of chiefly authority and the defenders of its subjects against the abuse of authority. They too were not always able to play both roles with success." Indeed, had they succeeded, the events leading to the "disturbances in the Provinces" in 1955–6 would never have occurred.

That the balance between the prerogatives of chiefs and the expectations of their subjects referred to above was altered by the establishment of the Protectorate seems obvious in the light of recent events, and it is the purpose of this study to document some of the changes that upset this balance. The relations between various positions in the administrative hierarchy were altered, bringing about some variation in the concept of chieftaincy itself. Of the sanctions of chieftaincy, that of force was changed in form and origin, while that of the supernatural was weakened through a variety of factors. The functions of the chief, particularly those of diplomatic and legal natures, together with the canons of eligibility for chieftaincy and the mode of selection of chiefs, as well as the emoluments of chieftaincy, have all been altered in a number of ways. It is necessary to consider each of these in some detail if the changing political system of the Temne is to be understood.

II

Today more than 500,000 Temne inhabit approximately 10,500 square miles.[7] According to their own traditions they have been organized into a variable number of chiefdoms ever since their migration into Sierra Leone.[8]

Each of these chiefdoms has a duly installed chief who is paramount within that area; the chiefdom is an independent political unit. With the formation of the Protectorate a splintering occurred that increased the number of chiefdoms, though this tendency was reversed with the introduction of the Native Administration system in 1937, as amalgamations were encouraged to form "viable units" in a politico-economic sense. The success of such amalgamations is dubious in some cases, judging by recent events.[9] Each chiefdom is composed of a variable number of subdivisions or sections, each of which in turn contains one or more villages or hamlets, a collection of houses formerly grouped into compounds. Each Paramount bears an heriditary title: Bai Yoso in Kolifa Mayoso, Masa Kama in Kolifa Rowala, Bai Kafari in Tane, and so on. There are regalia of varying complexity associated with each chieftaincy and rituals associated with the death, burial, selection, and installation of chiefs.

Within each chiefdom there are a variable number of subchiefs bearing different titles and having both administrative and ritual duties. The bifurcation of Temne country into "Muslim" and "society" chiefdoms is primary in this context, for in the former, subchiefs bear the title *Alimany*, while in the latter, that of *Kapr*, except where recent introductions have altered the traditional system.[10] The territory and population over which a subchief exercises control varies considerably, but is known as *aŋbap* or section.[11] A Paramount Chief could subdivide or combine sections as he wished and thus the number of subchiefs or sections in any given chiefdom fluctuated. In Kolifa Mayoso there were traditionally two sections but, after his installation in 1935, the last Bai Yoso subdivided each of these into three parts.

In the Kolifa area a chief-elect appointed his own *Kapr* chiefs, who were placed in *kantha* and initiated into the *Ragbenle* society with him.[12] The *Kapr* chiefs can be lumped into two groups, those bearing specific titles and those having no titles. The former were chosen from among the maternal uncles and maternal cross-cousins of the chief-elect, none

of whom belonged to his patrilineage (*ambɔnshɔ*) or patriclan (*ambuna*)
and most of whom took up residence in the chief's town. The latter were
normally resident in other villages and served as the chief's local representatives. Formerly the heads of founding, land-owning lineages [13] or
renowned warriors were selected, for by so honouring these men and incorporating them into his administration, the chief could in part forestall potential opposition. Usually the chief-elect kept any *Kapr* chiefs
of his predecessor, so long as they lived.

The number of "titled *Kapr*" chiefs and the titles given them by the
chief-elect varied widely from one chiefdom to another. Those commonly
used in Kolifa Mayoso were: *Kapr mɘsɘm, Kapr lɔya, Kapr sɔya, Kapr
fɛnthi, Kapr kiabin,* and *Kapr gbogboro.*[14] All of these served as emissaries or representatives of their chief and deputized for him in court.
Normally, they were his confidants, advisers, and trusted aides, though
there were exceptions,[15] and since they usually resided in the chief's
town, had a greater share of ritual duties. Each had a part in the installation and burial rites of their chief and specific duties as described below.

Kapr mɘsɘm: usually the chief's main adviser and intelligence officer, in charge
of sacrifices to the chief's sacred boxes and other ritual tasks. When his
Paramount dies, he rules as interim chief, first as *oboma,* "sick man," and
then as *Pa Rɔk,* until the installation of the next chief. He has the major
roles in the installation and burial rites of his chief, decapitating the corpse
and serving as chief mourner and guardian (*obariŋ*) for the chief's widows.
Kapr lɔya: generally an older man with a good knowledge of native law who
should advise his chief on legal matters and deputize for him in court.
Kapr sɔya: usually a member of the late chief's mother's lineage (*makara*) first
known as *aŋkapr ŋa ammaŋtɘr,* "*Kapr* of the tears," from his role as
mourner.
Kapr fɛnthi: entertains strangers and has charge of the cleanliness of the chief's
sacred things, the hut in which they are kept, and the chief's court building.
Kapr kiabin: usually the successor of *Kapr mɘsɘm* should the latter die.
Kapr gbogboro: a messenger who has special duties during his chief's installation.

The "non-titled *Kapr*" chiefs were formerly an integral part of the
administrative hierarchy; the Paramount's orders were channelled through
them, they judged certain legal cases, and enjoyed the prestige of being
"next to the chief." Remuneration came from court cases and gifts, often
in the form of land pledged or men pawned. Some became wealthy and
famous for their ability as jurists, and informants were unanimous that
it was an honour to be a *Kapr,* and that such men were highly respected.

This may have been the ideal, but in practice the ideal was not
always attained, for a Paramount Chief could use the position either as
a reward for those wealthy, mature men who had supported his candidacy, or as a means to ruin the representatives of groups that had op-

posed him. The former was simple patronage extended to supporters and "yes-men"; the latter was malicious revenge and gave rise to the generalization informants made that "a chief wants only wealthy men as *Kapr* chiefs in order that he can take more wealth from them." Of one old *Kapr* in Kolifa Mayoso it was said that he was a rich man when seized and placed in *kantha* and a poor *Kapr* when he came out.[16] While in *kantha* this man was accused on trumped-up charges of violating *Ragbenle məsəm* and heavily fined by the chief. He was asked to supply an inordinately large portion of rice, palm oil, and money for the Paramount Chief in return for the "honour" of having been selected (against his will, in this case). Even after installation the Paramount Chief continued to "take money from him"; his legal decisions in petty cases were reversed by the Paramount when appealed by one who had lost a case, and the *Kapr* was heavily fined in turn for not dispensing "justice." He was fined for not sending a full complement for labour on the chief's farms and for not keeping the bush paths in his section cleared. The Paramount Chief borrowed money from this *Kapr* and found cause for legal action without repaying him; the other *Kapr* chiefs tried the case secretly and cancelled the debt as a fine, for the Paramount suggested that they "watch out" if they did not give him "justice." Such extortion and corruption existed in other chiefdoms as well and is eloquent proof that the *Kapr* chiefs were hardly a check on the actions of a Paramount Chief in recent years. In practice most of them tried to ingratiate themselves with their chief, became identified with him, and in turn extorted for their own benefit when possible. Previously the position of *Kapr* chiefs was stronger, for they were empowered to kill their chief if he fell ill, and a wicked man was dispatched after the slightest decline in health or well-being. On the other hand, if a chief were on good terms with his *Kapr* chiefs, they would overlook a "temporary illness" so as to preserve what was for them a favourable *status quo*. The establishment of the Protectorate largely curtailed this threat to the Paramount Chief's authority, greatly weakened the position of each *Kapr*, and exposed the subchiefs to extortion.

Informants in the Kolifa area explained the reduced prestige of *Kapr* chiefs by saying that after the establishment of the Protectorate, District Commissioners dealt only with Paramount Chiefs or village headmen. When coming to a village the Commissioner asked for the headman, not the *Kapr* (who often would have been in another village), and so the village headmen were associated by the people with "Government business." Eventually village headmen were remunerated by the chief from Native Administration funds; the *Kapr* being paid only if he also served as a headman.[17] Little by little the prestige of the *Kapr* disappeared, as his position was undermined from both directions by Paramount Chiefs and headmen. Government, said informants, did not recognize the *Kapr* as a chief, though they should have since he had been in *kantha*. It is only too easy, of course, to see Government as a scapegoat, though undoubtedly some government policies were detrimental to the position of *Kapr*.

Each village has an elected headman who is subordinate to the section chief. In the distant past the Kolifa area was settled by Koranko and Temne hunters who, with their families, founded the first villages on the sites of hunting camps. The descendants of these founders and early settlers in turn established other towns and villages. Thus in each settlement today there are descendants of these first founding families, the head of each being termed *ɔgbɔŋli*, the old Temne name for the head (founder) of a village. Subsequently, such men were consulted by the Paramount Chief on difficult matters concerning the chiefdom as a whole. The number of such per village was variable, small settlements having only one, the chief's town and other large centres having several. In more recent times one *ɔgbɔŋli* in each village has been designated *ɔkɛrabump*, or "headman."

A headman is not placed in *kantha*, and to use one informant's words: "He is an ordinary man like ourselves, and not a chief." The position is an elected one, in contrast to that of *Kapr*, and the incumbent holds office so long as the adult males of the village feel that he does a good job.

The main duties of the headman are threefold: first, he serves as intermediary between chiefs and people; second, he is a judge who handles petty cases such as quarrelling and bodily or verbal assault; and, finally, he is a tax-collector. In return the headman keeps the small fines he levies for judging cases and receives a small remittance from the Paramount Chief each year from the tax. The amount of his remuneration depends entirely on the attitude of the chief towards him and may or may not be founded on the headman's honesty or efficiency. Headmanship all too often is sought by men who hope to use it to extort money from their fellow villagers. A man who is eager to occupy this position will secretly give small sums of money to the family heads of the town to influence their choice, and to the Paramount Chief, promising to do his bidding in return for sponsorship. Once selected, he remits a portion of the fines levied to the Paramount Chief in return for his backing. The chief gains financially from such arrangements and keeps up his part of the bargain by sustaining the headman's legal decisions when cases are appealed to him and by levying heavy fines on such appealers so as to discourage their challenging the headman's authority and decisions. That the villager responds cynically to such "justice" is not surprising. Other headmen, however, will try to serve as a buffer between the often illegal and harsh demands of the Paramount Chief and their subjects. Such men are badly treated by the chief, being heavily fined on faked charges, for turning in "insufficient tax" (the assessment in their villages being incorrect and high),[18] for turning over the tax late, and so on.

In the past, in the Kolifa area, wealthy slave owners established groups of slaves in small hamlets with either a junior kinsman or a trusted slave as headman. Such hamlets, generally known by the Creole term *fakai* rather than the Temne term *tagbom,* served as places of rest from work, and allowed the labourers to avoid the long walk from village to farm and back each day. Though they were inhabited all the year round, they were not considered to be villages, since they lacked secret society bushes and hence the funeral dances, without which burials cannot be made, could not be held.

Today there are fewer *fakai* since it is no longer necessary to hide from marauders, and the old slaves have either returned to their ancestral homes or moved into the villages and towns where life is more exciting. What hamlets remain are composed basically of members of one patrilineage, their affines, and a few outsiders whose farms are near by. Poor relations, pawns, children in training, and the descendants of former slaves, who have come to be regarded virtually as members of their previous master's patrilineage, are also found. The owner of the *fakai* rarely lives there, though it will bear his name, as *tagbom ta pa Kanka,* but rather he will reside in the village and act as intermediary between his *fakai* and the village headman. Few *fakai* in the Kolifa area even today have been assessed for tax, and their locations are kept secret from outsiders. The *fakai* owner collects food and money from the people living there and gives this contribution to the village headman, who in turn may share it with the family-heads of the village. The *Kapr,* if there is one in the village, the headman, and village elders keep the secret of the *fakai,* since in this way they benefit directly, whereas the Paramount Chief would return little or nothing from the tax if assessment was carried out. The people in the *fakai* and the owner prefer this system, since it costs them less per "taxpayer." When a village headman was caught concealing potential taxpayers in this way by the Paramount Chief or his clerk, and this was a favourite accusation by dissidents, he was generally removed from office; a *Kapr* found guilty of the same offence could not, of course, be deposed, but he would be fined heavily and his words would carry less weight with his chief.

The subchiefs, particularly those resident in the chief's town, the chief's close male relatives, the *aŋbɔŋli,* the heads of the founding families of the various towns and villages, and the *aŋkɛrabump,* the village headmen, most of whom are usually *aŋbɔŋli* also, comprised what many informants regarded as the chief's advisory council. In practice, however, formal meetings of all seem never to have been held, the chief consulting merely one or two men of his own choice. In 1937 the Tribal Authorities Ordinance formally provided for the establishment of a Tribal Authority consisting of the Paramount Chief, his subchiefs, and "representatives of the villages." The membership and size of the Tribal Authorities, however, varied considerably from one chiefdom to another until efforts at standardization were introduced in 1956. As a check on the chief they were of dubious value, since in practice few members would speak out against the chief, who in turn largely depended on a few chosen individuals for advice and assistance.[19]

With the establishment of the Native Administration system the formal position of Chiefdom Clerk came into being, the only position in the system having literacy requirements. Prior to this most chiefs had had clerks or secretaries, some of them employing men in such capacities even before 1900.[20] The clerk's duties are essentially to help the chief in the mechanics of administration by keeping court records when desired, making the tax assessments and helping in the collection, issuing receipts and summonses, and serving as the chief's secretary when, as is often the case, the chief is illiterate. Little has succinctly referred to the clerk as "manager of the chiefdom," and has written of the anomalous position of the clerk, who wields considerable power in return for a small salary and low status.[21] Usually the Chiefdom Clerk is retained by a newly elected chief, since he is the best adviser on the administration of the chiefdom, on how to avoid trouble with the District Commissioner, on what are the factions in the chiefdom and the best way to deal with them, and so on. Once oriented, however, the chief will usually hire a new clerk, a man he feels he can trust.

In the maintenance of law and order each Paramount Chief appoints a number of Chiefdom Messengers, though this practice was "legalized" by ordinance only in 1952. They are appointed by the Paramount Chief in conjunction with representatives of the Tribal Authority; hence they are in practice the chief's private police force. Ranks of private, corporal, and sergeant have been adopted in imitation of the former Court Messenger Force. Pay is low, and the turnover in personnel throughout the year is large.[22]

III

At the time of his installation the new Paramount Chief asks the assembled members of the *Ragbenle* society two questions: "what am I going to eat," *Koma ediye*, to which the reply is given, "you have us to eat," *Sama madi*, and "who will do the work for me," *Kana mɔyonami mɔpanthe*, the answer being "we will do it for you," *San sɔtɔyonamu*. It is from this set of questions, informants insisted, which the *Ragbenle* answer on behalf of all the people of the chiefdom, that the chief gets his actual authority.[23] More than these questions, however, is involved in "buying the chieftaincy," a procedure found throughout the eastern part of Temne country. Everything the chief pays is embraced in the phrase *aŋkala ŋa kawai rabai,* "money paid for the chieftaincy." The ceremonies extend over four days and mark the close of the *kantha* period for the chief. The payments, consisting of money and goods, are carried from the chief in the *kantha* house to the visiting Paramount Chiefs who are in the town *barri,* by *Pa Mela* the chiefdom *ɔkrifi.*[24] The explanation given is that each chief must buy his *masəm,* "taboos," from the Paramount Chiefs present at the time of installation.

On the first day the chief pays for the title of *Namasa,* his head wife in most cases, and of *Nakama,* if his head wife must bear this title.[25] This gives her equal rights with the *Kapr* chiefs to sacrifice to the box containing the chief's "sacred things," the *akuma ka masəm,* which ultimately is kept in the *akama ka masəm,* the chief's "sacred hut." It is said that the chief-elect sends bridewealth for her to the visiting Paramount Chiefs, who are hazily conceived as being her family. On the second and third days the chief-elect sends further payments to the visiting chiefs, but these are regarded as the dowry of *Namasa,* provided by her new family, the chief-elect's. In this part of the ceremony, it is explained, *Namasa* is to be married to the chiefdom *masəm* or to the deceased chiefs; there exist wide differences of opinion on what actually occurs. It is said that *Namasa* holds the chief's *masəm* while he is in *kantha.* On the fourth day, or even on the third, according to some, the chief-elect buys his own *masəm,* and that of his *Kapr* chiefs. For *Kapr masəm,* he buys the right for this man to stand in his stead when he dies, that is, to assume the title *Pa Rɔk* and rule as interim chief. In addition he pays varying sums for each of the societies in his chiefdom: *Pɔro, Ragbenle, Bundu,* and whatever lesser ones exist. Subsequently each of these must give a small present to the chief whenever they wish to carry on their ceremonies, and whenever a member is initiated or dies. When a society member dies, his or her family must pay 1s. to the chief for violating his *masəm.* Since he has paid for them, the chief is referred to as the "owner of the societies," and in return he acts as their patron-protector in relations with the population in general, and more recently with Government. As part of the fourth-day ceremony, children and adults gather together in a number of groups each representing a trade: hunting, fishing, trapping, and others. The chief buys these trades, and henceforth collects a tribute from those who practise them. Thus a hunter has to give the chest, one leg, and the liver of each large animal killed to the chief, as well as the skin, teeth, and claws of all leopards, and the skins of all deer killed. The leopard, the "royal animal," is *masəm,* and these parts of it are viewed as the chief's since he has paid for them; deer skins are used to cover the places where other people sit at the chief's house. A share of fish caught is also due to the chief, as are parts of the animals that are trapped. In return the chief intercedes with the family of anyone killed in these enterprises, and more recently with Government, so that "accidents" are not construed as murder and charges not made for compensation. Traditionally the chief rewarded a hunter with a small quantity of gunpowder.

The chief also pays to acquire the regalia from *Pa Rɔk* at the time of installation and the right to wear it in the future. He also buys the right to transfer the sacred box containing the sacred things from *kantha* to his new dwelling and to sacrifice to it hereafter; it is with this payment, said informants, that he bought "the full rights of a chief as defined by native law to levy fines in chief's court." At this time he buys his own chief's *mɔsɔm* and the rights to income from the violation of these *mɔsɔm*.

It is through "buying the chieftaincy," then, that a Temne actually becomes a Paramount and in a sense "owns" his chiefdom and his people, as the Temne express it. The "chief's portion" of all that is produced is generally recognized and was formerly rendered him without question. "He and the country are one," as Ture [26] wrote, in a mystical linkage.

Though traditions vary, the Temne once apparently inhabited parts of the Futa Djallon plateau in what is now the Republic of Guinea; the date of their arrival in Sierra Leone is uncertain.[27] A mystical relationship with "Futa" still remains, and it is said by some that when a chief is in *kantha* he journeys to Futa where he "acquires wisdom." *Nafuta* is so named because she is the "wife" who returns with him from Futa and helps cook for him in *kantha;* she also sits over his corpse when he dies and "returns to Futa." Ture [28] speaks of "the mystic chain binding him [the chief] to predecessors and successors alike," stressing that by it "he [the chief] is as immortal as our race" and that upon his death "he will return to Futa whence he came. . . ." A deceased chief is spoken of as having "returned to Futa," and Paramount Chiefs, *Kapr* chiefs, and also officials of the *Pɔro* and *Bundu* societies speak of their life before installation as "when I was in Futa."

The relationships between a chief, his predecessor, and his successor are underlined concretely in Temne custom. The skull of his predecessor is kept in the chief's sacred box to which daily sacrifices are made in the hope that the deceased chief(s) may bring all manner of success to the living. Upon his death a chief's head is severed from his body by *Kapr mɔsɔm, Kapr bana,* or *Korgba,* to be kept in the sacred box of his successor; the chief's body is buried, or otherwise disposed of in accordance with tradition in his particular chiefdom, along with the head of his predecessor. The line of chiefs and the connexion with Futa are thus perpetuated.

Much has been written of the sacred aspects of Temne chieftaincy, a complex that sets apart Temne chiefs from their neighbouring Mende, Limba, Koranko, and Susu counterparts. Little has phrased it as follows: ". . . the Mende chief is a purely secular figure, lacking the ritual sanctions with which chiefly authority is associated among the neighboring

Temne people. . . ." [29] In the north-western part of Temne country, however, where the secret societies do not install chiefs, this traditional non-Muslim, non-Christian complex is not found, and as Thomas puts it: "In Sanda country, corresponding to the subordinate position of the chiefs, the *məsəm* and the customs generally are of minor importance." [30]

Essentially it is the possession of *məsəm*, acquired by purchase at the time of buying his chieftaincy while still in *kantha,* that sets a Temne chief apart and makes him more than an ordinary man. *Məsəm* is best translated as "forbidden" or "tabooed," and a distinction is made between behaviour and objects that are "forbidden" and those that are "bad" or "evil" (*aləs*).[31] Only the *məsəm* connected with the Paramount, however, are of concern here, and these can be subdivided into prohibitions on the chief's behaviour and prohibitions on the behaviour of others towards the chief. The combination is known as "chief's *məsəm*," and was referred to as the "chief's holiness" by literate informants, this latter phrase again indicating the mystical, supernatural aura that surrounds a Temne chief.

Certain events or actions on the part of anyone are regarded as violations of the chief's *məsəm,* and offenders or their families were formerly fined the sum of £4; today no fines can legally be collected. Thus it is forbidden to fight, jostle, or pummel a man in the chief's presence. Certain types of deaths fall in this same category: drowning is said to spoil the water, while homicide spoils the soil; both are regarded as violations of *məsəm,* whether accidental or wilful, as are attempts to drown or kill. To be killed by an alligator or a leopard similarly violates the water and the soil, and hence the chief's *məsəm* too, though a common rationalization was that such deaths happened only to careless people. To die of snake-bite or falling from a palm tree is also regarded as resulting from carelessness and is a violation of the chief's *məsəm,* as such deaths weaken the chiefdom. For a mother to die in childbirth deprived the chief and his chiefdom of her productivity and perhaps of that of her child, thus rendering her husband and family liable to the fine for violation of chief's *məsəm.* Not to render to the chief what is rightfully his of the kill of a leopard is also a violation of *məsəm.* A man responsible for burning a house or field is similarly guilty, whether the act is deliberate or accidental. The death of any initiated member of society "owned by the chief" is a violation of *məsəm,* the fine in such cases being only 1s.[32]

A chief is forbidden to see *roləŋk,* the burial place of chiefs, the prohibition taking various forms in different chiefdoms, and can neither uncover his head nor eat in public unless he has held the *kabɔk,* "crying ceremony," in mourning for all previous chiefs. Two Paramount Chiefs should not shake hands, nor should a chief exchange clothing with another man or eat from the same basin with him. No chief should look in his sacred box or a house or village that has been burned. In addition to such "chief's *məsəm*," each Paramount Chief must observe "*Ragbenle məsəm*" as any member of that society; the most important of these are not to eat new rice before sacrifices have been offered, or to eat millet and some other secondary grains.

This is not an exhaustive list of prohibitions on the chief but it is sufficient to indicate how his freedom of action is hampered; few individual məsəm seriously impede the chief's behaviour, but the entire body together is a decided inconvenience. For this reason, chiefs in recent years have tended to pay large sums of money while in kantha to free themselves from those məsəm that might prove embarrassing in the presence of Europeans or seriously hinder their mobility and convenience.[33] A chief's məsəm in the broad sense of prohibitions of others' behaviour as well as on his own actions is commonly spoken of as his "native staff," [34] since his authority and the respect that must be shown to him derives from it. A chief deprived of his Government Staff is still a chief, and will be treated as such as long as he lives, since he has his məsəm. Thus traditionally there is no mechanism for deposing a chief, and Government innovations in this line seem strange to the Temne.[35] Some recently installed chiefs have paid to alter their məsəm and this is viewed with alarm; such men not being regarded as "full chiefs." This recognition of this secularization of chieftaincy is often phrased in terms of a comparison, that Temne chiefs are becoming like Mende chiefs, that is, chiefs without məsəm. The fact that some modern Temne chiefs do not possess or observe the full məsəm of their office lowers their prestige in the eyes of the villager and thus undermines their authority.

The supernatural sanctions of the chieftaincy are weaker today as a result of activity by Muslims and Christian missionaries and the more general changes that have taken place in Temne culture. That many chiefs today have managed to evade some of their məsəm is itself indicative of these changes. Yet the mystical aura surrounding the chieftaincy remains; Temne may criticize a particular chief and even work to have him relieved of some of his responsibilities, but they do not question the chieftaincy itself. Today the incumbent may be vulnerable, but the office remains inviolate and unquestioned.[36]

IV

Traditionally it was the chief's responsibility to maintain law and order within his chiefdom, and to protect his people from external enemies. "A chief is a peacemaker," as an informant put it, one who should maintain good relations between individuals and chiefdoms. External relations between chiefdoms involved both diplomacy and war before the organization of the Protectorate. The accounts of old men living today and the legends of the past are insufficient, however, for more than the crudest outline of the political system at that time. In each chiefdom there were a number of men, usually heads of lineages and often but not invariably subchiefs, who were sufficiently powerful and wealthy to supply men, weapons, food, and magical protection for a war party. Such a man was known as "war chief," ɔbai urafa, even though he himself did no fighting and apparently rarely accompanied his men on actual raids. The forces in the field were led by warriors, aŋkurgba, hired by the war chief for this purpose. Many of them were mercenaries from distant places who had built up fierce reputations.[37]

It is said that many Paramount Chiefs were also "war chiefs," who hired warriors secretly to raid other chiefdoms or tribes and bring back spoils to them. Such chiefs took what they wanted by raiding others and did not tax or levy their own people since this would have caused dissension. The loot of raids consisted largely of slaves and food,[38] though the prestige to be gained was perhaps an equal incentive. Nevertheless, it was mandatory for a Paramount Chief to hire warriors and finance raiding parties when needed, either by himself or with the aid of his "war chiefs." When force was unsuccessful or inadvisable, a chief would send to Paramount Chiefs who were neutral to arbitrate. On occasion a Paramount Chief would take it upon himself to make peace "for the good of all," first sending one of his Kapr chiefs with a small gift to each side indicating his wish to make peace. If both sides agreed, he would go in person, though at the head of his war chiefs and warriors for protection if his efforts were in vain. If neither side agreed to arbitrate he would generally not press the matter. If one side agreed, he would go to the other and attempt to persuade it. When peace terms were acceptable, each side supplied animals and all would "eat oath" over the agreement; the peacemaker swore both sides with his swearing medicines that they keep his peace.[39] The settlement was thus explicitly sanctioned by supernatural means and implicitly by the armed might of the peacemakers.

At times all efforts at peace failed, entire chiefdoms were evacuated, and the chieftaincy lay vacant for extended periods. Such was the case in Kolifa Mayoso, Yoni Mabanta, and other chiefdoms in the area at various times in history. Powerful, successful chiefs attracted such refugees, who, if they received land and permission to settle from him, could be counted as loyal followers. The successful taking of slaves, of course, strengthened the economic basis of a chiefdom by increasing the labour force where land was plentiful.

The relationships between a Paramount and his war chiefs are said to have been cordial, and in the historical legends the Paramount's authority usually seems to have been absolute and final, though whether this control resulted from his position as chief or, as was often the case, as senior kinsman or patron of outsiders whom he permitted to settle, is difficult to determine. Many of the war chiefs in the Kolifa area were apparently patrilineal kinsmen or affines of the Paramount. I learned of

no defections of war chiefs and their dependants from one Paramount
Chief to another, most informants finding this inconceivable. More information is needed, however, before any definitive statements can be made
regarding the power structure between Paramounts and their war chiefs,
though there are indications that the latter served to limit a Paramount's
autocratic inclinations and functioned as a last court of appeal.

With the establishment of the Protectorate the problems of maintaining their chiefdom against others no longer burdened Paramount Chiefs.
Government, sanctioned by seemingly overwhelming force, virtually out-
lawed war and raiding as means of settling disputes. This signalled the
end of the war chiefs and warriors, and all but destroyed their influence
over the Paramount since it had depended largely on force. Inter-chiefdom
disputes were settled through arbitration before Government, and the
Paramount's role in dealing with external affairs was limited to representing his people at the installation or funeral of another chief, or in disputes
with Government over questions of tax or of deaths in the *Pɔro* bush,
and getting Government to finance roads and so on.

In pre-Protectorate times only Paramount Chiefs had the legal right
to inflict capital punishment or sell into slavery [40] those guilty of particular crimes. Owing to the comparative lawlessness of the period, however,
subchiefs and even the heads of families frequently risked it. "To carry
him to the bush," *akɛra kɔ robɔŋko*, is the phrase used to refer to the one-
way trip for execution, and it is said of one executed that "he has gone
to wash," *kobuko ropɔŋ*. The family of the man executed had to pay £4
for violation of the chief's *mɔsɔm*, since the spilling of blood "violated
the ground."

In his role as judge, a Paramount Chief formerly dealt with murder,
arson, theft, kidnapping, "witchcraft," disputes over land tenure, and a
number of minor crimes. Murder in particular [41] was likely to provoke
inter-family or inter-lineage feuds and in such cases the chief conducted
investigations himself, trying to arrange punishment and compensation
so as to prevent a vendetta. In cases of accidental murder or manslaughter,
the killer would normally go immediately to the compound of the Paramount Chief for sanctuary and to explain what happened.[42] The chief
fined such a man and arranged with the victim's family to accept compensation from the killer's family. Such compensation varied with respect
to the circumstances of the killing, the relative wealth and prestige of
the kin-groups involved, and the status difference of the murderer and
his victim. Goods, money, and slaves were commonly given, and on occasion a free man or woman was sent to the victim's family to serve as a
labour substitute. Such a person, however, was not formally adopted and
could never inherit land.[43] The murderer's family supplied a cow so that
both parties and the chief could "eat oath" that the affair had been settled
to everyone's satisfaction. If the murderer was not executed he would

generally remain as a member of the chief's household where he had sanctuary for his own safety and to prevent a revenge killing that would lead to a vendetta. In cases of manslaughter the killer's family often gave a slave to the chief. Such a person was known as *sela*, "agreement," and seems simply to have served as a constant living reminder that the affair had been settled. Banishment or selling into slavery were also common punishments in such cases. Should a murderer or one guilty of man-slaughter run away and escape, he or she was free to return without fear of litigation if the matter had been settled by compensation. The fear of revenge, however, seemed to keep such return visits brief and secret.

The investigation of homicide was conducted under the leadership of the Paramount Chief; bodies were brought to him for identification,[44] and where the identity of the murderer was not known the chief fined the inhabitants of the section where the body was found for the violation of *məsəm*, thus providing an incentive for these people to identify and apprehend the murderer. Investigation began with a search for the mur-derer and for witnesses. Murderers were said to shun groups of men and thus made themselves suspect. Clues such as blood-stained clothing were sought, but in the absence of such leads a list of suspects who might have had a motive was drawn up. The past actions of the victim were reviewed, and those with whom he had quarrelled and was not on good terms were held as suspects and stocked in the chief's compound. The heads of the families of these suspects would then try to vindicate their kinsmen by presenting alibis supported by witnesses and ordeals. Those who accused a suspect and those who were witnesses for him took an oath on swearing-medicines in court, permission to swear being granted to the victim's family by the chief. In the absence of apprehension and/or suitable "proof" of guilt, the unknown culprit was sworn, the success of the medicine being acknowledged by a confession or by further divination.

In the event his Paramount Chief's legal decision was unacceptable to him, a plaintiff had the right to appeal to a second or even a third Paramount Chief in some areas but not in others.[45] One informant said that if Bai Yoso gave you a bad decision you could go to a neighbouring Paramount Chief, explain the case to him, and if you could convince him that you were wronged, he would send one of his *Kapr* chiefs back with you to Bai Yoso. This *Kapr* would ask to have the case reopened, and the retrial would be held in his presence. Bai Yoso would consent to do this if he were on good terms with the chief who sent the *Kapr*, and the plaintiff, of course, would make his plea only to a chief who was on good terms with Bai Yoso.

In the event of a case involving men from two chiefdoms, the plaintiff will inform his chief, Masa Munta, for example, that he is going to Mayoso for a case with "a citizen of that country." Masa Munta would then send a representative with him, usually a *Kapr*, together with a "shakehand" or gift for Bai Yoso. This representative would hear the case and report all to Masa Munta, including his opinion on whether or not justice had been served. If the decision was felt to be unjust, Masa Munta could send back his representative to complain and to suggest that a third, presumably impartial, chief retry the case. Furthermore, a plaintiff who had been wronged could swear Bai Yoso secretly if he were certain of his innocence, and informants generally agreed that in the past a chief feared to give an unjust or unfair decision lest he be sworn by such an innocent man.

While the above system with the ultimate appeal to the supernatural operated in times of relative peace and goodwill, it seems to have been more common to seek the sanction of force in the event of an unjust or unliked decision. Thus one informant said that formerly the only way to get justice was "to go to war with the chief," though this could be done directly only when you had a large powerful lineage behind you. Members of less powerful groups went to a war chief with a "shakehand" and asked him to obtain justice for them. The warrior chief heard the case, and if he agreed that the Paramount had made a bad decision and the chief refused to alter it, the warrior chief would threaten him and secure a change in the original decision by force. If the Paramount agreed to change his decision, and thus keep peace in his chiefdom, he forfeited any fines originally collected.

The employment of this system of appeal to a war chief depended first of all upon the relations between plaintiff and war chief and second between the Paramount and the war chief. Certainly the mere existence of the system was a check on arbitrary autocratic behaviour on the part of a Paramount, unless his war chiefs supported him in a conspiracy "to ruin the chiefdom"; I heard no intimation that this was ever the case. If a war chief were unscrupulous and felt powerful enough to challenge the Paramount and his supporters, he might seize such an excuse to cloak sinister motives for power in the mantle of "justice." A "good" war chief with the interests of the entire chiefdom at heart would accept such a case only if he was convinced there had been a bad decision or if the bonds of kinship or personal regard overrode his feelings for justice. The relative wealth of the plaintiff was also a factor, for a large "shakehand" was said to be a powerful incentive to a war chief. On the other hand, the Paramount would influence his war chief's estimation of the merits of the original decision by making a valuable present along with a request that he should not aid the plaintiff in reopening the case. Since the Paramount was usually wealthy and the plaintiff generally poor, the system seems to have been rarely employed. War chiefs, it was said, were proud of their might and boasted that they could go and seize what they wished at any time; for such men to indulge in petty bribery seems inconsistent with this characterization. Furthermore, few war chiefs were sufficiently strong to challenge all their counterparts at once; hence it was to their advantage to keep the "home front" stable; to help a man reopen a case and to champion him would make an enemy of the Paramount, who would take steps for revenge with the assistance of his other war chiefs, some of whom, motivated by jealousy or dislike, would probably eagerly support him.[46]

After the formation of the Protectorate, restrictions were placed on the Paramount Chiefs with regard to the types of offences over which they had jurisdiction and the penalties they could impose.[47] The infliction of unlawful punishment rendered the chief and members of his court liable to the legal consequences and, by order of the Governor, withdrawal of their jurisdiction over criminal cases. According to informants, the "treaty chiefs," those who had signed the protective treaties upon which the Protectorate was based,[48] were dealt with more leniently, or, as they phrased it, "were given more authority." Bai Yoso of Kolifa Mayoso, Bai Kafari of Tane, and Bai Simira of Bonkolenken Mayapo were among the chiefs in the Kolifa area who reputedly were granted more comprehensive jurisdiction. In practice, the District Commissioner removed the more serious cases from the hands of the chiefs; today these are handled in the Magistrate's Court.

While it was no longer possible to appeal a Paramount Chief's decision to a war chief, at least the wealthy could now appeal to the District Commissioner, though there seems to have been considerable reluctance to do so. Chiefs, it was said, became more careful in trying cases since they feared reversal of their decisions by the higher court. If this happened repeatedly, the chief was censured by Government, and perhaps forbidden to conduct court, a severe blow to his prestige and an embarrassment to everyone in the chiefdom. Whether or not the administration of justice improved cannot be incontrovertibly demonstrated, and the opinions of informants varied widely whenever this question was discussed. The crucial point is that in the past there was greater use of swearing medicines to determine guilt. While one educated Temne said, "I would prefer to swear; there is foolish case (litigation), but there is no foolish *sasa* (swear)," another of comparable background stated that "a man can protect himself from swears but not from justice" (law administered by the District Commissioner). The assessment of the administration of justice is determined by the relative faith of informants in swearing medicines and in the court system, and there are strong advocates of each.

V

Great local differences are found in the criteria for eligibility to the chieftaincy where kinship is concerned. Generally one of two situations prevails: either two or more lineages, *aŋkunte* [49] of a ruling clan, *ambuna*, provide the Paramount Chief in rotation, or lineages of two separate clans supply the ruler alternatively.[50] In the latter case one clan is often non-Temne, and has "rights to the chieftaincy" as a reward for military aid rendered to the once single ruling clan in war. In Port Loko the Kamara and Bangura clans alternate in supplying the Paramount Chief,[51] while in Kolifa Mayoso there are four *aŋkunte* which have furnished chiefs.

The Mayoso system will illustrate the *aŋkunte* rotation. Traditionally the chiefdom was founded by a hunter, *Kɛfita*, who had four wives. One son of each of these wives ruled in turn and thus the four *aŋkunte* were founded. The list of chiefs bearing the title Bai Yoso is found in Table 1; *Kɛfita* himself does not seem to have been a proper chief.

Chiefs (1), (2), (3), and (4) were sons of the four wives of *Kɛfita*. The rotation of *aŋkunte* thus established was repeated for chiefs (5), (6), and (7). The eighth chief should have been from *aŋkunte* Bon Poli, but the rotation was abrogated and this is explained in the following manner. An uncle of Bai Yoso Magbile (7), Pa Barewa by name, seduced another man's wife and, when nominated by a diviner, denied guilt and refused to pay "woman damage" charges. The husband of the woman then placed a secret "swear," *akutu*, on the chieftaincy so that any Bai Yoso would die quickly after installation. Bai Yoso Kolifa (8) was taken from the Mayoso *aŋkunte* since there was no acceptable male in Bon Poli, but he died just a year after his installation. The *Ragbenle* society divined the cause of death, and explained to the members of the four *aŋkunte* that this *akutu* would have to be removed lest all subsequent chiefs suffer the same fate. To so remove an *akutu* is an expensive proposition, and the *aŋkunte* refused to select candidates either out of fear of the *akutu* or hesitancy or inability to supply the money to remove it. The eventual decision was

TABLE 1. *Paramount chiefs and aŋkunte affiliation, Kolifa Mayoso*

Order of Rule		Paramount Chief	Aŋkunte
1	Bai Yoso	Chanta	Mayoso
2	Bai Yoso	Sesegbe	Robunkie
3	Bai Yoso	Satimaka	Magbile
4	Bai Yoso	Bon Poli	Bon Poli
5	Bai Yoso	Bonka Seri	Mayoso
6	Bai Yoso	Karanki	Robunkie
7	Bai Yoso	Magbile	Magbile
8	Bai Yoso	Kolifa (?–1903)	Mayoso
9	Bai Yoso	Masang (1904–18)	Magbile
10	Bai Yoso	Ka Na Gbonu (1921–35)	Bon Poli
11	Bai Yoso	Karanki (1935 on)	Robunkie

that Magbile should supply the next chief, since the actions of a member of this *aŋkunte* had brought about the situation. Thus Bai Yoso Masang (9) was elected, as he was the only member of Magbile with sufficient wealth. Apparently he was successful, since he ruled nearly twenty years. My examination of lists of chiefs in other chiefdoms indicates that the traditional rotation of *aŋkunte* was abrogated in most cases, often before the founding of the Protectorate.

The question arises whether or not membership in a particular clan, *ambuna,* automatically gives a man the right to seek chieftaincy wherever his clan rules. Thus, while clan Kamara [52] supplies chiefs in Kolifa Mayoso and alternately provides chiefs at Port Loko, most informants in Mayoso denied that a Port Loko Kamara had the right to seek the Mayoso chieftaincy, since "he is not a citizen of the country." Local residence, they said, was also necessary.

A number of Paramount Chiefs in the eastern part of Temne country, both now and in the past, seem not to have been local residents. Investigation showed, however, that such men were always the sons or grandsons of local residents who proved their patrilineal relationship satisfactorily and who were not disqualified on grounds of non-residence though some had been away more than 40 years, having been born in the far reaches of Temne country. It appears, then, that there is no residence requirement determining eligibility for chieftaincy, but that the kinship requirement does not cover all members of a clan, *ambuna,* but only particular lineages of it.[53] There have been charges and countercharges in many recent elections of "outsiders" trying to bribe members of the *aŋkunte* to provide the next chief to falsify genealogical evidence and to show that they are really members of this group.[54] That large bribes are so employed would appear to indicate the reality of a lineage requirement for chieftaincy.

Traditionally, in most Kolifa chiefdoms, a dying chief passed his ring to the head of the *aŋkunte* that was to supply the next chief, and this man was generally his successor. *Kapr məsəm* was present when this was done, and the practice, informants stressed, was a safeguard that *Kapr məsəm* (*Pa Rɔk*) was not bribed to designate the wrong *aŋkunte*. On occasion the chief died or was killed without having an opportunity to pass on his ring, and thus it was necessary to determine his choice through divination to corroborate *Pa Rɔk*'s announcement of the dying chief's death-bed selection. The *Ragbenle* go to the burial place of chiefs, *rolɔŋk,* where they divine, by means of *asanka,*[55] the late chief's choice of *aŋkunte* to supply his successor. When all have returned to town, each *aŋkunte* supplies money and wine to be sacrificed to the ancestors by *Pa Rɔk,* and the *Ragbenle*. Some of the wine is drunk as an oath by *Pa Rɔk,* so that if he does not announce the correct *aŋkunte* the ancestors will kill him. This is known as *akane maruba,* or as the "*maruba* ceremony," [56] in which, after *Pa Rɔk* has recited the history of the chiefdom, he makes the awaited "true" announcement and goes swiftly and secretly to another village lest the members of the disappointed *aŋkunte* do him bodily harm.[57]

After the establishment of the Protectorate, the selection of the *aŋkunte* to provide the next chief was also made known to the District Commissioner by *Pa Rɔk*. Disappointed candidates, informants generalized, then wrote letters to the District and Provincial Commissioners saying that *Pa Rɔk* had been bribed [58] to announce the wrong *aŋkunte*. Eventually other Paramount Chiefs, known as Assessor Chiefs and appointed by the Provincial Commissioner, arrived to determine whether or not *Pa Rɔk* had acted correctly by interviewing members of the various *aŋkunte* while under oath.[59] The indicated *aŋkunte* then selected a candidate, usually the recognized head of the group, who received a "government staff" before being placed in *kantha*. It is said that the *aŋkrifi ŋa arabai*,[60] "spirits of chieftaincy," appeared to the man who would become chief in his dreams, but while this must have been personally reassuring, it did not guarantee selection, for the mischievous spirits had the habit of appearing to more than one man. In recent times, the choice of an individual to be chief was less often unanimous, and Provincial Commissioners had more difficulty persuading candidates with little backing to withdraw and support their older kinsmen. In practice, several men from each *aŋkunte* presented themselves as candidates, and guided by the list of past chiefs, their *aŋkunte* affiliation, and the advice of Assessor Chiefs, the Provincial Commissioner endeavoured to eliminate first *aŋkunte*, and second individual candidates from the selected *aŋkunte*. When the list of candidates had been reduced as far as possible, the Tribal Authority usually agreed to vote and to accept the result of that vote. There was an understandable reluctance on the part of Provincial Commissioners, however, to award a staff if the vote was close.[61]

Members of ruling houses adamantly condemned the change from the old selection system to what they phrase as the "election of the chief" today. Elections brought bribery and corruption, they argued, and the candidate who could pass out the biggest bribes to the Tribal Authority, the Assessor Chiefs, and, formerly, to the Court Messengers present would secure the chieftaincy. Such arguments are unconvincing, for it was the breakdown of the traditional system and its sanctions that brought on the "election of the chief," rather than vice versa. The changes in the system for selecting a chief came about as only one facet of culture change in Temne country. Formerly the heads of extended families or lineages controlled the wealth of the entire group, and there were few grounds on which their juniors could challenge their overall authority. The increase in opportunities to obtain money, the fact that often heads of families were unable to pay the increased tax required, together with other factors, lessened the authority of such men over their junior kinsmen and dependants. One result of this, in royal families, was that juniors disputed with their seniors the right of candidacy for chieftaincy. When such younger men and even "outsiders" could offer sizeable bribes, some of their elders yielded and the traditional system all but disappeared. Representatives of Government, apparently, had recourse to "elections" of one sort or another in self-defence as an accommodation to a changing situation.

The effects of these changes are well illustrated in the attitudes towards the office by those eligible to hold it. In pre-Protectorate days chieftaincy was shunned and a man had to be persuaded to take office. The father of one of my informants ran away and hid when it seemed likely that he would be selected, and had to be seized and installed by force. Explanations for this state of affairs varied. Some stressed that the office yielded few tangible benefits; others, that there was too much responsibility involved in trying cases and looking after a chiefdom and that these overbalanced the prestige and personal satisfactions to be gained. The personal inconveniences involved were emphasized by others: the hindrances of observing the chief's *məsəm*, the necessity to sit through long legal wrangling, the boredom and confinement of a *kantha* period that might last more than a year, or the often prohibitive cost of buying the chieftaincy. Fear of a short reign or, more correctly, fear of being killed by the subchiefs at the time of some minor illness was frequently mentioned. During the *kantha* period a brief ceremony takes place in which the chief must put his hand, after it has been treated with medicine by the *Ragbenle,* into a bowl of ginger seeds and withdraw it; the number of seeds adhering to it indicates the number of years the chief will reign. The *Ragbenle* would see to it that this prediction came true, and old informants who had seen the ceremony laughingly recounted how the chief's hand shook with fear at this determination of his future. The "indignities" of the funeral ceremonies where the corpse of a bad chief would be dragged along the ground and mocked by those who disliked him were also cited. This reluctance to accept the office except under pressure, however, may have been feigned in part so that a man could be certain he was acceptable and liked by all. That he was drafted by the people was proof of their confidence in him and their willingness to obey him.[62]

Since 1930, however, there has been little reluctance on the part of eligible (and often ineligible) candidates to seek the office actively. Members of royal houses speak of "fighting for chieftaincy," and it is evident that the position is highly valued and sought after. One of the striking aspects of recent "elections" is the ever-increasing number of candidates. In the 1935 elections in Kolifa Mayoso five candidates contested; in the 1947 election, the first for the amalgamated chiefdom Kolifa

Mamunta-Rowala, there were twenty-six candidates, and in other recent elections in this area the number of candidates fell between these figures. There are many reasons for this reversal in attitude towards the chieftaincy; most of the old fear of assassination is gone, and it is possible now to evade the more restrictive *məsəm* and to cut short the *kantha* period. More important, however, is the possibility of making money out of the chieftaincy; the emoluments of office have increased tremendously. In view of this change in attitudes toward the chieftaincy, it is necessary to consider the sources of income for the incumbent.

VI

Before the establishment of the Protectorate a chief's income arose largely from tribute which seems to have been willingly paid. The "chief's share" of foodstuffs produced, known as *aŋsakəli arabai*, was an accepted thing and was given out of respect. After the harvest each village would give rice, salt, fowls, and a sheep (*akaba*) to provide for the chief, this gift being known generally as *akaba*. When the chief arrived in a village he was given food from each house before his hammock-boys could "put down the hammock," *aŋtura maka*. Something additional was then given as "greeting," *aŋbətr*, to learn why the chief had come and what he desired of them. When the chief left the village he received an *alimne*, "goodbye," from the village, another from the *Kapr*, and another from each rich man; these gifts again consisted of rice, fowls, sheep, a cow, or country cloth. In time such tribute in kind was replaced by cash, and by the mid-1920's the amounts had become reasonably standardized in the Kolifa chiefdoms at 4s. per house to "put down the hammock," 4s. to 10s. per village as a "shakehand," and £1 per village as a "goodbye." The separate "goodbyes" of rich men and *Kapr* might total as much as £15 in more recent years. The four royal *aŋkunte* generally provided rice in turn for the chief's sacrifices to the ancestors. When, on rare occasions such as the installation ceremony for a neighbouring Paramount Chief, additional provender was needed, the chief would ask his subjects, through the *Kapr* chiefs, to contribute, but he could demand nothing.

Another major source of income lay in fines of violators of the chief's *məsəm*. Such fines, collected by the *Kapr məsəm*, were automatic [63] in the event of death in the chiefdom occurring from a number of causes. Any listing must of course vary with the different *məsəm* of particular Paramount Chiefs, but the principal ones effective in Kolifa Mayoso were six in number: death from the bite of a snake, leopard, or alligator, by drowning, by falling from a palm-tree, or in giving birth.

In the chief's role as judge he acquired further wealth, the amount depending upon the nature of the offence and the relative wealth of the guilty party. Similarly, the chief could fine a village or section if he found that the bush paths were not cleared, or that bridges were missing or in bad repair.[64]

Traditionally the people of a chiefdom built and maintained a house or entire compound for a newly installed Paramount Chief; the building and maintenance of a Government Rest House was only an extension of this pattern. When the chief made his farm he would ask the wealthy men of his chiefdom to send some of their labourers to help him, but in pre-Protectorate times, informants stressed, he could not demand levies of chiefdom labour for his own use. Further labour was forthcoming in that men in debt borrowed money or food from their chief, leaving a kinsman or slave with him as security (pawning). Similarly, a man who had committed accidental homicide and taken sanctuary in the chief's compound would remain there as a retainer-labourer out of fear of revenge. Carriers and hammock-boys were provided by each village through which the chief passed on his travels.

Since he had "purchased" the societies when "buying his chieftaincy" the chief received gifts from each of them both before and after an initiation session. This tribute consisted of money and foodstuffs, a portion of it again going to the *Ragbenle* society for their sacrifices to the ancestors. Somewhat similar tribute was forthcoming from hunters, who gave particular portions of any large animals they killed plus all leopards' teeth and skins to the Paramount Chief, who in turn gave a small sum of money or some gunpowder to them. Not to do this was regarded as a violation of the chief's *mɔsɔm* and carried a fine.

Informants insisted that in pre-Protectorate times chiefs were "good," that they were loved and respected, and that corruption and extortion became rampant only with the coming of the British. These same informants on different occasions, however, provided ample documentation that excesses occurred then as well as in more recent times. With the establishment of the Protectorate new demands were made on the Paramount Chief by Government: rest houses had to be erected, house tax had to be collected, chiefs had to travel more outside their own chiefdom, and so on. The chiefs needed more income than the percentage of tax remitted by Government for their service as tax-collectors realized. With the spread of a money-economy the need was seen for cash rather than foodstuffs, except where the latter could readily be converted into money. Gradually chiefs increased their requests for tribute, representing them as demands, and putting their trust for support in Government, Court Messengers, and the District Commissioner if their people objected. The villagers, awed by the seemingly overwhelming power of Government, which was in terms of native law often arbitrarily used, submitted, though not always without protest. Pleas to the District Commissioner in those days, said informants, were ignored, for the Paramount Chief told the Commissioner simply that his subjects could not grasp what Government wanted and that when he, the chief, tried to implement Government policy, be it tax-collecting, making new paths, or planting new oil-palm trees, they objected. In general, District Commissioners, hard pressed for time and lacking capable assistance, supported the chiefs. The Paramount Chief came to be regarded in many cases as a part of Government, for the chief and the Commissioner always referred to one another as "my good friend," and all too often the chief's actions appeared prejudicial to the best interests of his subjects, individually or collectively.

In time, however, the District Commissioners became more aware of how and where the chiefs were obtaining their income, and of the sometimes extortionate means they employed. In the mid-1920's efforts were made by District Commissioners to reach agreements with Paramount Chiefs whereby some of their traditional sources of income, tribute levies, and some fines would be limited. Though such agreements were "signed" by both Paramount Chief and Tribal Authorities in the presence of the District Commissioner, and were at least at the time of the signing read publicly, the abuses by the chiefs continued and increased. Beginning in 1937, Native Administrations were established in one chiefdom after another.[65] After due consideration of notes taken by Government officers before the establishment of a Native Administration, the Cox Commission wrote that their intention ". . . was to commute tribute payments to the chiefs and their rights to forced labour on *manje* farms for an annual cash payment and it may be accepted that wherever a native administration was established those two rights were extinguished and chiefs enjoyed regular cash incomes, small at first, but showing a regular tendency to rise." [66] Though many of the traditional sources of income were thus legally surrendered with the establishment of a Native Administration, if not before, most chiefs seem to have continued to exercise their "traditional rights." Graft and corruption increased until, in large part, they brought about the "tax strike" of November 1955 to March 1956.

What were these excesses on the part of Paramount Chiefs, and what changes in their emoluments took place? The answers to these and similar questions would vary from one chiefdom to another; not all chiefs were equally guilty of graft in kind or degree. Informants in Kolifa Mayoso stated that *akaba*, the annual village gift or tribute, disappeared early in the reign of Bai Yoso Masang, that is, around 1905, when the chief began to move further abroad and there were more travellers asking for his hospitality.[67] A chief with an empty box (without funds) was summoned by Government and had to ask for *alimne*, "goodbye," over and over again, it was explained. The Temne word *alimne* came to mean "levy" when the chief demanded particular items.

"Shakehands," "putting down the hammock," gifts, and "goodbyes" continued, though increasingly currency came to be used. Fines for violation of the chief's *masam* also continued, though, since the chief no longer scrupulously observed his personal *mɔsɔm*, the villagers' attitudes seem to have changed in this regard. Thus in Kolifa Mayoso when a man's son died from snake-bite and the *Kapr* came to demand compensation from him for the violation of *mɔsɔm*, the man told him to collect from the snake since he, the father, had not killed his son. Furthermore, he added, instead of coming to him with his hand outstretched for compensation he should sympathize with him over the loss of his son.[68] The amount of tribute demanded from the secret societies was increased, and officials in *Bundu* and *Pɔro* had to pay for special licences to hold initiations; only a fraction of such fees, like those obtained from hunters, fishermen, dyers, and so on, found their way into the treasuries of the Native Administrations in recent years. Unlawful levies for foodstuffs and money increased and were collected for various purposes: to finance the attendance of the chief at the installation or funeral of a neighbouring chief, to finance portions of the chief's own *kantha* and installation expenses, to enable a chief to attend a District Council meeting, and, most recently, for the elaborate festivities accompanying the installation of a "non-official," that is African, President of a District Council. Frequently these and other reasons given for special levies were false and the money collected went into the chief's personal coffers.[69] Similarly, unlawful additions to the annual tax were collected and utilized by the chief. Tax was assessed by the chief's representatives, the Chiefdom Clerk, the subchiefs and members of the Tribal Authority, for non-existent or ruined houses, and after the establishment of a "head tax," for individuals not legally subject to the tax, namely those under age, females, some who were deceased, and even some fictitious individuals who never existed.[70] To rectify such "errors" in tax assessment a "beg" or gift was necessary, part of this going to the Paramount Chief and part to the assessors. That the chief added substantially to his income by such manipulation of tax-collecting cannot be doubted, and my Mayoso informants repeatedly stressed that illegal levies and taxes were driving villagers out of chiefdoms where such excesses were great into the towns and the chiefdoms where violations were less flagrant.[71]

Chiefdom labour levies for work on the chief's farm, *kamanta*, first came into being about 1905,[72] replacing *akaba*, the traditional tribute. The beginning was innocent enough; the chief's people would make a special large farm for him so that he could meet his increased expenses without making special food levies which could bring hunger to those on the margin of survival. With the passing of the years and the rise in rice prices, however, the chiefs came to look upon this farm as a money-maker; its size was increased and hence calls for chiefdom labour were heavier and more frequent. When the chief lacked sufficient land himself it was only too easy to obtain it in pledge, or seize it on a dubious decision in his own court. A chief can farm where he likes in his own chiefdom provided he gains permission from the landholder, and this would not be refused him as he is the "owner" of the chiefdom. At times labour levies were made every second or third day, and the people were unable to prepare their own farms properly. As indicated above, many in Kolifa Mayoso migrated, leaving their family land to which attraction was great, to escape. Some chiefs used labour levies to have pretentious houses built for themselves, others to have rice or palm kernels carried to market for them. Fines were collected from those who failed to appear for the labour levy, and in recent years such fines were arbitrary and exorbitant in many cases.

Court fees and fines have always been a source of income for Paramount Chiefs and with the breakdown of traditional checks on the chief's power they have provided an ever-increasing revenue. Extra-judicial fining as part of "settlement out of court" has become an accepted thing, and the suspicions that many of the "charges" imposed by the chief in such cases would not stand up in an impartial court following Temne law are justified. Such fines are viewed as a compulsory "beg" and regarded by the populace as preferable to being summoned into court and tried either by the accuser, the chief, or his henchman. Irregularities within and by the chief's court seem to have increased as their revenue-raising possibilities were realized. High court fees were collected from both parties and then no verdict given. Adjourned cases were not re-opened unless a large "beg" was forthcoming; as the Cox Commission also learned, such a "beg" was realistically termed "waking up the *barri*." Bribes were accepted in return for a favourable verdict; this, plus the partiality of the chief's court, brought on the cynical regard for the "justice" dispensed there that was so evident in many informants. Settlements out of court were regarded as preferable, whatever the merits of the case, and such fines were often appropriated *in toto* by the Paramount Chief.

With the establishment of Native Administrations new possibilities of extra-legal revenue were realized. The "sitting fees" for members of the Tribal Authority that sat as "bench" with the Paramount Chief were appropriated by the latter; those deprived of their legal remuneration did nothing, fearing legal action by the chief on the grounds that they did not dispense "justice." Only a fraction of each fine levied reached the Native Administration Treasury according to one informant who had served as a Chiefdom Clerk.[73]

Not only money but also land and labourers could be obtained through the court. My informants explained that in Kolifa Mayoso court fees were set so high that most people could not pay them, but that the stipulated £5 to £10 could be borrowed from the chief if a son were pawned or land pledged. Such creditors, it was insisted, "had no hope for winning the case" for they could not cross the chief's palm with a "beg," and the chief would put either the labourer-pawn or land-pledge to his own use. The chief, it was pointed out, kept his own money (the court fee), the pledge or pawn, and ultimately the fine charged. If a man did not have a pledge or a pawn he could mortgage his future rice or groundnut harvest, albeit at rates considerably below market value at harvest time.[74]

Thus in devious ways the chief was able to increase his income through autocratic action. The traditional emoluments proved insufficient to finance the chief in his new role, and with the power of Government apparently behind him and the breakdown of the traditional checks on autocracy, the chief could and did graft extensively. This rather lengthy though still incomplete cataloguing of excesses is not presented as an indictment of chiefs in general,[75] but rather to illustrate the extent of the ramifications of culture change in the area of the chieftaincy. The traditional checks and balances in the Temne political system were largely eliminated, for a variety of reasons, yet nothing comparable appeared in their place. The chiefs, still sanctioned by Temne religious beliefs and with the additional support of Government's power behind them, used their position for personal economic gain, pursuing too well, perhaps, the changing values of the times.

VII

Having outlined the concept of chieftaincy, the administrative hierarchy of the Temne, and the roles of the Paramount Chief, we must now consider, by way of summary, the power structure, that is, the checks and balances in the political system and the changes that have taken place in it during the time period under consideration. In the past, a man who felt he had received an unjustifiable adverse decision in the chief's court could follow various courses of action. Provided he had sufficient wealth, he could have appealed his case to a "war chief" or another Paramount Chief. Perhaps more common in the past and certainly the more usual procedure today is some recourse to supernatural means. The use of swearing medicines was usually secret, for if word of it reached the chief he would take steps to protect himself, by supernatural means, and employ a counter-medicine. Traditionally chiefs had very powerful medicines and in addition had the prestige and wealth to hire outside practitioners to work against those who would harm them. Nevertheless, the belief was strong that swearing medicines employed by a man who had been wronged were especially powerful, and fear of such was said to have been a powerful deterrent on a chief's behaviour. To swear a particular chief required great courage since the counter-medicines would be powerful; only a severely wronged man with a just cause would dare make the attempt. "Swearing the chieftaincy" so that each chief-elect would die soon after installation occurred in various chiefdoms in the past.[76]

When several men had received adverse decisions in court or when the chief's autocratic behaviour had embittered an appreciable segment of the population, other courses of action were available. First, attempts were made to get subchiefs, *Ragbenle* or *Pɔro* society officials, or renowned warriors to champion the cause. Warnings were given to those subchiefs who "had the ear of the chief" and were his close confidants and advisers, that unless the situation improved, drastic steps would be taken. In the past, provided that some of the subchiefs and *Ragbenle* officials could be won over to the people's cause, such warnings usually had the desired effect, for the chief feared assassination. At the same time threats to employ swearing medicines were made, and passive resistance of various kinds was employed. The threat of withdrawal of military support on the part of the war chiefs was another important deterrent.

When opposition to the chief was general, or, one surmises, if the majority of society officials were united in feeling, action would be taken through the societies, the *Pɔro*, *Ragbenle*, and *Bundu*. Recourse was had to the powerful society swearing medicines and the *Ragbenle* officials hindered the chief by refusing to aid him in ritual matters. If this was ineffective and the opposition was united and included the majority of prominent men in the chiefdom, the tyrant was assassinated by the *Kapr* chiefs and *Ragbenle* officials or poisoned or killed by *Pɔro* officers employing supernatural means.

After the establishment of the Protectorate, however, the sanction of Government behind the chief greatly altered the power structure. The chief, in the role of mediator between Government and his people, was not so easily intimidated by threats of violence. In general, Government was suspicious of the societies, especially *Pɔro*, and their power, and opposed them by ordinance and by warning. The chief was "owner-patron" of the societies and defended them against Government if a death occurred during initiation, or if parents protested against the seizure of their offspring for initiation. Frequently the chief protected the societies by keeping secret from Government such illegal actions, and subsequently used the threat to expose their practices to Government to influence the conduct of society officials.

In one of the Kolifa chiefdoms during the early 1940's, the Paramount Chief gave a number of dubious decisions in court and increased levies for labourers on his farm. Those he had treated especially harshly complained to the *Ragbenle* officials, who met with the chief, his *Kapr* chiefs, and some of his relatives in the *Turuma*, the *Ragbenle* bush, explained the situation to him, and advised him to mend his ways lest the people rebel. Many, they pointed out, had already left the chiefdom

with their families and settled elsewhere. The chief, however, was unmoved, and some time later the *Ragbenle* society held another meeting
with him where he reputedly threatened to summon those of his subjects
who were recalcitrant to the District Commissioner's court. Public sentiment grew against him when labour levies were called so frequently that
the people could not attend to their own farms properly and feared they
would be unable to pay the increased tax. The leaders of the people then
took their grievances to the District Commissioner, who ruled against
them, largely on the basis of the Chiefdom Clerk's sworn testimony that
village headmen had hidden people or reported them dead when he tried
to make the tax assessment. No further efforts were made until, two or
three years later, the chief raised the amount of tax and made a huge
farm by means of excessive labour levies. The prominent men of the
chiefdom, including many of the *Kapr* chiefs, then held a series of meetings in the *Pɔro* bush in which they agreed to refuse anything the chief
asked; those who weakened under the chief's threats were to be punished
according to *Pɔro* law. Powerful oaths were administered on *Pɔro* medicines that nobody reveal prematurely the plan of action agreed upon,
and that nobody backslide. Ultimately a delegation met the chief and
told him that they would no longer provide labour for his farm or pay tax
in excess of that stipulated by the laws of the district, and that they were
saying "goodbye" to him before taking their case to the District Commissioner. Letters were written to Government by the Chiefdom Clerk, who
now supported the people's cause, pointing out the chief's excesses.

Government backed the chief and urged the people to be patient
and give him another chance. A few days later the chief seized one of
their leaders on the charge that he had abused the chief's mother and
took him quickly to Magburaka. The people sent a party in pursuit, led
by the Chiefdom Clerk, but they were repulsed by a party of villagers
from the chief's mother's town, who seized them and brought them to
jail in Magburaka, where they were imprisoned and heavily fined by the
regent chief. As they were poor and unable to pay the fines, most accepted their chief's proffered loans, pledging bush and pawning kinsmen
as security. An appeal was made to Government, the case investigated,
and the chief instructed to "beg" his people with £30. This he did not do,
and the people again lodged a complaint against him, the case being
tried by another Paramount Chief. Many people were poor and in debt
to the chief, however, and these feared to give testimony against him;
hence he was awarded the decision. Embittered by the situation, the
people retaliated by petitioning Government directly for permission to
carry out *Pɔro* initiations, refusing to pay the chief the fee that was rightfully his ever since he had "bought the chieftaincy." Permission was
granted and the initiations completed when the chief went to Government and charged that "some boys" had been killed in the bush. My in-

formants insisted that the chief spent over £300 in bribes for "witnesses" to support his charge. Court Messengers were sent to arrest the people's leaders who insisted that, since they were *Pɔro* members too, they all go into the *Pɔro* bush and investigate the situation. The Court Messengers accepted as true the testimony they received there under *Pɔro* oaths and ordeals, and when the case was tried by the District Commissioner he awarded the decision to the people.

Encouraged by this success, the people sent a letter to Government, signed by all the Tribal Authorities demanding the removal of their chief. Action was deferred until the tax was collected, and in the meantime an appeal was made for contributions to supply a "Spitfire" for the Royal Air Force. Many villagers were too poor and indebted to contribute, while certain others saw this as further extortion by the chief, therefore the amount collected was small in comparison with the generous amount donated by the chief, who then appeared, one suspects, in a better light in the eyes of Government. Insults and breaches of respect then became more frequent on both sides. A hunter took the "chief's share" of a buffalo he had killed to a subchief rather than to the Paramount and was fined for this breach of *mɔsɔm*, the fine being upheld when the case was appealed.

Matters came to a head soon after the chief's house was burned down. The chief accused the leaders of the opposition, but they in turn denied this and said he started the blaze himself. The confessed arsonist, a poor man, testified that he had been hired by those accused, but they retorted that the chief had bribed him to perjure himself. The case was tried by another Paramount Chief who had requested the task of bringing peace to his "brother-chief" and his subjects (some say because the chief in question bribed him); though the accused swore themselves on a number of swearing medicines, none died or fell ill after several weeks in jail, indicating that they were innocent. Nevertheless, each received a sentence of five months' imprisonment for arson. Further disputes were settled only when the chiefdom was amalgamated with another and the chief in question placed in the role of "speaker" or assistant to the other Paramount Chief.[77]

It is evident in the above account that the societies, *Ragbenle* and *Pɔro*, no longer control and censor the chief's behaviour as they did in former times. Informants insisted that a chief such as this would have been killed by the medicines of these societies in the past, but that such means were not employed for fear that Government would investigate a chief's death and perhaps bring a murder charge against the people's leaders and the society officials.[78] For the same reason no attempt was made to poison or strangle the chief, for the *Ragbenle* feared the consequences.

The balance of power had shifted markedly, for, while some of the traditional checks on an autocratic chief had been negated, those supplied as replacements by Government do not seem to have functioned well, at least in this case. With the chief in a stronger position the people could counter with only limited means. Some migrated, but this meant the loss of access to ancestral lands. Others employed passive resistance of various kinds, but the chief exacted vengeance on those who refused to render labour and those who, like the hunter or the group who sought permission from Government to hold a *Pɔro* initiation, tried to deprive the chief of what was his traditional right. Complaints and petitions to Government, informants generalized, had been useless in this case, for "Government favours chiefs." Rebellion, too, was ineffective, in view of Government's power, until it broke out simultaneously in many chiefdoms during the "disturbances" of November 1955 to March 1956.

NOTES

1. The materials on which this paper is based were collected during the period September 1954, through July 1955, in Sierra Leone, where the writer conducted ethnographic and demographic investigations as a post-doctoral fellow of the National Science Foundation (Washington, D.C.); supplementary aid was granted by the Program of African Studies, Northwestern University (Evanston, Illinois). Grateful acknowledgment is extended to these two bodies for their support. The writer is indebted to Professors M. J. Herskovits, W. R. Bascom, and Roland Young, Mr. G. C. Guy and Mr. F. Clendenen for reading and commenting on this paper; their suggestions were most valuable. The opinions expressed, of course, are those of the author alone. Parts of section VI were read as a paper entitled "Changes in the Emoluments of Temne Chiefs" at the 56th annual meeting of the American Anthropological Association in Chicago, December 1957. Thanks are due to the Program of African Studies, Northwestern University, for a contribution towards the cost of publishing this over-long article.

2. In November 1953 Kolifa Mayoso was amalgamated with Kolifa Mamunta-Rowala; my data apply chiefly to the area that was formerly Kolifa Mayoso.

3. Banton, 1955, p. 241, has reached the same conclusion. For an account of the *Ragbenle* society, see Dorjahn, 1959.

4. Colson, 1958, p. 42.

5. The problem is a common one throughout Africa. For an excellent account see Fallers, 1955 and 1957.

6. Mair, 1958, p. 198.

7. Estimates taken from McCulloch, 1950, pp. 47 and 50.

8. Laing, writing of 1822, states that there were four districts in Temne country, each under one supreme chief. Chiefdom boundary maps are available in Dorjahn, 1959, p. 159, and McCulloch, 1950; the latter source includes a list of chiefdoms (pp. 99–101) as of the late 1940's.

9. Sierra Leone, *Report of Commission of Inquiry into Disturbances in the Provinces* (November 1955 to March 1956), 1956, p. 151. Hereafter cited as "Cox Report."

10. Sayers wrote that "the true office or title of 'Kap'r' is in the main only found in chiefdoms where the Poro Society flourishes" (footnote to Langley, 1939, p. 67). This is generally true, but there is no specific connexion between *Kapr* chiefs and the *Pɔro* Society. A *Kapr*, however, must be a member of the *Ragbenle* Society in the Kolifa area.

11. The section system has been adapted to the urban situation in Magburaka and other predominantly Temne towns, though *Kapr* chiefs and headmen have less authority where the Paramount and representatives of Government are more readily accessible. The presence of sizeable minorities from other tribes is an additional complicating factor; in Makeni and Magburaka the larger minorities were represented by "tribal headmen" whose positions were broadly similar to those described by Banton, 1954 and 1957, pp. 71–72, for Freetown.

12. The *kantha* period is one of retreat, in which the chief-elect and his subchiefs are confined in a hut or compound while the *Ragbenle* instruct them on various matters. Dorjahn, 1959.

13. At least in the Kolifa area, certain lineages came to have the hereditary right to provide the *Kapr* in a particular section; informants remarked that formerly *Kapr*-ships were hereditary in the patrilineal line.

14. Banton, 1955, pp. 241–3, lists a number of other titles, on which I have the following data. *Kapr kuma*, in Malal and the Bombali chiefdoms, cares for the chief's sacred house lest its contents be stolen. *Kapr wanda* was a title used in Malal and in Magburaka by the last Masa Kama. *Kapr sapɔ* was used in Yoni Mabanta during the reign of Fula Mansa Aŋsapɔ, who, according to tradition, used to entertain several of his wives in succession each night; a wife as she left him gave the key (*sapɔ*) to his next choice. *Kapr sapɔ* had nothing to do with the key, apparently, but only bore the title. *Kapr wusǝm* was a local official in Makari-Gbanti. *Kapr bana*, the "great" or "big" subchief, was a title used in the Kunike, Tane, and Bonkolenken Poli chiefdoms for a man who played an important role in the installation and burial of chiefs as well as serving as doctor. The *Kapr Kawan*, whom Banton calls "chairman of assemblies," may be the same as the *Pa Kwaŋ* of Mayoso and the Kunike Chiefdoms. *Kwaŋ* means "chair," and it is said that the chief leans on this man when "buying the crown." *Pa Kwaŋ* is selected because he is wealthy, and may or may not be related to the chief. He supplies wealth when that of the chief is exhausted and in return often sits in chief's court as adviser in big cases, yet in the Kolifa area he is not placed in *kantha* and is not known as *Kapr*.

15. During the reign of Bai Yoso Masang, a certain man had a court case with the chief and verbally abused Bai Yoso. When Bai Yoso Kanagbonu was installed, he selected this man as his *Kapr mǝsǝm*, so that he might "realize the responsibilities of a chief." Relations between the two were never good, and the man was a subchief in name only.

16. Usually the chief did not extort money from his titled *Kapr* chiefs, though in particular cases he might do so. All the *Kapr* chiefs in Kolifa Mayoso were relatively poor men in 1955.

17. I was unable to validate such statements except in Kolifa Mayoso, though in all probability this was true in other chiefdoms as well. My interpreter, a native of Port Loko, stated that there both *Alimamy* and *Santigi* were remunerated but that village headmen were not paid by the Government. Mr. Guy (personal communication) writes that the title *Alimamy* was recently introduced in some chiefdoms in Tonkolili and that these men do receive payment.

18. For an example of how this was accomplished, see Appendix I of the Cox Report, 1956.

19. Cox Report, 1956, p. 172.

20. These men were educated either in the Colony or in mission schools in the interior. Paramount Chief Bai Kur, M.B.E., of Kolifa Mabang, served as such a clerk in Yoni Mamela as a young man. I am indebted to G. C. Guy for this information. Fyfe, 1956, has indicated the extent and forms of European and Creole influence in what is now the Protectorate area.

21. Little, 1951, p. 210. Among both the Temne and Mende the elders look down upon the clerk as a "boy," though they recognize that he often has more influence with the chief than they do individually or as a group. My informants stated categorically that a wise man would present a gift to the clerk as well as to the chief in order to assure success in court. In this respect and others the clerk has taken over some of the roles played previously by the chief's traditional adviser-assistants, *Kapr məsəm, Kapr loya,* and so on. The clerk's sanctions are not traditional, however, being entirely the power of Government.

22. Cox Report, 1956, pp. 196–7. My field notes contain accounts of one Paramount Chief who asked for and received "gifts" or "kickbacks" of one-half the pay of a messenger in return for appointing the man. It was understood that the messenger could make up the difference in petty graft. Since 1957 their pay has been improved and Government has taken steps to control recruitment, training, discipline, promotion, and dismissals.

23. Formerly these questions were asked in public though now it is done in secret lest word of them reach Government, who might interpret them literally. One informant explained that formerly a chief had to observe more prohibitions (*məsəm*) including not to plant rice or eat bush yams, dried cassava, millet, or guinea corn, and that thus a chief could never support himself. Therefore, since he would depend on the largesse of others for sustenance after his installation, he was permitted to ask the indicated questions.

24. There are many types of *aŋkrifi* or "spirits." The chiefdom *ɔkrifi* usually bears the name of the ruling clan, or if there are two clans alternatively supplying the chief, the name of the clan in power. Formerly the spirit was impersonated by a masked dancer who also served as the chief's messenger and had the power to try petty cases. *Mela* is an archaic form of *Kamara*, the royal clan in Kolifa Mayoso.

25. *Namasa* is a title given to the chief's head wife provided she was virgin when she came to the chief, or to one of her co-wives who fulfils this requirement if the head wife does not. If ineligible to be *Namasa*, the head wife is given the title *Nakama*, "mother of the chief's house."

26. Ture, 1939, p. 95.

27. McCulloch, 1950, pp. 50–51.

28. Ture, 1939, p. 95.

29. Little, 1951, p. 184.

30. Thomas, 1916, p. 27. It is possible that the adoption of Islam brought an end to a traditional complex whereby a society performed the ceremonies, but I could discover no evidence that this actually happened.

31. Thomas, 1916, p. 69, indicates the same distinction and gives examples (69–79) of the various types of *məsəm*.

32. Perhaps because the *Pɔro* society was introduced to the Kolifa area by the Sherbro, and had no part traditionally in the political system, *Pɔro* initiations are regarded as violations· of the chief's *məsəm*, the society paying the fine through the *rabiŋa* of that session. *Bundu* and *aŋbiro* (boys' circumcision, unrelated to *Pɔro*) do not pay this.

33. Bai Kafari of Tane and Masa Kama of Kolifa Mamunta-Rowala both altered the *məsəm* traditionally associated with their office and title. In former times, it must be remembered, there were more *məsəm*, and they were more restricting and carefully observed.

34. This is figurative, since in pre-Protectorate times an elephant's tail or some other material object was used as a staff.

35. Once secured, *məsəm* remain throughout life, and a chief remains chief as long as he lives. Deposition is impossible, and the only solution, if a chief becomes undesirable, is to kill him. Mr. Guy writes that "even though some modern chiefs have ignored or eschewed their *məsəm*, and have since been deposed by Government, it is still considered impossible to elect other Paramount Chiefs in their lifetime to replace them" (personal communication).

36. The Cox Commission stated that: "All our inquiries have demonstrated the respect in which the office of chief—if not the office holder—is held" (Cox Report, 1956, p. 150). This situation may be unique in Sierra Leone, as Loveridge, 1957, p. 115, has remarked. Yet Elias, 1956, indicates that it is the general rule for Africa and cites exceptions to it.

37. Gbanka is an example. He was a Loko man who fought for various Temne and Mende Chiefs, was crowned in Yoni as Fula Mansa Gbanka, and eventually was betrayed and murdered by Temne and Mende together for the common good. Stories of Gbanka and literally dozens of other warriors abound in the Kolifa area.

38. The greatest boon of the Pax Britannica in Temne eyes was the fact that a man could be certain of enjoying the fruits of his own labours, for during the "tribal wars" of the nineteenth century and before, a warrior-band might seize the crops for itself. A levy system under such conditions was out of the question.

39. Thomas, 1916, p. 25, recounts that "in olden days" a chief might spend £15 to £20 to compose differences by giving presents to both sides. My informants insisted this was not true and that the only presents given were relatively small "shakehands." They pointed out that a chief and his retinue on a peacemaking expedition were fed, once they arrived, by their host, and received presents rather than gave them. As a mediator, the chief would certainly channel payments or gifts between the warring sides.

40. The Temne rarely used selling into slavery as an alternative to capital punishment, believing that while he lived, the guilty man could conceivably return and continue in his ways. Historically the Temne sold slaves to European traders and thus Mende, Koranko, Limba, and Loko found their way to the New World, but few Temne seem to have been exported. *Vide* Sayers, 1927, p. 14.

41. Lack of space prevents consideration of cases other than homicide.

42. Murder, whether accomplished or attempted, is regarded as a serious crime, *kapɛs,* a term which also includes intercourse with a woman who is suckling (this is believed to change her milk and bring death to the child) and rape, when the woman is unwilling or prepubescent.

43. Thomas, 1916, p. 155, states that in Sanda country such a person was known as *Kagbɔl raboma,* "sweeper of the grave," and was adopted into the victim's family. This is followed by the statement that: "If a girl was handed over, one of the brothers might marry her." The phrase "sweeper of the grave" was never used in the Kolifa area.

44. The concealment of a corpse, as reported by Thomas, 1916, pp. 155–6, was done only in time of war according to my informants, for word of it might leak out and those who buried it be accused. In addition, the victim's kin should not be deprived of their duty to bury the corpse and their right to obtain compensation from the murderer.

45. According to Thomas, 1916, p. 154, one Paramount Chief could reverse another's decision, but there is the possibility, as Fenton has suggested in another context, that Thomas was referring to the situation in "one of the four Sanda chiefdoms which were more or less subordinate to the fifth, Sanda Magbolonto" (McCulloch, 1950, p. 62). One of my informants said that in pre-Protectorate times any decision given by the chiefs of Kolifa Mabang, Kolifa Mayoso, or Kolifa Mamunta could be appealed to the chief of Kolifa Rowala, since these areas had once been at least nominally under his control. The same legal situation for appeals was in effect between the smaller Bonkolenken chiefdoms and Bonkolenken Yele. I am inclined to favour Fenton's interpretation of Thomas. The question is an important one as regards the paramountcy of chiefs.

46. Informants were unable to provide case material on the possibility of intervention by either another Paramount Chief or war chiefs from outside the chiefdom in question. Such intrigues are not beyond the realm of possibility.

47. Essentially the "Native Court" had jurisdiction to administer the estates of deceased persons, to hear and determine civil cases except those involving two or more Paramount Chiefs or Tribal Authorities involving title to land, or a case of a bad trading debt involving a licensed trader, and to hear and determine all criminal cases other than: cases of murder, manslaughter, rape, pretended witchcraft, person raiding, dealing in persons, cannibalism, robbery with violence, inflicting grievous bodily harm, cases relating to the "subversive societies" or arising out of factional or inter-tribal disputes, cases involving impersonation of Government employees, and so on. In his court a chief could not inflict punishment involving death, mutilation, or "grievous bodily harm or imprisonment" with or without hard labour for a period ex-

ceeding six months, or a fine greater than £10 in amount or value. The "constitution and jurisdiction of native courts" is outlined in section 7, cap. 149 (Native Courts Ordinance) in the *Laws of Sierra Leone* (vol. ii). I am indebted to Mr. G. C. Guy for this information.

48. Many chiefs did not sign treaties themselves, sending a subchief instead; thus not Masa Kama, but subchief Bai Kump signed for Kolifa Rowala. The motivation for such substitutions seems to have been largely fear and the fact that Paramount Chiefs traditionally employed envoys when dealing with external affairs. The Queen (Victoria) of England, it was pointed out to me, did not sign the treaties, but only her representatives.

49. The word *aŋkunte*, usually translated by literate Temne as "house" but more correctly as "lineage," is employed only with reference to subdivisions of a ruling clan. *Ambɔnshɔ* or *aŋkabilɛŋ* are the usual terms for lineage.

50. McCulloch, 1950, p. 61, has summarized the situation in a similar manner.

51. Frere, 1926, p. 70.

52. Sayers, 1927, pp. 104–8, lists the ruling clan or clans in most of the chiefdoms in the Northern Province.

53. My informants stated that all Kamara are related, else "we would not have the same name," and some assured me that all Kamara were descended from one individual. "Clan feeling," however, is all but non-existent, and the most important large kin groups are sub-clans or lineages localized in one or neighbouring chiefdoms. Government merely obliges a candidate to prove direct descent in the male line from a former chief.

54. In some cases, of course, such bribes are accepted even though the supporting witnesses do not present the desired falsified genealogical evidence.

55. This is a method of divination in which the corpse of the deceased or some part or representation of it is placed on a bier carried by two men on their heads. The deceased guides the movements of the carriers and thus answers the questions asked.

56. *Akane maruba* means "to reveal the truth," that is, the true *aŋkunte*. *Ruba* means "ink" or "ink-pot" and refers to the item used by the "Mori-man" when he writes out excerpts from the Koran to serve as charms. Both Muslim and non-Muslim Temne place great faith in such charms and regard the Koran and the ink used to reproduce parts of it in this way as truth.

57. It seems certain, in view of these safeguards and the attitudes attributed by informants to the parties concerned, that no generally known and accepted system of *aŋkunte* rotation was observed, at least in the Kolifa area. The selection of the *aŋkunte* to supply the next chief seems not to have been as predetermined as many Temne stated, for the histories of most chiefdoms showed omissions and aberrations from the earliest established cycle.

58. The Tonkolili District files contain many examples.

59. Swearing medicines were used, or the Koran, if the witnesses were Muslim. Every attempt was made by Government to adhere to the rotational system which had usually been previously abrogated. Generally the District Commissioner visited at least once to check on proceedings. To prevent claims that neighbouring Paramount Chiefs took bribes, or favoured friends and rela-

tives, Government came to select as Assessor Chiefs men from the far borders of Temne country. No non-Temne chiefs were selected as they would be unfamiliar with procedures. A difficulty arose when it was traditional to have particular neighbouring Paramount Chiefs present and Government forbade this.

60. Formerly it was believed that these spirits elected the chief before his identity was made known. If they liked a chief, they would help him to become powerful and famous. The phrase is a generic term for all spirits, and the masked dancers who embody them, of the society that crowns the chief, be it *Ragbenle, Ramɛna, or Pɔro.*

61. The margin of victory necessary seems to have been quite elastic, depending on local circumstances. Some informants insisted that a literate candidate on good terms with the Chief Messenger would be selected if he polled the most votes even if these were not a majority, while a non-literate candidate, especially if not friendly with the Court Messengers, would not be chosen even if he had a substantial plurality, or even majority. That there may have been a preference, initially, on the part of the Government for literate "educated chiefs" is understandable, but the charge of deliberate manipulation of the voting remains unproved to the writer's satisfaction. The people themselves seem to have wanted literate chiefs, in some cases, feeling that they would bring more rapid development.

62. The Cox Commission has drawn what is essentially the same conclusion (Cox Report, 1956, pp. 190–1).

63. The amount of the fine varied from decade to decade, being in the 1930's in Kolifa Mayoso £4 for the Paramount Chief; £1, four fowls, one bottle of palm-oil, one yard of white satin, one bottle of rum, one head of tobacco, and a varying amount of rice and salt had to be given to the *Ragbenle* society for their sacrifices to the ancestors. The fine was paid by the parents and family of the deceased.

64. In practice the chief would halt his journey under such circumstances, summon the *Kapr* and village headman responsible, fine them, and demand and get immediate action.

65. The first Temne chiefdom in Tonkolili District to receive a Native Administration was Yoni Mamela in 1939 (G. C. Guy, personal communication).

66. Cox Report, 1956, p. 152. *Manje,* the chief's farm, was known as *kamanta* in Temne.

67. In the years following the formation of the Protectorate, "rascals from Freetown," impersonating Government officials or their clerks, toured parts of the Protectorate demanding money, food, and women from the chiefs on numerous pretexts. In 1953 an impostor appeared in Mayoso claiming to be the Colonial Secretary's chief clerk on a secret fact-finding mission before the meetings on amalgamating Kolifa Mayoso with Kolifa Mamunta-Rowala. He stipulated that for a price (£200) he could assure Bai Yoso that he would emerge as Paramount Chief of the amalgamated chiefdoms.

68. It was not recalled whether or not his arguments convinced the *Kapr,* but the Paramount Chief was unmoved and took him to court. The District

Commissioner ruled that the man should not pay, on the basis of an old "agree-ment" between Bai Yoso and the Government, but told the father to "beg" the chief with a small gift that he be not publicly disgraced by losing a case.

69. For example, see the Cox Report, 1956, pp. 154–5. Traditionally there had been no distinction between the chief's personal coffers and the "chiefdom treasury"; nor, with the establishment of Native Administrations, it seems, was such a distinction drawn in practice.

70. Further data on irregularities in connexion with the assessment for tax can be found in Chapter VII of the Cox Report.

71. There are other reasons for the rural-urban migration in the Protec-torate though this is a major factor. Chiefs were reluctant to make levies in the towns and tax-assessors were wary of grafting where complaints were more likely to find their way to the District Commissioner's ears and the presence of literate, politically conscious individuals brought about a greater awareness of what was legal or illegal. Some sections of neighbouring Bonkolenken chief-dom served as a "tax refuge area" for many years: the assessment there was greatly under-enumerated and Government surveillance negligible. My gene-alogies confirm a sizeable migration from Kolifa Mayoso to Bonkolenken during the last two decades.

72. Communal labour on a village, section, or even chiefdom basis for repairing bridges, paths, and so on, was practised long before 1905, but it was only then that chiefs demanded labour levies to work on their own farms. Such farm work, in lieu of *akaba*, was at first welcomed by the people. The chiefs, it seems, took advantage of the situation for their personal enrichment. It must be remembered that the chiefs suffered heavily when the establishment of the Protectorate put an end to their slave labour force.

73. For a more detailed consideration of irregularities in chiefdom courts and extra-legal abuses see the Cox Report, 1956, Chapter XVIII. I have not considered petty graft, which was indulged in by many Kolifa chiefs. My in-formants gave detailed accounts, observing that such practices ought to be beneath the dignity of a chief.

74. A loan to pay court fees was secured in one case at 5s. a bushel for husk rice and 3s. a bushel for groundnuts; the market prices at harvest time that year were £1. 2s. for a bushel of husk rice, 7s. 6d. for a bushel of ground-nuts. Impoverished men could get rice on credit from the chief when needed, returning at harvest time two bushels for each bushel received.

75. Many chiefs continued as good, benevolent rulers, grafting from time to time to be sure, but not to the point of impoverishing and ruining their chiefdom for personal gain. One can, I think, excuse a degree of illegal action when there were no legal mechanisms by which a chief could obtain the revenue to maintain his traditional position and fulfil new duties.

76. In Kolifa Mayoso (*supra*, p. 127) a particular chief's uncle wronged a man and the chief did not intervene, thus prompting the man to "swear the chieftaincy." James, 1939, p. 115, indicates that this was once done in Koya chiefdom.

77. In the unsettled weeks during the first two months of 1956 when the "tax riots" occurred in much of Temne country, the villagers threatened their

ex-chief with violence and demanded money from him. Fortunately, the District Commissioner was able to rescue him from what might have been a dangerous situation. (Geoffrey Guy, personal communication.)

78. Two young men, pawns of the chief, did try to employ bad medicine but were discovered. They had acted, however, independently and on personal motives.

REFERENCES

Alldridge, T. J. 1901. *The Sherbro and Its Hinterland*. Macmillan & Co. Ltd., London.
Banton, M. 1954. "Tribal Headmen in Freetown," *Journal of African Administration*, vi. 3, pp. 140–4.
———— 1955. "The Ethnography of the Protectorate," review article of McCulloch (1950), *Sierra Leone Studies*, n.s., No. 4, pp. 240–9.
———— 1957. *West African City*. Oxford University Press, London.
Beatty, K. J. 1915. *Human Leopards*. Hugh Rees Ltd., London.
Colson, E. 1958. "The Role of Bureaucratic Norms in African Political Structure," *Systems of Political Control and Bureaucracy in Human Societies*, Proceedings of the 1958 Annual Spring Meeting of the American Ethnological Society, edited by V. F. Ray.
Dorjahn, V. R. 1959. "The Organization and Functions of the *Ragbenle* Society of the Temne," *Africa*, xxix, 2, 156–70.
Elias, T. O. 1956. *The Nature of African Customary Law*, Manchester University Press, Manchester.
Fallers, L. 1955. "The Predicament of the Modern African Chief," *American Anthropologist*, lvii, 2, 290–305.
———— 1957. *Bantu Bureaucracy*. W. Heffer & Sons Ltd., Cambridge.
Frere, N. G. 1926. "Notes on the History of Port Lokko and its Neighborhood," *Sierra Leone Studies*, Nos. i–iii, pp. 63–70.
Fyfe, C. H. 1956. "European and Creole Influence in the Hinterland of Sierra Leone," *Sierra Leone Studies*, n.s., No. 6, pp. 113–23.
James, J. W. 1939. "Temne Constitutional Law, with especial reference to the Koia Chiefdom," *Sierra Leone Studies*, No. xxii, pp. 112–19.
Laing, A. G. 1825. *Travels in Western Africa*. London.
Langley, E. R. 1939. "The Temne; their Life, Land, and Ways," *Sierra Leone Studies*, No. xxii, pp. 64–80.
Little, K. L. 1951. *The Mende of Sierra Leone*. Routledge & Kegan Paul Ltd., London.
Loveridge, A. J. 1957. "The Present Position of the Temne Chiefs of Sierra Leone," *Journal of African Administration*, ix, 3, pp. 115–20.
Mair, L. P. 1958. "African Chiefs Today," *Africa*, 28, 195–206.
McCulloch, M. 1950. *Peoples of the Sierra Leone Protectorate*, Western Africa, Part II. Ethnographic Survey of Africa, International African Institute, London.
Sayers, E. F. 1927. "Notes on the Clan and Family Names common in the Area inhabited by Temne-speaking People," *Sierra Leone Studies*, No. x, pp. 14–108.
Sierra Leone. 1956. *Report of Commission of Inquiry into Disturbances in the Provinces*. Crown Agents for Oversea Governments and Administrations.
Thomas, N. W. 1916. *Anthropological Report on Sierra Leone*, Part I, Law and Custom. Harrison & Sons, London.
Ture, A. B. 1939. "Notes on Customs and Ceremonies attending the Selection and Crowning of a Bombali Temne Chief," *Sierra Leone Studies*, No. xxii, pp. 95–103.

E. M. Chilver and P. M. Kaberry

FROM TRIBUTE TO TAX
IN A TIKAR CHIEFDOM (1960)

This historical reconnaissance is not concerned with the economic consequences of direct taxation or its relation to the dogma of colonial self-
sufficiency but rather with what McPhee calls its "political, moral and
social nature." A revenue system reflects not only the circumstances in
which the authority of governments is exercised, but some of its ideal
premises—a truism which can be illustrated from the tax history of British
West Africa in general and by the comparison of the Northern and Southern Nigerian systems before the post-Amalgamation reforms of Lugard
and his successors. Since direct taxation is an aspect of colonial administration which affects members of a tribal society regularly and generally
and demands a voluntary or enforced accommodation, its study in a particular tribal area may provide some useful insights to students of social
change. Where the tribal society already has a system of tribute or provisioning, the introduction of a different system presents the colonial
Government's native agents with problems of reinterpretation as well as
procedure.

This paper deals with the accommodations made to direct taxation
by Nsaw, a Tikar chiefdom now some 60,000 strong in the Bamenda
grasslands of the Southern Cameroons. Their accommodations involved
experiments with the political devices at their disposal, on some occasions under direct pressure from the Administration, on others in response
to economic events. The limits on experimentation were set by the traditional delegation of authority and the traditional patterns of political
behaviour in Nsaw, but within these limits ingenious accommodations
were made. The first made to German direct taxation was temporary:

SOURCE. E. M. Chilver and P. M. Kaberry, "From Tribute to Tax in a Tikar Chiefdom," reprinted from *Africa*, XXX, 1, 1960, pp. 1–2, 17–18, by permission of the
International African Institute. Copyright E. M. Chilver and P. M. Kaberry.

tax demands were met by the collection of gifts from those who could afford them, namely the lineage heads. As German administration became firmly established and apparently permanent, the institutions concerned with mobilizing the resources of the country for the provisioning of the chief and for war were called into action, and were employed for the collection of direct tax until very recently. . . .

CONCLUSIONS

The taxation imposed by European administrations demanded a territorially based organization for census, regular collection, and enforcement. There were two possibilities open to the Nsaw ruler. One was to base taxation on the compound, using the lineage heads to collect and remit taxes through designated intermediaries to the palace. The other was to use the *manjong* organization. In the first two collections in German times, the Fon relied on the lineage heads, the only persons with some convertible wealth which could be readily tapped. In 1911, after the Germans had increased the tax quota, the lineage heads complained of difficulties. The same thing happened after the introduction of lump-sum assessment in 1929, and the slump which followed it. In both cases the Fon reacted in the same way: he placed the responsibility for collection and enforcement on *manjong*. Why did he do so? The reasons put forward are hypothetical, but they are consistent with what we know of the Nsaw polity.

In the first place it must have become evident to the Nsaw by 1911 that the German tax quota was to be a regular burden, a tribute rather than a war-indemnity. In this respect it resembled the regular prestations due from every man in Nsaw rather than the irregular gifts expected from persons seeking prestige and honours. Regular prestations were within the sphere of competence of *manjong* and *ngwerong*, but, of the two, *manjong* possessed a state-wide membership and jurisdiction. Moreover, as between *manjong* and the lineage heads, it was *manjong* which enjoyed the right to enforce obligations by fines and distraint, and to enforce them in relation to a weekly time-table. Like *ngwerong's*, its authority was impersonal. Even though a lineage head would have been supported by the Fon in exposing a tax-defaulter to penal sanctions, it would have been contrary to lineage values for the former to have done so. In entrusting tax-collection to *manjong* Fon Bifon showed he had a shrewd grasp of the instrumentalities at his disposal.

The introduction of the sliding-scale system in 1946, which again involved assessment and collection by lineage heads, was unpopular with them. Their control of their dependants had by now seriously diminished owing to the expansion of trading opportunities and mission influence: at that time they were no longer the economic leaders; and they had been deserted by some of the most energetic members of their lineages. The very reason that lay behind the Administration's desire to impose the sliding scale—increasing diversity of the economy—made them the less capable of complying with the requirements of the new system. The compromise proposed by the *takibu* council, a higher flat rate all round, offered increased revenues while avoiding a collision between the traditional and modern elements in Nsaw society.

Since the post-war expansion of the Cameroons' economy, several important changes have taken place: the increase in the number of persons wealthy enough to pay individually assessed tax, the entry into coffee farming by men of all ranks (including lineage heads, councillors, and *manjong* officers) for whom time is now money, and an increase in the social services. These changes have also affected Nsaw attitudes to tax-commission and taxation.

Tax-commission, for long wholly retained by the Fon, was, in Nsaw eyes, a substitute for tribute from sub-chiefs; Nsaw proper did not regard the Fon's stipend as a substitute for tribute to him, but as a token of the Government's recognition of his position as a paramount chief. After 1937 the tax-commission was shared between the Fon and his sub-chiefs and his subordinate collectors in Nsaw proper. By 1958 direct tax was £1 per head; and the commission of 5 per cent. was shared between the Fon and his collectors. As far as the latter were concerned the commission amounted to no more than a few pounds, in some cases a few shillings; but there was a significant difference in attitude on the part of the sub-chiefs and the collectors in Nsaw proper. For the former the right to commission and the custody of nominal rolls was a political symbol and was believed by them to confer a far greater degree of officially sanctioned authority than the Administration intended to accord. By contrast, many of the *manjong* officers set less store by the commission, which in any case had never symbolized their political claims against the Fon. At one time there was general agreement among them that "The Fon should take all" and redistribute according to the Nsaw conventions of reward. But attendance at *manjong* meetings is falling off because men have other calls on their time. The work of collection is consequently becoming more wearisome, more akin to the work of the Native Authority service but without its regular pay, perquisites, and security. The *manjong* officers, once honoured warriors and hunters, resent being forced into the role of tax-bailiffs and a few have already refused to carry out their duties.

Until quite recently direct taxation was regarded as tribute to a suzerain. When, for example, a Nsaw pagan lord was told of the German surrender in 1945 his first question was: "Will the Germans pay tax to the British?" The most important change in the Nsaw attitude to taxation over the last decade has been the general realization of its connexion with the provision of local services. This realization has, in turn, focused Nsaw interest on getting what they consider a fair share of these services locally, and in promoting local development schemes for which they are willing to supply free labour through the *manjong* organization. It has also called into question the propriety of the Fon's statutory role as Sole Tax Authority, and led to the discussion of other means of maintaining his traditional dignities which will not expose him to public criticism or legal action.

J. A. Barnes

INDIGENOUS POLITICS AND
COLONIAL ADMINISTRATION
WITH SPECIAL REFERENCE TO AUSTRALIA (1960)

LOSS OF INDIGENOUS SOVEREIGNTY

In an age of crumbling empires, when many former colonial territories are becoming politically independent, it may still be instructive to study the processes by which empires and nations have been built up. What political forms have been involved and how have they been modified and developed? The new nations of Africa and Asia now emerging have political structures that bear a generic resemblance to the established democracies and dictatorships of Europe. These forms of organization seem to be a necessary requirement for membership of the United Nations, and are widely held to be essential if there is to be a flexible industrial and commercial economy, centralized administration and widespread literacy. None of the United Nations enjoys an entirely subsistence economy or relies only on communication by word of mouth. They all have courts of law, standing armies and at least the beginnings of a bureaucracy. In particular, all the United Nations are nations, or states; there are no stateless societies among them. Thus they are drawn from only one broad category of known and possible political structures, a category which has come to dominate the world scene. Many other forms of political life are known from the past and have been described for the more remote parts of the world at the present time. Those people who follow these other forms of social organization we call by a variety of terms of which "tribal" is perhaps the least presumptuous. Tribal political structures have declined both as the tide of empire rose in the nineteenth century and, for different reasons, as these same empires now wither

SOURCE. J. A. Barnes, "Indigenous Politics and Colonial Administration, with special reference to Australia," reprinted from *Comparative Studies in Society and History,* II, 2, 1960, pp. 133–149.

away. Erstwhile tribal peoples have either been absorbed into existing economic and political systems of Western type or sooner or later have copied them for their own use. Much has been written about the recent adoption of Western forms of organization by nations newly independent. Here I shall consider what happened, and in some places is even continuing to happen, to primitive political life under colonial impact at a stage when independent nationhood was either a very distant vision or not an objective at all. In particular I shall compare conditions in aboriginal Australia and Australian New Guinea with other parts of the world.

Most tribal people now live in some kind of association with Europeans or with others who have adopted at least the technology if not the social institutions of Europe. With few exceptions Europeans and tribesmen form plural societies in which the two main segments of the population differ in ways of life, values and customs. In general political power is divided unequally; the Europeans are conquerors and the tribesmen are conquered. There are few tribes who can still make war on their own account, or who are interested in making war only against their tribal neighbours. In the political life of modern states the ability to make war is a good test of sovereignty; if we extend the notion of warfare to include feuding and organized revenge the test works fairly well for the tribal world. Almost everywhere except perhaps in parts of New Guinea and South America legitimate war-making has become the prerogative of those few political entities which recognize one another as sovereign states. There cannot be more than about a hundred of these in the whole world. Warlike acts by other groups or by individuals are categorized by these sovereign states not as war but as revolt, rebellion, insurrection, sedition, terrorism, banditry, brigandage, mutiny, piracy, faction fighting, or murder. In the struggle for political independence, these are terms of denigration, not euphemisms; terrorists and bandits are not accorded the privileges of prisoners-of-war. Two or three hundred years ago, not to go back further in time, there were many more war-making bodies than there are now. Warfare was an activity much less coordinated than it now is and the right to make war was more widely recognized. In those days the nations of the West made war on peoples who had not yet been brought under Western control. Where warfare was avoided, treaties were made between high contracting parties who in formal terms were assumed to be equally free and sovereign, even if one party was in fact a European leviathan and the other a non-European midget.

The trend has been for tribal peoples to lose their sovereignty to the West. In many other aspects of social life, tribesmen have adapted themselves to conquest by a bewildering and fascinating variety of responses. Yet in political affairs a uniform trend is quite clear; despite small and shortlived exceptions, tribal political systems have been in retreat. In very many instances it is still possible to study as a going concern the contemporary economic system of a tribal or erstwhile tribal group, or its kinship structure or its religious beliefs. Only in a limited sense can one study its political system. There is almost always some *pax* (*britannica, australiana,* or the like) which has to be assumed and whose existence affects profoundly the doings of the people being studied. Eyewitness accounts of primitive warfare belong in the main to the nineteenth, not to the twentieth, century (cf. Turney-High, 1949). Even when warfare does now take place, it is usually what we might term "one-sided" war, in which although one side sees itself at war with an external enemy the other regards the disturbance as merely domestic trouble requiring police action.

ANALYTICAL FRAMEWORK

The widespread erosion of tribal political systems provides our data. Although the general trend is manifest the process of erosion has not been uniform. We therefore ask if there are any systematic variations in the process as between one tribal people and another, one historical epoch and another, one mode of conquest and another. For a preliminary analysis, this complex question can be simplified by considering only two main variables. Indigenous political systems can, without too much injustice, be divided among three categories; the diverse processes of White conquest can, with perhaps rather more injustice to the facts, be arranged into four phases.

Fortes' and Evans-Pritchard's "Introduction" to *African Political Systems* (1940, pp. 6–7) provides a convenient classification of tribal systems generally. Firstly there are those groups of food gatherers who live in small politically-autonomous units. I shall mention the Bushmen of southern Africa, the Australian aborigines and the Siriono of Brazil. Secondly there is the category of primitive states, typified by the Zulu, Ngoni, Ashanti and Nupe, in which there is centralized authority and other attributes of statehood. The size and precise location of a primitive state often seems not to be determined by the environment, so that portions of the unit frequently break off to join neighbouring states or to found new independent states. There are other primitive states where, although control of the unit is disputed and its boundaries fluctuate, the unit itself remains relatively intact. An example is the Barotse empire in Northern Rhodesia. Thirdly there are those stateless agriculturalists where there is no centralized authority. Examples are the Nuer, Tallensi, the Plateau Tonga and the peoples of the New Guinea Highlands.

The other variable, phases of conquest, provides four categories (Barnes, 1955, pp. 169–170). We distinguish the presence or absence of a colonial administration and of settlement involving the alienation of substantial portions of land. If both an administration and settlers are absent, any dealings that the tribal society may have with a Western country are regarded by both as external affairs. This phase prevailed in the early days of White settlement at the Cape of Good Hope, in West Africa until the late nineteenth century, in the Pacific during the voyages of exploration, and in North America before treaties began to be made.

Treaty-making usually marks the end, or one possible end, of this phase. A treaty between a conquering Western power and a tribal society usually differed in two respects from the treaties generally made between two Western nations. Almost all treaties with tribal peoples were agreements that the Western power should take the tribal group under its protection. In the heyday of imperial expansion in Africa after the Berlin West African Conference of 1885, British agents were provided with a supply of printed treaty forms which could be completed with the names of chiefs and tribes they met with on their travels (cf. Hanna, 1956, frontispiece; Perham, 1956, p. 671). Because of its content each tribe usually made only one treaty; there was never opportunity or occasion for another. This generalization is not true of North America, where the indigenous tribes were regarded, at least in the eyes of constitutional lawyers, as foreign nations with whom treaties could be made even after they had been in close contact with White settlers for many decades. Treaty-making was usually followed by the arrival of one or more representatives of the conquering or colonizing power, from the solitary Adviser or Resident, as in an Indian princely state, to the complete apparatus of Agricultural Departments, Magistrates, Labour Officers, and the like as in many an African colony.

Colonizers did not always make treaties before they arrived. Sometimes agreements of a less formal kind were made, as with the Ngoni of northern Nyasaland. Sometimes the colonial power extended its influence gradually and more or less peacefully, as in Australian New Guinea or Eastern Samoa; or it followed on the heels of military conquest, as with the Fort Jameson Ngoni, the Maori, the Ashanti, and the Kaffirs of eastern Cape Province. Whether the colonial administration established itself peacefully or by force, it usually introduced a regime of what we may term administrative paternalism.

Administrations were not always in the van; sometimes the settlers were ahead. On the northern frontiers of the Cape settlement during the eighteenth century, and in most of Australia most of the time from 1788 until, say, 1900 European settlers on the moving frontier were in contact with the indigenous inhabitants and of necessity had to take the law into their hands even as they took the land with their own hands. Colonial administrations operating without the complication of settlers have on the whole been paternalistic, and often benevolently paternalistic, towards the tribal people they have conquered; settlers have on the whole been forced to take a much shorter-term view of their own interests. They have had to concentrate on securing control of the land they wished to exploit, and on defending their property and stock against the attacks of the indigenous inhabitants. In varying measure, depending on the particular type of enterprise on which they were engaged, they have tried to secure their labour supply, either by establishing friendly relations with the local people, or by kidnapping, capturing, recruiting or enslaving enough labourers to suit their needs. These actions may lead to conflict between the frontier settlers and the administration, as in British North America after 1754 (Collier, 1947, p. 197).

Administrative paternalism may well be combined with White rural settlement. The colonial administration is then concerned not only to maintain law and order, but also to regulate conditions of employment for the tribes and to protect them against excessive exploitation. However, the real change in the regime does not usually come about until the indigenous inhabitants of the country begin to earn money in ways other than as unskilled plantation or farm labourers, and begin to spend their money on things other than the limited range of Western consumer products provided in the plantation store. A considerable degree of political and social autonomy is possible under a paternalistic regime; the tribal population can be left to govern itself provided the peace is not disturbed. With the growth on the one hand of industrial production with its demand for a stable urban indigenous proletariat, and for a wide market for its consumer products and, on the other, of native entrepreneurs and petty industrialists, this measure of autonomy becomes impossible. The indigenous peoples begin to find that, in political affairs at least, they have to struggle on a national scale. In Australia, the numerical preponderance of White over aboriginal, and the inelectable frontier quality of most of the interior of the continent, obscure the emergence of this last phase of White conquest, which we may term industrial integration. In New Guinea this stage has not yet been reached. But it can be seen clearly enough in the condition of the Maori in New Zealand, the Bantu in South Africa, and even the Hawaiians in Hawaii.

This analytical scheme overlooks two factors which locally have sometimes been of great importance. In the first place, missionaries have often acted independently and far in advance of administration and settlers. After the mission has gained converts, a quasi-colonial administration arises, relying mainly but by no means exclusively on supernatural sanctions but less inclined to leave well alone (cf. Gann, 1958, Chap. II). Secondly, the scheme recognizes only those settlers who seek large tracts of land. In some parts of the world the invaders have been mainly interested in gaining mineral wealth, and have left the natives in undisturbed occupation of most of their land while demanding a secure labour supply.

But large-scale mining has usually taken the administration along with it, as for example in the New Guinea Highlands. Where traders, as distinct from miners and settlers, have gone ahead of the colonial administration, as notably in West Africa, the process of conquest has usually remained in the first phase, of external relations, although in the past some traders did settle down to establish small empires on their own account where the indigenous inhabitants were weak.

FOOD GATHERERS

Let us now turn to the simplest type of indigenous political organization, as found among food-gatherers.

In most parts of the world, peoples who still relied on this simple technology had been subject to pressure from their pastoral or agricultural neighbours long before a Western administration or Western settlers appeared on the scene. They had already been forced into the less attractive portions of the environment, into the jungles or deserts or arctic wastes. These marginal areas were seldom of immediate interest to the Western invaders, and the small numbers of hunting and collecting peoples were left to live their own lives with little direct interference from outside. Thus in territories where head-taxes have been applied to the agricultural population, we often find that the swamp, desert and jungle dwellers are exempted. It is usually more difficult to introduce modern facilities, such as schools, roads and dispensaries, in such areas than in closely settled regions, and the small number of individuals served by these facilities makes them relatively more expensive. The environment does not lend itself to cash cropping, and the small numbers of people do not constitute a reservoir of labour for Western enterprises. Hence interaction with the invaders takes place only on the periphery, if at all. Unfortunately small bands of nomads living at a low level of technological development and existing often on the edge of starvation are not only hard to administer but also hard to study; detailed information is slight about the way in which Western assumption of sovereignty over the country inhabited by people of this kind affects them. It seems that Bushmen in South-west Africa, Bechuanaland and the Rhodesias are still left very much alone, despite the seventy years or more that their territory has been under Western sovereignty. Pygmies in the Belgian Congo and the related peoples of the Great Rift Valley in Tanganyika seem also to govern their own affairs, or rather to be in a position to continue to do so if they do not wish to settle down under the wing of a mission or government post and abandon their semi-nomadic ways. The Siriono of Brazil studied by Holmberg were in a similar condition. The response of such peoples to Western intrusion, and indeed to approaches from other non-Western peoples with a higher technology than their own, is to flee. So long as the deserts are large enough and contain some wild life and water, or the jungles deep enough, the old way of life can be continued.

Under these conditions, it would be surprising if any great changes in political organization took place. The density of population and the maximum size of the local food gathering group are controlled by the environment, and are likely to decrease rather than increase under the new conditions. There is no improvement in communications. Hence we would scarcely expect that centralized authority would develop, or that the size of the political unit would extend beyond the small band. So long as the people remain subsistence hunters, no large-scale organization is likely to emerge. If the Administration appoints its own nominee as headman, it has to find some way of ensuring that his followers do not melt away when he endeavours to enforce his authority over them for there are few sanctions at his disposal other than the force that he may be able to call upon from the Administration. As we know to our cost, it is difficult to send punitive expeditions into the jungle.

Just as the food-gatherers do not adapt to the invasion, so the invaders do not adapt to the presence of the primitive food gatherers. The hunters merely flee, and invaders merely reject or ignore the hunters. Thus in Formosa the Chinese did not attempt to administer the food-gathering peoples of the interior, but were content to confine them in a demarcated area (cf. Okada, 1955, p. 382). In South Africa the Bushmen, who were hunters, became the hunted. Similar procedures were adopted in Australia. Elkin comments: ". . . a semi-nomadic, food-gathering, and therefore scattered people, with neither settled villages, anchored gardens, nor centralized organization, has no . . . points of resistance to the newcomer and his ways, nor means of recovery. Moreover, the obvious absence of these features gives the invader (settler, administrative officer, or missionary) the impression that the natives are almost cultureless and that whatever he does can interfere but little with them. Therefore, he is very unlikely to respect native ways, customs, beliefs and values, or to adjust to these his method of economic, administrative or spiritual invasion. He sees no objective symbols of their existence." (Elkin 1951, p. 165.)

ABORIGINAL AUSTRALIA

When the colonization of Australia by the British began in 1788 conditions were unusual in that peoples living by hunting and collecting were spread over the whole of a continent. There were no indigenous pastoralists or agriculturalists who might have gradually pressed the aborigines back into the less hospitable and fertile parts of the region. Furthermore the culture of the aborigines differed from that of many other food-gatherers. People who live in intimate dependence on the natural environment build up an elaborate body of knowledge and lore about flora, fauna, localities and natural phenomena. The Australian aborigines developed an unusually strong attachment to specified sites, and the policy of flight in the face of invasion was not so readily open to them. On the other hand, each aboriginal community was linked with many distant localities by a systematized elaboration of interpersonal ties. The White invaders gradually pushed back the frontiers of settlement in much the same way as, for example, the Bantu had pushed back the Bushmen and other pygmy and pygmoid groups in Africa a few centuries earlier; but in the face of this movement Australian aborigines did not retreat into the central deserts in the way in which, for example, the Siriono retreated deeper and deeper into the jungle in the face of advancing Brazilian settlement (Holmberg, 1950, pp. 62–63). The European invaders of Australia were not peasants and did not settle the country closely. Furthermore they were not subsistence cultivators or pastoralists, but were producing for a market and were able to employ labourers. In most parts of Australia the settlers were well in advance of the administration. The stage was thus set for the partial elimination of the aboriginal population, and its partial conversion to a peon class attached to White pastoral properties. The same process seems to have taken place in the Transvaal and in parts of Natal at about the same time in history. In Southern Africa the Bantu who came to live permanently on European farms were traditionally cattle-keepers and maize growers, not hunters, and hence perhaps fitted more efficiently into the sheep and cereal economy of their White overlords. They did not have the same tradition and recurrent need to go off on long journeys that affected aborigines in Australia. Politically the Bantu of the Transvaal had a tradition of centralized authority in fissile states. But when the Boer and British settlers invaded the high veld and the uplands of Natal, the indigenous population consisted for the most part of splinter groups of refugees who had been harried by the empire-building activities of the Zulu, Swazi and Southern Sotho. The White farmer offered protection of a kind to people accustomed to authority at a time when their own leadership was proving inadequate.

In both countries the administration eventually caught up and even overtook the settlers on the frontier. The administration asserted its monopoly to dispense justice and laid down conditions of employment. In neither country has anything substantial remained of indigenous political organization, either traditional or modern, despite the persistence of major cultural distinctions. In both countries the native population is dependent on the White economy principally as labourers, in Australia as casual unskilled labourers, in South Africa on a more permanent basis. Sovereignty has passed to the White government.

PRIMITIVE STATES

Where indigenous people live in a well-ordered state with powerful centralized authority, it is economical for the conqueror to govern through the native ruler. It is a mistake to imagine that this technique was created by Lugard in the 1900s, even if he invented the name Indirect Rule. The technique goes back to the Romans, if not earlier. The principles of the technique are clearly expressed in a memorandum written by Captain Thruston, a British colonial administrator in Uganda in 1897. He says:

It has always been the practice of England to govern her distant dominions, as apart from her Colonies, whenever feasible by the system of Protectorates; by which system their administrators are placed under a native Prince who governs by the advice of a native Protector. The advantages are obvious; for the people through force of habit, love for the person, or the prestige of his office, naturally submit to the orders of their Prince. The Prince himself through the instinct of self-preservation if through nothing else, usually willingly obeys the orders of his protector, and those orders are further disguised under the name of advice, and are conveyed in such manner as to as little as possible destroy his prestige or wound his susceptibilities. By this means pressure when it is necessary is brought to bear on one person only, the Prince, and not on the whole population. Even when the Prince withholds his ready cooperation from his protector, the cases of Egypt, of Zanzibar and of Uganda tend to prove that the system can still be employed with a full measure of success. (Cited in Low, 1958, p. 20.)

Most of the studies by social anthropologists of the political effects of conquest relate to primitive states. In describing decentralized societies, whether stateless societies or the political structures of food gatherers, it has been easier to ignore the results of conquest. Furthermore almost all these studies are concerned with the same phase of the process of conquest, that of paternalism (Barnes, 1954; Busia, 1951; Fallers, n.d.; Gluckman, 1940 and 1951; Hunter, 1936; Kuper, 1947; Mair, 1934; Mitchell, 1956; Schapera, 1956). We can state briefly the main features reported in these studies.

It is only with primitive states that a clearly demarcated phase of peaceful external relations is possible, forming a prelude to the introduction of administrative paternalism. There must be an effective indigenous ruler with whom the Western power can make a treaty of non-aggression, protection or trade. Conquest is often achieved when the invaders make an alliance with a legitimate but not dominant faction in the indigenous state; with Western help the faction achieves dominance. An indigenous ruler may be successful in utilizing Western assistance to conquer his neighbours. Resistance to invading pressure often promotes increased centralization of power. Once incorporated into the colonial administrative framework, the indigenous political structure, or rather that portion of it utilized by the conquerors, tends to become ossified. Territorial groups are utilized and non-localized groups ignored. Political units that formerly varied continuously in size and status are frozen or undergo discontinuous changes. New officials, particularly clerks, rise to power. Chiefs who formerly were highly competitive specialist politicians relying on popular support find themselves appointed to relatively secure and non-competitive administrative positions; they depend on the support of the invaders, and tend to lose touch with their people. Whereas in the past the chief legitimately favoured his kinsmen, in the new dispensation to favour a kinsman is nepotism and therefore wrong. If cash cropping develops, chiefs and other aristocrats may be able to utilize their traditional prerogatives to become comparatively much richer than their subjects; if labour migration is the main source of money, chiefs who have to stay at home may find themselves poorer than returned migrants. Dissatisfied subjects cannot flee to another chiefdom as they might have in the past, and it becomes necessary to set up some kind of council or assembly where popular dissatisfaction can find an outlet. Where some traditional assembly is utilized, membership is usually more sharply defined and more restricted than in the past. The new social order lacks the sanctions of the traditional religion, and Christian beliefs are usually not presented in such a way as to support the position of local rulers, new or traditional. The doctrine of the divine right of kings is not for export.

STATELESS SOCIETIES

The characteristics of primitive states under a regime of colonial paternalism are not our main topic. I am more concerned with food-gathering peoples and with stateless societies. However, in several parts of the world colonial administrations have assumed that all the native peoples under their charge were organized in states, and sometimes in states of a specified kind. In any colonial territory administered as a unit it is convenient to have a uniform system of native administration which can be applied by field officers wherever they are stationed and which can easily be adapted to territory-wide action. An indigenous model, if it appeals to the Administration, may be used even in areas where the indigenous political system is of quite another kind. Thus in Uganda where the British were impressed with the efficiency of the Ganda state system, Ganda models were used for the administration of other parts of the Protectorate. In some of these areas, the former political system had indeed been largely similar to that of the Ganda, but in other parts there had been stateless societies of various kinds. To make the conversion more thorough, the British appointed Ganda notables as paramount chiefs of these non-Ganda areas.

Another stateless society that has been treated as a state is the Plateau Tonga, an egalitarian matrilineal stateless people of Northern Rhodesia (Colson, 1948). Their territory was bisected by a railway line built a few years after they had been brought under British control at the beginning of the twentieth century. Land on either side of the railway line was alienated to White settlers who began to raise cattle, maize and tobacco, employing labourers from the Tonga and from more distant tribes. In the early stages of contact the British ignored the Tonga, for they were considered to be tributaries of the Barotse empire, with whom the British negotiated a treaty which, *inter alia,* transferred rights in Tonga country to the British in return for protection and payments to the Lozi. Later, Tonga villages, which had been and still are fairly fluid residential units, were made the basis of administration. Villages were grouped into small districts and a leader appointed to each district. Colson considers that the district leader was probably the indigenous ritual leader. In 1918 chiefs were appointed over larger areas. Some of the men selected as chiefs were ritual leaders or their descendants, others were rainmakers or leaders of rain shrine cults. A genuine effort seems to have been made to appoint those who had a traditional claim to chiefly office, for it does not seem to have been realized that indigenously there were no chiefs. Those appointed to office were succeeded by their heirs, for it was assumed that the position had been, or ought to be, hereditary. In this way small groups of matrilineal kin obtained a monopoly of office which had power over the whole chieftaincy. The government has not reached the point of intervening to alter the rules of succession they have themselves introduced and it seems that chiefly matrilineages may emerge in what was 50 years ago an egalitarian society. One chief has been given higher status than the others.

The people pay no particular respect to the chiefs, whom they call government chiefs. One reason for acquiescence in the present state of affairs is that the proximity of the railway line makes it possible for industrious and ambitious individuals to become relatively prosperous.

Native officials in new positions similar to the administratively created chiefs of the Tonga have no traditional models to guide their conduct. More importantly, in most stateless societies there are few institutionalized ways in which the community can exercise a check on their conduct.

Hogbin has shown how difficult it can be for an administrator to realize that one of his native subordinates is exceeding his powers, and how hard it may be to take effective action even when the administrator does realize what is happening. Indeed, in a stateless society, it may be almost impossible for a man appointed as headman or chief to carry out his duties efficiently in the eyes of the administration without at the same time exceeding his powers. He has the force of the administration behind him, but he has to assert his authority over his people and demonstrate to them that he must be obeyed; they do not automatically do what he says. His own definition of his role is unlikely to coincide exactly with the definition intended by the administration, and there is no traditional model for him to follow. Hence he is likely to do either too little, and be acceptable to the people but inefficient in the eyes of the administration; or too much and become a tyrant. Since his status is unprecedented, there are usually no traditional mechanisms for limiting his power. Since he is the nominee of the administration, he is bound to get its support, and often there is no effective way by which the common people can bypass the local autocrat and complain directly to the administrator.

Those appointed to recognized posts may have some traditional claim to office, even if it is to office lacking secular authority, as with the rain shrine priests who have become chiefs among the Plateau Tonga. Sometimes they lack any traditional legitimacy at all.

Hogbin has reported how in Malaita, where traditionally the leaders of district groups were men who owed their position not to descent but to their own success in organizing feasts, the Administration appointed Headmen who seem not to have been traditional, but were men who had had some experience of the constabulary run by the Administration. Maekali, one of Hogbin's main informants, had served in the Malaita constabulary for twelve years before being appointed Headman of a territorial division. In 1940 the Administration introduced a scheme of Native Councils and Native Courts. The councillors selected were in fact in many cases the traditional district group leaders but the Headman remained as President of the Native Court, and he acted as chairman of the Council (Hogbin, 1939, p. 143; 1944, p. 262).

Whatever the traditional form of political organization, the local representative of the colonial administration has to employ some members of the indigenous population full time in order to carry on the day-to-day business of administration. They may be employed as policemen, porters, clerks or even as administrative officers. No system of administration seems to be able to operate entirely without this buffer of local employees. It would be impossibly expensive to operate with only expatriate labour, whether or not it was thought to be in the best interests of policy to do so. The group of indigenous public servants, if they be so called, tend to identify themselves with their employers and to adopt in many respects the values and attitudes of the administration. They may be able to exercise a fairly complete control over the activities of their superiors, particularly if the expatriate administrator cannot speak the local vernacular (cf. Mitchell, 1944, pp. 153–4). The indigenous public servants are often able to exercise considerable power even when they are dealing with traditional primitive states. With stateless societies, there are usually fewer checks against the abuse of authority imposed from above, and their position is therefore likely to be even stronger. These same considerations apply to other individuals who gain the support of indigenous members of the public service.

AUSTRALIAN NEW GUINEA

In terms of this analysis, the chief characteristics of modern Australian New Guinea are that the indigenous political systems are very largely stateless, and that with some exceptions the administration is on the frontier, not the settlers or the missions. As in aboriginal Australia the traditional systems do not provide hereditary princes and rulers who might become the channels for implementing the policies of the Administration. The amount of force that can be deployed is much greater than in the conquest of Africa in the nineteenth century, where the colonizers were often operating months away from their bases, threatened by disease, with very vulnerable communications and difficulties of supply which kept their forces small. Hence in Africa for survival and success it was necessary to find local allies. These conditions have not applied so forcefully in New Guinea, despite the very rugged terrain and the insularity and hostility of the inhabitants. If they had, the conquest of New Guinea would be even more difficult than it is, for stateless peoples make poor allies.

Even stateless peoples have leaders; but their authority is usually transient, and may be restricted to one domain of social life. When an hereditary chief becomes the nominee of the Administration, it sometimes becomes an embarrassment to have to accept his son as his successor to the administratively recognized position. Traditional leadership, particularly if it is largely ceremonial, may be too determinate for the purposes of the Administration. On the other hand, in a stateless society, the problem may be how to give permanence to a leader who may have achieved his outstanding position in a traditionally acceptable manner but who is likely to be challenged in a few years' time. If, as in much of New Guinea, a leader owes his popular support to his success in giving feasts or in arranging ceremonial exchanges, how can he continue to enjoy public confidence when he switches his attention to such activities as seeing that pigs are not allowed to wander at will, or that the paths are kept clear, or that ill people are taken to the dispensary for treatment? If there are two conflicting systems of evaluation of his performance, to what extent can he continue to enjoy simultaneously the admiration of the administration and the people? In particular, in those societies where prowess in warfare is one of the most important criteria for positions of leadership, how can the former war leader become the upholder of the *pax australiana* and eschew indigenous warfare?

The answers to these rhetorical questions will no doubt be found as our knowledge of New Guinea is gradually built up by patient observation over the years. However, it is clear that very much more is involved than the loss of sovereignty. We can be sure of radical change in the way in which leaders are produced, and particularly in the way in which they are removed from their privileged positions. Unfortunately experience in Africa, in situations that are in some respects similar, is not very helpful in forecasting for New Guinea. In most territories in Africa, at least in British Africa, some indigenous societies were primitive states. The Administration assumed that it could rule through chiefs. Frequently there were chiefs, sometimes many more than the Administration could easily use. A uniform system of native administration was established within each territory, even though there were very considerable differences between one territory and another. Stateless societies were assumed to have chiefs, and gradually, under administrative pressure, did acquire them. The general administrative aim in Africa, at least until 1939, seemed to be to establish constitutional monarchies, even if the monarchies were sometimes matrilineal. The constitutional limitations were partly enforced by the conditions imposed on the chiefs by the Administration in return for its support, and partly arose from the weakness of their traditional claim to power. Conditions in New Guinea are different. On the one hand there are virtually no powerful hereditary chiefs; on the other the Australian Administration neither assumes that there are chiefs waiting to be discovered, nor intends to create chiefs where there are none. Indeed, it would be particularly interesting if, by some rather unlikely chance, in the areas yet to be brought under effective administration, there should be a fully-fledged primitive state, complete with permanent leadership, and an indigenous judicial system. A society of this kind would scarcely fit readily either into the existing pattern of government-appointed headmen (*luluais* and *tultuls*), or into the newer scheme of local councils.

But if not chiefs, then what? The distributed authority characteristic of statelessness is incompatible with the hierarchical administrative and judicial system which asserts a monopoly of executive and adjudicative power. Because of their lack of indigenous tribunals and hereditary leaders, the inhabitants of New Guinea are perhaps being brought into the new social order faster than if they had had traditional rulers through whom the policies of the Australian Administration might have been implemented. It seems clear that those who are recognized as leaders by the Administration act in many ways as if they were chiefs. They dispense patronage and justice and act as the initiators of many forms of social and ceremonial activity. But it is not clear to what extent they depend on maintaining a monopoly of access to the local administrator, or on fulfilling their obligations to the people for whom they have been made responsible. At the one extreme is Bumbu, sometimes paramount *luluai* in Busama, New Guinea, whose knavish exploits have been described by Hogbin (1946, 1949 and 1951, pp. 150–163). Bumbu forced villagers to work in his gardens, seduced unmarried girls, thrashed Christians who met for prayer and finally, by organizing a continuous series of dances, endeavoured to prevent his villagers from growing food at all. At the other extreme, to take an African example, we can cite the so-called Warrant Chiefs of the Gold Coast. Here, in the 1920s and 1930s, indigenous rulers who had been appointed or recognized by the British administration and who then lost the confidence of their subjects were frequently dismissed (Busia, 1951, pp. 105–109). To steer a course between these two extremes cannot be easy unless chiefs and others in positions of power are clear to whom they can look for support.

INDUSTRIAL INTEGRATION

In a fully integrated society, the traditional form of indigenous political organization ceases to be relevant. Groups of people can continue to manage their own affairs only so long as their affairs are mainly their own. Once a people begin to participate effectively in the economic and social life of a wider community, they cannot be kept out of its political life. Even if the indigenous population remains a sharply demarcated unit in the social structure, as for example with the Bantu people in South Africa, political activity by indigenous people still begins to form part of the political life of the nation. If power is concentrated at the centre, political activity must be aimed, directly or at several removes, at achieving control at the centre. Whether or not there is any continuity in leadership from the old to the new regimes is largely a matter of chance. It has been argued that stateless peoples can in fact adapt to major political changes of this kind more easily than those who have belonged to primitive states; new leaders, trade union presidents, bishops, priests and congress chairmen, can emerge without exciting opposition from the older hierarchy of paramount chiefs, clan leaders, and the like. However, aristocrats of the old regime do sometimes achieve positions of leadership in the new order, as for example the Hawaiian prince who was one of the first delegates from the Territory of Hawaii to the United States House of Representatives; he went as a Republican.

Where incorporation takes place without assimilation, as for example in South Africa, or with the Jews in the ghettoes of mediaeval Europe, some limited autonomy is possible and the cultural traditions of the enclave are one factor in determining the form that the internal organization takes. But even in this limited sense, indigenous political institutions depend on recognition by the wider society. Furthermore, in external affairs, the group and its leaders have to contend within the larger political system.

POLITICS AND ADMINISTRATION

In this paper I have tried to outline what seem to me to be some of the principal features of the process of conquest as affecting indigenous political systems of different types. I have incidentally endeavoured to fit aboriginal Australia and present day New Guinea into the scheme of analysis. The examples I have used have been selected casually, but I hope that they may suggest parallels and divergencies in other areas.

One important distinction to make, in discussing forms of political structure, is that between administration and politics. M. G. Smith makes the distinction between what he regards as two aspects of the wider category of government. He defines action as political when it seeks to influence the decision of policy.

Policy decisions define a programme of action, implicitly or otherwise. The execution and organization of this programme is an administrative process. (Smith, 1956, p. 48.)

Administrative action consists, according to Smith's usage, "in the authorized processes of organization and management of the affairs of a given unit." Whereas politics is a struggle for power, administrative action is "defined by authority, and is inherently hierarchic" (Smith, 1956, p. 49).

In a modern state we make a sharp distinction between professional politicians and administrators, and we do not expect, and do not find, the same qualities in the two categories. In the same way we make a distinction between political activity and administrative activity. Under almost any scheme of colonial administration, the recognized chiefs, headmen, and councillors, are intended to be mainly, if not wholly, administrators, like their superiors in the hierarchy. In the traditional society prior to contact, positions of leadership call for the exercise of political rather than administrative skill. In those well developed primitive states with a distinctive administrative and judicial machinery, as for instance in the Nupe and other West African kingdoms, the junior positions were mainly administrative; but even here the chiefs acted, and were expected to act, as political leaders. Official reports contain many instances where a chief or leader has shown that however courageous a warrior and adroit a politician he may have been he makes an ineffective subordinate administrator. But the difficulty of adapting a political élite to administrative tasks is not fundamentally a personal one. The difficulty lies rather in the method of recruitment. If leaders are selected because they are diligent in acquiring esoteric knowledge, as in aboriginal Australia, or because of their outstanding managerial skills, as in the Highlands of New Guinea, it is likely that few of them will be efficient or cooperative administrators.

Furthermore, loss of sovereignty does not remove the need for political leadership. In part the invaders supply, or endeavour to supply, all the leadership that is thought to be necessary. They debate with one another about how the indigenous people should be protected, exploited, or developed. The task of implementing the policies decided upon is left to the administrative hierarchy, from the highest colonial public servant down to the lowest village headman. In a fully integrated society, this division of function might work, but it can scarcely be expected to provide effective leadership when the mass of the people do not participate, even as spectators, in the policy-making process. Hence we have on the one hand the perennial crop of chiefs, headmen and others who become inefficient administrators because they endeavour to play politics; and on the other hand the development of native councils and similar institutions of local government, in which the indigenous people can argue with one another about alternative courses of action or inaction. The effectiveness of these new institutions depends in part on the extent to which they are truly political institutions, concerned with the control of power, and not mere debating societies. A native council that always acquiesces in the policies of the colonial administration cannot be an effective political instrument. One of the main practical problems facing any plural society composed of conquerors and conquered is to adjust to the unequal distribution of power and sovereignty. It has to ensure that despite the divergences of culture that divide its people the struggle for power can be carried on in political institutions that are effective and which enjoy the support of all sections of the community. The penalty for failure is more "one-sided" wars.

REFERENCES

Barnes, J. A., *Politics in a Changing Society* (Capetown, Oxford University Press, 1954); "Race Relations in the Development of Southern Africa," in Lind, A. W., ed., *Race Relations in World Perspective* (Honolulu, Hawaii University Press, 1955).

Busia, K. A., *The Position of the Chief in the Modern Political System of Ashanti* (London, Oxford University Press, 1951).

Collier, J., *The Indians of the Americas* (New York, Norton, 1947).

Colson, E., "Modern political organization of the Plateau Tonga," *African Studies*, vol. VII (1948), pp. 85–98.

Elkin, A. P., "Reaction and interaction: a food gathering people and European settlement in Australia," *American Anthropologist*, vol. 53 (1951), pp. 164–186.

Fallers, L. A., *Bantu Bureaucracy* (Cambridge, Heffer, n.d.).

Fortes, M., and Evans-Pritchard, E. E., eds., *African Political Systems* (London, Oxford University Press, 1940).

Gann, L. H., *The Birth of a Plural Society* (Manchester, Manchester University Press, 1958).

Gluckman, M., "The Kingdom of the Zulu in South Africa," in Fortes, M., and Evans-Pritchard, E. E., eds., *African Political Systems* (London, Oxford University Press, 1940); "The Lozi of Barotseland," in Colson, E., and Gluckman, M., eds., *Seven Tribes of British Central Africa* (London, Oxford University Press, 1951).

Hanna, A. J., *The Beginnings of Nyasaland and North-eastern Rhodesia* (Oxford, Clarendon Press, 1956).

Hogbin, H. I., *Experiments in Civilization* (London, Routledge, 1939); "Native councils and native courts in the Solomon Islands," *Oceania*, vol. XIV (1944), pp. 257–283; "Local government for New Guinea," *Oceania*, vol. XVII (1946), pp. 38–65; "Government chiefs in New Guinea," in Fortes, M., ed., *Social Structure* (Oxford, Clarendon Press, 1949); *Transformation Scene* (London, Routledge and Kegan Paul, 1951).

Holmberg, A. R., "Nomads of the long bow," *Smithsonian Institution, Institute of Social Anthropology, Publication no. 10* (1950).

Hunter, M., *Reaction to Conquest* (London, Oxford University Press, 1936).

Kuper, H., *The Uniform of Colour* (Johannesburg, Witwatersrand University Press, 1947).

Low, D. A., The anatomy of administrative origins: Uganda 1890–1902. (Conference paper, East African Institute of Social Research, Makerere College, January 1958.) [Cited by kind permission of the author.]

Mair, L. P., *An African People in the Twentieth Century* (London, Routledge, 1934).

Mitchell, J. C., "The political organization of the Yao of southern Nyasaland," *African Studies*, vol. VIII (1949), pp. 141–159; *The Yao Village* (Manchester, Manchester University Press, 1956).

Okada, Y., "Race relations in Formosa under the Japanese," in Lind, A. W., ed., *Race Relations in World Perspective* (Honolulu, Hawaii University Press, 1955).

Perham, M., *Lugard: the Years of Adventure, 1858–1898* (London, Collins, 1956).

Schapera, I., *Government and Politics in Tribal Societies* (London, Watts, 1956).

Smith, M. G., "On segmentary lineage systems," *Journal of the Royal Anthropological Institute*, vol. 86 (1956), pp. 39–80.

Turney-High, H. H., *Primitive War: Its Practice and Concepts* (Columbia, University of South Carolina Press, 1949).

L. Fallers

THE PREDICAMENT
OF THE MODERN AFRICAN CHIEF:
AN INSTANCE FROM UGANDA (1955)

The role of the modern African chief poses difficult problems of analysis because it is a role which is played out in a matrix of diverse and often conflicting institutions. Perhaps it would be better to say that the chief occupies many roles. On the one hand, he has a series of roles in the indigenous institutions of African society. On the other hand, he occupies roles in the imported institutions of colonial government. Of course, in various parts of Africa institutions of African and European origin have met under widely varying circumstances and have interpenetrated in varying degrees, but nearly everywhere the effect is confusing and bizarre. In Uganda, for example, if we were to visit a chief we might find him attending a committee meeting, helping to work out a budget for the coming fiscal year. If we ask for an appointment, we will be received in a modern office equipped with typewriters, telephones, filing cases, and the other apparatus of modern bureaucracy. If by chance we had called on another day, our chief would have been unavailable. He would have been meeting with his clan mates in the thatched hut of his paternal uncle, and the talk would have been of genealogical refinements and the wishes of the ancestors. If we are invited to have tea at the chief's house in the evening, we will be introduced to his several wives, and this may surprise us because we have heard that he is a pillar of the local Anglican parish and a patron of the Boy Scout troop. I have chosen a rather extreme, though not unreal, example. Reading the literature on the various areas of modern Africa, one is impressed by the patchwork character of the chief's social milieu. It appears to be a collection of bits and pieces

SOURCE. L. Fallers, "The Predicament of the Modern African Chief," reprinted from *American Anthropologist*, 57, 2, 1955, pp. 290–305.

taken at random from widely different social systems. Modern African society as a whole frequently gives this impression, but in the case of the chief the effect is heightened because his role is so often the meeting point, the point of articulation, between the various elements of the patchwork.

It is perhaps because of this confusing diversity of elements in the chief's social world that relatively few attempts to analyze his role in systematic terms are to be found in the social science literature on Africa. There are, of course, important exceptions, notably the papers by Gluckman and his colleagues of the Rhodes-Livingstone Institute on the village headman in British Central Africa (Barnes 1948; Gluckman, Mitchell and Barnes 1949; Mitchell 1949) and Busia's recent (1951) book on the chief in present-day Ashanti. Probably there are others. Generally, however, such published material as is available is of two sorts. First there is the large and growing body of official and semi-official literature dealing mainly with what might be called the ideal structure of African politics as conceived by colonial governments. Notable here are Lord Hailey's (1950, 1953) five volumes on the British dependencies and much of the content of the *Journal of African Administration*. This is the literature of what is called in British territories "Native Administration," and it is concerned with those institutions which are the result of explicit planning on the part of the administering power. Sometimes these institutions embody many elements of indigenous institutions; sometimes they are wholly, or almost wholly, new. Everywhere they represent attempts by colonial governments to erect intervening institutions, manned by Africans, between themselves and African peoples. Familiarity with this literature on native administration is of course essential to the student of African politics, but by its very nature it seldom reaches deep levels of subtlety in the analysis of political process. It is concerned with formal arrangements, with the ways in which power *ought* to flow, and it treats such arrangements in quite general terms, emphasizing that which is common to native administration over wide areas often containing great diversities of indigenous social structure. It seldom concerns itself with the ways in which such indigenous diversities combine with the formal, official institutions to form the real pattern of politics within a tribal or ethnic area.

The second type of material generally available is that gathered by anthropologists in the course of investigations into the traditional structure of African societies. Such studies are most often concerned with the role of the chief in the *traditional* political structure and tend to treat those features of his role which are the result of modern conditions as peripheral to the main focus of study. If the official literature on native administration looks at the chief as he *ought* to be, or as the District Officer hopes he will be tomorrow, the bulk of the anthropological literature looks at him as he was yesterday. There are reasons for this emphasis. Rightly or wrongly, anthropologists have frequently seen their primary task to be the documentation of the full range of variation in human society. They have therefore devoted themselves to the analysis of precisely those features of African society which existed before contact with Europeans. Modern developments are usually mentioned in monographs but most often only as representing the destruction of the integrated social systems which existed before. Judged by the task which they have set themselves—the analysis of indigenous institutions—the work of anthropologists in Africa has been of a high standard indeed, representing perhaps the richest body of monographic literature possessed by anthropology today. However, such studies do not often yield full analyses of the present-day role of the African chief.

The reason why we have so few adequate studies of the modern chief's role may be found, I think, in certain characteristics of the conceptual schemes commonly applied by students of African societies. African studies have been the home par excellence of structural sociological or social anthropological analysis, a tradition founded by Durkheim, elaborated by Radcliffe-Brown, and more recently applied so brilliantly to empirical research by Fortes and Evans-Pritchard. The virtues of this frame of reference are obvious and familiar to anyone acquainted with the real classics of social science which have been its fruits. Its primary concern is to analyze the ways in which institutions dovetail with one another to form an integrated whole—the ways in which, to put it another way, the institutional demands made upon individuals are harmonized so that the demands of institution X do not run counter to the demands of institution Y, but rather complement and support them. As a result of such studies we now have, for example, excellent detailed analyses of the relationships between political and religious institutions among the Nuer (Evans-Pritchard 1940, 1951, 1953) and the Tallensi (Fortes 1945, 1949).

The difficulty which arises when this point of view is applied to the present-day role of the African chief or, indeed, to many other features of modern African society, is that much of what we observe appears, as I have said before, to be a patchwork of diverse and conflicting elements. Institutions are constantly getting in each others' way, and individuals are constantly being institutionally required to do conflicting things. If our point of departure is a conception of the integrated social system, we can say of such situations only that "society has undergone disorganization" or that "cultures have clashed." We can say relatively little, I think, about why the particular kinds of disorder which we observe occur. Increasingly, however, we want knowledge of precisely this kind.

One key to the escape from this dilemma lies, I think, in a recognition that the notion of "social order" or "social system" can have two referents, both of which are quite valid, but which must be distinguished. One consists in order or system in the sense of harmonious integration, the notion which I think structural social anthropology has stressed. Order in this sense exists to the degree that institutions making up a social system mutually reinforce and support one another. The other referent is order in the sense that the phenomena observed may be subjected to systematic analysis leading to greater understanding by the analyst of the connections between events, whether these events relate to harmony or to discord. This meaning corresponds, I think, to the natural scientist's notion of "order in nature," leaving aside the philosophical question of whether the order really exists in nature or only in the scientist's head. In this latter sense, a society which contains major elements of disharmony or conflict may be studied just as fruitfully as one characterized by a high degree of internal integration. It would perhaps be better to say that the *disharmonious elements* of a society may be studied just as fruitfully as the harmonious ones, since presumably no society is ever either completely integrated or completely at odds with itself.

If I am right in thinking that there are these two possible conceptions of order or system in social life, then it follows that the second conception, that of social life as subject to systematic analysis without regard to its harmonious or disharmonious character, is the more fundamental. It is in the nature of a first assumption which we must make if we are to study the disharmonious elements in societies. The first conception then, that of order in the sense of harmony, finds its place in our frame of reference at the next stage and it defines a range of variation. The elements making up a social system will be harmonious or disharmonious in varying degrees and ways, and we will require concepts for talking about these various degrees and types of disharmony.

On the most general level, concepts of this kind are not hard to find. Delineating the elements involved in the *integrated* or *harmoniously functioning* social system has been one of the major preoccupations of social scientists, and lists of such elements may be found in almost any text or theoretical volume. All that is required in order to utilize such a list in the study of relative harmony-disharmony is to treat each of the characteristics of the integrated social system as subject to variation. Perhaps the most generally agreed-upon characteristic of the integrated social system is the sharing of a common system of values by its members. If the actions of the individuals who are members of the system are to be mutually supporting, these actions must be founded upon common conceptions of what is right and proper. Actions which are in accord with the common norm will be rewarded, and those which run counter to it will be punished. Sometimes it is useful to distinguish "means" from "ends" within the general field of common values. Or one may find it useful to distinguish between situations in which value integration requires actual sharing of common values and those in which it requires merely that values held by groups within the system be compatible. Further distinctions under this general rubric might be drawn, but it is clear that integration among the values held by its members is one of the characteristics of the harmoniously functioning social system. It is also clear, however, that in actual social systems the degree to which value systems are integrated is subject to wide variation.

A second general characteristic of the integrated social system is a sharing of belief or a common system of cognition and communication. Persons must share not only a common system of means and ends but also a common system of symbols enabling them to interpret each other's behavior, as well as other events, in a common way. For traffic to flow smoothly on a crowded street, drivers must not only share the common value of obeying the law, but must also interpret red lights and green lights in the same way. Again, however, the sharing of symbols is by no means always complete, and we may expect to find social systems in which malcommunication is a common occurrence.

Again, the integrated social system is one in which the motivations of its component individuals are to a high degree complementary with the shared systems of value and belief. Actually, this is merely the other side of the social coin. To the degree that values and beliefs are actually shared, persons will "want" to do the "right thing" and will believe the "correct thing" and will be responsive to rewards and punishments which nudge them in this direction. The common values and beliefs of the social system will be built into the personalities of its members so that they will be adequately motivated to do the things others expect them to do. Where the system of value and belief is held in common and its parts harmoniously integrated, persons will not be expected to do incompatible things. All this, however, is also clearly subject to wide variability in concrete social systems. Individuals may be insufficiently motivated to socially valued behavior, or they may have placed upon them conflicting social demands.

I have been at some pains to spell out a point which may seem obvious to some and irrelevant to others because I believe it has a direct bearing upon the prospects for fruitful research into the role of the chief in modern Africa. In many areas the chief lives in a disordered and conflict-ridden social world, and it is important, if we are to reach some understanding of this chief's position, that we be able to talk about this conflict and disorder, if I may so put it, in an ordered way. In many regions of Africa today, and indeed in many other colonial and semi-colonial areas, the situation is not simply one of two radically different social systems colliding head on and, as it were, holding each other at bay.

Though in some areas something approaching this situation may exist, it is not generally so. More commonly, African and European social systems have interpenetrated with the result that new social systems embodying diverse and conflicting elements have come into being. We must therefore be prepared to analyze systematically situations in which incompatible values and beliefs are widely held by members of the same social system, where individuals are regularly motivated to behavior which in the eyes of others is deviant and where other individuals have conflicting motivations corresponding with discontinuities among the values of the social system. We must be able to think analytically about these elements of relative disharmony and to determine their consequences for the functioning of such systems as wholes.

Something of what I have in mind may be illustrated by the situation of the chief today in the Busoga District of Uganda, where I have been engaged in field research under the auspices of the East African Institute of Social Research and of the Fulbright Program. Conditions in Busoga, and, indeed, in Uganda as a whole, have provided perhaps the optimum situation for the harmonious mutual adjustment of African and European social systems. The absence of extensive European settlement has meant that there has been little or no competition for land. The successful importation and cultivation on small peasant holdings of cotton, coffee, and groundnuts have provided a cash crop economy upon which a rising standard of living could be built without detriment to food crop cultivation. Administrative policy has stressed the recognition and gradual re-molding of indigenous political institutions without sharp breaks with the past. In this situation, European and African institutions have, indeed, merged to a striking degree, but the result remains a social system containing major elements of disharmony and conflict. In large measure, the role of the chief is the focus of this conflict.

Busoga was "discovered" by Europeans in 1862 and came under British administration in 1892; the temporal base line for the analysis of change in the Soga political system therefore lies in the latter part of the nineteenth century. At this time, Busoga was not a political entity. It did have sufficient linguistic and general cultural unity to mark it off from the other Bantu-speaking areas of southern Uganda so that in 1862 John Hanning Speke, the first European explorer of the area, was told that "Usoga" comprised the area bounded by Lake Victoria, Lake Kyoga, the Nile, and the Mpologoma River. These are the boundaries of the present-day Busoga District. (See map.) The inhabitants of the area, the Basoga, appear to have numbered some half-million. They were sedentary subsistence cultivators and livestock breeders, relying for staple foods mainly upon their permanent plantain gardens and plots of millet, sweet potatoes, and maize. The country is described by early travelers as being extremely fertile and closely settled, particularly in the south along the Lake Victoria shore.

Politically, Busoga was divided among some fifteen small kingdom-states, which varied widely in size but which shared a fundamental similarity in structure. The elements of this common political structure may be seen in three key institutions: *patrilineal kinship, rulership,* and *clientship.*

In its fundamentals, Soga kinship followed a pattern common in East Africa. Descent was traced in the patrilineal line, and kinsmen sharing common patrilineal descent formed corporate groups which were important units in the social structure. Kinship terminology was of the Omaha type. The most important unit formed on the basis of patrilineal kinship was the lineage, comprising all those persons within a local area who were able to trace the patrilineal genealogical relationships among themselves. This lineage group was important in landholding, through the rights which it exercised over inheritance and succession by its members. An individual was free to choose his heir from among his sons, but his testament was subject to confirmation or revision by the council of his lineage-mates, which met at his funeral. The lineage played a prominent role also in marriage. Most young men were unable to meet from their own resources the marriage-payment demanded by the bride's kinsmen and so had to depend for aid upon their lineage-mates. Such dependency gave the lineage at least a potential influence over its members' choice of marriage partner and an interest in the stability of marriage. Finally, the importance of the lineage in temporal affairs was matched and complemented by its role in relation to the supernatural. The most prominent feature of Soga religion was the ancestor cult, founded upon the belief that patrilineal ancestors maintained an interest in and influence over the well-being and good behavior of their living descendants. Common descent thus involved a common sacred interest in the ancestors, and this in turn, through the ancestor's graves, which were the focus of the cult, reinforced the lineage members' corporate economic and legal interest in the land.

Units other than the lineage were also formed upon the basis of patrilineal kinship. The individual homestead was located in space by the practice of patrilocal residence, and where extended family homesteads were formed, these took the form of a small lineage group composed of a man and his sons together with their wives and children. Beyond the lineage, groups of lineages which were known to be related patrilineally but which were unable to trace the precise genealogical links among themselves formed clans which were unified by a common clan name, common totemic avoidances, and the rule of exogamy. Patrilineal kinship thus defined a large sector of the individual's life; it controlled inheritance and succession, structured marriage, gave form to religion, and strongly influenced the spatial distribution of homesteads.

Soga society was not, however, a segmentary society in which unilineal kinship constituted the only principle of organization. Through the institution of rulership, members of many patrilineal groups were bound together to form kingdom-states in which membership was defined, not in terms of kinship, but in terms of territorial boundaries and common allegiance to the ruler. In each of the kingdom-states there was a royal clan or lineage (in the case of the royal group, clan and lineage tended to be coterminous because royal genealogies were better remembered), which was set above commoner groups as having higher rank and an inborn fitness to rule. The ruler's position was hereditary within the royal clan. He was the active head of the kingdom and the overlord of all other holders of authority. He was also the chief priest for, as the ancestors of commoner lineages were thought to both assist and control the behavior of their descendants, so the royal ancestors were in a sense *national* ancestors who took a similar interest in the affairs of the nation as a whole. The ruler, being their descendant, was supported and controlled by them in his conduct of national affairs and was the intermediary through whom they might be approached on behalf of the nation. Inherited regalia and a courtly style of living centering around an impressively constructed capital symbolized and enhanced the ruler's political power.

To complete this outline of traditional Soga political structure requires the addition of the third of the institutions noted above—that of clientship. The administrative staff through which the ruler in each of the kingdoms governed was recruited neither through patrilineal kinship in commoner lineages nor through membership in the royal group. The ruler's leading lieutenants—the prime minister and the chiefs of territorial divisions—were commoners bound to the ruler by personal loyalty. Often they were chosen from the many servant boys, sons of ordinary peasants, who were sent to serve in the palace and to seek social advancement. This mode of recruitment to positions of subordinate power was a partial solution to a problem which apparently afflicted most Bantu kingdoms in the Great Lakes region. All members of the royal group shared in some measure the inborn fitness to rule, but within the royal group there was no clear-cut rule of seniority. Throughout the kingdom there were princes —junior members of the royal group—in control of villages or groups of villages, and these persons were a potential threat to the paramount authority of the ruler. When the problem of succession arose, any member of the royal group who could command a measure of support might assert a claim to rulership and fighting not uncommonly broke out. The institution of clientship, through which commoners of administrative and military ability were raised by the ruler to positions of authority and thus were bound to him as personal followers, provided an administrative staff which could be trusted with power. Not sharing the inherited rank of the princes, they were not potential usurpers. At times of succession, the major clients under the previous ruler participated along with members of the royal clan in choosing a new ruler and thus exercised a disinterested and stabilizing influence upon the ambitious princes. They also acted as a check upon the ruler's power, since if he failed to govern within the limits set by custom they might combine in support of a rival prince and drive him from his position.

Traditional Soga society thus took the form of a hierarchy. At the top was the hereditary ruler—the paramount holder of authority and the central symbol of the kingdom's unity. At intermediate levels were the princes administering villages or clusters of villages and, counterbalancing them, the ruler's administrative staff of client-chiefs administering other villages or village clusters in the name of the ruler. Forming the broad base of the society were the communities of commoner agriculturalists organized into corporate patrilineal groups. Commoner and royal, kinsman and kinsman, patron and client, were bound together by highly personal rights and obligations. Subordinates owed superiors economic support through the payment of tribute, military support in war, the recognition of judicial and administrative authority, and personal loyalty. Subordinates in turn received paternalistic protection and aid.

The sixty years which have passed since the establishment of the British Protectorate in Uganda have seen the radical reconstruction of this political system, to a great extent as a consequence of explicit planning by the administration. Innovations were introduced gradually, however, and under circumstances which contributed greatly to the willingness of the Basoga to accept them. During the early years, little was changed in the formal structure of Soga political institutions, though their day-to-day functioning was substantially altered. Initially, the aims of the administration were limited to the establishment of "law and order," which meant an end to warfare, and the creation of a system of revenue and trade. In the pursuit of these limited aims, the indigenous political structure was simply taken over intact, given new tasks, and allowed to continue functioning under the supervision of administrative officers. The rulers of the various kingdoms continued to hold hereditary office and to recruit their administrative staffs through personal clientship. The judicial and administrative powers of rulers and chiefs were recognized, and even enhanced, by Protectorate legislation which made them statutory judges and gave them the authority to issue administrative orders having the force of law. They continued to be supported by tribute paid by the commoner population. In recognition of the authority of the colonial government, they were required to collect taxes, to assist in public works, and to submit their judicial decisions to review by administrative officers.

The one major structural innovation was the setting up of a District Council composed of the rulers of the several kingdoms.

Even during this initial period of limited aims, however, important developments were taking place within Soga society. Though the additional functions which were imposed upon the indigenous political structure were minimal, they involved one important change. This was the introduction of literacy. Tax collection involved bookkeeping and administrative supervision over the courts required the keeping of written records of litigation. Every chief or ruler now either had to be literate or required the services of a literate clerk. This development was made possible by, and in turn stimulated, the development of mission education. Soon the sons of important rulers and chiefs, and ultimately the rulers and chiefs themselves, were mission-educated and largely Christian.

The loss of political independence and the innovations which accompanied it were made much more palatable to the rulers and chiefs by the support which they received from the administration and by newly developed sources of wealth. As I have noted above, the position of the ruler or chief in traditional Soga society was not particularly secure. Warfare was more or less endemic and the threat of revolt served as a constant check upon the ruler's exercise of power. Now, not only were the traditional authorities backed by the superior power of the British administration, but they were also able to enhance their economic position. Cotton was introduced at about the time of the first World War and it soon spread rapidly as a peasant cash crop. Tribute could now be collected in cash or in labor upon the rulers' and chiefs' cotton plots. Within a few years there developed a new chiefly style of life, which included imported consumption items such as European-style clothing and houses, automobiles, and, incidentally, mission education, which required the payment of fees.

This early period thus saw the development of a new kind of elite position for the traditional political authorities in Soga society. With greater power and an enhanced wealth differential, they now stood above the common people in ways which had not been possible for them in pre-administration times. This situation was very rewarding to them. It goes far to explain, I think, why they were so very ready to accept the supervision of administrative officers and why, later on, they were willing to accept much more profound innovations in the political structure. They had in large measure committed themselves to the new conditions.

The initial period, characterized by limited administrative aims and by the building up of the traditional authorities, came to an end in the nineteen-twenties and -thirties. The new policy of the administration came to be one of remolding the traditional political system in the direction of European-style civil service bureaucracy and electoral democracy. In a series of stages between 1926 and 1936, tribute was abolished and the chiefs and rulers began to be paid fixed salaries from a native administration treasury. The loss of tribute was painful to the chiefs and rulers, not only because it meant a reduction in monetary income, but also because tribute was in itself an important symbol of their power and prestige. Nevertheless, in part for the reasons I have mentioned, the change was accepted. A further fundamental change was introduced which concerned the basis of recruitment to office. Over a period of years, the administration came to insist more and more upon the recruitment of chiefs upon the basis of objective competence, and during the nineteen-forties it became established that not only chiefs but also the rulers themselves, who had previously been hereditary, would be chosen upon this basis.

Since, at first, rulers' and chiefs' sons tended to monopolize the mission schools, "recruitment on the basis of competence" meant, essentially, recruitment of the most competent from this group. With more widespread education, the group from which chiefs were recruited became wider. Again, no serious opposition was encountered. What had previously been a hierarchy of hereditary rulers, princes, and client-chiefs thus became in a strict sense a hierarchy of civil service bureaucrats, recruited upon the basis of competence, increasingly as indicated by formal education; paid fixed salaries out of revenue from general taxation; subject to bureaucratic transfer and promotion; and pensioned upon retirement.

Within recent years, this bureaucracy has tended to proliferate, as the Uganda Government has pushed forward its policy of devolving more and more responsibility upon the native administration, now known as the African Local Government. The hierarchy of civil servant chiefs which replaced the traditional hierarchy of rulers and client-chiefs has been supplemented by specialist officials concerned with taking over from Protectorate Government departments responsibility for matters such as finance, public works, agriculture and forestry, public health, and law enforcement. Concerned that this bureaucracy not become an irresponsible monolith, the Government has also encouraged the growth of elected councils, leading up to a District Council which is responsible for advising the bureaucracy, framing legislation, and preparing an annual budget. The strength of this trend toward devolution of responsibility upon the African Local Government may be seen in the fact that the share of direct taxation allocated to the African Local Government treasury is now four times that collected for the Protectorate Government. In 1952, the African Local Government Budget called for the receipt and expenditure of more than a quarter of a million pounds.

During the period of British administration, Soga political structure has been radically altered by the introduction of new institutional forms, which have achieved widespread acceptance by the Basoga. The new civil servant chiefs are granted great respect and are popularly regarded as legitimate heirs to the former authority of the traditional rulers and client-chiefs. Appointment to the civil service is regarded as a highly desirable goal for the ambitious young man. The acceptance of new institutions does not mean, however, that a harmoniously integrated social system has resulted: In many cases traditional institutions which are in large measure incompatible with the new ones have survived. The result is a social system which shows major deviations from harmonious integration in its value system, in its system of communication and belief, and in the social personalities of its members.

Traditional Soga political institutions emphasized the value of particular personal rights and obligations, a pattern which Parsons (1951) has described by the terms *particularism* and *functional diffuseness*. Relations were particularistic in that they emphasized personal loyalty between individuals who stood in particular status relations with one another, for example, as kinsman to kinsman, patron to client, or royal to commoner. One owed particular loyalty to *one's own* kinsman, to *one's own* patron or client, or to one's ruler *as a person*. Relations were functionally diffuse in that they involved a wide segment of the lives of the persons involved. Kinsmen, for example, were expected to stand together as total persons and to take a legitimate interest in the most intimate aspects of each other's lives. A patron was similarly related to his client, as is indicated by the difficulty of distinguishing a political subordinate from a personal servant and by the common practice of linking client to patron through affinal ties. The basic virtue was personal loyalty between particular individuals.

The value system associated with bureaucratic organization is in most respects in opposition to this pattern. Here the guiding norm is, as Max Weber has expressed it, ". . . straightforward duty without regard to personal considerations. . . . Everyone in the same empirical situation is subject to equality of treatment" (1947:340). Relations in such a system are to be, in Parsons' terms, *universalistic and functionally specific*—universalistic in that universally applicable rules, and not particular statuses, are to be the determinants of conduct, and functionally specific in that they relate to specific contexts and not to the whole of individuals' lives. As a civil servant, one ought to treat everyone alike without regard to particular status considerations. One applies general rules and procedures. One's competence is severely limited to what are called "official matters" and one is enjoined not to become involved in, nor even to know about, the personal lives of those with whom one has relations *as a civil servant*. This norm of disinterested service is of course the constant goal of all Western political systems, and it was the aim which led the British administration to introduce the civil service system into Busoga.

In Busoga, these two value systems today exist side by side, and both are represented in major institutions. The patrilineal kinship system is very much a going concern, in large part because its stronghold, the traditional system of landholding, has remained intact. Corporate lineage groups continue to exercise jurisdiction over inheritance and succession and this keeps the ties of kinship alive and strong. The strength of kinship ties is, however, a constant threat to the civil service norm of disinterestedness. The wide extension of kinship bonds means that a chief is frequently put into the position of having to choose between his obligation to favor particular kinsmen and his official duty to act disinterestedly. He may, for example, be asked to favor a kinsman in a legal case or to exempt him from taxation. Again, the institution of clientship survives and leads a *sub rosa* existence within the civil service. Although formally civil servants are chosen for their objective competence, in fact opportunities may arise for building up personal followings of clients. Senior members of the African Local Government, through their influence with the administration, are able to exercise substantial influence over the appointment and promotion of subordinates and are thus able to build up personal political machines. I want to emphasize that *both* these value systems are institutionalized in Soga society and that both are accepted by most Basoga as, in a sense, legitimate.

The system of belief and communication is also a focus of disharmony within the social system. Relatively widespread primary education and exposure to mass communications media have produced a situation in which at least two sets of symbols and two views of the nature of the world are current in the society. Again, as in the system of values, it is not so much that different individuals interpret events differently as that the same individuals are trying to work with two sets of symbols at the same time. A chief may, for example, read a newspaper and have a good working knowledge of world politics, but he may still not be quite certain that Europeans are not cannibals or that witchcraft does not really work. Again, these disharmonies in the system of belief and communication center upon the chief because it is he who is most simultaneously involved in the two systems through his relations with European officers on the one side and with peasants on the other.

Discontinuities in the systems of value and belief are reflected in inconsistencies in the social personalities of persons playing roles in the system. Since both the civil service norm of disinterestedness and the personal ties of kinship and clientship are institutionalized, both are also internalized in the personalities of individuals. It appears to be the case, though it is somewhat difficult to think about, that chiefs and most other Basoga hold both value systems and both systems of belief at the same time. This results in frequent conflict, both between persons and within persons. In social interaction, an individual is likely to uphold the value or belief which seems advantageous to him in a given situation. The kinsman of a chief is likely to expect preferential treatment in court and to bring the pressure of the lineage group to bear upon the chief if such preferential treatment is not granted. The same individual is outraged, however, if someone else does the same thing. Similarly, a chief is likely to exercise "pull" through a highly placed patron, if he can, in order to secure promotion, but complains bitterly about such behavior on the part of others. A chief who is requested to exercise favoritism on behalf of a kinsman or a friend is put into a literally impossible position. Both his internalized values and the sanctions impinging upon him from society pull him in opposite directions. Whichever way he jumps, he will be punished, both by his own remorse at having contravened values which are part of his personality, and by sanctions applied by others.

One of the consequences of these conflicts and discontinuities is a high casualty rate among chiefs. Where conflicting demands pull him in opposite directions, it becomes very difficult for the chief to avoid falling afoul of sanctions. The administration, of course, strongly upholds the civil service norm. If a chief is caught engaging in nepotism or embezzlement, he is dismissed. But he may also be dismissed for upholding the civil service norm. If he offends a prominent superior by refusing to grant particularistic demands, he may find that charges of corruption have been "framed" against him, and he may be dismissed for the very thing which he has refused on principle to do. The poor communication prevailing between the Basoga and the administration and the consequent dependence of the latter upon senior chiefs for information make it unlikely that such fabrications will be exposed.

Thus, from the point of view of the chief acting in his role, the discontinuities in the Soga social system impose severe burdens. It is possible to view these discontinuities also from the standpoint of their consequences for the system as a whole. From this point of view, it would appear that some of the conflicts noted above act to stabilize the system in a period of radical institutional change. I have stressed the point that these conflicts do not consist primarily in discrete groups of persons holding opposed systems of value and belief; they consist rather in the *same persons,* to a great extent throughout the society, holding two incompatible systems of belief and value. They appear *in action* in the form of conflicts between persons. A chief acts in terms of the civil service norm of disinterestedness and he is punished by others who wish him to act in terms of particularistic obligations. The *persons* in such situations, however, are interchangeable; on another occasion, the same chief may act to fulfill particularistic obligations and may have sanctions brought to bear upon him by the same persons who now, however, wish him to act disinterestedly. This *taking into* the social personalities of individuals of conflicts which might otherwise express themselves in conflicts between discrete groups of persons acts, I suggest, to maintain some unity and stability in the system. Very often—perhaps most often—in societies under-going rapid change, the latter situation has developed. The society has divided into intransigently opposed factions or parties with the result that consensus can be re-established only through the defeat, often by violence, of one group by the other. Of course, which of these alternatives one considers "better" depends entirely upon one's value position.

I have described the Soga political system only in outline as an example of the sort of disharmonious situation which I think we must be prepared to study if we are to reach greater understanding of the present-day role of the African chief. The situation is of course much more complex than I have been able to indicate. If there were more time, I should like to say something about what appear to be some of the consequences of the kind of institutional dilemma I have described for the personalities of chiefs. There are indications that for chiefs who do contrive to avoid falling afoul of sanctions, and who remain in office, this success is achieved at considerable psychic cost. The East African Insti-tute of Social Research is currently engaged in a program of research into a number of contemporary East African political systems and we hope, through a combination of institutional and personality analyses, to throw some light upon the reactions of personalities to such situations as well as upon other aspects of political process in these systems.

I should like to add just a word about the situation which I have described in a comparative perspective. This situation, which in its broad outlines is typical, I think, of Uganda as a whole, is probably rather unusual in the broader African picture. In Uganda, there have been few occasions for open conflict between European and African social systems as such. Economic conditions have been beneficent and administrative policy has emphasized gradual and orderly, though steady, change. The result has been a really astonishing degree of African acceptance of things European and a readiness to plunge into radical institutional change. New institutions have been quietly incorporated alongside old ones and conflicts between new and old institutions have been taken into the personalities of individuals who play roles in them. At considerable cost to its component individuals, the social system has come through radical transformation without splitting into opposed factions and without a serious showdown with the European innovators.

Elsewhere in British Africa, two other types of situation appear to be more common. In the classical "indirect rule" territories, such as the Gold Coast and the South African High Commission territories, there was also, as in the early stages in Uganda, a recognition of indigenous political institutions, but it appears that there has been much less emphasis in those territories on remolding such institutions and on devolving new responsibilities upon them. The traditional political systems have been preserved in more nearly their original form so that when new political institutions do develop the traditional ones tend to be bypassed and to remain as centers of conservative opposition. Such a process seems to have occurred in Ashanti where, one gathers, the Youngmen's movement arose as a "progressive" opposition to the "conservative," government-supported chiefs and ultimately contributed substantially to a self-government movement which was even more hostile to traditional political institutions. Another type of situation seems to exist in areas such as the Union of South Africa, parts of Central Africa, and in Kenya, where policy has stressed the rapid adaptation of Africans to the requirements of European settler communities. There again one sees African societies split into conflicting groups: traditional authorities who have had little recognition and who have gradually lost position and influence, government appointees who are often looked upon by others as stooges, and, occasionally, charismatic leaders of radical movements who oppose both the others. Comparisons with French and Belgian Africa should prove illuminating, though I am too little familiar with those territories to attempt such comparisons. One has the impression, however, that the French policy of "assimilation" and the Belgian emphasis upon economic as against political development have produced situations substantially different from those found in British territories (see, for example, Delavignette 1950).

I should like to end with a plea for more empirical studies of contemporary African politics. The great complexity and diversity of political phenomena there provide a fertile field for social scientists of many interests and disciplines.

REFERENCES

Barnes, J. A., 1948. Some aspects of political development among the Fort Jameson Ngoni. *African Studies* VII: 99–109.

Busia, K. A., 1951. The position of the chief in the modern political system of Ashanti. London, Oxford University Press.

Delavignette, R., 1950. Freedom and authority in French West Africa. London, Oxford University Press.

Evans-Pritchard, E. E., 1940. The Nuer. London, Oxford University Press.

1951. Kinship and marriage among the Nuer. London, Oxford University Press.

1953. The Nuer conception of the spirit in its relation to the social order. *American Anthropologist* 55:201–14.

Fortes, M., 1945. The dynamics of clanship among the Tallensi. London, Oxford University Press.

1949. The web of kinship among the Tallensi. London, Oxford University Press.

Gluckman, M., J. C. Mitchell and J. A. Barnes, 1949. The village headman in British Central Africa. *Africa* XIX:89–106.

Hailey, Lord, 1950, 1953. Native administration in the British African territories. London, Her Majesty's Stationery Office.

Mitchell, J. C., 1949. The political organization of the Yao of Southern Nyasaland. *African Studies* VII:141–59.

Parsons, T., 1951. The social system. Glencoe, Ill., Free Press.

Weber, M., 1947. The theory of social and economic organization, ed. trans. T. Parsons. New York, Oxford University Press.

IV

The Creation
of Urban Ethnicity

M. Gluckman

TRIBALISM IN MODERN BRITISH CENTRAL AFRICA[1] (1960)

During the last twenty years, fourteen members of the staff of the Rhodes-Livingstone Institute in Northern Rhodesia have studied both tribes and urban situations in British Central Africa. In this lecture I discuss some of the results of our researches. I am going to concentrate on describing how we see the persistence of tribalism into modern times, in spite of the industrial revolution which has produced such great social changes. Our main argument is that in the rural areas membership of a tribe involves participation in a working political system, and sharing domestic life with kinsfolk; and that this continued participation is based on present economic and social needs, and not merely on conservatism. On the other hand, tribalism in towns is a different phenomenon entirely. It is primarily a means of classifying the multitude of Africans of heterogeneous origin who live together in the towns, and this classification is the basis on which a number of new African groupings, such as burial and mutual help societies, are formed to meet the needs of urban life. In both rural and urban areas, these affiliations to fellow tribesmen have to be analysed as they operate alongside new forms of association, such as Christian sects, political pressure groups, and economic groups. These new groups are clearly more important in the towns than in the rural areas. Persisting loyalty to a tribe therefore operates for a man in two quite distinct situations, and to a large extent he can keep these spheres of activity separate.

The study of whether tribalism is dying out, or persisting and growing in strength, was obscured in early British studies by a fundamental fallacy in sociological analysis. It is easily understood that Government administrators and missionaries should think of an African miner in the new copper mines as being the same man as he who left his tribal home

SOURCE. M. Gluckman, "Tribalism in Modern British Central Africa," reprinted from *Cahiers d'etudes africaines*, I, 1960, pp. 55–70, by permission of M. Gluckman.

a short time before. These men of affairs therefore considered that the African tribesmen who came to the towns were undergoing a process of "detribalisation," in which they were changed; and change here meant being spoilt. Worse than this, in the towns, away from the control of their chiefs, they fell gullibly into the arms of agitators. Most British administrators, and many missionaries, considered that Africans who tried to form trade unions or political associations, and Europeans who tried to help them, were subversive, corrupting the simple and honest tribesmen. I myself found that this attitude had persisted among administrators in Northern Rhodesia as late as 1947. I remember an intelligent Labour Officer, in the Department responsible for the relations between European employers and African labourers, telling me that things would be better if the Northern Rhodesian European Mineworkers Union went out of existence, and the problems of European mineworkers were handled by the Labour Department. As I say, we can understand that many administrators should fail to read the lessons of the last two hundred years of history, which show that modern industrial towns have everywhere produced specific types of associations arising from the needs of urban life, and hence that we must expect these associations inevitably to develop in Africa. It is important to remember that the early British administrators came largely from upper-class and middle-class country backgrounds, and hence knew little about the problems of industrial society. In Africa, they lived and ruled in vast rural domains, and the traditions of a paternalistic government looking after simple tribesmen developed there. Later administrators continued to be drawn from the same groups, with in addition sons of professional people. I met no administrator who was acquainted at firsthand with the problems of industrial life. All newly appointed administrators served their first years on rural stations, and thus were indoctrinated with the Government tradition that towns and mines were almost places of iniquity in an Arcadian tribalism, where the decent natives were exposed to luxurious temptation and seditious developments.

These doctrines were never, of course, explicitly formulated, but they ran like a thread through the approach of administrators to the problems of modern life, until the end of the War, and perhaps the advent of a Labour Government in Britain, brought some change.

It is more surprising to me that British and other anthropologists were to some extent influenced in a similar way, and I am not sure that all have yet escaped from these influences. Our anthropologists, like our administrators, were reared on the rural tradition of the tribes. For them, the tribe was the "zero-point," the start from which people changed as they came under urban and other Western influences: hence the starting-point of analyses was the original tribe and the original tribesman.[2] Correspondingly, when some anthropologists began to study Africans in the towns, they saw the problems to be studied as those arising from the adaptation of a tribesman to urban conditions, and formulated these in terms of a process of "detribalisation," which had to be analysed and measured as the tribesman slowly changed. This view of the problems seems to me to be implicit in the papers of some delegates who attended the conference on African urbanization at Abijan.

I have said that it is surprising that anthropologists should adopt this point of view, because the whole stress of our analyses lies on the difference between persons and the roles they occupy in the social structure. Furthermore, our theories stress the extent to which the social structure exerts pressure which controls the behaviour of the occupants of roles. Hence it has always seemed to me that we must approach the study of African towns dominantly by regarding them as towns: in short, the fact that Africans now live, for longer or shorter periods, in towns, will influence their behaviour far more than the fact that they come from tribal homes and cultures. An African townsman is a townsman, an African miner is a miner: he is only secondarily a tribesman. That is, I would anticipate that as soon as Africans assemble in towns and engage in industrial work they will begin to form social relationships appropriate to their new situation: they will try to combine to better their conditions in trade unions, and so forth. Of course, these Africans continue to be influenced by many factors arising outside the urban situation: the rapid growth of the towns and their own inexperience of towns, the constant movement of African labourers between tribe and town and between towns, and the tribal culture and life from which they come, as well as customary linkages and hostilities between different tribes. But even these tribal influences operate now in an urban milieu, and not in a rural milieu. Thus I stated in an early essay that "in a sense every African is detribalised as soon as he leaves his tribal area, even though he continues to be acted on by tribal influences. He lives in different kinds of groupings, earns his livelihood in a different way, comes under different authorities." [3] He walks on different ground, for roads and pavements may be paved; he draws his water from taps and his food from stores; etc. etc. He is ruled now not by District Commissioner and chief, but by District Commissioner and municipal authority and location superintendent and European manager. In my own view, therefore, it seemed essential to start analyses of town life by saying that the moment an African crossed his tribal boundary, he was "detribalised," outside the tribe, though not outside the influence of tribe. Correspondingly, when a man returns from the towns into the political area of his tribe he is tribalised—de-urbanised —though not outside the influence of the town.

The first study of a British Central African town was by the late Dr. Godfrey Wilson, first Director of the Rhodes-Livingstone Institute, in the mining town of Broken Hill.[4] Wilson formulated some of his main problems in terms of the changes in behaviour of African town-dwellers, according to the length of time they had resided in the town. His study is penetrating and important, but I consider it was still dominated by the tribal outlook I have been describing. My colleagues who followed Wilson in making studies of Rhodesian towns have approached these from the opposite point of view. That is, they have started their analyses on the assumption that they are dealing with town-dwellers, many of whom come from tribes and retain ties with these tribes. Here perhaps the most important books are Professor J. C. Mitchell's *The Kalela Dance*,[5] and Dr. A. L. Epstein's recent book on *Politics in an Urban African Community*.[6]

One main theme of Epstein's study is an analysis of how, during the growth of a copper-mining town, typical urban associations and industrial groupings ousted European attempts to work with authorities based on tribal affiliation. I summarise this history fairly briefly, and will then draw out some of the sociological implications which have been analysed by Mitchell and Epstein. When the copper-mine at Luanshya was established in the early 1930's, Europeans provided the managerial and skilled working force: the heavy labour was performed by thousands of Africans from tribes spread over British, Belgian and Portuguese territories. The mine, like many industrial enterprises in Europe's industrial revolution, had to provide both order and some social services for this heterogeneous population. Government's resources were not adequate for these tasks, and in any case both European and African mineworkers dwelt on the private property of the mine. The mine provided houses for Europeans and Africans, hospitals, recreational facilities, institutions to distribute food to the Africans. The Africans were housed in a vast compound under a Compound Manager (later called African Personnel Manager). He was responsible for the housing and welfare of the Africans, for dealing with their working conditions and complaints, and for maintaining order among them and settling their quarrels. In this work he was aided by African clerks, mine police, etc. Faced with thousands of Africans of different tribes, the mine officials, reasonably enough, thought that it would be wise to deal with them through representatives of the tribes as groups. Therefore the Compound Manager instituted a system of Tribal Elders. They were given special houses and robes. His idea was that the mine management could communicate with its African labourers through the Elders while the Elders in turn would inform the management of the wishes and complaints of their tribesmen. In addition, the Elders would see to the welfare of newcomers to the mine until these were allocated houses or found friends, a most important duty in a system of migrant labour with men moving constantly from tribe to town and back again, and between town and town, and between jobs in each town. Finally, the Elders acted as judges in the small disputes that arose between men and their wives. The Elders together constituted a Council. The people themselves welcomed this institution. Meanwhile a similar system was established in the Municipal Location which had grown up in the town, distinct from the mine's compound.

Most of the Elders or Tribal Representatives, chosen by the Africans themselves, were fairly closely related to the royal families of the tribes concerned. The authority system of the tribe was projected into the urban, industrial sphere.

This system of administration worked fairly well until, in 1935, there were major disturbances throughout the area of the copper-mining towns (which is called the Copper Belt). These disturbances arose out of African demands for better pay and working conditions. A strike began in two other mines, and the Superintendent at Luanshya asked his Tribal Elders what would happen in Luanshya. They assured him that there would be no disturbances there. The Superintendent asked the Elders to go among the miners and calm them, but one of the Elders, a senior man, was driven away from a meeting and accused of being in league with the Europeans. A mob stormed the Compound Office, and the Elders had to seek sanctuary within it. Clearly they had neither influence nor power within the strike situation. Yet after the disturbances, the Elders resumed their previous role. By 1937 there was some forty accredited Elders on the mine, and Epstein says that "the system of Tribal Elders operated satisfactorily in the main, and was appreciated by the mass of the people" (p. 36).

I have time only to touch on Epstein's analysis of the background to this development. He stresses the tribal background of the Elders— their frequent affiliation with the families of chiefs, their acquaintance with tribal customs and values, their skill in adjudicating in disputes, and so forth. Yet, in a way paradoxically, they came simultaneously to be associated with the European mine management. During the strike they were driven away as in league with the Europeans. Two important elements in their positions have therefore to be stressed. First, as tribal representatives, whose authority was based in the political system of the tribe, they had no connection with the situations in which African miners worked in the mine itself. Here the workers were organised in departments and gangs within which tribal affiliation was irrelevant; and it was in this situation that common interests had brought the miners to joint action in the strike. This was industrial action, and here tribal divisions and allegiances did not operate. So the Elders lacked all influence over the workers in this situation. But, secondly, in the administrative system the Elders had become representatives of the mine itself, in dealing with its workers, and hence when those workers came into conflict with the mine, they regarded the Elders as enemies. When the strike had ended, the Elders could resume their former role.

This position changed slowly until a second series of strikes broke out on the Copper Belt in 1940. There were disturbances, with shooting of miners, at Nkana mine, but none at Luanshya. At Mufulira mine a strike committee of seventeen men was set up to negotiate with the management. At all mines, the authority of the Elders was rejected, and the strike committee at Mufulira was the beginnings of a new regime which was to oust tribal affiliation as a basis for handling industrial matters among African miners. For eventually after the War, the British Government (now a Labour Government) sent out trained unionists to help Africans form trade unions. The development of trade unionism was present among the Africans themselves, but it was now encouraged by Government policy. Eventually, the African Mineworkers Union emerged as a powerful, organised, industrial union throughout the mining towns of Northern Rhodesia, negotiating with the management. As its last step on the way to power, the Union insisted that the Tribal Elders system be abolished, for the trade union leaders saw the Elders as a threat to their own authority, and as a means which the mine might use to oppose them. A referendum was held among the miners: 85% of the 35,000 miners voted, and of these 97% voted for abolition of the Tribal Elder system. The trade union had finally ousted the formal organised power of tribal representatives from the industrial field, though later I will describe how tribal affiliation continued to influence trade union politics.

The story of developments which Epstein gives for the municipal compound is similar, but not so clear-cut. He suggests that the monolithic structure of the mine with its centralised power over the working, residential, etc. lives of the workers, provoked the response of a monolithic African trade union, also catering for many aspects of the miners' life, and unable to tolerate any rivals. On the other hand, the municipal compound is inhabited by the employees of many different employers in various trades, by domestic servants, by independent tradesmen, and so forth. Hence there has been less pressure to combined action by Africans in trade unions, and less possibility of their organising thus. Nevertheless in the municipal compound also, developments have been similar to those on the mine. The authority of Tribal Elders, outside of the settlement of small disputes, has been steadily ousted by bodies including better educated and more profitably employed Africans, who have less connection with families of chiefs and who are more permanently settled in the town. Secondly, wherever the Government has set up administrative councils or even courts to help it deal with the heterogenous African population, a spontaneous opposition has developed in the urban population itself. The two processes have worked together, for the Government's policy has been based on the use of tribal affiliations, while the educated Africans have been insisting that leaders in the towns must be acquainted with urban ways of life, and need not be guardians of tribal custom. But here the position is far more fluid than on the mine.

Epstein goes on to point out that the dominance of the trade union did not eliminate tribal allegiances within the industrial field. To some extent, they have ceased to be so significant in industrial matters where the Africans are opposed in their interests to the European mine officials and management. But in matters between Africans, tribal affiliation is important. Thus elections within the union for official posts in the union have to some extent been fought on tribal lines: other tribes complained that the leadership was dominated by the Bemba tribe. And, at the other end of the scale, Nyakyusa tribesmen from South-West Tanganyika talked of forming a separate Nyakyusa trade union, though in practice they joined in a general strike. Epstein explains that the Nyakyusa are so far from home that during a strike they do not get support, as Northern Rhodesian tribes do, of food from their rural homes. In addition, they are mostly without their wives, so do not have women to cultivate gardens for them as additional support. But it is in the struggle for power in the leadership that tribal allegiances have most significance.

Nevertheless even here it is not straight tribal hostility and loyalty that are operating. During the early years of the mine, the posts open for educated Africans were largely taken by Nyasalanders, for the educational system in Nyasaland was earlier established and better than in Northern Rhodesia, and by Barotse, who were similarly advanced. The Nyasalanders had also early gained mining skill by going to work in Southern Rhodesian mines. Finally, Bemba, who are the nearest powerful tribe, had filled many of the minor authoritative posts on the mine. Hence while many Africans see the struggle for leadership on the mine in tribal terms, this covers a struggle between groups of different skill. After the firm consolidation of the trade union's power, a dispute began with the mines and the European trade unions not only for better pay for Africans, but also for the opening of better paid posts demanding higher skill. Hence the issue emerged, whether the union was to press for a few highly paid openings for a few well-educated Africans, or for much better all-round opportunities for the mass of relatively unskilled labourers. Out of this struggle, a new and militant leadership, more representative of the labourers, won many union elections. The struggle reached its climax when the mine management opened new skills to Africans and put them on a monthly salary, instead of payment by ticket of work done. It also insisted that they join a new and separate union, formed by salaried Africans and led by a Barotse. The old union came out on strike against this move; and eventually the Government, holding that this was a political strike, arrested sixty-two trade union leaders and deported them to their tribal areas.

The significance for us of this strike is that it brought into the open

the emergence within the African urban population of affiliations based
on what we can call "class principles." In the most recent struggle for
leadership of the union, and in the formation of the new union, we see
that there has emerged among the Africans a division of interests in the
industrial field. As soon as the trade union had consolidated its power
against the potential rivalry of old tribal leaders, its members (like allies
in other situations) split apart in pursuing independent interests. This,
perhaps, we might also expect from the history of Europe.

The division on class lines has what Dr. Epstein calls a "pervasive"
effect. It spreads into many institutions. For the ideal of a Europeanised
and civilised way of life is the ideal which the Africans now follow.
Professor Mitchell has examined the effect of this situation on the Kalela
dance. His analysis is based on the interpretation of how the general
social situation influences the structure and actions of a single dance
team. The Kalela dance is a very popular dance on the Copper Belt. It is
danced by teams of Africans who come from single tribes. During their
dances they mock other tribes, by alleging, among many unpleasant
habits, that they have loose, and even perverted, sexual lives. Thus on the
surface the dance proclaims proudly the virtues of the team's own tribe,
and derides other tribes. Yet the members of the derided tribes attend
the performance and laugh as loudly as any at the salacious wit against
themselves. Mitchell was struck by the fact that despite this surface of
tribal competitiveness, the dancers had named their hierarchy of officials
after the hierarchies of British military or civil dignity. Moreover, the
dancers did not wear tribal dress: instead, they were dressed in smart
and clear European clothes, and they had to maintain their tidiness and
smartness throughout the dancing. This was insisted on, although the
dancers themselves were mostly unskilled, and poorly educated, labourers.
From this point of view he interprets the dance as reflecting the aspirations of all Africans after a European way of life, or civilisation, and he
shows from other data how the values implicit here form a prestige scale
for all Africans. But, he argues, these unskilled labourers are not striving
through the dance to participate in the European part of Central African
society: this is cut off from them by the colour-bar. They are striving in
the dance to associate themselves with the new African élite. Mitchell
shows that in political activity, such as the African opposition to the
establishment of the Central African Federation, Africans of all classes
and tribes (except the Barotse who are protected by special treaty) united
against the Europeans. Internally, they are differentiated on a class scale,
which people are striving to ascend. This is one marked trend in the
towns, and it seems clearly distinct from tribalism.

Yet the dancing-team is a tribal team, deriding other tribes. Its
actions have therefore also to be related to a persisting significance of
tribal allegiances in the towns. Here Mitchell works out that tribalism in

the town operates as a primary mode of classifying the heterogeneous masses of people whom a man meets into manageable categories. With his fellow-tribesmen he can converse, and he shares their customs and way of life. In practice, Mitchell discovered that there was far less tribal inter-marriage in the towns than is usually assumed, so that a man marries the sisters and daughters of his fellow-tribesmen. More than this, by the use of social distance scales, Mitchell found that all the many tribes in the towns were grouped into several limited categories by other Africans, and that specific institutionalised modes of behaviour had developed between various tribal categories. Thus he discovered that joking relationships between tribes in this region had developed in modern times, and were not, as previously thought, traditional. Mitchell thus stresses that tribes in towns form categories by which people group one another, and this categorisation determined a lot of action in casual as well as intimate relationships. Both he and Epstein stress that in domestic situations, where as we have seen most marriages occur within tribes, tribal custom and practice are effective, though much modified by the demands of the urban situation.

In short, to understand the persistence of tribal links in the towns we have to assess their significance in relation to dominant forms of association, which are produced by the demands of the urban and industrial situation. The people live in towns, as workers, and they associate here in terms of common interests which override tribal divisions. But tribal loyalties may influence the internal politics of these urban associations, and political struggles in these associations may, from historical accident, be cast in tribal terms. In leisure activities and in casual intercourse tribalism, in various categories, forms a basis for classifying people. Tribal allegiance and custom dominate in the sphere of domestic life, so far as the situation allows. And in many towns, though not in the Copper Belt, associations of mutual help, funeral societies, etc. are based on common tribal affiliation. But class relationships are becoming increasingly important and, in Epstein's words, pervade every situation. It is worth adding that Epstein found in a later study in a commercial town, that former pupils of certain schools felt themselves to be linked together.[7]

Epstein concludes his study by stressing that in our studies of the new African towns we can find plenty of systematic regularities. These are obvious in that people live and go about their business within the towns in relative peace and absence of fear. Hence clearly there is some kind of working, integrated social system in these towns. But the social system must not be thought of as rigid, tight, or self-consistent. The social field of the towns consists of many semi-independent areas of life, in which people associate for specific purposes: to run a home and raise children, to be entertained with friends, to work and improve status, to achieve political objectives, etc. Different principles of social organisation may be effective in the various areas of relations. Hence a trade union can oust Tribal Elders, and with them tribal authority, from the town, without affecting tribalism as a category or even loyalty to a tribal chief in other situations. Let me stress, too, that this situation is not confined to Africans. Tribalism acts, though not as strongly, in British towns: for in these Scots and Welsh and Irish, French, Jews, Lebanese, Africans, have their own associations, and their domestic life is ruled by their own national customs. But all may unite in political parties and in trade unions or employers federations. Tribalism in the Central African towns is, in sharper form, the tribalism of all towns.

These urban studies all emphasize that tribal associations in these towns do not dominate political life. Tribalism is not an organized set of political relations. Here modern urban tribalism differs radically from tribalism in the rural areas. In the rural areas, under British rule, each tribe is an organized political unit, with a complex internal structure. At its head, in Central Africa at least, there is usually a traditional chief, with a traditional council of elders, and a system of villages and other political units. For here it has been Government policy to rule through the tribal organization. Government has thus lent its powerful support to the continued working of the African tribal political systems, as systems. We may also say that continuing, and in the sociological sense conservative, loyalty to chiefs has been important here. Moreover, since the new industrial and urban political associations develop in the towns, they only affect tribal allegiances indirectly. But we also consider that the tribal system in the rural areas serves new needs of tremendous importance to the modern African.

All Africans now want to earn money. They must have money to pay taxes, and they want it to pay for clothes and other European goods, and for schooling and other welfare services. A few of the Central African tribes have been able to earn this money by selling crops and fish; most of them migrate for longer or shorter periods to work in European enterprises, mainly in the towns. But they consider that they have little security in their industrial life. Housing as well as sentiment makes it difficult for them to rear children there; till recently, they could not own houses, which were tied to jobs, and this situation is only slightly changed; there is no provision for unemployment; sickness and accident compensation is very low; there is no provision for work by, or care of, the old, and there are few pensions, and those there are, are small. The insecurity of town employment is constantly brought home to them. All tribal areas have tales like the incident recorded by one of my colleagues, who, when working on the Zambezi River, one morning saw men appear on the other bank—the bank of another Territory. One of the men shouted for a canoe, and they were brought across. It was a policeman, repatriating an old blind man. He had left the tribal home thirty years before and never communicated with his kin: now, old and disabled, he was brought back to it, to be supported by whosoever would accept responsibility or feel pity for him. And finally all Africans remember the great depression, when the mines closed and thousands of them returned to their tribal homes—as millions of Americans were absorbed back into eking a living on the land in the same crisis. Industrial and urban life offers little security to the vast majority of African labourers, and for this security they cling to their land in their tribal homes. They mostly want to return home, and look forward to it, but in addition this security of land is an ever-present need in the total field where they make their living.[8]

We must think here of these tribesmen who get their money by going out to work as earning their total living in two widely separated areas. Basically they depend for security on the land, and many of them leave their wives and children to get their subsistence from the land. Here the old must live. Hence Watson says of the Mambwe on the border of Tanganyika and Northern Rhodesia, that they raid the towns for money. If the tribesmen are to exploit their land and to raid the towns, they have to spread their economic activities very widely, and if they are to do this successfully, they need to co-operate with others. In short, there needs to be a group of kin, some of whom go out any one time to earn money, while others remain at home and cultivate the soil and care for cattle—as well as wives and children. Some tribes seem to achieve this organised deployment of men more successfully than others, for a complex of reasons which Dr. Watson has examined, but which I cannot set out here for lack of time. Other tribes are markedly unsuccessful. But all turn to the land for ultimate support.

Land here is not an individual item of land which a man owns for himself and by himself. For he secures his rights to land in two ways. First, as a citizen of the tribe he is entitled to some arable and building land, and to the use of public pasturage, fishing waters, and wild products. Secondly, in all tribes except those who shift their gardens widely and have an abundance of land, he gets right to land from membership of a village and a group of kinsfolk. That is, a man's rights to land in the tribal home depend on his accepting membership of a tribe, with all its obligations. He holds land as a Barotse, and not a Lunda, and the tribe jealously safeguards these rights. You all know that under Bantu systems of land tenure, which we may summarise as pre-feudal, the chief has to distribute land to his subjects, and he often does so through a complicated social hierarchy. I examined the development of land-holding in all the Central and Southern African tribes, and found that in no case, as land got scarcer and hence more valuable, had chiefs expropriated to themselves an unreasonable quantity of land. Instead, they had in various tribes, as pressure on land increased, steadily legislated to safeguard the fundamental right of every tribesman to some land. Thus the first step, taken e.g.

among the Ngwaketse in Bechuanaland, was for the chief to take power to commandeer land allocated to a subject which he was not using, for distribution to the landless. Then the chief took power to take over for the landless people land which had lain fallow for a certain period: you will see that when this is done, the cycle of land degradation has begun. The final step is seen in Basutoland, where each family is restricted by law to 2½ acres. People get around these laws by various devices, of course, but the trend of development in the view of both the leaders and the mass of the tribes is clear. Every man who is a member of the tribe has a right to live and support his family on the tribal land.

I am sure that honest fellow-feeling and sympathy and justice have contributed to this legislation. But in addition those who remain behind have an interest in the work of those who go away to the towns, for they bring home the money which the people require. In a way, those who stay at home hold the land as security for support in money from those who go out to work. And those who go out to work pass money to those who remain, in payment for this security. So that they get security by their continued allegiance to the tribe, for they hold land from the chief in return for loyalty and support. Hence they adhere to their chiefs; and as they adhere to the chiefs, they accept with the chiefs, for the rural areas, the organized system of tribal political relations. Very few tribesmen wish to overturn the tribal political system as such, though new interest groups, and new élites, in the tribes may struggle for power in tribal councils. With acceptance of the tribal political system goes acceptance of many customs and observances built into that system.

In tribes where land is worked in co-operating groups of kindred, or where kin organise their departures to town as I have described before, security in holding of land also involves acceptance of kinship obligations, and with these of many other parts of the tribal culture. I cannot enter further into this part of our analysis, for my time is running out; nor have I time to deal with developments in tribes which earn money by fishing or selling crops.

We see, in short, that tribalism persists in the rural areas because of Government support, and because the tie to tribal land is of the utmost importance to a man. With this tie goes acceptance of the tribal political system with its culture, and of its smaller constituent groups with their culture. In short, tribalism in the rural areas consists of participation in a highly organized system of social relations, based strongly on the chief's rights as trustee for his people over the tribal land. Dependence on land and the social relations arising from this dependence, give modern Africans many satisfactions they cannot find in urban life, and also security against the vicissitudes of industrial employment. Tribalism in the towns is not such an organized system of political and other social relations. In the towns, specific urban-type groupings and industrial associations develop, and have ousted the attempts of Europeans to transplant African tribal authority systems to deal with urban-industrial problems. But tribal linkages and hostilities affect the struggles within these new forms of association, though sometimes they cloak struggles based on other principles. Tribal ties and attachments still dominate domestic life. And tribalism is a most important basis for grouping people into categories, which determine how a man treats those whom he meets casually. Some associations emerge in which fellow-tribesmen band together to help one another. But class linkages are also beginning to pervade the life and the culture of the new towns. In all these respects, African towns differ only in degree from any town, anywhere in the world probably. In crisis, common interests arising from industrial and urban association seem steadily to overcome tribal ties and divisions.

To some extent, though developments in urban and in rural areas affect one another, as I have shown, the specific associations of each may exist independently. Tribal Elders were ousted from the mines by the trade union, yet the leaders in this move treated a visiting chief with respect—until he tried to intervene in an industrial dispute. The Africans' lives are partly dichotomised, and they live in separate compartments— like other men. But there is a mutual influence, which I have not time to examine.

What, then, becomes of "detribalisation," the problem I raised at the beginning of my lecture? Perhaps my intellectual opponents are right, as well as myself. The African is always tribalised, both in towns and in rural areas; but he is tribalised in two quite different ways. As we see it, in the rural area he lives and is controlled in every activity in an organized system of tribal relations; in the urban areas, tribal attachments work within a setting of urban associations. Hence the African in rural area and in town is two different men; for the social situation of tribal home and of urban employment determine his actions and associations, within the major politico-economic system covering both areas.

POSTSCRIPT

I make three points which were raised in the discussion after my lecture:

1. Though I speak of the separation of the African's activities in town and tribal area, I do not consider that this is achieved without both social and mental conflict. Nevertheless, there is considerable resolution of this conflict through the separation of the spheres of activities.

2. The analysis made here is for Northern Rhodesia and Nyasaland, and developments elsewhere may well be different. Industrial and other urban associations have developed less successfully, e.g., in the Union of South Africa, where legislation obstructing these associations are

severe. In British Central Africa, until recently, Parliament in Britain had considerable influence on policy. In the Union of South Africa it appears that tribal affiliations in towns are more significant than in Rhodesia.

3. The whole situation of the chiefs is affected by the presence of both a superior Colonial Government and European settlers. Hence in the recent political crisis chiefs aligned themselves with urban leaders. The development of local self-government, not dominated by settlers, might here produce a radical difference, as in Ghana; for an indigenous Government may require to reduce the autonomy of tribes and hence the power of chiefs.

NOTES

1. Conférence prononcée a l'Ecole Pratique des Hautes Etudes. VIe Section, devant le groupe des étudiants de sociologie de l'Afrique Noire.

2. See essays in L. P. Mair (editor), *Methods of Study of Culture Contact in Africa,* Memorandum XV of the International Institute of African Languages and Culture, 1932 (here only I. Schapera and M. Fortes took the point of view I shall advocate). The view I am criticising emerges clearly in B. Malinowski, *The Dynamics of Culture Change* (Yale University Press, 1946); cf. my critical essay, *An Analysis of the Sociological Theories of Bronislaw Malinowski* (Rhodes-Livingstone Paper No. 16, 1948).

3. M. Gluckman, "Seven-Year Research Plan of the Rhodes-Livingstone Institute," *Human Problems in British Central Africa,* The Rhodes-Livingstone Journal, No. 4, December 1945.

4. *An Essay on the Economics of Detribalisation in Northern Rhodesia,* in 2 parts (Rhodes-Livingstone Papers Nos. 5 and 6, 1941 and 1942).

5. Rhodes-Livingstone Paper, No. 27 (1956).

6. Manchester University Press for the Rhodes-Livingstone Institute, 1958. See also his publications on the work of African Urban Courts, cited in his bibliography.

7. Unpublished lectures on Ndola.

8. The two works which stress this problem most for the region are: W. Watson, *Tribal Cohesion in a Money Economy* (Manchester University Press for the Rhodes-Livingstone Institute (due shortly), and M. Gluckman, *Essays on Lozi Land and Royal Property* (Rhodes-Livingstone Paper No. 10, 1943).

G. W. Skinner

THE NATURE OF LOYALTIES
IN RURAL INDONESIA (1959)

The great majority of Indonesia's people live in the hamlets and villages which dot almost every island of the archipelago. While it would be misleading to discount the significance of an urbanization rate which is relatively high for Southeast Asia or to minimize the great importance of cities and towns in the nation's social structure, the fact remains that most Indonesians reside in rural corporate settlements within which many of their most enduring social relationships and loyalties are contained.

It would be meaningless, however, to speak of *the* Indonesian village. The world of village Indonesia is divided, first of all, into the various cultural areas each of which is the homeland of one of the country's many ethnically distinct agricultural peoples. Several of the most significant differences within village Indonesia are closely associated with ethnicity, and in order to point up the relevance of these differences to the problem of loyalties, the papers in this symposium deal with the villages of five contrasting peoples. While there is greater justification for speaking of *the* Javanese villager or *the* Sumbawan village, it goes without saying that considerable variation is often found from one village to another even within an area whose population is ethnically homogeneous. A Sundanese village typical of the Sumedang area differs in many respects from one typical of the Sukabumi area, and the caveat implicit in this observation should be understood to apply to each of the following papers.

This symposium treats the interplay of the villager's local, ethnic and national loyalties. It would be gratifying to report that the participants found the concept of "loyalty" an incisive analytic tool or that we

SOURCE. G. W. Skinner, "The Nature of Loyalties in Rural Indonesia," from G. W. Skinner (editor), *Local, Ethnic and National Loyalties in Village Indonesia: A Symposium*, New Haven: Yale University—Southeast Asia Studies, distributed in cooperation with the Institute of Pacific Relations, New York, 1959, pp. 1–11.

have made any considerable progress in sharpening the concept to that end. Unfortunately neither is the case. The contributors are concerned in a general way with the villager's identification with various more or less inclusive sociocultural and sociopolitical groups and with the ties of allegiance and affect which bind him more or less strongly to individuals, institutions, causes and symbols at various levels in the political-administrative structure. It will be useful to draw a distinction among loyalties to an individual person, to a corporate group, and to a cause, which may be termed, respectively, *personal, group* and *programmatic* loyalty.[1] Beyond this, however, there is little point in attempting an analytical definition here.

Nevertheless, in order to provide context for the contributions to follow, there is reason, perhaps, for pointing up some of the more important factors relevant to local loyalties, to ethnic loyalties, and finally to national loyalties in village Indonesia. In this introductory paper I shall try to indicate briefly what these factors are, with special reference to the ethnic groups treated elsewhere in the symposium.

It is no simple matter to determine what a village is in many parts of rural Indonesia. There is not uncommonly a distinction between a larger administrative unit with little social significance, on the one hand, and a small though multifamily settlement within which face-to-face social relations and primary loyalties are largely contained, on the other. The situation, however, is seldom so neat, for there may be more than one level of supra-hamlet village-type administration, and some of these "political villages" may have considerable social significance. Many of these complications arose through tampering on the part of higher political authority. Originally the "social village" in simple form was probably characteristic of that part of the archipelago where sedentary agriculture was practiced. New settlements were sometimes established as offshoots of the old. In the relatively densely populated core of the Javanese Mataram kingdom, sub-settlements proliferated to the point where, at least by the eighteenth century, a village complex consisting of a mother village together with related hamlets was the rule rather than the exception. This natural village—"natural" since its growth was undirected from above and since it had become the focus of village loyalties for the residents of all component settlements—served as the major prototype of the administrative village now found in widely scattered parts of the country.

For purposes of administrative convenience and efficiency, the Indies government initiated a consolidation process which by the end of the nineteenth century had created *kalurahan* (Javanese) or *desa* (Indonesia)—as the village complex is called—throughout Java. In most Sundanese areas, the imposition of the *desa* administrative unit, coupled as it was with the development of wet-rice cultivation, provided the population with its first stable and sizable territorial social unit, but . . . even today the sense of identification with the territorial village group is not strong. In the part of Java . . . east of the Mataram core area, the original village unit (*dukuhan*) has retained its own social functions and *esprit de corps,* and village loyalties have by no means been entirely extended to the *kalurahan* unit.[2] In Madura, however, even though the *desa* complex is made up of discrete *kampong,* themselves often consisting of scattered farm settlements, the larger unit has come to be regarded as *the* local community by its members.[3]

In this century, the Netherlands Indies government initiated a new program further to consolidate and standardize rural administration. In Java small *kalurahan* were merged, and in parts of Sumatra and Borneo the process of consolidating hamlets into village units was begun. In the last decades of Dutch rule, villages in the directly ruled areas of Sumatra and Borneo were grouped into *negeri* or other units more or less comparable in size to the Javanese *kalurahan.*

Throughout most of East Indonesia, however, there was less manipulation of village units. In the greater part of Sulawesi (Celebes), Maluku (Moluccas) and Nusatenggara (Lesser Sundas), the Indies government concluded agreements with local rulers whose territories were recognized as self-governing states (*swapradja*). In these indirectly ruled areas, the lower administrative structure was not standardized from the center. Whereas in most of western Indonesia the village complex (*desa, kalurahan, negeri,* etc.) was the meeting place between the central administrative system and the governed, in most of eastern Indonesia, the meeting place was at a considerably higher level, that of the *swapradja.*[4]

For much the same reasons which motivated the preceding regime—though there is now much talk of *desa*-level autonomy—the government of independent Indonesia has endeavored to continue and extend the process of village consolidation. This policy was made clear as early as 1948 in the official clarification of the decentralization law of the original Republic, and new legislation in 1957 (Law No. 1) predicated the extension of autonomy to the lowest level on the consolidation of traditional village or hamlet units into *desa* of adequate size. In spite of the present artificiality of the "government village" in Bali or the *gabungan* unit in Sumbawa, as described in the papers below, the government is determined to strengthen them and infuse them with social significance for the villagers.

For present purposes it may be useful to define as "local" those loyalties focussed at or below the highest unit whose administrative officer is selected or elected by the villagers from among themselves. Joint participation in the selection or election process in itself gives the unit in question some social significance and generally implies a good deal more. By this criterion, the highest local unit in Bali is the hamlet (together

with the non-territorial local units described by Mrs. Geertz), in Sumbawa the single-settlement village, in Java proper the *kalurahan,* in Sundanese Priangan the *desa,* and among the Toba Batak the *negeri.* So
specified, it is probably a safe generalization to say that the villager's
strongest loyalties at the present time are local, that the objects of his
most enduring loyalties are local individuals, groups and causes.

These loyalties are variously structured, as the following papers
abundantly attest, but it is perhaps useful to note that most of the traditional loyalties are related to the kinship structure, religious organizations, or the civil-*adat* [5] administrative hierarchy. The kinship structure
is an important focus of local loyalties where unilinear kin groups are
present—among, for instance, the Balinese, Batak and Minangkabau.
Where the kinship structure has territorial or religious significance, kin
loyalties will be accordingly diffuse. Likewise, the religious and civil-*adat*
structures are not always so discrete as appears to be the case in the Sumbawan or Toba Batak village; they may be intermeshed in various ways,
as in Bali and Madura, or a separate religious structure may be entirely
obviated. The relative importance of personal, group, and programmatic
loyalty at the local level and the degree to which village social structure
has room and even need for new organizational forms, as distinguished
from new content for old forms, are major variables in village Indonesia
directly relevant, as most of the following papers show, to the development of national loyalties. If there is any moral here, it is that the problem of loyalties in Indonesia cannot be understood apart from social
structure of the local community.

Regional levels, if we may so designate those between the administrative village or its equivalent and the nation, are no great focus of village loyalties. There are several reasons why regional loyalties as such
are relatively unimportant to the villager. In the first place, all administrative officials serving at levels from the province down to the sub-
district, just above the *desa* or its equivalent, are appointed by the center
from among the civil-service employees of the Ministry of Interior.[6]
Consequently, insofar as regional administrative levels are of significance
to the villager, they are often a focus of national rather than specifically
regional loyalties. This generalization needs qualification in the case of
several regional administrative units which were formerly indirectly ruled
swapradja and whose traditional rulers have continued as civil heads
under the unitary state. The Special District of Djokjakarta, headed by
Sultan Hamengku Buwono IX, provides the outstanding example of a
regional focus of loyalties which are clearly neither local nor ethnic nor
national. This situation, however, results from a combination of several
factors unique to the person of the sultan and to the special history of
the region. On the other hand, it is notable that villagers in western

Sumbawa see the capital of the regional *swapradja*, also headed by the former sultan, as the locus of new national institutions and influences.

Second, in areas where regionalism or "provincialism" is marked, it has flowed from basic policy differences between politicians and other leaders from the outer islands, on the one hand, and the central government in Djakarta on the other.[7] Although such policy matters directly affect his welfare, they are not ordinarily within the cognizance of the average villager. Even if, say, provincial leaders in Medan presented a united front to Djakarta, even if they fought the "good fight" in the interests of the local people, the Toba Batak villager would not thereby feel any closer to his fellow provincials, the Karo and Simelungun, Bataks, the Malays, or the immigrant Javanese. At least for the average villager outside Java, ethnic loyalties, being closer to his normal sphere of action, take priority over allegiance to any region not coterminous with his ethnic area.

Finally, and perhaps of greatest importance for this symposium, in moving from local up into regional levels of the sociopolitical structure, the villager almost immediately and universally encounters leaders and officials, groups and causes, which are predominantly town- and elite-oriented. The administrative officials are town-bred, often not from the local area, and of markedly superior educational attainment and social status. Organizations based at regional levels are largely urban in character, and their leaders are seldom farmers. The councils (DPRD or *Dewan Perwakilan Rakjat Daerah*) at the *kebupaten* level, even in areas where they were popularly elected in 1957, consist largely of townspeople identified with the civil service or following other urban-type occupations. As a recent student of regional autonomy puts it, the autonomous *kebupaten* "serves the interests of the elite, which has never belonged to, or has escaped from, the *desa*." [8] Above the local level, the villager is hard put to find leaders who genuinely identify themselves with the values of the rural population. Barriers of class, occupation and urbanism, then, tend to inhibit the extension of the villagers' loyalties to intermediate "regional" levels except when these are perceived as the focus of national or ethnic loyalties. These factors help explain why the contributors to this symposium seldom find it necessary to refer to regional as against either ethnic or national loyalties.

If we now turn to the ethnic loyalties of the Indonesian villager, it becomes necessary to specify what is meant by "ethnic" in the Indonesian context. The relevant Indonesian term is *sukubangsa*, which generally denotes an indigenous group characterized by a distinctive culture, with particular reference to language and *adat*. In the absence of definitive and comprehensive field surveys, it is difficult to estimate the total number of *sukubangsa* found in Indonesia, but even if we limit ourselves to discrete ethnic groups larger than 100,000 persons and speaking mutually unintelligible languages, the number exceeds 35. The three largest of these groups are the major indigenous peoples of Java and Madura: the Javanese (est. pop. in 1956: 36 million), the Sundanese (12.5 million) and the Madurese (5 million). The next largest ethnic groups are the Minangkabau (2.7 million), whose home area is the province of West Sumatra, and the Buginese (2.4 million), whose homeland is in south-western Sulawesi. Eight more ethnic groups fall in the size range from two million down to 750,000, including the Balinese (1.6 million) and the Toba Batak (950,000). The Sumbawans . . . rank about thirtieth in size among Indonesian *sukubangsa,* numbering approximately 135,000 in 1956.[9]

Given the cultural and linguistic distinctiveness of the typical Indonesian ethnic group and its concentration in a geographic region, the *sukubangsa* would appear to be a logical focus for the individual's loyalties. But when compared, say, with the new nations of Africa, ethnic loyalties in Indonesia are somewhat less prominent. In many parts of Indonesia, the villager seldom sees his *sukubangsa* as a major focus of either group or programmatic loyalties. There is considerable variation in this regard, however, and it may be useful to point to several factors which affect the intensity of ethnic loyalties among the various Indonesian peoples.

The historical, administrative and political integrity of the group is obviously relevant. Not since the Dutch began nibbling away at the Mataram kingdom have the Javanese had any political or administrative unity. During the last century of colonial rule, the Javanese were divided among four native states and, in the directly ruled part of the island, three provinces. So too, under the Republic, the major provincial boundaries on Java cut through Javanese areas rather than separate them from neighboring ethnic groups. The Sundanese must reach far back into history for a symbol of ethnic unity, the Padjadjaran kingdom, and at the present time whereas almost 94 percent of the country's Sundanese live in the province of West Java, only some 77 percent of that province's population is Sundanese. The Madurese ethnic area is far larger than the island itself, and more Madurese live in Java proper than in the residency of Madura. Similarly the Toba Bataks, who have never enjoyed political unity, form a bare quarter of the population in the recently truncated province of North Sumatra in which they are concentrated. In precolonial times, the Balinese and the Sumbawans were both divided among competing overlords, and only in recent decades have they achieved administrative unity at levels which may eventually become autonomous.[10]

On the other hand, there is probably some significance in the fact that the home areas of several of the *sukubangsa* with greatest ethnic awareness and group loyalty were largely coterminous with a single administrative unit under Dutch rule, thus providing a political-administrative focus for the group. This was the case, for instance, with the Atjehnese (the Government of Atjeh) and the Minangkabau (the West Coast Residency). In each case the Indonesian government attempted to obliterate these ethnically significant boundaries by submerging the old unit in a larger province, but ethnic loyalties and regional pressure of one kind or another have recently caused Djakarta to re-create the former units as the provinces of Atjeh and West Sumatra.

More important than the matter of administrative boundaries is the nature of intergroup contact. Ethnic awareness is intensified by inter-ethnic contact, and ethnic loyalties come to the fore only when the members of the group recognize common interests vis-à-vis others. It is notably those ethnic groups whose members during the last half century of Dutch rule were most mobile and most avidly in pursuit of scarce ends in the larger society which are outstanding today for ethnic loyalties bordering on chauvinism. The Buginese and Minangkabau were tradi-tionally mobile before Dutch contact, the former as sailors and seagoing traders, the latter as itinerant merchants. Minahassans, Ambonese, and Toba Bataks became mobile through the vagaries of colonial history— Christianization, population pressure on the land, and peculiarities of governmental policy. In somewhat different ways, social organization among each of these peoples is centrifugal, to borrow the term used by Mrs. Geertz; it expels the most ambitious and venturesome of the young men and, to a lesser extent, women into the larger society. For example, at the time of the 1930 census, over ten percent of all Minahassans, Ambonese and Buginese lived outside their respective home areas.[11]

Such ethnic groups are not only exposed to other peoples, they are thrown into competition with them. Under the colonial regime, and in the independent republic as well, the Ambonese, Minangkabau, Minna-hassans and, to a lesser extent, Toba Bataks have, along with the strate-gically situated Javanese, been disproportionately successful aspirants to positions of higher status in the modern, national and urban sector of society. But competition has been intense, frustration not uncommon, and the process has sharpened not only ethnic loyalties but also ethnic ani-mosities.

These remarks have considerable relevance for the loyalties of Indo-nesian villagers. To begin with, insofar as the villager is immobile and in situ, he tends to take his *sukubangsa* for granted. His ethnic awareness develops in response to the degree and nature of contact, vicarious or actual, with other groups. The amount of actual contact is, of course, not unrelated to the size of the group and to the location of the village near the center or at the periphery of the ethnic area. The villager in Central Java may never have laid eyes on a non-Javanese Indonesian, and he is correspondingly less conscious of his Javaneseness than is the villager who migrated from Java to South Sumatra. The amount of vicarious contact is related to the centrifugal force of the local social structure. Those who leave to seek their fortune in the larger society usually return to their native villages at least for visits, and in telling of their experiences with other peoples, they heighten the ethnicity of the stay-at-homes. This kind of influence is largely absent in a centripetal social structure such as that of the Balinese.

The degree of urban influence is another factor directly relevant to the villager's ethnic loyalties. Ethnic consciousness is accentuated in an urban setting. Given the heterogeneity and competitiveness of townspeople, it could hardly be otherwise. As Mrs. Palmer points out, it is the cities that support Sundanese ethnic organizations and breed interethnic animosities. The urban job hunter is quick to resent the disproportionate employment of other groups, and almost as quick to rely on ethnic favoritism within his own. Toba Bataks and Minahassans, who fifty years ago were barely aware of one another, today play out bloody feuds in the streets of Djakarta. The competition among *sukubangsa* has led to more than one attempt by town-bred leaders to solicit support in the countryside. As it is, villages near ethnically heterogeneous cities tend to be more strongly oriented toward their ethnic group than are those more remote, and as urban influences continue to penetrate villages, the intensity of ethnic loyalty—and antagonism—may be expected to increase.

At the present time, however, the villager's ethnic loyalties do not in most cases contravene his national loyalties. As the following papers suggest, national identification takes the form of personal loyalty (most ubiquitously to President Sukarno), group loyalty (to the Indonesian state or people), and programmatic loyalty (most prominently to the nationalist cause). In regard to the latter two forms, participation in the struggle against non-Indonesian outgroups for nationalistic political and economic causes has been a major factor shaping national loyalties. If the Javanese villager identifies himself more readily with the Indonesian state than does the Balinese, and the latter more readily than the Sumbawan, the contrast may flow in part from the different roles played by each in the Revolution. The government inevitably falls back on antiforeignism (with Indonesian citizens of foreign descent seldom clearly defined as members of the ingroup) in its efforts to minimize ethnicity among indigenous Indonesians and maximize national loyalties. Although mass media seldom directly touch the average villager, the great nationalistic campaigns have indirectly penetrated even the most remote village. A villager who may never have met a Dutchman or a foreign Chinese is by now likely to feel himself in some way a participant in the struggle for West Irian and, perhaps, even in the fight for a "national economy."

A more deep-seated and durable basis for national loyalties in the

Indonesian village is provided by education. Village schools—and Mr. Goethals reminds us that by no means even all administrative villages have them—are part of an educational system centralized in the Ministry of Education in Djakarta, and the Ministry aims at making responsible Indonesian citizens of all public-school pupils. The medium of instruction, at least beyond the first few grades, is Indonesian, a standard language developed from Malay and identified with no one *sukubangsa*. The Indonesian nation has been well served by the fortunate circumstances which made it unnecessary to adopt Javanese as the national language. (One need only think in this regard of India, Burma and Ceylon.) Textbook writers are not always able to find historical symbols identified with the Indonesian people as a whole, as opposed to one or another of the major *sukubangsa*, but in terms of contemporary symbols, the nation has an easy edge over most ethnic groups.

The introduction of the electoral process into village Indonesia in 1955 has had profound effects on the structure of loyalties. The election campaigns brought the Indonesian state into the immediate awareness of the villagers and in general fostered national loyalties of all kinds. The first elections were for *national* bodies—Parliament and the Constituent Assembly; they were accompanied by citizenship education undertaken by officials in the *national* civil service; and the related campaigns were waged for the most part by *national* parties. The 1955 elections gave millions of villagers for the first time a sense of participation in the main stream of national life.

It seems a little odd to Americans that in Indonesia religious affiliation is considered a completely respectable basis for political parties whereas *sukubangsa* affiliation is not. There are few overtly ethnic parties, and only one of these—the *Partai Persatuan Daya*, a party of the Dyak peoples in West Borneo—has achieved any considerable success. The dysfunctional aspects of political ethnicity for national integration are obvious.[12] Ethnic groups are particularistic in orientation and diffuse in their obligations, and if ethnic roles are merged with political roles, the result can only be the compounding of favoritism and corruption in government. Even more alarming to national political leaders is the problem of separatism, which has recently become a serious threat to national unity. Whatever the origins of dissident regionalist movements, given the geographical concentration of the various *sukubangsa*, appeals to ethnic loyalty can serve as a powerful weapon of their leaders.

But political ethnicity has its functional aspects as well. The identification of minority ethnic groups each with a single party could help circumscribe Javanese dominance in a governmental structure with no second chamber. More important for our purposes here, a system of parties based on ethnicity could serve to develop the villagers' national loyalties (at least as well as religious parties) *without* exacerbating schisms in the village or the rural countryside. In all of the villages treated in the following papers, competing national parties have, in the course of the election campaigns, divided either one village or hamlet from another or one group from another within the village. The cross-cutting of ethnic group and even village with party politics may heighten national loyalties as opposed to ethnic and local loyalties, but at what price to local social stability?

In point of fact, several ostensibly national parties function as ethnic parties. For instance, at least 75 percent of the IPKI vote (544,803 in December 1955) was cast by Sundanese, and approximately 70 percent of the PERTI vote (465,359) was cast by Minangkabau.[13] PERTI illustrates the relevant possibilities in this regard, for in several remote areas of rural West Sumatra, it is the only party which has organized the Minangkabau villagers. A truly national party occasionally functions in the same way in ethnic areas where particular combinations of social, religious and historical factors give the party a near monopoly of rural support. The *Nahdatul Ulama*, for instance, comes near to being *the* party of the Madurese villager. It is questionable whether the latter's national loyalties are any weaker in consequence, whereas a very obvious consequence is that his local world is far less rent by factionalism than is its Javanese counterpart. In many parts of Indonesia village unity has been sacrificed at the altar of national integration.

As it stands, most of village Indonesia has been penetrated by a number of national political parties, and the result has been not only the development of new loyalties to national institutions and causes, but also the restructuring of local loyalties. Herbert Feith, whose analysis of the 1955 elections followed intensive fieldwork, warns against one-way interpretations of the relation between social structure and political process: "However strongly one emphasizes the importance to parties of associations with previously existing social groups and centers of social power [in Indonesia's village areas], it should in no way be thought that campaigning was merely the political rubber-stamping of a previously existing pattern of authority."[14] In many cases, the elections created new social roles, elevated new local leaders, or left in their wake new organizations. In the process the social structure was permanently altered and local loyalties realigned in the significantly different ways described in the following papers.

And what about the future? Much depends on the way in which the basic autonomy law of 1957 is implemented and on the final results of the debate as to the role of political parties and popular elections in the national political system. If local autonomy is ever introduced on any scale at the so-called "third-level"—that of the *desa,* consolidated *desa* or, as envisaged by many Ministry of Interior officials, that of the subdistrict—and if interparty competition is curbed and new national elections indefinitely postponed, then local loyalties may well be extended and reinforced. Should the rural population gain any real representation in the elected councils (DPRD) at the *kebupaten* level, the villager might acquire a focus for regional loyalties supplementing and growing out of more traditional, strictly local loyalties. But whatever happens on the national scene, the process whereby the villager's local loyalties are infused with national significance or redefined in national terms will probably be accelerated.

National loyalties are not so well developed in the Indonesian village as in the villages of some other Asian countries where revolutionary programs of national reconstruction have captured the imagination of the rural population. National identity in Indonesia is still in large part defined in terms of what Indonesians are not and who they oppose. Only the government can provide the focus for national loyalties of the constructive, programmatic kind, which are at present weak in the villages. In the meantime, village schools, the lower reaches of the administrative system, and nationally oriented political organizations are rapidly increasing the villager's awareness of his nation and forging new ties between the farmer and the state.

The implication of the following papers is that ethnic loyalties have not assumed alarming proportions in the villages. It is possible that inclusion in this symposium of villages in still other ethnic areas of the outer islands might have modified this impression. In any case, there is no guarantee that ethnicity will not become more important as a consequence of the same modernization process which must underlie the consolidation of national allegiance. As the villager is brought closer to the national stream, his contact with representatives of other ethnic groups will increase. As he learns more about his country, he will become more conscious of his *sukubangsa's* distinctiveness within the total ethnic composition of the nation and of the existing distribution of privileges among the different groups. Since to a considerable extent "national" influences are urban influences, the invidious ethnicity of the cities may be exported in some degree to the villages. In particular, if the villager's rising expectations are continually frustrated, he may direct his aggression toward other groups—not only the Dutch and the Chinese, but other *sukubangsa* as well. There are dangers here, and it may well be that ethnic loyalties in a politicized and invidious form will grow in intensity before national loyalties triumph. Recognition of the dangers, however, will help rather than hinder Indonesia's audacious experiment to create unity out of diversity.

NOTES

1. See Harold D. Lasswell and Abraham Kaplan, *Power and Society.* London: Routledge and Kegan Paul, 1952, pp. 24–25.

2. Robert R. Jay, "Local Government in Rural Central Java." *Far Eastern Quarterly,* 15, 2 (February 1956), pp. 219–20.

3. For a comparative discussion of territorially-based communities throughout Indonesia see B. Ter Haar, *Adat Law in Indonesia.* New York: Institute of Pacific Relations, 1948, pp. 62–74.

4. John D. Legge, *Problems of Regional Autonomy in Contemporary Indonesia* (Cornell Modern Indonesian Project, Interim Report Series). Ithaca, 1957, p. 4.

5. *Adat* refers to indigenous custom, which may have the force of law.

6. The five levels of regional administration are, in the most nearly standard terminology, the *propinsi* (province), *keresidenan* (residency), *kebupaten* (regency), *kewedanan* (district), and *ketjamatan* (sub-district). The system is by no means completely standardized throughout Indonesia, however. It will be noted, for instance, that in the residency of Tapanuli, under which the Toba Batak *negeri* described by Mr. Bruner falls, the level of *kewedanan* is dispensed with. In Nusatenggara province, in which Sumbawa falls, the residency level is omitted, the *daerah* being equivalent to the *kebupaten* and the *swapradja* to the *kewedanan*.

7. For an informed and provocative discussion of the relative importance of political, economic and ethnic factors in outer-island "provincialism," see Chapter 5 of Gerald S. Maryanov, *Decentralization in Indonesia as a Political Problem* (Cornell Modern Indonesia Project, Interim Report Series). Ithaca, 1958.

8. Legge, *op. cit.,* p. 61.

9. Population estimates for 1956 are based on projections of the 1930 census data by administrative unit and *sukubangsa* (Nederlandsch-Indie, Department van Economische Zaken, *Volkstelling 1930,* 8 vols. Batavia, 1933–36.) in accordance with the 1956 registered population by administrative unit (Indonesia, Biro Pusat Statistik, *Penduduk Indonesia.* Djakarta, 1958.) All demographic statistics or estimates subsequently cited in this paper or in the editor's footnotes are drawn from or based on these sources.

10. The ethnic area of the Sumbawan *sukubangsa* is now roughly coterminous with the *swapradja* of Sumbawa: 94 percent of all Sumbawans live in this unit, and 86 percent of the indigenous population is Sumbawan. In the case of Bali, the island is now an administratively unified *daerah,* over 97 percent of whose population is Hindu Balinese.

11. In these computations, the home area of the Minahassans was defined as the Division of Manado, of the Ambonese as the Division of Amboina, and of the Buginese as the Government of Celebes and its Dependencies.

12. In writing this paragraph I have profited from reading "Ethnicity and National Integration in West Africa," an unpublished paper by Immanuel Wallerstein of Columbia University.

13. IPKI stands for *Ikatan Pendukung Kemerdekaan Indonesia* (League for the Upholding of Indonesian Independence), and PERTI for *Pergerakan Tarbijah Islamijah* (Islamic Education Association). For an analysis of the regional support of political parties, see Herbert Feith, *The Indonesian Elections of 1955* (Cornell Modern Indonesia Project, Interim Report Series). Ithaca, 1957, pp. 57–62.

14. *Ibid.*, p. 37.

M. Freedman

THE GROWTH
OF A PLURAL SOCIETY
IN MALAYA (1960)

The idea of a "plural society" was formulated by a British student of the political economy of Southeast Asia.[1] It has come to irritate some sociologists and find favor with others.[2] In this article [3] I begin by assuming that we know roughly what is meant by the term, and after a brief analysis of the social structure of Malaya, I try to show how I look upon Malayan society as "plural."

Malaya does not form one political community, for it is divided into the Federation of Malaya (an independent territory within the Commonwealth) and the State of Singapore (an internally self-governing territory of the Commonwealth). Before the post-war changes the country fell into three kinds of political territory: the Straits Settlements (a Crown Colony), the Federated Malay States (four States under British protection), and five Unfederated Malay States (under British protection). Each Malay State was headed by a Ruler (in most cases a Sultan) and administered by a civil service staffed at its higher levels by officials from Britain and by Malays. The political pattern was colonial.

But the colonialism of Malaya was greatly complicated by its ethnic divisions. We can get some idea of these divisions by a glance at demographic history.[4] Today there are some 7,750,000 people in the country; before 1850 the total population numbered perhaps 600,000. Malaya began its modern history as a set of petty States populated (with the exception of the aborigines in the jungle) by Malays and small settlements of other Asians. Among the latter the Chinese were the most important; they formed both trading communities (largely urban) and groups of tin-miners. From about the middle of the nineteenth century Chinese immigration increased sharply and continued up to recent years.

SOURCE. M. Freedman, "The Growth of a Plural Society in Malaya," reprinted from *Pacific Affairs*, XXXIII, 2, 1960, pp. 158–168.

Indian immigration began on a large scale as a result of modern rubber-growing. At the present there are in Malaya as a whole some 3,500,000 Chinese and about 850,000 Indians. The Malays have built up a modern population of roughly 3,400,000, partly by absorbing immigrants from the area we now know as Indonesia.

Already we are faced by two different patterns of immigration. The Chinese and Indians who arrived in Malaya have remained Chinese and Indians, not only in the eyes of census-takers but also in culture, social organization, and political status. In contrast, "Indonesian" immigrants have found their way into that part of the population which British policy regarded as enjoying primacy of occupation and political rights. A Malay is an individual who speaks the Malay language, is a Muslim, and displays a culture which, for all its variations, is clearly recognizable. To be assimilated into this politically privileged part of the population a non-"Indonesian" immigrant had to abandon one way of life and assume a new one, of which the practice of Islam was an important element. A few Chinese and Indians have in the past crossed this bridge, and doubtless a few still do; their antecedents are no more significant for their present status as Malays than are those of the many Chinese babies adopted by Malays. But the movement across the line into Malaydom has never been considerable.

Malays, Chinese, and Indians together make up 98 percent of the country's population. The Chinese are more numerous than the Malays, but since the population of Singapore (about 1,500,000) is predominantly Chinese, the Malays are the largest ethnic community in the Federation. Partly because of the different age-structures of Malays and Chinese, the latter are increasing at a higher rate, and it may be that after another generation the two communities in the Federation will be of equal numbers.

The plural society which has grown up in Malaya may be conveniently analysed into four spheres: political, economic, social, and cultural. Again as a matter of convenience, we may speak of three "societies"—Malay, Chinese, and Indian. But these are merely preliminary to a more realistic view of Malayan society as a whole.

Malay society today can be traced back in a straight line to the characteristics it displayed when, in the last quarter of the nineteenth century, the British began to interfere actively in the affairs of the Malay States. (Before that period the British had for the most part remained politically within the Straits Settlements.) Each State was ruled by a member of a royal family who was "invested with attributes of supernatural power and dignity." [5] He exercised very limited powers of central government. The State consisted of a number of districts, each ruled by a chief who came of a family long connected with the district. Together the district chiefly families "formed a more or less united ruling class of the whole State." [6] Beneath the district chief and the class from which he came were the mass of the people, the peasantry; their inferiority was political, social, economic, and cultural. (In these and the following generalizations I am greatly simplifying the facts and must therefore do violence to a complex reality, especially in regard to the State of Negri Sembilan which was organized on the basis of matrilineal kinship groups with political functions.)

There was little marriage between the peasantry and the aristocracy (the chiefly class), except in so far as aristocrats took minor wives from among the people. The relation between the chief and his people was in principle one in which strong authority was matched by submission. The chief exacted *corvée*, was likely to help himself to any significant surplus accumulated by the peasant, and occasionally took village women for his household. Moreover, the chief kept up the numbers of his entourage (both for domestic and agricultural labor and for fighting purposes) by bringing men into a form of servitude known in English as "debt-bondage." On the other hand, the economic and political realities of Malay life were set against a system of grinding oppression, for men who were pushed too hard could run away to establish themselves in the district of another chief or even in a different State. Land was plentiful, and since the wet rice fields relied upon rainfall and on merely temporary and simple irrigation works, there was little capital investment in land. A man could pull himself up and move without great economic loss. It seems likely that at this period of Malay history there was considerable movement of population.

Under British control the Malay States underwent an economic revolution, but while the Malays benefited from the development, they were only in small measure its direct agents. The reason lies, at least in part, in the way in which economic enterprise had been linked into the traditional Malay political and social system. The peasants lived in an economy in which money was used for some exchanges; they bought part of their foodstuff and a range of household necessaries; they sold some of their agricultural produce and materials collected in the jungle. But Malay trading on any considerable scale was conducted by the chiefs who derived revenue from taxes imposed on goods in transit through their territory and, in some cases, from Chinese miners (at this time the main exploiters of Malaya's tin). Some chiefs entered into partnership with Chinese tin-miners. There was very little investment by Malays in public works or productive enterprises, apart from what was staked in Chinese mining.

Beginning in the 1870s, British rule modified the political role of the chiefs; the economic aspect of their activity was accordingly reduced, and the Malays as a whole ceased to play a significant entrepreneurial part in the economy of their country.

British control bureaucratized the Rulers and their chiefs. It raised the Ruler from his traditional status of a chief among equals to that of an elevated king; at the same time it turned him into a kind of constitutional monarch. The chiefs were pensioned and some of them made administrative officers. State Councils were set up. Courts of law were instituted under European magistrates, often assisted by Malays. The districts were put under European and Malay officers. Public works were undertaken and an educational system devised.

Western and Chinese enterprise turned the country into a hive of economic activity, but Malays took no conspicuous part in it. They refused generally to sell their labour on mines and estates. But even so their role in the new economy was by no means unimportant; the peasantry adapted itself to producing cash crops (especially rubber and coconuts) on small-holdings. By taking advantage of the limited educational opportunities offered, some peasants' sons were able to move into the lower ranks of the civil service and something like a rudimentary Malay middle class emerged on the basis of the administration. On the other hand, the traditional class system persisted in its main outline within the new framework. The old aristocracy was now the new administrative class, some of its former personal links with the people being transmuted into bureaucratic relationships. Since the Second World War the old aristocratic class has shown its leadership in the organization of Malay nationalism, within which Malays of all classes have demonstrated their attachment to their political privileges and their eagerness to keep the Federation in some real sense a Malay country.[7] The compromise worked out within the dominating political alliance in the Federation since Independence is an attempt to push these Malay nationalist ambitions as far as they can go without upsetting the communal balance. I return to this matter later.

In modern times Malaya has seen the rise of cities and towns, but except in the administrative section of urban life the Malays have not taken a great part in this new kind of society. They are to be found disproportionately in the less developed parts of the country. European control was first established along the western side of the peninsula and it was here that the greatest economic growth took place. Chinese and Indians are today overwhelmingly concentrated in a strip about fifty miles broad along the west coast. Here too there are many Malays, but their greatest concentrations are in the extreme northwest, where the Chinese west-coast strip thins out, and in the extreme northeast, where very few Chinese and Indians are to be seen. The vast majority of Malays are still villagers (cultivators and fishermen) and it is largely for the interests of countrymen that their leaders speak in debates on economic and political matters.

The cultural lines of demarcation have remained and, in some respects, been strengthened. The Malay language in its literary form is hardly known to non-Malays (except for a handful of Western Malay scholars); it is a possession which Malays have not abandoned in favour of English, despite the fact that Malay administrators have been educated in English. It may be that Malay will one day become the main cultural and political language of Malaya; for the moment, in its developed form, it is the mark of the Malays. Islam and the customary ways of Malay life (affected as they certainly have been by the modern world) are valued things which Malays see as central to their civilization and as indispensable to their survival as a people. Islam is certainly crucial to the solidarity of the Malays, having advanced both in organization and in intensity since the coming of colonial control. It has been bureaucratized and made sensitive to the currents of Muslim thought in the greater world. The Islamic orthodoxy which now begins to be seen as an important political factor has one of its roots in the pilgrimages and Muslim missionary activity conducted under the *pax britannica*.

The development of Chinese society and Indian society in Malaya has been very different. They are *nova*, lacking continuity with a Malayan traditional past. The Chinese population is by origin predominantly rural, but its pursuits in Malaya have been so commercial and industrial as to keep it either urban or, when rural, of a rather urban cast. Chinese filled the growing towns which were called into being by the expansion of trade, first in the Straits Settlements and then from the last quarter of the nineteenth century in the Malay States. They supplied skilled and unskilled labor in enterprises promoted both by Western capital and the capital they themselves accumulated and invested. They set themselves up as the traders and shopkeepers of Malaya *par excellence*, collecting, distributing, and acting as sources of credit. Some of them became exceedingly rich, so that in purely economic terms the Malayan Chinese were diversified from millionaires to coolies.

The reasons why the Chinese have been economically successful in Malaya are complex. In the earlier immigration there were experienced traders who laid the foundation for the greatly expanded Chinese activity of later times. The great mass of the Chinese arriving in Malaya, however, have been farmers and artisans rather than men of commerce, and the business success which many of them enjoyed must have been due to their general understanding of the uses of money and the manipulation of men in relation to money.[8] As immigrants they were inclined to be energetic and adventurous; when opportunities were created in Malaya, there were Chinese to seize them.

Chinese tin-miners were present in considerable numbers when the British intervened in the west coast States. During the last quarter of the nineteenth century Chinese economic power in the Malay States was firmly based on the control of mining and a monopoly of the State revenue farms. In the present century many Chinese have prospered in the rubber industry. Chinese have penetrated into nearly every corner of the economy, being conspicuously absent only in rice cultivation and the higher levels of the administration. They are too large a part of the population to form a homogeneously middle-class group—unlike many of their congeners in other parts of Southeast Asia; during this century some three-quarters of them have been "working class," but the commercial and industrial middle class has been predominantly their preserve.[9]

The urban proclivities of the Chinese are marked. Nearly 54 percent of them were classed as urban in the 1947 census. Before the Pacific War there were Chinese on estates and mines, on rubber small-holdings, on vegetable-gardens, and, as shop-keepers, in Malay villages; the pre-war depression drove larger numbers out into the countryside in search of a living, a movement which was intensified by the Japanese occupation. Many of these newcomers to rural life in Malaya, scattered here and there, remained beyond the scope of administration after the end of the war. When the Communist uprising began in 1948, Chinese in the countryside were widely involved in the moves and countermoves of the guerilla fighting; a plan to resettle large numbers of them was drawn up, and by the 1950s the whose aspect of rural Chinese life in Malaya had been changed by the establishment of the so-called New Villages.[10] About one-sixth of the total Chinese population of the country was involved in this transfer. One of its social consequences was to produce, for the first time in Malaya, a series of nucleated Chinese villages. Behind the barbed-wire perimeters clearly defined Chinese rural communities were forced into being. A political result of the change in settlement was that communications between the rural Chinese and leaders of the wider Chinese community were greatly facilitated, so that, while the security ends of the administration were served, a contribution was made to the development of pan-Malayan Chinese organization. It may well be that the New Villages have come to stay; if they survive, they will greatly help Malayan governments in their cultural and political control of the rural Chinese.

The Chinese did not arrive in Malaya in groups which could readily produce traditional leaders. Organizing themselves in relation to the economic roles for which they had been cast, they built up a social system in which leadership went to rich men and status depended directly on economic power. The Chinese evolved no class system comparable to that of the Malays. They were both physically and economically mobile. In any one area of the country they grouped themselves on the basis of interlocking associations which gave them the means of exercising control within their own ranks and of dealing with the outside world represented by Malay and British officials. During the nineteenth century their self-government rested primarily on secret societies, which brought

Chinese into conflict with one another and at the same time held them together in the face of non-Chinese.[11] In more recent times the associations giving Chinese society its form and chains of command have been more various; among them, Chambers of Commerce, trade associations, and organizations recruiting on the basis of like territorial origin in China (a species of *Landsmannschaften*) have been the most important.

When the emigrants left China in the nineteenth century to go to Malaya and the other overseas settlements, they were not ambassadors of Chinese culture. They went generally against the wishes of the authorities at home and were fired by predominantly economic ambitions. If they had business dealings with Malays or Europeans, they acquired enough colloquial Malay to make these transactions possible. There was no place for them in the main political framework of the country, and its values and symbols remained largely alien to them. The Chinese were linguistically differentiated among themselves by the several (and for the most part mutually unintelligible) "dialects" of their language; and these linguistic divisions were built into the associations and groupings which came to constitute Chinese society in Malaya. A small section of the Malayan Chinese, tracing its origin to the early settlement in Malacca, into which non-Chinese women had been incorporated, has in modern times maintained a Malayanized version of Chinese culture and spoken a somewhat sinified Malay colloquial. It is an exception to the rule that, insofar as Chinese culture has survived in Malaya, it has preserved its essentially southern Chinese peasant character—despite the adoption of *Kuo-yü* and modern styles emanating from China.

Of course, social and cultural consequences were to flow from modern nationalism in China. The "homeland" became a focus of political interest. A modern school system was created by the Chinese themselves which adopted *Kuo-yü* (the Chinese "national" form of Mandarin) as its medium. Chinese in Malaya became conscious of forming part of a Chinese nation, both politically and culturally. It is one of the instructive paradoxes of modern Malaya that the nationalist "school" culture of the Chinese has been strongest in the very period when they have been preparing to take their place in a Malayan nation.

The education of the Chinese has not, however, been entirely Chinese. Many children have passed through the "English" school system which in modern times has culminated in the University of Malaya. It is wrong, nevertheless, to ascribe all the westernizing elements in Malayan Chinese life to the "English" schools (for in one sense the Chinese schools have been more westernized than their "English" counterparts, bringing in modern influences via China), and it is a mistaken view of Malayan Chinese society which makes a sharp division between the Chinese-educated and English-educated sections of the community. The two forms of education overlap, often in the same family, sometimes in the same individual.

I have given drastic summaries of Malay and Chinese society in Malaya. If I am even briefer on Indian society, it is because the subject has been little explored rather than because I am trying to reduce a great body of knowledge to a simplified statement. The vast majority of Indian immigrants were Tamils from south India, brought over to work on estates. Historically and economically their place in Malaya has been bound up with the development of the rubber industry. Today Indians outnumber all other employees on rubber estates, and they hold a similar position on practically all other kinds of plantations. A common form of Indian local community in Malaya has, in consequence, come to be a body of workers on an estate, housed and supervised by an industrial concern. Indians are prominent in many other areas of the labour market. On the other hand, some south Indians as well as immigrants from other parts of India have taken on commercial roles in the Malayan economy which resemble some of those of the Chinese. Indian shopkeepers are to be found in Malay villages and a significant proportion of rural credit has come from Indian sources. There are large numbers of Indians in the towns, both in the trading middle class and among workers, skilled and otherwise. They have produced a number of professional men and many clerks, both in government service and private employment.

Some among the Indians (including those who may now regard themselves as Pakistanis) are Muslims. This has given them a ritual meeting-ground with the Malays, and intermarriage has sometimes taken place as a result. But while Malay society has absorbed a few Indians in this fashion, the line between it and Indian society has remained sharply defined. Within the ranks of the Indians several Indian languages are spoken; these languages, and to some extent the cultures associated with them, have been perpetuated in schools specially provided for Indians or set up by themselves, the dominant language (for simple numerical reasons) being Tamil. As with the Chinese, however, significant numbers of Indians have gone through the "English" school system.

The Malayan Indian population is no longer dominated, as it was before the Second World War, by the coming and going of labourers from south India. It is now more highly stabilized in the country, politically as well as socially, the government of India having encouraged Malayan Indians to make their political home where they live.

We may now start to consider Malayan society as a whole, discarding the useful fiction that it is a plurality of societies. None of the individual "societies" has been politically autonomous; the British and the Malays have between them exercised the major political control, limiting one another in its application; Chinese and Indians have had to manoeuvre within the framework of overriding Malayo-British control. Nor can we continue to assume that each "society" has in reality constituted a unit. Have Malays, Chinese, and Indians been valid groups?

As far as the first two are concerned (for I am reluctant to commit myself on the Indians), we are certainly dealing with meaningful cultural categories, all the members of which regard themselves as belonging to a kind of ethnic community. But it does not follow that each community is an organized entity. In recent times the Malays, through the agency of a dominating political party, have built up a hierarchy of power within their own ranks which allows us to speak fairly realistically of a unified Malay group within the setting of national politics. This is the end-result of a process which began with the impact of colonialism on a set of independent Malay States. Before the Pacific War the Malay community, despite the early signs of pan-Malay nationalism, was essentially a plurality made up of units defined by State boundaries.

The Malayan Chinese have not attained the same degree of unification. The emergence of the Malayan Chinese Association notwithstanding, there is no single political party in the Federation which has welded all Chinese together. Structurally they are too loosely linked, economically and ideologically they are too diversified, to allow a single hierarchy of power to form among them. And yet today they are closer to unity than ever before. The resettlement in New Villages has simplified the lines of communication among a large section of the Chinese. The political developments of the last few years have rested on a widely accepted assumption that the first steps in Malayan democracy must be taken by means of an electoral alliance between the dominant Malay party (UMNO) and a single Chinese and a single Indian party (MCA and MIC). The rights of Chinese and Indians have had to be defended against both the nationalism of the Malay party forming the major unit in the alliance and Malay elements outside it which press for an Islamic and highly Malayized polity. These are conditions which favour a heightening of Chinese unity and a clearer definition of power within the ranks of the Chinese.

If, however, we ignore these recent developments and fasten our attention on the position as it was before the Pacific War, we see a different picture. The plural society then consisted not of ethnic blocs but of ethnic categories within which small groups emerged to form social ties inside and across ethnic boundaries. In any one locality a balance was struck between the interests of Malays, Chinese, and Indians. A rich and influential Chinese in one of the States, for example, maintained his position vis-à-vis Chinese and non-Chinese partly as a result of his relations with Malay power-holders. Before the intervention of the British an agglomeration of Chinese power (as in the case of the tin-mining "wars" in Perak between rival Chinese camps) bore directly on the struggles between Malay contenders for power. The shifts of power within Malay ranks affected similar shifts among Chinese, and vice versa. The routinization of the political system brought about by the British prevented the repetition of such wide movements, but the continued interlocking of the interests of Malay and Chinese power-holders forbids our looking at Malay and Chinese "societies" as though they were discrete entities, the existence of one failing to influence the fortunes of the other. The ties between local groups of Chinese and local groups of Malays could be determinants of the organizational features of both.

Malaya was and remains a culturally plural society. Paradoxically, from a purely structural point of view, its plural nature is more marked today than ever before. Nationalism and political independence in their early phases have tended to define, on a pan-Malayan basis, ethnic blocs which in former times were merely categories. Then the social map of Malaya was, so to speak, made up of a kaleidoscope of small culturally defined units rearranging themselves in accordance with local conditions. "The Malays" did not interact with "the Chinese" and "the Indians." Some Malays interacted with some Chinese and some Indians. But as "Malays," "Chinese," and "Indians" come to be realized as structural entities on a nation-wide scale, they can begin to have total relations with one another.

The conservatism which predominates in the political life of the Federation (and which differentiates it from Singapore and other parts of Southeast Asia) is an aspect of the balance between the structurally defined ethnic groups. The compromise which has been worked out on the political plane between Malays, Chinese, and Indians within the Alliance puts a premium on caution in the manipulation of economic and social change. It encourages moderation and damps down an enthusiasm for radical policies. The threat to the present balance from the extremism represented by the relative successes of the Pan-Malayan Islamic Party in 1959 and from other stirrings of ethnic and ideological opposition could lead either to a determined effort to maintain the compromise (if necessary by a retreat from electoral democracy) or to a dismemberment of the Federation as we now know it.

The compromise in the Alliance has an important economic aspect. There is in Malaya no neat hierarchy of Furnivallian "orders" endowed with specific economic functions. The Asian "immigrant" population does not sit squarely in the middle of the occupational pyramid performing only intermediate economic roles. Chinese and Indians are distributed over a wide range of economic functions, while in the period since the end of the Second World War a sizeable number of Malays have appeared in the ranks of industrial employees. On the other hand, capital and economic skill are highly concentrated in Chinese and, to some extent, Indian hands. Further economic development of the country is likely to strengthen the economic position of the non-Malays, unless some socialist formula is devised. Moreover, Malays wishing to enter more fully into the commercial and industrial life of the country come up against the difficulty of finding their way into networks of economic relationships which are composed of the personal ties between Chinese or Indians. Yet Malaya, when judged by Asian standards, is a prosperous country and it is conceivable that solutions to its economic problems will not appear so difficult as those to its political problems.[12]

The cultural face of the political compromise is, superficially at least, uncomplicated. Malay is ultimately to be the national language and is now to be taught in all schools. But the Chinese and Indian schools remain, although their curricula are Malayanized. There has been no attempt to "assimilate" the non-Malays; the emphasis has been put upon a common language (which will not exclude others) and a general minimum understanding of Malayan institutions. For the time being the cultural compromise appears to work.

One of the disadvantages of the notion of the plural society, as Morris has pointed out,[13] is that it tempts us to argue from cultural and "racial" appearances to social realities. Through most of its modern history Malaya has shown important cultural and "racial" divisions, but these divisions had not created cleavages running the length and breadth of the society. The social ideals of Malays, Chinese, and Indians were different and their interrelations governed by narrowly defined political and economic interests; but there was no framework for the massive alignment of ethnic forces. In the Federation of Malaya the attainment of Independence has furnished conditions for such an alignment. Malays, Chinese, and Indians are forced to confront one another and pushed into speaking for their own ethnic communities on a national scale. But of course the ethnic alignment is not complete; there are other cleavages in the society (some within ethnic groups, to weaken them; others marking divisions across ethnic groups). The political compromise of the Alliance will presumably go on working as long as it can keep within bounds the realization of the principles on which it is based; it could be destroyed by the logic of the communalism which it imperfectly enshrines.

NOTES

1. See J. S. Furnivall, *Netherlands India, A Study of Plural Economy,* London, 1939; "The Political Economy of the Tropical Far East," *Royal Central Asian Journal,* Vol. XXIX (Parts III and IV), July–October 1944; and *Colonial Policy and Practice, A Comparative Study of Burma and Netherlands India,* London, 1948.

2. See especially H. S. Morris, "The Plural Society," *Man,* Vol. LVII, August 1957, article 148; J. Rex, "The Plural Society in Sociological Theory," *The British Journal of Sociology,* Vol. X, No. 2, June 1959; and M. G. Smith,

"Social and Cultural Pluralism," *Annals of the New York Academy of Sciences,* Vol. 83, article 5, January 1960.

3. Based on a paper submitted to the Fourth World Congress of Sociology, Stresa, 1959, and on a paper read in a series on Malaya at the Seminar on Constitutional Problems of Multi-Racial Countries, Institute of Commonwealth Studies, University of London. I am grateful to the Chairman of the Seminar (Professor Kenneth Robinson) and other members for their guidance and comments.

4. The standard work on the Malayan population is T. E. Smith, *Population Growth in Malaya, An Analysis of Recent Trends,* London and New York, 1952.

5. J. M. Gullick, *Indigenous Political Systems of Western Malaya,* London School of Economics Monographs on Social Anthropology, No. 17, London, 1958, p. 21.

6. *Ibid., loc. cit.* For general historical background see D. G. E. Hall, *A History of South-East Asia,* London, 1955.

7. On nationalism in Malaya see T. H. Silcock and Ungku A. Aziz, *Nationalism in Malaya,* Institute of Pacific Relations, New York, 1950.

8. See M. Freedman, "The Handling of Money: A Note on the Background to the Economic Sophistication of Overseas Chinese," *Man,* Vol. LIX, April 1959, article 89.

9. The general scene is described in V. Purcell, *The Chinese in Malaya,* London, 1948.

10. The best work known to me on this subject is E. H. G. Dobby, "Resettlement Transforms Malaya: A Case-History of Relocating the Population of an Asian Plural Society," *Economic Development and Cultural Change,* Vol. 3, October 1953.

11. The latest published work on the secret societies is L. Comber, *Chinese Secret Societies in Malaya, A Survey of the Triad Society from 1800 to 1900,* Monographs of the Association for Asian Studies, No. VI, Locust Valley, N.Y., 1959. I have attempted to give a sociological interpretation of secret societies and other forms of association in "Immigrants and Associations: Chinese in Nineteenth-Century Singapore." *Comparative Studies in Society and History,* III, 1, Oct. 1960.

12. For a recent survey of economic questions see T. H. Silcock, *The Commonwealth Economy in Southeast Asia,* Durham, N.C. and London, 1959.

13. *Op. cit.*

R. L. Sklar

THE CONTRIBUTION
OF TRIBALISM TO NATIONALISM
IN WESTERN NIGERIA (1960)

Tribalism is the red devil of contemporary Africa. It was condemned by nationalists at the first All-African Peoples Conference as "an evil practice" and "a serious obstacle" to "the unity . . . the political evolution . . . (and) the rapid liberation of Africa." [1] The case against tribalism rests mainly on the premise that tribal movements thrive on ethnic group loyalties which undermine wider loyalties to emerging national states. Moreover, tribal loyalties are supposed to entail implicit attachments to traditional values and institutions which are thought to be incompatible with the requirements of social reconstruction.

These assumptions are questioned in this article which is limited to the discussion of two manifestations of tribalism in southwestern Nigeria. The first, pantribalism, is a vigorous offspring of modern urbanization and the distinctive expression of ethnic group activity for the most politically conscious members of a new and rising class. The second, communal partisanship, is endemic to rural areas and old towns where traditional values are paramount and the socially cohesive ties of traditional authority are binding upon the people. Both manifestations of tribalism have given impetus to the growth of mass political parties and the movement for national independence.

It will suffice as background to outline briefly the political setting of Nigeria, a nation of some 35 million people (according to a dated census), and to identify the main tribal groups and the major political parties. Nigeria is a Federation of three political Regions, each of which has a Legislature and an Executive Council headed by a Premier. In every Region a single "nationality" group of culturally related tribes [2]

SOURCE. R. L. Sklar, "The Contribution of Tribalism to Nationalism in Western Nigeria," reprinted from *Journal of Human Relations*, VIII, 3/4, Spring–Summer, 1960, pp. 407–415, by permission of *Journal of Human Relations*.

is numerically preponderant: The Yoruba in the Western Region, the Ibo in the Eastern Region and the Hausa in the Northern Region. There are three major political parties: the Action Group, the National Council of Nigeria, and the Cameroons (N.C.N.C.), and the Northern Peoples Congress; they control the Governments of the Western, Eastern, and Northern Regions respectively. The Action Group is the official Opposition in the East and in the North; the N.C.N.C. is the official Opposition in the West and operates through an ally in the North; the Northern Peoples Congress is restricted to persons of Northern origin. The Northern Region, however, contains about 54 per cent of the population of Nigeria, and the Northern Peoples Congress emerged from the federal election of December, 1959 with 142 of the 312 seats in the Federal House of Representatives, followed by the N.C.N.C. with 89, the Action Group with 73, and 8 members who are independent of the major parties. Presently the Federal Government consists of an N.P.C.-N.C.N.C. coalition with an N.P.C. Prime Minister, while the Action Group forms the Federal Opposition. Nigeria is destined to achieve independence within the British Commonwealth on October 1, 1960.

PANTRIBALISM

The Yoruba People, or "nationality," of Western Nigeria comprise a number of tribal sections that have a long history of conflict with one another attributable largely to precolonial effects of the slave trade. Pan-Yoruba unity was an ideal fostered by a twentieth century elite of educated men and women who followed entrepreneurial, professional, managerial, and clerical vocations in new urban areas, principally in the commercial centers of Lagos and Ibadan. In 1944 a group of Yoruba students and professional men in London organized a Pan-Yoruba cultural society called *Egbe Omo Oduduwa* (Sons of the Descendants of Oduduwa).[3] Four years later the society was inaugurated in Western Nigeria at a conference attended by illustrious Yoruba personalities who claimed to follow the example of pantribal organization set by other tribes and nationalities, in particular the Ibo people of Eastern Nigeria. It is not improbable that the founders of the *Egbe Omo Oduduwa* were motivated by interests that were political as well as cultural. Most of them were politically-oriented men of the new and rising class—lawyers, doctors, businessmen, civil servants, and certain far-sighted chiefs—who perceived that the locus of economic and political power was not local but Regional and national. In 1950, leaders of the *Egbe Omo Oduduwa* were among the principal organizers of a new political party called the Action Group, which came to power in the Western Region as a result of a general election held the following year. It was the chief aim of the founders of the Action Group to overcome the ingrained particularism of the Yoruba tribes and weld them together behind a political party that would serve their common interests. In the rural areas and in traditional towns of Western Nigeria, chiefs are among the most influential leaders of opinion, and the fate of a political party may hinge on the extension of their support. The Action Group applied that principle and reared its mass organization largely upon the foundation of support by traditional authorities. Two powerful inducements attracted various chiefs into the fold of the Action Group: some of the chiefs were nonparochial in outlook and responded to the cultural appeal of Pan-Yoruba unity; others were impressed by the political and economic power of the pantribal elite and embraced the new party with enthusiasm or with resignation to the new facts of political life.

The rise of the Action Group in the city of Lagos attested to the efficacy of collaboration between a traditional authority and the pantribal elite. Lagos, the capital of the Federation, is a Yoruba town that burgeoned into the principal port and main commercial center of Nigeria. Prior to 1954 it was administered under the Western Regional Government. The population of Lagos may be said to comprise three main ethnic categories: the indigenous Yorubas, the nonindigenous Yoruba settlers, and other settlers who are non-Yoruba. Traditional values weigh heavily upon the indigenous community while the values and social perspectives of the settler groups are primarily nontraditional. For about 25 years prior to 1950, Lagos local politics pivoted on the rivalry between a majority of the Yoruba indigenous community and the main body of Yoruba settlers. When the Action Group was organized in 1950, it derived its following in Lagos mainly from the Yoruba elite, most of whom were settlers. The vast majority of indigenous Yorubas and most of the non-Yoruba settlers favored an older party, the National Council of Nigeria and the Camerooms (N.C.N.C.). Within a few years of the inauguration of its Lagos branch, the Action Group managed to obtain the support of a majority of the Yoruba indigenes, an achievement that was due largely to the efforts of the *Oba* (Paramount Chief) of Lagos. The latter was an enthusiastic proponent of pan-Yoruba unity and he applied his influence among the indigenes effectively in behalf of the Action Group.

Everywhere in the Western Region, leaders of the Action Group solicited the active co-operation of traditional chiefs. Those few chiefs who were hostile to the party or obstructed the implementation of its policies courted jeopardy. A celebrated case of opposition by one paramount chief, the ex-*Alafin* (king) of Oyo, created a general impression throughout the Western Region that no chief could stand against the Government Party and survive. Oyo was once the capital of an extensive Yoruba empire, and the *Alafin* is one of the most exalted of the Yoruba chiefs. However, the ex-*Alafin* was a conservative chief of the old order whose relationship with the Action Group deteriorated rapidly soon after that party came to power. Supporters of the *Alafin*, including nontraditionalists who opposed the Action Group for political reasons, formed an Oyo Peoples Party and decided to affiliate with the N.C.N.C. In September, 1954, there was an outbreak of partisan violence at Oyo in the course of which several people were killed. The Regional Government held the *Alafin* to blame and suspended him from office; eventually he was deposed. In this context the substance of the issue at Oyo is irrelevant. What matters to us is the fact that a powerful chief was suspended by the Government and banished from his domain upon the recommendation of a committee of *Obas* (Paramount Chiefs) at a joint meeting with the leaders of the *Egbe Omo Oduduwa*. The Action Group may have resolved to banish the *Alafin* in any case, but the Egbe, technically a pantribal cultural organization, supplied a moral sanction from the most respectable elements in Yoruba-land, including the *Alafin's* traditional peers.

It must be emphasized that the Action Group as a political party, and the *Egbe Omo Oduduwa*, as a cultural organization, are technically distinct organizations. In theory the *Egbe* is nonpartisan and its relationship to the Action Group is wholly unofficial; in practice its service to the Action Group is beyond compare. The two associations are virtually inseparable in certain rural areas where the traditional chiefs bless them both in the name of the cultural and political interests of the people. Frequently, the pantribal organization is employed to settle disputes between Yoruba personalities, in particular among chiefs, that might otherwise embarrass the Action Group. Occasionally, it has been utilized by the pantribal elite, as in the extreme case of the ex-*Alafin* of Oyo, to coerce a recalcitrant chief. In general, the *Egbe Omo Oduduwa* functions as a crucial link between the Action Group, the chiefs, and other men of influence to facilitate the implementation of party policies (including policies affecting the position of chiefs), with a minimum of difficulty or resistance.

COMMUNAL PARTISANSHIP

Communal partisanship, unlike pantribalism, implies the affirmation of traditional value. Yet the nationalistic parties have relied upon it for mass support in areas of traditional habitation. The Government Party of the Western Region has enlisted communal partisanship by means of a systematic program involving the co-operation of chiefs. However, there are examples of communal partisanship emerging in opposition to the Government Party and persisting in defiance of the communal chief. Two such cases, at Benin and Ibadan, are examined here.

Benin, the capital city of the Edo people, provides an example of conflict between a traditional community and a rising class. The Edo are a minority group in the predominantly Yoruba Western Region. Some years ago, Edo men of wealth and high social status formed a Benin branch of the Reformed *Ogboni* Fraternity,[4] an exclusive society founded at Lagos by rising class Yorubas who were inspired by the example of European freemasonry. At first, membership in the Lodge was restricted to the town elite, i.e., professionals, businessmen, employees of firms, and leading chiefs. Subsequently, the Lodge was transformed by its leadership into a political machine and opened to all administrative and business officials, both high and petty. From 1948 to 1951 the *Ogbonis,* under a dynamic leader, dominated the administration of the Benin Division to the chagrin of its traditional ruler, the *Oba* of Benin, and the distress of the people. *Ogbonis* are reported to have controlled the tax system, the markets, the police, the courts, access to the firms, etc. It is said that the members of the Lodge could violate the law with impunity, and that they enjoyed special privileges in most spheres of political and economic activity. By 1950 *Ogbonism* had become synonymous with oppression. Moreover, the people of Benin identified it with the bugbear of Yoruba domination, and their anxieties mounted in 1951 when the principal *Ogboni* leaders affiliated with the Action Group, a new political party under Yoruba control. Meanwhile, non-*Ogbonis* formed a popular party, known as the *Otu Edo* (Benin Community), dedicated to defend tradition and the sacred institution of *Oba-ship* against the alleged encroachments of usurpers. In 1951 the popular party swept the *Ogbonis* from office in local government elections and defeated them soundly in contests for the Regional Legislature.

However, the vindication of traditional value by the electorate did not restore the political supremacy of the *Oba.* His attempts to control the *Otu Edo* were frustrated by progressive leaders of that party for whom the cause of tradition had been an expedient means to further nationalistic and other political ends. Since the *Ogbonis* were partisan to the Action Group, the leaders of the *Otu Edo* resolved to affiliate with the N.C.N.C. The *Oba* spurned the thought of affiliation with either national party. His primary interest was the creation of a new state in the non-Yoruba provinces of the Western Region where *Edo* influence would be dominant, and he organized an independent party to attain that objective. But it is perilous for any chief to stand against the party in power. In the words of an official report, commenting on the case of the ex-*Alafin* of Oyo, to which we have referred: "The shadow of one great Chief, now deposed and in exile, lies across the foreground of every Chief's outlook today."[5] In 1955 the *Oba* made his peace with the Western Regional Government; the Government endorsed the idea of a non-Yoruba state in principle, and the *Oba,* in turn, agreed to join the Government as a Minister without portfolio. A small minority of the Benin people who supported him against the *Ogboni* menace to his authority now followed him into the Action Group; but the vast majority remained loyal to their communal party, the *Otu Edo*. Their reverence for Benin tradition and the institution of *Oba*-ship (Chieftaincy) persisted, but they condemned the incumbent *Oba* (Paramount Chief) for his switch to the party that was associated in Benin with *Ogbonism* and class interest.

Our second case of communal partisanship, at Ibadan, capital of the Western Region, reflects an underlying conflict between urban settlers and sons of the soil. Ibadan, with a population of nearly 500,000, is the largest African city on the African continent. Urbanization at Ibadan exemplifies the two sector pattern of development that is typical of traditional towns. A vast majority of the people dwell in the teeming indigenous sector; they live in family "compounds" of more than one hundred people in most cases, subject to the traditional authority of a family head. An average Ibadan man divides his time between the town and the rural districts, where he cultivates cocoa on family land. Men of initiative from other towns and villages have settled in the new sectors of Ibadan for commercial and occupational reasons. Among them, the Ijebu people are the most numerous. The Ibadan and the Ijebu are neighboring Yoruba tribes; traditionally they were rivals and in recent years the historic antipathy between them has been revived by economic competition. In 1950 the indigene-settler conflict reached a climax over issues involving land ownership and local representation. The non-Ibadan group formed a Native Settlers Union to press for the rights of settlers both to acquire landed property in Ibadan on a freehold basis and to stand for election to the Ibadan local government. These demands were supported by the pan-Yoruba tribal association.

We have observed that in 1951 the Action Group triumphed in the Western election and became the Regional Government Party. It is pertinent to this discussion of Ibadan politics that the Action Group leader, an Ijebu Yoruba, was the General Secretary of the pan-Yoruba tribal union and a highly successful barrister resident of Ibadan where he was a legal adviser to the Native Settlers Union. Six Ibadan indigenes were elected to the Western House of Assembly on the platform of an Ibadan Peoples Party. Following the election, five of them declared for the Action Group and one was appointed as a Minister in the new Western Regional Government. The Ibadan chiefs and people reacted sharply. For several years the trend of events had run against their perceived interests; Ibadan chiefs had been shorn of their traditional prerogatives by a number of administrative reforms; acres of cocoa plants belonging to Ibadan farmers had been destroyed by the Government in a well-intentioned but costly and unpopular attempt to check the spread of a contagious blight; Ibadan lands were acquired by settlers who supported various objectionable reforms; and a settler personality had suddenly become the leader of the Government. In 1954 the single elected member who did not join the

Action Group organized an Ibadan tribal party with the support of the chiefs and the leaders of an Ibadan farmers' movement. The new party, called the *Mabolaje,* which means in Yoruba, "[Do] not reduce the dignity of Chiefs," affiliated with the National Council of Nigeria and the Cameroons. Swiftly the *Mabolaje* established its supremacy in Ibadan; eventually its leader became the First Vice President of the N.C.N.C. and Leader of the Opposition in the Western House of Assembly. Only a small minority of the indigenous rising class embraced the populist *Mabolaje.* The great majority of entrepreneurial, professional, and educated men of Ibadan gravitated to the Government Party. Furthermore, in 1955, an Action Group supporter was elevated to the head chiefship of Ibadan, whereupon most of the chiefs and aspirants to chieftaincy, who require the endorsement of the Head Chief for promotion or recognition by the Government, transferred their support from the party named in their honor to the party in power. As at Benin, the loss of the citadel of chieftaincy did not weaken the party of traditional value, and the dominance of the *Mabolaje* at Ibadan has been evinced at every election of recent years.

At Benin and Ibadan, communal partisanship emerged as a reaction to the political drives of a rising class. In Benin the new class was wholly indigenous; in Ibadan it was mainly a settler class with an indigenous component. In both cases the outlook of the indigenous rising class was supratribal, which led it to embrace a political party that the people at large identified with interests which they regarded as being inimical to the values of their communal traditions. The tribal parties affiliated with a rival national party, in both cases the National Council of Nigeria and the Cameroons. They are properly termed tribal party affiliates because their respective memberships are confined to the indigenous communal groups of Benin and Ibadan. Nonindigenous supporters are considered to be partisans of the N.C.N.C. at Benin or the N.C.N.C.-*Mabolaje* Grand Alliance at Ibadan, but not of the *Otu Edo* or the *Mabolaje* per se.

The ordinary follower or member of a tribal party in an area of traditional habitation is likely to regard it as an extension of the social order to which he is spiritually, sentimentally, and spontaneously attached. In his mind, and in the minds of others with whom he habitually associates, the party is endowed with the values of the traditional order. Partisanship of this nature is communal in the classical sense.[6] It implies the ideal of an integrated system of values involving the combination or synthesis of political, spiritual, and cultural values into a unified moral universe similar to the symbolic universe of traditional society.[7] Consequently, supporters of a communal membership party are apt to view opposition to that party by a member of the community with moral indignation and to punish it as antisocial conduct. Of course, the concept of communal partisanship does not correspond exactly to the psychology of any particular individual. It does not apply at all to the leadership of the tribal parties of Benin or Ibadan which was drawn primarily from the rising class, mainly from those populist and radically disposed individuals who rallied to the popular cause in principle or in consequence of a perceived advantage. The nature of their partisanship is properly termed associational rather than communal; it implies rational, deliberate affiliation without ritual significance in affirmation of a political belief or in pursuit of a personal goal.[8] Owing to the influence of radical leaders, communal participation parties have assimilated nationalistic principles within their codes of traditional values. A prime example is the *Mabolaje* of Ibadan, which was conservative with respect to administrative reform but radical with respect to political nationalism, i.e., the movement for independence.

CONCLUSION

In Western Nigeria most rising class elements in every tribal and nationality group are drawn by their interests into the fold of the party in power. By and large, ethnic affinities are outweighed by class interests, as an Ibadan where most of the indigenous rising class joined their social peers among the settlers within the Government Party. Prudent chiefs normally go along, since the Government Party controls the system of appointment and deposition. In 1958 only one member in 51 of the Western House Chiefs (a co-ordinate chamber of the Regional Legislature) was identified as a supporter of the Opposition Party, while 31 elected members out of 80 in the House of Assembly belonged to the Opposition.[9] Furthermore, Nigerian chiefs in general are associated with the economic as well as the political interests of the rising class, and the number of chiefs in business is legion. Progressive chiefs and other culturally conscious members of the enlightened minority required an ideological nexus of their ethnic and class values that would supply a rationale for their nontraditional and supratribal interests. That need was admirably satisfied by the theory of pantribalism.

Within its defined cultural sphere, pantribalism is cosmopolitan and consistent with the affirmation of nontraditional interests or the negation of traditional interests that obstruct the policies of the pantribal elite. Pantribalism like Jewish Zionism, is innately secular, and produces a sense of "national" identity among peoples who are ethnically or tribally diverse but culturally related. The pantribal spirit was ardent in the breasts of those who felt the most urgent need for unity beyond the parochial confines of their tribes. These were typically men of the rising class to whom the conditions of colonial rule were least tolerable. When their perspectives rise above the stage of ethnic "nationality," pantribalism may be expected to lose its class distinction and the magic of its political appeal.

Communal partisanship is a social and psychological form of party-type tribal movement in areas of traditional habitation where the integral values of traditional society have not been transformed by the process of social change. In many cases local parties based on communal partisanship have been brought into existence deliberately by nationalists and rising class elements with the co-operation of chiefs. Occasionally, as at Benin and Ibadan, the emergence of communal partisanship has reflected the repudiation of a rising class by the people of a traditional community in transition where class structure is incipient and a lower class of psychology has not evolved. Most chiefs have a leading foot in the rising class, especially if it supports a governing party, and they are likely to disavow communal parties that are associated with the Opposition. At Benin and Ibadan, the nature of conflict was class versus community, rather than modern elements versus traditional elements or higher class against lower class.[10] However, rising classes herald the decline of old orders, and the transformation of classless communities into class societies is perceptible in the tendency of communal partisans to shed their traditional values and to adopt lower class perspectives.[11]

Throughout Nigeria, millions of tradition-bound people were drawn through the medium of communal partisanship into the mainstream of political activity where they accepted the leadership of progressive nationalists. Therein lies its historic significance. No nationalist movement or political party could have achieved independence for Nigeria without the massive support of the people, especially the rural masses and those millions who live in traditional urban communities. The British Government would not, in principle, have agreed to transfer power to a leadership group that was not broadly based. On the other hand, Britain could not, in principle or in fact, deny independence to popularly elected leaders who enjoy the confidence of a decisive majority of the people and insisted upon the termination of colonial rule. Communal partisanship, based on psychological commitments to the traditional values of tribal groups, was utilized by nationalist leaders to mobilize mass support in rural areas and old towns.

These observations will not restore tribalism to grace in Africa. But the devil deserves his due; and in Nigeria, at least, the contribution of tribalism to nationalism has been crucial.

NOTES

1. These strictures were applied to religious separatism as well as to tribalism. See the Resolution on Tribalism, Religious Separatism, and Tradi-

tional Institutions, adopted by the All-African Peoples Conference held at Accra, Ghana, December 5–13, 1958.

2. James S. Coleman has defined the concepts of "tribe" and "nationality" as follows: A tribe is "a relatively small group of people who share a common culture and who are descended from a common ancestor. The tribe is the largest social group defined primarily in terms of kinship, and is normally an aggregation of clans." "A nationality is the largest traditional African group above a tribe which can be distinguished from other groups by one or more objective criteria (normally language)." *Nigeria: Background in Nationalism* (Berkeley and Los Angeles: University of California Press, 1958), pp. 423–24.

3. *Oduduwa* is a culture hero and mythical progenitor of the Yoruba people. The principal founder of the society, who later became Premier of the Western Region and is now Leader of the Opposition in the Federal Government, expounded a theory of nationalism based on pantribal integration under the auspices of educated elites. See Obafemi Awolowo, *Path to Nigerian Freedom* (London: Faber & Faber, Ltd., 1947).

4. The traditional *Ogboni* was a politico-religious institution in certain historic Yoruba states. See W. R. Bascom, "The Sociological Role of the Yoruba Cult Group," *American Anthropologist*, 56, No. 1, Part 2, Memoir 63. (January, 1944), pp. 64–73; and Saburi O. Biobaku, *The Egba and Their Neighbors, 1842–1872* (Oxford: Clarendon Press, 1957), p. 6.

5. Colonial Office, Report of the Commission appointed to enquire into the fears of Minorities and the means of allaying them (London: H.M.S.O., 1958), p. 11.

6. Ferdinand Tonnies, *Fundamental Concepts of Sociology* (Gemeinschaft und Gesellschaft), translated and supplemented by Charles P. Loomis (New York: American Book Company, 1940), pp. 37–39, 67–70.

7. Cf. M. Fortes and E. E. Evans-Pritchard, *African Political Systems* (London: Oxford University Press, 1940), pp. 16–18. S. F. Nadel drew attention to the cohesive value systems of subtribal groups that we find operative in the case of tribal parties. *A Black Byzantium* (London: Oxford University Press, 1942), pp. 22–26.

8. Maurice Duverger utilized the concepts of Community and Association to distinguish between ideal types of participation. He observed ". . . the nature of participation can be very different according to the categories of members: especially does it seem probable that electors and members are not joined to the party by links of the same nature and that it is the Community type party that is predominant among electors, even in parties where members and militants belong rather to the Association type." *Political Parties* (London: Methuen & Co., 1954), pp. 128–29. Duverger's analysis of participation goes beyond the purpose of this paper to general theory of party classification.

9. Most chiefs are supporters and patrons of the Government Party rather than members in the technical terms. The fiction of their nonpartisanship in theory is still respected on occasion by party leaders and chiefs alike.

10. Needless to say, party division never corresponds exactly to sociological differentiation, but it is significant of most of the rising class and most chiefs who affiliate with a particular party in areas where popular sentiment is

to the contrary. In this paper competition between rising class and communal membership parties is not regarded as a manifestation of class conflict inasmuch as the tribal societies involved are not structured in terms of class. Anthropological studies of them generally describe communal societies of a corporate nature, segmented vertically by lineages and stratified by age grades and title associations. Chieftaincies may be vested in particular families; but the families of kings, chiefs, elders and titled men have not been differentiated in terms of social class.

11. This kind of change in perspective is evident at Ibadan and elsewhere, as at Enugu in the Eastern Region, where many of the communal partisans are employed as industrial laborers. In the Emirate states of Northern Nigeria, class structures are traditional and the class factor is fundamental to the analysis of competition between parties in that section. Rising classes in Northern Nigeria emerge within an existing class structure which they alter; rising classes in the part of Nigeria with which this paper is concerned emerge from classless communities which they transform into class societies. Since the new classes do not rise relative to other classes it might be preferable to term them emerging or emergent classes.

V

Class, Education, and Power:
The Emerging Class Structure

B. S. Cohn

THE INITIAL BRITISH IMPACT ON INDIA:
A CASE STUDY OF THE BENARES REGION (1960)

The British administrative frontier in India had widely differing effects
on the political and social structures of the regions into which it moved
from the middle of the eighteenth century until the middle of the
nineteenth century. It is impossible to generalize on the impact of the
administration, because the regions into which it moved differed in their
political and social structures, and because British administration and
ideas about administration, both in India and in Great Britain, changed
markedly throughout this hundred-year period.

This paper is a case study of the establishment of British administration in the Benares region [1]—an area which encompasses the present
districts of Ballia, Benares, Ghazipur, Jaunpur, and Mirzapur minus its
southern portion.[2] The concern is with the nature of the political system
before the establishment of British rule and the changes wrought by that
rule—who had power and how the power was administered; how the
British changed the political system; who administered for the new authority; and how a small group of Indians, whom I term the under civil
servants, benefited from their employment under the British. I will try
to show that, through the establishment of their legal, revenue, and
administrative systems, the British created new economic conditions; that
individuals who had the necessary training and who had the opportunity
to join the new administration capitalized on these new economic conditions, became wealthy, and bought land that came into a newly created
market through the administrative action of the British. A new class was
thus born in Indian society. It is this class which became the "respectable
natives" after its members had settled down as landlords. Discussions of
the effects of British rule on the Indian class structure have usually

SOURCE. B. S. Cohn, "The Initial British Impact on India: A Case Study of the
Benares Region," reprinted from *Journal of Asian Studies*, XIX, 4, 1961, pp. 418–431.

emphasized the role of the British and the new economic and social conditions which they created in establishing a new urban middle class; they have often overlooked the fact that the new conditions provided an opportunity for the creation of a new landed class as well. It is beyond the scope of this paper to describe and analyze the political role of this new landed class in late nineteenth and twentieth century India, except to point out the neglect of the origins, development, and role of the class in modern India.

POLITICAL OFFICIALS AND POLITICAL STRUCTURE IN THE EIGHTEENTH CENTURY

With the breakup of the Mughal Empire in the eighteenth century, three political systems emerged: the Mughal (national), the regional, and the local. The systems were interrelated; in some cases they existed side-by-side and in other cases they had a hierarchical relationship. Each system had a characteristic structure and realm of activity, as well as characteristic types of officials.

Mughal Political and Administrative Structure

The Mughal system, looking at it from Benares, was represented by the new state of Oudh, a conglomeration of regional and local entities, held together in the eighteenth century by the abilities and military powers of the Nawab Vazirs. The Nawab Vazirs had inherited some of the administrative structure of the Mughal Empire and a good deal of the theory of the administration. Many of the Mughal offices continued in operation: in the judicial branch of the service, *kāzīs* and *kotwāls,* and in the revenue service, *parganā sarrishtadārs.* The *kāzīs*—of which there were several grades, down to the level of *kāzīs* in *parganā* which are revenue subdivisions of *sarkārs* (districts)—theoretically had jurisdiction over most criminal and civil cases. In addition, they registered marriages for the Muslim population and certified documents.[3] *Kāzīs* had to be adult males, Muslims, and free. They had to be men of learning and scholarship in the Muslim law and religion. Often as part of their position they had the duty of leading the Friday prayers.[4] By the latter part of the eighteenth century, the position appears to have become hereditary within families; upon the death of the incumbent, his son or another male descendent would petition the sovereign for his installation in the office of his deceased relative.[5] In the late eighteenth century, when some of their judicial functions had been curtailed, *kāzīs* were paid by fees for attesting documents and registering marriages. According to early nineteenth century records concerning *kāzīs,* the British accepted the hereditary nature of the post, and the post was maintained to register deeds and marriages.

In the seventeenth century, the *kotwāl* was much like a chief of police in an urban center. His main function was the prevention of crime and the apprehension of criminals. But in Upper India, by the latter part of the eighteenth century, he functioned much as a city magistrate and tried cases, mainly of a criminal nature. A different type of person appears to have held the office of *kotwāl* than held the office of *kāzī*. For example, in late eighteenth century Benares City, the kotwalship was directly under the control of the Nawab Vazir of Oudh, not under the Raja of Benares who controlled most of the other aspects of the administration. Unlike the *kāzīs*, the *kotwāls* did not settle down and become hereditary holders of the office, tied to the local region. Rather, they appear to have been relatives or close followers of the Nawab Vazir; the position of *kotwāl* was looked upon as an important financial plum for a relative or friend.[6]

In the revenue service the *pargana sarrishtadār*, sometimes called a *kānūngo*, was the head record keeper of the *pargana*. In theory he was to provide a check for the imperial government on the activities of the revenue collectors.[7] The office was a hereditary one, with the skills and, more important, the records being passed from father to son. The *kānūngo* was paid by provision of a rent-free grant of land, which theoretically kept him free from the pressures of both the tax payers and the tax collectors. In reality, *kānūngos* appear in the late eighteenth century and in the nineteenth century as accomplices of the tax collectors. In 1796, there were 168 *kānūngos* in the Benares region. Judging on the basis of names, fifty-five were Kayastha or Baniya, twenty-two were Rajput or Bhumihar, seven were Muslim, and I couldn't make an ascription about the caste of thirty-seven.[8] The *sarrishtadār*, like the *kāzīs*, were local men, but in the Benares region at least, they were overwhelmingly Hindu, the largest group being Baniya or Kayastha.

It is important to note that while the Mughal-style officials—the *kāzīs*, the *kotwāls*, and the *kānūngos*—derived their functions and their offices from the Mughal system, they operated within the local and regional systems, and helped, in a tenuous way, to hinge the systems together.

Regional Political and Administrative Structure

The Nawab Vazir of Oudh, the inheritor of the part of the Mughal empire encompassing the Benares region, had little direct political power in the regional and local political systems. He held for awhile a few forts, and from time to time he tried to exercise his power through force of arms. But by the middle of the eighteenth century, the Raja of Benares, Balwant Singh, was successful in becoming almost independent of the Nawab Vazir of Oudh. The Raja paid a lump sum annually as his tax (tribute) obligation. He was occasionally pressured into providing some troops for the Nawab's army. And he still had to accept the Nawab's appointment of *kotwāls* and the continuation of the *kāzīs* and *pargana sarrishtadārs*.

The Raja built up his own administrative organization, apart from that which existed in the region under the Mughals. The main function of the Raja's administration was levying and collecting taxes and building a military force sufficient to control rebellious elements within the region and keep him as free as possible from the Nawab Vazir. The organization which the Raja built was not the type of civil service the Mughals had had or what the British developed in the nineteenth century. For the collection of revenue, he relied on officials who were independent contractors. They agreed to pay the Raja a lump sum for the right to collect the taxes of a certain *pargana*. They derived their profits from the difference between what they collected and what they had agreed to pay the Raja, plus certain recognized dues which they could collect.

In 1788, the Raja's revenue was collected largely by twenty-two *amils* (tax collectors).[9] Of these, seven—three Muslims and four Hindus—were responsible for approximately eighty-five per cent of the revenue demand. The Muslims, as far as I have been able to find out, were drawn from a group of civil servants who had no local ties initially, but were Persian in origin. They or their ancestors had migrated to India and had found employment with one of the local Rajas or Nawabs. The fortunate and clever ones were able to acquire capital and go into the profitable business of tax farming after a career of administrative duties. Three Muslim officials of the late eighteenth and early nineteenth centuries will serve as examples of the civil servants of Persian origin.

Mehendi Ali Khan, an *amil* under the Raja of Benares, had a long, checkered and eventually brilliant career. He was from Persia.[10] As a young man he went to Hyderabad. In 1782, his fortunes were apparently at a lob ebb and he was involved in the robbery of a Muslim holy man.[11] In 1788, he was in Benares where through his diligence and his knowledge of the tax system he became a principal source of information on the Benares tax and tenure system for Jonathan Duncan, then the resident. When Duncan was appointed Governor of Bombay in 1795, Mehendi Ali Khan evidently went with him. In the early part of the nineteenth century, Duncan used Mehendi Ali Khan for high level diplomatic missions to Persia.[12]

Ali Ibrahim Khan, although not a tax official, is another representative of this type. He was born in Patna of a Persian family and served several different Rajas of Bengal. Warren Hastings appointed him Chief Magistrate of Benares in 1782. He was well known to Hastings and the English in Calcutta at this time, having been a friend and advisor of Mir Kasim, Nawab of Bengal from 1760–63. Having survived the revolution of 1763 in Bengal, he became *diwan* (prime minister) to Murbarkk al Daula, Nawab of Bengal, during the period 1770–73.[13] In addition he was noted as a scholar and compiled a work on Hindustani poets.[14]

Ali Ibraham Kahn appears to have been as successful an official under the British as he was under the Nawabs of Bengal.[15]

Maulana Khair ud Din Muhammad of Jaunpur was a scribe who apparently never rose to the lucrative office of Mehendi Ali Khan or achieved the distinction of Ali Ibraham Khan. Perhaps he is more typical of the late eighteenth century official of Persian background. Maulana Khair was born in Allahabad in 1751 and received his education in Allahabad and Jaunpur, where he studied Muslim theology, law, rhetoric and astronomy.[16] He served as a teacher in Benares, as a scribe for the British in Allahabad, in Delhi in the Court of Shah Alam, and at the court of the Nawab Vazir of Oudh. In the later part of his life, he served as private secretary to James Anderson, the East India Company's resident at Scindhia's court, and as secretary to the English judge of Jaunpur. During his career he was an active scholar, writing several histories and works of literary criticism.[17]

Most of the non-Muslim *āmils* under the Raja of Benares appear to have been relatives or close associates of the Raja of Benares. Almost all appear to have been Bhumihar, the caste of the Raja. Several of the *āmils* held high posts in the Raja's household service, which probably meant that they were high-level advisers or assistants of the Raja.[18] The Raja was able to keep his civil service relatively small because of the function of the bankers of Benares City in relation to the collection and payment of revenue. All the revenue of the region passed through the hands of the bankers on its way to the Raja's treasury. Revenue was due from the *āmils* in monthly installments, but the *āmil* could collect the revenue from the payers only at the time of harvest. Therefore the *āmils* needed short-term notes from the bankers to meet the requirements of the Raja. Much of the function of the collector's office in relation to the revenue was actually in the hands of private bankers. Duncan commented, "The Schroffs can in fact in a great measure command the Raja and the Government itself with respect to the realization of revenue." [19] In a number of instances, banking and money lending in the late eighteenth century were stepping stones to āmilships. Although being an *āmil* was a riskier business than banking, the profits were higher, especially if one combined being an *āmil* with banking. Such a combination was enjoyed by Sheo Lal Dube, whom we will discuss later.

The Raja of Benares, Balwant Singh, theoretically was an officer of both the Nawab Vazir of Oudh and the Mughal Emperor in Delhi. He had a *sanad* (royal grant) granted by the Mughal Emperor and he paid revenue (tribute) to the Nawab Vazir. He could also be forced to provide troops for the Vazir and did at the Battle of Baxar in 1764. Politically, the Raja of Benares had to face in two directions. He fought a continuous and devious battle to become completely independent of the Nawab. He also had to keep in check lineages and local chiefs and rajas who had power within his province. The Raja did not have enough strength to exterminate the local power holders; even if he had, it would not have been economically or militarily a wise way for him to use it. The Raja's treasury came from land revenue paid by the local lineages and chiefs. The Raja did not have adequate administrative machinery to circumvent the local power holders and collect revenue directly from the cultivators. Similarly, he was dependent on the local lineages and chiefs for some of the troops he needed to maintain his independence from the Nawab of Oudh.[20] The Raja wanted to eliminate the more powerful of the local chiefs who might supplant him as the regional Raja, but he needed to keep the system going to maintain his own position.

Local Political and Administrative Structures

The local political system (as distinct from the regional, Benares, and the "national," Oudh) in operation in the eighteenth century was that of the little kingdom. In the Benares region there were three types—rajadoms, *jāgīrs*, and *tālukās*.[21] Each type of little kingdom had different types of local officials. The *tālukā*, which was a lineage-dominated political unit, for obvious reasons had a minimal development of official structure other than the *patwārīs* (keepers of village records). The *patwārīs*, although technically part of the old Mughal administrative structure, were the employees and servants of the dominant lineage in the *tālukā*. Members of the lineage, the "brotherhood" of the older British literature, were the tax assessors, tax collectors, police, and judges as far as the population of the *tālukā* was concerned. The *jāgīrs* were grants of tax-free land made by either the Raja of Benares, the Nawab of Oudh, or the Mughal Emperor to officials as rewards for service. The *jāgīrdār* had agents to collect the rent due him. Often the *jāgīrdār* was an absentee landlord.

The administration of local rajas, such as Saltanat Singh of Badlapur Taluka, the Raja of Raja Bazar, and the Raja of Aghora Burhar, was a scaled-down version of the administration of the Raja of Benares. The organization of Badlapur will serve as an example of a rajadom. Badlapur, a *tālukā* of seventy-four villages on the border of what was in the late eighteenth century the border between British territory and Oudh, was in the control of Saltanat Singh, a Bais Rajput.[22] Saltanat Singh had a fort at Badlapur, and received taxes (tribute) from the seventy-four villages. The Bais Rajputs were not the only Rajput lineage in the *tālukā*. For leaders and men for his army, Saltanat Singh relied heavily on other lineages as well. Some of his closest advisers and military leaders were the leaders of other lineages in the *tālukā*. His army had Ahirs and Pasis in it as well as Rajputs. Saltanat Singh had in his court, in addition to Rajput military chiefs, two Baniyas, one of whom was his treasurer and another who was responsible for the acquisition of foodstuffs for the army.

There was also a group of pandits in the court, and several professional bards. For their services to him, these officials were supported through land grants made by Saltanat Singh. Interestingly enough, even though the British in 1796 confiscated Saltanat Singh's personal lands and abrogated his *zamindāri* (estate) rights over the remainder of the *tālukā*, they recognized the validity of the tax-free grants made to the pandits and bards.[23] If we may use the term "official" in this type of political system, the officials were largely the allies or followers of the man or family who held power in the *tālukā*. They were not civil servants or military officers such as developed under the Mughals.

The local political system was based on the dominance of one lineage over a territory. The dominant lineage was usually Rajput, but was sometimes Bhumihar, Muslim, or Brahman. The territory was considered as belonging to the dominant lineage, both by the lineage itself and by other castes. In most cases the dominance was based on conquest or subjugation of the pre-existing population. In a few cases territories were granted by Mughal or pre-Mughal emperors for service. In other cases the *sanads* granted were a recognition of the local conquest. The dominant lineage exacted from its low-caste followers shares of their crops if they were cultivators or handicraft products if they were artisans. In return, it provided protection.

Thus in the eighteenth century these three political systems, with their three types of civil servants, existed in an articulated system dependent on mutual antagonism and a delicate balance.

BRITISH ADMINISTRATION AND THE UNDER CIVIL SERVANTS

In 1775, the British obtained sovereignty over Benares Province. But they did not exercise any direct political authority except to establish a resident. After Chait Singh's rebellion in 1781, when Warren Hastings replaced Chait Singh with his relative, Mahip Narain Singh, the British began to take a more direct interest in the administration of Benares.[24] But the power of the regional raja and the local chiefs and lineages was undisturbed. The British had only taken over the position of the national power, and were content to accept the payment of tribute that usually went to the Nawab Vazir of Oudh.

From 1788 to 1795, there was a brief transition period. At first the Raja of Benares had full rule, but much of the real administrative power was in the hands of a British resident (Jonathan Duncan) and two European assistants. By 1795, full British administration was extended to the Benares Province when Jonathan Duncan's five and ten year revenue settlements made on behalf of the Raja were declared permanent. An

English collector and several European assistants were appointed for all of the Benares Province (what is today five districts). Civil and criminal judges with European registers were appointed in Benares City, Jaunpur, Ghazipur, and Mirzapur. A provincial court of appeal with three European judges and a European register was established for the four inferior courts in Benares City.

In most general discussions of the development of British administration in India, little attention is paid to the question of what Indians joined the new administration. For Bengal and Upper India, most attention focuses on the development of policy. Even though Cornwallis made the basic decision that the administration was to be through British officers, it was obvious that much of the day-to-day routine work, and even much of the important revenue work, were to be in the hands of Indian under civil servants.[25] British district officials were faced with the immediate task of recruiting a large number of clerks, scribes, and peons. They also had to employ some Indians in responsible positions as *āmils* or *tahsīldārs* (local tax collectors), *sarrishtadārs* (record keepers and head clerks), and law officers.

Lower judicial employees in one district will serve as examples of the men who were recruited for the services. Jacob Rider, a man of long experience as an official in Bengal, was appointed judge in Ghazipur in September 1795. A month later he swore in the first group of Indians for his office. The *sarrishtadār*, in terms of his power if not of his title, was the most important Indian official in the English judge's office. He supervised the clerks, kept the records, and was the judge's principal native administrative assistant. The man appointed was a Muslim, known as a Persian scholar. He was the nephew of the last Indian judge in Ghazipur and had functioned as his uncle's *sarrishtadār*. Eight Persian writers were appointed. All were Hindus—three Kayasthas, two Baniyas, a Bengali Brahman, and two who were either Bhumihar or Rajput. Two had worked for the previous Indian judge and were recommended by him; three were from Lucknow and were recommended by Jewam Singh, a man who had served Rider when he had been posted in the Resident's office there. The head writer was a man who had served in the court in Benares. He had been deputed by the Benares Court to bring to Rider the records regarding Ghazipur which were in that court. Rider liked the manner in which the writer turned over the papers. He had him examined and found him to be competent in Hindustani and Persian.[26] This man was also to bring two other men from Benares.

In the Nagri writer's office there were also eight scribes: six were Kayastha or Baniya, one Bengali Brahman, and one to whom I cannot ascribe a caste. Of the eight, three were recommended by the former Indian judge, three by the man who had worked for Rider in Lucknow, and one by the man who had brought the papers from Benares. The other was the son of a man who had worked for Rider in Nadia (in Bengal). The *nāzir* of the criminal court was a local Muslim. The *maulavt* (Muslim law officer) was Omar Ullah, the former judge. The pandit (Hindu law officer) was a man trained at the Hindu college in Benares. He was recommended by the principal of the college. In this instance there were three principal sources of employees. One group had been associated with the former judge; another group was associated with the man who had brought the papers from Benares; and a third group comprised people who had worked for Rider or were associated with people who had worked for Rider.

A total of 350 Indians worked in the four district courts and in the provincial court, exclusive of native commissioners (small claim courts judges, of whom there were about 25 or 30). Out of these 350, approximately 40 earned about 25 rupees a month, 155 between 24 rupees and 10 rupees, and the rest below 10 rupees. There were 77 Indian employees in the Benares District Court. Their total wage bill was 1,020 rupees. The British judge's salary was 2,200 rupees per month.[27]

Some of the men recruited for the British administration were old civil servants of Persian origin; they had the skills, training, and experience which the British needed. But the significant criterion for employment appears to have been either acquaintance with a British officer or kinship or friendship with someone who was acquainted with a British officer.

The most important posts open to Indians at this time were in the revenue service. As *tahsīldārs* in the period until 1805, Indians had almost complete power over the police and the collection of revenue. Even after the British took over the direct administration of the Benares Province, tax collection at the local level was left in the hands of the old *āmils,* who were now called *tahsīldārs.* It was the duty of the *tahsīldārs* to collect the taxes from the revenue payers and to pass it on to the collector's treasury. They were not paid a salary, but an 11½ per cent commission on what they collected. They also had police powers and were responsible for the maintenance of law and order in the district. During the period from 1797 to 1805 there was an average of forty-four *tahsīldārs* listed on the books of the English collectors as being responsible for the collection of the land revenue. In reality two thirds of these tahsildarships were controlled by three men: the Raja of Benares, Sheo Lal Dube, and Devikinundan Singh.[28] During the period 1797–1805 they made huge profits out of their official positions, because in the first place, they were able to get more than their 11½ per cent profit through extortion and the use of their police powers, and, more important in the long run, they were able through illegal means to force lands to be sold for the arrears of revenue, and were able to purchase very profitable estates under fictitious names. Since the *tahsīldār* controlled the land records and the revenue records and knew well which estates were profitable to their owners because they were underassessed. And since they knew all the legal maneuvers and also had great illegal powers, they were able to acquire large estates in a very short time.[29]

In social origin, the three men were quite different. The family of the Raja of Benares were Bhumihars from a village in Benares District. His ancestor, Mansa Ram, had a small *zamīndārī* of a few hundred bighas and worked as a servant (official) for a local tax farmer in the early eighteenth century. As part of his job, he had to negotiate on behalf of his employer with Mir Rustum Ali, who was the officer under the Nawab Vazir of Oudh in charge of the Benares Province. He gained the confidence of Mir Rustum Ali, and was able to supplant his employer in his position. He continued as a confidential adviser and servant to Mir Rustum Ali. He dealt on Mir Rustum Ali's behalf with Sa'adat Khan, the Nawab. He was successful in again supplanting his employer, Mir Rustum Ali. In 1738 or 1739, just before he died, he was able to get his son, Balwant Singh, recognized as the zamindar of most of Benares Province, and to get him granted the title of Raja. Balwant Singh expanded and consolidated his hold on Benares Province. When he died and was succeeded by his son, Chait Singh, the family was established as the Rajas of Benares and as the paramount political power in the region. Chait Singh fell afoul of Warren Hastings and the East India Company and was driven into exile in 1781. He was replaced by Balwant Singh's sister's son, Mahipnarain Singh. The new Raja was young and inexperienced, and his mismanagement and the mismanagement of his advisers and officials led to the taking over of the administration by the British in 1795. The Rajas of Benares kept a sizeable area as their own *jāgīr*. With his capital and the experience he had gained by this time, the Raja was able to get control of a large number of amilships.[30]

Sheo Lal Dube came from a very poor Brahman family in Fathepur District. As a boy he went to Allahabad, where he took service as a night watchman for a jeweler. The jeweler came to depend heavily on Sheo Lal, who rose in his service. When he died, Sheo Lal took over his business. With the capital he acquired, Sheo Lal moved to Benares, where he went into the banking business in the 1780's. He dealt mainly with Kulb Ali Beg, one of the big *āmils*. Kulb Ali Beg, through the enmity of the Raja, was forced to over-extend himself in 1787. He could not meet his obligations and had to give up his amilships. Part of them were taken over by Sheo Lal Dube, who thus became under Duncan one of the important *āmils*. Duncan thought very highly of Dube, and evidently Dube did his job well. When the administration changed in 1795, Dube stayed on as an *āmil* in Jaunpur district. He was responsible for the death of Saltanat Singh, the Raja of Badlapur, who had been declared an outlaw for his failure to pay revenue and for his raiding activities along the

Oudh border. He was rewarded with the title Raja and was given Saltanat Singh's land. He expanded his operations widely in the period 1795–1805 and acquired large estates in Jaunpur and Ghazipur districts during this period.[31]

Devikinundan Singh was a Bhumihar from Ghazipur. His father had been an official in Allahabad, and in Benares, but it was the son who had the spectacular career. James Barton and John Routledge, who were collectors of Benares from 1796 to 1805, were corrupt. The chief corrupter appears to have been Devikinundan Singh, who controlled Barton through direct payment and by placing his own men in the key positions of Barton's staff. Barton and Routledge closed their eyes to the operations of the three leading *āmils*. Barton was finally tried by a commission of civil and judicial officers on over thirty counts of incompetency and corruption. The commission concluded that Barton had taken bribes and was incompetent in that he would not or could not control his subordinates. He was not prosecuted, because the Governor General's legal advisers did not think the evidence would stand up in the supreme court in Calcutta, where he would have had to be tried.[32]

Devikinundan's career did not stop in Benares. When Allahabad was ceded to the company in 1801, Devikinundan appeared there. Because of his experience and wealth he was able to get employment as an *āmil*. As far as the British collector was concerned, he was a model *āmil*, because he paid the revenue promptly and was able to dispose of troublesome taxpayers speedily, since he knew from his Benares experience all the regulations of the court system. In the space of a few years Devikinundan Singh had acquired about a tenth of the land in the district.[33]

The fraudulent land sales by means of which the early *tahsīldārs* had become rich were remedied by the 1820's. But through overassessment, poor management on the part of the zamindars, and internal disputes in estates held by lineages, land continued until the 1840's to come into the market in large quantities for sale for arrears of revenue. After the 1840's, land sales were either private action or sale by decree of court for the payment of private debts. Positions in government service, even at the level of clerks and scribes, continued to be highly attractive throughout the period. The kinds of people and the kinds of jobs changed. In 1833, through the establishment of the post of deputy collector, the upgrading of the *sadr amīns* and *amīns* (judges), and the establishment of what later became the uncovenanted civil service, it was hoped that Indians of high training and integrity would be attracted to the service. In the 1840's, however, there was more and more demand that the holders of these posts know English. Thus many of the posts came to be filled, not by Indians, but by Europeans, often born in India, and East Indians (Eurasians). They were of a different social class than the covenanted civil servants.

The numbers of those employed directly in the collector's office grew throughout the period under consideration. In 1805, there were 264 employees in the collector's office of Benares, 215 of whom earned below 10 rupees per month. It should be remembered that at this time there was only one collector's office for the five districts. The individual *tahsīldārs* had establishments as well, but it is impossible to estimate how many employees they had.[34]

Less than fifty years later, Jaunpur District, one of the four districts into which the Benares Collectorship had been divided, had 652 employees.[35] Throughout this period of expansion, one of the principal bases of employment was a connection with a British officer. In the district records, often in the letters informing higher echelons that a man had been employed as a clerk, it would be mentioned that he had been recommended by another officer, or that he had been employed by the English officer asking for his employment in another district. In petitions from Indians for pensions or favors, it is clear that Indian employees often spent a good part of their lives traveling from district to district with one English officer. The historian of the Mittur family, a Bengali family of prominence in Calcutta and Benares, is explicit in stating that it was the family connections with English officers, including the Colebrooke brothers, which had enabled them to obtain many posts as *dīwāns* and *sarrishtadārs*.[36]

Throughout the period, Indian officials continued to make large sums of money through illegal means. In Benares District in 1840, the acting collector became concerned about the way the revenue settlement was then being conducted in the district. Benares was permanently settled. The settlement officers were not assessing revenue, but only making a record of rights and drawing field maps. Still, much dislocation was being caused among the zamindars and cultivators. The collector examined the *patwārī's* records and the zamindars' records for the villages which had been settled—at this point about three fourths of the villages of Benares District. He found in the *patwārī's* records that 44,380 rupees were recorded as having been paid to the surveyors and settlement officials. This amount was illegal inasmuch as the charges which had been made against the villages for such things as food, presents, and fees were illegal. It represented the amount which the officials had been able to pass off as legal charges coming out of the village at large. It did not include amounts paid by individual cultivators or zamindars in the form of direct bribes.[37]

The Under Civil Servants and the Purchase of Land

The British created a market in land by making land revenue settlement permanent in 1795; by giving title to land to those whom the British considered zamindars; by using land sales to realize delinquent tax payments; and by failing to settle land rights within lineages which were recognized as zamindars. The first settlement was an uneven one; some holdings were overassessed and some were underassessed. Since the settlement was in perpetuity, those estates which were underassessed became extremely valuable properties. Until this point, land does not appear to have been a commodity in the European sense. Individuals and groups had had claims to shares of the produce of the land. Individuals and groups had controlled the land through exercise of military or other forms of power. Land had changed hands before the coming of the British, but it had usually changed hands by force. In a short period of time, the British eliminated the use of physical power except that which was derived from the East India Company's government. Courts were established to adjudicate disputes over land and determine rights to land. However, there were major differences in knowledge of and access to the new courts and administration.

The Indian officials were in the best position to understand and manipulate the new situation. They knew how the courts worked, because they worked in them. They knew which estates were valuable, because they kept the records and collected the taxes. Many of them acquired capital quickly through bribery and corruption. It became a simple matter for them legally or fraudulently to bring to auction those estates which were valuable because underassessed, and to acquire them for themselves.

In the first period of British rule, much of the land changed hands fraudulently. After 1820 the land continued to change hands, but it was largely due to the inflexibility of the revenue and legal system.

It is difficult to trace in specific instances the sources of money which were used to purchase land during the period. Of 205 land sales in the districts of Benares and Jaunpur on which I have data and which I have been able to analyze, the occupations of the purchasers were as follows: [38] Mahajan—58; Zamindar—48; Service—38; Raja of Benares—30; Other—4. The figures indicate that at least 38 of the purchasers were still in service—at this point, largely government service. There is no way of telling how many in the zamindar and mahajan categories were relatives of men in service, sons of men who had been in service, or men who had been in service and had retired.

An analysis of the data on the occupational origins of the holders of large estates in the Settlement Reports of Jaunpur and Ghazipur District of 1885 and 1886 is even more revealing. Twenty-three out of seventy-four of the holders of large estates owed their beginnings as landholders to a family member who had been in government service. Out of the seventy-four large landholders, almost forty per cent of the revenue paid by them was paid by government service families.[39]

By the middle of the nineteenth century, about forty per cent of the land in the Benares region had changed hands. The land went from lineages and local chiefs into the hands of under civil servants and their descendants, and to merchants and bankers. These groups formed the basis of a new class of landlords—different in outlook and background from the old landed interests. Often they were absentee landlords who managed their land through managers and who had little attachment to their land.

Under the old local system, land had been the basis of power; with land one could provide for followers. Once land became a commodity, power came to be based on economic considerations. Followers were not as important as income for the basis of social status.

Most of the old zamindars remained on the land. From the point of view of their old lower caste followers, they still had considerable power locally. Being old landlords, they still retained control over some land— their *sīr*, or home farms. They became tenants on some of the rest of their land. As long as they paid their rent regularly to the new landlords, and as long as there was no violence which came to the attention of the British officials, they could continue much as before. But from the point of view of the old regional political system, the old local power holders had sunk to the condition of tenants and cultivators. They counted for little with the new administration. They had no influence or status in the new status system which was based on economic position, education, and employment in new professions. The old landlords became peasants.

CONCLUSIONS

By the middle of the nineteenth century, after fifty years of British rule and seventy years of British influence in the Benares region, the political, administrative, and economic structure of the region had undergone marked changes. The three political systems which had existed side by side in the middle of the eighteenth century had been reduced to two. The main and all-powerful one, the British Government, had replaced the Mughal and regional governments with a salaried civil administration controlled from the provincial capital in Agra, the Governor General's staff in Calcutta, the Secretary of State for India, and the Parliament in London. This political structure was rapidly destroying the third or local system. In many *tālukās*, through the workings of the revenue and legal systems, the old landholders had been replaced by new groups who became landholders. In those *tālukās* where the old lineages still remained, or where descendants of rajas or jagirdars held some power, their actions were completely circumscribed by the regulations of the administration, who did not formerly recognize them as political entities. The old local system survived in spite of the new administrative system, but it survived only so long as it did not come into open conflict with the new system and so long as the old local powers could maintain their positions in relation to their tenants or followers.

A new landed class grew up during this period. One of the primary segments in this new class was those families which had acquired wealth through working for the new administration. The new type of lower administrator was different from his eighteenth century counterpart. In individual cases, a family tradition of government service may have carried over, but for the most part the British looked for a different type. In the period before 1840, a knowledge of Persian, the language of the administration, was a prime requisite for employment. Still the British seem to have turned to Kayasthas, Brahmans, Baniyas, and Bhumihars in Benares who knew Persian, rather than to the descendants of the old Persian-speaking and writing civil service families characteristic of the eighteenth century. Bengalis had a special advantage, in that they had had a longer contact with the British. A few learned English. But in the early nineteenth century, they also continued to learn Persian, as did Ram Mohan Roy as a young man, not as an intellectual exercise, but to gain employment under the British. After 1840, with a growing emphasis on the use of English in the administration, it increasingly was the Kayastha, Baniya, and Brahman, especially those in cities like Benares where English education was available, who entered the service and were able to get money to buy land. The Rajputs, who had been the main landed group from the sixteenth to the eighteenth centuries, along with some old Muslim families, steadily lost their land to this new group.

Before the latter decades of the nineteenth century, the group which I have been discussing did not form a class in the European sense of the word. But a new style of life was evolving in this period, and a new economic interest was emerging in the society which reached full development in the post-Mutiny period. Members of this group were referred to as "respectable natives." They were men of substance, in that they were large landholders and were big spenders in the maintenance of certain aspects of the pre-British culture. They supported the festivals, built temples and rest houses, dug wells, supported Brahmans and other learned men, and were interested in hunting, curio collecting, and in building the mansions which are a feature of Benares City, Jaunpur, and Mirzapur today. They sat on the municipal boards and district boards and provided much of the Indian opposition to the political aspirations of the rising middle-class English-educated urban Indians who gave the leadership to the nationalist movement.

NOTES

1. The research upon which this paper is based was carried out from January 1958 to July 1959 in the Commonwealth Relations Office Library, and

the Uttar Pradesh Central Record Office, Allahabad, while the writer was on a fellowship from the Rockefeller Foundation.

2. A brief outline of the history of the Benares Province can be found in Douglas Dewar, *A Handbook to the English Pre-Mutiny Records in the Government Record Rooms of the United Provinces of Agra and Oudh*, n.d., no place of publication, pp. 258–262.

3. For the duties of the *kāzī* see M. B. Ahmad, *The Administration of Justice in Medieval India*, Aligarh, 1941, pp. 120–123 and 173–176.

4. *Ibid.*, pp. 82–84.

5. India Office Library, *Bengal Civil Judicial Proceedings*, 6 April 1789, No. 6, "Translation of the Petition of Cauzy Tuckey Ally Khan."

6. India Office Library, *Home Miscellaneous Series*, Vol. 379, "Report by Mr. Beaufoy," p. 189; India Office Library, *Bengal Secret Consultations*, 13 Dec. 1775, Fowke to Hastings, LS 16 Nov. 1775; and Warren Hastings, *A Narrative of the Insurrection which Happened in the Zamendary of Banaris*, Calcutta, 1782, Appendix, Part I, p. 21, mispaged as 12.

7. Allahabad Central Record Office, *Miscellaneous Revenue Files*, Vol. 17, Basta 100, D. B. Morrison, "A Few Remarks on Mr. Jonathan Duncan's Settlement of the Benares Province."

8. Allahabad Central Record Office, *Benares Commissioner's Office, Miscellaneous Files*, Basta 98, Vol. 2, "List of Pargana Sarishtadars, 25 July 1796."

9. India Office Library, *Bengal Revenue Consultations*, 3 Oct. 1788, No. 24, "Raja Mahipnarain's Muffusil Settlement."

10. India Office Library, *Bengal Revenue Consultations*, Duncan to Gov. Gen. Consultation 3 Oct. 1788.

11. John William Kaye, *The Life and Correspondence of Major General Sir John Malcolm*, London, 1856, Vol. I, pp. 114–15.

12. *Ibid.*, p. 115.

13. Hastings, *Narrative*, p. 22; and C. A. Storey, *Persian Literature: A Bio-Bibliographic Survey*, Section II, Fasciculus 3, London, 1939, p. 700.

14. C. E. Buckland, *Dictionary of Indian Biography*, London, 1906, p. 10.

15. India Office Library, *Bengal Civil Judicial Proceedings*, Consultation 11 Sept. 1795 Duncan to Gov. Gen.; and Charles Ross, ed., *Correspondence of Charles, First Marquis Cornwallis*, Vol. II, London, 1859, p. 34.

16. Maulana Khair ud Din Muhammad, *Tazkirat-ul-Ulama or A Memoir of the Learned Men of Jaunpur*, ed., with an English translation by Muhammad Sana Ullah, Calcutta, 1934, pp. 74–82.

17. Storey, *Persian Literature*, pp. 521–22.

18. Allahabad Central Record Office, *Benares Commissioner's Office*, "Settlement Book from 1197–1206," Basta 48, Vol. 134B, "Settlement of Taluka Bhaysa Daoorawee."

19. India Office Library, *Bengal Revenue Consultation*, 3 Oct. 1788, No. 3, Duncan to Gov. Gen.

20. Hastings, *Narrative*, p. 44.

21. I have elsewhere discussed some of the aspects of the political and legal structure of a lineage-controlled *tālukā*. Bernard S. Cohn, "Some Notes on Law and Change in North India," *Economic Development and Cultural Change*, Vol. VIII, No. 1, October 1959, pp. 79–93.

22. The description of Badlapur and Saltanat Singh is based on Shri Aditya Narain Singh, *Biography of Saltanat Bahadur Singh, Talukadar of Badlapur,* a manuscript in Hindi. Aditya Narain Singh was a descendant of Sultanat Singh. A small landholder from Badlapur, he collected legends and stories regarding his ancestor and wrote the biography in 1952–53. One of the principal aims of the work is to prove that Saltanat Singh was the first freedom fighter in the area, and that at the time of compensation for confiscation of zamindari rights under the zamindari abolition act, his descendants should receive the compensation, and not the Raja of Jaunpur, who defeated Saltanat Singh on behalf of the British in 1796 and was rewarded with Saltanat Singh's lands. The work was translated for me by Shri Nath Singh.

23. In November 1958, the descendant of a Brahman who had at one point supported Saltanat Singh showed me a *dhānpatta* and the decision made by P. C. Wheller, the settlement officer of Jaunpur district from 1879 to 1886 in village Tiera, *tālukā* Badlapur. The Brahman had been rewarded with a *māfī* grant and the *dhānpatta* was the original grant. The settlement officer upheld the validity of the grant. Even though the grant had been resumed in 1842, when there was large-scale resumption of *māfī* lands, ownership of this land was attested to by the document, which the British ruled was a valid grant made by Saltanat Singh, who in the late eighteenth century had the right to make such a *māfī* grant.

24. See Hastings, *Narrative,* and C. C. Davies, *Warren Hastings and Oudh,* Oxford, 1939.

25. For the development of the administration, see B. B. Misra, *The Central Administration of the East India Company, 1773–1834,* Manchester, 1959; A. Aspinall, *Cornwallis in Bengal,* Manchester, 1931; D. Bhanu, *History and Administration of the North-Western Provinces, 1803–1858.* R. N. Nagar is one of the few who have examined the question of Indians in the civil service at this early period. See his "The Subordinate Services in the Revenue Administration of the North Western Provinces, 1801–1833," *Journal of the United Provinces Historical Society,* Vol. XV, Part 2; "The Tahsildar in the Ceded and Conquered Provinces, 1801–1833," *Uttar Pradesh Historical Quarterly,* Vol. II (n.s.), Part I, 1954; and "Employment of Indians in the Revenue Administration of the N.W.P., 1801–1833," *Journal of the United Provinces Historical Society,* Vol. XIII, December, 1940.

26. India Office Library, *Bengal Civil Judicial Proceedings,* 20 Nov. 1795, No. 22, Rider to Gov't.

27. *Ibid.,* No. 16. The figures are based on rough calculations, using the Benares District Court as the base from which the figures for the other courts are projected.

28. Allahabad Central Record Office, *Miscellaneous Revenue Files,* Basta 99, Vol. 12, "Kistbundi of the Land Revenue," Collectorship of Benares, F. S. 1210 and 1213; India Office Library, *Home Miscellaneous Series,* Vol. 775, R. O. Wynne, "Report on Jaunpur," August 15, 1815.

29. Allahabad Central Record Office, *Proceedings of the Board of Commissioners of Behar and Benares,* Vol. 9, Proceedings 21 Oct. 1816 LR No. 162, Report from Robert Barlow on Deputation to Badlapur; *Processings Sudder Board of Revenue N.W.P.,* 20 Sept. 1833, No. 28, G. M. Bird to Board;

Benares Commissioner's Office, *Miscellaneous Revenue Files*, Basta 101, Vol. 17, Letter of John Deane, Dec. 10, 1803; W. O. Oldham, *Tenant Rights and Auction Sales in Ghazeepoor and the Province of Benares*, Dublin, 1873.

30. Imperial Record Department, *Calendar of Persian Correspondence*, Vol. V, Calcutta, 1930, No. 1407, p. 306; Wilton Oldham, *Historical and Statistical Memoir of the Ghazipur District*, part I, Allahabad, 1870, pp. 100–105; Hastings, *Narrative*.

31. The details of Sheo Lal Dube's early life were given to me by his descendant, Yadvedra Datt Dube, the present Raja of Jaunpur. Dube's career under Duncan can be traced in A. Shakespear ed., *Selections from the Duncan Records*, Vol. I, Benares, 1873. For his later career, see references in foot-note 28.

32. On the Barton case, the report of the commission is in India Office Library, *Bengal Civil Judicial Proceedings*, 2 July 1807, Nos. 19 and 20.

33. Letter of M. J. Fortesque, Judge of Allahabad, in *Selections from the Revenue Records, North-West Provinces*, Vol. III, Allahabad, 1873, p. 22–24.

34. Allahabad Central Record Office, *Benares Commissioner's Office, Benares*, District Revenue Files, Vol. 125, File No. 2005.

35. A. Shakespear, *Comparative Tables of District Establishment in the North West Provinces 1852*, Calcutta, 1853, pp. 190–193.

36. For the Mittur family, see *An Account of the Late Govendram Mittur*, by a member of the family, Calcutta, 1869. For other evidence of the usefulness of the connection with an English officer, see R. N. Cust, "Report on a School for the Instruction for the Native Amlah," *Selections from the Records of Government*, Vol. III, Art. XXVII, Agra, 1855; Allahabad Central Record Office, Ghazipur Collectorate, *Copies of Miscellaneous correspondence*, 1820–27, Barlow to Tilghman, 5 June 1824; and *Proceedings of the Board of Commissioners in Behar and Benares*, April 1819, Middleton to Bd. Consultation, 3 April 1819.

37. Allahabad Central Record Office, *Benares Commissioner's Office, Benares*, Revenue Files, Vol. 61, File No. 369. For other evidence of corruption and of the large-scale corruption possible, see Panch Kauri Khan, *Revelations of an Orderly*, Benares, 1848; for a slightly later period, see Iltudus Prichard, *Chronicles of Budgepore*, London, 1893, new edition.

38. The figures are based on notices of the sale of land and on compilations of sales of land found scattered throughout the district records of Jaunpur and Benares in the Allahabad Central Record Office. These series are incomplete as to year; files for many years have been lost or destroyed, and within any given year it is impossible to know if all the files were kept.

39. W. Irvine, *Report on the Revision of Records in the Ghazipur District*, 1880–1885; and P. C. Wheeler, *Report on the Revision of Records in the District of Jaunpur from 1877–1886*.

A. W. Southall

DETERMINANTS OF THE SOCIAL STRUCTURE OF AFRICAN URBAN POPULATIONS, WITH SPECIAL REFERENCE TO KAMPALA (UGANDA) (1956)

GENERAL FACTORS

In this paper I use the example of Kampala to illustrate the main factors which may be supposed to determine the structure of African urban populations. I must point out that these are some of the preliminary results of a study not yet completed, and therefore a number of gaps remain to be filled.

A factor of wide significance seems to be the relation of the level of African wage employment to the general level of African economic development in a territory. This factor is closely linked with the relative size of the European population and with the positive or negative quality of the reaction of the territorial administration to African urban development. The populations of nearly all the larger African towns are stratified into layers which are very largely determined by race. This gives the urban community many of the characteristics of a caste structure. The layers are further differentiated internally, and this is most important in the case of the African layer, which is usually divided into a large number of very sharply distinguished tribal groups, showing varying abilities and inclinations in relation to the urban work situation.

The social organization of the tribe in whose traditional territory a town grows up is often of particular importance. It may largely determine the structure of the whole African community according to the degree of centralization in its traditional political system, the form of its descent groups and the extent of their localization, and the type of marriage and family system. The manner in which immigrant tribes are

SOURCE. A. W. Southall, "Determinants of the Social Structure of African Urban Communities, with special reference to Kampala (Uganda)," from UNESCO, *Social Implications of Industrialization and Urbanization in Africa South of the Sahara,* 1956, pp. 557–565, 568–577.

321

assimilated also depends upon their variability in these respects in relation to the local tribe. The system of land tenure is associated with the
same factors and strongly influences the pattern of urban settlement. Men
heavily outnumber women among groups immigrant to town, and the
precise effect of this unbalanced sex ratio again depends largely on the
family and marriage system of the local tribe.

The net effect of these interrelated determinants varies according to
the detailed system of urban administration into which the individual
has to fit, and its relation to the territorial administration and to African
local governments. Included here is the extent to which Africans are
segregated, administratively, legally or spatially, and the extent to which
they rent their housing accommodation from other Africans, and also
erect their own, or are compelled by administrative regulation or lack
of choice to live in accommodation provided by employers, governments
and municipalities.

Here are many dependent variables. I hope to show that the factors
mentioned give a reasonable frame of reference for the analysis of the
social structure of the Kampala African population and its comparison
with that of other African towns.

ECONOMIC DEVELOPMENT, EMPLOYMENT
AND URBAN POLICY

The Uganda Protectorate belongs to that group of territories in which
the general level of African economic development is comparatively high,
while the proportion of the African population employed in wage labour
is relatively low.[1] In Africa such a situation is closely correlated with a
comparatively small European population, especially settled population,
and with a comparatively negative and permissive policy towards African
urban development.

Thus, in Uganda, the majority of those Africans who are attracted
to the towns have been left to fend for themselves in finding house accommodation and in organizing their urban existence.[2] Such housing estates
or locations as have been built by either employers or the Government
have provided for only a minority. Where little administrative provision
is made for African urban life it naturally follows that little control can
be exercised over it. Where no special housing is provided for the majority, no particular area of land set apart for the settlement of urban
Africans, and no particular administrative organization designed for the
government of Africans in town, no compulsory system of registration or
pass-laws is possible.[3] There is no effective means of either knowing or
controlling the numbers or type of people coming to town.[4] Those without work cannot be identified or sent home. Another result is that the

areas in which most urban Africans settle tend to lie outside the statu-
torily defined boundaries of townships or municipalities.[5]

In this situation immigrants to town must depend heavily upon the
already existing African population around the town. The political structure, system of land tenure and social organization of the local tribe
becomes of great importance. For example, where the local tribe traditionally has a centralized political system, the assimilation of immigrants
is likely to take a form very different from that which it would take
where the structure of the local tribe is based on a system of localized
segmentary lineages.[6] The extent to which the holding of land is indi-
vidualized largely determines the flexibility with which it can be adapted
to urban uses. The pattern of marriage and family life which grows up
among urban Africans is influenced by the marriage system of the local
tribe because immigrants are predominantly male and the unbalance of
the sexes can be most easily remedied by recourse to women of the local
tribe. All these points will be illustrated in detail later when the tribal
structure of the African population in Kampala is analysed.

THE RACIAL FACTOR

Kampala is regarded as the commercial capital of the Uganda Protectorate as a whole. Mengo, the capital of the kings of Buganda, forms
a continuous urban area with Kampala itself in terms of density of settlement, but it lies outside the boundaries of the municipality of Kampala.

In 1952 the population of the municipality was estimated at 4,250
Europeans, 17,000 Asians and 16,800 Africans. However, urban conditions prevail beyond the municipal boundary, and to arrive at the total
urban population it is necessary to add at least another 30,000 Africans,
living in a narrow belt round the municipality, which also probably contains a few thousand Asians and a few hundred Europeans. There is thus
a population of about 70,000 living under urban conditions.

As in all towns, the population of Kampala is differentiated according
to status, low status being closely linked to low income and unskilled
labour, and high status to wealth and to the sources of political and economic power. But in Kampala the cultural symbol of race is the cause
of additional status distinctions, since persons who would otherwise be
considered to occupy the same status are in fact sharply divided by the
barrier of race. Racial barriers are the more noticeable because they run
sufficiently close to political and economic distinctions to be usually
identified with them in the public mind. The stereotype is that while
Europeans are politically dominant, through their control of the formal
political institutions, Indians dominate the economic scene, and Africans
hold the lowest status, supplying all the unskilled labour. Although there
are many exceptions to this stereotype, and there is no statutory colour

bar, but rather considerable administrative enforcement of non-discrimination, none the less racial divisions are actually institutionalized to a considerable extent. Europeans, Asians and Africans have to attend different schools, and unofficial members of the municipal council are selected on the basis of their racial origin. The very attempt to secure equality between the races in many situations emphasizes racial divisions. The average person of all three main racial groups tends to regard Europeans, Asians and Africans as a descending series of horizontal status layers, and treats members of the different races with condescension or deference accordingly. Where a person's position in the power system, and the network of his social relationships, belies this popular analysis, there is always considerable resistance on the part of most people to accept such deviation from the prevailing pattern.

The three racial groups are to a high degree endogamous. As some indication of this, in the 1948 census the coloured population of the whole of Buganda province was given as only 233, and although a number were probably missed, through being counted together with the other races, interracial marriage is certainly rare. It occurs most often in Kampala between the poorer Indian Moslems and African women who are either Moslems already themselves, or else readily adopt that faith for the purposes of such unions. The incentive is an economic one, for the shortage of housing accommodation hits the Indian group more severely than any other. They can often acquire accommodation more easily or more cheaply in the name of an African wife, and by this means they may secure a plot on which to build and be able to rent accommodation with great profit.

There are, in fact, wide status differences within each racial group. The real incomes of wealthy Ganda aristocrats are well above those of the lower economic levels of both the European and Asian groups. Some of them occupy important positions in Government bodies and state-sponsored corporations, as well as in both the Buganda provincial Government and the central political system of the Protectorate. The more successful members of the Asian group are far more wealthy than the high status Europeans as a whole, whether the latter are in government or in business. Such wealthy Asians not only thereby acquire a firm economic basis in relation to the status system within their own group, but their importance is also recognized in the official positions which some of them enjoy both in local and central government. The Mayor of Kampala is an Asian, and all Asians in positions of political importance are also to a greater or lesser extent drawn into cross racial social relationships which express and confer high status.[7] If we are to visualize a status system encompassing the Kampala community as a whole, we must view it as a somewhat amorphous one, with innumerable cross-linkages and overlaps, in which the members of each part are conscious mainly of the other parts with which they are in closest contact, rather than of the whole. The majority of those in the highest status positions are Europeans, the majority of those in the middle ranges are Asians, and practically all the lowest status positions are occupied by Africans.

On the other hand, the exclusiveness of the racial groups is such that, for many purposes, it is more realistic to treat them as having separate, though parallel, status systems, while the majority in each racial group occupies a significantly different range of the status scale applicable to the community as a whole.

I have spoken so far of the three racial groups, but each of them contains a number of ethnic subdivisions, some of which are closely linked to economic and status differences. In the European group these take the form of nationals of the various European states, and in the Asian group mainly of the different Indian castes and sects together with other groups such as Goans and Arabs. But I shall be mainly concerned with the numerous tribes which form the subdivisions within the African group.

The tribal heterogeneity is a complicating factor which always causes difficulties when the attempt is made to provide for Africans simply on the basis of their economic roles and general social status. It is responsible for tensions and hostilities, as well as outright failures in communication, between persons and groups whose similarity of economic and social position would otherwise be expected to bind them together on the basis of common interest. But, on the other hand, these animosities are the complement of the solidarity which still persists even in town between members of the same tribe. Without this solidarity it is difficult to see how the minimum of order and consensus could be secured among masses of largely illiterate and unskilled labourers, unused to the demands of town life, without much more detailed, costly and undesirable control and regimentation.

THE DOMINANT TRIBE

The Ganda owe their dominance not only to the fact that they are the local tribe, but also to the impressive development of their political system. The capital of the kings of Buganda drew all early European travellers to it, and this undoubtedly determined the location of the future town of Kampala.[8] It must therefore be placed among those towns which have a genuinely African origin.[9]

On the establishment of the Uganda Protectorate, the kingdom of Buganda became one of its constituent provinces, with Kampala as the headquarters of its Provincial Commissioner (now styled the Resident), with his British provincial administration. Meanwhile, Mengo remained the seat of the native government. The Ganda tribe had a long history of

centralized government under their kings, with their increasingly bureaucratic cadres of chiefs. This system was considerably modified and for-
malized with the conclusion of the Uganda Agreement of 1900 and the
inclusion of Buganda Kingdom as a province of the Uganda Protectorate.
The main structure of government has, since that time, been a hierarchy
of bureaucratic chiefs, at the levels of county, sub-county, parish and
ward. These chiefs are under the executive direction of the Katikkiro or
Prime Minister of Buganda, who is answerable to the Kabaka. The hills
of Mengo, Rubaga and Namirembe, on which are situated the headquarters of Buganda Kingdom, of the White Fathers' Mission and of the
Church Missionary Society, respectively, each form a parish in this system and the present Municipality of Kampala itself consists of three such
parishes.

In theory, responsibility for the government of the whole African
population of Kampala remains with the Buganda Kingdom, subject to
the advice of the Governor of Uganda, tendered by the Resident as his
agent. A system of local government adjusted to essentially rural conditions has thus during half a century become responsible for a very large
urban population which has grown up in its midst. The Principal Court
of the Buganda Kingdom has power to hear all cases except those which
concern "offences in consequence of which death is alleged to have occurred," [10] and certain other special types of case such as those involving
the Marriage Ordinance, the Uganda Agreement, or the Mailo Land
Settlement. Civil cases involving non-Africans cannot be heard, but criminal cases can be heard provided the defendant is an African. An appeal
from sentences of over five years' imprisonment, over 2,000 shillings fine
or from civil cases involving over 2,000 shillings in value lies to the High
Court of Uganda, and from all other cases to the Judicial Adviser to the
Buganda Kingdom, an official appointed by the Protectorate Government.

The court of the sub-county which contains about three-quarters of
the urban area is also situated at Mengo. This court has special powers
beyond those normal to sub-county courts, and appeal from it lies to the
Principal Court, not via the county court as is the case elsewhere in
Buganda. This sub-county court has power to impose prison sentences
of up to 18 months, or fines of up to 1,200 shillings, and it can hear civil
cases involving claims to the amount of 1,500 shillings or the equivalent
of 15 head of cattle.

The Buganda Kingdom also has its own body of police askaris to
enforce its order. But through deficiencies alike of organization, training
and personnel, this force appears increasingly inadequate to deal with
urban problems. The Ganda chiefs of urban parishes, finding these
askaris unreliable, tend to call in the Protectorate police direct.

Meanwhile, the local affairs of the municipality proper, especially
those of non-Africans, are dealt with by the mayor and municipal council,

with town clerk, treasurer, engineer and health officer as permanent salaried staff with their own departments. The Municipality has no police force of its own, and depends for law and order on the strong contingent of the Protectorate police which is stationed in the town.

From the point of view of the Buganda Kingdom, the municipality itself consists of three parishes and part of a fourth. Ten other parishes lying round the municipal boundary must be considered essentially urban, and this whole area may for convenience be referred to as Greater Kampala. It contains part of three sub-counties. All the latter belong to the same county, which is regarded as the most important in Buganda. One of the three sub-counties contains nine out of the thirteen parishes, and is known to the Ganda as the capital (*Kibuga*). It would be more logical if this sub-county, which actually has special powers, contained the whole area which could be counted as urban, instead of which this area is also split up between the two other sub-counties while, in addition, the sub-county of the capital contains some areas which are essentially rural.

Although the Ganda are the largest tribal group in this area, they form a minority in the total population. All the parish chiefs are Ganda, but some of the ward heads who assist them belong to other tribes. The administrative philosophy of the Buganda Kingdom here is that its duty is to teach Ganda custom to the foreigners. The parish chief holds court every Saturday afternoon, and often on other occasions to deal with cases as they arise. This court is only arbitrational, having no power to enforce its decisions. Any serious case and any case in which the decision of the parish court is not accepted by both sides has to be sent to the court of the sub-county.

As these parish chiefs rule populations of from two to three thousand, and the people are highly mobile, the parish chief has little chance of getting to know them all. Much depends on the ward heads, who are unpaid, and have varying motives for their official activities.

In rural Buganda the parish chiefs are supposed to be landowners in their areas, while the other landowners of the parish act as ward heads. If landowners are resident elsewhere their stewards act as ward heads in their place. Around Kampala neither the parish chiefs nor the ward heads are in fact local landowners. The parish chiefs are simply the lowest level of the bureaucratic, salaried, transferable executive staff of the Buganda Kingdom. The ward heads here are not even usually the stewards of landowners. They are persons chosen by the parish chiefs as having some standing in the area and as being able and willing to assist in the tasks of government.

In the central part of the urban area the ward head organization works on a basis which may be said to represent the transition between the traditional system of gift giving in return for services rendered and a modern system of graft and corruption. The main difference between the two, apart from the scale of operations, is that the graft and corruption is less and less part of any stable system of personal relations, and tends increasingly to frustrate some of the main objectives of administration. The main opportunities arise from such matters as the desire of illicit brewers to be left in peaceful pursuit of their occupation, the desire of prostitutes to avoid the very occasional round-ups of unattached single women, and the desire of many people to get houses built in spite of the building regulations. These opportunities attract people of low status and education to act as ward heads. They play an important part in collecting taxes and licences, and in maintaining law and order. Quite a number of cases are settled by arbitration before them, without even reaching the parish court. Parish chiefs endeavour to choose, among their ward heads, members of one or two of the main immigrant tribes, who may be able to exercise additional control over these foreign groups.

Beyond the central urban area there seems to be a zone in which the ward head organization has almost broken down. It is still not possible to get landowners of good local standing to act in this capacity, and the special urban opportunities do not form a sufficient attraction. The ward heads occupy a nominal and inactive position. Many parishioners do not even know who they are.

The administration of the urban area thus depends on three different sources of authority, the Protectorate Government, the Buganda Kingdom and the Municipality. The possibilities of confusion, overlapping and omission in this situation can easily be imagined. Enough has been said to indicate the important part played in urban affairs by the Buganda Kingdom, which is the modified government of the tribe within whose territory the town has grown. . . .

THE IMMIGRANT TRIBES

Some fifty or sixty African tribes are represented in Kampala. But most of these are present in such small numbers that nothing significant can be said about their differential reactions to the situation. They may be classified either according to their language and culture, or by differences of social organization and political system. Uganda, of course, stands at the cross-roads of nearly all the main linguistic groups of Eastern Africa, Bantu, Nilotes, Nilo-Hamites and Sudanics all being represented.

The most important groups of Bantu are, besides the Ganda themselves, the Toro, Nyankole, Rwanda-Rundi, Haya, Ciga, Gishu and Luhya. The first five belong to the interlacustrine group of Bantu, with their stratified societies and centralized political systems. The Ciga, Gishu and Luhya, of south-west Uganda, Mount Elgon and the Nyanza

Province of Kenya, respectively, were all traditionally without centralized government or stratified structure. Their political organization was
on a very small scale, and depended on localized lineages.

The Ganda naturally regard their own status as being somewhat
higher than that of all other African tribes who migrate into their territory. But they recognize a closer affinity with the other interlacustrine
Bantu such as Toro, Nyoro, Nyankole, Haya and Rwanda-Rundi than
with any of the rest. Intermarriage of Ganda with all these tribes is comparatively frequent in some part of the urban area. All these tribes pick
up Luganda with comparative ease. They are most likely to be distinguished from the Ganda by their lower standard of living in dress and
food and their lower education. The majority of them have no kinship
links or permanent interests to enable them to enter the Ganda status
system anywhere else but at the bottom. Among these tribes the Ganda
regard the Rwanda-Rundi as the lowest of all. They are, indeed, notor-
ious in Uganda for their poor physique and skill, which naturally results
in low wages and status. In this case the Ganda inevitably draw conclusions from an unrepresentative sample, for hardly any of the Tutsi, who
form the upper caste in Ruanda-Urundi, come to work in Kampala.

The marriage systems of these tribes differ in various details, but in
the urban context all seem to have been influenced like the Ganda in the
direction of increased frequency of divorce and of temporary unions.
The Haya are renowned as prostitutes in many East African towns. In
Kampala there is at least one marked concentration of these women.
Theirs is the most openly mercenary type of prostitution practised in the
town. Toro and Rwanda prostitutes are also very numerous, but they
tend to prefer temporary unions as opportunity offers, and to give their
services in the expectation of gifts instead for cash down as the Haya do.

The Nyankole are especially numerous as unskilled labourers. So
also are the Rwanda-Rundi, though the numbers of them actually working in town are far less than those in the Buganda countryside. The Toro
are particularly numerous as domestic servants, both the men as houseboys and cooks, and the women as children's nurses, called "ayahs"
locally as in India. Many of the latter circulate among the houseboys as
temporary wives. In domestic service the Toro have of recent years been
displacing the Ganda, as the latter move to jobs which are more in
accordance with their higher average education. Haya men dominate the
charcoal trade. This is an important activity, because most urban Africans
and many of the poorer Indians depend upon charcoal as cooking fuel.
It is a dirty job, and this is the reason always given by the Ganda and
other tribes for taking so little part in it. It yields remarkable returns.
A Haya goes to a forest in Buganda some 20 or 30 miles out of town,
burns charcoal there for two months while living very cheaply, then he
comes to town for a month to sell, and realizes a profit of as much as £30.

The Toro have established several large and concentrated urban tribal neighbourhoods, and there is also one of Haya. These consist of dozens of circular mud and wattle or grass huts, built close together on a single plot of land. The hut builders and owners pay a monthly rent to the landowner, and share their huts with several other men who either in turn pay monthly rent to the hut owner, or, being relatives, are permitted to live with him free. Few of these men have any wives or children with them. Each settlement contains a population of several hundred. Conditions of living are primitive, but a sense of tribal community is here secured which insulates these very poor labourers from the strangeness and inhospitality of urban life.

The other group of Bantu tribes represented by the Ciga, Gishu and Luhya, are also mainly found as unskilled labourers. The Ciga are one of the main suppliers of goat meat, walking the 300 miles from their tribal home to Kampala with large herds of a hundred or so goats at a time.

The largest group of Nilotes is that of the Luo, also from Nyanza Province of Kenya, and one of the most important groups in Kampala. Next come the Acoli of northern Uganda, with small numbers of Alur and Padhola. All these have strong localized segmentary lineage systems, most marked in the case of the Luo, who have no traditional chiefs with specialized political power, and less so among the rest, who have the institution of chiefship developed on a fairly small scale. The Luo stand out in striking contrast to the Ganda and all the interlacustrine Bantu. Their dark colour, heavy build and facial features often mark them out visually, and one often overhears either their bad accent in Luganda speech, or their Swahili or Luo talk where most others are speaking Luganda. They are noted as powerful workers. The majority are probably in unskilled jobs, but they are more willing than most tribes to do hard or unpleasant, dirty work in return for higher pay. They live fairly simply even when their earnings are high, and save money and send regular amounts to their wives and kinfolk at home, rather than spending all on fine clothes and luxuries. With the Ganda they have a reputation for fighting and hard drinking, but these things are difficult to measure precisely.

Luo bridewealth is high, usually amounting to a dozen head of cattle or more. Some Luo bring their wives to town, but most do not. But in either case their unions seem to be remarkably stable and also far more fertile than those of the Ganda and interlacustrine Bantu. There seem to be no Luo prostitutes in town. Some of the men in town without their wives go to prostitutes of other tribes, and this pattern of stable marriage with occasional prostitution contrasts with that of a succession of temporary unions which characterizes many of the Bantu tribal groups in town. Agnatic kinship ties are very strong among the Luo, and it is frequent to find brothers or classificatory brothers living together in town, sometimes as many as six to a room, sharing their rent expenses and keeping a common menage. The number of pagans among the Luo is higher than in any of the big tribal groups.

The Luo are noticeably prominent in occupations requiring some manual skill and, sometimes, muscular strength. Thus they are frequently found as mechanics, bricklayers, carpenters and cobblers. They have also, like the Ciga, established a considerable trade in goats, which they find it profitable to bring by train from Kisumu to sell in Kampala. Some of them also deal in chickens by the same method.

The Nilo-Hamites are represented chiefly by the Teso, though there are also a few Karamojong, while the Lugbara and Madi are the only Sudanic-speaking groups which are of any importance in Kampala. Though the patterns of social organization of these Nilo-Hamites and Sudanics differ radically in detail, all alike lack any specialized political institutions. In their tribal home the Sudanics live in very small groups of only a few hundred persons, all of which were traditionally independent and hostile to one another. The political community of the Teso was also very small; but there was some organization of relationships on a wider basis since all the kin groups of a locality united periodically to perform the ceremonies by which people passed up the age set system.[12]

The Teso, like the Luo, include many pagans and a lower general level of education. Most of them are unskilled labourers, though a few have set up small businesses of their own, such as laundering. The Lugbara are probably the most pagan and illiterate of all the tribal groups in town. They are almost exclusively unskilled labourers, sought after for their strength. They are noted among other tribes, and even among themselves, as hard drinkers ready to fight at the least provocation. All other tribes regard them as barbarians. Their facial scarifications mark them out, and they are also distinguishable by the whistled codes through which they communicate with one another at night.

Most of these non-Bantu tribes tend to react similarly against the air of superiority which the Bantu adopt towards them. For their part, they regard the Bantu in general, and the Ganda in particular, as a degenerate lot, afraid to fight, unable to get and rear many children and riddled with venereal disease.

Tribal associations have not so far played a very important part in the structure of the urban life. They are now being to some extent artificially fostered by the activities of the Community Development Department. Those who could benefit most by such organizations are usually least able to organize them. The strongest tribal organization in town has probably been the Luo Union. It has at times helped destitute Luo to return to their homes, and has tried to prevent any Luo women acting as prostitutes. The Gishu also have a tribal association, although they are not a very large group. The Rwanda-Rundi have also had quite a flourishing organization, which runs social functions from time to time. The Toro in Kampala arranged a party to welcome the Mukama or King of Toro on his return from a visit to England.

It is possible that segmentary societies, like the Nilotic Luo and Bantu Gishu, are more apt to organize themselves in a new context than tribes which are used to being organized within the framework of specialized political institutions. Or it may be that urban tribal groups, which are drawn from the lower ranks of political centralized societies, are more likely to organize themselves when they are free from their traditional political framework.

EDUCATION, OCCUPATION AND INCOME AS FURTHER
FACTORS OF SOCIAL DIFFERENTIATION

The mass of urban Africans start off in town as members of their respective tribes, relying heavily on such kinsmen as are also in town, or failing these, extending something of the attitudes of kin towards any of the same language and culture as themselves. Since there is an ever flowing stream of new migrants to town, the kinship system of each tribe, its type of marriage and family life, its expectations as to the political ordering of society and the sources of cohesion, are all of continuing importance. Thus, on a horizontal plane, there is dependence on a series of tribal social structures of different types, each offering varying possibilities of adaptation to urban needs. The urban community is based on highly dispersed kinship and descent groupings of an *ad hoc*, ephemeral kind. Residence is usually based initially on the use of tribal and kinship ties as a jumping-off ground, followed by the hunt for jobs and the adjustment of residence to the location of work in conjunction with the enjoyment of such amenities as offer. One must suppose that, as his familiarity with urban existence increases, and his economic status improves, the individual becomes less dependent on his tribal background for his sense of security, and more and more on relationships developed with neighbours, with work mates, and with those whose interests are similar to his own.

The general pattern of residence seems to depend on economic distinctions, though these still follow tribal differences fairly closely. Of the 30,000 unskilled labourers employed within the municipality in firms with five or more employees, little more than a tenth live within the municipality. Three-fifths of them live in the belt immediately surrounding the municipality, which for convenience is referred to as Greater Kampala. This belt lies within two and a half miles of the centre of the municipality. The rest of the unskilled group live beyond this limit, but very few beyond four miles from the centre. Two-thirds of this whole unskilled group belong to tribes other than the Ganda. The main body of African residents within the municipality consists of domestic servants, and those in the quarters provided by the East African Railways, the Uganda Police and the African Hospital. Thus, broadly speaking, the Africans who live within the municipal boundary are those for whom quarters are provided by their employers. The rest live beyond this boundary, but as near to it as possible, because they cannot afford bicycles or any other form of transport to and from work.

The better paid workers, of whom the clerks make up the largest group, live mainly further out than the two and a half mile zone, remarkably large numbers coming in on bicycles, and the best paid on motor cycles, from as far as ten or even twelve miles away. The majority of this group are Ganda. They try to combine urban employment with rural residence. This solves the problem of food supply, money expenditure on food being begrudged where it can possibly be avoided. The great objective of this group is to acquire *mailo* land and so to enter at least the bottom of the class of landed gentry. With the appreciation of land values near the town they are driven further out to get hold of land at a reasonable price. Those who cannot afford *mailo* try to obtain plots under customary tenancy, but this too is difficult near the town, and high premiums have to be paid.

The better paid workers of tribes other than the Ganda form a special group. There is nothing to prevent them, as natives of the Protectorate, acquiring either *mailo* land or customary holdings from the Ganda. But very few have done so as yet. Presumably they do not feel sufficiently settled in Kampala to invest their savings in land which would form too strong a tie in preventing them from returning to their tribal homes. These people therefore, like the unskilled labourers, try to rent accommodation as near the town as possible. It is with them that accommodation provided by the Government or by employers is particularly popular.

It is only the wealthiest section of the Ganda who can afford to live near the town and in their own land and housing. Most of them belong to the principal Ganda families, who received land in the original distribution of *mailo* and took care to secure part of their allotment in plots near to the town and to their own capital of Mengo. Ganda who, without these hereditary advantages, have by education and ability achieved high incomes, struggle to secure at least a residential plot within two or three miles of the town.

It would be wrong to suggest that all urban Africans are consciously engaged in a struggle for status. The lower their skill and consequently their income, the more loosely are they tied to the urban economy, the more pressing is the struggle for mere subsistence and the less their interest is likely to be in their long-term social position in the urban community. In the higher economic strata there are many, as in most societies, who accept passively the status conferred on them by their hereditary position, their education, occupation and wealth, for their interests are not solely concentrated on competition for prestige or power. But the urban social structure is a network of status positions, based on a mixture of partly conflicting and partly maladjusted tribal systems, increasingly modified by the manipulation of new types of economic and political power together with the associated status symbols. The only coherent status system for the Kampala African population is the much modified status system of the local Ganda tribe, and Africans who achieve significantly high status outside this are as yet so few as to be regarded as anomalous. The question of great interest and importance is whether any status system alternative to that of the dominant Ganda is likely to result from the aspirations of non-Ganda whose education and ability brings them high economic status. This is unlikely to occur unless non-Ganda begin to manipulate the *mailo* land system for their own purposes in large numbers, or if they become so numerous and successful in business and the professions that local landholding ceases to be the chief determining factor in the wealth and way of life of higher status Africans as it is today.

TECHNIQUES OF STATUS MANIPULATION

Some further description of the techniques used by those who wish to improve their status in the Ganda society which dominates the African community in Kampala are of interest. Although the traditional Ganda status system may have permitted a somewhat unusual degree of mobility, it is regarded by most Ganda as a system of considerable rigidity. There was the Kabaka and royal family in relation to whom all were commoners (*bakopi*). But within the commoner group there was the distinction between chiefs or nobles (*bami*) and commoners proper who formed the free peasantry. Then, of course, there were the slaves who have now disappeared. The Kabakas were able to substitute political chieftainship increasingly for clan authority, and to change hereditary chiefship in the direction of an appointed bureaucracy. The path to greatness was upbringing in a great household, and all tried to send their children to be reared as pages in the households of their most important relatives, on either the father's or the mother's side. The Kabakas sometimes preferred slaves for advancement above the members of great families, because the former lacked kinship ties or local security acted as some guarantee of faithful service. Besides this, service to the Kabaka was a very risky career often leading to violent death, and many great chiefs sent slave boys to serve the Kabaka as if they were their own sons, fearing to expose their own flesh to such danger. Hence foreigners often rose to positions of importance and founded new great families which came to be accepted as Ganda, and were adopted into the Ganda clan system. The origins of powerful Ganda families are thus far more diverse than appears on the surface. However, the degree of accepted mobility was not sufficient to prevent the Ganda aristocracy appearing as a clearly defined and exclusive class. Through all the changes of the period in which the British Protectorate was established, this class remained intact, despite the vicissitudes of individual families. It was difficult for outsiders to marry into the important families, and the 1900 allotment of land in the form of big estates for all chiefs increased class exclusiveness by putting it on a firm economic basis which continued until the big estates began to break up after about 1930 and the rate of change began to increase. The fragmentation of estates by both inheritance and sale blurred the distinction between landowners and landless peasantry, while increasing education, new material wants and new ideas led to the weakening of family discipline and the increasing possibility of cohabitation, both within and without formal marriage, between men and women of widely differing status.

The traditional technique of having children reared in the households of important relatives is still widely practised, but for many its importance is reduced by the interruptions of school attendance, as well as the many new techniques of social advancement which have now become possible.

The idea is deeply rooted among the Ganda that advancement comes from personal sponsoring rather than as the natural reward of merit. One who seeks advancement must therefore pay court to those who have power to confer it on him. He may adopt the sycophantic method of flattering his patron and all that he stands for, while vilifying everything else. In this he will manipulate already existing factions such as the long standing division between Catholics and Protestants in Buganda. He will also invent and circulate slanderous rumours about the opponents of the faction he has chosen, while attributing the actions of his own side to the noblest motives.

The great officers of the Ganda state keep open house, and it is legitimate for anyone to attend upon them, entertaining them with a ready flow of conversation and retailing all the interesting news of the day. After such a visit a chicken can be sent the next day to express thanks to the great man for the attention he paid to his client. After repeating this process several times the client could reasonably invite the great man to go and drink beer at his home. Thus a social relationship is built up, and as time goes on the client can beg his patron for favourable consideration when lucrative jobs fall vacant, again accompanying his supplication with a gift such as a goat, or sometimes with a much more valuable present such as a plot of land.

The most important persons nowadays cannot be visited straight away in their homes by those who do not know them. But, supposing, for example, the prospective patron is a successful business man, the client can simply go to his shop and enter into light conversation. After doing this several times the patron will ask the client's name. The latter seizes on some opportunity to deepen the relationship, as by asking some favour such as begging the patron for a lift home in his car when he knows that he is going the right way. Such an incident again gives the opportunity for sending a present in gratitude to the patron the next day.

Or the client can discover the haunts of his patron, such as a dance club which he may frequent. Then he goes there and attaches himself to the man and buys him beer. He can get into his company at football matches and gradually acquire a reputation for moving in the right circles. If he is wealthy he can even make his charity serve his own advancement. Although he did not go to the right school and so cannot belong to the old boys' club of which his patron is a member, he can intimate his willingness to contribute to its funds and can attend many of its functions.

All these practices are no doubt indulged in by some ambitious individuals. Two points stand out in this connexion: the great importance of a ready tongue, which is an art highly developed in Ganda society, and the necessity of wealth. Without wealth none of these techniques can lead to the desired end of a relationship of equality with a person of high status. Ingratiation without the backing of wealth can only lead to a position of accepted dependency, except when, by working hard for a patron, the client is able to secure an office in which he will be able to better his economic position. There are still a number of semi-comic figures in Buganda, most often in the entourage of members of the royal family. They enjoy great licence in the company of important persons to whom they give entertainment, but cannot be said themselves to achieve high status.

Wealth must therefore be considered the essential preliminary to the acquisition of high status in Buganda. As already pointed out, the Ganda are themselves far better placed for the acquisition of wealth. With the present level of development of professional skills in the African population, the securing of property in land offers a means of enrichment which far outweighs any other occupation, more especially around Kampala where land values have multiplied themselves many times during recent years. As yet the members of other tribes have entered this field very little. During the present century the landed class of Ganda have developed a distinctive civilized way of life of their own. They live in large houses of many rooms, constructed in permanent materials. They own cars. They dress in public in the best modern European clothes.

They send their children to expensive boarding schools. They drink European liquors. This way of life tends to constitute a social barrier between them and those who cannot afford it, and there are extremely few Africans of other tribes in Kampala who can do so. It is said that even a foreigner, who is wealthy, can without great difficulty go to the major domo of the royal palace, present him with the customary gifts, and persuade him to get the Kabaka to visit him in his home and be feasted by him.

Wealth is above all important in relation to marriage, which many regard as the most important seal of assimilation to high status in Kampala African society. Again, it is said not to be too difficult to negotiate for the hand of one of the Ganda princesses. But they are not in fact regarded as the best matches, and what is much more difficult is to marry into one of the great commoner families. Among these latter, a father scrutinizes a suitor's character, antecedents and way of life most strictly before giving permission for his daughter to marry him. Until recently they only approved of intermarriage within their own circle of families, or to the great chiefs of Busoga and the neighbouring kingdoms of the interlacustrine Bantu. Some aristocratic Ganda still cannot bring themselves to countenance intermarriage with neighbouring tribes because they remember these people only as slaves and servants in their fathers' households. On the other hand many daughters now do not wait for their father's permission and contract irregular unions with men whom they choose for their personal qualities rather than their status, though wealth is important here.

It may be said then that the higher grades of professional, clerical and skilled workers belonging to tribes other than the Ganda are at a distinct disadvantage in the Kampala African community. The urban social structure so far provides them with no effective alternative status ladder equivalent to the one which would be more easily available to them if they belonged to the Ganda tribe. This category of people seems to be the least favoured in the urban African community in relation to its economic importance, and it is surprising that this has not already led to any particular disaffection. Presumably it is because members of this social group have not yet overcome their tribal heterogeneity in order to achieve any common front on the basis of its economic position. These people probably find themselves faced with several conflicts. Their ethnic origin ties them to their poor and unskilled fellow tribesmen in town, yet, being away from home they have no local roots and rarely any effective organization as a group. At the same time they already resent the exclusiveness of the Ganda with all their special local advantages, even while they feel a strong solidarity with them over against the non-African population.

NOTES

1. This proportion was only 10 per cent in 1949, when firms employing more than ten were taken into account. In 1952, when the enumeration was directed at all known firms employing more than five persons, the proportion was 12 per cent. (See *Reports on the Enumeration of African Employees in Uganda*, 1949 and 1952, East African Statistical Department.)

2. Up until the second world war, the Uganda Government devoted little attention to the housing of urban Africans, except in the case of its own employees. The war held up further developments. Between 1945 and 1948 some £60,000 was spent by the Government on African housing in the whole of the Uganda Protectorate. In 1949 £75,000 was spent on General Housing Estates not exclusively reserved for Government Staff, and by 1952 this figure had risen to £274,000. But the total accommodation so provided throughout the Protectorate still amounted only to quarters for 2,400 employees. The actual population living in the two Kampala Housing Estates in 1953 was about 2,400 including women and children. It may be said that from 1952 the Uganda Government has been planning a detailed and comprehensive urban housing policy, but those affected by it remain so far a very small minority.

3. The *mailo* land system would, in any case, make such controls extremely difficult to enforce.

4. This situation would be regarded as unusual in some parts of Africa, but it must be remembered that in Europe it would be quite normal.

5. This was true also of Jinja, the second town in Uganda. However, in 1950, in anticipation of the hydro-electric scheme and industrial expansion, the township boundary was extended to include some peripheral areas of African settlement so that it was said that 30 per cent of the African population was living within the township but under "village" conditions. See C. and R. Sofer, *Jinja Transformed.*

6. The township of Kisumu, capital of the Nyanza Province of Kenya, might prove a good example of this. The local tribe, the Luo, has a localized segmentary lineage structure without any specialized traditional political authorities. Members of other tribes attracted to Kisumu cannot be incorporated politically into Luo society as in the case of the Ganda, but they are more likely to form small enclaves on their own, which are largely independent of the Luo social system and local government organization.

7. Status within the Indian community is complicated by the fact that different castes and sects may, like different African tribes, have varying views as to the symbols which confer high status. There is thus a more and a less inclusive status system, and some individuals may play the one off against the other, manipulating the one which suits them best.

8. Kampala may be said to owe its origin to a grant of land on Old Kampala Hill, made to Lord Lugard in 1890 by Mwanga, the Kabaka or King of Buganda. Lugard, as an officer of the Imperial British East Africa Company, established a fort on this hill while trying to secure a peaceful settlement between the warring factions of Moslems, Catholics and Protestants in Buganda. The Catholics and Protestants had already been established on Rubaga and

Namirembe Hills, respectively, by grants of land from Mwanga's father, the great Mutesa I. Kampala, Rubaga and Namirembe are all hills adjacent to Mengo Hill, on which Mutesa had built his capital. A sketch map of this capital by Sir Apolo Kagwa, which is claimed to be accurate, shows a cluster of 1,271 huts, so that it must have been a considerable place. The native capital of Buganda has remained on Mengo Hill ever since Mutesa's day, and this is the main fact responsible for the growth nearby of Uganda's principal town of Kampala.

9. Many of the West African towns belong to this category. Bulawayo is one of the few examples in southern Africa. It might well have grown up in the same way as Kampala, for evidently the presence of the capital of the Ndebele kings was primarily responsible for its location. As in the case of Mengo and Kampala, missionaries were the first Europeans to make their head-quarters there. But the flood of European adventurers seeking to exploit the mineral resources led to armed conflict with the Ndebele in which Bulawayo was captured and the Ndebele king fled. After another unsuccessful Ndebele revolt the tribal organization was broken, and ceased to be a determining factor in the situation. See B. W. Gussman, *African Life in an Urban Area*, part I, pp. 1–2, Bulawayo, 1952.

10. See Uganda laws.

11. See A. C. A. Wright, "Notes on the Iteso Social Organization," *Uganda Journal*, vol. IX, no. 2, p. 57.

P. Mercier

PROBLEMS
OF SOCIAL STRATIFICATION
IN WEST AFRICA (1954)

The study of problems of social stratification in colonial societies has only recently been undertaken. Similarly, the dominant theories regarding the sociology of dependent peoples [1] have taken form only in recent analytical studies whose possibilities have not yet been fully explored.[2] As for particular theories that attempt to define a limited number of concepts and which are needed to bridge the gap between a general theory and specific on-the-spot investigations, they are still lacking in many instances. Terminology often remains tentative and hesitant; a number of terms are used having no precise object of reference. For example, in his conclusion to a very interesting study of an urban complex in West Africa,[3] the author notes the confrontation between "a new class structure" and "an old class structure." But nothing in his description enables us to determine what meaning he assigns the word "class" within the context of the present-day city. Even less can we determine under what conditions he applies the term to traditional social groupings (and yet that is a very sensitive adjustment . . .). One cannot take too many precautions in using such concepts which have been for so long the object of important efforts at definition.[4] We would find such a lack of precision more difficult to understand in the framework of a study concerning a Western society.[5] It therefore seems important to us to determine the specific problems which are posed by a study of present-day social stratification in West Africa, and particularly in an urban environment.[6]

Certain recent writings of varying interest provide a contribution to this study.[7] Difficulties in terminology are quite noticeable in the use, separately or simultaneously, of such words as: class, category, group, grouping, etc., without ever getting to the root of the problem. In general,

SOURCE. P. Mercier, "Aspects des Problèmes de Stratification Sociale dans l'Ouest Africain," reprinted from *Cahiers internationaux de sociologie*, XVII, 1954, pp. 47–65.

and with varying degrees of circumspection, the social strata that are identified are placed along an axis of social change, giving each a content of increasing Westernization. (We are dealing here only with the African population.) Consequently, they are defined by a collection of criteria whose homogeneity is either affirmed or taken for granted. This collection of criteria is sometimes treated, out of a desire for simplification, as a single criterion.[8] The most obvious example of Westernization is the adoption as a criterion of the educational level, in the European sense of the term. Education is thus made the essential basis for distinction among the social strata.[9] It is not to be denied that this is an important yardstick, and we shall have occasion to come back to it. But this distinction comes too close to the popular meaning of the term—whether made by European or African members of the colonial society—for us not to feel obliged to study it very carefully.[10] The critical remarks prompted by a study of these several texts enable us to define the outlines of the analysis that is to follow:

1. The "evolution of the African population" clearly cannot be viewed as a thing apart. It is indispensable to situate the facts analyzed into the entire global picture and not simply to suggest the latter by implication. The relationship of the colonizer to the colonized,[11] in its various forms and despite whatever changes it has undergone in recent years, is an essential fact of this situation.[12] The concept of a colonial society, understood as a whole and necessarily regarded as such, is well perceived by K. Little even though he did not elucidate all its consequences.[13] The concept is only touched upon in the writings of such men as G. Grévisse and J. Ghilain, but we may attribute that fact to the Belgian colonial thesis they adopted rather than to scientific preoccupations.[14]

2. The meaning of the term "social class"—used as a word with its popular connotations (rather convenient, in fact), or else taken from a politico-social vocabulary that has become very vague [15]—is rarely clarified. An important attempt at conceptualization is still in order. Moreover, the observer, who is nearly always a European, does not always avoid being contaminated, more or less completely and more or less consciously, by the points of view of the colonial system within which he operates, points of view which, more often than not, are less than objective.

3. The strictly sociological aspects of any given facts are usually overlooked in favor of their cultural aspects. Even K. Little's concept of "the socio-cultural grouping" is not entirely free from this criticism. The explanation lies in a tradition of ethnographic research which is slow to expand its scope of inquiry. To be sure, we can discern a tendency, perhaps a temporary one, in the differentiation of African populations into several cultural environments of a more or less sharply defined character. Facts of this nature deserve careful examination. But attention must first be given to factors regarding the formation of groups, if there

are such, that can be compared, more or less directly, with social classes—
not only on the level of the basic and immediately recognizable White-
Black split, but also on the level of each of the constituent elements within
the colonial society.

4. There has been a consequent neglect of the study of facts concerning tensions and antagonisms.[16] And yet these facts are of utmost importance on the two levels we have just mentioned. They form a tangled
skein more or less complicated depending on the particular context in
which they appear (the relative numerical importance of the European
element, the degree of detribalization, the existence of groups other than
Europeans and Africans, etc.). Their study, in short, cannot be separated
from a study of the facts of "the growth of consciousness." To borrow for
a moment K. Little's expression, can we place the various "socio-cultural
groupings" that one finds within a colonial population on a scale of
increasing consciousness of their status of dependency?[17] And to what
extent are the members of these groups, if indeed these groups are objectively definable, conscious (in a positive manner or by an attitude of
opposition) of their membership within such groups, a consciousness that
would give them the potential characteristics of a social class?

Investigations that we have carried out in French West Africa (some
of which are still in preparation) have enabled us to evaluate the numerous difficulties one may encounter and to fill in some of the details of
these remarks. It appears that the use of the term "social class" risks
completely falsifying the picture in the great majority of cases. At the
very most we may, in some instances, speak of social classes in gestation.[18]

The first step in any research in this area consists in defining, according to their most prominent characteristics, the various categories into
which the population is divided. This was the first objective in the works
we have mentioned. But these studies were not completed, or only
partially so, by any attempt at interpretation. Consequently, the identification of these categories with the groupings themselves was, on the
whole, an alleged rather than a proven fact. The problem is a complex
one. We do not claim to do more than set forth some of its fundamental
data, bearing in mind that the problem has presented itself, and continues
to do so, under various aspects depending on the context of each particular colonial situation. We have concerned ourselves primarily, but not
exclusively, with urban studies undertaken in Senegal.

The researches, carried out in particular among the population of
Dakar,[19] were quite extensive at the outset, but they led us to define and
delimit a series of socio-professional categories enabling us to exploit our
documentation more effectively and use it for theoretical purposes. Certain
behavior patterns were found to be constant or dominant in each category.
Broadly speaking, the observed behavior could be divided into two pat-

terns. On the one hand, behavior which is essentially conditioned by membership in a single ethnic group or by adherence to a religion shows rather negligible variation from one social-professional category to another.[20] On the other hand, we found behavior patterns more or less independent of these factors and which can be taken as characteristic of the various categories. Rarely did there appear any sharp cleavages between them. Accordingly, demarcation lines have been made only for the convenience of our analysis. At first glance the categories were divided between two poles of attraction. We may roughly define these as tradition, in the one case, and Westernization in the other.[21] The divisions were of different kinds, however, according to the criteria employed—the structure of the family group, the role of new types of structural groupings, their way of life, their leisure time activities, etc. We can thus deduce only the existence of two groups as defined by these elements. As a matter of fact, the socio-professional categories overlap heavily. Social mobility remains high in a population whose majority is but recently urbanized.[22] Nearly half the individuals investigated were sons of farmers, and subsequent researches enabled us to note the fact that at least three quarters of them were grandsons of farmers. Already we discover certain social crystallizations. First on the workers' level: among those studied whose fathers were workers, 60 percent were likewise workers; [23] next on the level of salaried employees, civil servants, members of the teaching profession, doctors, etc.: among those whose fathers belonged to any of these categories, 75 percent remained therein.[24] We must not try to read anything more into these figures than the simple expression of the process of urbanization in a society only beginning to approach the limits set for its development.[25] Two categories were only precariously urbanized: unskilled laborers and, to a lesser degree, tradesmen.[26]

Here are the facts we have retained for an initial summation of the characteristics of our socio-professional categories:

Their style of life discloses considerable variations which are not always a function of the level of their economic resources. It is clear that other factors intervene: the more or less steady persistence of traditions of hospitality and of mutual family assistance,[27] the degree of "evolution" of women, etc. Only a few features of their style of life will be used here by way of illustration. Food remains a basic and traditional element in every category although certain European foods (bread, condensed milk, and preserves) have been adopted even by the least Europeanized. Only the categories of salaried employees and senior civil servants and of the liberal professions [28] are found to have blended the two traditions more fully. The same tendency is observable with respect to the material things of life: personal comfort, etc. For instance, new demands for furniture are everywhere in evidence, even among manual laborers.[29] Here again the change is a complete one only in the two categories just mentioned. Changes in living pace and the organization of home life are less pronounced. The use of leisure time is an important criterion. Among new types of entertainment, the cinema has penetrated every category, but its importance tends to decrease somewhat among the more Europeanized groups in which an element of choice exists. On the other hand, sports (whether individual or spectator sports) play a minor role among unskilled workers, tradesmen, and skilled workers, whereas they have become an important pastime among salaried employees and civil servants.

A study of the structure of kinship groups makes possible the study of a wide range of situations. This is an essential criterion for studying the extent of disintegration in traditional social structure.[30] In the city, the single household and a small-sized family tend to coincide. But this tendency is only fully realized in the categories of the higher-level salaried employees and senior civil servants, and among members of the liberal professions,[31] while among unskilled workers, domestics, tradesmen, artisans, and skilled workers, the tendency to traditional family regroupings is still very much alive.[32] The occurrence of "family parasitism" as an obstacle to higher living standards is very much in evidence. One important category occupies an intermediate position comprised of junior civil servants and lower-level salaried employees. This category is very disparate in composition and there is very little correlation between living standards and style of life. There is not a high correlation between these facts and the monogamy-polygamy dichotomy. Polygamy remains an ideal for the great majority of the Islamized population,[33] an unattainable ideal in any of the styles of life below a certain economic level. Hence we find an increase in the number of polygamists as we move from the level of unskilled laborers, through skilled workers, to master craftsmen, from lower salaried employees to those in higher positions, and from small tradesmen to big businessmen. Only among the liberal professions do we note a strong tendency toward monogamy independent of any ethnic, religious, or economic factors. A study of opinions regarding polygamy among younger groups presents a more finely shaded picture: the dominant preference in favor of monogamy includes the higher-level salaried employees and senior civil servants, and, to a lesser degree, lower-level salaried employees and junior civil servants.[34]

A study of the *outline of networks of voluntary association memberships* clearly reveals significant differences. As to the role played by a common ethnic membership in cities of a primarily heterogeneous character, we will have more to say later on. Ethnic ties and kinship ties, which are inseparable, seem to assume their maximum importance among tradesmen and among the farmers and fishermen who have become city dwellers. We are concerned at the moment with the role of groups organized for a particular objective. If the categories are placed in the following order—farmers and fishermen, common laborers and domestics, artisans, skilled workers, lower-level salaried employees and junior civil servants, higher-level salaried employees and senior civil servants, and members of the liberal professions—then the variations among them can be outlined as follows. The percentage of individuals belonging to a political party is high in all cases—more than 40 percent.[35] A rather surprising fact is the slight and progressive decrease in this percentage from one category to another.[36] The curve is just the reverse for trade-unions. We note the significant fact [37] that unions play a less important role among manual laborers than among the other groups. The same holds true for cultural associations as well as for sports and recreational organizations.[38] We come back to a diminishing curve, though less pronounced, in the matter of associations of a religious nature, or those with a purely ethnic basis.[39] And lastly, we point out that the average number of groups to which members of each category belong increases regularly from one category to the next in the sequence we have given. The category of tradesmen has been given a place apart. As a very composite group, it contains several different levels. We discover the great importance attached to membership in a political party and to an ethnic association, and the very minor role played by any other type of association.

As for *the preservation of the ethnic group as a social framework,* we limit ourselves in this matter to the variations of two simple criteria which, nevertheless, have proved to be very significant. First the question of inter-ethnic marriages: [40] they are uncommon (less than 20 percent) among farmers and fishermen, ordinary laborers and tradesmen, but they assume an increasing importance as one moves from lower-level salaried employees and junior civil servants to members of the liberal professions (from 35 to 45 percent); artisans and skilled workers form an intermediate group. A study of the composition of groups of friends produces a curve in the same direction, although one less sharply defined. One notes the increasing importance of friendships between persons belonging to different ethnic groups, friendships formed at work, at school, among neighbors, or by a common membership in some organization or other.

Lastly, *the frequency and nature of conflict situations,* in which individuals, family groups, etc., find themselves are extremely variable. The socio-professional categories have permitted us to determine an initial arrangement of typological classifications. The remainder of this article will set forth certain features of our schema.

Such then are the results one may expect from a first attempt, purely descriptive and, as such, indispensable. But what is the sociological reality of these important differences in behavior? The variations we have indicated are continuous from one level to the other in the African population. Only in certain cases have limitations been set. Moreover, they do not coincide with the areas envisaged. But are there groupings within these limits to which mutually antagonistic conditions might give an initial sociological reality? A study of attitudes and opinions prevailing in the colonial society permits our first approach to this problem.[41] In the African population the awareness of a division or an opposition between two or more groups is not sharply felt except in extreme cases as, for instance, when the antagonisms coincide with ethnic divisions.[42] Less pronounced in the other cases, the intensity of such feelings varies with the stages of colonial history [43] and diminishes to the point of disappearing altogether in times of grave crises. European opinion, for its part, tends to regard as an established fact a fundamental opposition between the *évolués* and the *non-évolués*—and, on another level, between the villages and the rural areas, still tradition-bound. But this opposition is also subject to the same variations, somewhat slower in reaction.[44] We shall touch again on these attitudes and opinions as well as on the conditions responsible for them.

In any event, we find ourselves in the presence of a hierarchy based on social status and regarded as such by the population as a whole. The various categories, and the professions which in the eyes of the masses symbolize them, can be arranged in an order of increasing prestige corresponding to the order we adopted in the preceding paragraphs. Some interesting facts were gathered in the cities of Senegal at the time of our inquiries regarding the desired choice of professions for children. The clarity and determination of intentions were greater among those who had acquired a relatively high level of education. But everywhere we found the same answers dominant. In addition to "the civil service" (with no further specification), the most frequent answers were: teacher, professor, doctor, lawyer, and less frequently, engineer. The answer "worker" was very rare, even among those who had not attained the level of a skilled worker. Consequently, there is a generally admitted scale of social positions.[45] Those with the greatest prestige are: salaried employees, civil servants, and the liberal professions.[46] This scale corresponds closely to types of social situations and to specific facts creating tensions which, as we shall see, can take perceptibly different forms of expression according to circumstances.

We must emphasize, first of all, the fundamentally *ambiguous nature* of social status and individual rank (and even that of groups). The ambiguity is discernible in both the European and African populations comprising the colonial society.[47] Among the former, it is an important obstacle to the maintenance of groups based on class distinctions, and it acts to prevent the appearance of such groups among the latter. At the very outset we posed the problem concerning the frame of reference within which are located the facts of social stratification we proposed to examine. There is not however just one, but rather several, frames of reference to be considered. Groups and individuals are placed simultaneously into several social systems, of varying degrees of influence, whose structures are heterogeneous and whose social values are radically different.

In the African population in particular, individual statuses result from numerous determining factors, sometimes contradictory, whose relative importance varies greatly according to circumstances. Until now we have been looking at the problem in the context of the colonial society, properly speaking. In that society the relationships resulting from the domination originally established have favored the birth of a new social stratification which *seems* to lean toward a class-minded society (based on profession, standard of living, style of life, etc.). But these relationships in themselves act to impede the establishment of a diversified system of classes. However, the traditional patterns of African society, even if in the process of breaking down, remain much more than vestigial remnants in West Africa. Traditional values can reassert themselves on occasion with sufficient strength as to cause more recent statuses, and eventually any groups established outside the older frame of reference, to lose their importance, temporarily at least.

Finally, with the advance towards political autonomy and the process of "decolonization" proceeding in various parts of Africa, we can see a third framework taking shape, one that is not yet clearly definable, the image of an African society liberated from European supervision.[48] Whether one considers the fixing and recognition of the status of individuals or groups or whether one considers the eventual crystallization of reasonably stable social strata, it is important to distinguish three component elements in each specific situation and three sources of social values. Their respective roles vary according to time and place. Value conflicts within groups, or even within individuals, offer useful vantage points from which to observe the deeper causes of tension. These conflicts deserve greater attention and study. Thus, for example, in addition to the ambiguous social status of the individuals involved, we see the precarious situation of "groupings"[49] which certain authors thought they had defined and covered rather summarily under the term "social class."

The partition of colonial society along racial lines, whether or not officially admitted, a partition confirmed by a policy of segregation,[50] remains a more important sociological fact than any other type of separation into more diversified groups. In a moment of acute crisis, it becomes the overriding factor tending to obscure any internal antagonisms within either of the two groups in confrontation. The study of such crises is essential.[51] There is an immediate return to unity in the African population. The feeling of being threatened provokes reactions of generalized violence.[52] Simultaneously, the European community recovers a temporary state of homogeneity and reflects a common outlook.[53] Class differences disappear, and generally accepted rules of morality give way to a greater sense of urgency.[54] We may think of it as the expression of a two-class system corresponding to colonializers and the colonial population whose relationships to each other are those of capital to labor.[55] If this comparison has been enormously helpful in attempting to visualize the colonial situation, it is also too general in nature to be regarded as the only tool to be utilized.[56] For one thing, we must not overlook internal tensions in both populations which, at certain moments in colonial history, may assume a greater measure of importance. And also we must examine the cultural aspects of the situation: African cultures remain unfamiliar to the vast majority of Europeans.[57] Among Africans we note either the spontaneous adherence to traditional values as a means of protection (more or less vaguely regarded as such)[58] or else, in another type of situation, the utilization of these same values (experienced at the moment in a very different way) as symbols of resistance to the colonial social order.

Meanwhile, every study of social stratification in colonial society must be accompanied by a study of racial relations.[59] This has only been hesitantly touched upon in the case of West Africa.[60] Yet one can discover in such a study a very wide range of situations depending on the numerical importance of the European population, its make-up (occupational and class structure), etc. Recently, an extreme situation has occurred in the large cities: in Dakar, for example, Europeans comprised about 10 percent of the total population. Its composition had undergone profound changes since the last war. The spread of occupations and classes from whence they come has enlarged and diversified. The opportunities of gaining admission to any particular class had become progressively more restricted.[61] Class disappearance, in the sense we noted above, remains only a theoretical possibility in everyday life.[62] Once again we are in the presence of situations of an ambiguous nature. For instance, the first investigations conducted in Dakar seemed to indicate, among workers and European artisans, a greater degree of fraternization with Africans[63] (on and off the job) and at the same time, a quicker tendency to evoke racial prejudices.

As a matter of fact, competitive situations have arisen in the field of employment between Whites and Blacks. This is an important element in the urban picture, particularly in Senegal. The problem of "the poor white," which has been studied elsewhere, is discernible here, to some extent, in its initial stages. The number of European men (and women) occupying subordinate positions, specialized or non-specialized, has increased in recent years[64]—a fact that has had certain repercussions. A new kind of African unemployment has appeared which we might call unemployment from competition.[65] Resentments arise reinforcing those occurring in other areas of society. The attempts by African and European workers to redress their grievances in the employment field have been carried on independently of each other, when they are not actually directed against one another (given the existing differences in status and salaries). Europeans, in this instance, find themselves on the defensive, taking a conservative position.[66] Trade unionism expresses in depth this almost complete separation of Africans and Europeans. Outwardly the unions reject separatism. Most trade-unions are affiliated to various metropolitan federations: C.G.T., F.O., C.F.T.C. But in reality, the union activities of European workers, both executives and white-collar workers, operate almost entirely outside these organizations and take the form of independent unions. Grievances and strikes are never carried out jointly. On the other hand, we have observed that the socio-professional categories to be found in closest proximity in the African population are only occasionally unionized. Trade unionism among the African population of Senegalese cities appears to be a clear indication of the growth of consciousness of the colonial situation.[67]

This consciousness is increasingly discernible, as we have seen, from one category to the other in the scale that we adopted. Outside influences (intellectual, political, trade-union, etc.) have intensified this consciousness more rapidly among salaried employees, civil servants, and members of the liberal professions (and to a lesser degree among the workers). Their reactions in the face of colonialism have become progressively differentiated from those of the masses whose eventual resistance took essentially passive forms characterized by a reversion to traditional values (specifically African or Islamic). Yet at the same time, the attitudes and collective goals they established for themselves led them to give ever increasing attention to the ties linking them with the masses. The post-war break in the rhythm of colonial evolution was accompanied by a significant change in outlook and orientation among the élite groups. Before the war, people spoke freely of the cleavage between "the masses and the élite." [68] In French West Africa the élite accepted, more or less willingly, a position in the context of "assimilation": the awareness of belonging to a society occupying a minority status remained a confused one. It aimed more at dissociating itself from the masses than at exercising leadership. This cleavage has been reduced. Accordingly, on the level of intellectual reactions, there has been a more or less theoretical re-evaluation of "tradition" in its various aspects, juridical, religious, etc.; in its extreme form we can observe the creation of new myths resurrecting ancient values in a more or less confused manner.[69] On the level of more immediate and spontaneous reactions, we note that the post-war relaxation of certain forms of colonial power brought about a global reaction against all the imposed features of colonialism (a renewal of religions, of secret societies, a rejection of outside cultures, etc.), and this reaction, widespread among the masses, extended to the élite groups as well. Thus in certain parts of Dahomey, values that were regarded as characteristic

of the élite and which presupposed at least a formal disavowal of traditional religions, were momentarily wiped out. It was only a crisis. However, the incompatibilities that tended to divide the African population
and to give the Westernized élite (and consequently the "mass" of the
population) the appearance of a social class, were almost completely
eliminated. Whenever there is a rapid acceleration in the rhythm of
history, the most Westernized elements are forced to make adjustments
that are sometimes painful.[70] Let us put aside extreme examples. Even
in a less tense situation the symptoms are present. For example, a return
to the use of African names in Christianized populations or (among very
Westernized elements) a return to the use of the mother tongue in the
education of their children. Thus we see in French territorial possessions
the movement leading from an acceptance to a rejection of assimilation,
from what might be called a "mystique of equality" to a mystique of
independence. A study of the changes in attitudes among the élite,
changes occurring at an accelerated pace, therefore appears essential.

Meanwhile, conflicts and antagonistic situations have not always
disappeared. They persist particularly in extreme cases, in which the
categories we have noted coincide within a heterogeneous population to
different ethnic groups. Thus in Kumasi (Gold Coast), M. Fortes has
pointed to a close parallelism between ethnic origin, living standards,
the degree of Westernization, etc.[71] He observes the rare instances of
contact and the scornful reactions between people of different social
levels. We are in the presence of authentic social groupings, structured
and placed in opposition to one another. But we are aware that this
situation takes place in a context appreciably different from that of a
true class structure.[72] Such situations occur frequently in the coastal cities
of the Gulf of Guinea, Cotonou, for example—and above all in rural
areas.[73] They are much less discernible in the cities of Senegal where
most large ethnic groups are to be found on all the social levels that we
defined.[74] The various social classifications are still open, and their tendency to assume the nature of structured groups is less noticeable. Ethnic
attitudes and attitudes associated with a new social status do not reinforce
each other reciprocally. On the contrary, cleavages based on ethnic differences can reappear at any moment during any collective type of action.
A study of the degrees of cohesion among ethnic groups in a mixed
environment and of the persistence of specific behavior patterns therein
seems to us most essential. In our first surveys of the city of Dakar, we
included a few criteria concerning ethnic cohesion: in particular the
relative importance of inter-ethnic marriages and membership in associations with an ethnic basis. Significant variation appeared in terms of the
numerical importance of the group within the city, its distance from its
place of origin, and certain special factors peculiar to a closed society
(racial prejudices, religion, etc.).

New statuses and the different degrees of prestige associated there-with can cause antagonisms within the same ethnic group, creating con-flicts with older statuses based on traditional value systems which have not yet been completely superseded. Hence we discover a new kind of ambiguity, one that is more clearly discernible in a rural milieu. A study of the relations in Dahomey between the hereditary élite and those known as the *akawé* ("those who can write"), a rather vaguely defined group, furnishes many examples of this ambiguity. Mingled with the desire to share in the different type of prestige accorded the other group, we find evidence of a desire to revert to their own ancient value system. We note the development of more or less open struggles for modern forms of power.[75] The attitude of the traditional aristocracy varies with time and circumstances: thus, in the Gold Coast, after having been the leaders of what we may call pre-nationalist movements,[76] the aristocracy hesitated between a conservative position [77] and active participation in the na-tionalist activities of recent years.[78] This ambiguity reflects, moreover, a similar condition affecting the political and ideological positions of new élites.[79] Conflicts of this sort are obviously much less apparent in urban environments which are more or less outside the bounds of old customs (*"extracoutumiers"*). But individual situations can be very complex, espe-cially in regions where the social system originally included caste groups. Belonging concurrently to a lower caste and to a new category carrying social prestige, or inversely, is at the root of many antagonistic situa-tions.[80] In each instance we discover compensatory attitudes which de-serve to be studied: the role of tribal pride, the contemptuous reactions toward those of lower castes, etc.

We have presented only a few aspects of the problems raised by a study of concrete situations. We perceive the main directions and out-lines to be followed in conducting detailed surveys. On the whole, colo-nial societies are societies with only *a very slight degree of integration,* and the gulf separating Europeans from Africans is such as to preclude the possibility of seeing an organized and diversified system of classes come into being. Cultural heterogeneity remains fundamental.

Consequently, individual status in colonial society—and especially in the African population—cannot be defined by any single approach to the problem. Status hierarchies which coexist are frequently in a state of tension. We are dealing with societies already highly differentiated, especially in an urban environment. But differences that appear important, both on the plane of social observation and on the plane of conscious awareness among the members of these societies, can disappear more or less completely, more or less instantaneously, or never play more than a secondary role.

The division of the African population into social categories, while a valuable concept for general study purposes, cannot be directly interpreted in terms of classes.[81] No doubt these categories may tend to crystallize into groups with class characteristics in certain sociological—and ideological—types of colonialism (and according to the stage of colonial development). The expression of an acute consciousness of a situation of dependency is reflected on different levels according to these types. And finally, there are numerous gaps and interruptions in the evolutionary development of the colonial society. We noted one such in the changes in meaning of the category designated "élites." It is in the light of this context one must interpret the ambiguous aspects characterizing individual statuses.

(Translated by Robert A. Wagoner, State University of New York Maritime College.)

NOTES

1. We have preferred to adopt this term which is more concrete, as used, for example, in our brochure written for the general public and published by the *Institut français d'Afrique noire, Les tâches de la sociologie,* Dakar, 1951. We prefer it to the "sociology of dependency" as used by G. Balandier (in the *Cahiers internationaux de Sociologie,* XII, 1952).

2. Of course there have been precursors; the studies of contacts and cultural changes have produced valuable collections of data. But a specific sociology in this domain has only appeared since the last war. The contribution of our friend G. Balandier has been indispensable.

3. K. A. Busia, *Report on a Social Survey of Sekondi-Takoradi,* London, n.d.

4. One of the most recent and fruitful attempts is that of G. Gurvitch. Cf. *La vocation actuelle de la sociologie,* Paris, 1950. And his course: *Le concept de classes sociales de Marx à nos jours,* Paris, 1959.

5. However, such lack of precision is to be found. See, for instance, the critical article by L. Gross, "The Use of Class Concepts in Sociological Research," *The American Journal of Sociology,* LIV, March 1949, pp. 409–421.

6. The Sociology Section of the Institut Français d'Afrique Noire, which we are in charge of, has undertaken a series of studies on urban centers in Senegal (Dakar, Thiès, Saint-Louis du Sénégal). The publication of our results will not begin before the end of 1954.

7. K. Little, "The Study of Social Change in British West Africa," *Africa,* XXIII, 4, Oct. 1953, and "Social Change and Social Class in the Sierra Leone Protectorate," *The American Journal of Sociology,* IV, 1, July, 1948. J. J. Maquet, "The Modern Evolution of African Populations in the Belgian Congo," *Africa,* XIX, 4, Oct. 1949. J. Ghilain, "La naissance d'une classe moyenne noire dans les centres extra-coutumiers du Congo belge," *Bulletin de l'Institut royal colonial belge,* 1952, 2, p. 294–301, various writings by F. Grévisse in the

bulletin of the C.E.P.S.I.; and many other texts that raise the question, if only by alluding to it.

8. If we adopt the distinctions in the interesting study by L. Gross, these essays would fit into the conceptual framework which he defines thus: "subdivision of a population into class intervals constructed according to the degree to which individuals possess more or less amount of a single quality," unlike the "substantive" use of the word *class* (*op. cit.*, p. 410).

9. Proletarians, *évolués,* and Europeanized groups of J. J. Maquet, *illiterate* and *literate natives* of K. Little, etc.

10. We will refer again to the position of Europeans who make a broad distinction between *évolués* and *non-évolués.* The position of even the least "modernized" Africans, for example, the Somba of Northern Dahomey, is comparable with regard to the inclusiveness of these terms, if not to their content: *bènitisoo* (black men) *bèpèisoo* (the blacks of the whites).

11. That it must be considered in order to achieve even a summary definition of the problems facing a sociologist specializing in Africa is a fact clearly demonstrated by G. Balandier in the various articles he has published in these *Cahiers.*

12. The progressive disappearance of colonial structures, for example in the Gold Coast, will doubtless lead to a reformulation of certain problems.

13. Nevertheless, he perceives to some extent, and in a valuable way, the relationships between the various "socio-cultural groupings" comprising the colonial society. Cf. K. Little, *op. cit.*

14. It is an article of a concrete, practical nature that we have quoted by way of illustration; other writings of a more scientific nature are also found marked by a particular set of colonial assumptions.

15. Note the use of the terms "middle classes," "professional classes," etc. in numerous writings. We will deal with the justification K. Little gives for using the term "class."

16. From a reading of the article by J. J. Maquet one might even doubt the existence of any tension whatsoever between the colonial power and the colonial population.

17. G. Balandier attempted to establish such a scale by classifying the types of behavior expressing reaction to the presence of a colonial power. (*Cahiers internationaux de Sociologie,* XII, 1952, p. 54 ff.)

18. This expression is used in a somewhat different sense and context from those found in G. Gurvitch's article, "Groupement social et classe sociale," *Cahiers internationaux de Sociologie,* VII, 1949, p. 40.

19. Cf. P. Mercier, *Un essai d'enquête par questionnaire dans la ville de Dakar,* a paper given at the Conference on the effects of industrialization and urbanization in Africa, Abidjan, 1954 (in process of publication), and: "*Groupes de parentés et unités de voisinage*" in *L'agglomération dakaroise: quelques aspects sociologiques et démographiques,* I.F.A.N., Dakar (in publication).

20. This factor takes on considerable importance in the case of Moslems. Hostile reactions to foreigners are more easily aroused among them in times of crisis. Such reactions remain entirely sporadic in French West Africa.

21. Note that urban life in Senegal is also a factor in Islamization, at least among the less settled elements.

22. Cf. *Un essai d'enquête par questionnaire . . .* , *op. cit.*

23. In spite of the prestige accorded to office work, the civil service, etc. as noted below.

24. The question of living standards is a factor here.

25. However, the critical point is near at hand: an absence of employment opportunities for young people who have completed their studies or have acquired specialized training. Cf. *infra.*

26. In these two categories, seasonal workers are numerous. They come from all parts of Senegal, even from the French Sudan and Guinea, and the permanent population itself is unstable.

27. Extending even to the most distant relatives of the kinship group, defined broadly (lineage). Their maintenance in town creates situations described in the somewhat debatable term of "family parasitism."

28. This term is simply a convenient one to designate members of the teaching profession, the medical profession, etc. As for salaried "employees and higher civil servants," we refer to those having a specialized function that carries responsibility.

29. Estimates of "basic necessities" (*le minimum vital*) often lag behind the expanding concept of what is required. For example, a mat to sleep on is all that is classed as "a basic necessity" for an unskilled laborer, while in fact he acquires a bed as soon as he can afford it.

30. Ethnological studies have underscored the great importance of kinship on groups in African societies. Sometimes it is the only basis of social structuration.

31. We disregard here certain secondary factors, a cause for minor variations' attitudes peculiar to certain ethnic groups, the importance of ties with the region of one's origin, etc.

32. Within the limit of financial possibilities (the maximum number of persons who can be supported by a given number of wage earners), and even beyond this limit: the standard of living is below the average living standard in this category.

33. The Islamic press vigorously challenges criticism from the Christian press by insisting on the fact that polygamy is inseparable from the Moslem religion—although in fact in Senegal it has been simply a transposition of traditional polygamy into a new context.

34. However, a certain ambiguity will be found in attitudes and opinions on this subject. Certain individuals may have chosen monogamy for themselves but defend the principle of polygamy in the framework of a general defense of African values. We are dealing here with reactions of a cultural nature in opposition to the colonial situation. Cf. *infra.*

35. As for the Socialist Party, (SFIO), the only one for which we have available statistics, we must note that Senegal is among the five most important federations in terms of the number of party adherents, ahead of the majority of metropolitan departments. And its members are largely concentrated in the cities.

36. We have already mentioned in previously quoted studies the somewhat traditional character of the political party in Senegal, and especially in "the four communes" where elective systems have been in existence the longest. Only a few parties with a very limited following remain groups making radical demands.

37. We will deal with this fact elsewhere in this article.

38. We find a direct correlation here with the level of instruction in French.

39. The part played by other groups, such as veterans' organizations, is far less significant.

40. An earlier study on this subject can be found in *L'agglomération dakaroise . . . , op. cit.*

41. Its value should not be over-estimated. We are aware of the excessive nominalism to be found in certain American studies of "social classes," based solely on research of this nature. Nevertheless, it allows us to group various indices of change that occur with the passing of time in certain deeply rooted situations.

42. Cf. *infra.*

43. We will return later to the question of the lack of continuity in African history.

44. It is noteworthy that, in the current stage many official points of view tend to assume, more or less explicitly, the existence in the overall colonial society of a working class, a middle class, a bourgeoisie, etc. Hence we find, for instance, appeals to fraternal ties between African and European elements on the same social level, etc. They differ appreciably from the opinion commonly held by the European population. The optimistic Belgian theses belong in this same category even though the social and legal context, etc., is different. We see here an aspect of mystification in the Marxist sense of the term.

45. The problem of the persistence of traditional statuses, which may or may not be in opposition to the statuses, will be commented on in the concluding portion of this article.

46. A direct consequence of the first stage of the colonial period in which serving the white man in the civil service was regarded as a form of compensation for a status of dependency.

47. We are thinking here primarily of cities like Dakar where we find a large and diversified European population.

48. We must recall the very great influence beginning to be felt in French West Africa from the progressive emancipation of the Gold Coast.

49. The important critical study by G. Gurvitch in his already mentioned article, reprinted in *La vocation actuelle de la sociologie,* indicates how cautious one must be in using this term.

50. There is no such policy in French West Africa. Nevertheless, certain *de facto* segregations do exist. Cf. *L'agglomération dakaroise . . . , op. cit.*

51. For example, the crisis of a period of rupture in the immediate postwar era when institutional changes were interpreted among the mass of the population as a sign of the white man's departure.

52. A riot like the one at Porto-Novo (Dahomey), which we witnessed in 1950, permitted a rather complete analysis of that particular situation. It was

a question of incidents triggered by the death of an African employee suspected of robbery and subjected to a brutal interrogation. The employee was later found to be innocent. At the center of the disturbance were the victim's relatives, neighbors, and co-religionists, but the entire city sympathized with them. After the demonstrators had been dispersed by force (and not without suffering casualties in their ranks) attacks occurred against any European (or anyone working directly for Europeans) who might be walking about the streets. (It should be noted that the attacks were not very vicious.)

53. In certain cases one finds improvised structures: vigilante groups, etc. This is not only characteristic of a colonial situation, properly speaking, but is equally true of any opposition to the reactions of a minority.

54. As was the case in Porto-Novo: disregard for the rules for maintaining order, temporary prevalence of an opinion favoring general use of force, false testimonials, more or less deliberate, during the investigations conducted after the outbreak, etc.

55. Not only in the writings of Marxist sociologists, but also in studies of Christian orientation, such as *Peuples et civilisations d'Outre-Mer* (*Semaines sociales de France*, 1948), and in various articles in the review *Esprit*, etc.

56. Certain American sociologists have also advanced the notion of caste, a notion that is not applicable. Cf., for instance, the discussion by G. E. Simpson and J. M. Yinger in *Racial and Cultural Minorities: An Analysis of Prejudice and Discrimination*, New York, 1953.

57. With the consequence of derogatory judgments in most cases: see, for example, the importance of such concepts as *"se bougnouliser"* (said of a white man who adopts, in whole or in part, the way of life of the Blacks) and *"se rebougnouliser"* (said of an African who had *évolué* and then re-adopted, in whole or in part, his traditional way of life). These words are tending to disappear among "young colonials," but the opinions they reflect are slower to disappear.

58. An extreme case is that of ethnic groups whose history is a chronicle of their efforts to resist outside influences, first those of the black empires and later those of the colonialists, a history in which we find a very conscious desire, clearly expressed by many of their leaders, to preserve the homogeneity of their culture as the indispensable condition for survival; "custom" is viewed as identical with their "nature" as men—a position which, of course, can only be temporary.

59. Although the demarcation line between the two populations does not coincide exactly with the color line. In the category of the whites we find the West Indies, even very dark ones, and certain groups of mixed-bloods. In the bush, for instance, the overriding notion is that of "the white man's function," the white man's style of life (differences in "custom" are far more important in African eyes than the color of one's skin in expressing differences in nature between Blacks and Whites). African reactions of a purely racist nature are of very recent occurrence, when they exist at all.

60. It was developed first in areas where these relations are particularly tense, in South Africa for example.

61. There exists, for instance, in Dakar a "high Society" that is fairly exclusive. It is noteworthy that the Europeans who are supposed to be the

leaders of Dakar society minimize these separations or disregard them altogether. We need only read certain articles on the welcome "one" receives in Dakar in which to discover the survival of what has simply become a myth about colonial life; or else read the report of a Dakar journalist in a colonial magazine in which we find social life in Dakar restricted not only to the elements of the European population, but to the more exclusive membership of Dakar high society.

62. It is revealed in the compulsive need to adopt an attitude in opposition to "the Other": incidents in public places, etc.

63. The observation is made only on the basis of the first results of a survey currently in progress. Fraternizing with Africans appears most frequently among those we may call lower middle class intellectuals.

64. At a faster rate, no doubt, than the development of the economic and administrative life of Dakar.

65. A number of young Africans about to complete their general or professional studies are already potentially unemployable.

66. And in extreme cases they develop feelings of frustration. These feelings have come to the surface in certain areas and at certain times. Cf. the post-war period when new legislation was interpreted by many Europeans as a liquidation of the classical colonial system. It was common, oddly enough, to hear Europeans speaking as if *they* were an oppressed minority.

67. This situation is manifested on different levels according to circumstances. It is for this reason that the word "nationalism," used to describe these general processes, appears much too limited in its connotations. The phenomenon can appear on the political plane (nationalist parties, properly speaking, although this word, even thus qualified, is not unambiguous); on the economic plane (as the platform for basic demands in French West Africa where nationalist parties as such cannot be legally organized). And on the religious plane (for instance, in South Africa where neither free political expression nor free labor movements are permitted).

68. And certainly facts of antagonism, of mutual misunderstanding, of exploitation, etc., could be and can still be observed. But colonial opinions tend to overestimate these facts in order to reassure the Europeans of their need to maintain an attitude of protectors of the masses and, at the same time, to confirm European belief that the élite groups are not representative. Actual situations have changed much faster than opinions. . . .

69. As, for example, the myth of negritude among the intellectuals, a notion that did not originate with the Africans. We should note in this connection that messianic movements play a far less important role in West Africa than in central Africa.

70. Of considerable significance in this connection is an interview with an African from a territory particularly troubled at the present time. Having studied in Europe, this African had thought it possible to establish membership in a class based on other criteria than membership in a certain racial and ethnic group. ("Class" in his mind was defined as a style of life, a certain level of intellectual attainment, etc.) He was unable to achieve what he regarded as a step forward and admitted that he could only "return to his people." But to do what was expected of him (and he was under pressure from political

organizations to do so) meant changing his food habits, clothing, esthetic principles, etc., all of which seemed particularly painful to him.

71. Cf. M. Fortes, R. W. Steel, P. Ady, *Ashanti Survey,* 1945–6: "An Experiment in Social Research," *The Geographical Journey,* CX, 4–6, April 1948.

72. One must note also the existence of such populations as the "Creoles" of Sierra-Leone, the "Brazilians" of Dahomey, etc., blacks or mixed-bloods who had returned from America and who, down to the present time, have constituted a closed type of society comparable to a caste system. But here again we do not have an authentic caste system.

73. For example, in the northern areas of the Gold Coast, Togo, and Dahomey, etc. Civil servants, salaried employees, and often skilled workers come from the coastal regions and continue to be regarded as foreigners, an attitude reinforced by their higher standard of living, their partly Western way of life, their reactions of contempt, etc. It is easy to mobilize in these areas "anti-South" reactions (outbreaks in Niger, Northern Nigeria; the usual political defeats sustained at the polls by candidates "from the South" in elections in Dahomey, Togo, and only recently, in the Gold Coast).

74. Thus in Dakar groups native to the town or coming from nearby regions (Lébou and Wolof) are not to be found exclusively within the categories having a higher standard or a more Westernized way of life. The Lébous comprised 9 percent in our investigations. They ranged from 8 to 11 percent in all categories (but they included many more farmers (25 percent) and fewer unskilled workers (3 percent), an understandable fact since they are landowners). As for the Wolofs, broadly speaking, they comprised 43 percent in our investigation, and they were to be found in all categories, ranging from 33 to 50 percent. Only a few ethnic groups, generally of minor numerical importance, were distributed less evenly because of various factors.

75. In Dahomey, for instance, following the establishment of new institutions in 1946, the traditional chiefs formed a protective association, but it was one in which their interests proved too divergent to enable them to undertake any common program of action. They attempted, but with mixed success, to ensure election mandates for themselves through the use of intermediaries.

76. The Fanti Confederation of 1868, etc.

77. Which becomes the only defensive position when new political leaders accuse them of compromising with the colonial régime.

78. For example, in the campaign to boycott British goods (1948) which hastened the recent political evolution of the Gold Coast.

79. Cf. the article by Rupert Emerson, "Paradoxes of Asian Nationalism," in *The Far Eastern Quarterly,* Vol. XIII, no. 1.

80. Which have been apparent since the beginning of the colonial era during which, in many regions, it was the children of the lower castes who were sent to school as an expression of passive resistance.

81. Most American approaches to the notion of class cross this hurdle too easily. They disregard the specifics involved and end up with a system of classes that is simply "a social-status continuum or gradient along which the atomized status-bearing objects are arranged." (Cf. O. C. Cox, *Caste, Class, and Race,* New York, 1948.)

T. Hodgkin

THE AFRICAN MIDDLE CLASS (1956)

That middle classes, in some significant sense of the term, have emerged, or are emerging, in most African territories, and that politically this middle class is of actual or potential importance, seems pretty generally agreed. Beyond these two basic propositions, or basic platitudes, there is obscurity. What exactly does one mean by the "middle class" in the context of contemporary Africa? To what extent did anything in the nature of a middle class exist in parts of pre-European Africa? What problems are posed by the existence, alongside of a nascent or developing African middle class, of a middle class of "strangers," Lebanese and Syrians, Indians, Pakistanis and Goans, Greeks, Portuguese, and Europeans in general? What is the approximate numerical strength and economic status of the middle class in the various African territories? Has it developed any specific forms of organisation? Are there any discoverable external signs, or mental attitudes, by virtue of which members of the African middle classes can be differentiated from the rest of society? Is there any correlation between the size, economic status, degree of organisation and consciousness of common interests, of the middle class in a given African territory and the development of political nationalism? To try to answer such vast questions in any generalised way would be ridiculous. The most that it seems possible to do is to make some tentative comments.

As Mr. Lewis and Mr. Maude remark, quoting John Stuart Mill, in their classic, *The English Middle Classes*, it is not necessary "to aim at a metaphysical nicety of definition, where the ideas suggested by a term are already as determinable as practical purposes require." There does,

SOURCE. T. Hodgkin, "The African Middle Class," reprinted from *Corona*, VIII, 3, 1956, pp. 85–88, by permission of the Controller of Her Britannic Majesty's Stationery Office.

however, seem to be a rather basic distinction between the term "middle class," used as the equivalent of the French *bourgeoisie,* referring to those who either own on a substantial scale, or are engaged in professions, like the law, that are connected with owning, or, like medicine, enjoying a well established social status; and the term as equivalent to *classe moyenne,* referring in the main to relatively small-scale entrepreneurs, traders, the less exalted ranks of the salariat, etc. It is clear that the African *bourgeoisie*—large property owners, lawyers, judges, doctors, senior civil servants, and what Mr. Burnham calls "managers"—is as yet infinitesimally small. This remains the case even if the category is enlarged somewhat to include wealthy representatives of specifically African occupations, such as that of *marabout* or religious leader. It seems probable, too, that the largest concentration of African *bourgeois* in Africa south of the Sahara and north of the Union is to be found in British West Africa; and that wherever there is a rapid expansion of university education, combined with Africanisation of the public service, this class will tend to increase. In any case mere numbers do not necessarily provide much evidence as to political importance. There were, I suppose, relatively few *bourgeois* in eighteenth century France.

In contrast with this rare *bourgeoisie,* the *classe moyenne* is a general African phenomenon. The development of an African middle class, in this second sense of the term, with all its internal gradations, has been a necessary consequence of the growth of towns, the diversification of the economy, the expansion of bureaucracies and the spread of western education. About the importance of the last factor as a basis for social differentiation all commentators seem agreed.[1] In fact some have even argued that the level of educational attainment—primary, post-primary, teacher-training, university—is the sole objective criterion of social status in contemporary Africa. This I doubt. Any working classification must surely take account of the semi-literate or self-educated farmer, middleman, contractor, lorry-owner, trader—an employer of labour, enjoying a relatively comfortable standard of life, with European-style furnishings and equipment. He regards himself, and is regarded, as belonging to a class apart, which can only be described as the middle class. But it remains true that "within a society in which illiteracy is still a dominant fact, to be educated constitutes a privilege which opens the door to non-manual jobs, and guarantees immediate prestige."[2] Though the African middle class, in this second sense, is wider than the category variously described as "educated," "graduates," "*évolués,*" "*lettrés,*" "*certifiés,*" they are perhaps its most important single component.

From an economic standpoint this category, the educated salariat, is at the same time relatively rich and absolutely poor. Europeans tend to stress the former aspect of the situation; the African middle class themselves stress the latter. In French West Africa, for example, it has been estimated that *fonctionnaires*, who constitute 3 per cent of the total population, receive nearly 14 per cent of the national income.[3] But those who, on grounds of education and occupation, would be classified as middle class in Africa, often, of course, earn salaries which would be regarded as "sub-proletarian" in Western Europe. In Brazzaville M. Soret has suggested that about 12 per cent of the employed population might reasonably be regarded as middle class; but he points out that only one per cent receive salaries of more than Fr. CFA. 24,000 per month, more that is than a French worker's minimum wage (taking the French African franc as roughly equivalent, in actual purchasing power, to the metropolitan franc).[4] (It would be interesting to have comparable figures for the income levels of the African salariat in other major towns.) It is, moreover, a commonplace that the more an African earns, the more his extended family commitments increase—so that the money income of a member of the African salariat is not necessarily a good guide to his own, or his restricted family's, actual income.

What are the political implications of facts of this kind? It has been argued that, correlated with this ambiguous economic status, at the same time privileged (in comparison with the mass of Africans), depressed (in comparison with the European and Asian middle classes), and precarious (given intermittent unemployment, indebtedness, etc.), there develops a kind of political ambivalence—a tendency to oscillate between support for moderate and radical policies. In the present state of our ignorance this is, I suspect, little more than a bright guess.

The external signs of belonging to the African middle class seem fairly universal (except insofar as "cultural nationalism," in one or other of its forms, has introduced a complicating factor): living in a solid European-style house, equipped with solid European furniture; wearing European clothes (for everyday use, at least); eating European food; listening to the wireless; reading the newspapers; membership of social and sports clubs, old boys' associations, literary societies, progressive unions, etc.; participation in, and direction of, political organisations— where these are permitted to exist. (The great majority of African members of the major representative bodies—*Assemblées Territoriales, Grands Conseils*, and Houses of Assembly, other than Houses of Chiefs—in French and British West Africa are, naturally, drawn from the middle class. The 300-odd candidates for the 1954 general election in the Gold Coast consisted almost entirely of professional workers of various kinds, clerical workers, traders and entrepreneurs, and a few farmers.) Attitudes—the subjective signs of middle-class membership—are more difficult to assess. A new individualism, an interest in getting on in the world (not merely in the economic sense)? A passionate belief in the value of education as the key to achievement (for oneself, one's children, one's people)? The importance attached to the concept of "progress," and to a "progressive" outlook in relation to such matters as marriage, the family, religion? A certain consciousness of social superiority and separateness? These are no more than suggestions. Even if there is a discoverable common pattern, there are also clearly wide variations within the pattern.[5]

Two points in conclusion, which require discussion, but must be made here somewhat dogmatically. First, there were certainly regions of pre-European Africa, particularly those in which well organised States existed, where the concept of a "middle class" (referring to craftsmen, councillors, military captains, heads of families, for example) had a definite, though different, meaning: whether the new middle class has any links with the old seems doubtful, but would be worth investigating. Second, nationalism, in one of its aspects, clearly expresses the dissatisfaction of an emerging African middle class with a situation in which many of the recognised functions, and rewards, of a middle class—in the commercial, professional, administrative and ecclesiastical fields—are in the hands of "strangers," whether European or Asian. The demand for African control of State power is in part a demand for unrestricted access to these functions.

NOTES

1. See, for example, K. R. Little, *Structural Change in the Sierra Leone Protectorate* (*Africa*, XXV, 3, July, 1955).

2. Georges Balandier: *Developpement d'une Classe Moyenne dans les Pays Tropicaux et Sub-tropicaux—Aspect Social.* (Document de Travail pour la 29e Session d'Etudes de l'Institut International des Civilisations Différentes—Londres, 13–16 Septembre, 1955).

3. *Bulletin de l'Union Française*, 29 March 1955.

4. Marcel Soret: *Formation d'une Classe Moyenne en Afrique Equatoriale Française.* (Document de Travail pour la 29e Session d'Etudes de l'Institut International des Civilisations Différentes.)

5. See the discussion of this topic in Georges Balandier, *Sociologie des Brazzavilles Noires*, pp. 159/160.

W. F. Wertheim and T. S. Giap

SOCIAL CHANGE IN JAVA, 1900–1930[1] (1962)

The choice of 1900 as a starting point for the study of subsequent developments in Java has a certain significance. It singles out a definite turn in Dutch policy concerning the Netherlands Indies for a special consideration of its ultimate effects on Javanese society. In Dutch colonial history, the turn of the century stands as a symbol for a shift from a "liberal" toward an "ethical" policy. The Dutch "liberal" politicians whose ideas gained ascendancy in the Netherlands about 1870, had expected that a system of free enterprise would result in the free economic development of the population of Java. The example of efficient management given by European plantation-owners was expected to be followed by Javanese farmers, who were supposed to be as susceptible to economic stimuli as Europeans once the legal barriers to economic freedom were removed. About 1900, however, there was widespread disappointment as the Javanese peasantry appeared not to have responded to the spur of economic freedom. If anything, economic welfare had declined rather than increased since the inauguration of a liberal policy. As a reaction, a new "Ethical Policy" was conceived which placed the interests of the native population in the forefront and was intended to protect them from the onslaught of Western enterprise. Dutch industrialists, who wished to see the market for their textile products expanded, were strongly in favour of a policy which would increase the purchasing power of the Javanese.[2]

The character of "Ethical Policy" as a reaction to the liberal period was decisive for its eventual shape and content. It was not meant as a radical departure from the economic principles adopted during the liberal period. Capital investment in commercial crop plantations was

SOURCE. W. F. Wertheim and T. S. Giap, "Social Change in Java, 1900–1930," reprinted from *Pacific Affairs*, XXXV, 3, 1962, pp. 223–231 and 240–247.

still considered of primary importance for the promotion of general welfare. Any deliberate attempt to bring about a more radical transformation of the overall economic structure, as for instance by means of the development of industries, was still out of the question as will be shown in greater detail below. The change aimed at by Dutch politicians was mainly one of emphasis. Whereas formerly the accent had been upon Western enterprise, while native farming was largely left to itself, there was now a greater awareness of the need to protect the native farmers against the impact of Western capitalism, and to foster native production in order to promote general welfare. It was understood better than previously that economic development among the Javanese population would not ensue automatically from formal freedom. But there was still a common belief among the Ethical Policy-makers that a number of rather simple coordinated devices introduced by government agencies would suffice to set in motion the economic forces needed to bring about the intended development, with improved general welfare in its wake.

The devices advocated by one of the main initiators of the "Ethical Policy," the lawyer C. Th. van Deventer, included irrigation, reforestation, education, an improved credit system, provisions for public health, and resettlement of peasants from densely populated Java in the open spaces of the "Outer Islands." What was needed to effectuate the new policy, according to van Deventer, was, above all, *money.* "Money! That is the indispensable oil with which the Indies machine will have to be lubricated before it can be got over the dead point." [3] As a device for getting the money needed for the new policy van Deventer proposed to use a large portion of the wealth earned in the Indies, which in the past had been largely transferred to the mother country.

To the contemporaries the new policy, which propagated a kind of "welfare state," seemed radical and to a certain extent even revolutionary. It was inaugurated in the Netherlands, not as a bone of contention in the political party strife, but as a common program of parties politically rather distant from each other. It was formulated in terms of a new era to be introduced in the Eastern colony and in subsequent years fulfilled with a measure of energy and consistency.

A certain doubt as to the appropriateness of designating this period as one of rapid development only rises when one surveys the results of the ethical policy at the end of the period which was entered in an atmosphere of high hopes and optimism.

The welfare policy, inaugurated about 1900, aimed at an improvement of the material condition of the Javanese villagers. In order to achieve such improvements, the Netherlands Indian government had to rely upon the traditional pillar of official policy, the Civil Service. The usual way of handling village affairs by the Javanese officials in the lower rungs of the civil service hierarchy, the heads of districts and sub-districts (*wedanas* and assistant-*wedanas*), had some autocratic traits. The villagers had acquired, in the course of an age-long history of authoritarian rule, a habit of unquestioning obedience to the numerous demands made by the representatives of a colonial government or the Javanese princes. At the village meetings where the *wedana* or assistant-*wedana* was present, the official transmitted the commands of higher authorities. The villagers were expected to approve all he said, answering back being considered a sign of bad taste.

When, about the turn of the century, a new welfare policy was initiated, the same lower officials had to be relied upon for introducing all kinds of innovations into the Javanese village communities. It was not surprising that these innovations were largely introduced in the same aloof, authoritarian way those officials had been accustomed to in transmitting new regulations on taxes or services. *Perintah halus* (gentle commands) became the usual method for promoting welfare.

Whatever new device was to be introduced—an improved irrigation system, better village roads, new planting methods or fertilizers, innovations in the field of sanitation, the construction of village schools—the easiest way to get things done proved to be the use of the "gentle command." The villagers nodded approvingly when the officials came and proposed that the village community should adopt a certain innovation. The village chief understood that he had to comply with the *perintah halus* received from above. The burden of implementing the innovation had to be shouldered by the common villagers in the traditional form of communal work to be executed in behalf of the *desa*.

In 1927, Professor J. H. Boeke argued in an epoch-making lecture [4] that the "Ethical Policy" had met with failure. The Reports on the Economic Enquiries of 1924 [5] led him to conclude "that the cultivator eats a bit more than before the [first World] War, but food of somewhat lower quality, and with its production surplus is able to buy slightly fewer imported goods than before the war." This situation had arisen despite the spending of over 158 million guilders in the course of a quarter of a century on irrigation works alone. According to Boeke, the main weakness of the Ethical Policy consisted in the stress it laid upon definite objects to be achieved by the welfare measures. This "objective" welfare policy could only be pursued by making use of the traditional authority of the Civil Service. *Perintah halus* had to be used to induce the villagers to comply with the official projects. As they did not understand the aims and the significance of the innovations, they responded passively in their customary way to the gentle pressure. Insofar as the pressure lasted, the project was duly fulfilled. But as the villagers did not feel actively engaged in the project, there was no sense of responsibility needed for lasting results. Often the innovation was due to a hobby or a whim of some enthusiastic Dutch civil officers. As soon as he was transferred to another district, which was likely to happen within a few years, the temporary advance was bound to go to waste.

Boeke attributed these failures to the fact that the Ethical Policy aimed at achieving quick results for the mass of the population. In his opinion any improvement not properly understood by the people concerned was bound to fail. Real successes could be achieved only by a "personal approach" based on patient education and persuasion. Such a system, however, could not work on a mass scale, but should be directed toward those individuals who showed themselves, for example by better farming methods, more susceptible to rational advice. In this "personal approach" the welfare officers, according to Boeke, should bypass the Civil Service which was accustomed to working in an authoritarian way. But such a policy could, in his opinion, never hope to attain quick results. Therefore, the welfare policy should not primarily aim at achieving definite "objects" but at slowly changing the mentality of the rural population.

There was certainly some exaggeration in Boeke's analysis of the situation in Java at the end of the "ethical" period. But in concluding that many Javanese villagers were not actively participating in the welfare measures undertaken on their behalf he was fundamentally right. The Ethical Policy had not evoked any real change in the mentality of the mass of Javanese villagers. They were generally distrustful of the measures introduced from above and not explained to them in the proper way. Even in the field of education the well-intended measures were, at first, little appreciated by the mass of the people. "Gentle command" had, again, to be used to induce the parents to send their children to the village school.

In general, all well-intended measures were bound to fail if they were not based on an already existing, consciously felt, need of those concerned. Where such a need was lacking, the response of the population gave the impression of a general inertia.

Another cause of stagnation was the prevalent pattern of population growth. Since 1800 the population of Java has grown at an amazing rate, from some 6 million at the start of the nineteenth century to about 28 million in 1900. During the period 1900–1930 the population continued to increase: at the 1930 census over 40 million were counted in Java and Madura. The population increase did not imply, however, a structural change in Javanese society. Even before 1800 the typical Javanese landscape showed the familiar picture of densely populated valleys where rice was cultivated on irrigated fields, alternating with mountainous regions covered with forest. Throughout the nineteenth century population growth had not led to an essential change in the type of agriculture, except for the opening up of large tracts of mountainous waste land for tree-crop cultivation under Western management. The fabulous population increase, however, was largely absorbed by extending the traditional *sawah* (irrigated ricefield) cultivation to many more regions, and by further intensification of the type of agriculture practised from times immemorial. Thus, the *sawah* pattern prevalent mainly in Central Java gradually spread to large areas in East and West Java, including mountainous areas such as the Preanger plateaus. Regions such as the Kediri and Malang Residencies were densely populated between 1875 and 1885. Large irrigation works built by the Netherlands Indian Government stimulated the spread of the usual type of Javanese settlements over ever wider areas. The new villages were modelled after the familiar pattern known from the land of origin, and the village structure as such did not appreciably change. Nor did agricultural technique alter significantly, production *per capita* remaining approximately the same.

In areas where *sawah* lands were leased by sugar plantations from individual peasants or village communities, under a system which periodically left the land free for rice cultivation by the original Javanese occupant, no intrinsic change in traditional agriculture was any longer evident. The impact of the Western plantation, which provided hardly any other employment for the peasants than as unskilled manual labourers, made the traditional type of agriculture, if anything, more rigid than before, because of the ensuing scarcity of land.

During the period 1900–1930 the process described above was still clearly in evidence. The Ethical Policy did not produce an intrinsic change in the village structure, as it continued to lay stress upon the plantation economy as the mainstay of economic welfare. Irrigation works, often mainly undertaken in the interest of sugar plantations, promoted a further spread of the *sawah* pattern to the eastern and western extremities of Java. For example, the Krawang region, not far from Jakarta, became a rice granary during that period. Boeke has rightly termed this process one of "static expansion"; the process of production had not technically developed, but had been extended over an ever-widening territory. "Java is filling up, and when it is full to the brim, this static expansion will still continue, only it will be transferred to the adjacent lands by means of colonization."

Rural overpopulation and a continuing fragmentation of land holdings has equally affected the social structure of the Javanese village. Karl Pelzer has summarized the findings of a few Dutch investigators as follows: "In 1903, . . . of all those holding land in individual hereditary possession or having fixed shares of communal land, 70.9 percent had less than 0.7 hectare, another 18.2 percent from 0.7 to 1.4 hectares, 7 percent from 1.4 to 2.8 hectares, and only 3.9 percent had more than 2.8 hectares." [6] But around 1930 the parcelling of land had proceeded much further. "According to a study by Burger comparing conditions in 1868 and 1928, in the *desa* of Pekalongan, regency of Pati, residency of Djapara-Rembang, the average peasant-proprietor had from about 0.7 to 1.1 hectares of *sawah* in 1868 but only 0.5 hectare in 1928.[7]

An increasing number of mouths had to be fed from the produce of a given territory. Partially this difficulty could be met by further intensification of the traditional forms of agriculture. Plots of land previously yielding one crop a year were made to yield two; where two crops were usual a third was added. But as the average landholding diminished production per man remained at the same level. Increasing the productivity *per capita* by introduction of new tools would cause insuperable difficulties to those who did not possess enough land to live from its yield. Additional work had to be performed for the richer landowners—for example at harvest time when all the women from the village were entitled to join in reaping the harvest by cutting the rice stalks, in order to get their share in the produce. A landowner replacing the traditional rice knife (*ani-ani*, with which the stalks are cut ear by ear) by a scythe in order to save labour, would place himself outside the village community.

Thus, the social system prevalent in the villages could be termed one of disguised unemployment. The generally accepted value-system resisted any innovation or technical improvements, as they would mean misery and distress for a significant proportion of the villagers. Clifford Geertz has termed this social system one of "shared poverty."

Rather than a concentration of land holdings and a disenfranchised proletariat, there has occurred a fractionization of both the land tenure and labor rights side of the equation so that the structure can contain more people . . . ; thus complicated tenancy, subtenancy, renting and subrenting patterns have developed which allow a greater number of people to claim a small portion of agricultural output from a single piece of land. Such a social structure, its agricultural base growing more and more labor intensive, holds an increasing number of people on the land through a pattern I have called elsewhere "shared poverty," a kind of supersaturated solution of land and people sustained at a level of living only slightly above subsistence.[8]

Owing to their general character, the welfare policies of the Netherlands Indian Government during the period under review, instead of contributing to a dynamization of Javanese village society rather increased the rigidity of the traditional *desa* structure.

The heavy emphasis on irrigation at the expense of other kinds of capital improvement in agriculture—e.g. those concerned with stimulating a medium scale mixed farming pattern of wet and dry crop cultivation plus animal husbandry—encouraged the development in Modjokuto of the classical Central Javanese pattern by recreating the environment to which it is adaptive. By utilizing native-owned land in a monocultural manner and reserving diversification of capital intensive commercial agriculture to "waste" land where peasant living patterns were not directly involved, the plantation companies encouraged an essentially anti-developmental, self-defeating form of land use on the part of the Javanese. It was (and is) anti-developmental despite—particularly after the disappearance of the plantations—the great diversification of native crops, because it implied a steady increase in labor intensification (and so of population density) up to some high and probably still unreached limit and maintenance of the largely uncapitalized (except for irrigation), two and a half to five acre "Lilliputian" farm characteristic of so much of Java. Like the Culture System before them, which they so much resembled, the sugar plantations brought on a rise in population and in food production which so nearly matched one another that *per capita* income was probably virtually constant.[9]

A further factor adding to the rigidity of the traditional social structure is to be found in the colonial type of social stratification. In the course of the nineteenth century a class structure had developed in Java which could be termed a "colour caste" system. About the turn of the century the whites were firmly entrenched in a position of complete supremacy. Together with the socially somewhat inferior Indo-Europeans (Eurasians) they formed the "European" group occupying all key-positions in government, including the civil service, the army, the police force and the judiciary. In private enterprise even Indo-Europeans were hardly to be found in higher staff functions. Intermediate and clerical functions in government offices and private firms were also largely occupied by Indo-European staff, owing to their advantage in the educational field. Intermediate trade of a middle-class character was mainly concentrated in the hands of "Foreign Orientals"; among whom the Chinese group was by far the largest. The great majority of the "native" population group was relegated to small farming or to menial work as cheap labour in Western plantations or in urban sectors, such as public works or industry.

Outside the "principalities" of Solo and Jogjakarta the only significant groups distinguishing themselves from the mass of the population were the *pryayi* (aristocracy) and the *ulama* (Moslem scribes). The former dominated the Indonesian sector of the dualistic civil service under a colonial system of "indirect rule," while the latter were either serving as mosque personnel and advisers at the government courts, or occupied an independent position as religious teachers (*Kiyahi*).

Within the Javanese villages there had always been some social differentiation, based on landownership.

First comes the group of villagers who own both fields and garden land plus a house on the latter. They are known as *gogols*. The *gogol* is a "full peasant" in the sense that he has all the rights that a member of the *desa* may have and also shares in all the burdens. In the next lower group are the *stengah gogols*, or "half peasants," who own garden land and houses, but no fields. The *menumpangs* are villagers who own houses, which, however, stand on the garden land of others. Still lower in rank are the villagers who live in others' houses and own neither house nor land of any kind. These are called *kumpulans* or *nusups*. The numerical proportion of these various groups is a good indication of the crowded condition of a village. If a *desa* or a whole district is divided into small holdings and has a large number of *stengah gogols, menumpangs,* and *nusups,* we may assume that the population exceeds the carrying capacity of the land. The excess population must rely in part or wholly upon wages for their livelihood.[10]

But as landlordism of the type prevalent in several Asian countries was largely absent in most parts of Java (only the Preanger showing a significant exception), the villagers, whether landowners or tenants, were equally to be reckoned among the "mass of the population" separated by a wide gulf from the upper caste of Europeans, who kept themselves in their large mansions and select clubs aloof from the main body of Javanese society.

During the period 1900–1930 some factors were operating to affect the rigidity of the colonial caste structure. Both economic development and education opened the way to social mobility for significant numbers of Javanese, particularly in the urban sphere. (These factors are discussed in greater detail below.) On the other hand, the traditional "colour caste" structure blocked a full realization of the potentialities opened by the dynamic impact of modern colonial rule. According to an analysis by Mr. Ph. Levert,[11] in the sugar plantations and factories the Indonesians were all but relegated to menial or minor administrative tasks. Clifford Geertz argues that "by keeping their labor force maximally seasonal, their wages low and preventing mobility for Javanese upward through the ranks of their organization, the plantations encouraged the formation of a very large partial proletariat composed of worker-peasants who were neither wholly on the 'pre-capitalist' nor wholly on the 'capitalist' side of the dual economy, but who moved uneasily back and forth between the two in response to the movement of sugar prices." [12] This policy was one of the main factors responsible for what Geertz calls "the plantations' re-enforcement of the traditional village way of life."

Again, the general atmosphere created by a colonial stratification according to race was one of the factors preventing a rapid transformation of Javanese society throughout the Ethical Policy period.

If we take into account the above factors making for increasing rigidity in the social system, should not the period be termed one of stagnation instead of accelerated development? Some dynamic developments did occur, however, during the Ethical Policy period but such processes were much less directly influenced by the new Dutch policy than had been expected by its initiators. And in as far as Javanese society was transformed, the development took a quite different course from what had been foreseen by the leading Dutch politicians at the turn of the century.

The inadequacy of the conceptual framework in which the Ethical Policy period is visualized as a consistent sequence of events was clearly demonstrated by Professor Resink's attempt to conceive a different frame, in which the period of accelerated growth is reduced to the years 1908–1928.[13] Resink, in so doing, tried to demonstrate that insofar as dynamic processes occurred they were produced by intrinsic social forces often in conflict with the colonial government's proclaimed aims, rather than by forces set in motion by policy-makers in the Netherlands.

In our opinion, the two viewpoints can be combined into a consistent whole. It is useful to view the Ethical Policy (ending with the world depression of 1930) as an entity if one wants to assess the prospects of a program of "rapid development" initiated by a colonial power. It is instructive to see how far such a well-intended policy may be frustrated by the rulers' aloofness from the mass of the population. The Ethical Policy took for granted the existence of certain economic needs which in reality had first to be aroused among those for whom the measures were intended. On the other hand, it is interesting that in spite of those limitations such a program may set in motion a number of social developments, some of them intentionally (for example by extending popular education), others unintentionally (for example the rise of nationalism stimulated by the very formation of a class of educated people). To quote Raymond Kennedy, in Indonesia as everywhere else education functioned as "dynamite for the rigid caste system of colonies." . . .

Around 1900, Islam was looked upon by many Western observers, and even by a good many Indonesians from the *pryayi* élite, as a stagnant religion. Islam as practised at that time in Java was fettered by age-old traditions and burdened with a cumbersome heritage of medieval scholasticism. The "Ethical" politicians expected that liberal education would succeed in transforming Indonesian society. But a "modern Indonesia, by definition, could not be an Islamic Indonesia nor an Indonesia ruled by the *adat* (customary law); it would have to be a Westernized Indonesia." [14] But as a reaction to Western influences, and particularly to widespread missionary activities by the Dutch Protestant Church, Indonesian Moslems responded with a vigorous countercurrent in the shape of a preponderantly urban Islamic renaissance movement. By adapting their own value-system, as expressed in Islamic religion, to the requirements of a modern world, the Moslem reformists succeeded in unleashing a movement of rapid development without abandoning their spiritual basis and their identity as true Moslems. Both in its political form as a pre-nationalist movement (*Sarekat Islam*) and in its cultural aspects as a movement for spiritual and social reform (*Muhammadyah*), Islamic modernism embodied at the same time a dynamic response to and a vigorous protest against the Ethical Policy. [15]

The importance of Western education for the period under review is also undeniable. One of the striking facts about the growth of education was that, while the creation of village schools did not evoke a wide response (as they did not meet a live demand within the Javanese village community) the supply of other types of schools education lagged far behind popular demand. School education became, especially among broad sections of the *pryayi* class, a key to upward mobility on the social ladder. All types of schooling which provided the diplomas required for government positions were in high demand. Frequently, private initiative was in advance of the government in providing such educational opportunities, or remained active by supplying facilities for many children excluded from entrance to government schools or attracted by the better educational level achieved at certain private schools. In the field of education especially religious organizations of a denominational character were very active, among them the Protestant and Catholic missions, masonic organizations and the Islamic reform movement, *Muhammadyah*.

This mushrooming of Western-type schools produced a surplus of clerical skills. To quote Furnivall, "The schools meet the demand for officials and subordinates in administration and Western enterprise and produce a supply in excess of the demand." [16] Even those attending agricultural or technical schools tended to look for employment in the clerical sphere, which was more lucrative than native agriculture or crafts where there was little scope for the skills acquired at school. Moreover, a "feudal" tradition made many young people favour types of employment in accordance with the social value-scale which placed clerical work definitely above manual labour.

The graduates of these schools began to compete primarily with those groups (such as Eurasians and Menadonese or Ambonese Christians) who had achieved during the nineteenth century a near-monopolistic position in the field of government administration. The large numbers of educated Indonesians working in the ever-extending government offices and large concerns under Western management became a major factor in upsetting the clear-cut colonial caste system in existence about 1900. Higher education provided in the Netherlands or in Java also began to threaten the traditional stratification system within Javanese society by creating a class of "new *pryayis*" in possession of certificates affording them a social and economic status at least equal with that of "old-style *pryayis*" who were still mostly employed in the civil service. An academic degree could assure its holder the *ius connubii* within the highest levels of Javanese aristocracy. Likewise, the spread of Western types of education among girls contributed to a collapse of the traditional social structure, emancipating many young women from their position of relative inferiority. In general the traditional stratification according to birth was gradually being replaced by one based on individual achievement.

Besides this widespread demand for the type of education promising entrance into government service, there were other groups aspiring to social advance for their children along a different road. Among the Chinese group, mostly occupied in commerce and other middle-class functions of an independent character, a desire to see their children admitted to government service was, before the world depression of 1930, all but non-existent. On the other hand, that group decidedly needed better and more advanced education than was provided by the colonial government at the end of the nineteenth century. Therefore, an organization (*Chung Hua Hui Kuan*) was formed providing educational facilities on a *Chinese* cultural basis. Even after the government had reacted by creating primary schools (with Dutch as a medium of instruction) especially intended for Chinese children, the private Chinese schools continued to absorb large numbers of children from the lower trading class, whose parents were not able to pay the high entrance fees for the Dutch-language government schools.

In the same way, around 1920, the *Taman Siswa* organization was founded to provide education on a national basis for Indonesian children. The *Taman Siswa* schools were not intended to prepare new applicants for the government service, nor did they accept governmental subsidies. Again, to a certain degree, both the *Muhammadyah* and the *Taman Siswa* schools embodied at the same time a response to and a protest against the official educational policy by providing educational facilities along lines different from those supplied by the colonial authorities.

In the cultural field, too, dynamic developments occurred but they followed a course much at variance with the assimilation policy advocated by the founders of the Ethical Program. The Indonesian language became a vehicle for expressing cultural, political and social aspirations in accordance with current trends all over the world but generally in conflict with the colonial legacy, even if clothed in an "Ethical" cloak. The modernization of the Malay language in order to adapt it to modern society was a process in which the Indonesians themselves led the way, though *Balai Pustaka* (the government Agency for Popular Literature) stimulated the development. In the *Taman Siswa* schools and other similar institutions attempts were made to adapt the Indonesian cultural heritage to modern life, and at the same time to imbue the expression of Indonesian culture with a nationalistic, anticolonial spirit. Both the Westernists and the revivalists among the Indonesian intellectual youth were above all anti-assimilationists.

The developments described above were largely urban-centered and affected the countryside only superficially. Nevertheless, the rate of change in village society during the period under review should not be underrated. But in the Javanese villages it was most of all the continuing penetration of a money economy which affected the traditional social structure. This thesis may appear to contradict the previous argument that the Ethical Policy period was one of stagnation and inertia in the villages, the only responses being static expansion and a system of shared poverty which amounted to an increasing rigidity of the traditional structure. To this objection we could reply that the general picture as outlined above retains a certain validity against the background of the Ethical Program but should be revised by adding a few fine shades to bring out its relative insufficiency. The trend toward stagnation is only one part of the story.

First, the picture holds mostly for typical *sawah* (irrigated ricefield) areas where Western sugar plantations added to the rigidity of the economic system. But Java presents great regional differences which account for significant deviations from the general pattern outlined above. For example, areas not too far from large towns were much more influenced

by factors radiating from the urban centres than distant regions. Likewise, the Preanger area (where landlordism was increasingly in evidence) more directly felt the influences of a penetrating money economy
than regions where parcellation of land was steadily proceeding despite
the official restriction upon sub-division of allotments under a system of
"communal" ownership.

Second, the process of levelling termed "shared poverty" does not
exclude the possibility that individuals respond positively to the stimuli
of an expanding money economy. Many Javanese in the villages undoubtedly attained a more dynamic attitude toward economic life, among them
those who migrated to a city and profited from the better opportunities
for economic advance. Others were attracted by non-urban centres of
Western enterprise, such as sugar factories and found employment there
as full-time semi-skilled labourers. But the village society also afforded
some opportunities for individuals of more than average energy, as small
traders, cart-drivers or tailors. Agriculture offered opportunities for some
who were keen to profit from the advice given by officials of the Agricultural Extension Service; after about 1920 this service had applied the
"personal approach" method advocated in 1927 by Professor Boeke as a
general means for promoting welfare.[17]

Accordingly, social differentiation was probably greater in 1930 than
it had been in 1900, as is suggested in the regional surveys undertaken
by van der Kolff and Burger. The former sees some indications that from
1900 to 1922 economic life had been developing in a more individualistic
direction. "It might prove that the higher class had advanced. In that
case there is always this gain to be booked from a dynamical point of
view, namely that in an amorphous mass a definite differentiation has set
in, which is the beginning of all progress, including increased prosperity."[18] Burger's data, comparing a few Central Java villages as they had
been in 1868–69 with the situation in 1928–29, also point in the same
direction.[19]

Profession	Number of individuals occupied			
	Desa Pekalongan		Desa Ngablak	
	1868	1928	1869	1929
Tailors	–	7	–	7
Goldsmiths	–	5	–	2
Carpenters	–	–	–	2
Traders	–	36	–	29
Cart-drivers	–	7	–	11

The village schools and "continuation schools," despite the primitive
level of instruction which was restricted to the three R's, also helped to
open up new opportunities for those young people who wanted to improve their social and economic status. Moreover, the existence of the
village schools, where young teachers (largely of lower *pryayi* origin)

wielded an authority which often surpassed that of the elders in the village, and were entrusted with inculcating in both boys and girls skills of which their parents were ignorant, was in itself a factor undermining the traditional social structure and its underlying value-systems.

Still, the characterization of the situation in the Javanese villages as one of stagnation remains valid insofar as the above individualizing and dynamizing effects were, for the time being, restricted to a minority. As Boeke has pointed out, with a certain amount of exaggeration, the dynamic forces in the villages did not affect the mass of the population. Those profiting from a "personal approach" were only the happy few. And while an increasing social differentiation helped a few individuals to rise on the social scale, to the rapidly growing mass of the population the impact of a money economy meant a harder plight, increased indebtedness and dependence on the *beati possidentes,* and a growing tendency "to share food equally when one had it and to share its absence equally when one did not have it." [20]

The following table, based on an official report from 1926, provides a rough picture of the social stratification system in the Javanese countryside at the end of our period.[21]

	Percent of total population *	Household income per year (*in guilders*)
Officials, native chiefs, teachers of religion	4.0	
Permanent workers in European and Chinese enterprises	2.4	370
Wealthy farmers	2.5	1,090
Middle class farmers	19.8	300
Poor farmers	27.1	147
Share-croppers, having no property of their own	3.4	118
Labourers on native holdings	12.4	101
Native wholesale merchants and industrialists	0.3	1,130
Retail dealers, artisans	5.9	248
Coolies	19.6	124
Miscellaneous	2.6	–
	100.0	

* From this table we can calculate that the landless peasants and coolies amounted to 37.8 percent of the village population; by adding the poor farmers or semi-proletarians we arrive at a total of poor people amounting to 65 percent.

Despite the existence of a few factors making for increasing rigidity in the traditional village social structure, the general tendency was one of decay of the existing communal ties. The introduction of a money economy transformed many relationships based on mutual aid into contracts of a financial character. Greater mobility loosened the existing bonds between the individual and his village community. Several customs in connection with land-ownership or cattle decayed, and the social status of the elders, the traditional upholders of the ancient *adat*, crumbled. Yet, at the same time, the first beginnings of a new collective consciousness became visible. The rise of all kinds of trade unions and voluntary organizations was mainly an urban phenomenon but the influence of this organizational growth radiated from the towns into the countryside. One of the most striking phenomena was the rapid expansion of the *Sarekat Islam* movement among the Javanese peasantry. The huge following that this organization was able to collect within a few years (allegedly over two million) was a sign that new collective ties of an organizational kind were in accordance with a deeply felt need among many villagers. The religious tinge of this new bond appealed to the existing value-systems at the rice-roots level. As a prenationalist movement, *Sarekat Islam* at the same time gave vent to a general desire among the peasantry to identify themselves with those defending their own value-systems against the colonial government and its representatives.

One of the striking facts about this rapid expansion of the *Sarekat Islam* movement was the readiness of the peasantry to accept the leadership of an urban class of Western-educated people. This proved that the old-style aristocracy, by its association with colonial rule, was gradually losing its grip upon Javanese society. On the other hand, the traditional opponents of the aristocracy, the rural *kyahis* (religious leaders), could retain their influence only by joining the urban-led Islamic organization.

Another sign that new collective ties were beginning to replace the old communal bonds, was provided by a rapid rise of a trade union movement, in particular among the workers in the sugar plantations. This incipient proletariat of peasant origin, uprooted by the impact of wage labour, was the first to organize on a large scale. Despite the usual weaknesses and shortcomings of these young organizations, their rapid growth was again a sign of a new social consciousness, directing itself against the very economic forces which had called this new labour class into existence.

Finally there is one dynamic development within Javanese society which we should not overlook. At the turn of the century, group cohesion among the inhabitants of Java, as a rule, did not extend beyond local or familial boundaries. Where there was a broader group-consciousness, it seldom extended beyond speech-groups, such as Javanese, Sundanese or Madurese. The only spiritual bond linking Indonesians from different parts of the archipelago together, and all of them to the outer world, was the Islamic faith. Despite the many divisions within Islam, with its manifold schools and mystic sects, there was an underlying unity of the *Ummat Islam*, the community of all Moslems. But this latent unity was not yet expressed in adequate organizational forms.

The same phenomenon was prevalent among minority groups such as the *totok* Chinese who were also mostly organized on a local base and divided according to speech-groups. Even among the Indo-Europeans (Eurasians), who were a rather mobile group within the archipelago owing to the fact that many of them worked in government offices and were subjected to frequent transfers, local differences and group allegiances were in evidence.

When the government started to create representative, consultative or legislative bodies, they were first of all established in the local sphere in order (as it was stated) to educate the Indonesians in political affairs in a sphere which did not extend beyond their supposedly rather limited outlook.

The spontaneous growth of a group-solidarity, rapidly extending to a nation-wide scale—which could be also termed a development from a restricted "particularism" toward a quasi-"universalism"—was one of the most striking developments during the period. The first group to organize itself on a broader, more-encompassing basis, were the Chinese. The formation of the *Chung Hua Hui Kuan* in 1901 is a case in point. Lea Williams has discussed many aspects of this broadening base of Chinese group life during the period from 1900–1916.[22] The traditional organizations, based on separate speech-groups or assuming the underground form of "secret societies," were replaced by all kinds of modern unions, encompassing the Chinese living throughout Java and uniting into nation-wide organizations. This trend could be distinguished both among the China-born *singkehs* and among the Indonesia-born *peranakans*. Among the Indo-Europeans the trend toward large nation-wide organizations became equally apparent. The best-known organization of this type was the *Indo-Europees Verbond* (1919), though it already had predecessors in such movements as the *Indische Bond, Indische Partij* and *Insulinde*.

Among the Indonesians, the creation of *Budi Utomo* (1908) was highly significant. Though inaugurated by Javanese, it did not choose *Javanese* as its medium, but *Malay*. This choice was a symbol of a desire to encompass all the people in Java regardless of their speech-group. A few years later *Sarekat Islam* was established as a nation-wide organization. In it Islam still was functioning as a pre-nationalist ideology, but by 1930, after both the organizations on a religious basis and those on a Communist basis had met with serious set-backs and the Communists had even suffered a major defeat in the suppressed rebellions of 1926–27, nationalism was finally adopted as the leading ideology for the time being.

In the same vein, all kinds of organizations (cultural, religious, youth groups, women's organizations) were increasingly conforming to the pattern of nation-wide group life.

Meanwhile, the colonial government had been forced to create avenues for the expression of nation-wide political aspirations and to abandon its policy of "local education towards self-government" by creating the *Volksraad*, first as a consultative and later as a legislative body. The rapid development of nationalist feelings had made the establishment of this body overdue as early as 1918. All attempts to introduce an "assimilationist" policy were crushed by the rising tide of nationalism.

These were a few among the most striking signs of a progressive dynamization in Javanese society. The period between 1900–1930 can thus be rightly called a period of "rapid development." But the development was largely independent from, and in certain respects opposed to, the forces which had originally formulated a reform program. All the dynamic processes mentioned in the previous pages tended to combine into a strong nationalist movement, Western-inspired as far as ideology was concerned but at the same time directed against the very colonial power which had produced the new forces unwittingly and unwillingly. "Western education and welfare legislation, however well intended they had been, had combined in unloosing a whirlwind of unexpected and highly perturbing repercussions which seemed to threaten the very foundations of colonial society. The tides of change, in other words, were running faster than ever before, but they were to all intents and purposes spilling over the banks chartered by the proponents of the Ethical Policy." [23]

The ultimate cause of this devious and even abortive development, however, should not be exclusively sought in the fact that the Ethical Program was formulated by a colonial government aloof from the population for whom the policy was intended and defending economic interests partly opposed to those of the masses. A further cause may have been the fact that the Ethical Program, despite its more or less revolutionary appeal, did not aim at a wholesale transformation of Indonesian society. The changes it attempted to bring about were of a partial nature and did not affect the totality of the economic and social structure. As a consequence, dynamic processes outside the scope of the Ethical Program could develop in sectors of the Javanese society which had been completely left out of consideration by the Dutch policy-makers, and were liable to unleash forces aiming at a total transformation of the society. The experience of the 1900–1930 period in Java thus appears to bring additional support to the thesis elaborated by Margaret Mead [24] that overall change may, under certain circumstances, occur with less friction than partial change.

NOTES

1. This article, published with the permission of the Institute of Social Studies, The Hague, is based on two discussion papers originally prepared by the authors for students in the Java Seminar at the Institute during the period 1958–60. The seminar formed part of a larger research program on problems of rapid social change in underdeveloped countries based on a working-paper drafted by Dr. C. A. O. van Nieuwenhuijze. One of the primary aims of the project was to study processes of social change in terms of the initial program formulated by the innovators at the start of the period of guided accelerated change.

2. See J. S. Furnivall, *Netherlands India: A Study of Plural Economy,* New York, 1944, p. 247.

3. C. Th. van Deventer, "A Welfare Policy for the Indies," in *Indonesian Economics: The Concept of Dualism in Theory and Policy,* The Hague, 1961, pp. 261–62.

4. J. H. Boeke, "Objective and Personal Elements in Colonial Welfare Policy," *Indonesian Economics, op. cit.,* p. 265 ff.

5. *Verslag van den economischen toestand der Inlandse bevolking,* 1924 (2 vols., published in 1926).

6. Karl J. Pelzer, *Pioneer Settlement in the Asiatic Tropics,* New York, 1948, p. 166, based on C. J. Hasselman, *Algemeen overzicht van de uitkomsten van het welvaart-onderzoek, gehouden op Java en Madoera in 1904–05,* 1914, Appendix R.

7. Karl J. Pelzer, *op. cit.,* pp. 166–167, based on D. H. Burger, *Rapport over de desa Pekalongan in 1868 en 1928,* Economische Beschrijvingen I, 1929, p. 8; and on idem, "De desa Ngablak (Regentschap Pati) in 1869 en 1929," *Koloniale Studien,* Vol. XVII, 1933, p. 232.

8. Clifford Geertz, *The Social Context of Economic Change: An Indonesian Case Study,* M.I.T., Cambridge, Mass., 1956, p. 13. See also his "Religious Belief and Economic Behavior in a Central Javanese Town," *Economic Development and Cultural Change,* Vol. IV, 1956, p. 134.

9. C. Geertz, *The Social Context, op. cit.,* pp. 43–45.

10. Karl J. Pelzer, *Pioneer Settlement, op. cit.,* pp. 165–66.

11. Ph. Levert, *Inheemsche arbeid in de Java-suiker-industrie,* 1934, pp. 107 ff., 295.

12. C. Geertz, *The Social Context, op. cit.,* pp. 41–42.

13. G. J. Resink, *Java 1900–1930,* paper prepared for the Institute of Social Studies, The Hague, 1950.

14. Harry J. Benda, *The Crescent and the Rising Sun,* The Hague, 1958, p. 26 (discussing Professor Snouck Hurgronje's views).

15. This view has been elaborated further in W. F. Wertheim, *Indonesian Society in Transition, op. cit.*

16. J. S. Furnivall, *Colonial Policy and Practice,* Cambridge and New York, 1948, p. 404.

17. *Indonesian Economics, op. cit.,* p. 36.

18. G. H. van der Kolff, *The Historical Development of the Labour Rela-*

tionships in a Remote Corner of Java as They Apply to the Cultivation of Rice,
New York, 1936, pp. 36, 41.

19. D. H. Burger, *Rapport over de desa Pekalongan in 1868 en 1928,*
Economische Beschrijvingen I; *idem, Vergelijking van den economischen
toestand der districten Tajoe en Djakenan (Regentschap Pati, Afdeeling Rem-
bang)*, Economische Beschrijvingen IV, p. 55 ff.

20. Clifford Geertz, "Religious belief," *loc. cit.*, p. 141.

21. J. W. Meijer Ranneft and W. Huender, *Onderzock naar den belasting-
druk op de Inlandsche bevolking*, 1926, p. 10; Wertheim, *Indonesian Society
in Transition, op. cit.*, p. 112.

22. Lea E. Williams, *Overseas Chinese and Nationalism. The Genesis of
the Pan Chinese Movement in Indonesia*, 1900–1916, Glencoe, Illinois, 1960.

23. Harry J. Benda, *The Crescent and the Rising Sun, op. cit.*, p. 36.

24. Margaret Mead, *New Lives for Old*, New York, 1956.

VI

The New Network
of Voluntary Associations

P. Lloyd

CRAFT ORGANIZATION
IN YORUBA TOWNS[1] (1953)

Everywhere in West Africa contact with Western economy has brought changes in the technology of the indigenous people; today, side by side with the old man chipping away at a block of wood, making an image or a mask, and the weaver with his horizontal loom producing yard upon yard of narrow cloth strips to be sewn together into huge, flowing robes, sit the tailor making khaki shorts on his treadle sewing-machine and the carpenter nailing together planks for doors and window frames. In the traditional craft industries a father hands on his knowledge and skill to his sons; thus some crafts become the preserve of certain lineages. The sudden impact of the new technology did not give the craftsmen an opportunity to adapt their work to the new machines and tools; new men were recruited who had never been craftsmen and thus today the numerous tailors, carpenters, builders, and their like are not related to their fellow workers by blood ties; but, independent as these workers may appear, they are usually united to their fellow craftsmen by bonds of economic agreement whereby their work is strictly regulated. This study will attempt to describe the organization of the traditional crafts in some Yoruba towns and to show how the new crafts have formed guild organizations which preserve many of the functions of the older craft organization, but have a structure based not upon the lineage but upon the territorial divisions of society.

The Yoruba today have one of the most diversified economies of West Africa. Even before the arrival of the British their craft industries, such as blacksmithing, weaving and wood-carving, had reached a high level. More recently the cocoa trade has brought new wealth to the re-

SOURCE. P. Lloyd, "Craft Organization in Yorubu Towns," reprinted from *Africa*, XXIII, 1, 1953, pp. 30–44, by permission of the International African Institute. Copyright P. Lloyd.

gion and has enabled the Yoruba to buy European machines and tools, bicycles, sewing-machines, hair-clippers, saws, chisels, etc. The flow of these imports began within the memory of middle-aged men; its volume has been steadily increasing with the expansion in cocoa-growing and the rise in the export price of the crop. Cocoa was first planted at the turn of the century but it was not until the late 1930s that many towns in the Oshun and Ekiti divisions became important producers. In those years the price paid to the farmer was often only £20 a ton; today it is £170. Not the whole of Yoruba country lies within the cocoa belt but those areas outside it are benefited by the export of foodstuffs to the cocoa belt and to the big towns. In every town the older crafts linger on; a few flourish; alongside them is a fantastic medley of small producers, making hundreds of articles for the Yoruba home. Today there is hardly a village without a sewing-machine.

The Yoruba are rapidly becoming an urban people. For a century at least they have lived in large agglomerations to which people were driven by wars, the inhabitants of which are predominantly farmers; it is not without justification that the term "village" has been applied to such settlements irrespective of their size. But today the fine administrative buildings, shops and market stalls, produce stores and rooms for crafts-men, give them the appearance of towns, and the glamour of the town draws many young people away from the villages. The size of the towns has an important effect on the formation of craft organizations. The number of craftsmen that a community can support is limited; a village of 5,000 people could support very few, for not only is the population small, but it is poor—wealth is located in the larger towns where one finds the Royal Courts, traders, and clerks. Two or three craftsmen may, it is true, make agreements among themselves; but it is when the number reaches twenty or more that one finds guilds with elaborate rules. The organizations described here are typical of large towns and not of small villages.[2]

TRADITIONAL CRAFTS

The traditional crafts for men are blacksmithing and silversmithing, wood- and calabash-carving, weaving; one may also include hunting, drumming, and medicine-making, for these occupations tend to be limited to certain lineages. House-building, which was formerly performed by the prospective owner, his kinsmen, and friends, is now the work of specialists. Two features characterize these crafts: tools are many but always simple; workers are almost always united by ties of kinship, members of a lineage following the same craft and sharing a common work-place.

Technology

The number of craftsmen in any town is highly variable. In Iwo there are almost 40 blacksmiths in 6 different compounds; in Shaki and Ado there are slightly fewer, and in the latter town there are no large compounds engaged in the work. Iwo has 200 weavers; Shaki only 50 and Ado 10; in Ado it is the women who weave most of the cloth, using the vertical loom; the men weavers in Ado are all immigrants from Oyo. In Shaki the women, too, weave on the vertical loom, but there are few women weavers in Iwo. Wood-carving is a dying art—there are less than 10 carvers in each of these towns. Only Iwo has calabash-carvers; a line-age with about 15 carvers migrated from Oyo where the craft head-quarters remain. Drummers are professional only in Oyo towns where one hears the instruments sounding praises of chiefs throughout most of the day and night. There are probably over 100 drummers in both Iwo and Shaki but only 5 in Ado where it is not the custom to sing praises in this way. Today, when almost every farmer has a "dane" gun, it is diffi-cult to judge how many men are hunters by profession and how many have never been initiated into the secrets of the bush. The large com-pounds of weavers and blacksmiths are common in Oyo country; they do not seem to exist in Ekiti for this was not only, until recently, one of the most backward parts of Yoruba country but the settlements are small.[3] Within the Oyo towns one is often told by a lineage head that his lineage was founded by a man from Old Oyo. If this is true, it would appear that in the past these crafts were centred in the large metropolitan towns which possessed a well-developed hierarchy of chiefs. Even today it is rare to find a male weaver in a small village and, although there is usually a local blacksmith, most of the requirements of the people are supplied by the town.

In each of these craft industries the tools are of simple construction; all can be made locally. The smiths use a variety of hammers which, in former times, they would make themselves; their bellows were made by the wood-carvers. The wood- and calabash-carvers have a complex range of knives and adzes but all can still be purchased from the local black-smith for a few pence each. The parts of the weaver's loom can be made by the craftsmen themselves from materials found locally. Blacksmiths, weavers, and calabash-carvers have a special work-hut built by them-selves; wood-carvers usually work at home. Not only are the tools simple but the capital outlay on raw material is low. The craftsman usually pro-duces his goods to order, the customer paying part of the price in ad-vance. Blacksmiths produce hoes and knives for casual sale but they never hold large stocks. Each man purchases his own raw material, usually in the local market. He sells his product direct to the consumer,

or gives it to his wife to hawk round the town during the day or sells it
in the night market himself. The technology of these crafts is so simple
that there is no necessity for large-scale co-operation either for production or marketing.

Each of these craftsmen regards his craft as his principal occupation,
for which he was trained, and which gives him status in the town.[4] No
man may pursue two crafts. While the crafts are defined by such broad
categories a man is hardly likely to acquire skill in two; but a division
often occurs among the smiths where work in black metal—iron—is distinguished from work in white metal—silver and brass—and both are
distinguished from the work of tinkers and gunsmiths. In some towns
these three groups remain united within one organization; in others they
are divided into two or three organizations. Most craftsmen have small
farms on which they grow a considerable proportion of their food; within
any lineage one may find some craftsmen who spend nearly all their time
at their craft while others have almost lost interest in the craft and prefer
to farm.

Organization

In each of the crafts mentioned above a father taught his children to
follow his own occupation, and thus there are lineages in which all the
members ply the same craft. Theoretically a lineage should retain its
craft for all time; but this is an ideal pattern which many factors have
blurred. Yoruba towns are composed of lineages whose heads today claim
that their founders migrated from other towns within the last five centuries; thus in Iwo there are six compounds of blacksmiths each belonging
to a different lineage and each with its own town of origin. In some cases
old men will state that a certain man living in the last century started a
craft and that members of the lineage segment descended from him have
followed the same craft. Small villages rarely have any craft workers except a blacksmith who can perform emergency work. Such a smith is
usually a member of a lineage in the village; he will teach only one of his
children to succeed him. Rarely would a lineage of a large town send one
of its members to live in a village and so keep the craft confined to a
minimum number of lineages. Other crafts are rapidly declining. Carvers
are still needed to make pestles and mortars and the occasional image;
but nobody wants their type of doors and lintels today—one goes to the
carpenter instead. While the weavers must now compete with European
cloth, their position is still assured, for the big gowns made of local cloth
which give such prestige are no longer worn by chiefs alone but by
anyone who can afford them. But whether the craft is flourishing or in
rapid decline it remains the preserve of certain lineages.

Craft Training

The training of a young craftsman differs little in principle from that of the farmer's son. A son is trained by his own father or, in the absence of his father, by his father's brother or his own elder brother. It is not uncommon for a boy to go to his mother's brother to learn the craft of his mother's patri-lineage, for it is felt that the boy will have some craft blood in his veins. In the old days it was unlikely that a craftsman would adopt and train a boy unrelated to him. Today, however, some blacksmiths do take boys who are strangers to the lineage, and pay apprenticeship fees to the master. No man would ask a fee for training his sister's son. In most crafts there is work for a small boy—he runs errands, pumps the smith's bellows, washes calabashes, sweeps the floor, winds cotton on to the reels. By watching his father he learns and by the time he reaches the age of sixteen he will have enough knowledge to perform most tasks and needs only a little practice. By Yoruba law a father is expected to set up his sons in life—he must provide land, tools, and the first wife. The farmer gives his son a small plot of land on which the boy may work in the evening for his own gain (the work being known as *iʃεalε*); [5] the father retains his right to the boy's labour during the earlier part of the day. Similarly the craftsman still expects his son to work for him; he will give him set tasks each day and only when these are completed may the boy work for his own gain. The father must provide bride-wealth for his son but the boy should earn pocket-money to pay the contributions to his social club (*εgbε*),[6] for presents for his girl friends and for his own luxuries. Whereas a farmer retains the labour of a son until marriage, the young craftsman tends to leave his father at an earlier age. There is no ceremony to mark the freedom of the boy although his tools would probably be ritually consecrated. After his freedom the boy will, of course, continue to live in his father's corner of the huge rectangular compound and he will probably eat with his parents until his marriage. His freedom gives him little enhanced status in the lineage where age, marriage, and the birth of children are the important criteria.

Lineage Organization

There is little economic co-operation among craftsmen within the lineage. This is unlike the Bida industries described by Nadel where group labour (*efako*) is important.[7] With a simple technology there is little place for variations in skill and in any case it is not necessarily the older men who are the most adept. A man needs to have one or two small boys to help him; the young unmarried man could easily find these among his junior siblings. The craftsmen do, of course, perform minor services for each other; they will take in orders for one another and buy materials from a distant market. But the organization which binds together the many small units of production is of paramount importance.

In every compound the eldest man of the dominant lineage is known as the *Bale;* a craft compound is no exception.[8] The *Bale* is the director of lineage policies, the arbiter of disputes. In the craft compound his authority extends to all matters affecting the craft industry as well as the social life of the lineage. At the same meeting the craftsmen will decide about their marriage disputes, farm land, prices, the maintenance of high standards of work or the repair of the common workshop. Some craftsmen, notably the smiths, carvers, and hunters, worship Ogun, the god of iron and war; other lineages have their own deities which may be associated in a lesser degree with the craft. In both cases the deity is regarded as belonging to the lineage and propitiatory rites addressed to it are carried out by the *Bale*. There is no division in the minds of the craftsmen between their social and economic activities.

When members of any craft are to be found in more than one lineage, the *Bale* of one lineage is *ipso facto* the head of all the craftsmen throughout the town or district. His authority extends, normally, as far as that of the king of his town; the calabash-carvers are exceptional; their head, living in Oyo, has jurisdiction over craftsmen in Ibadan and Iwo; but in this case the craftsmen of the three towns acknowledge a common ancestry. The title [9] which accompanies headship is kept by one lineage which claims that it was given to them by an early king of their town. To the compound of this craft head come most of the craftsmen from all the other lineages for a meeting held every sixteen days. Today, some craft meetings are held monthly, a European calendar having been adopted. No work may be done on the day of the meeting by any of the members. At the meeting are discussed the affairs of the craft: prices, disputes, new techniques, and marketing. Disputes which cannot be settled in the meeting are taken to the king's court for judgement. Every citizen of a town pays an annual tribute to the king, usually in food crops; the craftsmen give products of their own making—hoes, knives, wood plates, gowns, medicine, etc. These are carried to the house of the head craftsman who forwards them to the king, receiving in return a small gift of palm wine and kola which he distributes at the meeting. If the king needs anything produced by the craftsmen he will inform their head who will arrange for its production. He will not be charged for the work but should give some small present in return for it. The craft head is rarely a titled chief but he enjoys many of the rights of one and is permitted to have direct access to the king. This inter-lineage organization is, of course, concerned solely with craft matters. Social affairs of the members are not discussed at the meetings, and any lineage head would refer a marriage dispute in his compound not to the craft head but to his own quarter chief. Only in matters affecting the craft does the meeting have jurisdiction.

Inter-lineage meetings are found in most of the crafts. They are most regular among the blacksmiths of Oyo. The carvers had such a meeting in the past but, with the decline in the numbers engaged in the craft, the custom has fallen into disuse. The weavers today rarely seem to combine at any level higher than the lineage. This may be because of their great numbers; it may be a heritage of the past when their work was much less important to the town than that of the blacksmiths—the makers of munitions—for whom co-ordination between themselves and some link with the king was necessary during a century of prolonged wars. The hunters have an inter-lineage meeting; they are still, in Oyo towns, the night guards and police of the town as well as the killers of game. Drummers and native doctors, too, are organized in inter-lineage meetings, but here again the tendency is for the inter-lineage meeting to disappear leaving only a series of lineage meetings. Today kings are less unapproachable than in the past and a lineage head need not fear to visit his ruler himself.

The organization of the traditional crafts is thus inseparable from the lineage structure. The weekly meeting, held in the house of the *Bale*, is the forum for the discussion of all matters affecting the craft and it is the *Bale* who is the co-ordinating link between the numerous independent craftsmen.

MODERN CRAFTS

Among the new crafts which have developed in recent years are those of the goldsmiths and guilder-smiths—the latter make cheap ornaments of brass resembling superficially the work of the former. Silver-smithing must be included since, in some towns, where this work has not been carried on by the blacksmiths, young men have joined the craft and set up a modern form of organization. Similarly, we must include tinkers and gunsmiths. There are also sawyers, who fell trees and cut them into planks, and carpenters; tailors, barbers using scissors, comb and clippers, builders, shoemakers and other leatherworkers, washermen, and bicycle repairers.

Technology

In most towns far more men are engaged in these new crafts than on the traditional forms. Including apprentices, there are in Iwo 40 goldsmiths, 120 carpenters, 400 tailors, 50 shoemakers, 80 barbers. In Ado these figures are probably higher in relation to the size of the town; in Shaki they will certainly be much lower.

Every craftsman must first acquire some tools or machines which are not made in his home town. Most are manufactured in England and must be purchased with money. The tailor needs a sewing-machine costing

£25; for £5 a barber can buy a full set of instruments and a carpenter the basic tools of his craft. Shoemakers need leather imported from Northern Nigeria, needles, and shoeblocks; the washerman needs a charcoal-burning iron. In Europe one would find much of this equipment in the average home; in Nigeria this is not so. One must rush to the tailor if one's clothes are torn; only the bicycle repairer has the simple tools for mending a puncture; women can wash their husbands' clothes but are unable to iron them, so the man usually gives all his larger garments to the washerman. The craftsmen have fostered the belief that only a person trained for many months in one of these crafts can perform the work, and thus keep as much of the work for themselves as possible. It will be clearly seen that in very few cases do the technical processes involved in using these tools require more than one man, and since the tools are so costly one rarely buys more than one set. Carpenters and builders, however, can usually employ several men simultaneously and may in fact be obliged to do so. But on the whole we do not find that the technology requires the setting up of large labour units.

With the modern crafts the worker must be a specialist; he may not engage in two crafts at any one time (although some youths do wander from one to another to find the occupation which best suits their temperament). Here, too, most craftsmen possess farms although the young men who take up the craft as their livelihood are usually those who have the least inclination to farm. The modern craftsman has insufficient capital to undertake any work without a definite order—he rarely builds up a stock of goods. The shoemaker is an exception; but the tailor with one machine would probably need nearly £400 to buy cloth to provide him with work for six months. Shirts and shorts are usually needed urgently, while the weaver can keep his customer waiting for a costly gown; the modern craftsman must stay near his shop if he is not to lose business to a neighbour. So he usually sits in his shop all day and works for one-third of the time. Every town has too many craftsmen for the greater part of the year; it is only at Christmas and at the Moslem Sallah that there is a flush of spending and work for all.

The traditional craftsman had his organization designed for him in advance; he simply used and adapted it. His modern counterpart, not being related to his fellow workers, found no such organization but designed one which would give him a similar feeling of security in a world where competition might make life precarious.

Organization

The modern craftsmen have set up a guild system [10] which strikingly resembles craft organizations in medieval Europe, although it is difficult to see how the Yoruba guilds could owe their formation to any influences from outside. The first guilds were probably formed near the coast in

Ijebu Province and in the larger towns: Lagos, Abeokuta, Ibadan. As men trained in these towns moved back to their home towns to work they probably carried the idea of the organization with them. But there is nothing in the structure of the guilds to suggest that craftsmen in the smaller provincial towns would not have set up guilds without the example of those in the larger towns.

In Iwo the first guild—that of the carpenters—was founded in 1925; that of the goldsmiths followed a few years later. During the 1930s their number increased rapidly both in Iwo and in other towns. The initiative in forming a guild came from the members and not from kings and chiefs; one craftsman would visit his fellow workers, call a meeting of them, and the guild was born.

This Structure of the Guild

In 1945 the literate secretary of the Iwo Carpenters' Union wrote in his minute-book the following aims of his guild:

Reasons for having a meeting:

1. To know one another outside one's work and to love one another.
2. To make arrangements on our work and to be of unanimous voice.
3. To make merriment with each other in joy and to sympathize with those in sorrow.
4. To meet every eight days [11] to make a true judgment on the work that comes to our company.
5. To keep the laws of our work, not to quarrel and not to fall into using bad medicine due to trouble over getting another man's work.
6. To contribute money to help when we have strangers or when we have a case in our work.[12]

The guild laws followed:

1. To meet every eight days. 2. To meet from 10–12 a.m. 3. To fine a member 1/- if he is 20 minutes late. 4. A carpenter who starts work on a house must pay the *Bale* 1/-. 5. A carpenter who steals another man's work must be fined £2. 10s. 0d.[13] 6. A carpenter who goes to the house of a deceased person must be fined 10/-.[14]

The officers of a guild are the head, known variously as *Bale* or *Baba Egbɛ,* and the secretary (*akɔwe*). The head may be the eldest man practising the craft; or the first man to practise in that particular town; or he may be elected by the members and have neither of these qualifications. In each of the first two cases a traditional principle is invoked: that of the supremacy of age, as within a lineage, or of prior settlement. The third case involves a new principle, that of election of a person on his merits alone. In Oyo towns the first two principles usually seem to be adopted except in those guilds where most of the members are comparatively young. In Ekiti election is far more common, especially in the newer guilds. In all cases it is the members of the guild who choose their head; this choice must be ratified by the king but he is unlikely to object. The title is not, of course, hereditary in any one or any series of lineages. The secretary is often the one member of the guild who is literate in either Yoruba or English. In most cases a man is appointed to be the official messenger of the guild head.

The first rule of all guilds is that every craftsman, whether master, journeyman, or apprentice, must be registered with the guild, must attend meetings, and must pay his dues. This applies also to strangers who may come to work in a town for a few weeks only. Failure to register can lead to a confiscation of the tools of the offender. Most craftsmen questioned about this rule said that breaches could never occur; but in 1930, in Iwo, a carpenter came to the town to work on a house without first reporting to the guild head. The guild head reported the matter to the *Oluwo* (king of Iwo) who in turn summoned the man to his palace. The carpenter refused to appear, whereupon the *Oluwo* imprisoned him and later expelled him from the town.

Apprenticeship

Continuity in a modern craft is ensured by the apprenticeship system.[15] Most of the craftsmen whom one sees at these new occupations are still young. Their own children—if indeed they are married—are not old enough to be taught a craft and in fact little pressure is put on them to follow their father's trade. The craftsman must therefore train youths who are not of his lineage and are possibly not related to him at all. Parents will put a son to learn a craft when he reaches the age of sixteen or more years. There is no definite rule on age but the contrast should be noted between this practice and that of the traditional craftsmen who allow their children to play in the workshed at an early age. Unlike the traditional craftsmen whose worksheds are within the compound, the modern craftsman often works away from home, renting a room overlooking a busy street to which his children are less likely to follow him. It would be untrue to state that kin ties do not count in choosing a master for one's son, but skill and integrity do appear to be the more dominant factors. The father or guardian of the boy will sign a contract with the master stating the length of the apprenticeship and the fee payable. The following document is a typical example: [16]

This is to certify that I, the undersigned, by name I. A. of M. compound do hereby submit my boy, by name A. A. of N. compound, Iwo, to Mr. S. A. (bricklayer) for the purpose of learning the art of bricklaying under the mastership of the said S. A.

The boy, by name A. A., shall be under the mastership of S. A. for a period of twelve calendar months or a year clearly. I also agree to pay the sum of two pounds ten shillings out of which the sum of one pound is paid as cash advance.

Feeding allowance shall be carried out by the master while all other expenditures such as clothing shall be my own lookout. Tools shall be provided to the apprentice on the completion of his course by me I. A.

I hereby promise most faithfully to pay the fee of his course correctly on completion, or if he deserts I shall pay accordingly.

I the said S. A. do hereby promise faithfully to teach A. A. the art of brick-laying to sound standard for the period of one year as under agreement. I shall also carry out his feeding affairs for the length of time that he shall be under my mastership.

Dated and signed in Iwo, today the   day of   1949

(Signed)   Guardian I. A.

Master S. A.

A scale of apprenticeship premiums is usually laid down by the guild but a master may make concessions to his friends. The principle is that the longer the apprenticeship the smaller shall be the premium; for, as masters often say, "in the first year a boy will play, in the second year he learns, and in the third year he will work for me." The premiums vary also when a boy lives with his master who is responsible for all or part of his feeding and clothing and may even agree to provide tools for the boy on the completion of his training. An example of the scale of premiums is provided by the Bicycle Repairers' Union in Ado where, for a six months' apprenticeship, the premium was £3, for a year's course £2, for a two-year course £1 and for a three-year apprenticeship no premium was payable at all.

The apprentice is usually between the ages of fifteen and twenty years and unschooled. His duty at first is to do simple and menial tasks for his master, running errands and often working on his farm. Many seem to spend their whole period as "small boys." The master ought to teach the boy the trade and if he is literate he may well teach him the rudiments of writing and arithmetic. All the work done by the boy belongs to his master; the apprentice receives no remuneration for his work. Most masters will allow boys to do odd jobs for their own relatives in slack periods and to keep whatever they may earn in this way. At the end of his term of apprenticeship the boy should be fully qualified; at this stage the master often gives him all the work to do—unpaid—while he is free to take up public duties in the town and so enhance his prestige. When a boy first joins his master he will be introduced to the guild, the members of which are the arbiters in any dispute between him and his master. At the end of the apprenticeship the boy will hold a small cere-mony at which he is given his freedom. The boy's father must provide beer and cigarettes, kola and palm wine for the members of the guild assembled in his house. The guild head will bless the boy and read to him the guild laws. The father is usually responsible for providing a son with tools after his freedom. In some cases, especially with carpenters or goldsmiths, the young man will receive a few tools from his master.

As soon as the boy has tools there is nothing to prevent him from becoming a master himself. If he cannot buy enough tools or if he fails to attract customers the new craftsman will hire himself to masters with a full order book as a day-labourer. Wage rates are fixed by the guild according to the type of work done—roof building on a two-story house earns a high rate—and according to the tools brought by the worker— the journeyman with his own hammer can receive 5s. a day, without tools he receives 4s. a day. Every journeyman hopes to save or borrow enough money to buy his tools and there has not yet arisen a permanent class of craftsmen owning no tools. The apprentice usually manages to become a master, with or without his own apprentices, and to maintain his independence.

The Work of the Guilds

Economic functions. One of the prime functions of a guild is to maintain a reasonable standard of work in the craft. This is difficult and is not satisfactorily carried out. There is no system whereby an apprentice must produce his "masterpiece" before being granted his freedom. Many boys leave their masters before they are properly trained and thus the standard of work tends to fall. There is no organized inspection of workplaces to seek out shoddy work. The guild simply censures a member if a customer complains about his work.

The guild determines the rules of apprenticeship; it recommends, if it does not actually fix, the premiums. It is responsible, in theory, for seeing that the boys are well trained. It settles disputes between masters and apprentices and will not allow apprentices to run from one master to another, or allow the masters to encourage such action without its express permission. There are no rules governing the number of apprentices which a master may train at any one time. The upper limit is usually fixed by the prosperity of the master—when he is earning nothing he cannot feed his apprentices, who then abscond. Some carpenters have as many as ten apprentices, but the number of craftsmen with more than five is small. The guild also fixes the wages of journeymen and the conditions of their employment.

The guild fixes prices of workmanship (the raw material is usually paid for by the customer as a separate item). Within a town the craftsmen are able to maintain the set prices. A rich man may be persuaded to pay a higher figure: that is his loss; the guild member will only be accused if he robs the poor. Lower prices are often paid by friends and relatives— this too is legitimate. Prices are not fixed in relation to the amount of labour expended on the article. They are low on the commoner types of article, high on those which will reflect the wealth and prestige of the owner.

The guild settles all disputes, whether between members or between craftsman and customer. It stops members from stealing work from each other; the carpenter who cannot fulfil his contract, because of absence due to sickness or death in his family, is protected against his neighbour who would like to take over the work. Customers who prove awkward may find that the guild has itself arranged who will complete the work, sometimes giving the contract to several craftsmen and inviting them to charge the maximum prices. Such a case occurred in Iwo in 1949 when a wealthy trader objected because a carpenter failed to build his house in the specified time. The guild also protects the customer against the craftsman who receives an advance payment for his work and then fails, without good reason, to complete the contract and is unable to refund the money. In judging cases between members the guild will order one or both parties to the dispute to pay a fine which will be used to buy beer to be consumed at the meeting. Disrespect to a guild head or to his official messenger merely aggravates any offence and will result in heavier fines. Any person who is dissatisfied with the judgement of the guild may appeal to the king. If a guild member is accused by some person outside the guild and, in the opinion of his guild, the charges are unfounded, the guild head will intercede on his behalf and the members' contributions will be used to fight the case in the king's Court.

Most guilds levy a small weekly contribution to cover normal running expenses; the guild head and secretary are unpaid.

Political functions. The guild head, as stated earlier, must be approved by the king; but he holds no position in the hierarchy of chiefs. There is no official ceremony of installation. The head is not admitted to council meetings of the chiefs but he may approach the king directly. The members of the guild are represented politically through the heads of their lineages. The king is arbiter in all disputes brought to him on appeal, and refusal to obey the judgement of the king is punished by expulsion from the town. The traditional craftsmen paid annual tribute to their king in kind; this is more difficult for the modern craftsman, especially those whose work is in the nature of personal service. Moreover, the young men dislike paying tax as well as tribute and, since the former is now compulsory (and is used to provide the salary of the king), they neglect the latter. A guild head is usually responsible for bringing his members before the Tax Assessment Committee, for ensuring fair assessment, and for collecting the tax money from the members. Work for the king is usually done without payment. In Ado the *Ewi* (king of Ado) asked the head bricklayer to supervise the building of the new two-story house in the palace. In Iwo the *Oluwo* annually calls on the head tailor to come and work inside the palace with several of his guild to make gowns for the mallams at the end of Ramadan. In both these cases the king provides the materials but does not pay for the workmanship.

Other functions. The guild member still retains full membership of his lineage and suffers no disabilities by joining another organization. Most forms of social security are still organized by the lineage, not by the guild. The guild does not undertake to care for its members in sickness or old age; neither does it function as a bank, lending money to members for tools. It takes no interest in disputes over a member's wives or land. (But a member may not seduce the wife of a fellow craftsman; this would cause enmity within the guild!) There is often merriment at guild meetings; if any member has a ceremony in his family the rest will be present, contributing the usual money and drinking as much as the host will allow.

Variations in Guild Structure

The guild pattern is similar in all the three towns studied but within each town there are some guilds which are powerful, others which are weak. Of all the guilds those of the carpenters seem to be the best organized. Perhaps this is because their members tend to be better educated than those of other crafts; it is more likely to be due to the complex nature of the work—the construction of all the woodwork in a two-story house— and the high costs involved. Other guilds associated with house-building— those of the painters and bricklayers—are also strong. Tailors usually have the least-developed guild organization. Often there appear to be too many of them in one town and a meeting of those of one quarter is the highest unit; but even these meetings are sporadic, especially in the slack seasons. In other guilds the meetings are poorly attended, in spite of the threat of fines, but the organization definitely exists and could quickly be strengthened if the need arose.

FUTURE DEVELOPMENTS IN CRAFT ORGANIZATION

To what extent do these craft meetings encourage or prevent developments either in technical processes or in the organization of the industry? The processes used in the traditional crafts seem similar throughout Yoruba country; only in local designs do variations appear. There seem to be few indications that any recent improvements in technique have been made; the exception, perhaps, would be the rise of gunmaking. But here, although many gunsmiths were originally blacksmiths, the tendency has been for them to break away from the lineage organization to set up a guild. The modern mechanic is seldom a blacksmith by birth; the weaver on the broad loom introduced by the European Textile Officer does not come from a weaving compound. None of these crafts has been able to undertake any of the modern technological improvements within its own sphere. The lineage meetings retain responsibility only for the crafts practised before the advent of the European. No young men are joining these traditional crafts from other lineages; only a few practise the craft of their own lineage. Inter-lineage meetings are becoming rarer and the discussion of economic affairs is only a minor feature of lineage meetings.

Within these crafts it is theoretically possible for one man to become an entrepreneur, buying raw material, giving it out to men to manufacture at a stated fee, and later selling the finished article. This would involve exploitation of one lineage member by another and would probably be resisted on social grounds. It seems to be of rare occurrence. Today one does find that a weaver may become engaged solely in such entrepreneurial functions, buying cotton yarn and silk from the big towns and supervising the manufacture of traditional gowns. This is largely because the best cotton can often be obtained only in the large towns which the illiterate weaver may never have visited and because the market for the gowns now extends as far as the Gold Coast. Bulk buying of motor parts is practised by the blacksmiths but they sell the scrap iron to their fellow workers and have no interest in its manufacture. Neither the weaver-trader nor the blacksmith-trader confines his activities to his own lineage members. There seems to be no indication that craft organizations based on the lineage will become stronger again, but plenty of evidence that they are slowly dying out, leaving the lineage meetings to discuss social affairs only.

It is difficult to predict the future of the guilds. The scientific knowledge of the modern craftsmen is so slight that one cannot expect them to make any technical improvements in their tools. Many craftsmen look forward to the day when they can afford to buy new tools and so employ more journeymen; this would create a new form of organization where the master would become an entrepreneur and his relationship with his workers would be that of employer and employee. Such a development is hampered because craftsmen lack capital; since the guilds do nothing to restrict entry into the craft, the number of workers grows, there is increasing competition, and today the less successful craftsmen are returning to farm-work. The guild laws do much to restrict competition between members; the Yoruba feel that it is immoral to prevent another man from earning a living in the way that he pleases. Finally, tribal social life, with its polygamy, feasts, and costly funerals, does much to prevent capital accumulation. Tribal values thus seem to be primarily responsible for the lack of development within the guilds and, while the guild laws remain unchanged, the labour unit will remain small.

SOME OTHER ORGANIZATIONS

Before leaving the guilds it might be appropriate to mention some other organizations existing in Yoruba towns with which comparison may be made. The women's crafts are spinning, weaving, dyeing, pot-making, and food preparation. These, like the men's crafts, are technologically simple and employ large numbers of women. All are carried out in the home with the exception of pot-making, which takes place in a common work-place; but even here each woman is an independent producer. Most women train their own children in their craft but, since marriage is patrilocal, the women soon become dispersed. They seem to have no form of organization which compares with that of the men. Today many literate women own sewing-machines; they teach young girls to sew, as a wifely accomplishment, though the girls seem similar in most respects to apprentices. But there is no evidence that the sewing mistresses have established a guild organization.

Women traders are, however, organized. In the markets the women selling one particular commodity sit together; their head is usually the oldest woman. These groups of women settle disputes, fix prices, and prevent the encroachment of one set of traders on another: those who sell leaves and peppers must not sell onions and vice versa. The market unions have many of the features of guilds; the women are not related one to another but they train their daughters before taking apprentices. These unions seem to be traditional. The modern traders in cocoa, palm kernel, and cattle have strong guild organizations of recent growth. The butchers usually arrange that each member kills the same number of cattle each day, thus preventing price cutting and consequent elimination of the weaker traders.

In Ekiti until recent times there has existed an age-set system. In the first place all men born in the same three-year period form one social club (εgbε); in the second place men between the ages of fifteen and forty-five years are arranged in four or five grades of ascending ages for the performance of public duties and war. In Oyo today there are no traces of this system; youths are banded together into clubs (εgbε), based on similarity of age, interests, and residence, but none of these criteria is so definitive that a man does not have considerable choice of which club to join. This system has now been adopted in Ekiti. The club has a leader, a member of the club elected for his personality. It also has an older man or patron (baba εgbε). These clubs are purely voluntary and may be dissolved at will. At weekly meetings are discussed the affairs of the town and the problems of the members; the club holds annual dances and will visit the house of any member performing a ceremony. Their strength may be indicated by the fact that many youths will attend a club meeting rather than a function connected with their lineage. These clubs are earlier in origin than the craft guilds and their rules for regulating attendance and behaviour at meetings and for social intercourse between the members seem to have been copied by the guilds.

Within these older social and economic organizations, together with those of the traditional crafts, are contained nearly all the features, both of function and morphology, of the new craft guild.[17]

CONCLUSION

The function of the traditional craft organizations was, and still is, to settle disputes, to regulate the relationship between producers, to fix prices, and to organize the payment of tribute to the king. The structure of these organizations was the lineage structure, the lineage meeting was the craft meeting; the craft head was the compound head, the oldest man in the lineage. The labour group was small, consisting of a father and his sons.

The modern craft guild has precisely the same economic functions as the lineage meeting: it too settles disputes, fixes prices, and organizes the collection of tax money; it regulates the relationship between the workers engaged in the production process. But the workers are drawn from all parts of the town by their common interest, and are not related by blood. The lineage no longer provides the structure of the organization. This is due to the speed at which the new crafts have developed. Even if the traditional craft organizations had been sufficiently flexible to absorb the new techniques—a point which itself is doubtful—their method of training could not have produced craftsmen quickly. A father will only train one or two sons in his lifetime; but a master who keeps two apprentices for a three-year course will train twenty craftsmen in thirty years. The form of organization adopted by the new crafts is similar in many ways to the social clubs; from them it seems to have copied the unrestricted entry and the rules governing attendance and behaviour at the weekly meetings and members' ceremonies. The guilds which elect their head do not, however, have a patron; they thus make a final break with the custom of respecting one's elders; no longer is it felt necessary to have the guidance of the older men. But the social clubs are not productive units and the relationship between their members is not economic. They are social meetings and the guilds have adopted their social features. The market-women's unions are similar to the guilds but the relationship between the persons within a single labour group is still that of mother and daughter.

The guilds are distinguished by one new feature. Apprentices and journeymen are not found in traditional Yoruba society; the relationship between these and the master craftsman is entirely new. In the traditional crafts the labour group consists of men whose relationship in the productive process is determined largely by their blood ties, ties between father and son. In other traditional spheres may be found slaves over whose persons the master had legal rights. The relationships between master and apprentice and master and journeyman are those of contracts which give the master the right to the labour of his worker within defined limits. The master has no blood ties with his apprentice or journeyman, neither has he the right to sell their persons. The guilds have devised sets of laws which regulate this new relationship.

The change from one form of economic organization to another always appears to be a slow process; in response to changes in technology a new organization is formed having most of the functions of its predecessor and a morphology similar to existing associations. The guilds are structurally similar to the social clubs and market-women's unions and their functions are similar to those of the traditional craft organizations. But the labour group is no longer composed of father and sons but of master and journeymen or apprentices; and this is a difference of overwhelming importance both in the craft industry and in society as a whole.

NOTES

1. The text of a paper circulated at a conference held in April 1952 at the West African Institute of Social and Economic Research.

2. There is considerable cultural diversity between the Yoruba subtribes. Material for this study has been collected from two towns—Iwo and Shaki—which are predominantly Oyo, and a third—Ado—which is in the heart of Ekiti country. There seemed to be no significant difference between the craft organizations found in these towns, and unless otherwise stated, their description will apply to all three areas. There seems to be little reason to doubt that a common pattern is found throughout the whole of Yoruba country.

Of the towns mentioned in this study Iwo has a population of 50,000 persons, Shaki—21,000 persons, and Ado—17,000 persons. Ado is in the heart of the cocoa-producing area; it is a trade centre and a political headquarters of Ekiti Division; the rate of literacy is relatively high and Christianity has progressed farther than in Iwo or Shaki. Iwo is on the edge of the cocoa belt and Shaki is far north of it; both towns are predominantly Moslem and education has made little progress.

3. Ado itself is in reality a union of three towns. Settlements of between 3,000–5,000 are common in Ekiti.

4. In a Yoruba town lineages are not ranked in hierarchical order; in this sense craftsmen are not given a higher or lower status than non-craftsmen.

5. *Iʃɛalɛ* = evening work; *iʃɛ* = work; *alɛ* = evening.

6. *Ɛgbɛ* = any type of club, meeting, or union.

7. S. F. Nadel, *Black Byzantium*, 1942, ch. xiv.

8. The lineage (*idile* = stem of the house) is a group of persons descended from a common ancestor in the male line; the compound (*agbo-ile* = group of houses) is the residence of the male members of the lineage, their wives, and unmarried children; the *Bale* (*baba ile* = father of the house) is always the oldest living male.

9. The head of a craft organization is known as the father of the craft;

thus *baba alagbɛdɛ* = father of blacksmiths. Sometimes the prefix *oni-* or *ɔl-*, denoting possession, is used; thus *ɔlɔde* = head of the hunters.

10. Nadel, *op. cit.*, has used the word "guild" for craft organizations based on the lineage or extended family where the labour group is formed of a man, his brothers, and sons. It seems preferable to use the word in the same manner as historians to connote the organization of crafts where the master-apprentice-journeyman relationship is typical.

The Yoruba use the word *ɛgbɛ* for guild; the semi-literates usually translate this as "meeting."

11. Eight days is, by Yoruba counting, a seven-day week. Meetings are held on Fridays or Sundays according to whether the members are predominantly Moslem or Christian.

12. A case is a legal dispute involving payments to chiefs for their arbitration.

13. Stealing work is the seeking to obtain contracts on which a fellow worker has defaulted.

14. One must not overtly seek for business and this includes visiting the relatives of the deceased to obtain an order for a coffin.

15. The Yoruba use the word *ɔga* for master; this term includes all types of employers. There is no specific word for master craftsman. The apprentice is *ɔmɔʃe* (*ɔmɔ* = boy, *ʃe* = to work), a term which includes all boys learning anything and also casual unskilled labourers. The journeyman is often called by the same English word; the only Yoruba equivalent is *alagbaʃe* = a labourer.

16. The contract was written in English by a public letter-writer whose phraseology has been retained. Names and date have been omitted to avoid any possible embarrassment to the parties involved.

17. The development of the craft guild from the clan or lineage is described for Europe by V. Gronbech in *Culture of the Teutons*, 1931, p. 35.

M. Banton

ADAPTATION AND INTEGRATION
IN THE SOCIAL SYSTEM
OF TEMNE IMMIGRANTS IN FREETOWN[1] (1956)

This paper presents a study of what is sometimes called detribalization—
the process by which tribal people, especially those who have left their
homeland and obtained paid employment in towns, are separated from
the social and cultural heritage of their tribe. But this is too superficial
a statement of the matter. It is necessary to define the problem in sociological terms before attempting a systematic analysis of the process.
Accordingly I shall start by describing the system of social relations
prevailing among Temne in Freetown, and shall examine the forces which,
over the past fifty years, have influenced its character. At the beginning
of this period relationships among the Temne immigrants appear to have
been relatively close and stable, but, from the 1920's, disintegrative tendencies became progressively more marked until, at the end of the 1930's,
the young men carried out a series of swift changes which resulted in a
more successful adaptation of the system and its closer integration.

A SECONDARY SOCIAL SYSTEM

The Temne immigrants who settled in Freetown had been trained
for living in their tribal societies; they brought with them, therefore, ideas
concerning the ordering of social life and the behaviour expected of
people occupying particular positions, and they tended to establish in
the town the social institutions and behavioural patterns which were
familiar to them. They looked to the social system, thus transplanted, to
fulfil most of the needs which it met in the rural environment, as well as

source. M. Banton, "Adaptation and Integration in the Social System of Temne
Immigrants in Freetown," reprinted from *Africa*, XXVI, 4, 1956, pp. 354–367, by
permission of the International African Institute. Copyright M. Banton.

those new needs that were closely related to tribal culture. The chief's office is of crucial importance to the traditional social system, but it cannot function in the town as it does in the country; the lineage cannot provide a principle of social organization among a population of immigrants having few ties of kinship with one another; traditional religious beliefs cannot maintain their hold in a technologically advanced society. New institutions have to be created and the system must be adapted to meet the new demands. Often, in circumstances similar to those of the Temne in Freetown, such adaptation is not achieved: those who try to introduce changes may be defeated by others with vested interests in the existing state of affairs, or they may be foiled by the logic of the system itself, if the practices which stand in the way of adaptation incorporate major cultural values. Attempts at adaptation may lead to fission or to a total assimilation of the system to its environment and its consequent dissolution. Unless the social system retains its distinctive character, it cannot be said that a successful adaptation has been achieved.

A second set of factors directly influences the integration of the system. In the new circumstances of urban living, tribal immigrants look to urban instead of tribal institutions to satisfy particular needs, most of which arise only in the new environment. Thus many Temne immigrants come to set greater store by their membership of trade unions or political parties, and the profession of Islam, which they share with other tribes, and to emphasize African solidarity in opposition to Europeans rather than Temne solidarity in opposition to other tribes. These factors operate to reintegrate the social life of immigrants round non-tribal foci; only indirectly do they make for the disintegration of the tribal group. But since Temne residents spend much of their day working and co-operating with non-Temne in the larger social system of Freetown, the separate Temne social system tends increasingly to become of secondary importance in their lives. It would theoretically be possible to extend the Temne system into these new social areas and create Temne trade unions, just as Catholics in some countries have created Catholic trade unions, but in practice little of this has occurred. In this way a tribal system, which in the country encompasses the whole social life of each member, in the town forms a secondary system in relation to the larger urban society. In such a situation there is the likelihood that the tribal system may dissolve. Nor, in the long run, can it hold at bay the disintegrative forces unless also its institutions are adapted to the demands of its new environment.

Thus, if a tribal social system is to survive transplantation into a new, urban, environment, it will have to be adapted to that environment without sacrificing its tribal identity. The two requirements, of adaptation and integration, are inter-related.

SOCIAL RELATIONS IN FREETOWN

During the seventeenth century the Temne took possession of the peninsula on which Freetown now stands. In 1787 much of this land was bought from them for the establishment of the Colony of Sierra

Population Changes in Freetown 1891–1953 by Principal Tribes

	1891	1901	1911	1921	1931	1947	1953
Creoles	17,815	16,505	16,716	15,791	20,970	17,331	17,000
Temne	2,897	4,494	5,007	8,358	11,405	–	19,000
Mende	1,015	2,291	2,557	4,094	3,828	–	11,000
Limba	693	1,423	1,611	2,941	4,960	–	9,000
Kru	1,234	1,903	1,551	4,744	4,460	–	7,000
Loko	115	198	382	775	1,633	–	4,000
Mandinka	1,256	1,037	1,021	1,461	1,352	–	4,000
Fula	244	270	289	499	1,119	–	4,000
Susu	1,434	1,417	1,311	1,346	1,450	–	2,500
Others	3,330	4,925	3,645	4,133	4,181	–	7,500
Total	30,033	34,463	34,090	44,142	55,358	64,576	85,000
							±5,000

Sources: 1891–1947, Censuses; 1953, Author's estimates.

Note: There are at present 28 Temne chiefdoms, with a total population of about 500,000, situated in the northern and central districts of the Sierra Leone Protectorate.

Leone. The first colonists were Negro settlers; in the nineteenth century their numbers were very greatly augmented by the settlement in the Colony of emancipated slaves rescued from the slaving vessels. Children of liberated Africans and the later descendants of the settlers came to be known as "Creoles." In the second half of the nineteenth century small groups of tribal immigrants settled in Freetown; at first these consisted mostly of traders and each of them led a separate existence under its own chief. In the last two decades of the century immigration of labourers from the hinterland increased and, as the table shows, the ethnic balance of the population gradually changed.

At the beginning of the twentieth century the system of social relationships in Freetown as a whole showed marked stratification. Europeans occupied all the most valued offices in state, church, and commerce. Creoles monopolized subordinate posts in the government service, while the more notable of their number won prestige at the bar, in medicine, and in holy orders. A few Creoles established themselves as merchants and others experimented in agriculture, but in neither of these avocations did they have any continuing success. At the bottom of the scale came the tribal immigrants or "natives" (a term which, in the peculiar circumstances of Sierra Leone, has a less opprobrious connotation than in some other regions). The Creoles referred to the tribal immigrants as "aborigines"—regarding them as hewers of wood and drawers of water—and with such roles the latter were for the time content. These racial distinctions were at first accepted, but they began to be called in question when individuals of subordinate groups attained positions comparable with those of their superiors.

During the early years of the twentieth century a number of mission-trained youths from the Protectorate obtained government clerical posts by open competition. The single native youth newly placed in an office staffed entirely by Creoles was subject to very considerable pressure, for his colleagues would give him none of the assistance he needed unless he identified himself with them outside the office as well as inside. He was forced to "turn Creole," that is, to adopt a Creole name and Creole practices, to associate with Creoles and forget his tribal friends. Passing into the Creole group may be adequately explained in this way, but to see its full significance it must also be considered from the standpoint of the tribal group. The possession of educational skills was at that time regarded as an attribute of Creoles and foreign to the Temne and other tribes. The possession of these skills, rather than the joining of the Creole group and the consequent forsaking of the tribe, was the departure from the norm. Since there was no recognized place for young literates in the existing tribal group, they were not hindered from turning Creole, and when they had done so they were renounced by their fellow tribesmen. The exclusion of young literates helped to maintain intact the tribal system with its illiterate elders.

Springing as they did from many different tribes, the Creoles tended to build their group round values and practices learnt from European administrators and missionaries. They spoke a form of English, wore European clothes and accepted many of the values of Victorian society; their social organization was centred on their churches, chapels, and ecclesiastical associations. They enthusiastically professed what, in the eyes of the native, was the religion of the white man. That the tribes in the immediate hinterland regarded the Creoles as black Europeans was demonstrated in the massacres of the 1898 rising. By this time some of the Protectorate tribes had been Islamized by immigrant Fula and Mandinka, though only to a slight extent. The vast majority of tribal people adhered to traditional beliefs that were bound to crumble before the advancing cultural and technological influence of the Europeans. Islam has, however, gained many more adherents than Christianity among the people of the Protectorate. Probably this is to some extent because the adoption of Islam tends to strengthen existing authorities in tribal life and entails relatively little change in the social system. Another factor which seems of considerable importance in Freetown is that Islam offers an alternative to the white man's religion and indeed stands opposed to the aggressive culture of the European. The migrant who settles in Freetown can draw relatively little support from the religion of his fathers and the pattern of relationships in the city presses him to identify himself with either Islam or Christianity. The overwhelming majority of immigrants have followed their headmen and elders in choosing the former. Islam offers them universal values that are viable in the western world, it offers them a distinctive set of prestige-bearing symbols and a world free from white domination. Thus Islam has acquired special significance in the inter-group relations, one consequence of which will be touched upon later.

Each of the tribal groups made a practice of electing one of their number to act as their chief and to arbitrate in their disputes. The Government found it convenient to support this arrangement and to extend official recognition to the persons so elected, since they were able thereby to exercise greater control over these separate and varied elements in the population. The Colony was a Creole area, subject to statute law on the English pattern, and Crown courts had no power to administer the native customary law of the Protectorate. So by the Tribal Administration (Colony) Ordinance of 1905 these chiefs were enabled to claim the title of Tribal Ruler and to exercise wide powers, dependent in theory upon government supervision. They were to apprehend malefactors, control immigration, explain government regulations, and were permitted to hold their own courts.

In the traditional Temne social system the chief is of central importance, for in both secular and sacred affairs his person symbolizes the shared life of his subjects; if the chief is strong and respected his people take pride in this, for his prestige symbolizes their unity; if he is weak, integration declines and the system functions less smoothly. In Freetown this is to some extent true of the office of Tribal Ruler or Headman whose incumbent is always in Temne and usually in English referred to as "chief." To be closely related to a chief or tribal high official, or to come from a respected lineage, still confers much prestige among Temne in Freetown. That a non-hereditary chiefship should enjoy government recognition and considerable privileges, has therefore been of the greatest importance for the vitality of the Freetown Temne social system.

DISINTEGRATIVE TENDENCIES

The Government failed to supervise the Tribal Rulers, who, left to their own devices, abused their powers. They were expected to conform to European norms of administration but they were given no training to this end. They tried to act as a chief acts in the Protectorate, for this was the only chiefly role they knew, but rule of this kind was unacceptable in a city and brought them into disfavour with the Government. The exercise of personal authority by chiefs is incompatible with municipal government, in which policies are framed with regard to commercial as well as personal interests, are referred to an electorate, and are administered by specialists on a basis of monetary accounting. To use power on a personal basis in a modern city is conventionally defined as jobbery, boss-rule, and so forth. Chiefship has no economic foundation in an urban setting like that of Freetown. The small stipends granted to Tribal Rulers in 1905 have not been increased in fifty years. Yet from the tribal standpoint it would be unthinkable for a chief even at this level to undertake paid employment; he can employ people in trade or agriculture but he very rarely has the capital for this. A chief must be available at all times to help his subjects. In the town the prestige of chiefship is overshadowed by that of other institutions, and its authority is sapped by their greater economic power. The Tribal Ruler could not fulfil the expectations of his subjects: he could not find employment for or offer hospitality to more than a fraction of those who went to him for assistance. Moreover most Tribal Rulers were illiterate and had not sufficient influence in administrative matters to help their fellow tribesmen. Weakness of this sort affects the whole system.

After the submission of an unfavourable report from a Commission of Inquiry in 1932 the Tribal Rulers were prohibited from holding courts; their powers were drastically reduced and their title was changed to that of Tribal Headman. This did not in itself have so disturbing an effect on the tribal system as might be expected because the nature of the change was only partly understood by the illiterate population. Power to administer native law was not transferred to the Crown courts and the new ordinance was not strictly enforced. Tribal Headmen continued to hold courts to decide "dowry palaver" and such like, in much the same way as before, except that to enforce their decisions they were largely dependent on their personal authority, the desire of the parties to reach a settlement, the litigants' ignorance of the Headman's impuissance, and the pressure of public opinion. As before, the Government made few demands upon them, so the Headmen did not find their official obligations conflicting with their own peoples' expectations of them.

Apart from the disruptive effects on the chiefship of administrative and economic factors, the urban situation creates new needs and emphasizes needs that used to be, but no longer are, met by lineage organization. Religious sentiment requires that a man honour his dead kinsmen. In the country a lineage will see to the burial of its dead, but when a man dies in Freetown he may have only two or three relatives in the city and they may not have the means to give him a proper burial.

New cultural and technological forces introduce new levels of achievement; people who attain to literacy, for example, want this to be recognized in tribal society. Some men desire positions of authority; others wish to align themselves behind chosen leaders who will protect and aid them in any difficulty. In traditional society the old men's claim to leadership was validated by their authority as mediators with the ancestors. With the decline of traditional religion and the shift of power to the young men some basis must be found for leadership roles. Young men who wish to choose their own brides want new forms of association in which they can meet girls and display themselves before them to their best advantage. Local conditions affecting persons following a particular trade, opposition between groups or personalities, all these cause people to associate for temporary or more lasting periods. Such new needs require the adaptation of the social system if it is to survive.

These demands early led to the creation of savings clubs and burial societies on Creole lines, but norms governing such forms of association were but dimly recognized and the early ventures were often brought to an unexpected end by the peculations of their treasurers. After 1918 the Temne in Freetown formed a succession of so-called "social societies" of a partly or wholly religious character resembling the so-called "literary societies" of the Mandinka. Such a one was the *Muktarimin* founded to commemorate the birthday of the Prophet. Although such societies could help to put on a firmer footing the organization of affairs relating to the mosque, and although the danger of embezzlement was lessened, these also enjoyed but a brief existence.

In so far as the Temne system failed to meet these demands for adaptation its integration was weakened and its chances of survival reduced. A different but no less serious threat came from the growing strength of non-tribal institutions. Individual Temne became acquainted with members of other tribes at work and in the districts where they lived. They found they had much in common with Africans whom they had previously regarded as foreigners. It seems as if in this sort of situation the recognition of an opposition of interests is more important for the building of groups than the discovery of similarities; as Balandier says of Brazzaville, "la parenté ethnique est plus efficace pour rejeter (ou refuser) l'étranger que pour provoquer l'organisation d'un groupement." [2] Tribal people felt themselves united in opposition to the Creoles, who sought to retain political supremacy, but they found common ties with Creole trade-unionists when there was trouble with their employers. Temne might say that they would rather be exploited by the British than by Lebanese, Indians, and Creoles, but the Europeans were an exclusive group, small but powerful, and the common bonds of all Africans subject to their rule came to acquire an overwhelming significance in social organization. Thus the longer an individual Temne resided in Freetown, the more completely he was drawn into the social system of the town, not merely as a citizen but as a member of a series of groupings. Of all these groupings (or regroupings, as they were from the point of view of the immigrant) the one which had the most disintegrative effect upon the Temne system was the grouping of tribal people as a whole. Immigrants from the hinterland tribes [3] were coming increasingly to accept Islam and the social values of the leading Muslim groups (notably the Aku [4]), imitating their dress and customs. The possession of a common religion opposed to the Christianity of the Europeans and Creoles gave this grouping a coherence and continuity which the others lacked. The wealthier tribal groups, such as the Fula and Mandinka, smaller in size and composed mostly of traders, were orthodox Muslims, and their notables were regarded with the greatest respect by the Temne immigrant. Islam, wealth, fine clothes, impressive ways, a certain arrogance in the possession of a distinctive faith, all went together. The Temne immigrant was drawn increasingly into this sector of the town's social system, for it possessed continuity and was a significant unit in the opposition between tribesman and Creole, African and European.

The tribal sector of the urban system was divided within itself, for the more orthodox and wealthy tribes, such as the Aku, Fula, and Mandinka, were accorded a higher prestige than the partly pagan and poorer groups, including the Temne. Being more completely Islamized than the Mende, Limba, and Loko, the Temne early became sensitive to their inferior standing. That strangers should look down on them was a particular blow to Temne pride, for the land on which Freetown stands was once Temne territory. They still regard it as theirs and claim for themselves the privileged status of those who own the land.

Because so little prestige attached to being a Temne, many ambitious young Temne joined the youth associations of the Aku and Mandinka, often learning the language and seeking to pass as members of these tribes. One of the younger Temne leaders has described this development in terms which make it clear that he was under no illusions as to its significance. He wrote:

The Temnes in the City were moving rapidly towards detribalization, some becoming Creoles and others Akus and Mandingoes. The first were the ones educated in English and others who were not educated but have come to Freetown to seek jobs. The reason for the exodus from the Temne tribe was the backwardness of the Temnes socially and economically. To be considered favourably was to call yourself a Mandingo, Creole or Aku. This protective measure was adopted in many forms, dress, language and in joining foreign dances. Consequently every bright looking Temne is lost to the other tribes and the word Temne is associated with the uncivilized people.[5]

An African does not lightly renounce his own tribe for another. Moreover, if a young Temne changed his allegiance the Temne group could not close its ranks and prevent further losses; when one man went it was an invitation to the others to follow. This was a clear threat to the survival of the system. The danger of complete disintegration could scarcely have been greater.

YOUNG MEN'S COMPANIES

The Aku associations to which the young Temne deserted were mostly of the nature of secret societies, such as the *Orjeh*. The Mandinka organizations represented a newer development and provided a basis of association which was destined to acquire greater significance. The crucial innovation had come in 1930 when the Tribal Ruler of the Mandinka returned to Freetown after a visit to French Guinea, bringing with him three *yelibas* (professional musicians) to introduce a new tune, the *Yankadde* (literally "Here is sweet"). A society was formed, the members of which met for the playing of the *Yankadde*, and for rehearsing and performing dances. To give this association a firm basis the members constituted themselves a benefit society and held collections for any of their number who were bereaved. Later, a group of Freetown-born Mandinka, who set no store on importations from French Guinea, established a rival society on similar lines which was called the *Tarancis* (from the French *trente-six*). The *Tarancis* songs and dances were easy to learn and soon became very popular. Some of the younger Temne leaders sought to counter the influence of these societies. The most notable of them, from whose manuscript I have already quoted, reviewed the situation as follows:

The serious educated Temne began to think about their tribe and to seek means for emancipation from this low prestige. The problem is very great as there is no means of approach. The Tribal Administration is effective only with the low educated classes; the better class of Temnes look with disdain upon their less favoured brothers. . . . The problem was made more difficult as the leaders of the Temne community were not educated and most of them were of limited means. Their appeals to the youths were ineffective.

When the writer says that the problem was great because there was no means of approach, he implies that it could not be solved within the existing framework—some new institution had to be created. This institution would have to accord with the aspirations of the young men and would therefore probably be opposed by the illiterate elders who would know that they had little chance of controlling it.

The first move towards the foundation of a Temne association that would meet these needs came from an illiterate goldsmith who gathered a band of young associates and approached a young Temne schoolmaster for assistance. The latter soon took over the organization of a society on the lines of the *Tarancis*, combining the functions of entertainment and bereavement benefit, which was named *Ambas Geda*. In Temne *ambas* means "we have," and *geda* is the Krio form of the English "together." The name expressed the feeling that "We, the Temne, have the people and we must collect them in," while its combination of Temne and English words unconsciously typified the blending of tribal elements with items taken from European culture. Such societies are known in Sierra Leone as *compins*, from the English word "company" which is also used to describe similar associations in Nigeria, Gold Coast, and Gambia.

The schoolmaster was an advocate of European education and ways. He had earlier exposed corrupt practices among the tribal elders, so he was supported by many young men who were dissatisfied with the lethargy of their traditional leaders. The old men regarded him as an upstart, while his association with an Ahmadiyya missionary had aroused the antagonism of orthodox Muslims in the tribe. Thus the conservative faction viewed the establishment of a society under this man's leadership as a dangerous development and attempted to suppress it. In this they failed, though a rival company was established which represented the conservative and ultra-Islamic faction among the Temne. *Ambas Geda* gained great popularity and many similar bodies were formed having close ties with the parent body. Here it was favoured by events over which it had no control, for the outbreak of war brought many immigrants to Freetown from the interior. Most of the new-comers were young men owing no obligations to the recognized Temne elders in Freetown. They had plenty of money to spend and liked to show off their new clothes at company dances. The influx of young workers added to the strength of the progressive and modernist faction within the tribe.

Company dances show signs of considerable European influence in their manner of dancing, the music, the instruments, the dancers' dress, the display made over smoking cigarettes, etc. Part of the time mixed couples dance together, which represents a marked departure from the traditional tribal dancing. The songs are in Temne. The companies offer entertainment much more likely to appeal to the would-be respectable youth than dancing round a masked "devil" in the street.

So far it might be thought that companies of the *Ambas Geda* type did not represent any very great advance over the earlier types of voluntary association which existed before 1940 and which continue to the present day. The companies had developed a technically more efficient form of organization; in the sphere of entertainment they had created new expressive roles, but in the more important sphere of the explicit benefits offered to members they continued the practices of the bereavement contributions clubs with only minor improvements. Yet the companies had a number of implicit or latent functions of a most novel kind and in this respect they differed appreciably from the earlier societies.

These functions may be detected not so much in the satisfactions they offered their members as in their effects in and upon Freetown Temne society. The companies tended to act, unconsciously and consciously, as a pressure group representing modernist elements among the Temne youth. Their members shared common values appropriate to a semi-industrial society and partially opposed to the traditional order, though they were ready to build upon the latter wherever they had opportunity. They believed in "civilization," meaning by this the adoption of many European and Creole practices. They were interested in machinery and new techniques, and scornful of superstition. The companies have attempted with some success to raise standards of dress and cleanliness. The discipline which they impose upon their members makes them more ready to accept discipline in other spheres, and by attempting to raise standards and organize recreation the companies have tended to reduce crime. Because young men and women of similar outlook were brought together at their meetings, many successful marriages between company members resulted. The companies deliberately sought to raise Temne prestige and thus they had a mission which the other sorts of association lacked. So, though the different companies and their various branches competed with one another in dancing contests and so forth, they thought of themselves as co-operating in a common enterprise intended to elevate their tribe.

The integrative functions of the companies in drawing the isolated immigrant into a group deserve special notice. The moral support which they give to members when bereaved is at least as important as the financial assistance. All members of the company are expected to be present at the wake held the first night after the announcement of a death, and some will come to the subsequent ceremonies three, seven, and forty days afterwards. In this way the company honours a member's dead and helps him to live up to the requirements of tribal culture. However, in the long run, it is probably the companies' adaptive functions which will prove to be the most significant, for they take the place of the lineage and translate new norms into patterns of action. The sense of obligation to fellow members of their clan and their lineage remains strong among the immigrants but, as the Temne group is composed of individuals from many lineages who have moved there independently, ties of descent are of limited use as a principle of organization. Thus the companies sanction and allocate new leadership roles in a situation where the old authority patterns no longer apply. They also express the increased political importance of the young men as a group, though there are no age sets or similar institutions in the traditional social structure of the Sierra Leone tribes.[6]

In situations of rapid change friction often arises from conflicting views as to the obligations of particular roles; this the companies avoid by basing their organization on the contractual obligations which members assume in the act of joining: the contract defines the member's new role. By a process of splitting up existing roles and admitting only particular candidates the companies reintegrate individuals into groups adaptable to new social demands.

INCREASED INTEGRATION

The growth of company organization among the Temne had the effect which the conservative elders feared. When, during the war, the post of Tribal Headman fell vacant the young men determined to put up their own candidate, finally nominating the schoolmaster who had taken the lead in founding *Ambas Geda*. Having announced his candidature this man then resigned from his office in *Ambas Geda* but kept in close touch with his supporters in the various companies and transformed them into the most effective party machine that Freetown has yet seen. Acting in concert they swept him into office. With them behind him, the new Headman was able to reinvigorate the political structure of the tribe, that is, the structure of section chiefs and other officials responsible to the Tribal Headman and his council. There are now two separate structures, of political offices and companies, both of which have their apex in the person of the Headman and founder of *Ambas Geda*. Section chiefs now, even where they do not owe their office to the new dispensation, take care to be on good terms with the companies in their territory.

The role of Headman has been transformed, most conspicuously in that the Freetown Temne now for the first time have a literate person in this office. The new Headman's influence is greater than that of his predecessors although they had wider legal powers. Having, on the one hand, a knowledge of how government institutions function and, on the other, the enthusiastic support of most of his fellow Temne, he is a more effective leader in his dealings both with outsiders and with his own people. It would be difficult for any illiterate to succeed to his post in the future. By taking to himself the title *Kande*, which is normally the prerogative of certain Paramount Chiefs, the Temne Headman asserted his tribe's claim to the ownership of the land on which Freetown stands and their claim to precedence over other tribes. His right to the title has not been challenged and appears to meet with approval among the Temne. The post of Temne Tribal Headman does not have the glory of that of Paramount Chief, but the influence which its occupant can bring to bear is by most standards greater. The Temne population of Freetown is larger than that of the average Temne chiefdom while the Headman's influence extends far outside the boundaries of the city to encompass most of the villages in the rural areas of the Colony. The Temne Headman entertains Temne chiefs when they visit the capital and sometimes acts on their behalf. He is Treasurer of the Sierra Leone Peoples' Party, serving on its executive, and thus articulating the tribal structure with national politics, for he occasionally calls section meetings to be addressed by a speaker of his party. He has influence with the working classes of nearly all the tribes, which may prove to be a valuable asset. This was recognized when, after the rioting in February 1955, he was appointed with two others to a special conciliation committee. It is interesting to note that in the official appointment he was referred to as "Chief"—a title to which in Government eyes he is not entitled, and which would never be used in an official reference to any of the other Tribal Headmen. In other respects he has pursued an independent course which may tend to set an example of westernized behaviour, for he often wears European clothes and behaves informally, dispensing with the trappings and bands of retainers with which traditional chiefs surround themselves. Though a Muslim, he has displayed considerable independence *vis-à-vis* the mosque. Thus, in one way and another, he has gained the support of illiterates, literates, and educated elements.

These changes have stopped the desertion of young men to other tribes and have so raised Temne prestige that the flow is in the reverse direction. Limba, Loko, Mende, Mandinka, and others, join Temne companies and Temne activities. The Temne Headman has now to be most discreet in many matters, for the other Headmen are jealous and suspect him of wanting to establish Temne paramountcy on an administrative basis. The tendency of ambitious Temne to pass into the Creole group has now been halted. After the last war a Temne, just returned from the United Kingdom after qualifying as a lawyer, started to "turn Creole," beginning by hyphenating his native surname with a Creole one. The Temne Headman was able to put a stop to this. Now the Temne tribal system in Freetown, and indeed the very notion of "being a Temne," is big enough to embrace new and powerful roles, such as barrister and Minister in the Government, which would previously have been disruptive. This has been achieved by elevating the status of the Temne Headman in the life of the town; because the chief's role is very important symbolically for the Temne, this has helped to increase the integration of this group. The young men succeeded in adapting this system to meet their expectations of it. They established it as a secondary unit within the larger urban society by defining its functions so that their membership of non-tribal groupings did not, within the immediate future, constitute a threat to the continued existence of the tribal system.

COMPANIES AS ADAPTIVE ORGANIZATIONS

The reason why the companies should have had so notable an influence upon the Temne group cannot be fully appreciated without a consideration of what they have to offer individual members.

It is not easy in Freetown to organize a company and to keep it running smoothly. Young Temne are not easily disciplined and are reluctant to recognize the authority of any Temne official placed over them. Partly for this reason, partly because of the methods of money collection and attendance at wakes, the optimum size of a company is about 70–90 members. The leading officials have to give a great deal of time and effort to their duties, and to maintaining control over members, so that their roles in the company are of great importance in their lives as individuals. Though a leadership status is specific to the association its prestige has tended to carry over to other situations and its incumbent is respected by persons who are not members of the association. In 1953 there were about thirty companies in active existence and at least another fifteen registered Temne friendly societies which resembled companies in certain respects. The total number of company members is limited not by the number of companies—for new branches can always be created—but by the number of suitable applicants. The better companies are very careful about whom they admit to membership and make inquiries into an applicant's background. One of them claims that it accepts less than half of the people who apply and that it keeps a watchful eye on its younger members: if they fail to go straight home after late meetings they are liable to be suspended from membership. The better companies also co-operate with one another, transferring members on their request, while if an applicant has formerly been a member of another company they will not admit him without first communicating with the one he has left.

A member of one of these stricter companies is more highly thought of than a man who belongs to one of the older, less sophisticated types of voluntary association. Prestige attaches to associations the more they copy certain European practices, the more Islamized they are, and the more they call upon valued elements in traditional Temne culture. Thus the young men's organizations form a continuum in prestige, with the companies at the top, moving downwards through *Orjeh* societies to informal dancing groups. This scale also represents the extent to which individual members accept new norms and are capable of living up to them.

The most striking feature of the companies' organization is the plethora of offices—in one extreme case there are half as many offices as members. This must be seen against the background of the previous paucity of offices in the Freetown Temne social system. In tribal society of the traditional order there is a limited number of prestige-bearing offices—chief, section chief, lineage head, etc.—to which no one normally succeeds before his hair has grown grey. Rural life is geared to a social system in which prestige is linked with age, so that the young men have no occasion to object to their subordinate status. A structure of this kind, however, is not in accord with urban life, where old age is not greatly respected and where the principal sources of prestige lie in the mastering of western technology and culture. Young men who have acquired some of these new abilities expect a commensurate status within the tribe. Thus there is a double demand: for if the new instrumental needs are to be met, new roles must be created, and to meet the young men's aspirations new prestige-conferring statuses have to be recognized. It is to be expected that this demand for new statuses will be greatest where social change has gone farthest, and this is supported by the fact that where companies have been formed in Protectorate villages they have far fewer offices. In Freetown, the higher a company is in the prestige scale the more offices it tends to have, suggesting that the more modernist members of these companies have an especial demand for prestige-conferring statuses. This relation deserves further investigation because it is to be expected that, after a certain point, people will be less flattered by high-sounding titles and the status of membership itself will be most valued; the conditions under which this occurs need to be studied.

The titles given to office-holders in the companies illustrate the selection and blending of elements from their traditional heritage, from the British administration, and from Islamic culture. The chief executive is the *Sultan* and his female counterpart the *Mammy Queen* (a name originally applied to Queen Victoria). Then there is a *Pa Kumrabai* who is a sort of patron having nothing to do with the day-to-day working of the company but to whom is taken any dispute that the officers cannot settle among themselves. He must be an older and widely respected person; he can be called upon to rebuke the *Sultan* or to convene the committee of senior officials and has rights analogous to those of the *Kumrabai* in Temne chiefdoms. Among other company officials are the *Judge, Doctor, Manager, Commissioner, Reporter, Bailiff, Cashier, Clerk, Leader, Conductor, Sister, Nurses, Provoes,* and *Collectors.* Most of these offices are duplicated on the male and female sides, though there is no formal division of companies into sex groups, and nearly all the officials have their deputies. At some meetings companies provide food resembling that served at European cocktail parties and there are formal regulations regarding the serving of officers. Referring to similar behaviour Nadel writes: "Psychologically, it has the significance of a substitute for thrills and achievements which normal life cannot offer." [7] Mitchell has called it "vicarious participation in the European social structure." [8] This is without question an important component in such behaviour but, from what I saw of the companies in Freetown, I am inclined to think that it places too much emphasis on the process of "westernization" and too little on the independent process of change in the tribal group.

The use of the term "westernization" conceals the important part played by Africans in choosing their own destiny. The same error is apparent in the assumption made by some French and Belgian writers that "*évolution*" is necessarily a process of approximation to European ideals. Each society evolves in its own direction and the Africans who seem most *évolués* at the present day may not be those to whom the historian of the future will apply the term. Leading Africans in British West African territories insist that they wish to develop their own distinctive culture. The growth of syncretistic religious movements in French and Belgian territory suggests that the situation there may not be so very different. The *évolués* are the most advanced representatives of a process of growth by which members of tribal groups and emergent nations select the cultural elements which appeal to them and modify their social systems. Viewed in this light the bizarre imitation of certain European practices is seen as part of a process, not of substitution but of selection, albeit one which *at the present stage* shows the assimilation of many European cultural elements.

In Freetown membership of associations at different points along the prestige scale appears to be an index of individual change and to indicate the extent to which the members are *évolués*, i.e., of modernist inclination. This deserves further study for its bearing on the problem of growth or social evolution in a restricted sense.

The significance of the prestige rating of associations was not fully apparent to me while I was in the field and I neglected to investigate the extent of consensus on this. I believe the Temne would be fairly agreed on the rating of different associations except in so far as any individual would probably exaggerate the prestige of an association to which he himself belonged. Most of the companies are Temne and more friendly societies are composed of Temne than of any other tribe, so it is probable that the Temne evaluation of different associations would be accepted, with additions, by other tribes from the northern districts of the Protectorate. The Kru and Bassa would disclaim interest in the matter. A Creole welfare officer told me there was a definite prestige hierarchy of associations, but he was the only person I ever heard refer to it so explicitly. It would be interesting to know whether the Mende recognize any such hierarchy, for they have no companies of their own.

The Temne companies have been copied by the Limba and there has been talk of the Loko forming one of their own, but to the best of my knowledge the Mende have never attempted to form such an association, though individual Mende occasionally join Temne companies. It is not easy to see why the two tribes should differ in this way, for the social circumstances of Temne and Mende immigrants in Freetown are very similar. It seems likely, however, that there is greater scope for private initiative in the traditional social structure of the Temne and more devolution of authority. The Temne chief was in olden times a semi-sacred figure, surrounded by powerful officials, and he did not exercise the personal rule of the Mende chief.

Temne and Mandinka companies have spread from Freetown to the Protectorate and branches have been established in the towns of the northern province and of Mende country. In the rural districts of the North they have been grafted on to the older communal working societies like the Temne *kabóthó* and the Limba *kuné*. These societies have a recognized place in the indigenous social structure; on their formation the leader pays a fee to the chief to notify him of the event, and he is held responsible for the society's actions. The societies till the land of their members' households and now most of them have their company names, titles, dances, and songs as well. Young Mende do sometimes, on their own initiative, form a band known as a *bémbé* which hires out its services for hoeing; it is a relatively recent institution which has never been employed for any other operation and now appears to be receding. *Bémbé* members are apt to behave irresponsibly and in some districts these groups have been broken up. The Mende look to the chief to deal with the sort of problems which elsewhere have led to the establishment of companies.

In this connexion it is interesting to observe that before the end of the nineteenth century the Kru brought with them to Freetown from Liberia the basic notions of a contractual association. From what we know of the traditional Kru social structure it was of a decentralized segmentary type with age sets, resembling that of the Ibo and Yakö. A working hypothesis may therefore be advanced that, other things being equal, the more devolution of authority there is in tribal societies the more rapidly do contractual associations like companies emerge. Comparative data on this from other regions would be most valuable.

NOTES

1. This paper is based on material collected in 1952–3 during a field study carried out with the aid of a grant from the Nuffield Foundation. A full report has been prepared for publication.

2. "Approche sociologique des Brazzavilles Noires." *Africa*, xxii, 1952, p. 29.

3. That is, excluding Kru and Bassa. These tribes migrate from Liberia for sea-going employment. Among them no religion other than Christianity is practised and they do not identify themselves very strongly with the partly Islamized tribes from the Protectorate.

4. Descendants of Yoruba liberated Africans who profess Islam and have constituted a separate community intermediate between the Creoles and the tribal people.

5. In a brief manuscript history of *Ambas Geda* prepared by the founder in 1953 for the writer.

6. Cf. "The 'meeting' serves as a method of . . . institutionalizing and giving recognition to these young men as a group." S. Ottenburg, "Improve-

ment Associations among the Afikpo Ibo," *Africa*, xxv, 1955, p. 13. Among the Nupe, the companies formed by youths resident in the towns strongly resemble the traditional age sets found in the villages. S. F. Nadel treats the two forms of association as fundamentally similar. He emphasizes their integrative functions: both serve to foster the solidarity of existing social groupings, and differences in their structure reflect differences between village and town society. *A Black Byzantium*, 1942, pp. 383–94.

7. Nadel, *op. cit.*, p. 391. See also p. 392: "A game it indeed is. These ranks let you enjoy fictitious contacts with a world of rank and power which you can never hope to enter in reality. Their upward trend, their incentive of competition, imply, not preparation or anticipation but pretence, imitation—substitution."

8. J. Clyde Mitchell, "Kalela: A Tribal Dance on the Copperbelt of Northern Rhodesia," unpublished MS.

C. Geertz

THE ROTATING CREDIT ASSOCIATION:
A "MIDDLE RUNG" IN DEVELOPMENT (1962)

*The building up of a variety of institutions, serving the purpose of promoting
individual savings, and organizing them and making them fruitful to the saver
and to the community, should be given a high priority in every development
plan. To be effective, the institutions have to be adapted to different individual
needs and possibilities and must fit into the community patterns; they must aim
at encouraging planned and "goal-directed" savings. Even if, at least in the
beginning, the financial results would not constitute more than a trickle of new
capital disposal, the effects in rationalizing attitudes and mobilizing ambitions
might be crucially important.*

> Gunnar Myrdal, in
> An International Economy (*p. 360*)

The necessity for a fundamental change on the part of the people of underdeveloped nations in their attitudes toward saving has been a recurrent
theme in discussions of the developmental prospects of such nations.
Unless aggregate national saving can be increased to cover, or at least
approximately cover, the growth in investment a developmental program
implies, persistent, run-away inflation will frustrate all efforts toward the
realization of such a program. Neither large-scale international capital
transfers nor improvements in the terms of trade can, in themselves, bring
about domestic capital accumulation in the absence of effective efforts to
raise the level of domestic saving, a hard fact of economic life summed up
in V. K. R. V. Rao's aphorism that capital is made at home.[1] In part, such
savings can be realized by means of taxation programs, the compulsory
sale of government securities, economies in government expenditure, and
other fiscal measures; but in the long-run these financial mechanisms will

SOURCE. C. Geertz, "The Rotating Credit Association: A 'Middle Rung' in Development," reprinted from *Economic Development and Cultural Change*, X, 3, 1962,
pp. 241–263, by permission of The University of Chicago Press. Copyright 1962 by
The University of Chicago Press.

not in themselves bring about the one change which is essential if development is to have a firm basis—a change in the propensity to save on the part of individual members of the population. Unless the basic savings habits of the people of a country can be altered, the prospects for sustained economic growth are dim indeed.

The reasons why the saving/income ratio of a particular country living above the subsistence level is what it is, rather than larger or smaller than it is, is dependent, as Henry Bruton has pointed out, on "the general pattern of mores and the social structure which govern all aspects of social behavior." [2] Consequently, it is evident that an effort to change the ratio demands an attempt to change the general pattern of mores and social structure. The main efforts along these lines have so far been of two general sorts: (1) propaganda drives asking individuals to save through buying government securities, or (2) the setting up of Western-type savings institutions: banks, savings cooperatives, and the like. [3] Neither of these efforts has been wholly ineffective, but both of them have tended to be disappointing: the first because deep-rooted customs yield very little to official sponsored exhortations to discard them in the interest of progress; and the second because the impersonality, complexity, and foreignness of the mode of operation of such "capitalist" institutions tends to make traditionalistic peasants, small traders, and civil servants suspicious of them. What seems to be needed, particularly in the early stages, is an institution which can combine local popular appeal with the sort of savings effects a developing economy demands; and institution which can act as an educational mechanism for a people moving from a static economy to a dynamic one, at the same time as it operates to bring about the restriction of increased consumption such a transformation implies.

It is the intent of this paper to describe and analyze one such institution found over a great part of that broad band of underdeveloped or semi-developed countries stretching from Japan on the East through Southeast Asia and India to Africa on the West: the so-called rotating credit association. [4] The rotating credit association, which assumes a remarkably similar form over a very wide geographical area, although to be sure with local adaptations and variations, will be shown to be essentially a device by means of which traditionalistic forms of social relationship are mobilized so as to fulfill non-traditionalistic economic functions. It will be seen, in fact, to be an "intermediate" institution growing up within peasant social structure, to harmonize agrarian economic patterns with commercial ones, to act as a bridge between peasant and trader attitudes toward money and its uses. The rotating credit association is thus an institution of the sort Myrdal rightfully demands: one which fits into community patterns and yet aims at planned and "goal-directed" savings.

I shall begin with a brief description of the rotating credit association as it is found in Modjokuto, a town-village complex in Eastern Java, Indonesia, which I studied in 1953–54.[5] The association is found in Modjokuto in its most elemental form, and the way in which it is integrated into the more general sociocultural pattern can, consequently, be quite explicitly demonstrated. Next, I shall review the general distribution and typical variations of the association in Asia and Africa, in an attempt to show more complex elaborations of the basic form, both in organization and in terms of its economic functioning. And finally, I shall say something about why this institution has arisen, the functions it fulfills, and the meaning it has for those who participate in it.

THE ROTATING CREDIT ASSOCIATION IN EASTERN JAVA

The basic principle upon which the rotating credit association is founded is everywhere the same: a lump sum fund composed of fixed contributions from each member of the association is distributed, at fixed intervals and as a whole, to each member of the association in turn. Thus, if there are ten members of the association, if the association meets weekly, and if the weekly contribution from each member is one dollar, then each week over a ten-week period a different member will receive ten dollars (i.e., counting his own contribution). If interest payments are calculated, by one mechanism or another, as part of the system, the numerical simplicity is destroyed, but the essential principle of rotating access to a continually reconstituted capital fund remains intact. Whether the fund is in kind or in cash; whether the order the members receive the fund is fixed by lot, by agreement, or by bidding; whether the time period over which the society runs is many years or a few weeks; whether the sums involved are minute or rather large; whether the members are few or many; and whether the association is composed of urban traders or rural peasants, of men or women, the general structure of the institution is constant.

In Modjokuto, the rotating credit association is called an *arisan*—literally, "cooperative endeavor" or "mutual help." Its form is of the most elemental sort: interest is not calculated, rotation is determined by lot or by agreement, membership tends to be small, and a separate staff of officers does not exist. The members simply come together and agree among themselves to contribute one or two rupiah every week or month, each one thus receiving ten or fifteen rupiah once during a ten- or fifteen-week or month cycle. Each person who draws the fund is responsible for holding the next meeting of the association in his home, and of providing food and coffee for other members. A meeting of an *arisan* is thus also a feast, a small gathering of friends, neighbors, and kin, and, particularly in the villages, is commonly viewed by its members less as an economic institution than a broadly social one whose main purpose is the strengthening of community solidarity. The primary attraction of the *arisan,* they say, is not the money you receive, but the creation of *rukun* (communal harmony) which occurs, the example of *gotong rojong* (mutual assistance) which is demonstrated.

Traditional Patterns of Cooperation and the Arisan in Rural Java

To the extent that it still exists, the traditional Javanese village is essentially a group of territorially integrated elementary families. Extended kin ties are of some importance, but the major unifying bonds are those of neighborhood, village, and village cluster. The very labor-intensive pattern of rice cultivation necessitates concrete mechanisms of inter-familial cooperation, as does, of course, the crowded, nucleated-village settlement pattern, and these mechanisms of cooperation are all geographically based. What has developed, consequently, is not so much a general spirit of cooperativeness—Javanese peasants tend, like many peasants, to be rather suspicious of groups larger than the immediate family—but a set of explicit and concrete practices of exchange of labor, of capital, and of consumption goods which operate in all aspects of life—in rice field cultivation, in house building, in irrigation, in road repairing, in village policing, and in religious ritual. This sense for the need to support specific, carefully delineated social mechanisms which can mobilize labor, capital, and consumption resources scattered thinly among the very dense population, and concentrate them effectively at one point in space and time, is the central characteristic of the much-remarked, but poorly understood, "cooperativeness" of the Javanese peasant. Cooperation is founded on a very lively sense of the mutual value to the participants of such cooperation, not on a general ethic of the unity of all men or on an organic view of society which takes the group as primary and the individual as secondary.

This general model of rotating cooperation among families appears in all fields of traditional peasant life. The land tenure pattern is, for example, based on the myth that the contemporary occupants of the village are all descendants of its original founders. These founders are said to have cleared the forest from the village site and to have built the first rice terraces in a cooperative labor fashion, with the result that their descendants have all inherited equal use rights to the land. The land is, consequently, divided into equal plots and distributed among these descendants of the founders. In some villages the plots are actually rotated among these citizens every year or two; in others they remain with the same holder in perpetuity, though they cannot be alienated in any way and can be forfeited if the holder commits a serious crime or leaves the village. Since, in the original system, only such land-right holders could participate in the choosing of village leaders, political, economic, and—

as the peasant-citizens are also family heads—kinship elements were fused.

Labor relations are, in the traditional pattern, organized in a similar fashion.[6] The two major types of cooperative labor are "group work" and "exchange work." In group work, a whole neighborhood applies its labor to certain labor-intensive tasks: clearing a man's fields, erecting his house, etc. In such a pattern all the nearby neighbors are invited and are obligated to come, and the host provides a large feast at the close of the work. In "exchange work," several households work on each other's land in turn. Reciprocality is exact and specific, and usually work is returned within a short period of time.

Even the central religious ritual in the villages—the *slametan*—reflects this rotating communalism pattern. The *slametan* is a communal feast given in the home of one family for six or eight geographically contiguous families who are represented, as in political and economic contexts, by their male heads. Again, the feast may be prepared in the "group work" fashion, with the neighbors and (especially) relatives pitching in collectively, both in the cooking and in contributing the food. More commonly, however, the women of the host family prepare the feast, and the expectation is that over a period of time the giving of *slametans* will balance out among all the families of the neighborhood.

Today, the purely traditional pattern of life exists in full force only in the very isolated villages; in the Modjokuto area, the complex of intrusive factors summed up, somewhat inexactly, in the term "urbanization" has very noticeably weakened it. In addition to the "communal" land inherited from ancestor-founders, there is now simple private property which may be sold outright for cash—though the tendency is still to sell it within the village. In addition to the traditional labor patterns, there is wage work—though this tends still to follow the obligations and expectations implicit in the older cooperative forms. And the contribution to the host at the *slametan* is now mainly in cash, rather than in kind—though close friends are still expected to be willing to help with the work. The Javanese village is thus moving fairly rapidly into the world-wide economy, and it is in terms of such an incipient stage of commercialization that the *arisan* seems best understood—it is a link between the largely unmonetized economy of the past and the largely monetized economy of the future.

In the villages, *arisans* are usually formed by a local group of three or four householders through a common agreement, and other households are then invited to join. The order in which the fund is drawn by the various members is fixed, in most cases, by simple agreement: the originators of the *arisan* come before the later joiners, and the latter draw in terms of the order in which they signed up to participate. Usually a secretary to keep the records is elected; sometimes someone to call the people together to the weekly meetings at the home of the recipient of the previous week is also chosen. Sometimes, too, a very small sum is taken out of the fund and given to these "officials" as a token payment, but they have no other special role in the association. Twenty to thirty members is a typical size, one to five rupiah (i.e., a fund from twenty to one hundred fifty rupiah) the usual size of the contribution.[7] At the end of the twenty- or thirty-week (or month) cycle, the *arisan* simply disbands, though it may soon be started up again with more or less the same personnel. Individuals may belong to several *arisans* at the same time, and they may hold multiple shares in a single *arisan*. Most members claim, actually, that the social, cooperative aspects of the associations—the small parties that accompany them and the sense of neighborliness they stimulate—are more important than the economic aspects: that they are closer to the *slametan* ritual pattern than, say, to the cooperative labor patterns, in the sense that their symbolic, expressive aspects have precedence over their technical, instrumental aspects. Nevertheless, as the cash needs of the peasantry grow ever and ever more intense, *arisans* become more and more important as strictly economic institutions, as mechanisms for mobilizing cash resources of essentially the same type as those which were, and are, used to mobilize land, labor, and consumption resources in traditional village society.[8]

Urban Arisans *in Java*

This tendency for *arisans* to become more and more specifically economic rather than diffusely social institutions becomes even more apparent among the inhabitants of urban compounds, or *kampongs*, within the town of Modjokuto. The *kampong* type of settlement, which is characteristic of town and city life everywhere in Java, is, essentially, a reinterpretation of the village pattern in terms of the denser, more heterogeneous, less organically integrated urban environment. Most of the well-to-do, fully urbanized members of the town elite live in stone houses along the streets, while the "lower class"—manual workers, petty craftsmen, small traders, or simply unemployed—live behind them within the blocks which the street grid outlines and the stone houses partially enclose. The land of the whole block is owned by one or two people—quite commonly, but not necessarily, one of the people in the stone houses facing the street. Small bamboo houses, of the same sort as common in villages, are placed haphazardly in crowded profusion on this block, often with very little space between them, so that the result is a rather fetid, unhealthy atmosphere. The people who live in these houses represent, then, a semi-urban, semi-rural proletariat, the members of which, though they have been forced to adopt many of the social, political, and economic patterns of the town, still cling to many of the values and beliefs of the village.

The *arisan* becomes, among these people, an extraordinarily popular institution, most particularly among the women, who hold the purse strings in any case. Almost every woman belongs to several; they are a constant topic of conversation and interest; and even children often form small ones—with ten or fifteen cent contributions—among themselves. Further, though feasts are held as in the villages, and the average size of the funds is only slightly larger, the *arisans* are seen much more in terms of their practical, instrumental importance, as mechanisms for the effective use of one's income, than is the case in the villages. One structural characteristic which points up this difference is the fact that almost all urban *arisans* decide on the order with which the individual draws the fund not by agreement but by lot. Thus the members are essentially gambling for the interest, a fact of which they are quite conscious. Nor is the sum involved insignificant. If the going monthly interest rate in the community is, say, 10 percent, then the man who "wins" first in a 12-member, ten-rupiah association which meets monthly gets an interest windfall (ignoring feast costs) of 66 rupiah, while the last man is out a theoretical 66 rupiah which he would have had if he had lent his 110 rupiah out on the open market in the same pattern.

The centrality of this factor in the minds of the members—in contrast to the relative unimportance of it in the villages (where interest-taking is rare in any case)—is shown by the gambling attitude *kampong* people take toward the *arisan* and the intense interest they have in it. They desire very much to win the lottery as early in the cycle as possible, are very disappointed each time they fail to win and very elated when finally they do. This anxiety to receive the fund early cannot be traced simply to fear of default by other members, for default is quite rare, mainly because the members are all fairly close acquaintances, and so would be deeply ashamed to evade their obligations, but also because the weekly or monthly contributions are small enough that most people can meet them somehow or other. Rather, it must be traced to an increased sensitivity to and understanding of the economic aspects of the rotating credit association, as against its symbolic, ritualistic aspects, or, more exactly, to an increasingly commercial rather than agrarian orientation in economic matters.

Arisan membership is praised in the *kampongs* not merely in terms of its positive effect on social solidarity—though this is stressed too—but even more enthusiastically as a good way to save money. If one has a little cash one will certainly soon spend it; but if one deposits it in an *arisan*, one can build it up into a sizeable sum. With such a sum one can make larger purchases than would otherwise be possible, say, of a bicycle or a new set of clothes. Or, one can hold a traditional ceremony, a wedding for one's daughter, a circumcision for one's son, both of which tend to be expensive. Or, one can lend the money out again at a high interest rate. More rarely, one can go into trading or craft work with it as capital. Of course, one can also simply "throw it away" on trivialities as if one had not joined the *arisan* in the first place. But *kampong* people tend to agree that the *arisan* improves the level of individual financial responsibility, for people are more careful and thoughtful in spending a large sum than in spending many small ones. Another positive factor of the *arisan* is that it acts as a form of insurance: if one is the victim of a sudden misfortune—say theft, or illness—one can always persuade the other members to allow one to take the pool out of turn, an aspect of the association also important in the villages. The *arisan* is, then, an institution of growing importance in the wholly monetized economy of this culturally rather traditionalistic urban proletariat—at once a unifying ritual, an exciting game, an economically useful device, and a generally educational experience.

The *arisan* is also quite popular among the elite of the town, those who, for the most part, live in the stone houses along the streets. In this group it is almost always based on one or another of the dozens of sodalities, political parties, youth groups, labor unions, charitable associations, school societies, women's clubs, athletic associations, which have proliferated on the urban scene since the Revolution in 1945. This network of voluntary associations provides the main social structural context for society-wide leadership in post-revolutionary Indonesia. In Modjokuto the number of people active in these voluntary associations is only a small percentage of the total population, but the intensity of activity among these few is quite astounding. The number of committee meetings, conventions, demonstrations, charity drives, celebrations, and other such "modern" activities seems so great as to take up most of this group's free time. If there is not a school board meeting, there is a holiday celebration to be organized; if the women's club is not holding a charity bazaar, the labor union is meeting to discuss the latest government policies concerning railroad pensions. The velocity of activity is extraordinarily high, and as this group is, relatively speaking, small, the burden on them is rather great.

The *arisan* acts in this context, then, to support the solidarity not of the neighborhood group, but of the club, union, or party. The *arisan* is, in most cases, held after the usual business meeting, its explicit purpose being to attract individuals to the meetings, and to intensify the feeling of unity among them. If one is not present at the meeting one cannot win the fund, and club leaders say that clubs which have attached *arisans* get a much higher turnout than those which do not, for there is the added attraction that one might come home from the meeting with a sizeable bundle of cash. The purpose of club *arisans,* as one leader said, is to bring the members together in an informal, neighborlike setting, and so strengthen their friendship bonds and consequently the club. The older ties based on residential propinquity are thus being replaced by new ties of the same sort based on common club membership; there is a shift away from the dominantly territorial integration of the villages towards a form of integration in which ideological factors, the bases of the clubs, play a more important role. The *arisan,* the same leader said, is the "harmony" part of the club which makes the "business" part of the club, its central purpose, more effective. Also, however, the economic significance of the *arisan* is again more prominent than in the villages, and as the sums involved—funds may run as high as five hundred rupiah—are generally larger.

The final urban context in which the *arisan* is important is among the traders in the market.[9] Market *arisans* are the most clearly and specifically economic of all. No meetings are actually held, but rather an agent is selected who tours the traders' stalls to collect the contributions and award the fund. Further, most market *arisans* are daily rather than weekly or monthly affairs, and they tend to be more or less permanent, cycling over and over again (though individual members may, of course, be replaced). The order of drawing is fixed. After the cycle has rotated several times, the sense of getting the fund early or late is obscured: one simply draws it every thirty days, etc.; so that the idea that some people have a more fortunate position in the cycle with respect to interest windfalls is also lost. The number of members in market *arisans* tends to be very large, reaching nearly 200 in some cases and only rarely being less than fifty. Funds are consequently rather large, even though individual contributions are small. Thus, one *arisan* with a one-rupiah contribution had 187 members and so a 187 rupiah fund.[10] Sometimes, however, a smaller group of wealthier traders will form an even larger-scale *arisan.* For example, some 36 members of an Islamic trade cooperative contributed, at the same time, to a 5, a 10, and a 25 rupiah *arisan* every five days (the Javanese have a five-day market week), to yield a 180, a 360, and a 900 rupiah fund, which the recipients almost invariably used to buy textiles for resale. These *arisans* also never met, and one trader—smaller than the rest—had an almost full-time job simply keeping the records, making the collections, and distributing the fund. Here, then, the *arisan* has become an almost entirely economic institution, the diffuse "social harmony" element having dropped out almost entirely.

THE ROTATING CREDIT ASSOCIATION IN ASIA

The Javanese form of the rotating credit association, at least as it is found in Modjokuto, has, even within the market context, not developed to very complex levels of organization or of functioning. It remains a simple rotation pattern without interest calculations or elaboration of administrative superstructure. The available reports on similar associations in China, Japan, Indo-China, and West Africa,[11] however, show a generally more complicated pattern. In Asia, the tendency is toward the development of complex methods of calculating interest payments and of distributing those payments among the members of the association. In Africa, the tendency is toward the development of more complex leadership patterns and more differentiated internal organization and, consequently, toward increasing administrative costs.

Swatow, South China

The simplest pattern reported for Asia is that given by Kulp, for a village in the Swatow area of South China.[12] Here, a rotating credit association is always founded by an individual who needs a lump sum of cash for some particular purpose. The founder will contract, say, a fifty-dollar debt with ten people, and then pay it off by holding not ten, but eleven five-dollar feasts (the first one being that at which he receives his money), thus paying five dollars, or one feast, in interest. The ten creditors form a simple rotating system with five-dollar contributions and a fifty-dollar fund (including the contribution of the winner). In such a pattern, only the founder pays interest; his five dollars of "extra" feast-giving is theoretically divided as fifty cents among each of the other members over the whole cycle. This system is, obviously, very little different from the Javanese, and Kulp shows in detail how closely it is tied in with the traditional "familistic" orientation of the Chinese village.

Japan

Embree's description of the association in the Japanese peasant community, Suye Mura, where it is called a *ko*, introduces, however, a new element: namely, that of competitive bidding for the fund.[13] Again, Suye Mura *ko* are typically instituted by a single individual in need of cash. If he needs, say, 160 yen, he will gather together a group of his friends and ask them to make up the loan. If there are twenty such contributors, for example, each will put up eight yen, and the borrower will then repay the loan in twenty ten-yen payments, usually making two such payments a year. Thus he pays forty yen in interest over a ten-year period. If the sum borrowed or the number of contributors is larger, the repayment may not be completed for as long as twenty years, individuals dying in the meanwhile being replaced by their heirs.

But the simple repayment pattern acts only as the framework for a more complex economic organization. At each of the twenty repayment meetings, the members each make a secret bid on a piece of paper. The lowest bidder receives the ten yen of the original debtor, plus the sum he has bid, say, six yen, from each of the other members of the *ko*. If this were the first meeting, this would amount to 10 plus 6 × 19, or 124 yen. Once having received the fund, an individual contributes an automatic ten yen at each meeting thereafter. Thus, the interest the second man would pay would be 8 (the original payment to the borrower) plus 10 × 18 minus 124, or 64 yen. The process continues through the whole cycle, though toward the end the bidding may be zero or even minus (in which case the bidder pays the members who still have not drawn the fund). Embree gives, in somewhat different form, the following ideal model of a 21 member *ko* of this size:

Meeting	1	2	6	19	20	21
a. Bid	8 *	6	5	1	0	0 †
b. Number paying bid	20	19	15	2	1	0
c. Number paying fixed 10 yen	0	1	5	18	19	20
d. Total payment to "winner" (ab + 10c)	160	124	125	182	190	200

   * I.e., the original proposition.
   † I.e., no bid need be made; the last man wins automatically.

On the social side, however, the *ko* is almost identical to the *arisan*. Here, too, the man who won the fund at the previous meeting is responsible for providing his house and the necessary refreshments, and many *ko* are formed—they may be organized not only along neighborhood lines, but by age, sex, occupation, and the like—more for recreational than financial purposes.[14] As almost everyone belongs to at least one *ko*, and most people belong to several, the *ko* acts as an important integrative institution in the society generally, and is deeply involved in the traditional Japanese value system emphasizing village cooperation. Embree stresses the fact that the *ko* is but one of several traditional forms of mutual aid common in Japanese villages, including exchange labor patterns, reciprocal gift giving, communal house raising and repairing, neighborly assistance in death, illness, and other personal crises, and so forth. Thus, as in rural Java, the rotating credit association is more than a simple economic institution: it is a mechanism strengthening the over-all solidarity of the village.

Shanghai, Central China

In the system reported by Fei, from a village near Shanghai in the lower Yangtze valley, interest calculation becomes even more complex.[15] If, for example, the organizer of an association, which is called a *hui*, needs 140 dollars, he will gather 14 members to subscribe ten dollars each. The association will then meet twice a year for seven years, in the usual feasting pattern. At each meeting the organizer will repay ten dollars of capital and three dollars of interest. The man who "wins" at each meeting (he is chosen by lot) received, however, not 140 dollars, but half this, or seventy. At each succeeding meeting he will be a debtor and will repay five dollars of capital and one and one-half dollars of interest—i.e., half of what the organizer pays. A man who has not yet drawn the fund—Fei calls him a depositor—makes a contribution determined by the following formula:

The total fund − [the organizer's contribution + (the number of donors × the debtor's contribution)], all divided by the number of depositors.

Suppose at the fifth meeting the total fund is 70 dollars, the organizer's subscription is 13 dollars (10 capital, plus 3 interest; this is a constant). Each of the four members who have already drawn the fund, i.e., the debtors, must pay 6.5 dollars (5 capital, 1.5 interest; also a constant, though of course the number of debtors increases one each meeting), and there are nine depositors, i.e., men who have not yet drawn the fund. The man who has just this time won makes up the fourteen members of the *hui* in addition to its organizer. The equation for a single depositor's contribution at this meeting is thus:

$$\frac{70 - [13 + (4 \times 6.5)]}{9} \quad \text{or 3.44 dollars.}$$

This means that the 70-dollar fund is composed of a 13-dollar contribution by the organizer, a 26-dollar contribution by the four people who have already won the fund, and a 31-dollar contribution by the nine who have not yet won it.[16]

This system is sufficiently complex, Fei remarks, to be beyond the comprehension of the average villager, who has to invite the village head or some other notable to instruct him. Fei also emphasizes the manner in which a *hui* is built, in this family-centered society, around the kinship group: the nucleus of such an association is always a set of relatives. A man always approaches people who have consanguineal or affinal ties to him when he wishes to set up a *hui:* his father's brother, brother, sister's husband, mother's brother, wife's father, etc.; and these are under a heavy obligation to join or, if not, to find some of their own relatives to take their place. Thus a person with a large sphere of relatives has a better chance to organize a *hui* and so get financial support, than a man with a narrow sphere. Kin ties between members also, of course, reinforce the economic obligations involved, so that defaulting is rare, as it is in Japan. The usual purposes for starting such a society are ceremonial ones—to finance a wedding or a funeral—rather than productive ones, such as starting a business or buying a piece of land, the latter not being considered as proper ground for an appeal for a *hui*-type loan.

Peking, North China

Gamble's report on a semi-urban county in north China, just south of Peking, gives an example of a rotating credit association—of the auction variety—which fulfilled a more specifically economic, less diffusely social function.[17] Of the eight members of the particular association studied intensively for whom the information is available, four used the fund they received for business expenses or ventures, seven loaned it out to others, and only three used it for family expenses. Among the "good points" of the association mentioned by members were included—in addition to the universal comment that they promote friendship—such distinctly non-traditional ideas as that they encourage thrift and that they provide investible funds of a low cost, while among the "bad points" were listed the fact that sometimes members evade their obligations, and that the feasts were too expensive and uneconomical. The fact that, in most cases, the costs of each feast were born equally by the members points in the same general direction: toward the conclusion that traditionalistic ties were of less importance here, or could be less relied upon, than in the other examples which have been reviewed.

Even more striking is the fact that the founder of an association had to sign a written contract, in which all his obligations were spelled out in detail, and have it countersigned by two guarantors. Similarily, each member had to provide two guarantors before joining the association and had to sign a receipt for all funds received. But perhaps the most telling evidence of the essentially economic nature of the association in this area was the fact that Gamble's data for the whole ten-year cycle of an association he studied in detail (from 1917 to 1927), show a smooth linear increase in the amount received by each member as a percent of amount paid by him.[18] This indicates that the members were figuring a set discount rate for the money, relatively independently of any immediate needs for it such as a wedding or funeral. As a result, the interest rate remained more or less constant, around 1.5% per month (a low rate). It seems clear that this association was relatively businesslike and uninfluenced by traditional needs.

Vietnam

But perhaps the most clearly economic in function of the Asian rotating credit associations so far reported is the *ho* of Vietnam.[19] Traditional *ho* exist in the villages (*ho* means family, and, by extension, corporation or mutual association), operating according to the more broadly "social" pattern we have found elsewhere—the ties of friendship, kinship, and social status forming the integrative bonds for what is only secondarily or partly a specifically economic institution. As in Japan, some of them are even in kind—rice seedlings, etc. But in the urban areas of

Vietnam, the rotating credit association begins to approach a fully "businesslike" organization, an embryonic corporation.

The urban *ho* are run by professional managers (who, it happens, are all women), who are not actually members of the association and usually run several at the same time on a purely economic basis.[20] Each *ho* has a special firm name which must be notarized by the government; detailed books are kept of all transactions; and the obligations of all concerned are enforceable in the courts. In some of the more elaborate *ho*—organized among civil servants—one finds sealed bids, stamped receipts, acceptance of near monies such as promissory notes of Indian usurers, and a quite rational-legal set of statutes for governing the society, including default and bankruptcy procedures.

In general outline, the functioning of the *ho* is similar to that of the Chinese and Japanese auction-type associations, but there is a major difference in the role of the manager. Unlike the Japanese and Chinese cases, the manager does not set up the association in order to raise a personal loan, but as a straight business proposition. She takes one-third of the fund each time it is constituted, only two-thirds being distributed among the members, and she pays nothing in. Further, at the second meeting, the whole fund goes to her in full (i.e., without bidding). This fund she uses personally to make loans to members which are paid back in small increments—with the going interest rate included—in much the same manner as in the association itself. Such loans from the manager are called "given *ho*," in contrast to the "bought *ho*" of the normal revolving fund.

On her side, the manager is responsible for providing the feast each meeting in her home, for advancing the fund to each winner, even if collections have not as yet been entirely completed or if members who have drawn the fund have defaulted, and for keeping the books. Thus, the manager is a small-scale professional banker at the center of a complex network of credit ties. As Nguyen comments, successful managers

. . . must know how to select their clientele, having it well balanced between those with resources and those needing loans in order to balance the offers and demands for money; they must also know how to arrange things so as to be able to have the meetings gay, very short, and sufficiently elegant but using up only a reasonable portion of the profits. There are some women who manage two, three, and up to five *ho* simultaneously, and know how to manipulate the funds of all without a hitch.[21]

Another indication of the business-like nature of the *ho* is the fact that the gap between the open market interest rate and that of the rotating association is not so wide as in the traditional cases. The main advantage of the association over private money lending is not the difference in interest rate (though association rates are still a little lower), but in the fact that in private money lending "the money rests while the interest runs"—i.e., payments are not applied to the principle until current interest charges have been met in full—while in the association "the capital destroys"; i.e., part of each payment goes to discharge the loan, so that as long as one keeps up the relatively small payments he will sooner or later rid himself of the debt entirely. Genuine bondage to the association manager of the sort all too common to the private Indian or Chinese money lender evidently does not occur.

Pointing even more clearly in the same direction is the fact that each association usually has a core of several members who, well acquainted with the manager, merely make their payments regularly without coming to the meetings (they receive a money premium from the manager in exchange for their abandoned perquisites), the explicit understanding being that they will not receive the fund—which may grow as large as 2,000 Indo-Chinese dollars (300 American)—until the last few meetings. Thus, they actually are "backers" of the manager, her source of finance in offering loans to others in the earlier part of the cycle. In some cases, evidently, the time of loans for every individual in the *ho* is contracted with the manager ahead of time, so that the association becomes more a matter of a rationalized savings institution managed by a skilled promoter than a simple expression of communal solidarity and mutual aid.

The rotating credit association in Africa. The rotating credit association is also found in various parts of Negro Africa, most especially in the more commercially developed regions of West Africa, from where it evidently spread via the slave trade to the Caribbean, and perhaps to parts of the southern United States.[22]

The Bulu

A traditionalistic example of the rotating credit association in Africa, of about the same level of complexity as that of Modjokuto, is found among the Bulu of the French Cameroons.[23] As in all the African cases, no interest is calculated, and bidding is not found. The pattern is largely confined to the salaried laborers and civil servants in this only very slightly monetized society, but these sometimes put almost the whole of their salary into the pool, depending on cultivation (or that of relatives) for their day-to-day subsistence. The fund, when received, tends to be used for such customary needs as a dowry, or to buy consumption goods such as a bicycle, or, much more rarely, to set up a son in a trade or craft. The order of drawing is strictly determined by traditional notions of status—based on kinship and age—and members are almost inevitably related to one another, at least to the point of being members of the same clan. The economic aspects of the association are thus completely embedded in tribal social structures.

The Nupe

Nadel's description of the *dashi* of the Nupe in central Nigeria, a rather more developed group than the Bulu, introduces the note which is characteristic of most of the African systems: the very strong role the leader of the group plays in determining its mode of operation.[24] Among the Nupe, the head of the group decides the order in which the members will receive the fund. This man, called aptly enough the "king of the *dashi*," is usually a man of some reputation: for example, a well-known trader or the head of a craft guild. Especially able organizers are in heavy demand. As in Indo-China, the organizer does not himself participate in the association as a contributing/receiving member. He receives no payment, his only perquisite being that he is allowed to borrow from the fund occasionally for his own business needs, provided that the members agree and the original plan of the *dashi* is not disrupted. Also, he may receive gifts from a member who, without giving any "legitimate" reason for wanting to do so, wishes to collect at a certain time. A member who can, however, show a "real" need, from the traditional point of view (an illness, a funeral, a bride-price payment), need not pay a bribe to get his share when he wishes it; the head is obligated by custom to give it to him.

The Yoruba

The *esusu* of the Yoruba to the south and west of the Nupe follows an essentially similar pattern, except for the fact that the associations seem to reach a somewhat larger size than Nadel reports for the Nupe, running up to as many as 200 members, with cycles of four or five years.[25] This larger size evidently necessitates a somewhat more formal organization. Larger *esusu* are divided into four or more subgroups, called "roads," which are numbered (1st, 2nd, 3rd, 4th, . . .), each with its own sub-headman under the over-all headman. Collection for the whole group must alternate among the roads as well as among individuals, giving the following sort of pattern for the order of receiving payment:

Road	1st	2nd	3rd	4th
Order of payment:	1	2	3	4
	5	6	etc.	

Here we have a somewhat more "bureaucratic" form of the system, for the head of the *esusu* may not even be personally acquainted with all its members; his relations are mainly with the subgroup heads. The members pay in and take out through the agency of the subgroup head, and it is he who determines the order of the distribution of the fund among members of the subgroup. In this slightly more impersonalized form of the association, defaulting by members and embezzlement by leaders is a more serious problem. If a member defaults after he has received the fund, every effort is made to force him to pay. The over-all head attempts to coerce the subgroup head, the subgroup head the member. As a last resort, the over-all head may take the matter to court. Some heads insist that the first round of contributions be kept as a reserve against possible defaults. Another technique used by the subgroup head is not to give the whole fund to one member at a time, but to split, say, the first payment between Mr. A and Mr. B, and then again split, say, the 13th between these two, thus maintaining an individual in a "depositor" position for a longer time.

The reverse problem, the probity of the heads, is also more prominent than it seems to be in the less developed cases. In larger *esusu,* a diviner may be called in to select the various heads in an effort to find ones who can be trusted not to abscond. The members keep track of their payments and receipts by cutting grooves into the walls of their huts, but this method is not certain enough, or the members do not have enough confidence in their own figures, to prevent heads from embezzling one or two rounds. This much of a cut for the head is considered more or less unavoidable and is chalked up to administrative costs, "but it is unlikely that the *esusu* head could take a third round for himself during the cycle without being caught." [26]

The Ibo

The most thorough and incisive report on the rotating credit association in Africa is that of Ardener on the Mba-Ise, an Ibo group also in Nigeria.[27] The Mba-Ise area has no large towns or railheads, but population pressure is very heavy (1,000 per sq. mi.), leading on the one hand to a heavy outward migration, and on the other to land pressure of such an intensity that a man is fortunate if he can gain from one-third to one-half of his food requirements from farming. The result is that an elaborate trade economy is needed (based on the export of palm oil) to bring food in from the less dense areas to the north and south. "That the Mba-Ise has made the transition from a mainly agricultural to a predominantly trading economy successfully is due, to a large extent," Ardener argues, "to the growth and development of the [rotating credit association]." [28]

Here, the associations get even larger than those reported for the Yoruba. Ardener describes a one-shilling association, with 248 members of both sexes, divided into seven subsections, which meet every eight days (the Ibo have an eight-day week). Once every four Ibo weeks, shares are doubled to two shillings per person and two members receive a fund. Thus, each member pays five shillings in every thirty-two days and receives a fund when it comes his turn—once in four years and eight months—of £12/8s. Each member must have a senior man from his compound as a guarantor, who will agree, in writing, to continue the shares if the member defaults. These guarantees are kept by the association secretary and are upheld in court proceedings by the native bench. When a member receives the fund, he must sign or thumb-print a receipt for the money. Clearly, the size of the club, the length of the cycle, and the size of the fund combine to make this a fairly impressive example of long-term, "purposeful" saving—whatever the use to which the money is ultimately put.

The recipient of the fund has, however, certain overhead costs. First, he is required to supply six calabashes of palm wine for the other members. Secondly, he must contribute four shillings to the association loan fund. This fund, held by the association secretary, is constantly lent out in very small sums over short terms at the normal 100% interest rate. The fund increases rapidly—in the case at hand from £3/11s/0 to £17/19s/4.5d a year later, a 459% increase (!)—and is shared equally among the members at the end of the cycle, though some of it may be applied to a party for the whole association.

But the most important cost to the members is the 15–20% of the fund he must pay to the headman (or men) to get the fund. Here again, the headmen decide who shall get the fund at which time, and this is determined, in most cases, not on the basis of the headman's evaluation of the member's needs, but in terms of who offers him the highest bribes. Thus, the "interest" on the loans—about one-fifth of the going rate—goes here not to the lenders but to the headmen. It must be remembered, though, that the headmen are taking the risk of defaulters, in most cases, and are providing—with a membership of 250 or so—a genuine and necessary administrative service.

Nevertheless, there is a tendency for the associations to become top-heavy administratively. Associations tend to proliferate officers: councils are formed for general policy and money checkers appointed, as are food tasters and sanitary officials to judge the quality of the food at the feasts. In one one-shilling club with a £7 fund, there were two headmen, a secretary, a messenger, four chiefs, a sanitary man, and four food dividers. Each of these men drew money bribes and food payments, until the point arrived where the net fund was only £3, and the association dissolved in a fist fight. Evidently, breakdowns of associations due to the burgeoning of organization which raises administrative costs above a reasonable level are relatively common.

In any case, the rotating credit association is obviously of crucial importance in Mba-Ise society. In one subsection of a small lineage, Ardener found that six men paid an aggregate 90 shillings a month; the total fund to which they were contributing was £181/7s/6d. Only one of these six men received a regular wage of £2 a month, while the others were part-time traders, craftsmen, and, in all cases, farmers. Figures such as these must certainly damage theories about the intrinsic inability of peoples in "underdeveloped" areas to save.

Keta, Ghana

Thorough descriptions of the operation of rotating credit associations in African cities are, unfortunately, not yet available, but passing references to their existence and importance, both as specifically economic and broadly social institutions, have become increasingly numerous in recent urban studies in both West and East Africa.[29] That, when investigated in detail, such urban forms may show some of the same sort of movement toward increased economic rationality that their counterparts in Asia show is indicated by the association Little has briefly described for Keta, a town in Ghana, where for the first time we find an association in which the amount each member contributes and receives is not firmly fixed by rule, but fluctuates according to individual speculative assessments.[30] Composed of 400 members, most of them market women, the club raises a "loan" for one member at each weekly meeting. All the members present who have not yet taken the pot give as much money "as they feel they can afford," the amount they give being recorded in writing. The member receiving the collection as a loan is then given a list showing the amount of money contributed to it by each of the other members. As these various contributors in turn take the collection over the weeks, this former collector must contribute as much as the present collector contributed to his pot; i.e., if this week's collector contributed a shilling to my loan, I must contribute a shilling to his; if five shillings, then five shillings; while people who still have not yet collected continue to be free to give any amount they wish. All of this makes for a very much more calculating approach to the whole affair:

In a period of rising prices, those at the top of the list naturally have the advantage, but on the other hand, those who wait longer may receive more because the society's membership will in the meantime have increased. There is an element of chance in all this which adds spice to the normally dull business of saving, and this partly explains the society's popularity.[31]

But this increased sense for economic calculation does not, once more, imply the simple disappearance of the more diffusely social, solidarity-producing aspects of the association: when a member is sick, he is visited in the hospital; if he dies, his relatives are given £10 toward the cost of his funeral; and each week's loan raising begins with a round of community singing.

THE ROTATING CREDIT ASSOCIATION
AND ECONOMIC DEVELOPMENT

In a recent paper on the economic adaptation of oriental immigrants in Israel, S. N. Eisenstadt has attempted to demonstrate the manner in which "traditional value orientations" have been effective in supporting rather than hindering—at least in the early stages—such an adaptation to the highly rationalized Israeli economy.[32] On the one hand, customary family and kinship ties, authority relations, and religious views have remained very strong among the new immigrants from such "underdeveloped areas" as Yemen, Iran, and North Africa; while on the other hand, these immigrants have made an increasingly successful adjustment to the developed economic setting through the mediation of the agricultural cooperative. Within the cooperatives it has proven possible to integrate traditional attitudes with modern functions in such a way that the former actually support the latter rather than hinder them, and the latter react back upon the former to alter them slowly. A form of symbiosis between the "traditional" social structure of the immigrants and the more "rational" one into which they have been suddenly projected has made possible the immigrants' adaptation to the new economic and political tasks with which they are faced, while at the same time minimizing the strain of transition and social transformation. The agricultural cooperative may thus be seen as an "intermediate" institution which links traditional motivations to modern functions, serving at the same time to transform those motivations toward a more rationalistic basis; it "facilitates the learning of new skills, patterns of behavior, and value orientations, and makes possible some changes in the structural principles in the general direction of modernization, without undermining the basic cohesion and solidarity of the group." [33]

The rotating credit association is, I would argue, a similar intermediate institution, a product of a shift from a traditionalistic agrarian society to an increasingly fluid commercial one, whether this shift be very slow or very rapid.[34] It, too, mobilizes familiar motivations and applies them to unfamiliar purposes, while serving at the same time to reconstruct those motivations on a more flexible basis. The *arisan, ko, hui, dashi,* or *esusu* is essentially, then, an educational mechanism in terms of which peasants learn to be traders, not merely in the narrow occupational sense, but in the broad cultural sense; an institution which acts to change their whole value framework from one emphasizing particularistic, diffuse, affective, and ascriptive ties between individuals, to one emphasizing—*within economic contexts*—universalistic, affectively neutral, and achieved ties between them.[35] The rotating credit association is thus a socializing mechanism, in that broad sense in which "socialization" refers not simply to the process by which the child learns to be an adult, but the learning of *any* new patterns of behavior which are of functional importance in society, even by adults.[36] The theoretical as well as the practical interest of the association lies in its ability to organize traditional relationships in such a way that they are slowly but steadily transformed into non-traditional ones, as an institution whose functional significance is primarily to facilitate social and cultural change in respect to economic problems and processes.

In all the cases we have reviewed, the rotating credit association has been found associated with a lesser or greater penetration of an elaborated, and ultimately international, exchange economy into a primarily agrarian society. Such a penetration of commerce into a peasant society means that the society must, in the long run, change its whole form in such a way as to (1) set aside certain social contexts within which rational, economic calculation can legitimately be pursued; (2) distinguish these contexts from others within which it is morally reprehensible to so calculate; and (3) relate the two. This is essentially a process of social structural differentiation and reintegration. On the one hand, narrowly economic processes must be institutionally segregated from broadly social ones, and economic interests must be allowed to operate independently of non-economic constraints to a rather higher degree than formerly. On the other hand, these processes and interests must in some way be integrated with, or related to, the broader social framework—the more differentiated economic system must remain an integral part, a sub-system, of the total social system. This in turn implies that there must be a development of a "commercial ethic," a set of social values in terms of which the expectations and obligations within the economy itself can be stabilized and regulated, which ethic is, at the same time, but a "special case" of the general value system of the society as a whole, formulated with respect to economic functions.

In these terms, one can see the range of forms of the rotating credit association which have been reviewed, both in Modjokuto and in Asia and Africa generally, as representing, in an over-all way, a continuum ranging from more "traditionalistic" to more "rationally oriented" types. As one moves from the village *arisan,* the Japanese *ko,* or the Bulu example, toward the Indo-Chinese *ho* and the case Ardener reports for the Mba-Ise, or Little for Keta, one moves toward an increasingly formalistic, impersonal, specifically economic institution; a fact reflected in the declining importance of the ritualistic, solidarity-strengthening elements, in the increasing concern with the financial probity of members and leaders and the legal enforceability of obligations, and in the development of more complex patterns of organization and commercial calculation. The degree to which, in any given case, the rotating credit association is an institution with explicitly economic aims and modes of operation is an index of the degree to which commercial motivations, attitudes, and values have replaced diffusely social motivations, attitudes, and values as controlling elements in the members' behavior within economic contexts generally, the degree to which they have learned to discriminate between economic and "non-economic" problems and processes and to act differentially with respect to them.

The rotating credit association as an intermediate institution reflects, then, two contrary forces. There is a movement toward an increased segregation of economic activities from non-economic ones, a freeing of them from traditional constraints; while at the same time, there is a directly contradictory attempt to maintain the dominance of the traditional values over those developing economic activities, to defend the integrity of the less differentiated pattern. It is these contrary forces that the association is able, at least in many cases, to balance in such a way that severe disturbances of social equilibrium are avoided, even in a situation of fairly rapid social change. It permits, in the favorable case, a coordinated pattern of change in which the extension of commercial behavior, the relaxation of traditional constraints in economic matters, and the development of a specific commercial ethic can go hand in hand, thus avoiding either a suffocation of new forms of economic activity by non-economic values, or an undermining of non-economic values by the sudden intrusion of morally unregulated market forces. The socialization process of the individual has been likened to a man climbing a ladder:

> As he reaches up with his hands to rungs not previously within his experience, he does not immediately let go of the lower rungs on which his feet have rested. The process is rather something like this: he reaches up to a new rung, grasps it tentatively, and only when he is rather sure of its location and solidity does he venture to pull himself up and let the lower foot finally leave the lowest rung on which he has been supporting himself . . . Essentially we are saying that such a process is not possible if the climber is in touch only with two adjacent rungs of the ladder; there must be at least three; otherwise the uncertainties inherent in securing his grip on the unfamiliar top one of the series will not allow him to let go of the bottom one; he must have a "middle" basis of security on which he feels he can rely.[37]

It is suggested here, then, that the rotating credit society is such a middle rung in the process of development from a largely agrarian peasant society to one in which trade plays an increasingly crucial role.

In the less developed cases—the village *arisan*, etc.—the hold of the traditional values remains strong, but commercial activities are "symbiotically" fitted into them in such a way that these values actually help support the new forms of behavior, rather than simply smothering them. The essential problem at this stage is that specific economic norms (and skills) have not yet been developed and fully internalized, with the result that there is a tendency for economic processes to be carried on, in large part, unrestrained by "human" considerations. The rotating credit association makes it possible to use customary patterns of cooperation, mutual help, and communal responsibility to regulate the emergent activities. The fact that the members of the association all have neighborhood, kinship, or other particularistic ties with one another acts to prevent fraud and evasion. The fact that the money is delivered immediately upon collection to the winner, so that no one has to be trusted to hold cash belonging to anyone else for any length of time reduces the likelihood of embezzlement. The feasting aspect softens the harshness of the economic calculation aspects and prevents them from undermining customary ties. The form thus combines an activity functional to a commercial economy—the concentration of monetized resources in larger units—with a maintenance of traditional moral values.

But this pattern is obviously limited in the scale and complexity of commercial activity which it can support. It is confined to small numbers and simple forms of organization. Thus, in the more developed cases, the traditional elements weaken and the stress comes to be placed on devising legal and economic mechanisms of normative regulation—contracts, record-keeping, professional managers, stable discriminations between debtor and creditor roles, bureaucratic organization, and the like. The rotating credit association becomes more and more like a specifically economic institution, a "firm," with its own pattern of value integration. In this sense, the form is, perhaps, self-liquidating, being replaced ultimately by banks, cooperatives, and other economically more rational types of credit institutions. But these latter can only function when the differentiation of a specific economic pattern of norms has occurred—when courts will enforce contracts, when managers worry about their business reputations and keep honest books, and when investors feel safe in giving cash resources to debtors to whom they are not related. Cultural change of this sort takes place, however, in steps rather than all at once, and in the intermediary stages the association fulfills a valuable function in organizing traditional and rational economic attitudes in such a way that the process continues rather than stultifies or breaks down into anomie.

It seems likely, too, that the rotating credit association is merely one of a whole family of such intermediate "socializing" institutions which spring up in societies undergoing social and cultural change, not only in the economic, but in the political, religious, stratificatory, familial, and other aspects of the social system as well. The building of "middle rungs" between traditional society and more modern forms of social organization seems to be a characteristic activity of people caught up in the processes of social transformation. As a group, this family of institutions should be, consequently, of particular interest for students of social and cultural development, highlighting, as they do, some of the central tensions involved in such development and the sorts of mechanisms by means of which those tensions are resolved.

NOTES

1. Quoted in Myrdal, *An International Economy* (New York, 1956), p. 273.

2. "A Survey of Recent Contributions to the Theory of Economic Growth," unpublished paper. Center for International Studies, Massachusetts Institute of Technology, April 1956.

3. There have also been, of course, efforts at "direct saving" through the employment of surplus labor on capital-creating projects. Though important, there is an obvious limit to the effectiveness of this device, especially in libertarian societies.

4. Actually, many terms are used in the literature for this single type of institution: contribution clubs, slates, mutual lending societies, pooling clubs, thrift groups, friendly societies, etc.

5. The field work period ran from May 1953 until September 1954, and was undertaken as part of a group project of seven anthropologists and sociologists sponsored by the Center for International Studies of the Massachusetts Institute of Technology. I wish to express gratitude to Alice Dewey, Robert Jay, and the late Donald Fagg for contributing some of the data used in the paper. The writing of the paper has been made possible by a grant from the Ellis L. Phillips Foundation.

6. For a review of rural land tenure and labor relations patterns, see R. Jay, *Village Life in Modjokuto* (New York: The Free Press of Glencoe).

7. One rupiah equalled about 10 dollar cents at the official rate, and about three dollar cents on the open market, in 1953–54.

8. A description of the operation of the rotating credit association in another region of rural Java, that of a western fruit-growing village near Djakarta, where it is called *paketan* (probably from *pakat*, "to agree upon"), shows a pattern essentially the same as that of the Modjokuto area (S. Stanley, "*Paketan* and *Selamatan* in an Indonesian Fruit-Growing Village," paper delivered at the annual meeting of the American Anthropological Association, Minneapolis, 1960). In this village there are two types of associations: *paketan daging* and *paketan kawinan*. In the *paketan daging* (*daging*, "meat"), the aim is to purchase collectively a carabao for slaughter to celebrate an Islamic holiday. Of the pool, 150 rupiah is donated by the "winner" (order is fixed by general agreement) toward the purchase of the carabao, the remainder being kept for personal use in the ordinary fashion. In the *paketan kawinan* (*kawinan*, "marriage ceremony"), meetings are held only irregularly, occurring only when a member has a ceremonial need—an offspring's wedding, circumcision, etc.—which he uses the pool to finance. Such associations are very long-term affairs, with positions being inherited as members die. Stanley reports that the rotating credit association is one of the major integrative forces in this otherwise fairly loosely integrated village.

9. For a description of the market in Modjokuto, see Alice Dewey, *Peasant Marketing in Java* (New York: The Free Press of Glencoe, 1962).

10. *Ibid.*

11. The existence of rotating credit associations has been mentioned in passing, but not thoroughly described, for parts of India—Madras, for example— as well. See C. Notteboom, "Assistance Economique Mutuelle Systematisee dans L'Asie du Sud et de L'est," in *Orientalia Nederlandica* (Leiden, 1948), pp. 423–30.

12. D. H. Kulp, *Country Life in South China*, Vol. I, *Phenix Village, Kwantung, China* (New York, 1925), pp. 190–96.

13. John Embree, *Suye Mura* (London: Kegan Paul, 1946). *Ko* are, Embree reports, very old in Japan. A document mentioning them is found as early as 1275.

14. The "insurance" element is prominent again, too. For example, a number of silk growers who had experienced several failures formed a *ko* in order to hedge against future failures.

15. Fei Hsiao-T'ung, *Peasant Life in China* (New York, 1946), pp. 267–74.

16. As a matter of fact, the actual calculation is, for various reasons, a great deal more complicated than this. For a full numerical example of a *hui*, see *ibid.*, pp. 271–72.

17. S. D. Gamble, *Ting Hsein: A North China Rural Community* (New York: Institute of Pacific Relations, 1954), pp. 260–71. See also his "A Chinese Mutual Savings Society," *Far Eastern Quarterly*, IV (1944), 41–52.

18. It ran from a 51.6% low at the second meeting after the formation, to a 207.6% high at the thirtieth, or last, meeting.

19. Nguyen Van Vinh, "Savings and Mutual Lending Societies (*Ho*)," Yale Southeast Asia Studies, mimeographed, 1949.

20. Nguyen does note that "some ladies hold the *ho* not in order to do business, but to receive friends at their home, to show their well-kept homes, to demonstrate the talents of their daughters, sisters, sisters-in-law, or nieces of marriageable age; or to make people talk about their famous pastries or of the excellent cooking done in their homes, or maybe even to boast of the rather innocent talent which consists of delicately folding over the betel leaves of a beautiful yellow-green shade or to be able to bring out the shade of rose-gray in the meat of sliced areca nuts, to perfume their tea, etc." But most women, he says, simply make a lucrative trade of it, and that there are in fact, some, "like the dubious bankers of Europe, who are able through adroit approach to draw in the resources of honest housewives and who, one fine morning, depart without having invited their clients to a going-away party and without leaving behind their forwarding address."

21. *Op. cit.*

22. The new world cases are described in M. Herskovits, *Trinidad Village* (New York, 1957), pp. 76–77; and M. F. Katzin, " 'Partners,' An Informal Savings Institution in Jamaica," *Social and Economic Studies*, VIII (1958), 436–40. Katzin says the association is the most important single source of capital for petty traders in the Kingston area, but that minor government offi-

cials, domestic servants, and wage workers also form them; and she quotes Dr. Bernice Kaplan as reporting the existence of associations among American Indians in Peru. In West Africa, the form has been reported from Nigeria, the Ivory Coast, Ghana, and Sierra Leone; elsewhere in Africa from the Congo, the Cameroons, Uganda, and the Union of South Africa (see I. M. Wallerstein, *The Emergence of Two West African Nations: Ghana and the Ivory Coast*, Ph.D. thesis, Columbia University, 1959, pp. 170–71).

23. G. Horner, personal communication.

24. S. Nadel, *Black Byzantium* (London, 1942), pp. 371–73.

25. W. Bascom, "The Esusu: A Credit Institution of the Yoruba," *Journal of the Royal Anthropological Institute of Great Britain and Ireland*, LXXXII, Part I (1952), 63–70. Bascom notes that all the evidence points to the *esusu* being not a recent borrowing or innovation, but an ancient institution among the Yoruba.

26. Bascom, *op. cit.*

27. S. Ardener, "The Social and Economic Significance of the Contribution Club among a Section of the Southern Ibo," *Annual Conference, West African Institute of Social and Economic Research, Sociology Section* (Ibadan, 1953), pp. 128–42.

28. *Ibid.*

29. E.g., M. Banton, *West African City* (London, 1957), pp. 187–88—Freetown, Sierra Leone; C. and R. Sofer, *Jinja Transformed*, East African Studies No. 4 (Kampala, 1955), p. 108—Jinja, Uganda; and A. Southall and P. Gutkind, *Townsmen in the Making*, East African Studies, No. 9 (Kampala, 1956), pp. 162–63—Kampala, Uganda.

30. K. Little, "The Role of Voluntary Associations in West African Urbanization," *American Anthropologist*, LIX, 579–96. This association is actually but a local branch of a highly organized national association which has its headquarters in Accra, the capital.

31. Little, *op. cit.*

32. S. N. Eisenstadt, "Sociological Aspects of the Economic Adaptation of Oriental Immigrants in Israel: A Case Study in the Problem of Modernization," *Economic Development and Cultural Change*, IV (April 1956), 269–78.

33. Eisenstadt, *op. cit.* I have altered the tenses.

34. Arguing, loosely, that the rotating credit association is a *product* of a changing society does not mean that I think it arose independently out of a local configuration of forces in each case. Its presence may be due in most cases to diffusion, perhaps in all cases but one. But, as has often been pointed out, diffusion analyses really contribute rather little to the understanding of social functioning in themselves. For example, the absence of the auction pattern of the association among the Javanese in Modjokuto can hardly be attributed to a simple lack of knowledge of it, for the commercially more sophisticated Chinese in the same town, from whom the Javanese have borrowed many other traits, practice it. Certainly, some assumption about "functional fit" and differential levels of economic development must be introduced to account for the fact that this auction pattern has not diffused "across the street," so to speak.

35. For a full discussion of these terms, see T. Parsons, *Social System* (Glencoe: The Free Press, 1951), pp. 58 ff.

36. "The term socialization in its current usage in the literature refers primarily to the process of child development. This is in fact a crucially important case of the operation of what are here called mechanisms of socialization, but it should be clear that the term is here used in a broader sense than the current one to designate the learning of *any* orientations of functional significance to the operation of a system of complementary role-expectations. In this sense, socialization, like learning, goes on throughout life. The case of the development of the child is only the most dramatic because he has so far to go." *Ibid.*, pp. 207–08.

37. T. Parsons and R. F. Bales, *Family, Socialization, and Interaction Process* (Glencoe, 1955), p. 377.

L. I. Rudolph and S. H. Rudolph

THE POLITICAL ROLE
OF INDIA'S CASTE ASSOCIATIONS (1960)

It is one of the paradoxes of Indian politics that India's *ancien régime,* surely one of the oldest and most deeply rooted in the world, produced no reaction. In three-fifths of India the nationalist middle classes which emerged out of the British colonial experience aimed not only at independence but also at the transformation of Indian society. The Rebellion of 1857 is the only historical event in which the old order attempted to preserve itself, but its causes and objectives were so ambiguous that its meaning remains open to serious dispute even today. At Independence, the vestigial political expression of the *ancien régime,* the princely states, which covered two-fifths of India's territory, swiftly collapsed. This event was as much the result of the atrophied condition of the institutions and wills of the ruling order as of the skill with which the Indian Government (through Sardar Patel) managed the negotiations. Only a few minor local parties today stand for a full return to the rule of Brahmans and *Kshatryas* according to the precepts of *dharma* or traditional duty, and they are ineffectual.[1]

There is one perspective in which the absence of a reaction in the European sense is not surprising: within Hinduism, conflict (at the level of theology, philosophy and law) has generally been dealt with less by confrontation of adversaries, struggle and decision, than by compartmentalization, absorption or synthesis. And absorption appears likely to be the fate of the *ancien regime's* most central and durable institution—caste. Within the new context of political democracy, caste remains a central element of Indian society even while adapting itself to the values and methods of democratic politics. Indeed, it has become one of the

SOURCE. L. I. Rudolph and S. H. Rudolph, "The Political Role of India's Caste Associations," reprinted from *Pacific Affairs,* XXVIII, 3, 1955, pp. 235–253.

chief means by which the Indian mass electorate has been attached to the processes of democratic politics.

The appeal of India's relatively weakly articulated voluntary associations is confined to the urban-educated who are more or less attuned to the modern political culture. Caste, however, provides channels of communication and bases of leadership and organization which enable those still submerged in the traditional society and culture to transcend the technical political illiteracy which would otherwise handicap their ability to participate in democratic politics. Caste has been able to perform this novel role by developing a new form for political activity, the caste association (*sabha* or *sangham*). Caste associations were already visible in the mid-nineteenth century. Over the last forty or fifty years, they have proliferated, their number and strength paralleling the growth of political literacy. After Independence, it became increasingly apparent that they would be a central feature of Indian politics for some time to come.

The political role and characteristics of the caste association resemble in many ways those of the voluntary association or interest-group familiar to European and American politics. On the other hand, the caste association is distinguishable in a number of important respects not only from the voluntary association but also from the natural association of caste out of which it has developed.

Membership in a caste is completely ascriptive: once born into a caste, a man has no way to change social identity insofar as the social structure and cultural norms recognize caste.[2] Caste norms prescribe the ritual, occupational, commensal, marital and social relationships of members, and caste organization and authority enforce these norms within the group and with other caste groups. Caste members are culturally and socially quite homogeneous since they share the same occupation, social status and ritual position.[3] This social homogeneity results in a sense of exclusiveness and identity which tends to subsume all social roles to that of caste membership. The unit of action and location of caste has been, until recently, the sub-caste in the village or group of villages. Traditionally, it has been concerned with settling problems at the village level, both internally and in relation to other castes. At most, its geographic spread took account of the reach of intra-caste (endogamous) marriages which often extended to other villages, but the village unit was crucial. Leaders were hereditary, generally the senior members of a specific lineage group. Social integration, the relationship of the caste to other castes, was governed by *dharma,* the sacred and traditional prescriptions of duty which permeate Hindu life. Finally, its organization was latent, embedded in habit and custom, rather than manifest and rationalized.

The emergence of caste associations seems to have been associated with the spread of communications and a market economy under British rule.[4] On the one hand, these forces undermined the hold of the traditional culture and society as it was organized in relatively autonomous local units; on the other hand, they created the conditions under which local sub-castes could be linked together in geographically extended associations. Caste associations, particularly those of lower castes, frequently undertook to upgrade the position of the caste in the social hierarchy. They pressed for the extension of privileges and rights to the caste either by turning to the state or by emulating the social or ritual behavior of higher castes. Thus, for example, in the South, where the caste culture has been conspicuously dominated by Brahmanical norms, the rising castes have emulated those norms by "sanskritizing" their caste practices; they have encouraged vegetarianism, abstention from liquor, the adoption of Brahman rituals, and the prevention of widow remarriage.[5] Caste associations have often expedited and coordinated such emulative activities.[6]

When the caste associations turned to the state for furthering their purposes, their initial claims were aimed at raising caste status in terms of the values and structure of the caste order. But as liberal and democratic ideas penetrated to wider sections of the population, the aims of the caste association began to shift accordingly. Instead of demanding temple entry and prestigious caste names and histories in the Census, the associations began to press for places in the new administrative and educational institutions and for political representation. Independence and the realization of political democracy intensified these new concerns. Caste associations attempted to have their members nominated for elective office, working through existing parties or forming their own; to maximize caste representation and influence in state cabinets and lesser governing bodies; and to use ministerial, legislative and administrative channels to press for action on caste objectives in the welfare, educational and economic realms. Perhaps the most significant aspect of the caste association in the contemporary era, however, is its capacity to organize the politically illiterate mass electorate, thus making possible in some measure the realization of its aspirations and educating large sections of it in the methods and values of political democracy.

The caste association is no longer a natural association in the sense in which caste was and is. It is beginning to take on features of the voluntary association. Membership in caste associations is *not* purely ascriptive; birth in the caste is a necessary but not a sufficient condition for membership. One must also "join" the (*Rajput*) *Kshatrya Mahasabha* or the (*Jat*) *Kisan Sabha* through some conscious act involving various degrees of identification—ranging from attendance at caste association meetings or voting for candidates supported by caste association leaders, to paying membership dues. The caste association has generally both a potential and an actual membership; when it speaks, it often claims to speak for the potential represented in the full caste membership. While the purposes of caste are wide-ranging and diffuse, affecting every aspect of members' life paths, the caste association has come to specialize in politics. The traditional authority and functions of the sub-caste are declining, but the caste association's concern with politics and its rewards serves to sustain caste loyalty and identification.[7] This loyalty and sense of identification tend to retain the exclusive quality of the natural association; the caste association seems to have a more complete and intense command of its members' commitments than is usually the case with voluntary associations.

Since modern means of transportation and communication have had the effect of broadening caste, binding together local sub-castes which had been relatively autonomous into geographically extended associations, caste associations today usually parallel administrative and political units—states, districts, sub-districts and towns—whose offices and powers of legislation or decision-making are the object of the caste associations' efforts.

Leadership in the caste association is no longer in the hands of those qualified by heredity—the senior or more able members of the lineage group which traditionally supplied village sub-caste leadership. The "availability" of association leaders is conditioned by their ability to articulate and represent the purposes of the caste association, and for this purpose they must be literate in the ways of the new democratic politics. Men whose educational and occupational backgrounds assure these skills have moved into the leadership positions. The new leaders stand in a more "accountable" and responsible relationship to their followers; their position depends to a great extent on their capacity to represent and make good the association's claims.

Finally, at the organizational level, the caste association is moving away from the latent structure of caste, towards the manifest structure characteristic of the voluntary association. It has offices, membership, incipient bureaucratization, publications, and a quasi-legislative process expressed through conferences, delegates and resolutions. On the other hand, the shared sense of culture, character, and status tends to create a solidarity of a much higher order than is usually found among voluntary associations where the multiplicity of social roles and the plurality of interests of its members tend to dilute the intensity of commitment and sense of identification.

The caste association brings political democracy to Indian villages through the familiar and accepted institution of caste. In the process, it is changing the meaning of caste. By creating conditions in which a caste's significance and power is beginning to depend on its numbers, rather than its ritual and social status, and by encouraging egalitarian aspirations among its members, the caste association is exerting a liberating influence.

Liberties in the west have a dual paternity. They arose on the one hand from an assertion of political philosophy which placed the reason and interests of the individual in a central position. On the other hand, they were the end-product of a historical process in which the rights and liberties of a variety of corporate groups and orders in traditional feudal society were gradually extended to ever-widening sections of the population until many rights and liberties became available to all. In India, as formerly in eighteenth century Europe, one attack on tradition and the old order came from the modern middle classes who succeeded in writing into the new nation's constitution the values of eighteenth century liberalism.[8] But the modern middle classes' attack constituted only one aspect, and a formal and impersonal aspect at that, of the challenge to the old order.

The other challenge has come from the caste association; its successful assertions of privilege and rights are in many ways comparable to the extension of corporate feudal liberties which characterized the development of English liberalism. They are perhaps more truly indigenous assertions of liberties than the liberalism of the modern Indian middle classes. Thus, for example, the *Shanans,* traditionally low caste southern tappers of palm-wine (toddy), asserted as early as 1858 that their women had a right to go about with an upper cloth, even though customary rules restricted such apparel to the higher castes. After a series of riots, the Maharaja of Travancore was persuaded to concede the claim: "We hereby proclaim that there is no objection to *Shanan* women either putting on a jacket like the Christian *Shanan* women, or to *Shanan* women of all creeds dressing in coarse cloth, and tying themselves round with it as the *Mukkavattigal* (Fisherwomen) do, or to covering their bosoms in any manner whatever, but not like women of higher castes." [9]

The caste's assertion, which could be multiplied many times with reference to other issues (such as extending the rights of temple entry to lower castes), exemplifies the caste association's liberating role. It also suggests that the corporate assertion of rights challenged the old order at points in which the "liberal" modern middle classes took rather little interest. Indian analyses of these developments have tended to attribute the entire credit for such victories to the state which concedes the right rather than to the group which agitates for it—a point of view which gravely underestimates the role of liberating forces within the old society.

The very considerable extent to which caste associations are performing a liberating function has been obscured by the fact that the modern Indian middle classes tend to see caste (in any form) as a part of the old order which they hope to destroy. That a new social and political force clad in the institutions of the old order is to an extent collaborating in this activity, that caste is in a sense anti-caste, appears to them incomprehensible. Because the caste association presses home the interests of its followers, it is also seen as pursuing a form of group selfishness which is deplored in the name of social duty and discipline. Finally, the caste association is condemned along with other interest groups of both the natural and voluntary variety, by those economic planners, civil servants and political ideologues who deduce policy from theories of economic development, conceptions of the public good and utopian visions of a new society. Such persons see the goals and interests pressed by caste associations and other groups as self-interested, confusing and partial. That the public good should in some measure be worked out from the interaction and accommodations of many group purposes is seen as morally degrading, intellectually unsatisfactory or aesthetically displeasing. For them, the political community includes only the state on the one hand and the citizen on the other, with the state having an exclusive (or at least primary) role in the formulation and execution of the public good. They fail to see that associations, both voluntary and natural, have a vital role to play in the exercise of political freedom through group self-government which contributes to the process of finding an approximation of the public good, provides a means for furthering group purposes independent of, as well as supplementary to, the state, and helps to protect the liberties of both associations and individuals.

None of this is meant to imply, however, that the caste association is an unqualified asset in Indian politics. Its tendency to place group loyalties above merit and competence, and caste patriotism above the public interest, runs counter to both liberal and democratic values and jeopardizes the effectiveness of the government's vital functions. In the final analysis, the meaning of the caste association in politics is ambiguous. Up to the present its role has been seriously misunderstood and its positive contribution neglected.

The caste association's main impact on politics within the Indian federal system is at the state level. Caste associations do not generally extend across state boundaries. Castes do not, as a rule, include persons of different linguistic-cultural backgrounds, and most Indian states today are organized on a linguistic-cultural basis.[10] The interest groups which seem to be most effective at the national level are voluntary associations (such as trade unions or chambers of commerce which have national constituencies) and natural associations like linguistic-cultural subnationalisms and religious communities.

At the state level, the strength of caste associations varies with the numbers that a particular association can attempt to mobilize, with the degree of self-consciousness and effectiveness of leadership, with the degree of internal cohesiveness, and with the power of countervailing interest-group forces. The balance of these factors has to be assessed separately in each state. Thus, in Rajasthan, a state which was formerly part of Princely India, the power of the *Jat* peasant caste, which constitutes 9 percent of the population of that state, may be explained by the particular constellation of all these factors. In part, the *Jats* profit from vigorous and effective leadership. The untouchable *Chamars* in the same state approach the *Jats* in numbers, but are relatively ineffectual politically because their level of self-consciousness and the quality of their leadership leave them for the moment merely a latent political force.[11] Among the organized castes, the *Rajputs* (a warrior caste) have served to check the power of the *Jats* by the lively activity of their association. The *Rajputs* are numerous, ranking fifth among castes in the state with 6 percent of population, very self-conscious politically, fairly well-led, and they still retain some of the authority of their traditional caste and class rank as *Kshatryas* (warrior rulers who constituted Rajasthan's monarchical-feudal order until 1947). But the *Rajput* caste association has not been able to exploit its full powers, in part because its internal cohesion suffered when *Rajputs* who were great feudal landholders and those who were petty landlords disagreed on the acceptability of the post-Independence land reforms.

The *Jats*, in addition to benefitting from these dissensions among the *Rajputs*, are also able to capitalize on the relative backwardness of the state. With very little industry or commerce and with a very high level of political illiteracy, neither voluntary associations nor other caste associations are particularly strong. In Bombay and Madras, which are more advanced economically and have higher levels of political literacy, the countervailing forces, both voluntary and natural, are considerably stronger. In addition then to the natural limitation to caste political power inherent in the fact that castes generally hold a minority status (at both the national and the state level) there are other possible checks—lack of cohesiveness, a low level of self-consciousness, ineffective leadership and the countervailing power of other caste associations or interest groups.[12]

The caste association differs from the other natural associations found in India—tribal, linguistic and religious—in its relationship to the political community, i.e., the nation-state. Tribal, religious and linguistic groups on the Indian scene represent *potential* political communities, which may claim (and often have claimed) a separate political identity, either in the form of a sovereign state or an autonomous unit in a federal system.[13] Caste, and its political expression, the caste association, have no such aspiration. Caste is a part of Hindu society; its meaning as a social institution is found in the values of Hindu culture. In this sense, all castes share a common culture, purpose and identity. The caste association is concerned with the distribution of values, status and rewards within a larger unit of action. It does not have a sense of nationality or aspire to separate political identity. It would be foolish, however, to suggest that such a development is out of the question. A caste like the Rajasthan *Jats*, with a tribal rather than an occupational caste origin, with a reasonably identifiable territorial base and a fairly recent (eighteenth century) political history, might conceivably develop such aspirations. However, so far there is no evidence of such a development.

One of the key means in Indian democratic politics for "brokering" and integrating diverse social forces is the political party; at present, it is the parties, particularly the Congress Party, that link together the caste associations which tend to play so vital a role in state politics. The relationship of caste to party (i.e., to the institutional means of political integration) has been markedly different from the relationship of other natural associations to party. Party has subsumed caste, acting as a broker for caste association interests and accommodating in some measure its demands for representation on party tickets. In relation to other types of natural associations, however, the party has often been subsumed by them. The most outstanding example of this appeared in Bombay where the Samyukta Maharashtra Samiti and the Maha Gujerat Parishad (associations of the two linguistic groups of the state) subsumed the parties to their larger "national" drives for political identity.[14] So long as a religious, linguistic or tribal drive for political identity is in full swing, the party has been harnessed to it. The lesson of states reorganization in India, from the demand for Andhra state onward, was that the demand for linguistic-cultural autonomy through some form of separate political identity could not be compromised or accommodated, nor could the demand for religious-cultural autonomy and identity, as the case of the Muslims and Sikhs clearly indicates.

In their relationship to parties, caste associations play a role more akin to voluntary interest-groups than do the other natural associations. They have specific program and personnel demands which can be accommodated at the levels of policy formation, "ticket balancing" in constituencies and in the cabinet, and legislation.

The Vanniyars, or Vanniya Kula Kshatryas, illustrate the development of caste associations. They are primarily a caste of agricultural laborers, but also include substantial numbers of cultivating owners and petty landlords in Madras state. They make up slightly less than 10 percent of the population of Madras, but in the four northern districts of the state (North Arcot, South Arcot, Chingleput and Salem) where they are concentrated, the caste constitutes about a fourth of the population.[15] As early as 1833, the Pallis, as they were then called, had ceased to accept their status as a humble agricultural caste and tried to procure a decree in Pondicherry that they were not a low caste.[15a] In anticipation of a census-taking in 1871, they petitioned to be classified as Kshatryas high-caste warrior-rulers)—a claim which found support in their traditional caste histories if not in their then low occupational status. Twenty years later the community had established seven schools for its members, and an enterprising Palli who had risen to the status of a High Court vakil (lawyer) had produced a book on the caste, which he followed with another some years later, supporting the caste's claim to be *Kshatryas* and connecting *Pallis* by descent with the great Pallava dynasty.[16] Oral histories simultaneously were stressing descent from the traditional "fire races," which *Kshatryas* both north and south often claim as ancestors. This attempt to press history into the service of social mobility, to counter current ritual and occupational definition of caste status by a historically derived definition, has been a quite frequent practice among rising castes.

By 1901 the *Pallis* had not won any battles but everyone was aware of their efforts. The Madras Census Commissioner noted that "they claim for themselves a position higher than that which Hindu society is inclined to accord them," and added that they were attempting to achieve this status via "a widespread organization engineered from Madras." [17] The organization's sporadic seventy-year activities to make *Pallis* conscious of their dignified and glorious history was bearing fruit. Instead of giving the old name, *Palli,* many were beginning to refer to themselves as *Agnikula Kshatryas* or *Vannikula Kshatryas* (i.e. *Kshatryas* of the fire race). The associations of the caste were spreading and becoming increasingly effective in various districts, enforcing a higher "sanskritized" standard of social conduct:

They have been closely bound together by an organization managed by one of their caste, who was a prominent person in these parts . . . and their *esprit de corps* is now surprisingly strong. They are tending gradually to approach the Brahmanical standard of social conduct, discouraging adult marriage, meat-eating, and widow remarriage. . . . In 1904 a document came before one of the courts which showed that in the year previous, the representatives of the caste in 34 villages in this district had bound themselves in writing, under penalty of excommunication to refrain (except with the consent of all parties) from the practices formerly in existence of marrying two wives, and of allowing a woman to marry again during the lifetime of her first husband.[18]

When these new caste associations turned to politics at the turn of the century, their main target was the census office, for its listing of caste and caste descriptions became more "real" than reality itself, carrying as it did the authority of official imprint. Mr. J. Chartres Moloney, of the Indian Civil Service, having survived the decennial onslaught of petitions from castes who wanted to be reclassified, remarked in the Census of 1911:

The last few years, and especially the occasion of the present census, have witnessed an extraordinary revival of the caste spirit in certain aspects. For numerous caste *sabhas* have emerged, each keen to assert the dignity of the social group which it represents.[19]

The rising castes continued to persuade their members to give a new name to the census enumerators, and to persuade the census commissioners to list this new name when the old one bore some odium. They also urged the census officers either to revise the description of traditional caste occupations, where these were thought undignified, or to drop them altogether. The Madras Census dropped caste occupations in 1921 as a result of these pressures.[20] The effectiveness of the *Pallis* in influencing the official recorders on the one hand and their own members on the other was considerable. By 1931 the *Pallis* had disappeared altogether from the Census, and only the *Vanniya Kula Kshatryas* remained.

The explicit organization of the *Vanniya Kula Kshatryas* in an association called the *Vanniya Kula Kshatrya Sangham* dates back at least thirty years in some districts, although the 1901 census commissioner indicated that some organizational stirrings were visible then, and the efforts of 1833 indicate even earlier (probably sporadic) activity. The *Vanniya Kula Kshatrya Sangham* of North Arcot District held its 34th annual conference in 1953, and the South Arcot *Sangham* held its tenth in 1954.[21] For the *Vanniya Kula Kshatrya Sangham*, the district unit was initially more important than the larger, Madras-wide organization which developed somewhat later. In 1952, the *Vanniya Kula Kshatryas* published a volume,[22] the introduction of which gave expression to the *sabha's* attempt to build a sense of caste patriotism and solidarity which would make it a more effective force:

> The Vanniya Kula Kshatryas who till now were proverbially considered to be backward in education have made long strides in a short space of time and have come almost on a level with other communities . . . the community has not realized its deserving status in society. . . . A cursory view of the book will show every reader how many a desirable fruit of the community was veiled by the leaves . . . (it) will stimulate the younger generation to greater deeds and will fill the hearts of the older with just pride in the achievements of the community. . . .[23]

That the *Sangham* still had some work ahead may be inferred from the fact that it listed 298 names, or about .01 percent of the community, as holders of degrees or diplomas.[24]

After the war, when the electorate was expanding but had not yet reached the adult suffrage proportions which came with the 1952 general elections, the *Vanniya Kula Kshatrya Sangham* began to press the Congress Party state ministry with two demands: it wanted the appointments to the civil services (which are based on competitive examinations and merit) to reflect the *Vanniyars'* percentage in the population, and it wanted Congress itself, through party nominations, to assure the election of *Vanniyars* on a population basis to all elected bodies—municipal corporations, district boards, and the state legislature. The request was Jacksonian in its optimism concerning the universal distribution of the capacity to hold office. But it was not altogether unreasonable in view of the constitutional, statutory and administrative provisions both at the central and the state levels, which are designed to give special consideration to scheduled castes (untouchables) and backward classes (usually low castes) in the public services and educational institutions, and the Congress' known disposition to give some special consideration in candidate selection to "depressed" elements in the population. It assumed also that the authority of caste no longer depended on traditional rank but rather on numbers in the context of democratic authority. However, the Congress ministry of Madras did not respond favorably to the *Vanniyar* demand, nor did the nominating bodies of the Congress party. From that time, the *Vanniyars* decided that they could rely only on themselves, dropped the attempt to work through the Congress or any other party, and began to contest for public office as independents.

Their first major electoral efforts were exerted in district board elections in the districts where their greatest strength lay. In fact, the district boards became one of their main targets, not only because they represented a convenient geographic unit within which caste influence could be maximized, but because the subjects falling under the competence of district boards, especially educational and medical facilities and road building, were of the greatest local and political interest. In 1949, the *Vanniyars* did well in the district elections, capturing, for example, 22 of the 52 seats in the South Arcot District Boards and defeating many Congress Party candidates. They almost succeeded in electing the President of the board.[25]

In 1951, with the prospect of the 1952 elections before them, the *Vanniyars* convened a major conference of the *Vanniya Kula Kshatrya Sangham* on a state-wide basis. The conference resolved that the *Vanniyars* should contest the elections "in cooperation with the toiling masses," and formed a political party called the Tamilnad Toilers' Party. The leading spirits in the conference were men with modern and cosmopolitan qualifications rather than hereditary and traditional ones. Two of the most significant were Mr. N. A. Manikkavelu Naicker, a lawyer with experience in earlier state-wide party activities, notably the Swarajya Party, and Mr. S. S. Ramaswami Padayachi, a young man (33 in 1951), a high school graduate, Chairman of the Cuddalore Municipal Council, member of the South Arcot District Board and the man who was narrowly defeated for its presidency in 1949.[26] The names of Padayachi and Naicker, especially the former, provided an effective signal for caste solidarity in voting. Padayachi's youth is an interesting commentary on leadership patterns in castes coming to political self-consciousness; older members of lower castes generally do not command the necessary skills in communication and education for state-wide organization.

Organizationally, the conference represented a capstone in the expansion of the association, since it mobilized the *Vanniyars* on a state-wide basis. It sought at once to centralize control and to bring about a proliferation of operating sub-units, working toward a more rationalized campaign organization which could mobilize the potential membership. Mr. Padayachi was elected Chairman of the Central Election Committee,

established to supervise *Vanniyar* candidate selections throughout the
state, and District Election Committees were established for twelve
districts.[27]

Subsequently, the unified state-wide effort represented by the conference broke down when the caste *sabhas* of North and South Arcot
districts, which had always rested on local loyalties, failed to agree. The
Tamilnad Toilers as a party remained strong in South Arcot and Salem
under Mr. Padayachi's guidance, while the North Arcot and Chingleput
Vanniyars rallied to a second caste party, the Commonweal Party, under
Mr. Naicker.

At election time, the caste *sabhas*-cum-parties utilized the older
village organization, mobilizing *Vanniyar* village leaders to assure solid
caste voting for one or the other party. This mobilization device was
effective because it defined the electoral issues in terms meaningful to an
unsophisticated electorate: government services, especially roads and
educational and medical services, could surely be more firmly secured for
poor *Vanniyars* if men familiar with their plight (i.e., other *Vanniyars*)
were elected to office. Watching Nehru speak to uncomprehending thousands, one might assume that there is an unbridgeable gap between the
ordinary Indian voter and his government, but observers watching
village election meetings, in which local caste headmen engage in running
debate with aspiring or incumbent legislators, cannot come to the same
conclusion. Common caste background is not essential to these exchanges
but the fact that candidate and village headman often share a common
caste culture provides a context in which discourse is natural and easy.

The Commonweal Party, representing the older caste *sabha* of North
Arcot and Chingleput, which had no program to speak of (much less an
ideology), won six seats in the state legislative assembly, while the
Tamilnad Toilers, speaking for the younger South Arcot *sabha* and stressing a more leftist socialist platform, captured 19. This gave the *Vanniyars*
25 of the 190 seats in the legislature of post-1953 Madras, or 13 percent
(though they numbered only 10 percent of the population).

In the same 1952 General Elections, the Congress Party failed to win
a majority in the Madras state legislature, and in its search for enough
legislative support to form a cabinet, persuaded the six Commonweal
Party members to support a Congress ministry, but it could not persuade
them to join the Congress. In return, Mr. Naicker, the Commonweal
leader, was given a seat in the Cabinet, an event which delighted many
Vanniyars but won him public catcalls from the Tamilnad Toilers, who
decided to remain in opposition.[28] Shortly thereafter, the Tamilnad Toilers
also opened "negotiations" with Congress, presumably to see what offices
might be offered in return for support.[29] The negotiations came to nothing
until 1954 when Mr. C. Rajagopalachari, a Brahman statesman with a
long and distinguished history in the nationalist movement, resigned as

Chief Minister and was replaced by the shrewd and competent but less cosmopolitan and lower caste Kamraj Nadar. He had made his reputation as chief of the Madras Congress Party over more than a decade, and belonged to a large and prosperous peasant caste.[30]

The Tamilnad Toilers decided to support Mr. Kamraj's ministry, and Mr. Padayachi joined the cabinet, consisting of eight persons. Mr. Naicker too remained in the Cabinet, so that the *Vanniyars* could now call two of eight cabinet seats their own. Mr. Padayachi reported to the press that he was happy to see that the Ministry was so much more representative of the backward classes than any previous one. With two ministers in the Cabinet and cordial relations with Congress assured, the Commonweal and the Tamilnad Toiler parties were dissolved, their members joining the Congress.[31]

The procedure followed by the *Vanniyars* is not unusual. In Rajasthan, the (*Rajput*) *Kshatrya Mahasabha* pursued an almost identical tactic in 1952, campaigning successfully for the legislature, extracting not cabinet offices but concessions on land-reform from Congress, and then joining the party, which needed members to strengthen its very precarious majority. The *Jat* caste *sabhas* in Rajasthan very nearly did the same when many members in 1950 considered converting the Rajasthan branch of the *Krishikar Lok* Party into a *Jat* branch. But the *Jats*, with politically literate leaders and a self-conscious and effectively mobilized following, saw the expediency of infiltrating the weak Rajasthan Congress, gave up the idea of a separate party, and contested the elections for the most part under the Congress Party label.

Throughout this period, both before and after the dissolution of the two caste parties, the demands of the *Vanniya Kula Kshatrya Sangham* continued to find active expression. The *Sangham* had three primary objectives. The first was educational services. What was at stake were scholarships which might allow a village student to pay for room at the hostel of a distant secondary institution, fee concessions at institutions which still charged tuition, and reservation of seats for *Vanniyars* in institutions of higher learning. The second objective was places in the civil service; these conferred status as well as a job. The third was winning Congress "tickets" (i.e., nominations) for seats in lower governing boards as well as in the legislature and places in the cabinet. The *Sangham* was also interested in various economic services affecting *Vanniyars*. That they could hope for government help in several respects was clear from the fact that they had been officially classified as a Backward Class, that is, a caste above the Untouchable level but one whose status and condition was nevertheless so weak that it deserved special consideration under the policy of "progressive discrimination" which has been a central feature of Indian social policy.[32]

The way these demands were pursued and the responses of the two ministers to them is apparent from the proceedings of *Sangham* meetings and conferences. Shortly after his appointment in 1954, Mr. Padayachi explained to a *Sangham* conference why he had joined the Kamraj ministry when he had not joined the earlier one of Mr. Rajagopalachari. The *Vanniyars'* demands for educational facilities and representation in the civil services had not been met by the Rajagopalachari ministry, he said, and implied that he expected a more generous attitude from the Kamraj ministry.[33] At a North Arcot conference in 1955, he could report that the government had been doing its best to give school fee concessions, scholarships and employment preference to the *Vanniya Kula Kshatryas*.[34] At that time, 5 out of every 20 seats in the state civil service were reserved for "qualified candidates of the backward classes," in addition to the reservations for scheduled castes and tribes. These reservations were established by administrative order in cooperation with the Public Service Commission. (Unfortunately no figures are available on whether enough "qualified" candidates were found to fill these posts—formal reservation and actual seats filled by members of backward classes have by no means always coincided.) [35] In any case, Mr. Padayachi apparently kept an eye on the situation, and presumably his and Mr. Naicker's views on how this difficult problem might be handled were always available to the government. The frequency with which both men reported to *Vanniyar* meetings indicates that they considered themselves to some extent special agents of *Vanniyar* interests; drawing a line between this role and their role as cabinet members responsible for the formulation and administration of public policy is of course difficult.

The quality of the *Sangham's* economic demands is illustrated by another North Arcot conference, addressed by Mr. Naicker in 1953. The resolutions present a striking illustration of the fact that the *Vanniya Kula Kshatrya Sangham* operated as an economic interest group—one might expect similar resolutions from western farm groups in the U.S. They urged better irrigation in North Arcot district; electricity for agricultural areas; better roads; expansion of the Krishna Pennar multi-purpose water project; relief to tenants for rain failure; and (recalling the fact that many *Vanniyars* were tenants and laborers) making tillers owners of the soil.[36]

Negotiations with the Congress concerning the number of nominations which would be given to the *Vanniyars* in local board elections became very lively late in 1954, just before the District Board elections. One result of the negotiations concerning seats in North Arcot was the promise, given by the officers of the state Congress Party, that once the District Board was elected, it would choose a *Vanniyar* chairman. This promise came in response to *Vanniyar* pressure to extend to District Boards the principle of "communal rotation" in the selection of officers, a principle which has long been recognized in the Madras Municipal Corporation Presidency. In this case, the promise caught the state party in a difficult situation: the non-*Vanniyar* Congress Party members of the North Arcot District Board, many of whom belonged to the higher caste of *Reddiars,* saw no reason why they should be bound at the district level by negotiations carried on by the state party with the *Vanniyars.* They accordingly decided not to vote for a *Vanniyar,* and elected a *Reddiar* president, in cooperation with non-Congress members of the board. The Madras Congress Party, knowing that they might not be able to count on *Vanniyar* support in the general elections in 1957 if they did not keep faith with the *Vanniyars,* took strict disciplinary action and suspended a number of the recalcitrant *Reddiar* members from the party. According to the newspaper report:

> Sri Karayalar (President of the state Congress organization) said that indiscipline in Congress ranks should not be tolerated as it would weaken the organization. . . . In the North Arcot case, Sri Karayalar said, the idea was that the Presidentship this time should go to a member of the Vanniyar community as in South Arcot. All along the Reddiars had been presidents there. The Vanniyar community had supported the Congress in the Board elections and the understanding all along had been that the Congress nominee for the Presidentship should be a member of the Vanniyar community. . . .[37]

Throughout this period, the *Sangham's* organizational structure was being elaborated and expanded. Local branches sprang up in many places, often at the level of smaller administrative units such as *taluks* (districts) and towns. Usually one of the ministers graced the occasion with his presence.[38] At all these sessions, the ministers and others sought to strengthen the *Sangham's* solidarity, to increase the sense of unity and of mission. Mr. Padayachi reminded a conference that his ministership was the result of the united efforts and sacrifices of the community over a long period, and the caste flag was ceremonially unfurled at the 34th annual conference of the *Sangham* at North Arcot.

It is clear that today the *Vanniya Kula Kshatrya Sangham* plays an important role in Madras politics. Village subcastes persist, but their relative role in the new democratic culture is gradually declining. It is the caste associations (*sabhas* or *sanghams*) which have given caste a new vitality, and it is political democracy which has transformed caste and enabled it to play its paradoxical role in India today. Rather than providing the basis for a reaction, caste has absorbed and synthesized some of the new democratic values. Ironically, it is the caste association which links the mass electorate to the new democratic political processes and makes them comprehensible in traditional terms to a population still largely politically illiterate. Caste has been able to play this curious political role as bearer of both India's *ancien régime* and its democratic political revolution by reconstituting itself into the *sabha,* with characteristics of both the natural and the voluntary association, of caste defined in terms of both *dharma* and democracy.

NOTES

1. Not even the *Jan Sangh*, strongest of the right-wing parties, espouses such a program. It is much more a rightist radical party than a traditionalist one.

2. Alternative status systems which parallel that of caste are also visible in contemporary India. See for example S. C. Dube, *Indian Village*, London, 1956, pp. 161–6; see also our discussion of aspects of this problem in "Indian Political Studies and the Scope of Comparative Politics," *Far Eastern Survey* (XXVII) No. 9, September 1959, pp. 134–8, where articles by Sushil Dey, Baij Nath Singh, Evelyn Wood, John T. Hitchcock, Henry Orenstein, Alan Beal and Edward B. and Louise G. Harper are analyzed. These articles appear in Richard L. Park and Irene Tinker, eds., *Leadership and Political Institutions in India*, Princeton, 1959.

3. Occupational heterogeneity of castes is already well advanced, however, in towns and urban areas. The materials of the older caste ethnographers indicate that the breakdown of social and occupational homogeneity was apparent in the nineteenth century. Both Edgar Thurston, in his *Castes and Tribes of Southern India*, Madras, 1909, and William Crooke in his *The Tribes and Castes of the North West Provinces and Oudh*, Calcutta, 1896, bear this out.

4. See M. N. Srinivas' articles bearing on the issues raised here: "A Note on Sanskritization and Westernization," *Far Eastern Quarterly* (XV), August 1956; "Caste in Modern India," *Journal of Asian Studies* (XVI), August 1957.

5. It may be that "sanskritization," while also practiced in the North, may offer less compelling emulation patterns there than in the South because of the strength of *Kshatrya* norms in many areas.

6. The caste association has not been alone in this type of activity. More parochial village caste groups have also pursued emulation as a vehicle for improving status, sometimes successfully. See for example the progress of the Boad Distillers, in F. G. Bailey, *Caste and the Economic Frontier*, Manchester, 1957. But McKim Marriott has pointed out that any caste group operating in an intimate local setting, where relative status positions are well understood and jealously protected, might have trouble advancing itself by emulation: "A mere brandishing of Brahmanical symbols by a well-known village group can scarcely hope to impress a village audience in its own parochial terms. . . ." See his "Interactional and Attributional Theories of Caste Ranking," *Man in India* (39), April–June, 1959. Conversely, the caste association, operating in the wider, more impersonal setting of a district or a state, may encounter less resistance to its emulative claims because in the wider setting there is no clear standard for assessing its "true" position.

7. For confirmation of these and other points, see also Selig Harrison, "Caste and the Andhra Communists," *American Political Science Review* (L), June 1956; M. L. P. Patterson, "Caste and Politics in Maharashtra," *Economic Weekly*, (VIII) 29, July 21, 1956.

8. They also included the often conflicting values of popular sovereignty and political democracy and the "socialist" goals of economic and social justice.

9. Edgar Thurston, *Castes and Tribes, op. cit.*, Vol. VI, p. 365.

10. Bombay and Punjab are exceptions. Castes with approximately similar origins do exist in different states. *Jats* live in the Punjab, Uttar Pradesh and Rajasthan. But inter-state organization is weak both in caste structure and in the caste associations.

11. The *Chamars* profit from the reservation of seats for untouchables in the Rajasthan legislative assembly; but even this crutch is not enough to make them influential in the absence of able leadership.

12. Of course India's constitutional structure, including the party system, also plays a crucial role. Space limitations prevent an exploration of this facet of the problem.

13. Many religious groups (the Christians and the post-Independence Muslims) and many tribal groups (the Bhils for example) have not in fact posed such problems of integration. But others have, at various levels: the pre-Independence Muslims sought and found their political identity in the nation-state of Pakistan; the various Indian linguistic groups successfully pressed for a political identity and some measure of autonomy within the federal system; the Naga tribes rebelled in an effort to gain some form of political identity; and the Sikhs found a measure of political identity in the compromise achieved in the Punjab legislature whereby two intra-state Regional Committees with broad recommendatory powers were established for Sikh and Hindu legislators respectively. See Joan V. Bondurant, *Regionalism versus Provincialism*, Berkeley, 1958, pp. 114–124.

14. See Marshall Windmiller, "The Politics of States Reorganization in India: The Case of Bombay," *Far Eastern Survey* (XXV), No. 9, September 1956, pp. 129–143; and Phillips Talbot, "The Second General Elections: Voting in the States," American Universities Field Staff, New York, 1957 (India, PT-6-1957).

15. These figures are necessarily tentative because they are based on the 1931 census, the last Indian census to enumerate caste. At that time, the *Vanniyars* numbered 2,944,014 and almost all of the *Vanniyars* were located in those parts of Madras which remained with the state after Andhra was detached in 1953. Presumably the *Vanniyar* population has increased substantially since then, at a rate not too different from the average population increase. In Chingleput, North Arcot, Salem and South Arcot there were 2,349,920 *Vanniyars* in 1931 in a total population for these districts of 8,810,-583. See *Census of India*, 1931, Vol. XIV, Madras, Part II, Imperial and Provincial Tables.

15a. On this and some of the material which follows, see Thurston, *op. cit.*, Vol. VI, pp. 1–28.

16. T. Ayakannu Nayakar, *Vannikula Vilakkam: a Treatise on the Vanniya Caste*, 1891, and *Varuna Darpanam* (Mirror of Castes), 1901.

17. *Census of India*, 1901, Madras, Part I, Report, p. 171.

18. W. Francis in *Gazetteer of South Arcot District*. Cited in Thurston, *op. cit.*, Vol. VI, p. 12.

19. *Census of India*, 1911, Madras, Part I, Report, p. 178.

20. *Ibid.*, Vol. XIII. This successful agitation reflected the fact that some castes were abandoning the traditional occupations. They presumably felt that

from a descriptive point of view this fact deserved recognition. Even where the caste still kept to its traditional tasks, the census description (i.e., "*Shanars* are oil pressers.") carried a normative implication. From the point of view of mobile castes, the census looked like a new agency for sacred classification, an impression hardly alleviated by the fact that Brahmans, the traditional compilers of sacred classifications, tended to dominate the Indian cadres in the bureaucracy. In a society in flux, the problem of maintaining "objective" official social records becomes particularly difficult.

21. *Hindu* (Madras), June 18, 1953; *Mail* (Madras), June 21, 1954.

22. *Graduates and Diploma Holders among the Vanniya Kula Kshatrya*, Triplicane, Madras, 1952.

23. *Ibid.* Introduction.

24. A diploma holder is about the equivalent of an American high school graduate, while a graduate is one who has finished college. It is probably safe to assume that most of those listed were diploma holders rather than graduates.

25. See interview with S. S. Ramaswami Padayachi, a prominent *Vanniyar* leader, in *Mail,* April 27, 1954.

26. *Mail,* April 13, 1954; *Indian Express* (Madras) April 14, 1954.

27. *Mail,* October 13, 1951.

28. *Indian Express* and *The Hindu,* May 13, 1952.

29. *Mail,* October 21, 1952.

30. The *Nadars* were formerly called *Shanans* and were once oil pressers. See Thurston, *op. cit.,* Vol. VI, pp. 363–378. Their caste *sabha* was influential in getting the old, odious name replaced (in 1921). They persuaded the census authorities to drop traditional caste descriptions, since many had moved out of oil-pressing, which had low status repute, into agricultural, commercial and financial pursuits. Mr. Nadar's strength is based on a combination of long service with the nationalist movement and on the faith which lower castes repose in him as "one of them."

31. *Mail,* July 30, 1956. The parties were in fact dissolved before 1956. At that time, the election commission merely recognized their dissolution officially.

32. Progressive discrimination, especially in the services, was already a policy of the old Justice Party governments in pre-Independence Madras.

33. *Indian Express,* April 28, 1954; *Mail,* May 30, 1954.

34. *Mail,* January 5, 1955.

35. See Government of India, *Report of the Backward Classes Commission* (3 Vols.), Delhi, 1955, especially Vol. 1, p. 131.

36. *Hindu,* June 18, 1953.

37. *Mail,* November 20, 1954.

38. Thus, the first conference of the North Madras *Vanniya Kula Kshatrya Sangham,* the conference of the Uttiramerur sub-*taluk Sangham,* the tenth annual meeting of the South Arcot *Sangham,* the second annual conference at Perambur, and a conference at Ayyumpet. See *Hindu,* May 23, 1955; *Mail,* June 21, 1954, and January 10, 1956; *Indian Express,* July 23, 1956.

VII

Changing Religious Institutions:
Links to Nationalism

R. Bastide

MESSIANISM AND SOCIAL
AND ECONOMIC DEVELOPMENT (1961)

It is fashionable these days to examine the question of relationships between religion (or religions) and the development of underdeveloped countries (or between religion and the type of government to be found in these countries: e.g., democratic, socialist). The problem has given rise in recent years to numerous studies by the World Council of Churches and, even more recently, to a United Nations debate in UNESCO. The question cannot be scientifically resolved by starting with a definition of religion, which is something necessarily subjective, even were we to try to do so by setting aside all the difficulties inherent in the notion of "development," a concept so laden with different value judgments and ethnocentrism that we long for the much more scientific concept of acculturation. All that the sociologist can hope to do is to examine the various kinds of correlations that have been established *de facto* between any given religious phenomenon and a given form of social development. And this is no easy matter since the correlations vary according to the global situations within which they occur, and because the situations themselves are modified with the passing of time. What we propose to do in this article (in a manner doubtless somewhat schematic) is to discover and analyze, with respect to the facts of messianism, one of these correlations or, more precisely, to set forth the general outline of a method capable of serving as a basis for this type of research.

In talking about messianism (or as it is preferably called nowadays, milleniarianism), we intend to speak only of colonial messianism. But its study is all the more interesting since it will enable us to make a fruitful comparison thereafter with the historical forms of messianism and thus

SOURCE. R. Bastide, "Messianisme et Développement Économique et Social," reprinted from *Cahiers internationaux de sociologie*, XXXI, 1961, pp. 3–14, by permission of the Presses Universitaires de France.

allow us to evaluate certain hypotheses of Marx, Engels, and their disciples, who hesitate between two concepts. On the one hand, they have justified messianism as the only possible form of resistance, given the structure of agriculture production, and they credit it with allowing exploited groups to become fully aware for the first time of those who were exploiting them. Yet on the other hand, Marxists have also condemned messianism as a force diverting the energies for resistance among exploited groups by turning them away from the arena of the material struggle and shunting them off into a region of religious myths, thereby delaying the rise of a class struggle as the exploited population becomes mired down in a morass of theological doctrines. These two concepts, moreover, are not necessarily contradictory. Indeed, they may well be complementary. However, we shall not undertake to analyze the confrontation between historical facts and the facts of ethnography. Is it true, as some maintain, that messianism does not occur among peoples who live by hunting and gathering and is found only in conjunction with the appearance of agriculture? An inquiry into this question would lead us too far afield. It would entail a discussion of specific cases, such as that of the Guaranis whose messianism antedates the colonial era and is therefore beyond the scope of our subject as we have just defined it. But even so, we believe there will appear, in the wake of our discussion, a certain number of possibilities for comparison between Marxist concepts and colonial messianisms. The reader will easily discover them for himself.

Before undertaking our own appraisal of the problem of relationships between messianism and development, we must first of all recall briefly the progress of informed opinion in this matter. Messianism was originally considered a pathological phenomenon. Not only did observers stress such manifestations as visions, trances, and anything else that might cause one to regard its leaders merely as persons mentally and emotionally unbalanced, but they also emphasized the consequences resulting from milleniaristic or messianic preaching: bloody revolts, collective suicides, and what appeared to be wild dreams and imaginings. The fact is that these early studies were the work of missionaries, colonial administrators, and doctors rather than of anthropologists or sociologists. Messianism was defined as a caricature of Christianity, a Christianity defined in turn as the best means of Westernizing a colonial population (see, for example, the conclusion of R. Allier's book on *La psychologie de la conversion*)—or else messianism was defined as a religious syncretism combining Christian and pagan elements, thereby effecting a return to a primitive mentality with detrimental results to one's intellectual development, the latter defined as the Westernizing of underdeveloped peoples. Administrators saw in messianism a refusal or an inability on the part of the natives to integrate into new and more productive forms of economy, a refusal to become creators of wealth. And lastly, doctors denounced the existence of sick groups as a danger to the mental health of the entire population, a view fashionable at that time in the field of psychiatry.

But during recent years a radical change has come about simply as a result of a change in perspective, by identifying oneself not with the colonialist's point of view, but with the point of view of the colonized population. The attempt has been made to understand the latter's motivations and to examine the effects of messianic movements on the colonial régime itself. The name of Balandier is associated in France with this new outlook. His books and articles on the Bakongo situation have shed light on the role of messianism as a form of resistance to the domination and exploitation of colonial peoples by the colonial powers when the road to political resistance is blocked and there remains only the religious channel in which to express opposition to the régime. He shows us how messianism, by reorienting individuals from their ancient allegiance to clans (which are crushed and destroyed by colonialism) into an adherence to a particular religious faith, has laid the groundwork for nationalism, inaugurated a new kind of social order, and restructured a disintegrated society. Accordingly, Balandier has seen in messianism not what was previously noted—mental derangement and the effects of a disordered imagination. Instead, he has perceived a response—and an adequate response—to a very real situation. Analogous ideas can be found with respect to other messianic movements in other parts of the world. Fred Vogt speaks of movements of adaptations to new stimuli produced by the whites, and A. Wallace speaks of the adjustment of ancient values to new requirements. Certainly, as Worsley says regarding the Cargo cult, the Dead do come back. Their early return as saviors is awaited, but they do not come back as Papuans. They return as White Men, that is to say, with the skills, knowledge, and power of the Whites. Consequently, this cult is not simply an expression of traumatisms; it is an effort to find a solution to new needs and demands: how to benefit from the desirable goods and skills of Europeans while at the same time escaping from European control? And no doubt in this kind of solution native myths are utilized, like those of the culture Hero or the land of one's Ancestors, but then we do the same thing. We, too, use ancient experiences to solve new problems that arise. In all these theories then, messianism clearly appears as something essentially rational rather than irrational. It reflects a reasoned judgment and interpretation following paths comparable to those of Western thought. Messianism is a theory based on real facts, clearly understood by everyone, and in terms of which certain rules of action and behavior are formulated.

Even in the domain of religious life, changes in points of view are slowly beginning to develop. Lanternari, for instance, discerns in colonial messianism not what was seen previously, a caricature of Christianity, but contrary to Christianity, a logical application of religion to indigenous societies. Christianity in effect brings to people, who think in terms of "We" rather than "I," a condemnation of the "We" concept. Seen from this angle, messianism is an attempt to redeem native culture (which explains the importance given to the struggle against "fetishes"), for a Black does not conceive of saving Man without saving his Culture, since man in his society is always integrated into a culture, and he cannot visualize himself without that culture. The result is that, fundamentally, the members of an indigenous population, who know no other kind of social life than the communal type, have a better understanding of the Christian solution for their problems than European missionaries who come from individualistic societies.

This reaction by contemporary sociologists and anthropologists has been a salutary one. It has exposed the positive side of messianism which was previously overlooked. Their conclusions may be summed up as follows: messianic or millenarian movements are not so much movements of retreat and escape into the imaginary as they are bonafide attempts at a rational solution for problems posed by contact with the whites. They are doubtless syncretistic movements, but this syncretism should be regarded less as a bastardizing of European elements, lost in the flux of traditional elements originating in a remote past, than as an initial movement toward acculturation, toward an acceptance of new values. They are the elements of changing mentalities, of Westernization that are revealed in this new conception of messianism. Prophetism, messianism, and millenarianism are indeed actions causing a rupture in the social fabric, but they are not merely a rupture with European society. They also reflect a sharp break, and even more so, with traditional society. In the last analysis what is rejected from Europe is not the many new and desirable things European cultures have introduced, but only, for the most part, the system within which these contributions have been made, namely, the colonial system. We must add that this new conception does not minimize the emotional and traumatic elements which characterize messianism, but there is discernible among certain anthropologists a curious tendency to give these traumatic manifestations secondary consideration. They see them more in terms of a social break with ancient traditions than in the destructuration produced by a culture clash. The new order arising from the ruins of the old one demands a clean break with the old rules of exogamy, and the prophets of the new order, like magicians in certain societies, must first violate the taboo of incest, an act that produces guilt complexes with all their traumatic consequences.

Despite its brevity, the foregoing résumé is, we believe, sufficient to indicate our point of view as expressed in this article (a view concerning correlations between messianism and social and economic development), namely, that messianism, far from being a hindrance to the advancement of peoples in under-developed countries, is, on the contrary, a crisis of growth. And at the same time that it represents an initial awakening, a conscious awareness on the part of pariah groups, as Max Weber has written, and is a first manifestation of a refusal to accept colonialism (a fact that has been especially emphasized). Messianism also represents a first step in the direction of social change and an acceptance of new economic and social values. But have we not tended to underestimate the negative features of this kind of reaction, however justified and necessary the movement may be? Have we not tended to gloss over its negative side? We must consider that possibility.

In this connection a few preliminary remarks are necessary. The question of relationships between the positive and negative factors in the development of messianism certainly does not lend itself to any single general solution. There are bases for distinguishing between colonial messianism (a "folk" messianism) and urban messianism (which is a response to industrialization, to the formation of a proletariat, or to the proletarianization of certain sectors of the middle classes). "Folk" messianism appears as a violent reaction to change imposed from without and is aimed at maintaining the status quo, whether it be the reaction of the civilization of the Brazilian *sertão* against the civilization of the coastal areas, the monarchical and Catholic *sertão* against the republican and secular society along the coast (Euclides da Cunha), or whether it is the reaction of the *Contestado*, the form of resistance taken by popular and "*folkloric*" Catholicism against Roman and urban Catholicism (Maria Isaura P. de Queiroz). In every instance "folk" messianism was opposed to social change, either preventing it or retarding it. Urban messianism (whether of the Western variety so familiar to us in France from the works of H. Desroche, or whether it is the black messianism among former slaves in North America) presents positive factors of change, of original and constructive solutions in response to economic difficulties, poverty, the breakdown of early capitalistic societies, or economic depression. And for that reason it has even been compared with utopian socialism. But by allowing this development of a privileged group as a group of the "chosen few" who cut themselves off from the rest of the world (which they define as the domain of Satan), the positive elements in the movement were rendered incapable of becoming the leaven of a new society. Accordingly, it should be understood that our observations about colonial messianism are not to be generalized and applied indiscriminately to other forms of messianism.

Colonial messianism itself appears in a thousand different forms. Attempts have been made to reduce them to a few specific types, but it seems to us that these alleged types are very often only historical moments in messianic development with the result that any given moment can be classified in such and such a category, depending on what stage it happens to have reached in the course of its evolution. Not that colonial messianism fails to offer a collection of general facts that serve to define and characterize it by comparison with other forms of messianism, but these general facts acquire specific and different characteristics as they develop within social structures, characteristics that vary from one ethnic group to another as different mythologies are drawn upon by the various ethnic groups. If, as we have said, this messianism (or millenarianism) is a response to a contact situation, then this response will necessarily vary with the nature of the contact, and we know how frequently colonial policies have changed. Consequently, the problem of correlating messianism with a country's economic and social development does not offer a common, single solution. The problem must be the subject of as many studies as there are instances of messianism. To limit myself to two illustrations: in the former French Congo the Matswaist Church of Kinzonzi continues the same policy of conducting strikes against the independent and native government of the country as it did against the French colonial government, just as if independence had never been granted (the Kinzonzi use the pretext that this independence was not the work of the Messiah, and for very good reason, since he was dead). The Matswaist Church rejects census-taking, the payment of taxes, and hospital care for medical cases. The Congolese government has therefore been obliged to take measures against its adherents in much the same manner as the former colonial government had done: arrests and imprisonments. On the other hand, in the New Hebrides the messianic movement was transformed into a progressive political party. The dream of a return of the Dead Ones was not abandoned, but their return has been projected into such a distant future that it offers no obstacle to initiating reforms, and unlike the situation in the Congo, millenarianism in this instance is a positive factor at the present time with respect to the economic and social development of the country.

And lastly, messianisms (or millenarianisms) evolve as conditions evolve and constitute an adaptation to the changing situation with the result that the positive or negative factors in messianic development vary according to the particular moment in time that one chooses to examine the phenomenon.

The reaction in defense of messianism, which has characterized sociological thought these past ten years (the principal arguments for which we have already summarized), corresponds in our judgment to a particular moment in scientific thought, the moment of "decolonization." It is quite clear that this reaction was justified at the time, for messianism was the first truly effective form of resistance to colonialism and the first conscious manifestation of nationalism, however veiled in appearance. There was a need, therefore, to emphasize the positive factors in its development, the creative dynamics in the dreams and imaginings of the

millenarians. But with the process of decolonization now under way, the
question has arisen whether that which was true of the movement would
continue to be so. Would not its negative features—previously unnoticed
or scarcely discernible—reappear at this juncture in the history of underdeveloped peoples and reassert their preponderance over its positive
features? Without entering here into a critique of the concept of development which would lead us too far afield, we must note that there is a
return at the present time to a stage similar to the one that marked the
beginning of colonialism, and that science, the servant of society's needs
(whether capitalist or Communist), is returning to her ancient doctrines.
In the United States, as in Russia, evolutionism is reappearing and shov-
ing aside all theses of cultural relativism that might gravely risk interfer-
ing with the general desire for exploitation of the earth's resources and
for an accelerated rate of industrial productivity. The evolutionist viewpoint has restored to favor the notion of a progress oriented along the
lines of Western values. This return to evolutionism (which was once
emphatically condemned), even if forced to appear under different guises
in order to gain scientific adherence, could furnish an excellent illustration for the sociology of knowledge. In effect, the return to evolutionism
is an imposition on our thinking caused by a collective or international
desire for (social and economic) development. It constitutes the rational
justification for such development and, to some extent, suggest its theory.
But with this return of evolutionism, it is quite probable that we will also
witness a return to the condemnation of messianism, using the same arguments and the same reasons that were advanced at the outset of colonialism. Messianism is likely to be denounced as a roadblock to progress,
as an obstacle to the birth of a new mentality, as a resistance to change
and development. An examination of the negative factors of messianism
which we claim to present will not, so to speak, repudiate the thesis which
set forth and emphasized its positive aspects, for both the positive and
negative appear alternately, depending on the particular moment in question. Messianism cannot be studied and judged *sub specie aeternitatis,*
but only in terms of historical circumstances.

These preliminary remarks have enabled us to realize the importance
of precautions that must be taken when wishing to establish correlations
between the facts of messianism and those of social and economic development. It is necessary to take into account the originality of each
movement as well as the situation and the moment in time in which the
phenomenon operates. But in a brief article such as this we cannot follow
each movement, one after the other. We must limit ourselves to general
considerations and underscore certain negative factors which threaten to
play a greater role as colonialism disappears.

Economic and social development presupposes a mentality that we
might call Promethean (to use the happy expression of G. Gurvitch). In

using this term we are thinking not so much of the idea of sacrilege (for primitive societies have a place in their culture for sacrilege), or of man's struggle against nature, but rather of man's perpetual state of dissatisfaction in the face of results already achieved and of his desire to push ever farther into the unknown. In short, we have in mind the feeling that history is never at an end, that there are no limits to the future, and that the latter is eternally open to new conquests. Messianism does indeed reflect an initial awareness of history, but it is the awareness of a closed and finite history. If we define the mythical thinking, so important among underdeveloped peoples, as an archetypal and cyclical kind of thinking (with M. Eliade, for example), one that consequently imposes a repetition of the same gestures and rigid types of behavior, then messianism represents in many respects a definite break with this kind of thinking. But it is merely the substitution of a long cycle for shorter ones. The cyclical factor remains. The contact between indigenous populations and the white man produced such a state of social instability that traditional creeds and rituals were found incapable of reestablishing the former social equilibrium. The need arose to invent new gestures, new rites and ceremonies, in order to escape from social chaos. It was necessary to re-create the world once again. That is why messianism abandons the short cycle which, year after year, repeats the myths of one's origins.

But in order to extricate oneself from the horrible chaos into which white men had plunged the traditional social order, what better way to accomplish this than by appealing to the very ones who had formerly created this traditional order—Ancestors and cultural Heroes? The ritual to be announced by the Prophet will have as its purpose the recalling of one's Ancestors or heroes as Messiahs, or as restorers of the Golden Age. And that is why if the short, annual cycle is abandoned, it is for the purpose of replacing it at once with a longer cycle—and not for the purpose of introducing a linear view of history. Since creation can only be a re-creation, human effort is to be diverted from the task of producing goods or saving money, the essential prerequisites of any economic development. Messianic movements appear as movements for the consumption and destruction of goods, flocks, and harvests, not as movements for the accumulation of wealth. And human effort is also diverted from social development, whether the latter is seen as the establishment of a democratic or Communist régime, or as the creation of a new Third World type of régime. This is because in a long cycle, just as in a short one, the model to be emulated is provided by the past (even if this past is borrowed from Western culture, as in the case where indigenous messianism is based on the Bible, the movement is not forward-looking). The positive elements from the standpoint of social and economic development—the break with the short cycle, the first steps in acquiring a sense of history, the need for a collective effort to create new responses and behavior patterns—all these elements, which come into play at a given moment, cease being effective to the extent that the cyclical mentality is not broken in favor of the Promethean outlook.

Much has been made of the syncretistic nature of colonial messianism. And by syncretism we do not mean here (simply) material syncretism, the admixture, for example, of Christian elements with traditional elements. We are thinking rather of what we propose to call "formal" acculturation, that is to say, an acculturation that affects the very structures of the mind and the emotions. In effect, messianic syncretism is seen as a mélange of the traditional mentality (magic thinking) and the Western mentality (observation and the formulating of hypotheses). Early missionaries who spoke of a caricature of Christianity, like former colonial administrators who spoke of collective insanity, were looking only for the vestiges of traditional thinking, for the remnants of a native paganism. On the other hand, the reaction which occurred at a later date emphasized the new features to be found, the intellectual changes, and the rational aspects of messianism. But in neither instance must we forget that messianism is syncretistic, and that consequently, it contains aspects simultaneously favorable and unfavorable to the possible development of underdeveloped countries. If manipulated from the outside by intelligent leaders who convert the movement, for instance, into a political party, messianism can become a form of apprenticeship to new ways of thinking and acting on the part of the masses. But if allowed to develop without direction of any kind, or if the movement is persecuted and repressed, the result will be a greater preoccupation with magic thinking, and with the fantasies of a dream world at the expense of useful human endeavor. Instruction and awakening of the mind or its stultification? We see today messianic movements that are hesitating between these two tendencies which syncretism had, for a moment, brought into harmonious balance. Will Amerindian messianism, for instance, having gone beyond the stage of the Ghost Dance, lose itself in the cult of the imaginary with Peyotism, or will it give birth to pan-Indianism with the Church of Oklahoma? Will Bakongo messianism join other sects in seeking a more potent magic than that of ancestor worship, or will it retain its dynamism along with some of its other sects, a dynamism formerly directed against the European occupation and one that can now be directed against that heritage of colonialism, the arbitrary frontiers between the former Belgian and French Congos and Angola, for the purpose of changing the political map of Africa?

There is a third fact which emerges from almost every recent study made on the subject of messianism, namely, the transition from a movement to a religious sect. Now the characteristic feature of a sect is its detachment from the rest of the world and its ultra-conservatism, its resistance to change. By virtue of its own duration, messianism passes from revolution to conservatism. Under these circumstances there is reason to fear that the same qualities which were positive at a given moment in history will cease to be so at another moment. The revolt, which proved useful against the colonial régime and helped in winning independence for the country, represents a threat to order itself when it becomes crystallized and rigid after independence has been achieved. We have seen this in the case of the Church of Kinzonzi. In a Congo now become independent, this church maintains watchwords and slogans that were meaningful only when the country was a colony. We have already defined messianism as a reasoned response (even if in appearance it seems remote from our own notions of rationality) to a troubled socio-logical situation, and we have described it as an adjustment to a changing situation. But history does not stop. Changes continue to follow one an-other, and old situations become modified. By transforming itself into a sect, the movement paralyzes its faculty for adjustment, a faculty observ-able at the outset of any messianic movement. Its members continue to react with the same responses although the problems have become new and different.

To be able to judge of the possible relationships that may be estab-lished in the near future between the facts of messianism and those of development, there is one final point that must not be forgotten, one to which we have referred in a recent article in these *Cahiers,* and that is the connection between messianism and utopia. The concept of utopia has given rise to contradictory views, to violent criticisms (as when Marx-ists speak of utopian socialism), and it has also elicited enthusiastic sup-porters (as with Auguste Comte, for instance, who equates the idea of utopia in the political domain with that of the hypothesis in the scientific domain, an anticipation of the future, or as with a Mannheim who com-pared it with ideology and laid great stress on its revolutionary force). The fact is that every utopia is perhaps a utopia of escape and a utopia of reconstruction (to borrow Mumford's expression). It is one of escape insofar as it corresponds to a need to flee from a reality that we find painful by building for ourselves a dream world, and it is an effort at reconstruction in the sense that it begins at the point where a political and social critique is called for. Messianism, like utopia, does include its share of political and social criticism on which contemporary anthropolo-gists and sociologists have placed such emphasis. It also includes that pronounced tendency to escape into a veritable dreamland of milk and honey as in cults of cargo ships, airplanes, or helicopters. This movement of escape—let us not forget the fact—can also include its positive side from the standpoint of social and economic development, for this utopian land of milk and honey includes the goods and advantages brought by the white man—minus his presence. Consequently, it is an admission and an acceptance of new requirements born from the contact with a more "progressive" civilization, and hence the escape is simultaneously a criticism and a reconstruction, a criticism of ancestral economic traditions and a reconstruction, or at least an appeal for a new kind of world, different from the old one. It is nevertheless true that messianism, like utopia, constructs "a false universe, complete and self-contained" (Ruyer). The elements of political and social criticism, of an acceptance of a desire for development among underdeveloped peoples and which are the symptoms of an acculturation and even of a Westernization of their minds—these elements must not blind us to that dangerous aspect of messianism, its retreat into the dream world and the irrational—obstacles to any kind of social effort, which is a slow and difficult process by definition.

But we do not wish to conclude on this pessimistic note. For messianism still has a lesson to teach us. The problem that occupies the best minds in countries recently elevated to the status of independence, and which are henceforth masters of their own destinies, is certainly the question of national development, but a development that also preserves the best within their own traditions. Does this development necessitate a radical change in a people's mentality and sensibility, a total conversion to Western thought, or will it be possible to accept new values, whether they come from the East or the West, by incorporating or molding them into traditions that have their roots in the distant past of any given race? In Africa, as well as in Asia, they dream of this marriage between the old and the new. Very well then! Messianism may be regarded as an attempt, not too successful perhaps, but an attempt nonetheless which deserves to be studied. It represents an effort to sift and filter values, introduced by Europeans, through the various forms of local mythologies or, if you prefer, to pour new wine into old bottles, just as it is an attempt (and this is even more significant) to adjust ancient systems of values to new needs and requirements. It is possible that certain suggestions offered in this study may be kept in mind and put to advantage by new leaders in the newly independent nations.

(Translated from the French by Robert A. Wagoner, State University of New York Maritime College.)

G. Shepperson

ETHIOPIANISM
AND AFRICAN NATIONALISM (1953)

International press reports on movements of Negro revolt and nationalism all over Africa today prompt reflection on one of their earlier phases, often called Ethiopianism, in which Americans, particularly Negroes, played important parts. The topic might well be introduced with a quotation from one who has figured much in the recent world press in connection with the "Mau Mau" disturbances in Kenya: Jomo Kenyatta. He writes: "During the last fifty years various religious sects have appeared in Africa. The most popular and one which conforms with the African secret societies is Ethiopianism." [1] But Kenyatta uses Ethiopianism here almost as vaguely as do many Europeans, whom he has so often condemned for their ignorance of African culture.

Strictly speaking, the term ought to be applied only to some aspects of the independent African church movement in South Africa, whose origins may be traced back to the 70's of the nineteenth century and earlier. Colour bar inside white churches, the search for avenues of personal advancement amongst a growing group of "educated" Africans, vague feelings of nationalism amongst peoples whose traditional institutions are being undermined—all combined to spur groups of Africans to seek at least a partial independence in their own churches. The movement came to a head first among the Wesleyans with the establishment of a tribal church in 1884 by a Tembu Wesleyan minister, Nehemiah Tile, and reached its first peak in 1892 with the founding of the Ethiopian Church (Psalm 68:31, "Ethiopia shall soon stretch out her hands to God") by another Wesleyan minister, Mangena M. Mokone. It was almost inevitable that the South African Ethiopian Church should seek affiliation with the American Negro body with which it had so much in common:

SOURCE. G. Shepperson, "Ethiopianism and African Nationalism," reprinted from *Phylon*, 14, 1, 1953, pp. 9–18.

the African Methodist Episcopal Church. This was achieved in 1896 when James M. Dwane, another ex-Wesleyan, visited the United States; and was consummated in 1898 when the A.M.E. bishop, H. M. Turner, made a five weeks' triumphal tour through South Africa. The independent Bantu church movement in South Africa by 1912 had created at least seventy-six separatist churches, which in the next thirty years were to swell to over eight hundred.

It would be false, however, to give the impression that this movement was dominated by quasi-respectable secessions from European Wesleyan and nonconformist churches. To anyone familiar with the course of the Wesleyan Revival in Great Britain, other, less respectable developments would seem to have been in order. The British revival movement canalized a great stream of social discontent not only into the austere and respectable chapels but also into many strange, apocalyptic forms of religion which threatened at times to burst through the banks of social control. For the South African native separatist church movement, such a phase may be said to have begun about 1904 when the first Africans were baptized into the Christian Catholic Apostolic Church in Zion, a body which had started in the United States. The more respectable form of separatist church had now a rival: a visionary, pentecostal, "Zionist" group at the mercy of the individual spirit and at the same time swayed by its own great powers for organizing Africans into "communities." These groups were often as secret as the traditional societies of the tribe and, to many white politicians, much more dangerous. It seems to be this type of Ethiopianism which Kenyatta had in mind.

Thus, at least two uses of "Ethiopianism" may be singled out: the one embracing secessions from the main stream of nonconformist churches in South Africa, usually Wesleyan, Baptist or Free Church, which often emphasize their independence of the European by associating themselves with kindred bodies amongst American Negro churches; the other representing new types of churches of an apocalyptic character, which often find their origins in the missionary efforts of similar American groups, white and Negro. The term "Ethiopianism" may be used unhesitatingly about the first group and, as the Kenyatta quotation shows, it is often used for the second. More and more, however, "Zionist" (an equally unfortunate expression) is being applied to the second group. Despite over half a century of controversy and attempted definition, it is still common to find "Ethiopianism" (a word which suggests one limited corner of Africa), used as a generic term for the whole of the African separatist church movement. On the other hand, it is no longer used so regularly as a loose synonym for African nationalism as it was about thirty years ago.[2] The growth of specific African nationalism, especially in West Africa, has put a stop to that.

Yet, in the early stages of West African nationalism, expatriates in

Britain often utilized the term for support in a general struggle that was only just becoming specific. One West African writing before the First World War could raise "Ethiopianism," a term which had very particular ecclesiastical origins in South Africa, to the general level of

a struggle between those who recognize the claim to equal participation in social and political rights with others and those who for themselves and their order assert a certain fictitious superiority of race, and claim for it as a consequence of causes, however accidental, exclusive and special privileges.[3]

However, other West Africans limited the term to Africa and refused to spread it, Garvey-like, to wherever the Negro was to be found. One of them wrote: ". . . it is not so much Afro-Americans we want as Africans or Ethiopians." [4]

Although West Africa has seen many apocalyptic, prophet-led movements along the "Zionist" lines of the secondary use of the term, it does not appear to have had much Ethiopianism of the kind characterized by secessions from the nonconformist white churches. The only exception to this may be in Sierra Leone where the Creoles appear to have played the role of a traditional white ruling class.[5]

This suggests that Ethiopianism of the truest type appears mainly in those parts of Africa in which there have been fairly large European or European-influenced ruling classes, effective colour bars, and—because of missionaries and administrative exigencies—groups of "educated" Africans. A European ruling class permanently resident in the areas concerned seems to be the most important part. Its absence in West Africa would, then, account for the comparative lack of the Ethiopian phenomenon there and would also explain why it appears in its most characteristic form in South Africa.

Another factor which should be cited is the dominance of Protestantism, particularly of a strong Calvinist form as in South Africa. Protestantism, as the early stages of the Reformation in Europe showed, sows powerful seeds of sectarianism. The marked element of Baptist and Protestant missionaries in the Belgian Congo, sometimes loosely considered a Roman Catholic colony, makes one wonder why the phenomenon is not seen more there. Perhaps the reason is to be sought in the character of Belgian colonial policy which, although quite determined on the subordinate status it assigns to the African, is also clear on the necessity of allowing him some measure of social mobility. However, there seems to be more than enough of the "Zionist" type of Ethiopianism in the Belgian Congo, as the Kimbangu and Kitawala movements indicate.[6]

South Africa, then, appears as the typical location of the first and most characteristic type of Ethiopianism. Yet concentration upon South Africa should not obscure another part of Africa where it has been much in evidence: Nyasaland or British Central Africa. This is strange in view of the traditional links between South Africa and this area from the 50's of the nineteenth century when Livingstone began to push the traditional missionary frontier of South Africa north of the Zambezi to Lake Nyasa—introducing at the same time as the Scottish Calvinist missions much of the spirit of the Protestant ethic in trade—to the end of the century when "Blantyres" or African labourers from Nyasaland began to appear in the South African gold mines.

If in South Africa the African Methodist Episcopal Church had been the body around which African separatism in the main grouped itself, in Nyasaland this role, to a much lesser extent, seems to have been played by the American National Baptist Convention. Its station, the Providence Industrial Mission, under John Chilembwe, its African pastor who had been trained in an American Negro Baptist seminary, became a focus for native separatism there. As in South Africa, the main elements amongst the Africans attracted to this movement seem to have been those who had received a certain amount of education at the hands of missionary bodies and who felt their newly-created aspirations blocked by the dominant European ruling class.

Yet the "Zionist" type of Ethiopianism was not lacking in Nyasaland. It was one of the first parts of Africa to be influenced by that distinctive brand of African nationalism and American apocalyptic sectarianism loosely known as "Watchtower." This was first manifested in a great wave of pentecostal revivalism, working within the orbit of the American Watch Tower Society, which an African named Elliot Kamwana stirred up in the west-central part of Nyasaland between 1908-9. A long time before "Watchtower" (Kitawala, Chitawala) had become feared by Europeans in South Africa, the Rhodesias and the Belgian Congo, its Nyasaland followers were bringing upon themselves the penalties of the law and the persecutions of society which the "Witnesses" seem to suffer wherever they go, east or west of the Iron Curtain.[7]

Bracketing these two forms of Ethiopianism in Nyasaland with their counterparts in South Africa brings out some important similarities. The first is its original political implications for both countries. For South Africa, one result was the loss of four thousand African lives in the suppression of the Bambata rebellion of 1906[8] and the waste of another hundred and sixty-three when the charge of Enoch Mgijima's "Israelites" against the police was stopped at Bulhoek in 1921.[9] For Nyasaland, the consequence was the overthrow by 1910, although mainly by peaceful means, of Kamwana's "Watchtower" movement and his arrest and deportation; and, on a more serious scale, the Native Rising of 1915, led by John Chilembwe himself.[10] Though there was no great loss of life in this rising, it had to be suppressed forcibly and on a smaller scale occupies in Nyasaland the place of the Bambata rebellion in South African history. The suppression of both of these movements in South Africa and Nyasa-

land marked the end of a distinct phase of Ethiopianism, in which religion and politics had tended to reinforce each other to almost revolutionary ends, and the opening of a new epoch in which their paths had a
tendency to diverge, forcing political activity into more secular channels.

A second similarity is the role of a much-neglected Englishman in
South African and Nyasaland Ethiopianism. This was an English missionary, Joseph Booth (1851–1932). An earnest and honest "seeker after
Truth," whose impractical sincerity often earned for him the appellation
of fanatic, Booth founded at least seven industrial missions in Nyasaland
and got himself deported on numerous occasions for circulating amongst
the Africans peace petitions critical of European rule. He seems to have
spent many of the intervals after deportation in South Africa and in the
United States. He came into contact with many American protestant sects
and was for at least eighteen months, after a personal visit to Pastor
Charles Taze Russell in Philadelphia in 1906, official Watch Tower agent
in Cape Town. The centre of a bizarre triangle of forces from Nyasaland,
through South Africa, to the United States, Booth is one of the most
overlooked figures in the "Africa for the Africans" movement. He kept
the pot of Ethiopianism boiling in South Africa and Nyasaland. Though
his remote influence on the Chilembwe Rising in Nyasaland in 1915 has
been noted, his effect on the chain of events leading to the Bambata rebellion in Natal is usually passed over. He had founded there in 1896 a
short-lived body, the "African Christian Union," with Afro-American
ideals of Christian self-help, industrial cooperation and independence.
Despite its short life, this was one of the first effective manifestations of
native discontent in Natal. The full web of his connections is difficult to
trace, though he appears to have introduced some American Negroes
with Ethiopianist dispositions to Africa and to have known some prominent Negro leaders on both sides of the Atlantic; Professor W. E. B.
DuBois is the best-known American representative and John Tengu
Jabavu, editor of *Imvo Zabantsundu,* the most prominent South African.
Some of Booth's sympathy for the Negro undoubtedly came from his
experiences in Richmond, Virginia, where he and his protege, John
Chilembwe, whom he had taken to America in 1897, were followed by
mobs of young whites and often stoned for consorting together. Yet he
was no uncritical admirer of the Negro, either American or African, and
left some testimony of this after his first rapture with the African missionary field had faded a little.[11]

It would be wrong to do more than indicate that he was an important
link in the South African and Nyasaland movements, for they were of
social, rather than individual, origins. The same applies to the third
similarity between these two movements: that is, the part played in them
by Americans, mainly American Negroes. And yet they have an obvious
formal importance. The Negro Wesleyans and Baptists brought the

prestige, finances and organizing experience of their parent bodies in America—though, as many of them were to learn, they were as much foreigners to Africa as were white missionaries, and like them, they had to start learning all over again the difficult art of proselytizing under very novel conditions. It was this which made them not always as welcome to many Africans as both sides had hoped. "Won't they sit down in their houses and read their books when they come out here and make us poor Bantu to do their work instead of themselves?" [12] This criticism of American Negro missionaries made by one African in 1897 had more than a grain of truth in it! But, more seriously, the charge was levelled against them of setting back the indigenous African's own movements by the use of alien tactics and methods. Perhaps, despite the characterization so often made of him as a South African "Booker T," John L. Dube (who seems at one time to have been associated with Booth and Chilembwe in the United States dangerously near to the fringe of "Africa for the Africans") was not far wrong when he said in 1904: "A great mistake has already been made in South Africa by some (American Negroes) who went there and preached to the natives, 'Africa for the Africans' and caused a great race feeling which it is hard to bear." [13]

But, whatever may have been the effect of American Negro missionaries in Africa, one thing is certain: they could not resist the call after the 1880's. About their individual motives, one may argue as long as one argues about those of white missionaries. One of the most powerful forces driving them to Africa at this time was a sentiment of post-Reconstruction Negro "manifest destiny." The A.M.E. bishop, H. M. Turner, delivered an address in 1896 on "The American Negro and the Fatherland" which almost out-Garveys Garvey.[14] For the Baptists, the Reverend Charles S. Morris, a Negro missionary on leave from Africa, speaking at the Ecumenical Missionary Conference in New York in 1900, sounded an even more authentic note of "manifest destiny":

> I believe that God in His providence has been intending and preparing the American Negro to assume a large place in the evangelization of Africa. He only has lack of formality and color prejudice. He is also immune from fever. . . . So, when I see the Negroes of our Southern states; people who came here naked savages, having no word of the language and no idea of God, and who to-day, are four millions in number, redeemed, regenerated, disenthralled, I believe that God is going to put it into the hearts of these black boys and girls in the schools of the South to go with the message to South Africa and to the rest of Africa and vindicate American slavery as far as it can be vindicated by taking across the ocean the stream of life.[15]

However, five years later, the Reverend Lewis G. Jordan, Corresponding Secretary of the Foreign Mission Board of the National Baptist Convention, was to sound a more sober note; [16] by this time, some of the initial enthusiasm had faded in the face of the many difficulties and problems; and, as some Europeans were putting it, the damage had been done.

The Bambata rebellion was close at hand during this period. It appeared also that native discontent was being accentuated in South and Central Africa by the fact that some Africans were beginning to show signs of dissatisfaction with the European native colleges which the missionaries had set up, and were starting to look to the Negro colleges of America for an education more in line with the aspirations of their leading educated elements. "It must result," wrote the editor of the *Rand Daily Mail*, "in the further introduction of ideas which cannot but widen the gap which already exists between the black and white races on the sub-continent." [17] And, as a South African missionary added, the "natives received impressions of an idealised America, which they took to be almost entirely peopled by Blacks . . . a new element brought by the descendents of the white people's slaves entered at that time into the minds of the Blacks of South Africa." [18]

How far such allegations are correct must wait a full investigation of the total effect of American Negro missionaries and their agencies on the complicated Ethiopian movement of South and Central Africa—and, no doubt, also, on the nationalist developments in West Africa. [19] Tentatively, one might say that American Negro influence accentuated tendencies already present in African church separatist movements, with all their political consequences, in the first stage of Ethiopianism from 1892 to 1921. But, if no American Negro had ever set foot in Africa, it is more than likely that Ethiopianism would have taken much the same course. However, the parallel courses of political and social movements amongst American and African Negroes at this time were affected by the superior position and prestige of the American Negro; it was almost impossible for them to remain apart. And so the American Negro entered Africa as missionary and uplifter. He added some of the confusion of his own political and social life to an already confused African political scene; this counterbalanced some of the advantages which his capital and organizing experience enabled him to bring to the Africans.

After this period, though the American Negro did not lose interest in Africa, the failure of some of the Pan-African scheming of the immediate post-1918 years, together with the decline of the Garvey movement and continual worsening before 1939 of economic conditions in America, introverted his horizon. For the African in the classical centres of Ethiopianism a similar process was at work—though he perhaps continued to think more about the Negro in America than the American Negro did about him.

Although the native church movement, on strictly Ethiopian and on "Zionist" levels, was to grow, much of its political fervour was spent. More and more it seemed to turn itself into a safety valve. Its only new lease on life was to come through an extension of the Watch Tower movement—a specifically African movement often parting company with the parent Jehovah's Witnesses, though using much of their literature and forms of organization. This development is by no means linked directly to the earlier forms of Ethiopianism, though it grew, no doubt, out of the main elements of their pattern. It threatened to become a mass movement in a way that even the most "Zionist" of the earlier forms of Ethiopianism never did. And it has been turning into something very different from the Witness organizations of America and Europe: its African content has been developed and asserted.[20]

This is a convenient place to stop and to ask, what sort of movements may be taking the place of Ethiopianism as an African political force? Is the answer to be found in the complete decline of the religious, particularly the foreign religious element? Certainly the words of Clemens Kadalie, Nyasa organizer of the first important South African trade union, the Industrial and Commercial Workers Union of Africa, in 1924, suggest this as a possible outcome: "I do not subscribe to any religion in the generally accepted sense of the term. In the words of Ingersoll: 'The world is my country: to do good is my religion.'"[21] (And this was a man who had come from the same country as Kamwana, first effective African protagonist of Watch Tower, and who had originally been under the same Christian mission.) Such an approach leads obviously into the field of totally secular politics and to militant, down-to-earth unionism.

On the other hand, there seems to be an alternative, though this may in itself be seen by some as a prelude to the completely secular approach in African political action. This is the stripping away of the last vestiges of traditional Christianity and the forcing back of the African upon ideologies which, while strongly influenced by European concepts and practices, spring from the heart of his tribal life. Such a development seems to be at work among the Kikuyu in Kenya to-day and its nativist spirit shows up well in the dedication to Jomo Kenyatta's own study of his Kikuyu people:

To Moigoi and Wamboi and all the dispossessed youth of Africa: for perpetration of ancestral spirits through the fight for African Freedom, and in the faith that the dead, the living and the unborn will unite to rebuild the ancestral shrines.[22]

Such an attitude has much in common with the initial phases of Chinese resistance to Europeans in the Tai-Ping movement of the late nineteenth century and to the early stages of Indian reaction to British conquest at the time of the Indian Mutiny. It is perhaps no accident that it has appeared in its most serious form in Africa first in a country which grew up largely after 1920 when, farther south, the real political influence of Ethiopianism had spent itself.

Whatever directions the new movements of nationalism and revolt take in Africa, it seems that Ethiopianism is finished as a basis for political action and that it is now no more than a sentimental, nebulous symbol around which the bitter memories and intentions of both races may on occasion group themselves. The foreign religious focus has been tried and found wanting.[23] It has not fanned the many flickers of revolt into a single clear flame but has paradoxically split them into even more tiny points of light—little flames threatening as much to burn themselves out as to come together in a single, general conflagration. To rake among the embers of Ethiopianism is to find a few sparks which may throw some light on the obscure roads into the African future—and also onto the byways of the past which make up a significant, if overlooked, section of the "glory road" of American Negro history.

NOTES

1. *Facing Mount Kenya* (London, 1938), p. 269.

2. For more recent works dealing with Ethiopianism, see especially: Bengt. G. M. Sundkler, *Bantu Prophets in South Africa* (London, 1948); Katesa Schlosser, *Propheten in Afrika* (Braunschweig, 1949); Edward Roux, *Time Longer Than Rope* (London, 1949). Earlier works and articles using the word in all its senses include: Maurice Leenhardt, *Le Mouvement Ethiopien au sud de l'Afrique* (Cahors, 1902); E. M. Green, "Native Unrest in South Africa," *The Nineteenth Century,* XLVI (July–December, 1899); Amos Burnett, "Ethiopianism," *The Church Missionary Review,* LXXIII (1922); W. C. Willoughby, *Race Problems in the New Africa* (Oxford, 1923); Allen Lea, *The Native Separatist Church Movement in South Africa* (Cape Town, 1926); Raymond Leslie Buell, *The Native Problem in Africa* (New York, 1928). Lloyd Allen Cook, "Revolt in Africa," *The Journal of Negro History,* Vol. 4 (1933) is also valuable. For further references, see subsequent footnotes.

3. Bandele Omoniyi, *A Defence of the Ethiopian Movement* (Edinburgh, 1908), p. 4.

4. Casely Hayford, *Ethiopia Unbound* (London, 1911), p. 173.

5. But cf. John H. Harris, *Dawn in Darkest Africa* (London, 1912), p. 288; Schlosser, *op. cit.,* pp. 239–293.

6. Cf. Schlosser, *op. cit.,* pp. 297–324; R. Wauthion, "Le Mouvement Kitawala au Congo Belge," *Bulletin de l'Association des Anciens Etudiants de l'Institut Universitaire des Territoires d'Outre-Mer,* Vol. 3 (1950).

7. R. D. MacMinn, "The First Wave of Ethiopianism in Central Africa," *The Livingstonia News,* Vol. 2, 1909, pp. 56–59. *Passim* to No. 2, April, 1911.

8. J. Stuart, *A History of the Zulu Rebellion, 1906* (London, 1913), pp. 97, 128, 420–1, 521, 512–537, etc. See also Roux, *op. cit.*

9. Roux, *op. cit.;* Sundkler, *op. cit.,* pp. 72–3.

10. George Shepperson, "The Story of John Chilembwe," *Negro History Bulletin* (January, 1952).

11. Cf. Frederick Bridgeman, "The Ethiopian Movement in South Africa," *The Missionary Review of the World*, XVII (1904), 434–8. This paragraph is based on materials from a study in progress too numerous to be mentioned individually. But I shall be pleased to supply individual references or to enter into correspondence on any of the points in this essay (particularly on Booth and Chilembwe), at the Department of History, The University of Edinburgh, Scotland.

12. Letter from Joseph Bismarck, *The Central African Planter*, Vol. II, No. 13 (March 1, 1897).

13. John L. Dube, "Are Negroes Better Off in South Africa?", *The Missionary Review*, XVII (1904), 583.

14. *Africa and the American Negro. Addresses and Proceedings of the Congress on Africa. December 13–15, 1895*, ed. J. W. E. Bowen (Atlanta, 1896).

15. *Ecumenical Missionary Conference* (New York, 1900), pp. 469–71.

16. "What the Brethren in Black Are Doing in Missions," *The Missionary Review*, XVIII, 599–602.

17. L. Elwin Neame, "Ethiopianism: The Danger of a Black Church," *The Empire Review*, X (1905–6), 264.

18. Edwin M. Ellenberger, *A Century of Mission Work in Basutoland* (Morija, 1938), p. 311.

19. Cf. for this particular gap in American Negro scholarship "The Contribution of the American Negro to Africa," especially p. 142, *Christian Action in Africa. Report of the Church Conference on African Affairs . . . Oberlin . . . June 19–25, 1942* (New York, 1942).

20. Cf. Schlosser, *op. cit.*, pp. 235–9; *Report of the Commission to inquire into the disturbances on the Copperbelt, Northern Rhodesia* (London, October, 1935, Cmd. 5009), pp. 42–51; Griffith Quick, "Some aspects of the African Watch Tower movement in Northern Rhodesia," and Ian Cunnison, "A Watch Tower Assembly in Central Africa," *International Review of Missions* XXIX (April, 1940), and XL (October, 1950), respectively. The official Watch Tower Bible and Tract Society's point of view on these matters may be found succinctly expressed in a pamphlet, *The Watchtower Story* (New York, 1948).

21. "The aims and motives of the I.C.U.," *General Missionary Conference of South Africa Report* (Lovedale, 1928), p. 128.

22. *Facing Mount Kenya*. Cf. also some stimulating points in Roland Oliver, *The Missionary Factor in East Africa* (London, 1952), pp. 280–92; especially footnotes to pp. 281 and 285 and penultimate sentence of p. 291. For the Dini ya Msambwa movement of western Kenya, see L. C. Wilson, *The Uganda Journal*, Vol. 16, No. 2 (September, 1952). For the effects of African church separatism on the complicated Kenya political scene, see L. S. B. Leakey, *Mau Mau and the Kikuyu* (London, 1952), pp. 90–92 and 113–114. According to Dr. Leakey, the church separatist movement among the Kikuyu received its impetus not from any colour bar in the white churches but from the European missionary attack on the custom of cliterodectomy. His succinct pages, while suggesting many parallels with all forms of Ethiopianism in South and Central Africa, suggest that Kikuyu separatism has rather different causes and

consequences from these particular movements. However, any general study of African church separatism would have to consider this carefully, for the Kikuyu resistance to European penetration into their culture is obviously a matter of prime importance for the future of the whole of Africa.

23. This thesis might also be extended to Islam as a "foreign" influence as well as to Christianity. E.g., the Mahdist movement in the Sudan and the character of the Islamic "prophets" in Africa. Cf. Schlosser, *op. cit.*, pp. 62, 221; also the anti-Islamic elements in revolts in East Africa against German rule, for which see, for example, R. M. Bell, "The Maji-Maji Rebellion in the Liwale District," *Tanganyika Notes and Records,* 28 (January, 1950).

J. Abun-Nasr

THE SALAFIYYA MOVEMENT IN MOROCCO:
THE RELIGIOUS BASES
OF THE MOROCCAN NATIONALIST MOVEMENT (1963)

Shortly after the First World War the Salafiyya group in Morocco became active in the political life of the country; and when in the 1930's a Moroccan nationalism along European lines appeared, it had as its leaders men who had been active members of the Salafiyya circle and retained their allegiance to the Salafi ideas which had formed the starting points of their social and political attitudes. The Moroccan nationalist movement and its struggle against the French until independence was achieved in 1956 have been studied and commented upon by European and American scholars working in the field.[1] Though aware of the importance of the religious foundations of Moroccan nationalism, these scholars have not given the Salafiyya religious movement before its appearance in the limelight of political life its due importance. The present paper deals with some aspects of the original Salafiyya religious movement.

The political and social attitudes of the Moroccan nationalists which crystallized in the period between 1930 (the date of the Berber *dahir* or law) and 1956, were superstructures based on the ideas of the Salafiyya group. The Moroccan Salafis, like their counterparts in Egypt at the end of the nineteenth century, upheld the religious tradition of *al-Salaf al-Salih* (the good or pious ancestors), and recognized the Qur'an and the *Sunna* of the Prophet as the only acceptable bases of religious and social legislation. That the Salafiyya group in Morocco could develop into a politico-social movement might be explained in terms of the nature of Islam itself, as well as of the following facts about the Moroccan scene at the beginning of the twentieth century: in Morocco at this time political questions were still reducible into religious ones: the French army

SOURCE. J. Abun-Nasr, "The Salafiyya Movement in Morocco: The Religious Bases of the Moroccan Nationalist Movement," reprinted from *St. Antony's Papers*, 16, 1963, pp. 90–105, by permission of Chatto & Windus Ltd.

of invasion, which imposed the Protectorate on the country in 1912, was viewed as a Christian army aiming to suppress Islam and replace it by Christianity, and not merely a colonizing one seeking material profit and glory for France. The co-operation of Muslims with the French was therefore judged equivalent to apostasy (*ridda*) and not merely political treason.[2] The French policy of introducing the culture and way of life of France on a wide scale into those countries of which the French took political control increased the susceptibilities of the Muslims in Morocco (as in other parts of the Maghrib), and added to their concern about their traditional way of life which they identified with their religion, in the same way that they associated French culture with Christian and not secular Europe. Furthermore, the co-operation of the Sufi orders with the French during the nineteenth and twentieth centuries in the three countries of the Maghrib, especially the Tijaniyya, Darqawiyya and Tayyibiyya (also known as Wazzaniyya or Tuhamiyya), compromised these orders in the eyes of the Muslim population. When the Moroccan Sultanate was divested of real political power by the French after 1912, and as the Sufi orders' subservience to the French cause became well known, the Salafis—who had already emerged as an important religious group in Morocco and had attacked the Sufi orders on theological grounds—became the natural champions of the rights and the cultural heritage of the Muslims in Morocco against the encroachments of the "infidels."

Islam in the Maghrib became tinged with Sufi influences in the eleventh century A.D., when the ideas of the leading Sufis in the eastern parts of the Muslim lands started to percolate into the Maghrib. The Sufi orders, some of which originated in the area itself, came to play important social and political roles in the life of its inhabitants. They became accepted by the Muslims in the area to such a degree that the distinction which had traditionally been drawn between Orthodox Islam and Sufism seems to have been blurred to the bulk of the Maghribi Muslims. The Sufi orders in North West Africa did not discard those elements in their beliefs and rituals which were incompatible with Orthodox Islam, but the majority of the Muslims in the area became oblivious of the discordant elements in the two systems. They came in fact to consider it religiously commendable to submit to the discipline of a Sufi order besides being conversant with the traditional Islamic subjects of learning; and it became customary to start eulogies on men of religion by describing them as having combined knowledge of the *Shari'a* with what they called the *haqiqa* (the esoteric truth of the Sufis). There also appeared the aphorism that "he who does not have a *shaikh* (meaning a Sufi *shaikh*) the devil becomes his *shaikh*," which also points to the co-existence between the Sufi way and the orthodox form of official Islam.

Besides the spread of the influence of the Sufi orders, an important aspect of Islam in the Maghrib during the past four centuries has been the deterioration of religious scholarship. A period of decline in religious studies in the Maghrib set in as from the fourteenth century, which coincided with the extension of the influence of the Sufi orders. Two instances of this decline interest us here, namely that Muslim jurisprudence came to be taught only in summaries in the leading mosque-universities in the area, and *tafsir* (the exegesis of the Qur'an) disappeared as a subject of study from the curriculum of the Qarawiyin University, the most important centre of Islamic studies in the Maghrib. Throughout North and Equatorial Africa, *al-Mukhtasar*, a manual of Muslim jurisprudence according to the Malikite rite prepared by the fourteenth-century Egyptian canon lawyer Khalil b. Ishaq al-Jundi, became the standard textbook for teaching jurisprudence in the Maghrib, thus replacing the more detailed books composed by the founders of the four rites of jurisprudence and the six canonical collections of Muslim traditions compiled during the eighth and ninth centuries.

The fundamentalism of the Salafis led them to condemn those beliefs and practices of the Sufi orders for which they could not find textual bases in the Qur'an or the prophetic traditions; and their desire to reorganize society according to the sacred law made them concerned about the stagnant state of religious studies. In consequence of this, the Salafi reformers in Morocco paid special attention to expurgating the Faith from Sufi influences, and to the revival of religious studies.

The first instance of what might be considered a Salafi tendency in Morocco dealt with the problem of the poverty of religious learning, as exemplified by the widespread use of *al-Mukhtasar* as a textbook of jurisprudence. The Alawite Sultan Muhammad b. 'Abdullah (1757–1790), whom the leaders of the Salafiyya movement in Morocco at the beginning of the present century considered the main precursor of their movement in the country, tried to replace *al-Mukhtasar* by more adequate books for teaching jurisprudence. He himself was an accomplished religious scholar, and spent a great part of this time studying the books of Prophetic traditions. It was through his great influence that interest in these books was revived in Morocco. He brought to Morocco from the eastern parts of the Arab Muslim countries copies of the *Musnads* of the great *imams* of the schools of Muslim jurisprudence and the major books of Muslim traditions and devoted a part of his time to their study, summoning to him every Friday after the evening prayer the leading traditionists in the country to discuss with them questions arising from his studies.[3]

Muhammad b. 'Abdullah's desire to revive interest in the original sources of Muslim jurisprudence, and his anxiety to have Muslims accept as the basis of the law only authentic Prophetic traditions, led him to undertake the task of collating the traditions in the six canonical books of Prophetic traditions in one volume which he finished in 1784 entitled *al-Futuhut al-ilahiyya fi ahadith Khair al-bariyya al-lati tushfa bi ha al-qulub al-Sadiyya.* He arranged these traditions according to the extent of the agreement among these authorities about their authenticity, giving first those traditions on which the six agreed, then those upon which five of them agreed, and so on. As an added precaution he rejected those traditions which were not connected in sound *sanads*[4] to one of the Prophet's companions.[5] Muhammad b. 'Abdullah's method may not constitute an infallible means of securing the authenticity of the traditions, but it shows his concern about establishing the beliefs of Muslims firmly upon the *sunna* of the Prophet.

Out of the four schools of Muslim jurisprudence, Sultan Muhammad b. 'Abdullah preferred the strictest, the Hanbali, which is the only rite recognized by the puritanical fourteenth-century theologian Ibn Taimiyyah and by the Wahhabis. In the preamble (*khutba*) of his book *al-Futuhat* he says, in the accepted fashion of introducing books in the Muslim world at the time: "Muhammad b. 'Abdullah, the Maliki by rite and the *Hanbali by faith* says. . . ." In a special section at the end of the book he explains what he meant by this statement, showing clearly his predilection for Ahmad b. Hanbal. He says that the latter's rite enables the Muslims to avoid submitting to the allurement of such illegal innovations in the faith as scholasticism (*'ilm al-kalam*). He says also in this section:

> "The way of the Hanbalis in their belief is easy to attain, is above false imagination and superstition, [and] is consistent with the beliefs of the doctors of the law in the time of *al-Salaf al-Salih.* May God help us live as they [the Hanbalis] live firm in belief, and enable us die as they do in faith."[6]

Muhammad b. 'Abdullah also discouraged the use of *al-Mukhtasar* in the teaching of jurisprudence, and preferred the older and more detailed books on the subject. In a decree dealing with the reform of instruction in the Qarawiyin, he ordered that *al-Mukhtasar* should not be used in teaching jurisprudence without detailed commentaries on it which he himself specified.[7]

Mawlay Sulaiman (1792–1822), Muhammad b. 'Abdullah's son who succeeded to the throne after the short reign of his brother Sidi al-Yazid, reversed his father's policy with regard to *al-Mukhtasar* and extolled its merits.[8] But at the same time he attacked the Sufi orders and their excesses, an action which made the later Salafis in Morocco look upon him also as one of the forerunners of their movement. One of Ibn Sa'ud's letters after his conquest of the Muslim holy places in 1806 containing an exposition of the theological bases of the Wahhabi movement reached Morocco about the year 1810. The Sultan seems to have looked with favour upon the Wahhabiyya; and in 1812 he sent his son Ibrahim to Mecca with a group of Moroccan scholars to perform the pilgrimage and discuss theological questions with the Sa'udis. The exchanges of opinion seem to have taken place in a friendly atmosphere, and agreement was reached between the Wahhabis and the Moroccan delegation on the main points raised. The Moroccans accepted the Wahhabi attitude regarding the interpretation of the Qur'anic passages dealing with Almighty God's qualities, which emphasized the necessity of accepting their obvious and literal meaning (al-zahir). If it is stated in the Qur'an that God "sat Himself upon the Throne," [9] a good Muslim, the Wahhabis like the later Salafis asserted, should not ask such questions as to what is the essence of the Divine Being who sits on the throne, and why and how He sat. He should only believe in the occurrence of the act of sitting without discussing the implications of this belief. This attitude was to form the cornerstone of the theological approach of the Salafiyya movement in Egypt as elsewhere. The Moroccan delegation also pronounced itself satisfied with the Sa'udi explanation regarding their attitude on the question of visiting the tombs of walis. The Moroccans had understood that the Sa'udis prohibited Muslims from visiting the shrines of all saints and of the Prophet's tomb without condition, and when it was explained to them that they forbade from visiting the shrines of saints only Muslims who did not perform the visit in accordance with the rules which they prescribed, and which were designed to prevent it from becoming an act of worship, the Moroccans concurred with them on the desirability of this precaution.[10] Mawlay Sulaiman himself later forbade the Moroccan populace to visit the tombs of saints. He also wrote a treatise in which he criticized the Sufi orders, warned the Muslims against the illegal innovations which they introduced and stated the rules which should govern visits to the shrines of saints.[11] The Sultan also delivered a speech in which he denounced the practice which some of the Sufi orders had of holding festivals (mawasim) on the birthdays of the founders.[12]

Sultan Muhammad b. 'Abdullah's endeavours to revive interest in the original sources of Muslim jurisprudence, and therefore his advocacy of a return to the early formative periods of Islamic history—which is the characteristic point of emphasis in the Salafiyya movement—and Mawlay Sulaiman's attack on the Sufi orders—which is another important part of the reformist programme of the later Salafis—remained isolated from the development of the Salafiyya movement in Morocco during the second half of the nineteenth century and the first half of the twentieth. They are important only in as much as they encouraged the later Salafis in the way of life to which they became converted through other means, and since the example of these two highly esteemed sultans served as a useful supplementary argument which the Salafis could use in their polemics with the advocates of mediaeval Islam in Morocco. The intellectual position of the neo-Salafiyya, as the movement which appeared at the beginning of the twentieth century has been conveniently called by its leaders, was formed by the influence of the reformers of the eastern parts of the Arab Muslim world, especially Muhammad 'Abduh.

At the end of the nineteenth century the ideas of the advocates of Salafiyya in Egypt started to spread in Morocco. A learned Moroccan called 'Abdullah b. Idris al-Sanusi (from the Berber tribe of Banu Sanus), who was a lecturer at the Qarawiyin University, was one of the earliest persons to introduce these ideas into Morocco. In the 1870's he went on the pilgrimage to Mecca, and on his return he was appointed by the Sultan, Mawlay al-Hasan (1873–94), as a member of the royal learned council [13] to attend the sessions on al-Bukhari's *Sahih*. In the meetings of the council al-Sanusi expressed the ideas which he carried with him from Egypt, advocating especially the acceptance of the literal and most obvious meanings of the scriptures and the strict observance of the *sunna* of the Prophet. He also argued in favour of the rejection of *ta'wil* [14] especially in the Qur'anic passages and Prophetic traditions dealing with the qualities of Almighty God. Al-Sanusi's views, especially his criticism of *ta'wil*, did not meet with the approval of the other scholars in the council among whom were two influential personalities of learning: Ahmad b. al-Talib b. Sudah, author of several books on the Prophetic traditions and Sufism and several times a judge, and 'Abdullah al-Kamil al-'Amrani al-Hasani, who enjoyed great prestige through being the maternal grandson of the Sultan Mawlay Sulaiman and the son-in-law of another Sultan, 'Abdullah b. 'Abdul-Rahman. Both these scholars were members of Sufi orders and upholders of Sufi practices and beliefs.[15] Al-Sanusi's critics accused him of subscribing to the views of the Mu'tazilites and of introducing illegal innovations (*bida'*) and of denying the existence of sainthood (*wilaya*). Their attacks were very vehement, and the Sultan did not interfere to restrain them, although he seems to have been rather sympathetic towards al-Sanusi since he did not persecute him as he would have done had the defenders of mediaeval Islam been able to win him over to their point of view. Al-Sanusi soon found the atmosphere of Fez disagreeable and emigrated. He travelled to Syria and Turkey, lectured in Damascus and Istanbul and returned to Morocco only after the death of Mawlay al-Hasan and the accession of Mawlay 'Abdul-'Aziz. The new sultan treated him well, and helped him settle in Tangier. Al-Sanusi travelled with Sultan 'Abdul-'Aziz after his abdication to Egypt and Syria; and when in 1910 al-Sanusi returned from this trip he remained in Tangier until his death on 7 October 1931.[16]

Not long after the setback which the Salafiyya in Morocco suffered in the defeat of al-Sanusi's attempt to propagate the ideas which he had imported from the east, the country had another champion of these ideas in the person of Abu Shu'aib al-Dukkali (1878–1937). Born at al-Sadiqat, a locality about fifty miles from Casablanca, al-Dukkali came from a family which belonged to the strong Moroccan Sufi order, the Darqawiyya.

In A.H. 1314 (A.D. 1896–7) he emigrated to Egypt to study at the Azhar. At this time the curriculum of this university had already been revised by Muhammad 'Abduh, and the latter's religious discourses were being published in the *Manar* and were the subject of commentary and discussion in Cairo. Whether or not al-Dukkali had any personal contacts with 'Abduh is not known; but his sojourn in Cairo brought him into touch with the intellectual atmosphere created by the Egyptian reformer. As a student Abu Shu'aib was outstanding, and when the Amir of Mecca, Sharif 'Awn al-Rafiq (d. 1905)—who himself was favourably disposed towards Salafiyya—asked the Rector of the Azhar to choose a student to conduct religious instruction and preaching in the Muslim holy town, al-Dukkali was chosen for the job. He remained in Mecca until A.H. 1325 (A.D. 1907–8), visiting Morocco twice in the meantime. On his return to Morocco in A.H. 1325 he was treated well by Sultan 'Abdul-Hafiz (1908–11), and remained the Sultan's guest in Fez for three years. He went once more to Mecca to bring his family back to Morocco, and on his return in 1911 he was appointed *qadi* in the town of Marrakesh; a year later he became Minister of Justice.[17]

Muhammad 'Abduh himself never visited Morocco although he visited both Tunisia and Algeria; but he seems to have corresponded with several Moroccans and his ideas were well known in the country independently of Abu Shu'aib's influence. When he wanted to select for publication by the Salafiyya press books written by earlier authors along lines acceptable to the Salafis, he wrote to the Sultan Mawlay 'Abdul-Hafiz and to Shaikh Idris b. 'Abdul-Hadi, who is reputed to have been the owner of the largest private library in Morocco, asking advice on the books which he should publish. When a great controversy flared up in 1903 concerning 'Abduh's *fatwa* which dealt with the question of whether the consumption of the meat of animals slaughtered by Christians was permissible to Muslims, known as the Transvaal *fatwa*, a Moroccan jurist called Muhammad al-Mahdi al-Wazzani (1850–1923), the Malikite *mufti* of Fez, wrote a treatise on the problem. He supported 'Abduh's attitude regarding the consumption of meat although he denounced him in the same treatise because of his attack on the custom of supplicating God through the intercession of the prophets and saints.[18]

Abu Shu'aib al-Dukkali's influence as propagator of Salafi ideas in Morocco was much greater than any remote influence which Abduh might have had. Through him Sultan 'Abdul-Hafiz was won over to the ideas of the Salafis and wrote a book in which he inveighed against the Sufi orders, condemning several of their practices and beliefs as being incompatible with the true Islam, and singling out the Tijaniyya order for a special criticism.[19] His impatience with the Sufi orders became evident when he had the chief of the Kittaniyya order, Muhammad b. 'Abdul-Kabir al-Kittani, tortured to death after the latter had undertaken serious seditious activity during the rule of ʿAbdul-Hafiz's predecessor—who had pardoned him—and later during ʿAbdul-Hafiz's own reign.[20] Through ʿAbdul-Hafiz's help, Abu Shuʿaib succeeded in adding to the curriculum of the Qarawiyin University the teaching of *tafsir;* this was indispensable if the Salafis were to have resort to *ijtihad* (individual interpretation), the door of which, they believed, contrary to the widely accepted attitude, was not shut. During the three years which al-Dukkali spent in Fez, he himself taught the subject in the Qarawiyin, and while there a group of enthusiastic disciples formed itself around him. It was to one of these disciples, Mawlay al-ʿArabi al-ʿAlawi, that he handed on the torch of the Salafiyya in Morocco.[21]

Mawlay al-ʿArabi al-ʿAlawi is now retired from public life although he is still in good health. He is a former member of the Tijaniyya order, whose beliefs he now vehemently criticizes. He was converted to the Salafi point of view through the influence of his master, Abu Shuʿaib al-Dukkali, as well as through the influence of his own reading, in which the writings of Ibn Taimiyyah and the articles of the *Manar* left the greatest impact on his mind. During the First World War he was introduced to the writings of Ibn Taimiyyah through *Kitab al-Furqan;* at this time the books of Ibn Taimiyyah were rarely sold or read in Morocco because of his invectives against the Sufi orders which were strongly entrenched in the academic circles of the country. This introduction to Ibn Taimiyyah's ideas induced him to search for other books by him and on investigation in Fez he discovered that shortly before the war a parcel of books sent from the Salafiyya press in Cairo to a merchant in Fez called Ahmad al-ʿAmrani, remained undistributed since very few people showed interest in them. Mawlay al-ʿArabi al-ʿAlawi procured these books at a nominal price and found among them Mahmud Shukri al-ʾAlusi's *Ghayat al-aman fi ʾl-radd ʿala al-Nabhani* and Ibn Taimiyyah's *al-Tawassul wa ʾl-wasila*. He distributed these books in Morocco, and through him many in that country came to know the ideas of the fourteenth-century Hanbali theologian. At this time *al-Manar* and *al-ʿUrwat al-wuthqa* were starting to have some circulation in Fez.[22]

Mawlay al-ʿArabi al-ʿAlawi continues to hold his Salafi views with unswerving conviction, and is still highly venerated by his disciples who are prominent in the politics of Morocco. This pleasant and dignified old gentleman, who is at once a religious scholar and an able political agitator, forms in his life and public career a bridge joining the Salafiyya movement which started with the work of the two religious reformers al-Sanusi and al-Dukkali, on the one hand, with the politico-religious and nationalist Salafi movement which emerged after the First World War, on the other. The task of leading the neo-Salafiyya movement after the First World War fell to a former student of his, ʿAllal al-Fasi.

The neo-Salafiyya differs from the old one in that whereas the aims of the old one were primarily religious—to improve the understanding of the precepts of Islam and their application—the neo-Salafiyya aimed at the establishment of a liberal political organization of society with a view to enabling Muslims to lead the good life, part of which was the correct exercise of their religion. The presence of the French in Morocco as rulers since 1912 explains this difference of emphasis. Before the Protectorate, religious and social reform had to come from the ruling class comprising the Sultan and his retinue of scholars and administrators, and had to be in harmony with the established framework of the society. This meant that the reformers had a very limited scope within which to operate: the absolute authority of the Sultan could not be challenged and consequently the establishment of democratic institutions was not conceivable, even if it was claimed that they were based on the Muslim law, as some of the leaders of the neo-Salafiyya claimed for their political programme. The organization of the regime of the Protectorate in such a way as to centralize all power in the hands of the French administrators enabled the neo-Salafis to demand political freedom without forsaking their allegiance to the Muslim head of their community. To a Muslim reformist movement like the neo-Salafiyya it was a welcome situation to be able to attribute the political ills of the country to the detested "infidel"; and although some of the leaders of the Salafiyya in Morocco (especially 'Allal al-Fasi, as seen from his book *al-Naqd al-dhati*) could see that the responsibility for a great part of the ills of the Moroccan society rested with the Moroccans themselves, this was not the prevalent attitude.

'Allal al-Fasi himself defines the politico-religious aims of the neo-Salafiyya movement in the following way: the movement, he says, aims at expurgating the Faith from all superstition, having for its purpose to educate the individual in the true Islamic principles, whose acceptance conduces to the welfare of the community in this life and in the one to come. It aims, therefore, at the reformation of society through the correct Islamic education of the individuals in it. Individual liberty is essential since only through it can communities choose their proper way of life; and organization in political parties and trade unions is also indispensable as a means of expression through which the community can attain its goals by legal and pacific means. According to 'Allal al-Fasi, it would be essential for the success of the Salafiyya movement that the Muslim countries should associate together in one political entity. The Salafis, he says, wavered for some time between trying to revive the caliphate along modern lines and attempting to create an Eastern league of nations; and finally they decided to work for a form of nationalism which should derive its spirit not from materialism but from religion. The Arabic language should become the common language of all the Muslim countries; through it the Muslim mentality would be unified, and its diverse elements brought together. The *Shari'a*, al-Fasi adds, should become the source of all modern legislation in Muslim states, and a modern form of *ijtihad* should be devised to make this possible. But *ijtihad*, he suggests, should be the prerogative of qualified deputies that the nation would elect and not, therefore, that of the *'ulama'*. But all this, he concludes, cannot be achieved if foreign domination in the country is not brought to an end.[23]

The Sufi orders, which had been attacked by the old Salafiyya movement in Morocco on religious grounds, were attacked by the new one on both the religious and political levels. These orders had been compromised in the eyes of the Muslims in the Maghrib through the cooperation of some of them with the French in Algeria and Tunisia during the nineteenth century. This fact enabled the Salafis to combine their religious and political objectives; it also made it possible for them to attack the French with impunity by directing their diatribes against the Sufi orders, the recognized allies of the French.

During the Rif War (1923–6), the Salafis in Morocco became organized in two main circles: one around Abu Shu'aib al-Dukkali in Rabat, and the other around Mawlay al-'Arabi al-'Alawi in Fez. The two groups co-operated with each other and endeavoured through lectures and articles which they published in Algerian and Tunisian newspapers to make their views heard. The group in Fez was more vociferous and active in its attempt to revive concern about Islamic culture and to counter French influence. The lessons of Mawlay al-'Arabi al-'Alawi in the Qarawiyin attracted a big audience, and were attended by several persons who were later to play important parts in opposing the French: 'Allal al-Fasi, al-Faqih Ghazi, Ibrahim al-Kittani and al-Mukhtar al-Susi, and others. In his lessons he attacked abuses of diverse natures: to show his discontent with the state of religious learning he criticized the use of *al-Mukhtasar* as a textbook for teaching Muslim jurisprudence. At the same time he and his disciples tried to give circulation to some of the books of Salafi tendencies which had reached Morocco from Egypt. Abu Ishaq Ibrahim b. Musa al-Shatibi's: *Kitab al-i'tisam bi al-kitab wa 'l-sunna* which had been published by the Salafiyya press in three volumes during the years 1913–14, reached Morocco at this time and became the object of commentary and discussion started by the advocates of Salafiyya. 'Allal al-Fasi launched at the same time a severe attack on the Sufi orders through the newspaper *Izhar al-Haqq* which was published in Tangier.[24]

The Salafiyya group directed at the end of the Rif War an attack on the Tijaniyya order, which was most clearly in the service of the French in Algeria, and whose leaders were accused of working for the French during the Rif War.[25] The attack at first took the form of a criticism of the doctrines of the Tijaniyya. Mawlay al-'Arabi al-'Alawi was the centre of the group which started this attack, and he had as a temporary ally the chief of the Kittaniyya order, 'Abdul-Hayy al-Kittani, who could not be described either as a Salafi or a Moroccan nationalist, but who sought to destroy the position of the Tijaniyya in the country because of the competition between the latter and his order. A chief of the Tijaniyya in the town of Marrakesh, called Muhammad al-Nazifi, in a small book entitled *al-Tib al-fa'ih* written to explain the Tijani litany *Salat al-Fatih*, stated that this prayer was a part of God's eternal speech, thus equating it in its origins with the Qur'an.[26] The book had long been printed and it circulated widely in Morocco, but it was chosen for the occasion merely as the target of the attack on the Tijaniyya and as a part of the Salafi campaign against the Sufi orders in general. The Moroccan Minister of Justice, 'Abdul-Rahman al-Qarashi, was persuaded to submit to the council of *'ulama'* of the Qarawiyin University in Fez a request that the council examine the statement made by al-Nazifi regarding *Salat al-Fatih* and express an authoritative opinion as to whether it offended against the religion of Islam or not, and if it did what punishment would be commensurate with the offence. Mawlay al-'Arabi al-'Alawi took an active part in the deliberations of the council, and it was through him that the extreme attitude of 'Abdul-Hayy al-Kittani and others who wanted al-Nazifi hanged was curbed. Realizing that a death sentence against al-Nazifi had little chance of being sanctioned by the French authorities, the council decided to produce a more lenient verdict which had a better chance of being executed. In a document dated 29th Rajab A.H. 1344 (11th February 1926) they recommended to the Minister of Justice, and through him to the Sultan, that al-Nazifi be strongly reprimanded and his books burnt.[27] No action was taken against al-Nazifi because of the protection of the influential Pasha of Marrakesh, Thami al-Glawi, who himself was a member of the Tijaniyya order. But the Salafis gained support in Morocco as well as in the neighbouring Muslim countries as a result of this *fatwa*. Salafi groups in Algeria and Egypt took up the attack against the Tijaniyya at once, a fact which serves to show the sympathy of the Salafi groups in North Africa for, and the connections which they had with, each other. Immediately after the learned council of the Qarawiyin passed its verdict, *al-Najah* newspaper which appeared in Constantine in Algeria published its text with a laudatory account of the attitude of the council of the Qarawiyin, calling its article: "The zeal of the learned men of Fez for the Faith." [28] *Al-Manar* periodical, the mouthpiece of the Salafiyya group in Egypt, also took up the attack against the Tijaniyya in its number for the 29th Sha'ban A.H. 1344 (17th March 1926). In Algeria the "Association of Algerian Muslim men" (*Jam 'iyyat al-'ulama' al-Muslimin*) reverberated with the echo of this *fatwa* a few years later. This association was founded in 1930 by 'Abdul-Hamid b. Badis (1889–1940) who had close contacts with the leaders of the Salafiyya circle in Morocco. The fifth congress of the Association which was held in the town of Algiers in March 1935 was attended by a deputy of the Salafiyya circle in Morocco, Muhammad Ibrahim al-Kittani; and in the sessions of the congress the speakers, especially the vice-president of the Association, Muhammad al-Bashir al-Ibrahimi, attacked bitterly the Tijaniyya.[29]

The proclamation of the Berber *dahir* on the 16th May 1930 was decisive in the transformation of the Salafiyya movement from an intellectual circle composed mostly of scholars into a popular political movement. In the midst of the agitation which resulted from the proclamation of the *dahir* 'Allal al-Fasi formed a secret society called "al-Zawiyya," which became the nucleus of the National Party and later the Istiqlal Party.[30] The Berber *dahir* placed the administration of justice in Berber areas in the hands of the *Jama'a* or customary courts, and provided for the application of the French criminal law among the Berber tribes. This meant that the Berbers were not to be subject to the system of justice as administered in Morocco in the name of the Muslim head of the community. The Pashas (governors) of the towns and tribal *qa'ids* in the country-side had dealt with penal and civil justice, and the *qadis* administered the *Shari'a* in matters of personal status and inheritance. The Salafiyya group, with their eyes firmly focused on the early periods of Muslim history, considered the promulgation of the law the first practical step towards the conversion of the Berbers back to Christianity. The ethnic and linguistic differences between the Berbers and the other elements of the Moroccan population were not considered by the Salafiyya circle sufficient to justify the promulgation of the *dahir*. This law constituted, according to their point of view, an attempt on the part of the French to resuscitate the period of *Jahiliyya* (the time of ignorance) which Islam is believed by its followers to have abrogated and superseded. To an orthodox Muslim the Berber *dahir* seemed to strike at the foundations of the Muslim society; consequently the reaction of the Salafis was immediate, violent and uncompromising. Immediately after its promulgation they aroused the feelings of the Muslim population by the recitation of the *Latif* prayer, one which is usually reserved for moments of national catastrophe.[31] The reaction of the Muslims outside Morocco was not less virulent. Shakib Arsalan, who opened an office in Geneva in 1930 to defend the cause of Muslims on an international level, visited Tetuan in that year and made contacts with the leaders of the Salafiyya group in the French zone of Morocco. Muslim religious circles in Egypt and elsewhere expressed sympathy with the Moroccans, and referred to the *dahir* as an act of religious imperialism.

The reaction of the Muslims of Morocco to the promulgation of the *dahir* showed the extent to which they still thought in religious terms, and how little they were prepared to tolerate any encroachment on their religion and culture in the name of the protection of minorities. Neither the French authorities, nor the Salafiyya group, was at this stage prepared to see the other party's point of view. But the promulgation of the *dahir* and the opposition to it were the beginning of the crystallization of the nationalist movement. Until 1930 the social and political programme of the Salafis was based on traditionally Muslim arguments; the nationalist movement which appeared after this date was a modern nationalist movement in its objectives and tactics, although its leaders presented their political programme inside a religious framework.

NOTES

1. The history of Moroccan political life after the Protectorate has been studied by several non-Moroccan scholars. Some of the better-known books on the subject are: R. Landau, *The Moroccan drama, 1900–1955* (London, 1956), F. Taillard, *Le nationalisme marocain* (Paris, 1947), and D. E. Ashford, *Political change in Morocco* (Princeton, 1961).

2. 'Allal al-Fasi, when speaking of the subservience of the chiefs of the Kittaniyya and Darqawiyya orders in Morocco to the French cause ('Abdul-Hayy al-Kittani and Habib al-Filali respectively), refers to them as *murtadds* (those who lapsed from the faith) and not *kha'ins*, as the Arabic political vocabulary would describe traitors. Whenever he uses the latter word, he invariably uses with it the former. See for example *Hadith al-mashriq fi 'l-maghrib* (Cairo, 1956), p. 20.

3. Abdul-Rahman b. Zaidan, *Ithaf a'lam an-nas bi jamal akhbar hadirat Maknas* (Rabat, 1929–33), vol. III, pp. 183–4.

4. Authorities relating the traditions of the Prophet.

5. Ibn Zaidan, *op. cit.*, III, p. 358.

6. Ibn Zaidan, *op. cit.*, III, pp. 358–9.

7. 'Abdul-Rahman b. Zaidan, *al-Durar al-fakhira bi ma'a thir muluk al-'Alawiyin bi Fas al-Zahira* (Rabat, 1937), pp. 60–1.

8. Ahmad b. Khalid al-Nasiri, *Kitab al-istqsa' li akhbar duwal al-maghrib al-aqsa* (Casablanca, 1954–6), vol. VIII, p. 67.

9. The Qur'an, X-3, XIII-2, XXV-59, XXXII-4 and LVII-4.

10. Ahmad b. Khalid al-Nasiri, *op. cit.*, VIII, pp. 120–1.

11. *Ibid.*, VIII, p. 124.

12. This speech was printed in 1933 by one of the active spokesmen of the Salafiyya in Morocco, Muhammad Ibrahim al-Kittani. It was distributed in the country so as to rally support to the petition which had just been submitted to Sultan Muhammad b. Yusuf by the professors and students of the Qarawiyin University in Fez calling upon him to interdict the festivals of the 'Isawiyya and Hamadsha orders.

13. The Sultans of Morocco held in the royal palace a council of the prominent scholars in the country to discuss important religious and legal questions, or merely to study the Prophetic traditions and Muslim jurisprudence. The Sultan himself attended the council and often conducted its proceedings.

14. Meaning the material interpretation of the Qur'an which deals with its content, as distinct from *tafsir* which means the external philological exegesis.

15. 'Abdul-Hafiz al-Fasi, *Riyad al-Janna aw al-mudhish al-mutrib* (Fez, A.H. 1350), II, pp. 77–80.

16. 'Abdul-Hafiz al-Fasi, *Riyad al-Janna aw al-mudhish al-mutrib* (Fez, A.H. 1350), II, pp. 81–5 and 94–5.

17. Muhammad Ibrahim al-Kittani, *Tala'i' al-yaqza al-maghribiyya aw Abu Shu'aib wa 'l-salafiyya*, MS., the author's personal copy, ff. 12–14.

18. 'Allal al-Fasi, *al-Harakat al-istiqlaliyya fi'l-maghrib al-'arabi* (Cairo, 1948); 'Abdul-Hafiz al-Fasi, *op. cit.*, II, pp. 48–50; and Muhammad Rashid Rida, *Tarikh al-ustadh al-imam* (Cairo, 1931), I, p. 716.

19. This book is entitled *Kashf al-qina' 'an i 'tiqad tawa' if al-ibtida'*, published in Fez in A.H. 1327/A.D. 1909.

20. 'Abdul-Hafiz al-Fasi, *op. cit.*, I, pp. 44–8.

21. Al-Kittani, *op. cit.*, ff. 16–17; and 'Abdul-Hafiz al-Fasi, *op. cit.*, II, pp. 141–3.

22. This information was given to the author by Mawlay al-'Arabi al-'Alawi himself during two working sessions he had with him in Fez in the month of November 1960.

23. 'Allal al-Fasi, *Al-Harakat al-Istiqlaliyya*, pp. 156–8.

24. Muhammad Ibrahim al-Kittani, *op. cit.*, ff. 4 and 5.

25. 'Abdul-Karim, the leader of the Rif uprising, accused the heads of the Sufi orders, after the collapse of his movement in 1926, of being themselves greatly responsible for the failure because they refused to co-operate. (See *al-Manar*, vol. 27, 1926, pp. 630–3.) A Tijani adventurer from Tunis called Muhammad al-Manubi al-Qitt carried in 1923 apocryphal letters to Lyautey in Morocco, claiming that he was given them by 'Abdul-Karim. In 1924 he was asked to deliver a message from the department of Native Affairs in French Morocco to 'Abdul-Karim, which suggests that the message which he carried to the French authorities in Morocco was taken seriously by the latter. Lyautey discovered the fraud around November 1924, when al-Manubi had already left. (See the documents on Muhammad al-Manubi in the Tunisian Archives, dossiers D.156.2 and D.156.21.) Muhammad al-Manubi was denounced by the leaders of the Tijaniyya in the mother *zawiya* of the order in 'Ain Madi (Algeria); and in the absence of any documentary evidence it is not possible to ascertain the extent of the latter's involvement in the politics of the Rif.

26. See Muhammad b. 'Abdul-Wahid al-Nazifi, *al-Tib al-fa' ih wa 'l-wird al-sanih fi salat al-fatih* (Cairo, n.d.), p. 11.

27. I have searched in Fez and among the paper of 'Abdul-Hayy al-Kittani, now in the Bibliothèque Générale in Rabat, but failed to find it. Mawlay al-'Arabi al-'Alawi, who supplied me with most of the information on the circumstances which led to the issue of the *fatwa*, believes that no copy of its text has been preserved anywhere. There is a mention of the *fatwa* in Mahmud Manashu's book which was written to rebut it: *Majmu' qam' al-ta'assub wa ahwa' a'da' al-Tijani fi' -lmashriq wa 'l-maghrib* (Tunis, 1926), pp. 3–4.

28. Mahmud Manashu, *op. cit.*, p. 3.

29. See *Sijil Mu' tamar Jam 'iyyat al-'Ulama' 'al-Muslimin al-Jazi' iriyyin* (Record of the Congress of the Association of the Muslim learned men of Algeria), published in Contantine, A.H. 1354/A.D. 1935, p. 25.

30. 'Allal al-Fasi, *'Aqida wa jihad* (Rabat, 1960), pp. 9–10.

31. Muhammad Ibrahim al-Kittani, *Min Mudhakkarati 'an al-yaqza al-maghribiyya*, MS., the author's private copy, ff. 8–9.

VIII

The Rise
of the Nationalist Movement

R. I. Rotberg

THE RISE OF AFRICAN NATIONALISM:
THE CASE OF EAST AND CENTRAL AFRICA (1962)

Now the British government having manifested itself as the leading power we hope it is going to extend more fully than it did before to all its British subjects irrespective of colour, race, or nation, the same equal rights, privileges, and advantages of freedom, liberty, and justice.

> Northern Rhodesia: Paramount Chief Yeta to Prince Arthur of Connaught, 31 March 1919.

Unless Justice be done, we can have no confidence in the pronouncements made on behalf of the British government that their primary object is to lead the African people along the path to self-government. What virtue can there be in self-government if the land on which and by which we live is alienated from us?

> An Appeal by Jomo Kenyatta addressed to James Griffiths (Colonial Secretary), 14 May 1951.

It is all too often assumed that African nationalism is a product of very recent manufacture. One supposes that World War II and its aftermath brought about new forces of change, loosely called "nationalism," which in a few short years swept African prison graduates into undreamed of positions of power and world importance. To some extent, of course, this presumption is correct: those elements of change unleashed by the war and by the subsequent estrangement of two of the victors did indeed accelerate the emergence of popular movements in Africa south of the Sahara. More rapidly than even the aspirants themselves could have hoped, colonial powers made it evident that freedom could be obtained for the agitation. Some achieved it incredibly swiftly; some are achieving it stubbornly. But the point of importance for our discussion is that the contemporary awareness of African political demands is simply belated recognition of a movement sixty or more years old. This article demon-

SOURCE. R. I. Rotberg, "The Rise of African Nationalism: The Case of East and Central Africa," reprinted from *World Politics*, XV, 1, 1962, pp. 75–90.

strates that the triumph of African nationalism since World War II is but
the final coordination and intensification of all the tangled strands of an
earlier, usually unrecognized, disaffection. It focuses on two of the main
ways in which this early nationalism expressed itself despite an inhos-
pitable environment. Analysis is limited to the case of East and Central
Africa, which has been less well studied than corresponding situations in
West Africa.

   One problem immediately arises: What do we mean by "African
nationalism"? Or, to put the question more usefully, what can we mean
by the phrase? Until recently nationalism in Africa has not meant a
"devotion to one's own nation," particularly since the borders of colonial
Africa were artificial and often divided tribes indiscriminately. Nationalism in Africa (the word was first used in English in 1844, and was given
wider currency when it described the program of the Irish Nationalist
Party in 1885) has also never meant a policy of national independence—
at least, not until recently.[1] African nationalism, critically defined, is not
the ethnic rebirth of Central Europe. Nor is it the pathetic cry of Wales
or Scotland. In its most precise sense there has simply never been any
African nationalism in the way that there was a Chinese nationalism after
Sun Yat-sen. In Africa there has been a common protest against white or
alien rule—anti-colonialism. Still, it would be wasteful to coin a new
phrase for a state of being that has results similar to historic nationalism.
We use "nationalism" in the way it is popularly used, in the way Africans
themselves use the term.

I

   It is a truism that without colonialism there would have been no
movements of protest. Nationalists of today, and their predecessors, all
ascribe the ills of their various countries to the oppression of colonial
regimes. Had it not been for the accident of European intervention, they
are wont to say, Africa long ago would have developed politically and
economically in ways conducive to the prosperity and contentment of
the peoples involved. Indeed, there is little doubt that the roots of African
nationalism may easily be found in the fertile soil of European conquest;
we would logically expect such to be true. The one serious deficiency in
this argument, however, is that we know far too little about the economic
consequences of imperialism and not enough about ways in which African
societies were developing before the onset of European rule.

   From the Zambezi to the Nile, whites came first as explorers and
adventurers, later as missionaries, administrators, and settlers. They found
a small number of strong chiefdoms and many small ethnic groupings.
The indigenous inhabitants enjoyed economies that were pastoral or
agricultural or that were dependent upon raiding and hunting. They

were linked, however tenuously, with the economy of the Indian Ocean via the ancient city-states of the coast. Slaves, gold, ivory, and iron were commonly traded for cloth or manufactured goods in these entrepôts.

The Western powers made their partition of East and Central Africa secure by outright conquest and by treaty arrangements often obtained by force. The pattern in nearly every case was the same. The Kaiser's or Queen's man promised protection and freedom from outside interference if the indigenous chief would sign over his lands and most of what were later considered his inalienable rights. Without realizing it, perhaps without even understanding the document he was signing, the chief proceeded to devolve upon Europeans his authority to decide allocation of lands, the application of tribal law, and the eventual policy-making role of the chief or headman himself. But if the indigenous ruler refused to accept a treaty or refused, like Chief Msiri of Katanga, to entertain the thought of foreign domination, he was speedily subdued. Military force was necessary to secure the colonies because even those Africans who at first had not objected to foreign rule began to regret its routine interference with their daily life. Chiefs saw themselves deprived of authority; the people were astonished to find that their new rulers were harsh and arbitrary.

What did colonial rule entail? Africans were taxed in each colony in order to raise revenues and in order to force them to work for Europeans. Africans were deprived of their lands and eventually restricted to crowded and less fertile reserves. They became subject to alien laws that were not always administered equitably. More crucially, Africans were deprived of elemental self-respect in their own country. They were made to carry passes or other forms of identification as a mark of their inferior status. The cruder forms of discrimination were perfected, especially on mission stations, and segregation of every variety was practiced.

Throughout East and Central Africa the indigenous inhabitants grew weary of insults and discrimination. They regretted low pay and regular tax increases, lack of representation in matters that involved their interests, and the onerous daily confrontation of race realities that can never be conveyed on paper. As Africans were absorbed into the urban labor force, they grew to understand white rule even more fully. They sought a betterment of conditions and learned to vent their frustration in the privacy of clubs and societies—the forerunners of congresses and modern political parties, by participating in the life of separatist Christian sects and chiliastic cults, and by the actual use of violence.[2]

II

The intermediate link in the causal chain that leads from the beginnings of colonialism to the negotiated triumph of radical African political parties was provided by those bodies that collectively may be called "associations." The term encompasses those voluntary groupings—clubs, societies, etc.—that are inherently political only in the wider sense, and those other organizations (African independent churches and labor unions) that often became vehicles of protest. Religious movements will be discussed in the following section. Labor protest also played its part in the rise of nationalism. The Copperbelt strikes of 1935 and 1940, the Tanga and Mombasa dock strikes before World War II, the formation of the Uganda Motor Drivers' Association, and recurring problems associated with the recruitment of plantation labor all reflected African dissatisfaction (with pay and housing for the most part), but more detailed research needs to be carried out before any conclusions may be advanced.

Associations, wherever they were formed, represented a precise response to the challenge of colonialism. They were both an urban and a rural response that to some degree "made it possible for Africans to recover . . . the sense of common purpose which in traditional African society was normally enjoyed through tribal organisations." [3] The white administrations subverted traditional means of obtaining satisfaction or redress for grievances, real or imagined, and thus made it all the more necessary for Africans to join together in order to protect and to further the interests of the otherwise unrepresented indigenous population. The Broken Hill Welfare Association of Northern Rhodesia, as its foundation, aimed to stimulate "cooperation and brotherly feeling, to interpret to the government native opinion on matters of importance, to encourage the spread of civilization, and to protect and further native interests in general." [4] These early mutual benefit societies were an imitation of similar white forms; settler pressure groups existed from the early decades of this century and their success was as easy to perceive as it was difficult to copy. [5]

The new associations were both tribal and atribal. In Kenya and Uganda the number of distinct ethnic organizations is indicative of the reinforcement white rule and urbanization have given to the traditional social structure. To name but the more prominent: Abaluhiya Central Association, Bataka Association, Arab Central Association, Luo Union, Ukamba Members' Association, Comorian Society, Karamoja Union, Kisii Union, Kipsigis Central Association, Kalenjin Union, Masai Association, Fighi Union, Maragoli Society, Meru Meru Society, and, not last by any means, the Thija Mwaniki and Muhisija Union. Similarly, some of the important tribes of Central Africa and Tanganyika have always fostered urban and rural groups that have acted as friendly societies and organs of political protest. The con-urban Copperbelt has always harbored various tribal affiliations; Livingstone, Bulawayo, and Johannesburg likewise have all had their Acewa Improvement, Lozi, Ansenga Young Men's, and Namwianga associations.

Tribal organizations were ideally situated to collate the grievances of their members and to seek to protect the collective ethnic interest. They were formed to preserve tribal loyalties in the face of inevitable detribalization in the cities or on distant farms. They tended to assist urban emigrants, to act as burial societies, or simply to serve as centers of social activity.[6] These groups were inevitably conservative. They frowned upon tribal intermarriage, on increased adultery (a product of the cities), and on the "alarming" rise in prostitution for profit. (The Luo Union sought to persuade government to deport all Luo unmarried women away from the bright red lights of the cities.[7]) Whenever land was alienated or other government measures posed a threat to the tribe, it was the tribal association, not the chiefs or elders (characteristically in government pay), which protested.

These associations were led by younger men who had drifted to the cities and who had found some need there for mutual succor within a tribal context. They saw their elders, usually less well-educated, as unable or unwilling to press the demands of the tribe. Gradually they sought redress for wrongs to their people. They learned the vulnerabilities of whites. They learned to deal with the white man on his own terms; they agitated, drove shady bargains, talked, and wrote. In the tribal and atribal associations these younger men amassed valuable experience in administration, negotiation, and in the manipulation and propagation of protest.

The most interesting and most radical of all tribal associations were those based on the grievances of the Kikuyu, Kenya's largest tribe. Whether labeled the Young Kikuyu Association, the Kikuyu Association, or the Kikuyu Central Association, Kikuyu organizations have always had much the same foundation. Indeed, in more recent times their members have been the core of the Kenya African Union and the present Kenya African National Union. The first Kikuyu organization dates from 1919, when a small group of urban Kikuyu met to discuss "matters affecting the interest of the Kikuyu people" and to form a "focus of tribal loyalty."[8] From this inception Kikuyu associations sought to prevent government actions inimical to Kikuyu. They unsuccessfully made representations to district and provincial commissioners, and to the governor himself. They prepared reams of propaganda for African as well as white consumption. Before long they were able to transform minor disaffections into major tribal involvements, simply on the strength of their network of local branches and the skill with which their leaders played upon the very real disillusionment of the Kikuyu.

The Kikuyu had been deprived of their land. From 1902, when Commissioner Sir Charles Eliot chose deliberately to encourage the settlement of white farmers on fertile lands north and west of Nairobi, Kikuyu holdings had been expropriated.[9] Their traditional system of individual tenure, earlier recognized by the government of the East Africa Protec-

torate (as Kenya was then called), was regularly ignored.[10] The settlers
took vast acreages—the most valuable 40 per cent of the African land
became the property of 2,000 whites—while Africans refrained from
requesting the return of alienated land. Instead they simply asked for
security of present occupation: "Our wish is not to claim the return of
the land now in the possession of Europeans, we realize that they must
now remain in occupation. We accept the present division of the land
between us and them, but we earnestly beg that our anxiety as to the
future may be finally removed and such legal security given us that we
need not fear the possibility of any further encroachment." [11] But legal
tenure was denied to them until after white farmers had ceased to enter
Kenya in large numbers.

Lower taxes, better education, improved medical services, and a
"voice in legislation affecting us" were other pleas addressed cogently,
but abjectly, to the government and to visiting commissions.

We pay large amounts annually in hut and poll tax but we see little coming
back to us in direct benefits.

Many laws are passed without our people having any say. We feel it is
only right that when legislation affecting us is contemplated we should have
the opportunity to say what we think about it. . . . Whites cannot speak for
us or reflect our views.[12]

These pleas were denied as regularly as they were put forward. Large-
scale alienation of land ceased, but tensions caused by insufficient land
were exacerbated as the Kikuyu population increased and as sections of
the Kikuyu reserve were overutilized. A second generation of militant
Kikuyu assumed the association leadership, and men like Harry Thuku,
the first Kikuyu nationalist, were distrusted for what had, after imprisonment, become their increasingly more moderate view. Jomo Kenyatta, a
leader in the pro-female circumcision imbroglio of 1930, was among the
first to assert himself within this context, but he soon went into voluntary
exile in Great Britain.[13] A decade of almost total stalemate readied Kenya
for Kenyatta's return, for an increasingly less obsequious approach to
government, and for a widening of the base of political support.

Voluntary, atribal groupings were even more direct precursors of
modern African political parties. They were wholly urban. They would
not have existed had it not been for the de-emphasis on tribal ties that
was apparent fairly early among the more educated, and more urbanized,
Africans. Clerks, teachers, capitãos (foremen), tailors, artisans, drivers,
and messengers were the leaders of welfare societies, recreation committees, and football clubs in Northern Rhodesia by 1935.[14] After 1928
these men had begun to meet together, to speak out against what they
believed were injustices, and to seek redress of grievances through channels that they had been taught were appropriate. Like nonconformists,
they preached a simple gospel and learned to speak and to debate in the

little societies constituted ostensibly for social reasons.[15] With utmost patience, they sought to influence their governments, which could easily deny them permission to meet. Although their methods were hopelessly ineffective, they tried diligently to obtain satisfaction by the passage of innumerable resolutions and by the presentation of frequent petitions to governors and chief secretaries.

What did these organizations want? There was no mention of self-government or independence: "We are here to make a recognition that should cement the existing friendship between the government, the settlers, and the Africans. Whatever we are going to discuss must be in line with the government because they are our fathers upon whom we should rely for our progress and welfare." [16] But there was much talk about the need for legislative representation by directly elected speakers. Most of the other demands were not directly political. They wanted improved sanitation: "We hereby resolve that the present compound latrines are in an obscene state . . . and it is doubtful in the present condition of the compound to expect Europeans interested in native development to visit native residents." [17] They wanted better boots and clothing to be supplied to prisoners. They desired markets in the urban compounds. They wanted better educational facilities and decent hospitals. They wanted the government to control dogs. And they wanted better housing and better burial grounds.

There were regular appeals for "justice"—that vague and undefinable benefit which they had been taught to expect from whites. So they asked, "Why is it only Africans who need to carry passes in their own country?" The trains do not provide places for Africans to eat or to purchase tea; the accommodation is not comfortable. "May we have improvements, please?" Query: "When a white man commits adultery with an African woman he is not punished. When a native is suspected of committing adultery with a European woman he is punished. Why?" Africans assembled to petition the police to cease assaulting prisoners, particularly those handcuffed to others. They asked for legal assistance to help them puzzle out the white man's court procedures.

Even in aggregation, there is little evidence that this form of constitutional protest ever brought about improvements. It did serve to air grievances publicly and to provide an avenue down which anger and frustration could be channeled nonviolently. The disaffection of the masses could be focused and verbalized and local associations could gradually join in concert. Individuals could conquer feelings of inferiority and begin to assert leadership; indeed, they accumulated that experience so necessary for an informed opposition. Most importantly, the associations afforded nationalist leaders informal professional training of inestimable value. Furthermore, the first modern parties had the heritage of numerous debating societies, and supposedly nonpolitical associations, on which to base their initial mass appeal.

Governments failed to deal realistically with these early associations. Civil servants were prohibited from speaking publicly or taking an active part in the associations. The associations were forbidden to discuss matters "entirely outside the scope of activities for which they were formed."

Native welfare associations should look after nonpolitical interests of detribalized natives resident in various townships. . . .

. . . welfare associations [are] not representative and government could not regard their views on political matters as representing those of the people as a whole.[18]

The governor of Northern Rhodesia suggested that the leaders of welfare associations, and the associations themselves, should be ridiculed and treated as errant children.[19] Alternately, government was exceedingly careful never to permit the associations to criticize the mine owners or white settlers and it regularly ostracized any whites who were wont to talk politics with the associations. Until World War II, government successfully resisted any amalgamation of African associations or the formation of any political parties of a territorial variety. And when they eventually were formed, government was unsure of the best ways in which to cope with them.

III

Colonialism almost everywhere in the non-Western world produced reaction, and where this reaction could not be expressed directly, or where healthy protest failed to bring about any appreciable amelioration, the conquered people expressed their rejection of colonialism religiously. Sundkler views the formation of African independent religious bodies as inevitable whenever there are no other outlets for protest available.[20] The Bantu quasi-Christian movements also permit those who are ambitious to come to prominence without direct reference to the colonial context. Furthermore, as Mair has rightly concluded, the separatist sects and prophet cults of Africa (like the related cargo cults of Oceania and the ghost groups of Indian America) demonstrate the need for "a religion that corresponds to widely held aspirations." [21]

In East and Central Africa one may differentiate two varieties of anti-colonial religion. The separatist sects have seceded from mission churches or have simply been formed by a small cadre of dissatisfied adherents. They emphasize African control of the present (not necessarily the future) and they model themselves on the prevailing Protestant mission form of organization (although the BaEmilio Church of the Sacred Heart of Jesus, of Northern Rhodesia, represents a Roman Catholic schism). These separatist sects have always asserted strong claims for African self-government within the congregational context.[22] They have baptized readily, revised the orthodox rules of mission Christianity to permit polygyny and beer-drinking and, wherever conditions were ripe, led overt, sometimes violent, and always abortive revolts against colonial authority.

The second variety, African versions of chiliastic cults so common to the Western world, depends on the inspiration of a prophet or a mystic.[23] Their members are converts from mission churches or from the ranks of nonbelievers. Their organization is loose and unstable, their dogma is frequently nonexistent, and their ritual is usually syncretic, spontaneous, and highly emotional. They emphasize confessions, faith healing ("Only pure water will do"), drumming, dancing, speaking with tongues, intercession by mediums and communication with ancestors or gods, divining, purification, elimination of sorcery and witchcraft, a fraternity of the elect who are sanctified by being "born again," and baptism by total immersion.[24] They are millennial. With the apocalypse will come a new and totally black Jerusalem. No longer will Africans be hewers of wood and drawers of water for the white man. These movements represent a reordering of daily life in preparation for the apocalypse and a structuring of a black godly pantheon or, in some cases, the deification of the local prophet as a Son of God to replace Christ or Muhammed in African minds.[25]

Religious separatism in Bantu Africa dates from the formation of the Tembu National Church in 1884.[26] By 1900 it had reached Barotseland, transmitted by Sotho evangelists, and Nyasaland, where it was furthered by the Australian evangelist Joseph Booth. The sequence of events that led via Booth to the formation of John Chilembwe's Providence Industrial Mission in Nyasaland, the first dynamic African separatist church in Central and East Africa, has been thoroughly described by Shepperson and Price.[27] By 1915 Chilembwe, backed by American Negro money, had brought about a unique religious experiment that was exclusively African. More intelligent or courageous than most other separatist sect leaders, or perhaps simply more persuaded of his own understanding of Africa's destiny, Chilembwe was active in opposing any government measures that he deemed an affront to Africans. He protested against the employment of African troops in Ashantiland, Somaliland, and against the Germans. He championed the cause of Nyasaland's landless proletariat. He opposed tax increases. Foreshadowing similar activity years later in Kenya, he established a chain of independent schools in the Shire Highlands (Nyasaland). Eventually he saw himself as the leader of an independent black Nyasaland, and he directed his Christian followers in a brief, bloody, and wholly unsuccessful rising against European rule.[28] Most other separatist churches have, since Chilembwe, confined their activities to more peaceful paths (governments have been more wary), although the Watu Wa Mngu in Kenya and the Lenshina movement of Northern Rhodesia have had clashes with the police.[29] Even where the independent churches have failed to demonstrate violently, they have remained in continual opposition.

Chiliasm in Africa is an American export. But Russell's "millennial dawn doctrine," [30] popularized by the Watchtower Bible and Tract Society, has been improved almost out of recognition by the African genius for the cult. Elliott Kenan Kamwana Achirwa preached the coming of the Kingdom wherein Africans would soon have full independence and control of taxes. The government would go. "We shall build our own ships; make our own powder, import our own guns." [31] Mwana Lesa, the self-styled Son of God, promised his followers immediate entrance into the select circle of believers and a reserved seat in the Garden of Eden. He proposed first to rid the earth of witches. At one performance a spirit seized him, ". . . for his eyes were red as coals of fire, and on his lips flecks of foam were appearing. He swayed and tossed his arms about like a mountain tree in the grip of a tempest, and the women of his retinue were swaying and moaning as though in fear and terror. . . ." [32] The African Watchtower movement that frightened Northern Rhodesia after World War I taught the immediate end of the world. It followed that there was no need to obey chiefs or government, to cultivate or to work; it was only necessary to be baptized—and baptism was easy—and to wait expectantly for the millennium. But in the meantime disobedience impelled conflict between white government and African anarchy. It led to warfare and to the eventual imprisonment of large numbers of tribesmen possessed of a simple eschatology.[33]

Government treated separatist sects and chiliastic cults with amusement, a measure of contempt, and some fear. Orthodox missionaries always sought to persuade their governments to forbid independent churches, and for long administrations limited the dissemination of religious propaganda and the spread of most independent African churches. In Northern Rhodesia the government unsuccessfully tried legal subterfuge to curb the influence of the Lenshina movement, and to eliminate the Ethiopian Catholic Church in Zion. Government feared the millennial movements more, however, and prohibited most Watchtower literature, censored the rest, and generally invoked sedition laws whenever prophets became too important. Prophets thereby became martyrs and objects of subsequent veneration by national political parties.

What has been the contribution of these religious movements to the development of African nationalism? Most important, the many cults and sects have helped to revive African self-respect. They have shown that change is indeed possible and that Africans are capable, given some solidarity, of asserting a measure of influence within the colonial context.

They have diffused new, often heretical ideas about the importance of Africans for Africa. They have provided an alternative to total submission to white power, and they have brought about ties that substituted mutual belief and purpose for traditional kinship arrangements. Together with the proliferation of associations, the religious movements helped to make possible the rapid rise of modern nationalist parties.

IV

The nationalist struggle for power, as distinct from plaintive requests for improved conditions, dates only from the formation of congresses or parties.[34] In East and Central Africa determined direct political assault on colonialism was a product of those forces unleashed by World War II and so neatly summarized by Hodgkin.[35] The prewar associations, usually local interest groups favoring gradualism and fearing militancy, were subsumed in the organization of new entities, the Kenya African Union, Uganda National Congress, Nyasaland African Congress, Northern Rhodesia Congress, and the Tanganyika African National Union. Younger and more aggressive men—a new elite—replaced traditionalists, the long-time champions of moderate change, just as they did in the Gold Coast, in Senegal, and in Western Nigeria.

The heritage of protest was the same as it was in West Africa, except that the rising leadership was less articulate, less well-educated, less accustomed to the ways of Western rule, and less free economically to risk anti-government activity. Hence the retarded pace of nationalism in East and Central Africa, particularly with white settlers added to the equation. Not until the 1950's did these nationalist movements demand self-government followed by independence. It has taken time, and the inspiration of events elsewhere in Africa, to bring about the rapid political change that shocks well-settled colonists and jolts foreign newspaper readers.

The post-World War II parties represent, for the first time, mass support. They have become highly organized, even bureaucratic. They have elaborate constitutions and emphasize their democratic procedures while, in fact, they remain oligarchic in the extreme. Branches have been formed and are wisely regarded as basic to the smooth and effective functioning of the particular national machine. The parties use every technique of modern propaganda to disseminate nationalism; they rely on the overseas press and television more than on the local, often settler-controlled, press and radio for a development of their "case" against the particular colonial government. Some parties keep permanent representatives in London, to influence the colonial government, and in New York, to fraternize with the Afro-Asian bloc at the United Nations. The party leaders make frequent visits to world capitals in order to dramatize their national struggle and to consult with others who have passed successfully through the same phase of revolt.

Only with the rise of a new urban middle class could full-time politicians, so necessary for the prosecution of modern nationalism, be afforded by those interested in change. Without them, of course, no mass parties would have been possible, and no nationalist movement would have remained unbought or otherwise uncompromised. Kwame Nkrumah represents the most illustrious of the early paid secretaries, but the efforts of Oscar Kambona of Tanganyika, Harry Nkumbula of Northern Rhodesia, and Dunduzu Chisiza of Southern Rhodesia and Nyasaland were equally important. Fund-raising, based on subscriptions, badges, flags, slogans, rallies, and the peripatetic campaigner in his gaily painted van or microbus, naturally follows, particularly after the franchise is broadened. The party is brought closer to the rural villager, both for internal party needs and in order to prevent whites from intimating that the nationalist groups represent only an urban elite. The more successfully the party can harness the rural and tribal element, the more it can become a truly atribal and national entity.

Gandhi and the Indian example persuaded the new nationalist movements that nonviolence was an efficacious weapon in their struggle against colonial rule. Indeed, they could publicly advocate little else, and financial and military weakness naturally made them press instead for rapid constitutional change. As a first step, nominated members of the legislative council must be replaced by elected Africans, then by a majority of African unofficials and, as the pace quickens and the demands intensify, by responsible government, self-government, and independence within the Commonwealth. Similarly, successive extensions of the franchise are requested until at last the parties can demand, and obtain, universal adult suffrage. As one would expect, the successful parties, at first extra-parliamentary, take advantage of any constitutional changes that afford them a reasonable chance of advance toward self-government. The 1956 elections gave the Nyasaland Congress a majority of the African seats and a certain encouragement to move rapidly toward a more anti-colonial position. Similarly, the tradition of African legislative representation in Uganda and Kenya made it easier, at first, for national movements in those countries to seek change through constitutional rearrangement. But in general they received relatively little encouragement from the governments concerned; not surprisingly, governments jailed leaders for sedition or for possessing prohibited literature (a Gandhi pamphlet in Northern Rhodesia). Nationalism became more aggressive in the face of white resistance to fundamental shifts in the power relationship. "Positive action"—the use of boycotts and strikes—came into vogue, interspersed before very long with violence—a violence that need not have been deliberately encouraged by nationalist leaders.

Over and above other factors, it was the charismatic leadership of a few men that caused modern nationalism to flourish after World War II. Jomo Kenyatta came home, leaving his wife and son in England. Dr. Kamuzu Banda encouraged and exhorted from afar. Harry Nkumbula returned from London. Oscar Kambona came to Dar-es-Salaam. Julius Nyerere of Tanganyika returned from Edinburgh. They were joined by others, but the encouragement of nationalism was, until recent years, primarily their contribution. They accumulated support with ease; the African grievances were many and evident, racialism was not unknown. In a relatively short time these leaders transformed their associations into modern mass parties. The people of Tanganyika, in 1961 the first to receive self-government and independence, campaigned for it from 1954, when Nyerere formed the Tanganyika African National Union. Nyasaland, which entered the stage of "responsible" government in 1961, had an African National Congress with modern aspirations as early as 1944. Uganda, which obtained self-government in 1962, experienced the birth of a national party only in 1953, after Great Britain had exiled the Kabaka of Buganda. A modern national party was evident in Kenya from 1947, after Kenyatta reasserted his leadership of the Kenya African Union. The onset of Mau Mau interrupted the growth of African politics in Kenya, but national parties were permitted to emerge again in 1956. In Northern Rhodesia the phase of modern politics began in 1951, when Nkumbula assumed direction of the African National Congress.

These various parties were the direct successors to the associations of an earlier era. Since 1920 the indigenous inhabitants of East and Central Africa had sought to ameliorate their colonial condition by organizing themselves in such associations or by participation in schismatic sectarian movements. But these were ineffectual avenues of protest. They were parochial. The African associations and sects sought improvement rather than change. The leaders requested equal opportunity within a white-dominated system, although, in some cases, these proto-nationalist movements idealized the traditional, pre-European society and sought to achieve it by a withdrawal. The early leaders did not envisage a radically altered society. They did not seek the political kingdom. Theirs was, in sum, a tentative approach adapted to the circumstances of colonial rule. But it did represent legitimate protest and it did provide the necessary bases for a later, "modernist" and more thoroughgoing nationalism. The parties drew their inspiration from the earlier forms of anti-colonialism. Their followers sought redress for the same grievances. But after World War II they wished to achieve a transformation; the parties sought the political kingdom in order to reassert themselves racially and in order to claim a national heritage originally stimulated by the European partition of Africa and later nurtured by colonial rule.

NOTES

1. Lord Hailey prefers "Africanism," and James Coleman gives "nationalism" restricted usage. For an excellent and thorough discussion, with further references, see Martin Kilson, "The Analysis of African Nationalism," *World Politics*, x (April 1958), 484–97.

2. There is no need to detail the "Maji-Maji" rebellion in German East Africa, the Nyasaland Rising of 1915, or any of a large number of less well-known revolts that have been a regular concomitant of colonial rule.

3. Thomas Hodgkin, *Nationalism in Colonial Africa* (London 1956), 84.

4. P. J. Silawe to Secretary for Native Affairs, 25 August 1930, SEC/NAT/ 324, National Archives, Lusaka.

5. See George Bennett, "The Development of Political Organizations in Kenya," *Political Studies*, v (June 1957), 113–30.

6. Cf. Simon Ottenberg, "Improvement Associations Among the Afikpo Ibo," *Africa*, xxv (January 1955), 1–28; and K. A. Busia, *Social Survey of Sekondi-Takoradi* (Accra 1950).

7. "The lit end of a cigarette in a woman's mouth is a sure sign of a prostitute plying for hire." Recurrent phrase in the minutes of the Ramogi African Welfare Association, 1945–1947. It is incorporated in the 1955 bylaws of the Luo Union, held *ultra vires* by the District Commissioner, Kisumu. Kisumu Archives.

8. Kikuyu Association to the East African Royal Commission, 1924. Kenya Archives.

9. ". . . in East Africa [I had] the rare experience of dealing with a *tabula rasa,* an almost untouched and sparsely inhabited country, where we could do as we will[ed], regulate immigration, and open or close the door as seem[ed] best. . . ." Charles Eliot, *The East Africa Protectorate* (London 1905), 3. For an excellent summary of evidence and relevant literature, see Martin Kilson, "Land and Politics in Kenya," *Western Political Quarterly,* x (September 1957), 559–81.

10. In 1897 the government admitted the principle of individual ownership of land and issued regulations respecting the sale of land by Africans. See Regulation No. 12 (1897), issued 8 July 1897. Copy in Kenya Archives.

11. Kikuyu Association Memorandum presented to the East African Royal Commission, November 1924. Copy in Kenya Archives.

12. Kikuyu Association to the East African Royal Commission, 1924.

13. George Delf, Kenyatta's unofficial biographer, was unable to talk with Kenyatta himself, but his book, *Jomo Kenyatta* (London 1961), is useful for a superficial outline of Kenyatta's life. Kenyatta was reluctant to discuss his early activities with me, but Thuku was both willing and articulate (11–12 September 1961).

14. For an early breakdown, minutes of 21 December 1935, SEC/NAT/ 311, National Archives, Lusaka.

15. Cf. L. F. Church, *The Early Methodist People* (London 1948); and J. L. and Barbara Hammond, *The Town Labourer, 1760–1832* (London 1917), ii.

16. Minutes of meeting of Welfare Societies at Kafue, 10–11 July 1934.

17. Minutes of Livingstone Welfare Association, 5 May, 7 July 1934.

18. Chief Secretary's circular minute, 4 September 1933, and Chief Secretary's minutes, 21 February 1946, SEC/NAT/311, National Archives, Lusaka.

19. Chief Secretary to Secretary for Native Affairs, 24 February 1931, SEC/NAT/321, National Archives, Lusaka.

20. Bengt G. M. Sundkler, *Bantu Prophets in South Africa* (London 1948), 297.

21. Lucy Mair, "Independent Religious Movements in Three Continents," *Comparative Studies in Society and History*, 1 (January 1959), 135. Cf. George Eliot, who writes of ". . . eager men and women to whom the exceptional possession of religious truth was the condition that reconciled them to a meagre existence, and made them feel in secure alliance with the unseen but supreme ruler of a world in which their own visible part was small."—*Felix Holt* (London 1866), 42.

22. The literature of separatism in Africa is extremely varied in scope and quality. In addition to Sundkler, see Katesa Schlosser, *Propheten in Afrika* (Braunschweig 1949) and *Eingeborenenkirchen in Süd und Süd-West Afrika* (Kiel 1958); F. B. Welbourn, *East African Rebels* (London 1961); George Shepperson, "Ethiopianism and African Nationalism," *Phylon*, xiv (March 1953), 9–18. See also Jomo Kenyatta, *Facing Mount Kenya* (London 1961), 269–79.

23. An excellent theoretical discussion is Bryan Wilson, "An Analysis of Sect Development," *American Sociological Review*, xxiv (February 1959), 3–15.

24. For some examples, see R. I. Rotberg, "The Lenshina Movement of Northern Rhodesia," *Rhodes-Livingstone Journal*, xxix (June 1961), 63–78.

25. See Raymond Leslie Buell, *The Native Problem in Africa* (New York 1928), ii, 601–12.

26. Sundkler, 38 ff. See also G. M. Theal, *Basutoland Records*, ii (Capetown 1883), 184, 229–31, 241 ff.

27. George Shepperson and Thomas Price, *Independent African* (Edinburgh 1958).

28. *Ibid.*, 265–320. Cf. Nyasaland Protectorate, *Report of the Commission Appointed . . . to Inquire into . . . the Native Rising within the Nyasaland Protectorate* [6819] (Zomba 1916).

29. Rotberg, 76.

30. Charles Taze Russell, *Studies in the Scriptures*, 7 vols. (Allegheny, Pa., and Brooklyn, N.Y., 1886–1904).

31. Quoted in George Shepperson, "The Politics of African Church Separatist Movements in British Central Africa, 1892–1916," *Africa*, xxiv (July 1954), 239.

32. Carl Von Hoffman, *Jungle Gods* (London 1929), 53. Also Frank Melland in *Glasgow Bulletin*, 14 January 1939.

33. The details are contained in ZA 9/2/2/2, Lusaka, and RC 3/9/5/29. Salisbury.

34. See James S. Coleman, "The Emergence of African Political Parties," in C. Grove Haines, ed., *Africa Today* (Baltimore 1955), 225–56.

35. Hodgkin, 142.

R. Emerson

PARADOXES OF ASIAN NATIONALISM (1954)

Sweeping and remoulding Europe in the 19th Century, nationalism has swept on in equally revolutionary guise to remould Asia in the 20th, and is now penetrating Africa. In the study of its impact and development almost every aspect of human society is involved, positively or negatively, and at least every social science discipline has its part to contribute to the analysis of an exceedingly complex whole. In the Asia of today and of the recent past we have a whole series of new nations coming forward to assert their claims in the world. A laboratory has been made available in which we can observe and analyze the growth of nationalism, catch it in its earliest stages and trace it through to its maturity, as well as at least noting in passing the countervailing forces of the past and present. The raw material, vibrant with a new and dynamic life, is there for our taking, and it would be tragic if we were to let it slip through our fingers without gathering it and subjecting it to the closest possible investigation.

Although the raw material is there, and in abundance, I would be the last to suggest that the task of analysis is easy or that we now have all the intellectual tools we need to carry it through. Much of what is glibly and habitually said about nationalism rests on a very slim foundation of positive knowledge and, more important, of precise and meaningful concepts. Much of what passes for solid scientific analysis is actually done with mirrors or with a sleight of hand which may deceive the unwary but should not be allowed to deceive the manipulator himself. One of the most seductive and elusive variants of this is the process of *ex post facto* reasoning: reasoning back from the fact of the nation to the things which must have caused it. Let me suggest two examples. Though it

SOURCE. R. Emerson, "Paradoxes of Asian Nationalism," reprinted from *Far Eastern Quarterly*, XIII, 1954, pp. 131–142.

often, and notably in some parts of Asia, is not the case, a nation is normally assumed to be a community knit together by a common language; but what is regarded for these purposes as a separate language and what as a mere dialect is actually likely to be decided after the fact on the basis of the national communities which come into effective existence rather than on any necessary and objective linguistic principles. With greater assurance we can assume a nation to be a community knit together by a common experience over a reasonably long past, shaping a common tradition and culture. But any extensive people has a host of traditions, historical experiences and even cultures, crisscrossing each other in almost every conceivable direction. Those which the observer is likely to put forward as constituting the inevitable national tradition, as integral to the national pattern of life, are those which fit the national mould as it actually develops, to the exclusion or minimization of those— equally real in historical experience—which cut across the nation, as on class or regional lines, or link it with other, external groups.

Behind this *ex post facto* process there often lurks the unspoken, but also unquestioned, assumption that the nations which actually appear on the world stage are, so to speak, divinely ordained and pre-determined entities which could not be otherwise than as they are.[1] But if one stands back from the stream of history and examines it with a somewhat quizzical eye, it becomes one of the most fascinating of pursuits to attempt to work out why the particular nations which have in fact emerged did emerge, as contrasted with the variety of alternatives which, under different circumstances, might have come to pass. This is far too large a topic for any real exploration, here. I suggest it as one worthy of far more attention than it has usually received. Particularly in Asia new nations have been created, and in some sense are still being created before our eyes but we have only scanty knowledge of the historical alchemy by which scattered fragments of peoples have been transmuted into communities responsive to the appeal of nationalism. What are the forces which shape the peoples who at some later stage come to feel themselves separate and distinctive nations? It is obvious that this is not, and by its nature cannot be, any sudden or even speedy process. Over long periods of time there must be a storing up in the minds of men of a folk sense of shared memories, of common patterns of life, which gives this particular people a deep and profoundly significant sense of sharing a common destiny from which all the rest of mankind is excluded. At what malleable stage in their history and under what circumstances do peoples become so deeply enmeshed in this particular community of the nation that

> In spite of all temptations
> To belong to other nations
> He remains an Englishman

It is an attractive theory, and one with a large measure of applicability, that the primary element in the shaping of nations is the existence at some malleable period in a people's history of a single political rule, of a common state structure or a reasonable approximation thereof, sufficiently long-lasting and deep-penetrating to make a permanent imprint on that people's social mind. The formation of the separate Philippine and Indonesian nations, despite a large original cultural and ethnic homogeneity, must be attributed primarily to the distinct colonial regimes to which they were so long subjected. Indeed, Quezon is on record as acknowledging that Filipino unity was largely a product of Spanish and American rule.[2] The unity of India is certainly not to be explained without some reference to the unifying force of the British regime—but the splitting off of Pakistan as a separate nation belies the notion that this theory is universally applicable. To understand the emergence of three nations in Indochina—if that is in fact to be the outcome—it is clearly necessary to go back to their ancient pre-French roots, but it is also in order to point out that French rule never really sought to unify them. As the dust gradually settles, will the present colonially-determined frontiers survive as the frontiers of nations for the considerable mélange of peoples stretching from Burma across Thailand into Laos and Cambodia and up into South China? What national allegiance or allegiances will emerge from the racial hodge-podge of Malaya, where one can only assume that differences were already so deeply imprinted that political unification in the colonial era could not have produced a single communal consciousness. Or, to raise historical "if's," what are the circumstances under which the diversities of China might have been exploited in such fashion as to produce not one, but several Chinese nations?

Part of what I have just been saying has already suggested the general range of issues which I should like to consider in this paper. Central to these issues is the fact that it is so clearly and strikingly the impact of the West which has brought to fighting consciousness societies which in their own roots derive wholly from non-Western sources. As I have suggested, in at least some of the colonial areas even the basic question as to which peoples are to be within and which outside the national community appears to have been determined by the lines drawn on the map by the imperial powers. It seems to me inescapable that in the future a great part of the inner dynamics of nationalism in Asia must derive from this profound contradiction within nations which derive from an ancient Asian past and yet have been brought to national awareness not only by the Western impact but even more immediately and insistently by the revolutionary appeal of their own native Westernizers.

The claim of any people to separate nationhood must rest primarily on the fact that over the centuries—in the Asian setting I should perhaps say over the millennia—it has developed an identity and way of life of its own. If it is no longer as fashionable as it once was to speak in Mazzinian terms of the peculiar mission of each nation in the divine harmony of the world, much the same is implied by the currently more palatable new-fangled terms such as national character, pattern of culture, or value structure. Without being highflown about it, what presumably drives a nation forward in its will to live and assert itself is that its members feel that they share among themselves goals, values, purposes, habits, and outlooks, shaped from an immemorial past, of which only they are properly aware and which only they can properly bring to bear on the conduct of their collective life.

Every nation which comes to awareness of itself inevitably searches back into its past to single out those things which are distinctive, which have brought it into separate existence, and which serve to demonstrate its unique and illustrious antecedents, be they real or largely in the realm of myth. In the first stage this search is likely to express itself most vigorously in the religious sphere in the form of a revival and perhaps purification of the religion of the country as a re-assertion of the integrity of the national culture and as a central symbol of difference from the Western intruder. At a later stage there is a turning away in the sphere of language from the alien-imposed European tongues, and an insistence on the adoption and use of a national language which will at once express the national soul and serve as an instrument of national unification. Everywhere there is an effort to re-establish contact with the national past. Sun Yat-sen and Chiang Kai-shek, in their different fashions look back to the majestic sweep of an earlier China, to the distinctive loyalties to family and clan, to the Chinese discoveries and inventions of past ages. Nehru rediscovers India, Gandhi seeks to build on the ancient Indian heritage, and many Indian nationalists, perhaps particularly in Bengal, turn back to re-explore the religious and philosophic grandeurs of Hinduism; as, later, their neighboring Pakistanis boast the Mogul Empire and the Islamic tradition. Indonesia comes to a new awareness of the empires of Srivijaya and Majapahit, of Borobodur, and of its heritage of music, dance, and art.

But it is a significant part of the paradox that a very large share of the credit for this re-opening of the treasures of the past must go not to the Asian peoples themselves but to the Westerners who have delved into the antiquities of India, uncovered the ruins of Angkor Vat, pieced together the ancient chronicles and monuments, and in this fashion presented the Asians with an ancestral past, with a rich store of national memories, which had almost slipped from the Asian mind. Indirectly there was the challenge to Asians of the presence of alien rule, bringing an assertedly superior alien culture; more directly there was the active work of Western scholars in recreating a partially forgotten past.

Nationalism, I have been suggesting, is in part necessarily a return to the past, to those things which distinguish this nation from the rest of the world. Yet who are the nationalists? In what parts and segments of the Asian societies do we find them? To put it negatively: the one place where we do *not* find them is in those parts of the society which are most obviously representative of the cultural heritage and way of life of the past. On the contrary, it is the persons and groups who are most characteristically the product of the Western impact who are the leaders, the storm troopers, and the usual rank and file of the nationalist movements. These are Asian nations which are being roused to life, but it is the disruptive force of the alien European encroachment and dominance which has brought new communities to birth out of the old societies, and the prime movers have been the people most divorced from their traditional worlds. The people who can probably be taken in some sense as the most authentic heirs and perpetuators of the ancient culture and traditions are the rural peasantry, who everywhere constitute the great mass of the population, and such of the old aristocracy as has been able to hold on; but it is very clear on the record that these groups have formed neither the leadership nor the mass following of Asian nationalism. As far as the peasantry is concerned this is, of course, by no means to say either that there have not been fringe segments of it which have been drawn actively into the nationalist movements or that, as nationalism has progressed and established itself, the peasants have not come to an increasing acceptance of it. But in general the evidence indicates that the rural masses, bound to their villages and continuing the traditional cultivation of their fields, have either been indifferent to the new currents or, at the best and belatedly, passive adherents to the nationalist creed. It is barely necessary to add that, of course, from time to time and place to place, the nationalists, like the Communists, have been able to make effective use of peasant grievances or upheavals, but with no necessary implication that the peasant actors themselves were either nationalist or Communist. The case is similar with the older aristocracy. Obviously certain members of it— I might cite the Sultan of Jocja and the considerably more equivocal figure of Bao Dai—have played nationalist roles, but in general it is a group which either has been pushed aside or destroyed by the colonial regimes or has become so tainted with colonial "collaborationism" as to have no nationalist standing.

On a geographical, as opposed to a class, basis of analysis, it was in the native states of India and, in lesser degree, of Indonesia that the old ways of life were carried on in contrast to the greater ferment of modernism in the more directly ruled areas; but these states tended to be backwaters, least touched by the nationalist stream. If one seeks the nationalists of Indochina it is not to relatively untouched Laos that one turns but to the deltas of the Red River and the Mekong.

Who are the nationalists? Certainly, as far as the leadership is concerned, they are almost exclusively neither of the aristocracy nor of the peasantry, but rather of what must be loosely and somewhat unsatisfactorily defined as the middle class. With only rare exceptions, leaving the special case of Japan aside, they are intellectuals or professional men with a very high degree of contact with and training in the Western world. Sun Yat-sen was a doctor who secured his lower education in Hawaii and his higher and medical training in Hong Kong. Gandhi, Nehru, and Jinnah were all British-educated lawyers. In the Philippines Quezon and Osmena were both lawyers with extensive experience of the West. Luang Pradit in Thailand was a Paris-trained lawyer. In Burma Aung San was a product of Rangoon University and a law student; Ba Maw studied at Cambridge and obtained a French law degree; Premier Nu studied at the University of Rangoon, turned writer, and—a somewhat odd occupation for a Buddhist statesman—translated Dale Carnegie's *How to Win Friends and Influence People* into Burmese.[3] In Indonesia Sukarno was an engineer by training; Mohammed Hatta a university student in Holland; and Sutan Sjahrir an intellectual and writer with an intimate acquaintance with the Western world and its thought. And so it goes up and down the list. The *Indonesian Review* in its issue for April–June, 1951, lists the educational background of the members of the Sukiman cabinet of 1951: for one no academic information was given, and the Minister of Religion received his education at a special Moslem institute; all the rest of the eighteen members of the cabinet had had either a substantial amount of or a full Western-style education; five had studied in Holland or elsewhere in Europe; six were law students; three were engineers; and two were medical doctors, including the prime minister. Surely these are men who, however much of the more ancient tradition they may carry with them, may properly be regarded as products of the Western world and its techniques and outlooks.

To trace down the nationalist following in similar detail is obviously a far more difficult matter because of the necessity of reaching into amorphous and anonymous masses of people. The general conclusion is, however, I believe unavoidable, that the groups and classes which have been most susceptible to infection by the nationalist germ are those who have been most sharply divorced from their old worlds by the impact of the new. Any listing of them must include the students who have enlisted in the nationalist cause with almost unbroken fervor. It would include many of the civil servants, and other elements of the rising middle class, of whom increasing numbers have economic interests which nationalism promotes and protects. An increasing mass following is contributed by the growing urban proletariat and, at least in many instances, by the uprooted workers on large-scale Western estates and plantations and in other Western enterprises, in mines and oil-fields—in brief, the workers in those employments which are least characteristic of the native society

and most characteristic of the new super-imposed Western society. It is
no accident that Sun and the Kuomintang after him found so large a
measure of financial and political support among the overseas Chinese
in Southeast Asia and elsewhere—a peculiarly uprooted element. We
have many of the bits and pieces from which a profile and sociology of
the nationalisms of Asia might be constructed, but I suggest that there
are many studies remaining to be undertaken which would give us a
vastly more detailed picture than we currently have of the inner structure
of the nationalist movements, and of the layers of the population in different countries which have successively taken part in them.

If we attempt to seek out the sources of inspiration of Asian nationalism we again move onto somewhat treacherous and uncertain ground,
since positive proof of intellectual influences and of the ancestry and
spread of ideas is notoriously difficult, but the predominant influence of
the West seems unquestionable. The very idea of nationalism is certainly
of Western origin, and there is every reason to assume that the mere
element of imitation in Asia is a powerful one. The strength of the West,
which enabled it to dominate so much of Asia, was a thing to be studied
and copied, and a major component of that strength, according to the
testimony of the West itself, was the existence of coherent and integrated
nations. The achievement and maintenance of national unity and independence were one of the central themes of the literature and political
tradition of the West to which the Asians were exposed. The writings of
Rousseau, Burke, Mazzini, and the great figures of American independence became familiar to them, and exercised among them the influence
which they had first exercised in the West itself. More recently a variant
strand of Western thought and political action—the Communist endorsement of national self-determination—has made its impact through the
doctrines of Lenin, Stalin, and their followers. The evidence of the direct
descent of the nationalists of Asia from those who propagated the nationalism of the West and hymned its praises is too overwhelming to allow
of any serious doubt.

This is not, of course, to seek at all to deny that the interactions of
the Asian nationalists on each other and the stimulus given to one country
by a neighbor are not of great importance; but it certainly appears to be
the case that even here the original spark is derived from Europe and is
passed on through an Asian intermediary, suffering, perhaps, some slight
sea change on the way. As the French Revolution is taken as the conventional date for the starting point of European nationalism, so the rise of
Japan, and particularly the Russo-Japanese War, is taken as the conventional benchmark for Asian nationalism. Sun Yat-sen points to the fact
that the new Japan, transformed into a first-class power, has caught up
with Europe and given the rest of Asia unlimited hope. "We once thought
we could not do what the Europeans could do; and we see now that

Japan has learned from Europe and that, if we follow Japan, we, too, will be learning from the West as Japan did." [4] But it is obvious from Sun's words that it is Europe which is the true and original model, and he was not averse to drinking directly from the springs of Communist Russia, which gave him both economic inspiration and the political technique of the centralized one-party state.

Particularly for the Vietnamese, so much more influenced by China than the rest of Southeast Asia, Sun himself, the Kuomintang, and later the Chinese Communists became sources of nationalist and organizational inspiration; and Sukarno pays tribute to the teaching of Sun. Elsewhere, and most notably in Indonesia in the interwar decades, Gandhi and the Indian National Congress were models to be studied and followed with respect; but nowhere can the nationalism of Asia be traced to Europe with greater assurance than in India.

The well-springs of Asian nationalism lie in the ideas and political example of Europe, and, despite the praise which, as I have indicated, was frequently heaped on the great past of the several nations, there have been very few among the nationalists who have had their eyes on a restoration of an Asian past rather than on the creation of a Western future. [5] Of the great leaders only Gandhi's name comes to mind in this connection, with his peculiar mixture of the modern world and of India's antiquity. In India this aspect of Gandhi's life and teaching has been carried on and exaggerated or distorted by the right-wing Hindu groups, such as the Hindu Mahasaba, but it is the modernism of Nehru which has carried the day. In China Chiang has in some measure preached a return to Confucianism and the time-honored tradition and structure of the older Chinese society. In Indonesia perhaps Darul Islam and some of the more traditionalist Moslem groups stand for an older world; and in Iran Kashani has stood up to challenge modernist trends; but the general drift is clearly modernist and Western.

Far from seeking a return to the past the bulk of the nationalists concentrate rather on bringing to their countries the dynamism, the Faustian drive, of the modern West. That there must be a certain ambivalence in their attitude lies at the heart of the paradox. They are attacking the West; they are seeking to get out from under Western supremacy; but it is the instruments and outlooks of the West which they would have their people master in order to substantiate their claim to an equal and independent status in the world. The nationalism of Asia is no mere xenophobic rejection of the alien disturber, no effort to restore a static and tradition-bound society, but to break with, or at least to build upon, the old traditions in such fashion as to infuse the nations of Asia with the dynamic power which has revolutionized the West.

There is, I believe, at least side evidence of this in the parallel which can be drawn between the development of nationalism in Asia and in the Western world. Although there are some who would deny that any such parallelism exists to a significant degree, I would be inclined to assert that, recognizing the many differences of time and place and circumstance, Asian nationalism has followed a course which coincides strikingly in many essential respects with the classic European models. It would take us too far afield to try to explore this argument in any detail, but I suggest that in Asia as in Europe and elsewhere nationalism has been the result of the forces which have characteristically shaped the contemporary world: the stress on individualism, the rationalist and scientific outlook, the commercial and industrial revolutions. It is a product of what one of the recent investigators of nationalism has termed a process of social mobilization [6]—the drawing of more and more people away from the traditional folk culture of village and market town into active participation in the larger society of the modern world. This has come about through the operation of such things as the spread of a money economy, the growth of wage labor, increasing urbanization, the development of communications, and the workings of a rationalized and more intensive governmental structure.

Metternich in the early 19th Century identified as the revolutionary and nationalist enemies of the old order he wished to preserve, the students, the professors, the intellectuals, and the lawyers: can we do better in identifying the leaders of 20th Century nationalism in Asia? Add to them more generally the rising middle class, the urban workers, and the uprooted peasantry, and you have the groups who have everywhere been the progenitors and the first adherents of the nationalist cause.

I shall leave aside one very baffling question which is, to my mind, all too infrequently asked and to which I have been able to find no satisfactory answer. Why is it that the groups involved in this process of social mobilization should so uniformly turn in the nationalist direction, pour themselves into the national mould? Considering all the other possible bases of community in the world, why should the nation have come to assume the centrality which it has? For example, it is apparent to the good Marxist that, while nationalism may be made use of for his purposes, the real allegiance of the working masses cuts sharply across national lines and is focussed on the solidarity of class—or, at least, it should. It would be interesting in this connection to dig deeper into the group and class make-up of the Communist as opposed to the more purely nationalist movements, and to see whether or not there is a significant difference in the elements to which they make their appeal; although it is evident on the face of it that such an investigation would be complicated by the large elements of nationalism which Communism in Asia has been prepared to absorb.

There is one further line of inquiry which I should like to pursue. What is the relation between the Westernized leaders and the mass of

the population which, in varying degrees in different countries and localities, has remained relatively untouched by the impact of the West? The
new elite in the contemporary Asian scene is obviously only a minority
and often a very small minority, and yet it claims to speak on behalf of
the whole of each of the nations. To the colonial administrator the gulf
between the Westernized few and the folk society was frequently one of
the justifications of his existence. Seeing himself as a better interpreter
and guardian of the interests of the unsophisticated native mass than
the clamorous Westernized nationalists, he was inclined to echo the
dictum of Lord Lugard in Nigeria that "it is a cardinal principle of British
colonial policy that the interests of a large native population shall not be
subject to the will . . . of a small minority of educated and Europeanized
natives who have nothing in common with them, and whose interests are
often opposed to theirs." [7] It was in large part the prevalence of this
attitude which led to the bitterest grief of the period of "liberation" after
the Second World War. Assuming that the simple masses would welcome
back their true friends and repudiate the Japanese- and Communist-
inspired betrayers of the real native soul and destiny, the colonial powers
sought to return to 1939. But, despite the great and undeniable gulf between them, the masses in fact gave their loyalty to their new national
leaders.

From the standpoint of the leaders the appeal to the masses of their
people was both a political necessity and, I believe, an inherent part of
the nationalist creed. To make headway against the colonial regimes or,
more broadly, against the imperial powers it was obviously necessary to
build upon a popular base, to enlist as large segments as possible of the
people in the political battles. Coming at it somewhat more abstractly,
the moral and political justification of their position, of their claim to take
over the guidance of their societies, was that they represented the entire
nation. What is the nation after all but the whole body of a people knit
together by special ties which distinguish them from the rest of mankind?
Hence, I suggest, nationalism has in it always a basic democratic element—a democratic element which is not wholly lost even when it is
debased into the plebiscitary totalitarianism of a Hitler or a Mussolini.

Under whatever conditions it may arise, nationalism, by its nature,
involves an appeal to, or, at the least, a reference to the people. Whether
the national claim is put forward against a ruler by divine right, against
a feudal hierarchy, against a conglomerate empire of the Hapsburgs, or
against a colonial regime, nationalism finds its *raison d'être* in the national people for whom it speaks. Furthermore, I would be inclined to
advance a tentative hypothesis to the effect that the democratic implications of nationalism are likely to be most effective, for a variety of
reasons, in the countries which have had the most intensive experience

of colonialism. Even apart from the fact that there has been a deep and direct indoctrination of the Westernized elements in the theory and creed of democracy, there are other important aspects. In the realm of actual politics there is the inescapable need to mobilize, to nationalize, the general populace. The colonial system has worked to destroy or to devitalize the older traditional, aristocratic leadership, and the new elite must establish its claim to power by winning the allegiance of the people whom it is helping to fashion into a nation. I would suggest that there is a more significant reality in the democratic claims and aspirations of the nationalist leaders of the ex-colonial countries of South Asia than there is in those of, say, Japan, Thailand, and Iran where the special circumstances and pressures of colonialism were absent. In the colonial countries the new leadership starts, so to speak, from scratch and has to make its way in the world with the aid of its constituents; in the others the mighty and the rich and landed groups have established positions, prerogatives, and privileges which the real practise of democracy might well threaten and overturn. Everywhere nationalism is used as an instrument to win and hold mass support. It would be my contention that in the countries emerging from the colonial era there is a greater and more effective intention to draw the masses into an actual share of political power.

In this sense nationalism is a unifying force, but I fear that it has also, and perhaps particularly in its democratic manifestations, a strongly divisive element. One authority has suggested that the nationalism of Asia, like its earlier counterpart in Europe, has had the effect of moving toward a territorial base, embracing all the people on the national territory within the nation: "Asia, like Europe, has discovered that modern governments can only function when all are citizens, and all citizens are of equal value." [8] In breaking down the loyalty to religion, caste, and clan, this is likely to be true; but it is also true that, as in Europe, the emergence of nationalism brings with it the emergence of national minorities as well. When the focal point of loyalty is the nation, the state having been created to implement the national will, and when issues are democratically posed for national decision, there is an inevitable tendency to sort out the national sheep from the alien goats. Under a pre-national authoritarian rule the question of membership in the national community may be largely irrelevant; in an age of nationalism it is likely to become the central question. When it is posed in India, a civil war flares up in which a Moslem Pakistan separates itself from the rest, and in Southeast Asia the Chinese, the Europeans and Eurasians, and others find themselves beyond the national pale. Malaya and, in lesser degree, Burma present the most striking instances of this trend. Where there is original unity, nationalism serves further to unite; where there is felt ethnic diversity, nationalism is no cure.

I find myself uncertain as to whether paradoxes are supposed to have answers or not. At all events, I do not claim to have them. The questions sprout up in easy abundance, but the answers are few and far between. We have the basic fact of Westernized elites which have taken command of Asian nations, but where they go from here is another matter. Even the elites themselves are inevitably torn by ambivalences. They cannot help but seek to re-integrate themselves in the national traditions, at the same time that they seek to revolutionize their societies into Western modernity. Casting off the control of the West and acutely sensitive to any imputation of inferiority, they are more than ever conscious of the need to draw on the West to build the strength and true equality of their nations. It is of more than symbolic significance that at a time when they seek to bring Western learning and skills to their people, they move toward the adoption of native national languages which must tend to diminish the ties to the West.

Prediction in the social sciences is always a hazardous matter, and it is even more hazardous today than yesterday. World wars and world revolutions have changed the old elements in familiar equations and brought in new ones whose values are still largely unknown. On the face of the record of what has happened in other comparable situations it is difficult to view the future of the newly risen Asian nations with any great measure of optimism, but in a world undergoing radical transformation there can be no assurance as to what constitute the relevant points of comparability and analogy. The experience of many other countries over the last century suggests that the most probable outcome is backsliding into a lethargy which pays little more than lip service to the ideals of progressive democracy, but this experience for the most part refers back to an era prior to the more recently fashionable mode of totalitarian dictatorships of the right and of the left. The case of China serves notice that Communist despotism may sweep away both lethargy and the proud hopes of liberal nationalism.

Nationalism is a response to the atomization of society, a turn toward a new form of community to replace old communities which are in process of being destroyed. In our day it is the nation which legitimizes the state; but what manner of nations are these which are being created in Asia? By any scheme of accounting they are communities which are all too evidently headed in several directions at once, built on a national unity which has in it more of diversity than of oneness. Will the leaders, holding firm to their democratic and progressive aspirations, be able to carry the masses with them and create a new and stable synthesis, or will they draw apart and form a separate governing caste wielding power for its own sake and enjoying the fruits thereof? Or will they be re-absorbed into a mass which refuses to surrender the ways of its fathers?

NOTES

1. This assumption receives explicit, if not quite unchallengeable, statement in a comment by President Sukarno to the effect that God Almighty created the map of the world in such fashion that even a child can tell that the British Isles are one entity—which might surprise the Irish—and that a child can see that the Indonesian Archipelago is a single entity stretching between the Pacific and Indian oceans and the Asian and Australian continents, from the north tip of Sumatra to Papua. *The Indonesian Review,* Jan. 1951, p. 13.

2. Cf. Joseph Ralston Hayden, *The Philippines* (New York, 1942), p. 21.

3. Cf. Virginia Thompson and Richard Adloff, *The Left Wing in Southeast Asia* (New York, 1950), p. 252.

4. Sun Yat-sen, *San Min Chu I* (Shanghai, 1929), p. 16.

5. An opposing point of view is stated by F. S. C. Northrop, *The Taming of the Nations* (New York, 1952), pp. 68–69, who contends that a study of developments in the Middle and Far East shows that the Muslims and Asians are not pursuing nationalist aspirations as the West understands them: "They are working toward the resurgence of their respective submerged civilizations. What Western reporters have described as the coming of Western nationalism to the Middle East and Asia is really the return of Islamic or Far Eastern ways and values. . . . It is culturalism rather than nationalism that is the rising fact of the world today." But Northrop immediately qualifies this statement by adding that the contemporary mind of Islam and Asia is also seeking to ingraft from the West the factors needed to raise the standard of living of the masses.

6. Karl W. Deutsch, "The Growth of Nations: Some Recurrent Patterns of Political and Social Integration," *World Politics,* Jan. 1953, pp. 168–196.

7. *Report on the Amalgamation of Northern and Southern Nigeria* (Lagos, 1919).

8. Maurice Zinkin, *Asia and the West* (London, 1951), p. 285.

M. L. Kilson, Jr.

NATIONALISM AND SOCIAL CLASSES
IN BRITISH WEST AFRICA* (1958)

INTRODUCTION

During the course of the past fifty years or so since the establishment
of colonial rule in British West Africa,[1] nationalism has registered striking
advances in this area and has even secured its major objectives of national
self-determination and self-government in the former Gold Coast colony
(now named Ghana). Political movements along "national" rather than
"tribal" lines, claiming, as we have already suggested, the rights of national self-determination and self-government, have emerged and have
succeeded in transforming a significant part of the way of life of West
African peoples and societies.[2] In this paper, we shall attempt to uncover
certain elements of the sources of West African nationalism, so as to
render its basic dynamics and character comprehensible.

It is clear to the student of African affairs that colonialism has been
the matrix out of which West African nationalism has arisen. Certain
distinct policies and practices of the colonial powers in West Africa (as
well as in Africa generally) have enabled African tribal communities to
embrace nationalism within a relatively short period. Firstly, the colonial

* A number of persons have assisted me, in one form or other, in the production
of this paper. I am especially indebted to Dr. Amon Nikoi, Third Secretary in the
Embassy of Ghana in Washington, D.C., for access, over a number of years, to his
impressive store of knowledge on West African nationalism. I also would like to
express my indebtedness to the following persons: Dr. F. Oladipo Onipede, Lagos,
Nigeria; Dr. James S. Coleman, University of California (L.A.); Dr. Sayre Schatz,
Hofstra College; and to Professor Rupert Emerson, Harvard University, whose lectures and seminars on colonialism and nationalism stimulated me to undertake this
study.

SOURCE. M. L. Kilson, Jr., "Nationalism and Social Classes in British West Africa,"
reprinted from *The Journal of Politics*, XX, 1958, pp. 368–387, by permission of the
Southern Political Science Association.

powers marked out their territorial estates in Africa by establishing rigid political boundaries, thereby placing diverse tribal and ethnic communities within specified politico-territorial formations and ruling them more or less as a unified group. Hence there emerged such politico-territorial formations as Nigeria and the Gold Coast, which were eventually to become the bases of operation for nationalist political movements. Secondly, the colonial powers supplied a significant segment among the tribal communities in their African territories with a *lingua franca* (*e.g.*, English, French), thereby enabling groups of persons within these communities to communicate with one another—as well as with the outside world and all that this implies—and eventually to lay the basis for common political and social action. Finally, the colonial powers supplied their subjects with a more or less common culture (especially through the establishment of Western education) which eventually enabled certain persons to surmount the parochialisms characteristic of the different, and at times antagonistic, tribal cultures. This last point, it should be noted, has been evidenced particularly by the emergent middle-class elements [3] in West Africa, for these elements have had the greatest and most intensified contact with the Western culture introduced into this area by the colonial powers. In spite of the heterogeneous tribal backgrounds of the persons comprising the West African middle class, they have successfully employed the social and political ideals and concepts derived largely, if not wholly, from their Western education and training in the mobilization of large numbers of their countrymen around the values of nationalism.

The foregoing sketch of the forces that have contributed to the emergence of nationalism in British West Africa remains inadequate without mention of the influence of European economic penetration on this process. The importance of the contribution of European economic penetration to the rise of nationalism in Africa has not always received the attention it deserves. On the basis of our own consideration of this question, it is suggested that, generally, in those areas where European or Western-type economic activity and enterprise (and with this Western education, especially higher education) have been fairly intensive, nationalism has been most advanced.[4] This thesis, of course, may be modified by the colonial policy and situation prevalent in any particular territory. Thus, in the Belgian Congo and in Southern Rhodesia where the industrial revolution has surged ahead most rapidly, the upsurge of nationalism has been rather slight. This can be attributed in part to the social, educational and political policies and situations operative in these areas. In both, higher or university education has been extremely limited, thereby delaying the rise of an educated and professional African middle class.[5] Furthermore, in Southern Rhodesia the racial policy has approximated *apartheid* as practiced in the Union of South Africa, and politics has been largely dominated by a European resident population. Nevertheless, in such British territories as Nigeria and the Gold Coast where economic enterprise, combined with higher education, has gone quite far, and where, in turn, an educated and professional African middle class has emerged, nationalism has made major advances.[6]

Since the last quarter of the nineteenth century, European economic activity (as well as the Western-type economic activity of Africans that has been stimulated by the European presence) has transformed a fundamental part of West African tribal societies.[7] With this transformation have emerged large towns and modern means of communication. The railroad, the automobile, the bicycle, the telephone, the radio, and the press have contributed in breaking down much of the isolation characteristic of tribal communities and have, in turn, accelerated the operation of forces effecting further change in these communities. Among the many consequences of this transformation of West African societies, one of the most important from the political standpoint has been the rise of what Professor Georges Balandier has termed new "social categories," i.e., new social classes.[8] In the course of the past thirty-five years, these classes have developed interests based not on the old tribal society and its subsistence economic system, but rather on the new socio-economic system characterized by commercial agriculture, trade, and industry. With their new interests at hand, and with elements of the necessary economic and political influence to serve them, these classes have been at the forefront of nationalism in West Africa. It is suggested, therefore, that the study of the rise of West African nationalism may be approached as a function of the rise of new social classes due to the general "social mobilization"[9] (to employ Professor Karl W. Deutsch's phrase) of West Africa by Western economic influences as well as political and ideological ones.

In the discussion that follows, we shall be concerned with the rise of the new social classes in West Africa and with the role of the African middle class in the emergence of nationalism in this area.

THE RISE OF NEW SOCIAL CLASSES IN WEST AFRICA

Prior to the advent of Western influences, West African society was a more or less static order within which social and economic change occurred at a relatively slow pace. Today, however, this state of affairs has changed significantly. The uniformity and stability in levels of social existence and modes of life characteristic of the traditional West African society have slowly given way to economic and class differentiation. A visitor to contemporary West Africa will immediately note the marked contrasts in types of social and human existence to be found there. Existing side by side will be seen Africans living the type of life characteristic of most Western countries, while the majority of Africans will be seen living a life of subsistence and adhering to much of the old, traditional patterns. As one observer has described the situation to be encountered by a visitor to contemporary West Africa:

> He can travel on trains and in motor-cars and airplanes, and stay at rest-houses equipped with electric lights and a flush toilet. He can visit African homes furnished in the latest western style. . . . He will see Africans working in shops, offices, and factories, growing crops for foreign consumption, and leasing and renting land. . . . On the other hand, he will also see a majority of Africans living in huts of wattle and daub and of grass, herding cattle, and cultivating their farms and plots with homemade implements, pounding their food in mortars . . . and worshipping ancient gods and spirits.[10]

Among the factors that have operated to produce the different levels of social existence in contemporary West Africa, perhaps the most fundamental one has been the rise of a money and an exchange economy.[11] The use of money to make money and the concomitant growth of production (agricultural, mineral, and, more recently, secondary) for the market has made it both possible and necessary to employ wage-labor. Thousands of Africans have been uprooted from their subsistence economies, and their existence has become dependent upon their ability to sell their labor.[12] As of 1954 there were over 300,000 wage earners in Nigeria, whose population numbered about 31,000,000, and some 648,825 wage earners in the Gold Coast, whose population was 4,118,450. As elsewhere in the world, the conditions of wage employment in West Africa have necessitated the movement of laborers to the towns and urban centers. In these towns and urban centers, life for the laborers has proven difficult. Slums have emerged with great rapidity, and such urban centers as Lagos and Accra "reflect the industrial revolution at its worst." [13] In order to lessen the negative effects of the new economic system upon themselves, as well as to protect and further their new interest and stake in this system, the wage laborers have, like their counterparts elsewhere, turned to trade unionism.[14] In so doing, they inevitably became involved in the nationalistic politics that took strong hold in West Africa immediately upon the close of World War II, and have since played an important role in the growth and spread of nationalism in this area.[15]

In addition to stimulating the rise of a wage-laboring class, the growth of a money economy in West Africa has given birth to a small but well-to-do group of African farmers who produce all sorts of primary commodities (viz., cocoa, palm oil, kernel, ground nuts) for foreign markets. Some of these farmers have gross incomes of over £700 per year and have attained standards of wealth that are high even by Western standards. For instance, Mr. P. C. Lloyd of the West African Institute of Social and Economic Research, Ibadan, Nigeria, has reported the following example of a wealthy Nigerian cocoa farmer:

The richest man in Ado-Ekiti today has an estate of approximately £50,000, he owns a shop, several lorries, two cars, many houses including the one in which he lives which has probably cost £3,000 to build.[16]

Similarly, in the Gold Coast, where cocoa has been the major export commodity, farmers have generally become a well-to-do group. As a member of the University College of the Gold Coast (now of Ghana) has reported:

> When the fact is kept in mind that out of a total estimated national income in 1951 of some £150 million, over £50 million was attributable to cocoa, and that many cocoa farmers have also other sources of revenue, such as food farming or forestry, the cocoa farmers as a group could be fairly described, from the point of view of income, as the "upper tenth" of the Gold Coast population.[17]

As has been the case with the wage laborers, the farmers have come to recognize their interests in the new economic system and have founded organizations, such as the National Farmers Union in Nigeria, to protect and further these interests. Through such organizations the farmers, like the wage laborers, have contributed morally and financially to the growth of West African nationalism, and have in more recent years played a direct and active part in nationalist politics, as evidenced by the rise of the National Liberation Movement in the Gold Coast in 1954.[18]

Finally, the impact of Western culture on West African society has produced an African middle class.[19] In this paper, we have made no attempt to define the concept of the middle class, and can only present an operational description of what is meant by this designation.[20] Thus, in general, to speak of a middle class implies the existence of two other classes: a lower class and an upper class. In the West African context, the "lower class" is the mass of African villagers or peasants who make their living by small-scale subsistence (and increasingly some commercial) farming. We also include in this social category the emergent wage-laboring class, whose general social status is not appreciably better than that of the African peasants. By the "upper or ruling class" we have in mind the small, but economically and politically dominant, group of European entrepreneurs, business administrators, senior colonial officials, district officers, and the array of lesser civil servants—what, in short, Sir Ivor Jennings has termed the "imported oligarchy." [21] Within this framework has emerged, over the past half-century, an African "middle class." It is suggested that in order to secure an adequate understanding of the social forces underlying nationalism in West Africa, it is best to view the West African middle class in rather broad terms. Accordingly, not only would we place African commercial and entrepreneurial elements —e.g., traders, timber merchants, money lenders, contractors—within the social category of middle class, but also such professional elements as doctors and lawyers. All of these middle-class elements have contributed to the development of nationalism in West Africa.

Within a relatively short period of time, the West African middle class, under the influence of an expanding money economy and the spread of Western higher education, coupled with the rise of the Western notion of individual initiative and gain,[22] has made impressive strides forward in both numbers and wealth. As early as the 1930's Miss Margery Perham could report on the status of the emerging middle class in Nigeria as follows:

> The place is evidence at once of the prosperity of Africans in Lagos and of the drive towards European standards of life which impels them. . . . Houses, built by African contractors, are worth £400 on the average, though some ran up to £1,000. . . . These houses, interior and exterior, have considerable social significance. The income-tax analysis suggests what classes are able to afford them, clerks, and especially Government clerks . . ., professional men, traders, transport contractors, surveyors, etc. . . . There are wealthy traders. One of these was recently President of the Chamber of Commerce, and his son and daughter were called to the Bar in London on the same day. . . . There are lawyers—fifty or sixty of them—some of whom are rich enough to send their children to school and university in England and to visit them there. There are editors and newspaper owners, journalists, bishops and archdeacons. There are elder statesmen such as Sir Kitoyi Ajasa, for many years a friendly adviser of the Government and a member of the Legislative Council.[23]

By the time of the outbreak of World War II there were, in the commercial sphere, some 100,000 African middlemen, who functioned as intermediaries between African primary producers and European trading firms. Today the average middleman has a net income of £650, while some large-scale operators have a net income of nearly £2,200.[24] As regards the professional group, the following report well represents their advanced status in contemporary West African society:

> A doctor who estimated his income for 1953 at about £6,000 has a house which can scarcely be distinguished from a British country mansion. . . . It has 20 rooms (to house 8 people), running water, 4 flush lavatories and 3 bathrooms. It is built of concrete and stone. The furnishings of the house follow the European pattern . . .: 10 beds with mosquito nets, 3 big tables, 2 small tables, 5 side tables, 21 chairs, . . . a refrigerator, . . . 117 pieces of crockery and glassware and so on. The family possess 3 cars, a radiogram, gramophone, sewing machine and typewriter; savings are kept in the form of investments, cash in the bank, and ownership of 4 lorries.[25]

Although the emergent middle class constitutes only a small part of the total population in West Africa, it has been, from a social and political standpoint, the most important class in the community. As a social élite in the African society,[26] the middle class has set imitable standards and patterns for the rest of the population, and in general has spearheaded the drive for modernity in this once isolated part of the world. Moreover, in its effort to both protect and advance its socio-economic and political status in a colonial situation, the middle class has turned to nationalism as one means for attaining these ends. Accordingly, in the remainder of this paper we shall consider West African nationalism as a middle-class phenomenon, and the important contributing role of the wage-laboring and farming classes in the development of West African nationalism has been omitted. Such an omission, however, in no way implies that these groups have not been essential components comprising the general social forces underlying the rise of West African nationalism.[27]

THE MIDDLE CLASS AND WEST AFRICAN NATIONALISM

Historically it seems that the commercial and educated middle class has been the organizer of nationalism, wherever found, as well as the bearer of the ideas underlying this phenomenon.[28] It was this social class which functioned as the driving force behind the rise of nationalism in eighteenth and nineteenth century Europe and in twentieth century Asia, and it has performed a similar function in the emergence of West African nationalism.

In West Africa the connection between the middle class and the emergence of nationalism may be attributed to three important situations that have been peculiar to the social position held by this class. Firstly, the middle class, and especially its professional component, has had a monopoly over the intellectual tools necessary for comprehending the complex forces that make for change in a society that is advancing towards modernity. It has thus been able rationally to manipulate these forces in its efforts to secure socio-political channels for advancing its status in a colonial society. Secondly, members of the middle class have had "the wealth and the influence necessary, and sufficient leisure to pursue a part-time political career." [29] Consequently, the work and financial effort involved in founding national political organizations and movements did not prove a serious burden upon the resources of the middle class. Thirdly, the professional and intellectual elements among the middle class were quick in developing an awareness of their interests in the new social system that emerged out of the Western impact, and of the relationship of these interests to the colonial situation. As the number of professionals increased with the advancement of the socio-economic status of the colonial society as a whole, it was inevitable that demands on the part of the professionals for greater and more attractive opportunities would also increase. At this point, however, a dilemma arose in the general colonial situation which Professor Balandier has posed in the following terms:

The colonizing power has created a situation involving profound social changes, but the control which it exercises imposes an upper limit to these processes. . . .[30]

This *upper limit*, as it were, which is inherent in the very nature of the colonial situation,[31] tended to hinder the fulfillment of the growing demands and aspirations of the professionals. Consequently, strong grievances were generated among them, grievances which placed the professionals in a conflict-relationship to the European elements who possessed effective social and political power in the colonial situation and hence determined, in the final analysis, the rate of advancement to be permitted to the professionals in particular and the middle class in general.[32] Faced, on the one hand, with this hindrance to their advancement, and motivated, on the other hand, by social and political ideas and values derived from their Western education, the professionals (in collaboration with the commercial middle-class elements who likewise found the colonial situation a hindrance to their further advancement) undertook to found political organizations and movements which eventually demanded full national self-determination and self-government. Thus, as we have suggested earlier, nationalism in West Africa has been, in large measure, the outgrowth of the demand on the part of an African middle class for free and unrestricted opportunities for social, economic and political advancement within a colonialistically dominated society. As one very able authority on African nationalism has put it:

. . . Nationalism, in one of its aspects, clearly expresses the dissatisfaction of an emerging African middle class with a situation in which many of the recognized functions and rewards of a middle class—in the commercial, professional, administrative and ecclesiastical fields—are in the hands of "strangers." . . . The demand for African control of State power is in part a demand for unrestricted access to these functions.[33]

In order to understand the many-sided aspects of the development of nationalism in West Africa, one must first recognize that, in general, the middle-class nationalists have viewed the colonial system not only as a form of administration or government superimposed upon them by a foreign power, but also as a *social order* within which certain more or less well-defined social relationships prevailed and permeated nearly every aspect of life (economic, social, political and cultural). More specifically, the middle-class nationalists have viewed the European élite of entrepreneurs, administrators, *etc.* within the colonial system as a ruling class for whose benefit and advantage the system was established and continued to prevail.[34] Accordingly, in their struggle against the colonial system, the middle-class nationalists were primarily concerned with undoing the dominant power position held by the European ruling class, as the first step towards the seizure of state power (or, in other words, the attainment of political autonomy) and through this the attainment of economic, social and even cultural independence. In this regard, the following statement by Dr. Kwame Nkrumah, the most eminent nationalist personality in post-war West Africa and now Prime Minister of the new state of Ghana, should suffice to demonstrate how the middle-class nationalists oriented their struggle against the colonial system:

This country must progress politically—indeed political self-determination is the means of further realisation of our social, economic and cultural potentialities. It is political freedom that dictates the pace of economic and social progress.[35]

On the socio-cultural side, West African nationalism has been characterized by demands on the part of its middle-class, professional leadership for full social equality and for the end of socio-racial discrimination practiced, or believed to have been practiced, by the European élite. These demands have been manifested most clearly in the cry of "Africa for the Africans"—a cry which has been an effective rallying point for the nationalists in their effort to secure support for their demands among the masses. Culturally, West African nationalism has been characterized by a movement to revive many of the old cultural patterns of African societies. In practice, this cultural revival has been expressed

. . . in the return to African names in place of European names, and to African cloth in place of tweed suitings; in a renewed concern for African music and dancing and plastic arts; and even, sometimes, in the substitution of palm wine for beer and whiskey.[36]

And in what may be called theoretical terms, this cultural-renaissance has been expressed in a movement on the part of nationalist intellectuals to "rediscover" the cultural history of ancient West Africa and has led to the construction of historical theories to demonstrate what is believed to have been the past as well as present greatness of African peoples.[37] The socio-political significance of these efforts for the development of West African nationalism is not difficult to understand. For one thing, the middle-class nationalists in West Africa, like their counterparts elsewhere, have recognized the need to produce "evidence" of a more or less continuous historical tradition to which the African masses could meaningfully relate themselves, and which, in turn, could serve as a symbol of national unity.[38] As Dr. Nkrumah's government put it when it first proposed adoption of the name "Ghana" for the future independent Gold Coast state:

It is clear the name of GHANA [the name of an ancient West African empire] serves the purpose of providing the people of the Gold Coast with a symbol of their national unity and a link with past history.[39]

Furthermore, given the fact that West African nationalism has emerged within a colonial setting, the nationalist politicians and intellectuals have found it necessary and desirable to combat the argument—stemming largely from sources favorable to colonialism—that peoples who have no known or "worthwhile" cultural history are incapable of governing themselves. As Dr. K. O. Dike, Nigeria's most eminent historian who was educated at the University of London, has pointed out:

> So long as the African is regarded as a man without a history, doubts concerning his ability to govern himself will find credence.[40]

As regards the political side of West African nationalism, the middle-class nationalists have sought an African official majority, as well as full ministerial status, in the Legislative and Executive Councils which govern their countries,[41] and have demanded ultimate control of the whole governmental apparatus. To this end, West African nationalists have resorted to the establishment of political organizations which may be said to have commenced, in an incipient nationalist form, with the founding of the Aborigines' Rights Protection Society in 1897–98. The history of the development of these political organizations (which, in the post-World War II period, were to become fullfledged political parties, due largely to the gradual but definite democratization of the organs of colonial government on the part of the European colonial power, which itself was responding, in large measure, to the pressures emanating from the nationalist political organizations) [42] falls outside the scope and purpose of this paper, save to mention, in brief, the middle-class nature of these organizations.[43] Commencing with the Aborigines' Rights Protection Society in 1897–98, the leadership, as well as the general socio-organizational basis, of West African nationalist political organizations was mainly, if not predominantly, middle-class in character.[44] The leadership positions in the Aborigines' Rights Protection Society were held, for instance, by such Western educated Africans as Mr. John Mensah Sarbah, who was the son of a wealthy Gold Coast merchant and who was the first African to be called to the English Bar in 1887, and Mr. Joseph Ephraim Casely-Hayford, who was called to the Bar in 1896. Being middle-class in status, it was perhaps inevitable that the leaders of the Society were to include in their political program aims which were consistent with, and promoted the advancement of, their particular socio-economic status. Thus, in the Constitution of the Society it was stated that its purposes were, among other things:

> . . . To promote a sound national educational policy with particular attention to agriculture, scientific and industrial training, and generally to facilitate the spread of industry and thrift in the whole country.[45]

Such a connection between what may be called class interest and political behavior is not always easily discernible.[46] However, it is suggested that a study of the development of nationalism in West Africa will reveal a close connection in this regard.[47]

To consider this theme in the development of political organizations in West Africa a little further: with the founding of the National Congress of British West Africa in 1921 we find a similar situation prevailing. The leaders of the National Congress were all middle-class in background. We have already mentioned Mr. J. E. Casely-Hayford, who was the most eminent personality in the National Congress; others were such middle-class Africans as Mr. T. Hutton-Mills, who was a member of the Gold Coast Legislative Council; Mr. J. Egerton-Shyngle, a Nigerian Barrister; Dr. H. C. Bankole-Bright, a physician and a member of the Legislative Council in Sierra Leone; Mr. Fred W. Dove, a well-to-do merchant from Sierra Leone; Mr. Edward F. Small, a member of the Legislative Council in the Gambia, and a number of other comparable middle-class persons. The political organizations that were founded in the late 1920's and the 1930's, which were now becoming more and more distinctly nationalist (e.g., the Nigerian National Democratic Party, which was founded in 1923 by Mr. Herbert Macaulay, who was a civil engineer and journalist, and the Nigerian Youth Movement, which was founded in 1938 by Mr. Ernest Ikoli, who was also a journalist and editor of a Nigerian newspaper, *The African Messenger*), also revealed a middle-class character in terms of their leadership and socio-organizational basis. This same pattern was to persist even during the post-World War II period, although now the middle-class nationalist political organizations were becoming more and more conscious of the necessity and desirability of securing a broad, popular base among the West African masses.[48] For, clearly, if the middle-class nationalist leaders in Nigeria and the Gold Coast were to convince the British colonial authorities that they *really* represented the "Nigerian nation" and the "Gold Coast nation," then it was imperative for them to make their political organizations as much "national" in character (*i.e.*, in terms of a nation-wide or mass support) as they possibly could. Furthermore, being politicians who were educated in the West and who had considerable knowledge of the techniques of Western politics, the West African nationalist leaders were well aware of the importance of sheer *numbers* in determining the success of a political organization in the attainment of its political objectives, particularly if, as has been the case in West Africa, these objectives were to be attained through constitutional means. Nevertheless, the post-war nationalist political organizations (and, more recently, political parties) were still characterized by a predominant position in them of middle-class Africans. For instance, the National Council of Nigeria and the Cameroons, which was founded in 1944–45, was under the leadership of Dr. Namdi Azikiwe, an American-educated Nigerian who became a wealthy journalist (owning a chain of over seven newspapers, among them being some of the most influential newspapers in West Africa) and banker, and Mr. Herbert Macaulay, whom we have already mentioned; the United Gold Coast Convention, which was founded in 1946, was under the leadership of Dr. J. B. Danquah, who was educated at the University of London, and Mr. George Grant, who was the wealthiest African businessman in the Gold Coast; finally, the Convention People's Party,[49] which emerged as a break-away-party out of the United Gold Coast Convention in 1949, was headed by Dr. Kwame Nkrumah, who was educated at Lincoln University, Pennsylvania (also the alma mater of Dr. Azikiwe) and the University of Pennsylvania. Although space does not permit us to consider in more detail the rise of nationalist political organizations in West Africa from the standpoint of their being not only dominated, in terms of leadership, by middle-class Africans but also as instruments for protecting and advancing, among other things, the class interests of these Africans, we should only like to point out again that a study of the development of West African nationalism does tend rather clearly to demonstrate this thesis.[50]

We now turn, finally, to the economic side of West African nationalism. For reasons of space, we shall confine ourselves to only one of the many economic arguments that have been utilized by West African nationalists in their struggle against colonial rule.[51] This argument has held that the economic aspect of colonial rule has hampered the implementation of any effective, thorough-going policy of industrialization and of general socio-economic development for the welfare of the peoples of West Africa. It is argued further and more specifically, that the colonial system, in its support of European enterprises, has restricted the growth of African industries so as to prevent them from competing with these enterprises. Thus, the nationalists arrived at the conclusion that to remove colonial rule is to open the way for the economic development of their countries in general, and for the growth of African industries in particular. In short, African economic prosperity was viewed as a function of the control of political power. As *The Accra Evening News*, the official organ of the Convention People's Party, has put it:

> As long as we remain under an imperialist government we shall continue to be poor, unemployed, ill-fed, ill-clad and continually oppressed, enslaved and exploited. Therefore to ameliorate our condition we can do nothing but ask for Self-Government Now.[52]

It should be noted, in this connection, that by emphasizing a functional relationship between economic development and state power, West African nationalists were able to attract the support of many African businessmen who expected the future, independent West African states substantially to assist their growth.[53] And as independence slowly but surely approaches, the nationalist governments seem to be keeping their word, for "both in Nigeria and the Gold Coast there are a variety of statutory institutions designed to promote African enterprise by providing credit for traders, farmers, industrialists, *etc.*" [54]

CONCLUDING NOTE

West African nationalism is now approaching its major objectives, especially in the sphere of political independence, and the now independent state of Ghana and the nearly self-governing Federation of Nigeria must face the momentous task of social, economic and political development along national lines. The new, unfortunately, cannot escape the influences and patterns inherited from the past. Accordingly, our ability to understand and to secure insight into the future course of events in West Africa is dependent in no small way on how well we have understood the past developments.

We have endeavored, in this paper, to uncover the sources of West African nationalism and to analyze aspects of its dynamics by employing the concept of social class as an analytical tool. Admittedly, our use of this concept has not given (nor was it intended to give) us a conclusive picture of the forces that have generated West African nationalism. We would only suggest that such may be more readily attainable with this approach than a number of other possible approaches to the study of West African nationalism. Thus it would be of much interest if further studies of African nationalism generally, and West African nationalism particularly, included material with which to test the usefulness of the approach employed in this paper.

NOTES

1. British West Africa encompasses the following territories: The Gambia, Sierra Leone, the Gold Coast (now independent), Nigeria, British Togoland (now a part of independent Ghana), and British Cameroon (a Trust Territory under United Kingdom administration). This paper, however, is concerned primarily with Nigeria and the Gold Coast, for it has been in these two territories that West African nationalism has made its greatest advance.

2. For a general background of these developments, see C. Grove Haines (ed.), *Africa Today* (Baltimore, 1955).

3. See *infra*, pp. 8 ff.

4. *Cf.* C. J. Hayes, "Nationalism," *Encyclopedia of the Social Sciences*, II (1933), 245; Paul Alduy, "La Naissance du Nationalisme Outre-Mer" in Colston Papers (ed., C. M. MacInnes), *Principles and Methods of Colonial Administration* (London, 1950), pp. 123–142.

5. *Cf.* Basil Davidson, "African Education in British Central and Southern Africa," *Présence Africaine* (Février-Mars, 1956), 110. ". . . Although few Whites in Southern Rhodesia are sufficiently well-read to know it, . . . this country . . . has failed to produce, since White invasion 70 years ago, a single African doctor, lawyer or qualified engineer." *Cf.* also Georges Balandier, "Social Changes and Social Problems in Negro Africa," in Calvin W. Stillman (ed.), *Africa in the Modern World* (Chicago, 1955), pp. 58 ff. Professor Balan-

dier notes that Belgian territories have, until very recently, shown "almost no opportunities for access to higher education."

6. For a valuable discussion of the effect of different colonial policies and situations on the rise of African nationalism, see Thomas Hodgkin, *Nationalism in Colonial Africa* (London, 1956), pp. 29–59. For a case study of the rapid advance of nationalism in West Africa, see David E. Apter, *The Gold Coast in Transition* (Princeton, 1955).

7. See The International African Institute (ed., Dayrll Forde), *Social Implications of Industrialization . . . in Africa South of the Sahara* (UNESCO, Paris, 1956).

8. Georges Balandier, "Conséquences sociales du progrès technique dans les pays sous-développés," *La Sociologie Contemporaine*, III (1954–55), 45.

9. See Karl W. Deutsch, *Nationalism and Social Communication* (New York, 1953).

10. Kenneth Little, "The Study of 'Social Change' in British West Africa," *Africa* (October, 1953), 274.

11. See United Nations, *Enlargement of the Exchange Economy in Tropical Africa*. Doc. E/2557ST/ECA/23 (New York, March 12, 1954); *Scope and Structure of Money Economies in Tropical Africa*. Doc. E/2739ST/ECA/34 (New York, May 1955).

12. See Georges Balandier, "Le développment industriel de la proletarisation en Afrique noire," *L'Afrique et l'Asie*, XX (1952), 45–53.

13. *Report of the Commission of Enquiry Into Disturbances in the Gold Coast, 1948*, Col. No. 231 (London, 1948), p. 68. See also Kofi A. Busia, *Report on a Social Survey of Sekondi-Takoradi* (Accra, 1950).

14. As of 1954, Nigeria had some 115 trade unions with a total membership over 150,000, and the Gold Coast had 104 trade unions with nearly 50,000 members.

15. See Thomas Hodgkin, "Background to Nigerian Nationalism: Nationalists and Economic Policy," *West Africa* (October 6, 1951), 919–920; "Towards Self-Government in British West Africa," in Basil Davidson and A. Ademola (eds.), *The New West Africa* (London, 1953), pp. 69–70.

16. P. C. Lloyd, "Cocoa, Politics, and the Yoruba Middle Class," *West Africa* (January 17, 1953), 39.

17. B. M. Niculescu, "Fluctuations in Incomes of Primary Producers: Further Comment," *The Economic Journal* (December, 1954), 730 ff.

18. See St. Clair Drake, "Prospects for Democracy in the Gold Coast," *The Annals of the American Academy of Political and Social Science, Africa and the Western World* (July, 1956), 78–87. See also "Politics in Ashanti," *West Africa* (May 7, 1955), 415; *Ibid.* (May 14, 1955), 437–438.

19. For background information on the rise of the West African middle class, see Kenneth Little, "The African Elite in British West Africa," in Andrew W. Lind (ed.), *Race Relations in World Perspective* (Honolulu, 1955), pp. 267–288; P. C. Lloyd, "New Economic Classes in Western Nigeria," *African Affairs* (October, 1953), 327–334; S. Leith-Ross, "The Development of a Middle Class in . . . Nigeria," in Institut International des Civilisations Differentes, *Développement d'une classe moyenne dans les pays tropicaus et subtropicaux* (Bruxelles, 1956), 174–183.

20. On the concept of the middle class, see G. D. H. Cole, *Studies in Class Structure* (London, 1955), pp. 78–100. On the problems of defining the African middle class, see Thomas Hodgkin, "The African Middle Class," *Corona: The Journal of Her Majesty's Overseas Service* (March, 1956), pp. 85–88.

21. Sir Ivor Jennings, "Approach to Self-Government," *Corona* (February, 1956), 61–62.

22. For the great extent to which African socio-economic behavior has followed an individualistic pattern typical of Western societies, see Dayrll Forde, "Education and Community in Africa," *Nature* (May 20, 1944), 606.

23. Margery Perham, *Native Administration in Nigeria* (May 20, 1944), 606, 256–257. For similar data on the Gold Coast, see A. W. Cardinall, *The Gold Coast*, 1931 (Accra, n. d.), pp. 170–176.

24. See K. D. S. Baldwin, *The Marketing of Cocoa in Western Nigeria: With Special Reference to the Position of Middlemen* (Ibadan, 1954), pp. 34–51.

25. W. B. Birmingham and D. Tait, "Standards of Living: A Comment," *Universitas* (University College of the Gold Coast, Accra, December, 1954), 8–9.

26. See S. F. Nadel, "The Concept of Social Elites," *International Social Science Bulletin*, VIII (UNESCO: Paris, 1956), 413–424. This number of the *Bulletin* is dedicated to a study of *African Elites*.

27. For an account of the role of wage laborers and farmers in the development of Gold Coast nationalism, see Amon Nikoi, *Indirect Rule and Government in Gold Coast Colony, 1844–1954* (Unpublished Doctoral Thesis, Harvard University, 1956), pp. 183–271.

28. *Cf.* Karl W. Deutsch, "The Growth of Nations: Some Recurrent Patterns of Political and Social Integration," *World Politics* (January, 1953), 168–196. *Cf.* also Royal Institute of International Affairs, *Nationalism* (London, 1939), pp. 15 ff., 239–240.

29. J. H. Price, "The Gold Coast's Legislators," *West Africa* (May 26, 1956), 324.

30. Georges Balandier, "Social Changes and Problems in Negro Africa," *op. cit.*, p. 63.

31. See Georges Balandier, "La Situation coloniale: Approche théorique," *Cahiers Internationaux de Sociologie*, Vol. XI (1951), pp. 44–79. See also Balandier, "Contribution à une sociologie de la dépendance," *ibid.*, XII (1952), 52–57.

32. Here, in short, is the origin of much of the conflict-situations that have characterized the emergence of African nationalism. For as Professor Kofi A. Busia of the University College of the Gold Coast has pointed out: "The conflict between the new literate elite [whom we have included within the middle class] and the European group [whom we have designated the ruling class] is a bid by the former to oust the latter . . . as wielders of political power [and] as a standard-setting group in the social sphere." (Busia, "The Present Situation and Aspirations of Elites in the Gold Coast," *International Social Science Bulletin* [cited above], 430.)

33. Thomas Hodgkin, "The African Middle Class," *op. cit.*, 88. *Cf.* James

S. Coleman, "Nationalism in Tropical Africa," *The American Political Science Review* (June, 1954), 412, 414.

34. The writings of Nigerian and Gold Coast nationalists are crowded with statements that clearly express their views on the nature of the colonial systems that rule their countries. See, *e.g.*, K.O. Mbadiwe, *British and Axis Aims in Africa* (New York, 1942); Obonu Ojike, *My Africa* (New York, 1946); Kwame Nkrumah, *Ghana: The Autobiography of Kwame Nkrumah* (New York, 1957).

35. *Gold Coast Weekly Review* (July 20, 1955). It is noteworthy that as early as 1903 Mr. Joseph E. Casely-Hayford, a Gold Coast lawyer and a leader of the incipient nationalist organization of this period known as the Aborigines' Rights Protection Society, maintained that: "If the Gold Coast were a country with free institutions, free from the trammels of Downing Street red-tapism, we should soon have good wharves and harbors, gas works, water works and railway communication, all over the country. Prosperous cities would grow up and knowledge would spread among all the classes of the people . . . for the material development of the vast wealth and resources of the country." J. E. Casely-Hayford, *Gold Coast Native Institutions* (London, 1903), p. 130.

36. Thomas Hodgkin, "Africa Finds Its History," *Spectator* (September 18, 1953), 290.

37. See Leopold S. Senghor, "L'esprit de la civilisation ou les lois de la culture négro-africaine," *Présence Africaine* (Juin-Novembre, 1956), 51–65; Senghor, "African-Negro Aesthetics," *Diogenes* (Winter, 1956), 23–38; Namdi Azikiwe, *Renascent Africa* (London, 1936).

38. *Cf.* K. Onwuka Dike, "History and African Nationalism," *Proceedings of the First Annual Conference of the West African Institute of Social and Economic Research* (University College, Ibadan, Reprinted March, 1957), 31–41. "It is my contention [writes Dr. Dike] that seemingly abstract considerations such as those of culture and history are as important as more material ones in building a nation. They are at the root of the question of self-government. If the African has no past heritage, and no future except by imitation of European ways at a pace which the European thinks safe, then the Gold Coast is destined to fail. But if the instinctive belief of the African in his traditions is justified, the ultimate emergence of West African states as independent modern nations cannot be doubted."

39. *Gold Coast Government's Proposals for Constitutional Reform* (Accra, 1953), p. 15.

40. K. O. Dike, "African History and Self-Government," *West Africa* (February 28, 1953), 177.

41. For the development of the organs of colonial government in Nigeria and the Gold Coast, see Martin Wright, *The Gold Coast Legislative Council* (London, 1947); Joan Wheare, *The Nigerian Legislative Council* (London, 1950).

42. See James S. Coleman, "The Emergence of African Political Parties," in Haines, *op. cit.*, pp. 225–256.

43. A study of the development of nationalist political organizations and parties in Nigeria and the Gold Coast may be found in Martin L. Kilson, Jr., "The Rise of Political Organizations and Parties in British West Africa" (to be published by *Éditions Présence Africaine,* 1958).

44. Given the very nature of the colonial situation in West Africa, as elsewhere, which provided higher education for only a small part of the population, it is not surprising that only that small class of Africans which secured this education would be able to partake in modern-type political activity. Furthermore, the advances in education and literacy, in economic activity and communication development, were for a long period limited largely to the coastal towns such as Accra, Lagos, etc. This uneven development in the general sphere of social mobilization (centering, initially, in the coastal areas and eventually advancing inland) inevitably operated to give the emerging middle-class resident in the coastal towns a near-monopoly on political consciousness and activity. And this situation was to persist well into the post-World War II period. Cf. G. B. Cartland, "The Gold Coast—An Historical Approach," African Affairs (April, 1947), 90 ff.

45. Text of Constitution, in George Padmore, The Gold Coast Revolution (London, 1953), p. 37.

46. Cf. Maurice Duverger, "Partis politiques et classes sociales," in Association Française de Science Politique (M. Duverger, ed.), Partis Politiques et Classes Sociales en France (Paris, 1955), 15–28. Cf. also Charles A. Beard, The Economic Basis of Politics and Related Writings (New York, 1955).

47. Cf. Nikoi, op. cit., pp. 218 ff.

48. For an idea of the broad, social basis that characterized the groups and organizations that comprised the National Council of Nigeria and the Cameroons, which was founded in 1944–45, see "Two Nigerian Lists," African Affairs (October, 1945), 164. For the Gold Coast's Convention People's Party, which was founded in 1949, see The Constitution of the Convention People's Party (Accra, 1949), reproduced in Nkrumah, op. cit., Appendix.

49. The Convention People's Party was the first soundly organized mass party in Tropical Africa. By 1955, the Party had a paid-up membership—at two shillings per member—of 1,000,053, and 2,885 local branches throughout the country (1,135 in the Colony, 1,043 in Ashanti, 204 in the Northern Territories, and 502 in Southern Togoland). This impressive membership was drawn overwhelmingly from the lower income and occupational groups—e.g., wage-laborers, low-salaried clerks, poor cocoa farmers, peasants, etc. Thus, to the extent that the Convention People's Party became a mass-organization, the influence and power of the African middle class, as such, within the Party became progressively less. At any rate, such lower-class groups as the wage-laborers were able, especially through their trade unions, to influence nationalist politics to a far greater degree than in any hitherto period in the history of West African nationalism.

50. It may also be of interest, in this connection, to note that as the colonial power slowly but surely retreats in face of the rising tide of West African nationalism and thereby throws open the major organs of colonial government to the Africans, these organs are largely filled by middle-class Africans. Dr. J. H. Price has demonstrated this rather clearly in his paper on "The Gold Coast's Legislators," op. cit., 324–325.

51. For additional arguments, see Thomas Hodgkin, "The Background to Nigerian Nationalism: Nationalists and Economic Policy," op. cit., 919–920.

52. Quoted in Thomas Hodgkin, *Freedom for the Gold Coast* (London, August, 1951), p. 8.

53. *Cf.* International Bank for Reconstruction and Development, *The Economic Development of Nigeria* (Baltimore, 1955), p. 21. "The need for self-help is not understood by the African businessman who looks to the government . . . for financial assistance in the expansion of his business. . . ." *Cf.* also Colonial Office, *Education for Citizenship in Africa*, Col. No. 216 (London, 1948), pp. 8–9.

54. "Credit for African Traders," *West Africa* (July 7, 1956), 473.

A. Hourani

SYRIA AND LEBANON (1946)

ARAB NATIONALISM

1

Out of the changes which have been discussed in the last three chapters, and the problems to which they have given rise, has grown the nationalist movement. Since this movement has for the most part taken an Arab rather than a specific Syrian or Lebanese form, it is necessary at the beginning to ask whether and in what sense the Syrians and Lebanese are Arabs.

Racially the Syrians and Lebanese are not of exactly the same stock as the Arabs of the Peninsula. The latter are mainly of the "Mediterranean" race, with some exceptions. In the Syrian desert and parts of the interior of Syria, the inhabitants are also mainly Mediterranean; but in the mountains the Mediterranean has been united with an "Alpine" element, to produce a "Dinaric" or "Armenoid" type. In most of the interior the population is a mixture of these two types, with the Mediterranean predominating.

Racial origin, however, is not of much influence upon popular judgement. When Syrians and Lebanese say that they belong to the Arab people, they mean that they possess the Arab heritage of language, history, literature and customs, and that they are conscious and proud of possessing it. The only exceptions to this are the Kurds, Turcomans, Circassians, Armenians and Assyrians, who together constitute only a small percentage of the population.

It would perhaps be more correct to regard the Arab people, of

SOURCE. A. Hourani, "Arab Nationalism" (Chapter VI) from A. Hourani, *Syria and Lebanon,* London: Oxford University Press under the auspices of the Royal Institute of International Affairs, 1946, pp. 96–104.

which the inhabitants of Syria and Lebanon form a part, as a group of peoples, which resemble one another in certain important respects but are dissimilar in others. The inhabitants of geographical Syria may be considered as constituting a single member of this group. They differ from the people of the Arabian Peninsula in that, while the latter are almost purely Arabic or "Semitic" in their ways of life and thought, in the Syrians the Arab has been mixed with other influences. They differ on the other hand from the peoples of Iraq, of Egypt and of the other North African countries in that while these too have been partly moulded by other than Arab influences, the latter have not been identical with the influences upon Syrian and Lebanese life. In Iraq such influences have been largely Persian and central Asian; in Egypt there was an indigenous civilization which was not entirely submerged by the Arabian influences; in much of the rest of North Africa there is a Berber race which has resisted all attempts to assimilate it. To these differences must be added those which spring from the mere fact of living in different regions possessing varying economic possibilities and subjected at times to very diverse historical processes.

It is possible to observe differences not only between the members of the Arab group of peoples, but also within each people. Physically and culturally alike, various elements within the people of geographical Syria represent varying blends of Arabic, of Aramaic and other Semitic, and of non-Semitic influences. Many such differences which formerly existed have in the course of time been levelled out and forgotten, but some of them still linger on, especially in mountain districts. For example, there are a few villages north of Damascus in which Aramaic is still spoken side by side with Arabic. What is more important, the Maronites and other Christians in northern and central Lebanon have not on the whole the same consciousness of being Arabs as the other inhabitants of the country. This is true also to a great extent of the Arabic-speaking Syrian Orthodox and Catholics and of the Alawis in the district of Latakia.

Thus the answer to the question which was posed above is a complex one. The Syrians and Lebanese are members of the Arab group of peoples; but they differ in some important ways from other members of that group; and they also differ among themselves in certain ways.

2

Although the Syrians and Lebanese have been Arabs in this sense for many centuries, it is only in the last two generations that an explicit nationalist movement has grown up.

Nationalism exists wherever two factors, which are to be found in some form in every society, take a particular shape and have a particular relation to one another. The one is the consciousness of solidarity: the sense that there is between the members of a certain group a special closeness of feeling, a special similarity of reaction, a possibility of understanding based upon the possession of common characteristics—language, customs, memories, real or imagined ancestry. The other is the will to work together for the attainment of a common aim in which all believe and for which all are willing to sacrifice something or everything. When this will derives its content from the consciousness of solidarity, and the members of the group take as their common aim the preservation both of that consciousness and of the characteristics on which it is based, nationalism arises. Political nationalism comes into existence when the attempt is made to achieve the common aim by means of the establishment of a State, which includes all the members of the group and of which the Government is imbued with the nationalist ideal.

In Europe, the idea of nationalism became an important political force during the nineteenth century. In one aspect it was a development of the idea that "the people" can and should be master of its own destiny: that the ordinary citizens of a State have both the right, and if effectively organized, the power to set up and to pull down Governments; and that Governments are only entitled to demand the obedience of the community which they rule if and in so far as they emanate from the will of that community. In another aspect it was the child of Romanticism, which was, among other things, the attempt to discover in Time and History what for the Christian belongs only to eternity: an adequate object of sacrifice and worship, a supreme purpose and consummation of human life. One type of Romanticism found what it sought in the community and the life devoted to the service of the community; and it was especially attracted to that type of community which is based on common memories and a common history.

3

Among the Arabs, nationalism in the sense defined above did not emerge until the later part of the nineteenth century. The sense of solidarity and pride in the Arab tradition had long existed; but they did not form the basis of a coherent movement until the West began to impinge upon the Arab world. Its impact had two effects, both of which worked together to produce the Arab movement. On the one hand, the West brought new dangers to the Arabo-Islamic life. On the other hand, far from destroying the Arabs' faith in their having a special part to play in history, it gave them fresh vitality and the promise of new strength. Arab nationalism may be defined as the resurgence of the will to live of the Arab people, produced by the action of the West upon it, and with the object of combating the dangers and realizing the benefits of that action.

It is true that the explicit aim of the nationalist movement in its first phase was not to come to terms with the West but to shake off the rule of the Ottoman Turks. But it was not simply a movement of revolt against an oppressor. The Ottoman rule was resented so much more bitterly than in the past, not because it was so much worse, but because it prevented the attainment of that new life of which the Arabs were becoming aware, and made it impossible for them to take what they believed to be their rightful place in the world. The overthrow of the Turkish régime, in the conception at least of the more thoughtful of them, would only be the beginning of their national effort. It would create the conditions in which it would become possible to face the real problems of their community. . . .

Most fundamental of all [these problems] was the danger of the complete destruction of the principles of loyalty upon which the traditional community had rested: membership of the family, the tribe and the religious community, respect for the past, the habit of obedience to the suzerain. Should they go and nothing take their place, the community might dissolve into a rabble of individuals without loyalties or the consciousness of belonging to a group. It was to avoid this danger that the nationalists endeavoured to arouse a consciousness of the common heritage of language, historical memories and customs shared by the Arabs; and to make that consciousness the basis of political action and ultimately of government.

A more immediate, although less fundamental, problem was raised by the penetration of Western goods and economic processes. This was beneficial in so far as it held out hopes of raising the standard of living of the people; but it dislocated the traditional structure of commerce and industry, and it threatened to place the economic life of the Arabs in the power of Western trading and concessionary companies. A similar process of dislocation was taking place in other aspects of social life. Here again much that was bad in the old order was being swept away, but also what was valuable was threatened. The process had a further effect: it emphasized, and made more unbearable, injustices and inadequacies which had formerly been accepted as inevitable or had passed unremarked. Thus there grew up the belief that social and economic Westernization was undoubtedly beneficial, but needed to be controlled and directed, and that a controlling and directing agency could not exist so long as the government was in the hands of foreigners who neither understood the needs of the Arabs nor cared primarily for their welfare.

A further element was added to the movement by the wounded pride which most Arabs felt when they considered the attitude of the West towards them. The Western Powers in act if not in word treated the Arab countries as if the desires and wishes of their inhabitants were matters of minor importance; individual Westerners showed only too often their contempt for a people who dressed, believed and thought so differently from them, and were so backward in the material arts. The contempt was no less wounding when it was concealed beneath a romantic admiration for the primitive or the exotic. It was the more unbearable to the Arabs because of their conviction that in essentials they were not inferior to the West, no less than because of their suspicion that in many other things they were indeed far behind the West and had much to learn from it. It gave rise to a desire to equal the West in those things on which the West set value, and to be recognized by the West as equals. Since the West set value upon the independence and power of the national State, upon economic prosperity and a certain ordering of social life, the Arabs too must be independent and powerful, and modern in their social organization.

4

Such were the factors which produced the nationalist movement. The movement was specifically Arab, aiming at the creation of an Arab nation and State which should include all branches of the Arab people, and not simply at the establishment of Syrian, Iraqi, Hejazi and other separate nations; and this for a number of reasons. The historic imagination of the Arab peoples had taken as its main and almost its only object the memories of the early Islamic period, of the orthodox Caliphs and their successors the Umayyads and Abbasids. Thus they were vividly aware that there had been a time when the Arabs had been conscious of themselves as a special community, and as a community had played a leading part in history. The thought of the solitary moment of history when the Arabs had been united in a single Empire, in which they had been the dominant element, overshadowed in their minds the memory of ages before and since. The revival of interest in Arabic literature in the course of the nineteenth century had a similar effect: coming to them through the medium of their own language, it aroused their pride and the sense of their own possibilities in a way which would have been impossible for the Greek culture of Syria or the pre-Islamic culture of Iraq. Then again the vision of a united Arab nation seemed to offer to a people becoming conscious of their weakness, and of the internal divisions which were the partial cause of it, a strength such as a Syrian or an Iraqi nation could never possess.

5

In the light of this analysis, it is possible to summarize the assumptions and aims of the movement.

The basic assumptions of Arab nationalism are: first, that there is or can be created an Arab nation, formed of all who share the Arabic language and cultural heritage; secondly, that this Arab nation ought to form a single independent political unit, both in the interests of the nation itself and in those of the world; and thirdly, that the creation of such a political unit presupposes the development among the members of the Arab nation of a consciousness, not simply that they are members of it, but that their being members is the factor which should determine their political decisions and loyalties.

The ultimate aim of Arab nationalism is to preserve and enrich the Arab heritage: to enable the Arabs to live in the modern world on an equal footing with other peoples, and to contribute to its civilization without being forced to break with their past. The political objectives of the nationalist movement are the independence of all the Arab lands; the establishment of some degree of unity between them; the encouragement of national consciousness; and the reorganization of the social and economic structure of the nation by means of a process of controlled and discriminate Westernization.

The movement of which these are the assumptions and aims is still at a comparatively early stage of development; and its ideals, although they have found their expression in patriotic rhetoric and poetry, have not yet achieved a reasoned and systematic exposition. But although Arab nationalism is still largely inarticulate and unformed, it does not spring only from passion and prejudice, nor is it confined only to the educated few who are its spokesmen. It is a movement with rational grounds and purposes, which, although they have not yet become fully explicit, exist implicitly and as motive forces alike in the mind of the peasant, who feels nothing but a vague unrest; of the educated townsman, in whom unrest has crystallized into definite emotions, desires and grievances; and of the politician, who expresses the emotions, desires and grievances in speeches and programmes. Although they might not be able to define and defend nationalism, they are all in some degree Arab nationalists.

Like all immature movements, Arab nationalism has not yet found its own authentic voice. It tends to imitate Western nationalism in its programme and its terminology. It is of great importance to make it clear that the spirit of the movement has not yet been definitely or adequately expressed. Its present form is not the only form which it could take. It is possible that if nationalism fails to obtain its explicit objectives, or even if it achieves them and its success is followed by disillusion, the feelings and desires which have given it birth will express themselves in different ways. Instead of a movement for an independent State and a modernized society there might be an outbreak of religious fanaticism, which would not help in the establishment of good relations between the Arabo-Islamic world and the West. Instead of a movement with rational purposes, there might arise one whose only ends were destruction and self-destruction.

6

Which of these paths Arab nationalism will take depends very largely upon the relationship which it establishes, on the one hand with Islam, and on the other with the West.

Although the movements of Arab and of Islamic revival lay emphasis upon different points it is impossible wholly to separate Arab nationalist feeling from Islamic feeling. In most Arabs the two tend to flow together; the movements of national and of religious revival are energized by the same complex of desires and emotions within the individuals who have created and who sustain them; and the ordinary Moslem Arab is not conscious of belonging in one aspect of his being to the Arab community, and in another to the Islamic, but rather of belonging to a single integrated "Arabo-Islamic" community in which he does not clearly distinguish the Arab from the Islamic elements. Even in analysis it is impossible wholly to separate the two. On the one hand there is in Islam no sharp distinction between spiritual and temporal, Church and State; and in consequence a movement of religious reform will have its repercussions in every sphere of social and political life. On the other, many Arab nationalists, especially of the older generation, would define the Arab nation partly in terms of the Islamic religion, which most members of the nation profess, and of which the Holy Book is written in Arabic; and they would therefore regard the preservation and revival of Islam as being among the aims of the nationalist movement.

What has just been said must be qualified in two ways. First, the secular view of life is becoming ever more widespread, especially among the younger generation and among those educated in Europe and America; and it is giving rise to the belief that it is better both for religion and for political activity if the two are kept distinct from one another. Thus it is possible to see the beginning of the idea of a secular nationalism, which rests upon elements of unity other than participation in a common religion; which aims at building a Westernized laic State; and in which therefore Moslems, Christians and atheists alike can join on a footing of equality. This lay nationalism is not consciously hostile to religion, although it is opposed to theocracy; but it is possible that at some time in the future it will come into conflict with Islamic orthodoxy.

Secondly, the connexion between Islam and Arab nationalism is perhaps emphasized less in Syria and Lebanon than in the other parts of Arab Asia. This is so not only because Syrians and Lebanese have assimilated Western thought more deeply than other Arab peoples and are more inclined to adopt modern Western secularism, but also because of the existence of an Arabic-speaking Christian element in the Syrian and Lebanese population. Moslem Arab nationalists cannot leave the Christians out of account in their plans for the future of Syria and Lebanon, and many of them sincerely desire Christians and Moslems alike to participate in the national community of the future. There are many Christians too who share the ideals of Arab nationalism; and indeed Syrian and Lebanese Christians were among the founders of the national movement, since they saw in the spread of the ideal of national unity the only way of escape from the religious differences which had for so long weakened their country. It is natural that Christian Arab nationalists should define the Arab nation mainly in terms of language, history, and race, and should draw a distinction, perhaps too sharply, between it and the Islamic community.

I. Potekhin

THE FORMATION OF NATIONS IN AFRICA (1958)

In recent years I have concerned myself almost exclusively with the study of the formation of nations in Africa (south of the Sahara).

I would first like to say what I understand by the word "nation."

A generally recognised definition of that word does not yet exist in world science. It is often used in an extremely arbitrary way and its content can be very different. Sometimes the word "nation" is used for a people without considering its level of social development. In that case the words "nation" and "tribe" are used as interchangeable terms. In the literature dealing, for example, with the Zulus at the beginning of the nineteenth century, we find the expressions "Zulu nation" and "Zulu tribe"; the twentieth-century Ashantis are sometimes called a nation, sometimes a tribe. Sometimes the word "nation" is used for the whole population of a given country, without considering whether they speak a common language or different languages.

Webster's *New World Dictionary* gives for the word "nation" the following definition: "1. Stable community of individuals, which has developed in the course of history, having a common territory, an economic life, a culture and a specific language; 2. Population of a territory united under the same government, country, state; 3. (*a*) People or tribe; (*b*) tribe of Indians in North America, belonging to a confederation, such as the ten nations; (*c*) territory of such a tribe."

If we understand that word in such a vague way, the problem of the formation of nations does not even exist: nations have always existed; they have existed everywhere, and as a result there cannot be a problem of the formation of nations. On the contrary, if the word nation has a definite sense the problem exists of how and when are they formed.

SOURCE. I. Potekhin, "The Formation of Nations in Africa," reprinted from *Marxism Today*, II, 10, 1958, pp. 308–314.

It is by no means an argument about words. To give a definition of a "nation" is of vital importance for the peoples. A nation is not an imaginary or mystical concept—it is a very real phenomenon, and as such needs an exact definition, without which it is impossible to understand the national question which plays such an important part in the life of the peoples of the present time.

STALIN'S DEFINITION OF A NATION

To study the problem of the formation of nations, I start from the definition given by Stalin as early as 1913. According to this definition a nation represents a definite human community, strictly outlined. Several human communities exist; but not all can be considered as nations. A nation has specific characteristics.

The first criterion or characteristic feature is a common territory. Without a common territory a nation cannot exist. The most vivid example is that of the Jews. Disseminated throughout the world for a number of historical reasons, they did not form a nation. The Jews, living in different countries, did not have in common any political, economic or cultural interests; many have for a long time forgotten their tongue and speak that of the people among whom they live. The Jews who established themselves in Israel do obviously form a nation; but I have not studied this question specially.

The second characteristic is a common tongue. Without a common tongue daily regular relations are not possible between individuals. If they speak different languages and cannot understand each other they are naturally unable to form a nation. The language is the expression of the soul of a people. Everybody loves his own language and prefers to speak it.

From their prolonged common existence within the same territory and their continued relations based on a common language, people acquire customs, habits and a way of life common to all, similar artistic tastes, and a single spiritual and secular culture. Great and small nations differ from each other not only in language but also in culture and psychology. Every nation has its national culture which it loves and respects. This is the third characteristic of a nation.

The fourth is a common economy, i.e., that all parts of a territory inhabited by a particular people are economically linked together. There is a geographical division of labour and a regular exchange of products, in a word a single national market. A common economy creates links between the people living in the different parts of the country shared by a particular people, and creates the necessity for regular relations between them—which encourage the disappearance of local language differences such as dialects and the development of a single national language with its permanent expression in literature. It is only as the consequence of a common economy that the common characteristics of a spiritual and secular culture can develop. A common economy makes a single unity of the territory of a nation and gives a concrete meaning to territorial unity. It is on this basis that a good understanding of the common political and economic interests of a nation are founded.

Such are briefly the four main or characteristic criteria of a nation. This does not mean that a nation has no other characteristics, but these four are the main and fundamental ones.

If we understand the word nation in this way it becomes clear that a nation can only come into existence under the capitalist system, and that nations are the product of capitalist development.

This means that nations have not always existed; they are born, and are only formed at a definite point in human history. Under the feudal system they did not, and could not, exist. They could not exist because there was neither a common economy nor a national market. Feudal society is characterised by a subsistence, not a profit-making, economy

This does not mean that under the feudal system the exchange of products did not exist at all and that there were no economic relations. No, an exchange of world products, economic relations, existed even under the primitive "commune" system. However, such relations were sporadic and not at all essential. Under the feudal system, economic relations between regions can or need not exist. Their non-existence cannot stop material production. This differs from the capitalist system in that economic relations have now become an essential condition of production.

A "NARODNOST"

We usually call the ethnic community living under a slave or feudal system a "narodnost." This word has no real equivalent in the West European languages. "Narodnost" comes from the word "narod" (people). From now on I shall use the word "narodnost."

The narodnost is an ethnical community of individuals who possess a common territory, a common language and a common culture. Unlike a nation, it has no common economy. Moreover the three first characteristics of a narodnost differ from the corresponding characteristics of a nation. The feudal system is distinguished by the division of the land into small or feudal principalities and, in some cases, by the absence of a central state authority. In the capitalist system national states exist, generally including within their boundaries all the territory inhabited by a particular people.

The existence of regional dialects of a common language is typical of the feudal system. In many cases there is even a single literary language, but by reason of the illiteracy of the majority of the people it is used only by the upper classes while the mass of the people speak various dialects. Under the capitalist system it is only when large-scale economic relations are established along with mass migrations from one district to another, and with the development of education, that the literary language comes to be used by considerable sections of the community, being transformed into a single method of communication, and regional dialects disappear little by little.

The same thing can be said of the common culture; it is only fully developed under capitalism.

Finally the narodnost and the nation have a different class structure. In the first case the feudal lords and their peasants formed the basic classes. In the second case we find the bourgeoisie and the proletariat.

In the primitive community there is no nation and no narodnost. The typical form of the ethnic community of the people was the tribe. What difference was there between a tribe and a narodnost?

A tribe is a classless community, while the narodnost is divided into classes. A narodnost forms when the change takes place from classless to class society.

A tribal community is based on blood relations: it is a community of people descended from the same actual or mythical ancestor. A narodnost is a territorial community, which includes people not on the basis of origin but on the basis of living within a given area: their geographical location in other words.

A narodnost grows out of the disintegration of the tribal community, of the mixing and merging of tribes and the emergence of classes. The mixing of tribes leads to the formation of a common language based on one of the tribal languages, while the others become regional dialects and finally disappear from history. The mixing and merging of tribes also lead inevitably to changes in the secular culture and psychology of the people: the tribal characteristics disappear and a single common culture emerges.

All these simultaneous processes have a definite economic basis which undergoes decisive modifications. The merging of the tribes and the transformation of the tribal system into a narodnost are based on the replacement of one form of productive relations by another. It is precisely at this period that the co-operative and mutual-aid relations characteristic of the primitive community system, where classes did not yet exist, are superseded by relations of exploitation, domination and subordination, characteristic of all social and economic class systems.

The period of the formation of antagonistic classes and of the state is also the period when the tribe becomes a narodnost.

There is no precise line of demarcation between feudal society and the commune system. The transformation of the primitive social system into feudalism takes place little by little over a long period. Even when feudal-type relations predominate there are generally some fairly clearly distinguishable survivals of the primitive commune. These survivals are very enduring, and can even be found in capitalist society.

Similarly there is no precise line of demarcation between the tribe and the narodnost. The transformation of the tribe into the narodnost also takes place little by little over a long period.

The survivals of the clan and tribe structure and organisation can subsist for a long time after the formation of the narodnost. At the same time they are but relics, old moulds with a new content. In this case the decisive role is not played by the mould but by the most characteristic and dominating social relations of the period in question.

STAGES OF DEVELOPMENT

To sum up: the ethnic community of the peoples goes through several stages of development: tribe, narodnost, nation.

The passage from one form to another broadly corresponds, but only broadly, to the development of the socio-economic systems: the narodnost is formed during the transformation of the primitive commune system into slavery or feudalism; the nation develops out of the passage from the feudal to the capitalist system.

In taking this interpretation of the term nation as a basis for our study of the ethnic development of the African peoples at the end of the nineteenth century and the beginning of the twentieth century, we easily reach the conclusion that there was not and could not be any nation in Africa at that time. It could not exist because there was no capitalist society.

In the African countries where more or less developed relations of a feudal type already existed, the transformation of the tribe into the narodnost was already taking place. There was clearly a narodnost in the case of the Egyptians, Moroccans, Tunisians, Algerians, Yorubas, Ashantis, Bagandas and others. The tribal organisation of these peoples, the Egyptians for example, had already completely disintegrated by this time, although still existing amongst other peoples.

In my book on the Southern Bantus, I made a special study of the development of the forms taken by the ethnic community of the Zulus, Kosas, Basutos and Bechuanas. I made detailed studies of the socio-economic system of the Southern Bantus at the beginning of the century, and submitted my conclusions to the Cambridge International Congress of Orientalists of 1954. I put them in this way: we see a picture of the primitive commune system at the last stage of development; the classical structure still exists but already has lost its first stability; private property exists and there are rich and poor, but without the community having split into antagonistic classes; the control of affairs is concentrated in the hands of wealthy dynastic families, but no state apparatus of coercion as yet exists. We conclude that the Southern Bantus were on the border-line between class and classless society: between a tribe and a narodnost.

THE ZULUS

I will deal more especially with the formation of the Zulu narodnost in the South African province of Natal. At the beginning of the nineteenth century there were about 100 independent tribes in Natal. There was no Zulu narodnost. There was no common Zulu language, but a multitude of tribal languages divided into two groups, the Tekela and the Ntungwa.

In the 1820's, Chaka, chief of the Zulu tribe, set out to bring all the Natal tribes under his rule.

Chaka's campaigns had an enormous influence on the Natal tribes. After being defeated, many tribes broke up and dispersed in different directions, giving rise to a mass tribal migration. Some disappeared purely and simply from the ethnic range of Natal, while others increased in number by absorbing newcomers from other tribes. The tribal structure being destroyed, the mixing of the tribes led to the formation of the Zulu narodnost. At the same time the old tribal divisions were replaced by a central authority based on armed force. This marked the beginning of the formation of the Zulu state.

"Independent tribes . . . ceased to be independent, the governing families were hounded out or exterminated, all the tribes without distinction were amalgamated and together they could be called the Zulu nation with Chaka at their head," wrote Bryant (A. T. Bryant: *Olden Times in Zululand and Natal*, p. 233).

In the same way as the Zulu tribe took the lead in the powerful process of unifying the tribes in a single state, so also the Zulu language gradually became the common medium of communication for all the tribes, and supplanted all the other tribal languages. The men of Chaka's army spoke a Zulu language of the Ntungwa group and as this army included adult men from all the tribes the Ntungwa language rapidly spread throughout the vast territory of Natal. According to Bryant the Tekela languages were retained for a certain time by the women but by the 1920's there only remained a few old women who spoke it (A. T. Bryant: *A Zulu-English Dictionary*—Maritzburg 1815, p. 60).

A long period of determined struggle by the Zulus against Anglo-Boer colonialisation then ensued during which the tribal structures disintegrated still further and the tribes intermixed still more.

At the end of the nineteenth century the Zulu narodnost, united in a common territory, language and culture, was already born in the territory of Natal.

The Kosas, Basutos and Bechuanas underwent a different process of transformation from tribe to narodnost, but nonetheless the process was concluded by the beginning of the twentieth century. This process is generally different for each people, and to give a general picture of the formation of the different narodnosts on the African continent the history of each people would have to be studied individually.

But not all the African people went through this process before the end of the nineteenth century, i.e., before European colonisation. In many regions, far from being any nations there was not even as yet a narodnost. Colonialisation found them at the stage of the primitive community with the characteristics of tribal organisation.

Colonialisation interrupted the natural course of the history of the African peoples and twisted the process of their ethnic development. At the present time it is very difficult to get a full appreciation of the stage of ethnic development reached by the African peoples. One thing only is clear: the process continues. In some regions the tribes are changing into narodnosts and in others existing narodnosts are becoming nations.

HOW TO STUDY THE CHANGES

I will now look at the methodology of the investigation of this process which I used as a guide in my work.

The first criterion of a nation is a common territory. That is why a study must start by working out the frontiers of the territory of the emergent nation, which must itself be based on the linguistic classification of the peoples. Here we find an obstacle that is difficult to overcome because there is not yet any unified and universally recognised classification of African languages. Each linguist puts forward his own classification, and I rather think that each seeks to outdo the other in producing a classification as complicated and imposing as possible. Johnston estimates that there are 226 Bantu languages; Van Bulk discovered 518 in the Belgian Congo alone, and it is further estimated that there are 700 or even 800 in the Sudan.

The linguistic map of Africa bears thousands of names indicating different languages. I am not a linguist but an historian, sociologist and anthropologist. It is difficult for me to criticise existing language classifications. I would, however, assure you that the real linguistic map of Africa is simpler than the linguists have tried to suggest. It is true that the linguistic divisions are a fact, and one which no scholar can deny or ignore since it is an irrefutable proof that for most of Africa neither nations nor narodnosts have yet emerged. The linguistic divisions reflect the tribal divisions of the people.

However I am equally certain that the picture of linguistic divisions given by the language specialist derives from their conventional linguistic approach to the work of classifying languages and their ignorance from the historic point of view. The development of languages follows the evolution of the tribal languages, then those of the narodnost and finally of the national languages. At a particular historical stage in the evolution of society the tribal languages become territorial dialects of the language of a particular narodnost, which later becomes the language of a nation. I don't think that the linguists take this important transformation sufficiently into account and continue to consider tribal and territorial dialects as independent languages.

At all events the assistance of linguists is essential in working out the territorial community of the nation. We can say here in general that any serious study of the formation of nations requires the co-operation of various specialists—historians, ethnographers, linguists and economists.

A further difficulty in defining the territorial community of a nation is that colonial frontiers do not correspond to ethnic frontiers. Many peoples, speaking the same language or languages so similar to each other that they can be considered as dialects, are cut in two by colonial frontiers, and different groups of the same people can be found in different colonies. This artificial division of the colonial frontiers is an especially great obstacle in the way of nations in formation, and especially in the case of neighbouring colonies belonging to different countries pursuing a different policy concerning the development of language and of culture. The most striking example is probably that of the Somalis who live in Somaliland under Italian, French or British domination or in that part which is included in Ethiopia. It is obvious that such a people cannot form a nation as long as the colonial frontiers which cut them into several pieces remain. The fact must not be excluded that the prolonged existence of such frontiers can divide a people into several related nations, i.e., separate nations can emerge in each portion formed by these frontiers. The history of mankind gives examples of a narodnost divided into several nations by reason of peculiar conditions. My own country is one. A long time ago, between the eighth and twelfth centuries approximately, there was a single old Russian narodnost with a common territory, language and culture. Later, different conditions determined by history and external factors in particular saw it divided into three parts, from which emerged three nations: Russia, Byelorussia and the Ukraine. Now each has its own national state.

There is another question in connection with the determination of a common territory. Following their policy of indirect government, the colonial powers keep the divisions into kingdoms, sultanates and chiefdoms. This is a particular form of feudal division which does not divide the common territory as it does not hamper the popular relations or the moving of people from a kingdom or sultanate to another. However, it prevents other criteria of the nation from maturing, and as a result is an obstacle to its formation.

A COMMON LITERARY LANGUAGE

Another characteristic of the nation is the community of language, the existence of a common literary language.

The object of the study of these criteria is to find the lines following which the languages develop, their structure becomes simpler and the tribal languages become territorial dialects.

The language of a narodnost or national language comes into existence when one of the neighbouring tribal languages, for a number of reasons, succeeds in spreading more widely than the others, becoming an inter-tribal language which supplants displaced languages. Through its triumph over the other tongues, this language becomes the literary language.

The course taken by this process is, due to historical conditions, very long, and wholly new in the African countries.

The major obstacle in the path of the creation of a single national literary language derives from the fact that the "official" language of the country is the language of the metropolitan country, English, French etc., and not the vernacular tongue. This is the language used for communication between people of different tribes speaking various tribal languages. This is the language of all gatherings, newspapers, radio stations etc. Scientific and fictional works by African authors are written in this language. An African wishing to make his way in the world beyond the confines of his tribe must firstly know the official language.

There are a good number of other difficulties confronting the formation of a national language. One is the ignorance of the mass of the people and thus the absence of a need for a literary language. A further difficulty derives from the feudal divisions which I have described earlier based on tribal particularism, the rights of the oldest tribesmen, an excessive devotion to local factors and sometimes a suspicion of anything concerning other tribes.

All these reasons show that the diversity of languages is of no value, since it holds up the development of a single national language based on one of the tribal languages.

Can a metropolitan language become a national language? Theoretically one cannot exclude such a possibility. Several English- or French-speaking nations can emerge. This does not contradict the interpretation of the term nation which I have put forward. Every nation must have a language common to all its members, but there is no reason why every nation should speak a different language.

The theoretical possibility therefore exists of the African nations being formed on the basis of European languages. This is, however, no more than a possibility which can scarcely become a reality.

As I have already said language is the mirror of the soul of a people. It is only in his mother tongue that man can fully express his real self. Language is an aspect of the culture of each people. Even the most perfect translation is no more than an imperfect copy of the original.

It is quite natural that the people should zealously conserve the right to speak their mother tongue.

I have dealt so far with the difficulties in the way of the development of African languages. There are, however, numerous other circumstances which help this development. In the first place there is the growth of the towns and the concentration therein of people belonging to many different tribes. A mass movement in search of urban employment influences the development of the languages by bringing them in contact and by mutually enriching their vocabulary and lessening the phonetic divergences.

In the last few years one has seen a growing interest amongst African intellectuals in linguistic problems. Associations for the development of African languages have been established. In some regions the question of standardising the writing of related languages has already been discussed. All this shows the extent of the national awareness, which reflects the objective process of national formation in the minds of the people.

COMMUNITY OF CULTURE

The third criterion of a nation is community of culture. The African peoples have created their own original culture for centuries—music and dance, songs and stories, sculpture and painting—their own clothes, buildings etc. The cultural heritage of past centuries is great and remarkable. This heritage represents a very rich store-house for the formation of national cultures.

Colonialisation has brought together in Africa two very different cultures—African culture and European culture. In some ways European culture was more advanced than the African. The Africans have assimilated something of this culture, and they should not reject the good elements which it contains.

However, this has come about in conditions wholly unfavourable to the development of African culture, which has been pushed into the background. Certain forms of African art and, in particular, certain artisan occupations have been forgotten and allowed to perish, while others have been adapted to European taste.

At the present time there are three different opinions amongst African intellectuals concerning the future paths of the development of African culture. Some would like to make European culture the basis of African national culture and forget the cultural heritage of the people. They describe themselves as progressive although to tell the truth I see nothing very progressive in it. Others would like to develop traditional African

culture and assimilate nothing of European culture. This group calls itself
traditionalist. Finally, the third group which describes itself as neo-
traditionalist proposes to establish a national culture on the basis of a
reasonable combination of elements from both African and European
cultures, taking the traditional African culture as a basis.

This reminds me of the controversy around the Russian national
culture in the nineteenth century. One section of the Russian intelligentsia
considered the original Russian culture as backward and almost barbarian
—preferring even to speak French rather than Russian. They suggested
importing Western culture and their representatives were called "zapad-
niki" (Westerners) as a result. Another part of the Russian intelligentsia
praised everything which was originally Russian and Slav in general,
including the backward aspects of Russian culture of the time. They
suggested closing the door against Western influence and constructing a
wall separating the country from the rest of the world. This group called
themselves the "Slavyonophiles." The Russian people did not take either
of these two ways. It built its national culture on the basis of its cultural
heritage, and took from the West what it considered worth while.

The national culture of the African peoples is developing in incom-
parably more difficult conditions, especially in the countries where a
policy of artificial assimilation is in vogue. There the peoples have to
defend their right to a free development of their culture.

Anyone studying the cultural community of a nation in formation
encounters complex problems. Culture itself is a complex and many-sided
phenomenon. It includes everything that is created by the hand of man
as well as his brain. National culture includes many local characteristics.
These local peculiarities exist even in the culture of old nations formed
a long time ago. They have their origin in the local characteristics of the
economic activities and the geographical situation and are therefore
inevitable. It is natural they take an important place in the culture of
nations in formation.

The tasks connected with the study of the process of formation of
the cultural communities of the African nations are particularly complicated by reason of the specific conditions in which these nations are
formed. The task of the scholar consists essentially in the necessity to
isolate from the immense variety of forms taken by the culture of a
particular people those which have already become the property of the
whole people and which have lost their local character. This task includes
determining what forms of the European cultures are already firmly
rooted in the customs and awareness of the people, and which are only
a temporary and superficial pastime of a part of the population.

Here I am touching on a critical question. Is it possible to speak of
the existence of a national culture if there is no more or less developed
literature in the national language and if there is not as yet any graphic

art, music or professional theatre? I do not think that is possible. The absence of these expressions of culture shows that the national culture is not yet in existence. There is a popular culture and a folklore. There are the materials which will serve to build a national culture. But the culture itself does not yet exist.

Only literature (novels and poetry etc.) and its more or less wide popularity amongst the masses completes the process of formation of a national language as the main expression of the national culture. Only the creation of professional art gives the national culture its perfection of form, its specific colouring and its truly national characteristics. If we try to estimate the level of development of the African on this criterion, we will have to recognise that the national culture of a good many of the African peoples is still at a certain stage of its development in spite of all the richness of its cultural heritage.

THE ECONOMIC COMMUNITY

Let us look now at the methodological considerations in connection with the last criterion of the nation, the economic community. The economic community of a nation comes into existence at the same time as a national market makes its appearance; if there is no national market there is no nation. In consequence study of this criterion comes back to the study of the national market. It is a purely economic problem. The main conditions needed for the formation of a national market are the geographical division of labour and the existence of developed exchanges on a profit basis within a capitalist mode of production.

Even a superficial knowledge of the economy of the African countries will show the presence of these conditions although not everywhere developed to the same extent. For example, capitalist exchanges in the African world are still relatively few and in some regions are still only at their beginning.

To my knowledge it can be said that the question of the formation of the national market is still completely unexplored. I do not know of any books devoted to this question. We know what is produced and where it is produced. We know what products and in what quantities are exported abroad. We know fairly well the foreign economic bonds but we know nothing practically of internal economic exchanges. It is to be hoped that economists will eventually study these internal relations.

As sparse as our information may be we can say that most of the African countries have no national market as yet or at the most they are only beginning to have one. To determine the degree of development of the national market it is necessary first to find the answers to two questions: 1. What part of the production is sold, i.e. what part takes the form of productive links giving rise to profit? 2. What part goes to the internal market and what part is exported? The economists of U.N.O. have made approximate calculations for some countries and I will mention the book *The Enlargement of Exchange Economy in Tropical Africa*, 1957. From these calculations one can see that in certain countries a considerable part of production is already transformed into profit, but it is mainly exported abroad. This is one of the characteristics of colonial economy. The colonies have become suppliers of raw materials for the metropolitan countries. This fact holds back the formation of a national internal market and thus hinders the development of the process of the formation of a nation.

The formation of the nations is accompanied by the development of national consciousness of belonging to the same people, and an awareness of national interest. Where nations have already taken shape each person is aware of belonging to a nation and is proud of it. The feeling of national pride is one of the deepest human feelings; an insult to national dignity is always taken as a personal insult.

The study of the process of national formation should include the study of national consciousness. One should point out how the consciousness of belonging to a tribe is replaced by the feeling of belonging to a larger ethnic community; how the people realise themselves to what nation and people they belong, how strong is the feeling of national dignity etc. But this is essentially a special and scientific problem which calls for special methods which I have no room to explain here.

S. Eisenstadt

SOCIOLOGICAL ASPECTS
OF POLITICAL DEVELOPMENT
IN UNDERDEVELOPED COUNTRIES (1954)

THE PROBLEM

This paper will present some hypotheses on the main sociological factors which influence political processes and institutions in underdeveloped countries. The future of democratic, representative institutions in these countries has often been debated, but most studies of these institutions have not been as systematic as others dealing with problems of economic development. Yet in many underdeveloped countries—whether of colonial, post-colonial, or independent status—the state plays a fundamental role in economic development and constitutes one of the basic factors influencing this development. Works on the political problems in Asia and Africa center mostly around the analysis and description of formal political institutions and basic political groups, and are often based on implicit assumptions as to the relative importance of some social conditions which may influence the stability and development of the new institutions.[1]

Certain basic themes seem to recur in most studies. One is the emphasis upon traditionalism manifesting itself in the organization of the society on a basis of authority. This traditionalism, accompanied by a low standard of living, seems to impede the development of democratic institutions and to favor authoritarianism.[2] Another theme emphasizes aspects of the problem of transition from a traditional to a modern society. Thus Scaliapino stresses the international economic and political tensions under which this transition has been made.[3] Emerson stresses such factors as

SOURCE. S. Eisenstadt, "Sociological Aspects of Political Development in Underdeveloped Countries," reprinted from *Economic Development and Cultural Change*, V. 4, 1957, pp. 289–298, by permission of The University of Chicago Press. Copyright 1961 by The University of Chicago Press.

lack of experience in governmental and administrative functions, the relative thinness of a modern Westernized elite and its dissociation from the traditional masses, the consequent lack of development of institutions of local government, and the continuation of traditional patterns.[4] The extent to which underdeveloped countries are internally divided is an other frequently stressed theme. The division between traditional and Westernized groups, on the one hand, and the division within the Westernized groups, on the other, producing many small parties, have been discussed repeatedly.

Thus while in most works on the political problems of underdeveloped countries assumptions are made as to the social conditions which may either impede or facilitate the development of modern political institutions, the assumptions are rarely systematized. Moreover, many analyses are consciously or unconsciously focused on the extent to which political institutions, especially on the formal level, deviate from the Western political pattern. Consequently, the internal dynamics of social and political systems is sometimes lost sight of, and the ways in which the societies—successfully or unsuccessfully—accommodate themselves to various aspects of modern political institutions, and evolve relatively new forms of political organization, is misunderstood. I shall try to outline, in a systematic way, some of the main sociological factors influencing the political developments in underdeveloped countries, and the social characteristics and internal dynamics of their political systems. I shall first list some characteristics which in varying degrees are common to most colonial societies, especially to countries which have attained independence. In the last part of the paper I shall list briefly some main characteristics by which these countries differ and shall present a few basic variables which should be taken into account in trying to explain these differences. (In this way this analysis may serve as a starting point for a series of researches in which these variables and some of the hypotheses implied in them will be tested out. This will have to be done in further publications.)

UNEVEN CHANGE IN COLONIAL SOCIETIES

A characteristic of this whole process of transition and change in underdeveloped societies is that it has been, and continues to be, unbalanced. Certain main elements of this lack of balance have long been recognized and more or less correctly attributed to the basic nature of colonialism.[5] Although many of the underdeveloped societies did not have officially colonial status, most of the changes have occurred under the impact of the clash with the West. As a result of this, these societies have been put in an inferior, dependent, and unbalanced position in relation to European powers. This situation, moreover, has been evaluated within a framework of European institutions and values. But in order to understand some of the dynamic problems to which this process has given rise, certain additional aspects of this uneven and unbalanced change should be analyzed.

The first major aspect is the lack of balance in processes of change and transition that can be found between the "central" level and the local level. Most changes introduced either directly or indirectly by the colonial powers (or by the "traditional" authorities of the independent societies which cooperated with the European powers) have been focused on the central institutions of the society. The most obvious changes were in the broad frameworks of political and economic institutions. In the political field, the introduction of unitary systems of administration, the unification or regularization of taxation, the establishment of modern court procedures, and at later stages, the introduction of limited types of representation, have greatly changed overall political structures and orientations. In the relatively independent states, innovation in military techniques was prevalent. The changes have introduced certain universalistic criteria, that is, orientations toward general rules and modern procedures. Even where various forms of indirect rule were practiced (as in many British South-East Asian, and particularly African territories), some change necessarily took place in political organization though this change was much slower than in cases of direct rule.

Similarly, many changes have been effected in the economy, notably the change to a market economy.[6]

Similar attempts to change the central foci of the institutional framework were made on a more limited scale in the educational field by endeavoring to provide new types of modern education for selected local elites.[7]

The common factor in these changes was their direction toward promotion of systematic change in the society as a whole. There was a more or less conscious awareness that such change was necessary (and presumably good), and that new general institutional structures and principles should be established. At the same time, however, the colonial powers (or indigenous traditional rulers) saw it as part of their task to effect these changes only within the limits set by the existing institutions and their own interests.[8]

This is manifest in their orientation toward change at the local level, i.e., the level of the village, community, or tribal unit. Here colonial or indigenous rulers attempted to contain most changes within the limits of traditional groups and/or to limit, as much as possible, the extent of any change. But many changes did develop within the local communities, as the literature on detribalization, social and economic disorganization in villages, and disorganization of the family indicates.[9] The important thing for our analysis is that the rulers tried, insofar as possible, to contain these changes within traditional systems, and most of their administrative efforts on the local level were aimed at the strengthening of the existing organizations and relations, at maintaining peace and order, and at reorganizing the systems of taxation. Thus, while the administration attempted to introduce innovations—particularly new taxes and improved methods of revenue administration—it tried to accomplish this within a relatively unchanging social setting, with the implicit goal of limiting changes to technical matters.[10] Here existed a basic contradiction: on the one hand, attempts were made to establish broad, modern, administrative, political, and economic settings, while on the other hand, these changes were to be limited and based on relatively unchanged sub-groups and on traditional attitudes and loyalties. This contradictory attitude could be found in most spheres of social action.

In the economic field, the major efforts were made to facilitate the functioning of a market-oriented economy—albeit of a very specific kind. This economy had to operate, as it were, without full development of new economic motivations, which would have disturbed the existing social order. In the field of education, where innovations were much less broad, there existed the tendency to impart rudiments of technical education without changing the system of values and aspirations.[11]

In economic and educational fields of action at least partial solutions could be found. Some indigenous groups found a place in newly established economic, educational, and professional organizations. Literacy grew to some extent, and the expectation of monetary rewards became customary and permissible for most groups.

Internal contradictions were most pronounced in the political field. Since the colonial powers or the indigenous rulers were interested in political loyalty, they aimed at maintaining a relatively passive type of obedience and identification, and were always ready, whenever possible, to utilize existing traditional loyalties or to transfer them to the new setting without much change in their basic social and cultural orientations.[12]

While the colonial powers and most indigenous rulers were interested in loyalty and were concerned with the transformation of certain institutional aspects—especially technical aspects—of the social structure, they wanted at the same time to base these innovations not on new types of solidarity and general political orientations and participation of the main strata of the population. Rather they tried to base the new political-administrative structure on orientations limited to technical, administrative changes for the bulk of the population, and on more general and active identification for a very limited and select group at the center.

The full dynamic implications of this unbalanced development can only be understood if some additional aspects of the unevenness of change are analyzed. These are aspects derived from the colonial or semi-colonial political situation. Most of them were present also in the non-colonial "independent" societies (China, Ottoman Empire, Arab states) but appeared in a different light, to be analyzed in more detail later.

The two chief results derived from the colonial nexus were (1) segregation between Europeans and natives, and (2) discrimination against the natives in most of the newly developed institutions. The extent of segregation and the intensity of discrimination varied in different institutional spheres and was often coupled with attempts to maintain the traditional native culture and even to idealize and romanticize it. The attempts at "segregation" and at minimal developments of a common framework were most prominent in the fields of politics and social solidarity; they were somewhat less so in the fields of administration and the economy. But the paradox of the situation was that the more overt attempts at segregation in the traditional as well as more modern spheres were gradually being given up, due to situational exigencies and as more and more natives were drawn into the modern spheres, the more acute became the discrimination against them in terms of the basic premises of these institutions.

Thus the basic problem in these societies was the expectation that the native population would accept certain broad, modern institutional settings organized according to principles of universalism, specificity, and common secular solidarity, and would perform within them various roles —especially economic and administrative roles—while at the same time, they were denied some of the basic rewards inherent in these settings. They were denied above all full participation in a common political system and full integration in a common system of solidarity. In other words, they were expected to act on the basis of a motivational system derived from a different social structure which the colonial powers and indigenous rulers tried to maintain. Quite obviously these societies faced acute problems of integration which could not be solved, except momentarily, within the framework of colonial or semi-colonial societies.

These processes of uneven change did not and could not stop at a given time and freeze, as it were, a society's development at a certain stage. Many such attempts were made—as is evidenced by the attempts at indirect rule, on the one hand, and by widespread efforts of indigenous rulers to limit changes to purely technical matters, on the other. But such devices could not succeed for long. The economic needs of the colonial powers and/or of the indigenous ruling groups, their growing dependency on international markets, and on the international political system and the changes within it, precluded any freezing of development at a given stage. Thus, all these processes tended to affect "native" social systems to an increasing degree and to draw ever wider strata of these societies into the orbit of modern institutional settings. Different countries are even today at different stages of development in this process. But the greater the tempo of these changes, the greater the unevenness and lack of balance, and the greater the problems of acute mal-integration the society has to face.

As has been shown earlier, these problems of mal-integration arose at various levels and in different social spheres—in the economic and ecological spheres, in education, in family life, and others. But they were necessarily most acute in the political and solidarity spheres; there the colonial or Western impact had undermined most of the old integrative principles and organizations both at the local and at the national level. While partial solutions could sometimes be found for economic and technical problems, their very partiality only tended to emphasize the alien political framework and the mal-integration in the solidarity sphere.

THE INFLUENCE OF UNEVEN CHANGE ON POLITICAL MOVEMENTS IN COLONIAL SOCIETIES

It is not within the province of this paper to analyze the various attempts by colonial powers to find solutions to these problems within the framework of colonial society. Our main concern will be to analyze the repercussion of these developments on the nationalistic political and social movements which have been of prime importance for the future of these countries.[13]

These movements have their origin in the dynamic situation of change, whose imprint can be discerned in their structure and development. Naturally, most of the nationalistic and social-nationalistic movements were especially sensitive to the manifestations of lack of balance and evenness of change. Yet, at the same time, they usually could not overcome easily the problems that this imbalance had created.

This sensitivity can be discerned in two basic characteristics of these movements: first, in their strong emphasis on new secular, modern symbols of solidarity and on their strong orientation towards solidarity-political activity (aiming ultimately at political independence); and second, in their attempts, especially in the later stages of development, to break through the "freezing" at the local level and to reach the broad masses of the population. But, at the same time—and this is most important for our analysis—the common bond which they tried to create with the masses was almost entirely couched in modern solidarity-political terms and did not emphasize the solution of immediate economic and administrative problems. The political symbols used were intended to develop new, ultimate, common values and basic loyalties, rather than relate to current policy issues within the colonial society. This emphasis was caused by their exclusion from effective power and by their fear of compromising the basic issue through participation in current affairs when opportunity arose.

A somewhat similar attitude can be observed in respect to economic, administrative and instrumental problems. Most nationalist movements did develop an economic ideology either stressing romantically the maintenance of the old village community or the necessity of state planning. All decried the injustices of the economic policies and discrimination of the colonial powers. But the nationalist leaders did not deal concretely with current economic problems or problems of daily administration. It is significant that members of the social groups among colonial peoples who participated relatively successfully in economic or administrative areas and who developed new types of social organization (as, for example, native business communities or membership in the colonial services) usually did not participate actively in the nationalistic movements and often were looked upon as traitors, or, at least, as "compromisers," by the members and leaders of these movements. The nationalistic leaders appealed to those groups of the population which were in an acute state of transition from the traditional to the modern setting, and which therefore suffered most from social disorganization, rather than to the groups which could adapt tolerably to the new institutional spheres.[14]

Thus, most nationalistic movements, though obviously opposed to the colonial regime, inherited from it some important social characteristics. On the one hand, the leaders attempted to formulate new symbols of solidarity which would transcend the limitations of the colonial situation and which were couched in modern nationalistic and universalistic terms. But at the same time, they did not make any special efforts to transform other spheres of institutional life and to solve the problems created there by the processes of uneven change. Although the nationalist leaders did not try to prevent the development of new types of social organization, they did not explicitly deal with problems provoked by these changes. They seemed to be content to base the new movement, within the instrumental fields, either on traditional types of attitudes and organization, or on transitory types of attitudes and motivations which were not fully stabilized. Their major assumption, common to many revolutionary movements, was that all of these problems would be more or less automatically solved once political independence would be achieved.[15]

The attitudes and social characteristics of these nationalistic movements are, of course, rooted in the colonial situation. They are closely related to the social origins and processes of selection of the leaders of the nationalistic movements and the relation of the leaders to the masses of the population. The leaders usually came from sectors of the more Westernized professional and intellectual groups, from among students, lawyers, journalists, most of whom had been directly exposed to Western values, had been active in some modern institutions, but either had not been fully absorbed by them, or, though indoctrinated with Western ideologies and values, could not accept their non-realization within the colonial setting.[16]

Most of the early leaders of nationalistic movements came from relatively well-to-do families. They had adapted themselves to some aspects of Western life, without entirely losing a foothold in their own traditions, and they rarely suffered from personal oppression.[17] However, at later stages, the ranks were swelled with unemployed semi-intellectuals, semi-professionals and semi-untrained groups.[18] These new men were mostly of urban origin; at least they grew up in the new urban settings which had come into being under the colonial regime. They usually did not have many direct relations with either the rural or the urban proletarian masses. Hence, they displayed a lack of understanding of many concrete economic problems of the masses, a limited grasp of political problems on the conceptual level, because of their narrow literary and professional background, and a strong idealization of the masses and of the village. Moreover, with the development of colonial economies and nationalistic movements, urban centers tended more and more to attract the more active elements from other parts of the colonies, with the result that the countryside was depleted of potential leaders. On coming to the towns, these potential leaders took up the symbols and orientations of the movement very quickly and often turned their backs on the acute problems of their groups or localities of origin. Whenever they returned to their points of origin, they tended to appeal in terms of overall solidarity symbols rather than in terms of specific concrete problems.[19]

The social peculiarities of nationalist movements produced various characteristics which have often been described in the literature. The emphasis on solidarity symbols, without attention on other aspects of social organization, has necessarily given rise to a relative lack of stability in the sphere of political organization itself. This is evidence by the divisions between different political movements and between the leaders of political movements and the more traditional powers in the society, such as tribal chiefs, princes, and colonial elites. Whenever competing nationalist movements developed within any one society, they became usually totally opposed to one another in terms of ultimate values and symbols of identification, and not merely in terms of differences over policies. This was not only true in the relations between modern and traditional forces, but also—and perhaps even more so—between the different modern groups, such as nationalistic, socialistic, communistic groups. Although on certain occasions all groups entered into uneasy alliances and coalitions—this did not change greatly their basic attitudes and their mutual ideological antagonisms.[20]

A further characteristic of political structures in colonial countries

is the relative weakness of various economic and professional organizations, e.g., trade unions, cooperatives, chambers of commerce, and the
talk of their mutual integration as well as their uneasy relationship with
the political movements. These weaknesses usually are of two kinds.
Either the economic organizations, whatever their strength, held themselves apart from one another and from the political movements, did not
participate in them, and thus did not exert their influence on them; or
they became entirely subordinate to the political leaders (especially in
the case of the Belfast movements) who did not take account of the
specific problems and needs of economic organizations.[21]

Another characteristic of colonial politics was the way in which
various interest groups, e.g., local merchants, exerted influence on the
administration or on political organizations in lower levels of government.
The most common techniques of exerting influence included various types
of lobbying, i.e., personal pressure, and sometimes attempts at bribery.
Whatever the exact nature and diversity of these activities, they were not
closely related to the major political movements and did not envisage
to any great extent the mobilization of public opinion. Whenever one of
these issues became important for political groups and public opinion,
it became transformed into an overall problem of political independence
and subsumed under the general solidarity symbols.

The combination of all these factors perhaps explains the importance
of the urban "mob" in the politics of many colonial countries—and the
parallel weakness of organized public opinion.

The different characteristics of the political process which we enu-
merated varied greatly from one country to another in their concrete
details and in their relative importance and intensity, and we shall later
distinguish some major types. But at this stage, a general analysis with
illustrations will have to suffice. The illustrations point out some inherent
weaknesses, or perhaps more accurately, the lack of balance in political
developments and organizations in colonial countries. All these problems
did not seem acute as long as the main issue was the attainment of political independence and as long as the movements were acting within the
framework of colonial rule which was responsible for the daily running
of the country. It was only when independence was attained, or when a
definite transfer of power was planned and realized, that all these problems became of crucial importance for the stability of the new political
system. In those countries which still retain their colonial status, the
former characteristics are still predominant in different degrees. Only in
those countries which have attained independence, or are in the process
of attaining it, or in those areas in which a traditional ruling group has
been supplanted by some more modern nationalistic elite (as in China,
or some of the Middle Eastern countries), all these problems are coming
to the surface.

NOTES

1. Among the exceptions see especially R. Emerson, *Representative Government in South East Asia*, Cambridge, Mass., 1955; and D. Apter, *The Gold Coast in Transition*, Princeton, 1956.

2. See Emerson, *op. cit.* See also E. Staley, *The Future of Underdeveloped Countries*, New York, 1954.

3. R. A. Scaliapino, "Democracy in Asia, Past and Future," *Far Eastern Survey*, Vol. XX (1951), pp. 53–57.

4. Emerson, *op. cit.*

5. Raymond Kennedy, "The Colonial Crisis and the Future," in R. Linton, ed., *The Science of Man in a World Crisis*, New York, 1945. See also Rita Hinden, ed., *Fabian Colonial Essays*, London, 1945, especially the essays by Fortes and Furnivall; and J. H. Boeke, *Economics and Economic Policy of Dual Societies*, New York, 1953.

6. See, for instance, Boeke, *op. cit.*

7. J. S. Furnivall, *Educational Progress in South East Asia*, New York, 1943.

8. It is not of interest for our analysis here to show the exact attitudes of different groups, leaders, etc. It is only the general trend of development that is significant.

9. See G. Wilson, *An Essay on the Economics of Detribalization in Northern Rhodesia*, Rhodes-Livingstone Paper 5, Livingstone, 1941. E. Hellman, *Rooiyard*, Rhodes-Livingstone Paper 13, Livingstone, 1948. G. Balandier, *Sociologie des Brazavilles Noires*, Paris, 1955. See also K. Davis, *The Population of India and Pakistan*, Princeton, 1951. See also the papers in Sections II and IV of *Contemporary Africa*, ANNALS of the American Academy of Political and Social Science, Vol. 298 (March 1955), and J. M. van der Kroef, *Indonesia in the Modern World*, Bandung, 1954, esp. Chs. 4 and 5.

10. See, for a good description, P. Griffiths, *The British Impact on India*, London, 1952, Section I; also J. Furnivall, *Colonial Policy and Practice*, Cambridge, 1948.

11. See Furnivall, *Educational Progress in South East Asia, op. cit.*, and also L. Finkelstein, "Education in Indonesia," *Far Eastern Survey*, Vol. 20 (1951), pp. 149–153; M. Read, "Education in Africa," *ANNALS* (March 1955), *op. cit.*, pp. 170–179; S. M. Naidis, *Economic Development and Education in India*, New York, 1952; B. T. McCully, *English Education and the Origins of Indian Nationalism*, New York, 1940.

12. See Griffiths, *op. cit.*; J. Furnivall, *Colonial Policy, op. cit.*; and W. F. Wertheim, *Indonesian Society in Transition*, The Hague, 1956, Chs. III, IV.

13. See, for a general description of these movements, R. Emerson, L. Mills, and V. Thompson, *Government and Nationalism in South East Asia*, New York, 1942; J. F. Halkema-Kohl, "Colonial Nationalism," *Indonesie*, Vol. VII (1953), pp. 35–61; J. S. Coleman, "Current Political Movements in Africa," *ANNALS* (March 1955), *op. cit.*, pp. 95–105; W. C. Holland, ed., *Asian Nationalism and the West*, New York, 1953.

14. See K. R. Bombwall, *Indian Politics and Government*, 1951, esp. Chs. IV, V, X, and XI; V. N. Naik, *Indian Liberalism—A Study*, Bombay, 1949, Chs. IV and XXI; Apter, *op. cit.*

15. See abundant material in Apter, *op. cit.*; and van der Kroef, *op. cit.*, Chs. 2 and 3.

16. See A. R. Desai, *Social Background of Indian Nationalism*, London, 1948, Chs. XI, XIII, XVIII. See also Emerson *et al.*, *op. cit.*; and Emerson, *op. cit.*

17. See the autobiographies and biographies of Gandhi, Nehru, Patel, and Nkruma. For a more general analysis see McCully, *op. cit.*

18. See Apter, *op. cit.*, Chs. 7 and 8.

19. *Ibid.*, esp. Ch. 8 for very pertinent illustrations.

20. See Emerson, *op. cit.*; Emerson *et al.*, *op. cit.*; G. T. McKahin, *Nationalism and Revolution in Indonesia*, Ithaca, 1953; C. A. O. van Nieuwenhuijze, "The Dar ul-Islam Movement in Western Java," *Pacific Affairs*, Vol. XXIII (1950), pp. 169–183. See also Coleman, *op. cit.*, and "The Emergence of African Political Parties," in C. G. Haines, ed., *Africa Today*, Baltimore, 1955, pp. 225 ff.; J. A. Curran, *Militant Hinduism in Indian Politics*, New York, 1951.

21. See V. Thompson, *The Left Wing in South East Asia*, New York, 1950; F. W. Galley, "The Prospect for Asian Trade Unionism," *Pacific Affairs*, Vol. XXIV (1951), pp. 296–306.

IX

Westernization, Cultural Revival, and the Rewriting of History

J. W. Fernandez

FOLKLORE AS AN AGENT
OF NATIONALISM (1962)

Hopefully there has been enough contact between humanists and social scientists in recent years and enough attempt at creating a common concern with common problems so that the one no longer entirely distrusts the cold and myopic eye of science peering into the literary intricacies of folklore and the other no longer thinks of folklore as a kind of folk entertainment, "a floating segment of culture," which is marginal to his main concerns. I cannot speak for the humanist, though I should imagine he has learned to put up with the sometimes heavy hand of the anthropologist or political scientist for the sake of the wealth of contextual crosscultural data he gets from him. But speaking for the anthropologists, I would be surprised if there are any of us left today who would not collect what oral narrative we could, exploiting to the fullest the potentialities of such data in arriving at explanations for the workings of society and culture. We recognize well enough that folklore functions within a social and cultural context whose cultural content and social integration it both reflects and determines. We should therefore find some agreement in regarding folklore as having efficacy in human affairs—as being an agent.

That folklore is an agent of particular vitality and potential in Africa is something that can hardly be denied by those who have been there. We have evidence for this in the many extensive collections of traditional verbal art from the different quarters of that continent, and most recently we have only to mention the Herskovits collection in *Dahomean Narrative*. But folklore is not to be seen only as a manifestation of tribal tradition now on the wane. It must be seen as an aspect of African culture that will enjoy *and* suffer the greatest exploitation for the sake of the

SOURCE. J. W. Fernandez, "Folklore as an Agent of Nationalism," reprinted from African Studies *Bulletin*, V. 2, 1962, pp. 3–8.

African future. This should surprise neither humanist nor social scientist for they both know well "how inviting, from its very nature the field of folklore is for those who wish to exalt national character and a national destiny." (Herskovits, 1959: 219.) We have watched it being used to these ends in countries as far removed as Ireland and Argentina, and now we see the same thing in Africa. We see, for example, how the concepts and the circumnambient mythologies of "African personality" and "negritude" depend in their expression upon authentic or reinterpreted African folklore. In the matter of migration legends alone one has only to read the work of one of the early African intellectuals to articulate these notions—Cheikh Anta Diop's *Nations Negres et Culture* (1948)—to realize how crucial to the arguments of these cultural pan-Africanists are the migration legends of the various African peoples. If this is not evidence enough that it is often from their rich folklore tradition that those who stress "negritude" and "African personality" take their identity, further confirmation may be obtained by studying closely the policies of new African governments in promoting research in the native population. If the author's experience in Gabon and Cameroun is any guide, funds allocated for such purposes are most willingly released for the kind of text collection which we would call folklore field research. There are many good explanations for this. New and unstable states are not anxious to explore profoundly either the maladjustments in the social organization or cultural manifestations of discontent in their populations. Peoples who have long felt that anthropologists and sociologists have emphasized their barbaric customs and tribal characteristics are unwilling to continue research in these directions and find in folklore a universal feature of human culture at which they excel. And finally, for non-literate peoples just becoming literate, the careful compilation and examination of mythologies, legends, and tales is one of the most obvious ways of re-discovering and having what the lack of writing had denied them—history. But whatever may be the reasons and rationalizations for this orientation toward folklore research and the folklore of African culture, the point to be made is that folklore has been, is, and will continue to be a dynamic aspect of African cultures. He who seeks to know Africa cannot ignore this any more than he would be able to understand Africans while ignoring the importance of the proverb and the trickster in their enculturative experience.

We examine in this paper the use of a traditional Fang migration legend as an instrument of political revitalization and regroupment. This legend, really a complex of legends all referring to what the Fang believe to have been the actual origin and migration experience of their ancestors, was seized upon by native nationalist elements for their own purposes. It became an agent of nationalism in this sense: it was hoped that, by placing emphasis upon this legend, a sense of community and political unity could be reinvoked in a dispersed and disorganized population. Colonial authorities were quick to perceive the nationalist implications both of the legend and the manner in which it was distributed.

The particular migration legend we study as agent belongs, properly, to the Ntumu dialect group of the Fang or Pahouin peoples of northern Gabon and southern Cameroun. But it is a legend that finds its counterpart throughout the various dialect groups of the Pahouin, and the elements common to all versions are numerous. In its traditional form this legend symbolizes the origin and migration experience of the ancestors from the northeast (nsi kwing) through a treeless savannah where there is little water, no game, and a constant shortage of food. At length the ancestors arrive at a great tree (adzap) which blocks their further passage. They are forced to chop a hole in this tree through which they then pass one by one to find themselves in a dense equatorial rain forest for which they lack techniques with which to deal. They soon fall in with the autochthonous pygmy peoples (Bukwé) who instruct them in the ways of the forest. Finally they build their own village, but family quarrels, which the various legends usually detail at length, commence, and minimal segments (ndebots) break away from each other, moving off to found what were to become the various dialect groups of the present Pahouin.

Some scholars of the western Bantu have examined the versions of this legend for clues to actual Fang history. Some maintain the legend gives clear evidence that the Fang originated in the area of the Bahr El Ghazal, in proximity to the present Azande, and were caught up and forced west and south by the Fulani expansion. Other scholars who seek evidence of Egyptian origins find this in certain versions of the legend. (Cheikh Anta Diop refers to it in this connection.) Though they speak a neo-Bantu language, it is true that the Fang are originally a Sudanic people of savannah origin. But it is the penetration of the equatorial rain forest, which is represented in the legend both symbolically and directly that most interests the Fang themselves. Genealogical research anywhere in Fang territory soon discloses that every one of the more than 150 clan traces its origin to Adzap Mboga (the pierced adzap tree), where in general the first ancestor in the genealogical line is supposed to have lived. The legendary account of ancestral difficulties in accommodating to the rain forest is heartily appreciated, for the Fang still do not feel fully at home in the forest and not only marvel at the pygmies in this respect but regard them as an important source of forest magic and medicine. As the Fang are a highly egalitarian and dispersed people, the legendary account of family conflict which originally led to their dispersion evokes for them a satisfying explanation for their fractionalism. In fact the legend is evocative enough that the nativist religious movements which have recently appeared among the Fang have taken the narrative and its symbolism directly into their mythology and ritual.

Thus the origin legend gives the Fang a satisfying explanation for their tentative accommodation to the rain forest and for the structural instability that has characterized their social and political life. At the same time by emphasizing their common origins it has persistently and almost single-handedly, I think, maintained a group feeling among all the Pahouin, a feeling which they might not otherwise have had by reason of their dispersion and growing dialectical separation.

In the colonial period the Fang give evidence of a number of different attempts at reconstituting themselves, for they well understood their dispersion was a weakness and that only through regroupment could they expect to exert influence in tribal and colonial affairs. Very likely all these attempts made use, in one way or another, of the origin legend. But the most recent and most important movement of this kind was the clan regroupment movement (alare ayong) of the late 40's and early 50's in southern Cameroun, northern Gabon, and Spanish Guinea. It is in the development of this movement that we have ample evidence of the political usefulness of the migration legend and its effect upon the populations involved.

The alar-ayong movement had its origins among the Ntumu and the Bulu, both Pahouin peoples of former French Cameroun living in an area heavily evangelized by the missions of the American Presbyterian Church. The Presbyterian Church, in the view of the colonial administration, was closely identified with all nationalist tendencies in this area, though it was clear that the church's commitment to those movements was ideological rather than moral or material. It does appear, however, that the clan regroupment followed closely the presbyter organizations employed by the Presbyterian mission in setting up church government among its converts (Alexandre, 1958: 68).

Most important, however, is the fact that the leaders of the movement searched in the various versions of the migration legend for a rationale upon which to regroup the clans. And they both actually found and pretended to find evidence, in the many varieties of the legend, for the reunification of clans on the basis of a common genealogical origin. Though they could find reasons in the legend for grouping all clans together into one unit, the regroupment leaders were content, since it involved questions of exogamy and certain resistant structural cleavages, to regroup usually no more than six clans under a new name said to be the legendary name of the matric clan. This new clan in turn was to be represented on a prebyter basis at the headquarters of the movement. Headquarters was identified, in a further use of the migration legend, with the symbolic tree, Adzap Mboga, through which all Fang had passed.

The rationale for this nationalistic movement of political regroupment thus adhered very closely to the migration legend. And in fact, when the movement sent its emissaries throughout southern Cameroun and into Gabon and Spanish Guinea they employed the migration legend as a password to gain the confidence of the population. Instruction on the operation of the alar-ayong movement, and in particular on the regroupment of clans, was given with the aid of the legend, for it was pointed out that according to it all clans now dispersed originally had common origins. If the particular legend of a clan under instruction gave no evidence of brotherhood with the clans to which it was said to belong, the memory of the elders was brought to task and the adequacy of the local legend impugned. It appears however that the haphazard regroupment of the clans at any cost was not the object of the leaders of the movement. And, indeed, they seem to have compiled carefully and studied closely the various versions of the legend in order to arrive at plausible regroupings of clans.

Nevertheless the migration legend suffered considerable interpolation and reinterpretation: fortunately we have several of these modern versions to compare with the traditional form. We even have an expanded literary version published in the vernacular in 1955 by the Presbyterian Mission Press of Ebolowa, under the title *Dulu Bon Be Afri Kara:* The Migration of the Children of Afri Kara (Ondoua, 1955). The modern versions and this literary version all show an attempt to bring the migration up to date to include the facts of colonial history as it impinged upon the Fang, as well as to amplify the early stages of the legend before the ancestors reached the great forest. The modern version traces the ancestors back to Egypt and to the other side of the Red Sea through which they passed as Moses escaped Pharoah's Host.

Though these modern versions contain no passages which could be interpreted as virulently anti-colonial and nationalistic, there are ironic statements about colonial exploitation. The good fortune of having passed over the Red Sea before the Suez Canal was built is demonstrated on the basis that had their ancestors been there at that moment of history, the Europeans would undoubtedly have put them to work to build it. Whether or not there was evidence in content, the various colonial administrations, particularly those of Gabon and Spanish Guinea, fully realized the uses to which this migration legend was being put and for a time considered it, especially its distribution in printed form, as being inimical to the interests of the administration. On the one hand the authorities of Spanish Guinea and Gabon of that period, a decade or more ago, were working hard to preserve the fiction of sovereign and separate colonial territories and they were bound to react strongly against any statement, such as the migration legend, that suggested the reality of common society and culture extending across arbitrarily assigned political boundaries. Such statement could only foster irredentist resentment. On the other hand, since this regroupment had its origin in Cameroun it was felt auto-matically to be contaminated with the rash of independence movements which characterized that territory and its special trusteeship status. It may already be difficult for us so soon after the facts to remember how strenu-ously and with what eternal watchfulness the colonial governments of the early 1950's worked to prevent this sort of contamination of their territories. Archives of the period indicate that some district administrators regarded the migration legend itself as having been wholly invented for the express purpose of subverting their sovereignty and contaminating their districts (Rolland, 1955: 4). The reason that the migration legend became one of the principal foci of administrative concern, rather than the other aspects of the regroupment movement for which it was simply the vehicle and agent, lay in the fact that representatives of the alar-ayong move-ment frequently posed as traveling troubadors or raconteurs, performing the old folklore and buying and selling the new, as is customary among the Fang. It soon became apparent to the administration that the migra-tion legend was the only item of folklore with which they were concerned.

Administration antagonism had little effect on distribution however, and by clandestine means the published form of *Dulu Bon Be Afri Kara* soon found its way into almost every northern Pahouin village. It became *the* source of tribal history, so far as the villagers were concerned, and the ethnographer working in these villages in 1958–1959 was hard-pressed to find a man who would recount to him a traditional version of the legend. If the elders had not learned the new version by rote, through having heard it read over and over by the young men in the council house, they would simply ask a young man to fetch the tattered pamphlet and read it to the European so that he should know the truth of the Fang past from that unimpeachable source, the printed word. Here at least is good evidence that the problem which baffles the student of European folklore, the interrelation between written and oral traditions, is becom-ing very much of a problem in Africa. And in the particular legend examined here it is already very difficult to extricate what was taken from a written source and what has always been a part of the oral tradition. Such confusions, though they compound the problems of the folklorist, greatly aid those who seek to put folklore to political use.

It should be clear from the evidence given that this migration legend was an important instrument of political regroupment in the hands of an early group of African nationalists. Changes in the content of the legend reflect, as we have learned to expect, the changes in the Fang social organization which were afoot at the time, changes in which the legend played an important role. As we expect to find in all folklore, the migra-tion legend gives voice both in its traditional and modern forms to the uncertainties and frustrations of the times while in the same breadth offering a message of integration and stability. That this is not an isolated and idiosyncratic example is made evident by the uses to which folklore is being put by present-day pan-Africanists in search of a personality.

REFERENCES

Alexandre, Pierre, and Jacques, Binet, 1958. *Le Peuple dit Pahouin.* Paris: Presses Universitaires de France.

Diop, Cheikh Anta, 1948. *Nations negres et culture.* Paris.

Herskovits, Melville J., 1959. Comments on "A theory for American folklore." *Journal of American Folklore* 72:216–20.

Herskovits, Melville J., and Frances S. Herskovits, 1958. *Dahomean narrative.* Evanston: Northwestern University Press.

Ondoua Engute, 1954. *Dulu Bon Be Afri Kara.* Ebolowa.

Rolland, M., 1955. *Le mouvement Fang au Moyen Congo.* Archives inedites—Centre des Hautes Etudes d'Administration Musulmane.

V. Monteil

THE DECOLONIZATION
OF THE WRITING OF HISTORY (1962)

Since Europe and America have become aware of the Third World, and since Africa and Asia have become aware of their situation (in the Sartrean sense of the word) and of their relationship to the rest of the world, it has become commonplace to ask whether all of African or Asian history ought not be redone. Because of prejudices of every sort, because of a persistent fondness for the exotic (for what Malinowsky so amusingly calls "hérodotages" [1]), and because of the internal contradictions of colonialism, has not the history of "colonial" peoples been falsified, and does it not remain falsified, mutilated, and consequently almost unusable? The superiority complex of the white man, the exclusive custodian of *civilization*—theirs, the only one there is, sometimes called "Christian," sometimes called "Western"—has not this attitude of superiority led the white population to reject *a priori* anything whose sources, facts, or opinions bear the hallmark of an indigenous origin? In short, has history been decolonized? And if not, what has been done thus far, and what more can be done about it?

The first solution, of course, is to produce a *national* history, established and published by Africans or Asians themselves, a history often treated by its editors as a kind of *committed* history—sometimes even as a "thesis" to be defended. Four recent examples, borrowed from India, Turkey, and black West Africa, reveal the tendencies, limitations, and dangers—if not the advantages of this passionate "approach."

In 1953 there appeared in English a work that quickly became famous: *Asia and Western Dominance* by K. M. Panikkar. The author, ambassador to Cairo at the time, is an Indian diplomat born in Malabar (1895), a former professor at the modern Moslem University of Aligarh,

SOURCE. V. Monteil, "La Decolonisation de la Histoire," reprinted from *Preuves*, No. 142, 1962, pp. 3–12.

and a graduate of Oxford University. Since its appearance, his book has been acclaimed a masterpiece by Anglo-American critics, and Nehru has recommended it. The method followed by K. M. Panikkar adheres to the Marxist point of view of "totality." The motives of European expansion in Asia are reduced to economic imperatives—which are, indeed, the undeniable truth, but which should not exclude recognition of certain spiritual factors especially evident in the case of Christian Missions. Critics have noted the Indian author's partiality for Russia, a country which "in fact, from the outset, showed that it did not share the superiority complex of Europeans in its relations with Asian peoples." Moslems benefited from a similar sympathetic attitude. The plurality of "the West" is unappreciated. Evangelical efforts are roughly handled. "The doctrine of a monopoly on truth and revelation is completely foreign to the Asian mentality." Clearly, a good deal might be said about the objectivity of the author's approach.

But the waters of the Ganges have been flowing for quite some time since René Schwab was able to write in 1950 (in his *Renaissance Orientale*): "Asia has entered European thought like an invisible interlocutor." Thank God! Asia can be heard speaking for herself. Still, one could wish that a return to original sources might furnish a reason for adopting positions that would cease being "positions of principle." Yet unfortunately, such is not the case. K. M. Panikkar has made no new contribution to our knowledge of facts or of mankind in general.

Since 1906 the works of Resid Saffet Atabinen, published in the French language, have sought to focus their attention on certain indispensable *Révisions historiques*—the title of one of his books that appeared in Istanbul in 1958. The Turkish writer endeavored to rehabilitate the memory of Attila and the Huns, regarded as frightful prototypes of "barbarians" by most European historians and, consequently, by countless millions of school children. Atabinen bases his history on a study of contemporary reports and documents (5th century A.D.) "reflecting a single viewpoint" since the caste of scribes in that era were members of the clergy, monks who kept chronicles. The author notes that Priscus is the only historian who had met Attila personally. He raises again the much debated question of the origin of the Breton Bigoudens and the traces left by the Alans in Rennes. The "scourge of God" seems to him in many respects more civilized than Charlemagne of later date. He sees in the Huns the ancestors of the Turks and Magyars, and he justifies Attila's implacable hostility to Rome on the basis of Roman decadence and Roman enslavement to flesh pots and circuses.[2] He reminds the reader that the Huns had a written language and that they left Europe with certain techniques still in use. If his biased point of view is clearly discernible and his etymological comparisons purely conjectural or unacceptable, we must grant him the merit of having gone "in the field" to verify his hypotheses and of having retraced, step by step, Attila's return itinerary from Orléans to Bregenz. In the words of Lucien Febvre (May 29, 1953), Atabinen's effort "is the forerunner of a great and necessary movement of historical reinterpretation."

Nowadays, Black Africa is the center of attention, and everyone wants to write its history—decolonized. A Senegalese, Cheikh Anta Diop, has sought to revise our perspectives with three startling works deriving from his doctoral thesis: *Nations nègres et cultures* (1955), *L'Unité culturelle de l'Afrique noire* (1959) and *L'Afrique noire précoloniale* (1960). He has written articles restating these themes; for example, "Intellectuals should study the past, not for the pleasure of doing so, but for the purpose of learning valuable lessons." (*La Vie africaine*, April 1960). From the outset, we are happy to see an African come to grips with his own problems and are thus prepared to give him an attentive and sympathetic hearing. Accordingly, we discover with interest echoes of the author's own personal experience. Unfortunately, such passages are all too rare. Cheikh Anta Diop almost never intervenes to bring us the benefit of an irreplaceable eye-witness account: "I was there. Such and such a thing happened to me personally." African societies are usually viewed through the eyes of Delafosse. There are quotations in superabundance, and the frequent references to Engels (1884) seem uncalled for. More recently there have appeared other works on Africa which are certainly better documented. The Egypt of the Pharaohs, and not his native Senegal, is C. A. Diop's favorite terrain, and yet he does not pass for an Egyptologist. Of course there is nothing to prevent a scholar from "hunting" elsewhere than on his own premises. But the amateur should be properly forewarned! For Cheikh Anta Diop, Negroes "were the first to invent mathematics, astronomy, the calendar, sciences in general, the arts, religion, agriculture, social organization, medicine, writing, technical skills, and architecture" (1955, p. 253). We note with regret that these affirmations claim to be based on history and linguistics. Both disciplines are subjected to rough treatment. These Senegalese *Wolof* (and why in the devil write Valaf for a word everyone pronounces Wolof?) do not appear, even in the traditions of the Senegalese *griots*, before the beginning of the 13th century. How could C. A. Diop find them in the Egypt of the Pharaohs? Idealizing the past and playing on words serve no purpose whatsoever: *germain* is represented as a Wolof word (1959, p. 178), and the Wolofs are alleged to have discovered America (p. 38). The author is clearly aware of the perils of his enterprise, for he admits (1959, p. 182): "Obviously, it would be ingenuous on our part to pretend to establish scientific certainties from such a vague comparison of African and Indo-European terms, especially when earlier examples of the African languages are so rare. We might even remind the reader that in linguistics it is always relatively easy to find comparisons between any two languages on earth; it is the reverse that is more difficult, to prove that two languages have no relationship to one another."

In offering this kind of criticism, do we run the risk of being taken for a "colonialist"? No doubt. But does not Cheikh Anta Diop run another kind of risk with the precarious premises of his intensely personal historical writings, jeopardizing the very cause he seeks to serve? As Raymond Mauny remarks in the *Bulletin de l'I.F.A.N.*, XXII, 1960, he risks discrediting the entire output of the new school of African historians by giving official sanction to a collection of errors and exaggerations which do an injustice to the Africans themselves. Happily, there are African historians from whom one can expect honest and dependable works firmly rooted in African cultures and traditions. Joseph Ki Zerbo is preparing in Ouagadougou a comprehensive study of the Mossi. Already in Bamako, Amadou Hampâté Bâ is pointing the way with an on-the-spot investigation conducted by a scholar solidly grounded in history, languages, and customs. His *Empire peul du Macina*, written in collaboration with J. Daget and published in 1955, is already out of print but in process of being republished (Mouton, Paris-The Hague). It deals with the Peul theocratic society known by the name of *dina*, a society which, from 1815 to 1853, dominated, structured, and produced the "Central Delta" of the Niger. Now in order to describe it, A. H. Bâ collected the oral traditions, still very much alive, by interviewing eighty-six Sudanese informants, marabouts, and traditionalists. The results surpassed expectations even if the method of presentation is occasionally confused and unscientific. We find in Bâ's study an authentic view "from the inside" of an African Moslem society which comes to life with its social structure, its behavior patterns, its motivating drives, its taboos, its laws, and its prototypes. The description of the founder of the *dina*, Cheikou Amadou (1775–1845), is in every respect like the one the "old men" had given to my father in Djenné sixty years ago: "He always kept his word; he took food only when he was truly hungry; he was known to have two wives (one of whom was his brother's widow) and a concubine literate in the Koran and in *fiqh* (Moslem canon law). His wife always called him Father of Amadou, according to custom. He earned his livelihood from selling hemp rope and copies of the Koran. The three fundamental virtues, in his eyes, were integrity, humility, and sobriety." There, in a few lines, we learn more than we would learn from long-winded rhetoric about the essential nature of "internal" conditions that guaranteed the success of one religion, Islam, in Black Africa—a religion that Richard Molard believed to have acted in history as "a cyclical stimulant for the societies of the Western Sudan."

It is apparent that the Marxist solution offers itself as the only one. In the first place, it is the creation of Soviet specialists themselves. In 1960, for example, *Présence africaine* published a volume entitled *Des africanistes russes parlent de l'Afrique* ("Russian Africanists speak about Africa"). B. I. Sharevskaya hardly spares Cheikh Anta Diop, accusing him of advocating "the development of ancestor worship and a state re-ligion"—which proves "of what intellectual aberrations even people with highly developed minds are capable out of ignorance of Marxist method-ology" (p. 126). There follows a debatable contention: "The wealth of African culture was not accumulated as a result of its ties with religion, but rather in spite of those ties." I. I. Potekhin expresses some construc-tive ideas on the formation of African nations and on the delay affecting language development caused by colonialism—although on this last point the British example in Nigeria is especially deserving of praise. Strictly historical interpretations are due once more to B. I. Sharevskaya for whom "the basic notion of Benin religion lay in beliefs and cults reflecting the process of the formation of classes and the development of the State," (?) and especially to D. A. Olderogge whose views are set forth in a biblio-graphical summary of his studies of the Songhay and Hausa states, and of the State of Bornu: "The author criticizes the prevailing opinion, according to which social relationships of the kind based on slavery had played the leading role in these States. . . . In the Middle Ages feudal-ism had already become a reality in the western Sudan where it was the dominant system." Similarly, "contrary to a number of Western scholars who consider the uprising led by Uthman dan Fodio (in 1804) either as a struggle between two peoples (the Hausa and the Fulani) or as a religious war, the author points out that the movement was joined by Hausa slaves and by farmers held in feudal serfdom who rose up against their exploiters, but that the fruits of victory fell into the hands of the Fulani feudal nobility."

Clearly, these are not first-hand investigations resulting from original studies of source materials, but are simple compilations, placed in a different light, it is true—and moreover one that is perfectly legitimate. But these limitations are not necessarily those of all African specialists in Communist countries. One has nothing but praise, for instance, for the honest and well-documented publications of Tadeusz Lewicki, who has shrewdly exploited in Cracow the collection of Arab manuscripts brought to Poland at the beginning of this century by Z. Smogorzewski, and which provides a valuable contribution to the history of Sudanese relations with businessmen and North African *Ibâdite* missionaries during the Middle Ages. Several of his articles have been written and published in the first instance in excellent French. On the other hand, the *Histoire de l'Afrique noire,* (of which) the first volume (with maps and illustrations) has just appeared in a French translation in Budapest (1961), discloses nothing new nor heretofore unpublished. The author, Professor Endri Sík, is described as "an eminent Africanist" in one of those appended notes to "please insert." In his introduction he rejects the expression "Black Africa" which he finds "racist and obscurantist." He explains how important it is to escape from "the labyrinth of imperialist lies and hypocrisy" and from "the misrepresentations of reactionary historians." He denounces "the monstrous historical crimes . . . of world capitalism." After dismissing "three erroneous manners of treating African history"—the struggle between colonial powers; units or colonies; "native" peoples—Endre Sík suggests that it must be examined and described "for each period of history according to the sectors in which history actually unfolded." He concludes with the declaration that "not a single historical work by a bourgeois author can be used with complete confidence." Of course allowance must be made for a sometimes hesitant translation or one that is curiously influenced by the Russian language: page 104, the Jewish traveler from Andalusia, Benjamin de Tudèle (12th century) is baptized *Tudelski.* The important and recent Portuguese editions of manuscripts relating to the Age of Discovery are apparently unknown to the author. It is true that works published in Bissao (Portuguese Guinea) are very difficult to come by. Sík's "survey" of "peoples of Black Africa up to the 15th century" (pp. 45–97) is so rapid that hasty generalizations are inevitably present. Every sentence conveys the feeling that the author is "an ivory-tower Africanist," less concerned with original research, starting from oral and written *sources,* than with supporting "the theses of Marx, Lenin, and Stalin in the domain of historical sciences" (p. 19). Does Africa really need this sort of thing?

In 1960 a Frenchman, J. Suret-Canale, and a Guinean, Djebril Tamsir Niane, published their *Histoire de l'Afrique occidentale,* printed in Czechoslovakia. A new edition, revised, enlarged, and very well illustrated, was brought out in 1961 under the auspices of *Présence africaine.* Far from offering "official lies," this joint enterprise sought to be "faithful to historical objectivity and to the cause of Africa." Indeed, its virulent anticolonialism ends up by defeating its own efforts at objectivity: "Colonialism accomplished nothing except in serving the commercial interests of the slave trade" (p. 108). Nowhere do we find the dialectical relationship of the colonializer and the colonized. There is no sense of moderation. No European is regarded as being intentionally progressive. As Charles-André Julien would say, it is a fine example of *totalitarian anticolonialism!* But there is an even more serious drawback to this work. The "historical" positions adopted by the authors are generally a mere echo, a simple reflection of outmoded theories (in spite of everything, there *has* been progress since Delafosse and 1912 . . . .). Thus we find Koumbi Saleh given as the (only) capital of a *single* empire of Ghana, and the latter is confused with Wagadou of the Soninké. And yet these mistakes had been rectified and placed in proper focus, especially by Charles Monteil in *Les Ghana* (1951) and *La Légende du Wagadou* (1959), two works apparently unknown to the authors of Conakry. The tendentious presentation of the empires of Mali (either from failure to understand or from ignorance of the *sources*) results in similar errors. All this is the more regrettable since thousands of African school children will thus learn as historical truths the inaccuracies and fantasies of Europeans who are either in too great a hurry to check their facts or else enjoy indulging their personal whims. We could cite many more examples of this sort of thing. Nor can we understand why the great explorations of the 19th century are limited to the English and to Barth (pp. 94–98). Are Frenchmen reduced to René Caillé for the purpose of eliminating in retrospect even the memory of their existence?

To get a clear understanding of this sensitive subject—"the decolonializing of the writing of history"—would it not be better to choose as an illustration the Soviet Union? Did not the homeland of Communism inherit from Czarist Russia Asian territories peopled with diverse minorities, generally Moslem, which are today "integrated" into the U.S.S.R. as autonomous regions or federated republics?

The problem is thus posed in Moscow, as elsewhere, of objectively evaluating *non*-Russian national history and of formulating a dialectical judgment on the colonial expansion of Czarist Russia. We may consider the official positions adopted in this matter as being divided into three stages. Until 1933 the Pokrovsky school unalterably condemned all imperialist conquests as an *absolute evil* for the colonial peoples. Down to the end of World War II, the question was asked whether the imperial yoke was but a *relative evil* compared with the traditional yoke of feudalism. Since 1948 the theory of an *absolute good* has won out owing to the fact that the revolutionary influence of the Russians has come to play a decisive role. It seems there is even a letter written in 1851 in which Engels declared to Marx: "Compared with the Orient, Russia has played a progressive role." Consequently, any reminder of historical circumstances that might harm "Stalin's friendship between peoples" is to be condemned. Three examples will shed light on this new interpretation of history. The quotations are, of course, taken solely from Soviet sources.

For several years the Republic of Kazakhstan was the scene of an ideological conflict, culminating in 1950, on the question of the national history of the Kazakh people—Turkish Mongols, nomadic and Moslem. As early as 1930 grave "nationalist" errors had been committed by N. Asfendiarov, but it was the *History of the Soviet Socialist Republic of Kazakhstan,* published in Alma-Ata, in the midst of the war in 1943, that ignited the fuse. Did it not contain the statement that "Russia has been the most dangerous adversary of Kazakhstan"? A second edition (1949) reflected the views of a book written by the Kazakh historian Bekmekhanov (1947): *Kazakhstan during the Years 1820 to 1840.* In this book Khân Qâsymov is described as "a popular chief (leader), almost revolutionary," and his insurrection against the Russians is portrayed as "a movement of national liberation." The storm broke December 26, 1950. An important article in *Pravda*, "The History of Kazakhstan in the Light of Marxist-Leninist Doctrine," sets forth in proper fashion "the profoundly progressive significance" of the annexation of Kazakhstan to Russia—between "the first three decades of the 18th century and the 1860's." "Soviet historical science stresses the progressive nature of anticolonialist movements. But one should not confuse popular anticolonialist movements with those that have been organized for petty goals of class status and are instigated by an aristocratic clique of the feudal nobility who also happen to be dissatisfied with the policies of the Czarist regime, but for different reasons." Alas! the "pernicious nationalist-bourgeois ideas" of Bekmekhanov have gained adherents, and the Soviet press must continually deal with these serious deviations: *idealizing* the past leads to a falsification of history. The theory of the "single stream," in particular, fails to distinguish in popular poetry the elements that truly represent the people and those that merely express the ambitions of a feudal aristocracy. Unfortunately, two years after the 1950 article in *Pravda*, "not a single study has appeared in the field of Kazakhstan history, economics, or literature. . . . Monographs are no longer being published. Scholars are demonstrating an incomprehensible timidity" (*Kazakstanskaya Pravda*, 28 December 1952).

The Shâmil affair offers a second example of the difficulties encountered in producing a history that is both Marxist and national at the same time—hence doubly "decolonized." Shâmil, a Moslem Avar prince of the Caucasus, led the struggle against the Russian colonial conquest from 1827 to 1857. For more than thirty years everyone regarded him, as did the *Great Soviet Encyclopedia* of 1934 (Vol. 61, pp. 801–806), as "a great democratic leader, celebrated for his heroism," and history books proclaimed the "rightness" of his cause in resisting the Russians. On May 14, 1950, there appeared an article in *Pravda* attacking an Azeri Turk historian, Haydar Huseynov (recipient of the Stalin Prize, 1949), for having eulogized Shâmil, and the article refers to the latter as "an imperialist agent," the instigator of a movement "profoundly reactionary and hostile to the great Russian people." In July 1950, Baghirov, First Secretary of the Communist Party of Azerbaijan, declared in Baku that "Shâmil was a sinister brigand, an oppressor of his people, a feudal tyrant, and a tool of Anglo-Turkish imperialism." In the intervening years, destalinization has restored Shâmil's name to good repute. The critical review, *Voprosy Istorii* ("Problems of History"), acknowledged in 1956 that the *Murîd* movement was "essentially progressive and revolutionary." In April of the same year the Soviet Turk, Baghirov, a Communist since 1917, was executed for "complicity with Beria, for acts of terrorism, treason, and participating in a counter-revolutionary organization." Shâmil had "liquidated" his adversary.

There remains a third and final illustration, as reassuring as the previous one—the question of legends and national epics. Each Soviet "nationality" has its epic poem: the *Alpamysh* of the Uzbeks; the *Keroghly* of the Azeri Turks; the *Dédé-Korkut* of the Turkmen Republic, and the *Manas* of the Kirghiz Republic, etc. Regarded as works permeated with "feudalism" and "religious fanaticism," they were made the target of a violent campaign of systematic disparagement that reached its climax in 1952–53. The *Manas* affair in particular provoked intense agitation in Kirghiz. This thousand-year-old epic, dear to the hearts of the Kirghistani, was still regarded as the *Iliad of the Steppes* in 1941. In 1952 Russian censors began to condemn its pan-Islamic and feudal aspects and its racial and religious hatred of the Chinese, "a proud and friendly people." The defenders of *Manas* were condemned in spite of the moving appeal of Ali Tokombaev, the Kirghiz national poet and a member of the party's central committee. "There is nothing in common," he noted, "between the horsemen of *Manas* and Soviet aircraft." His compatriot, S. Musaev, added (*Qyzl Qyrgustan*, 13 April 1952), "If we must outlaw *Manas*, let us also outlaw the Russian *Tale of Prince Igor* and the *Bylines*, for these works are as reactionary as those I am defending."

Everyone at that time was familiar with Stalin's fondness for the national epic of Georgie: *The Hero in the Leopard's Skin*. At the same moment that *Manas* was expiring, *Literaturnaya Gazeta* (14 June 1952) was denouncing *The Song of the Incursions* (*Pesn'o Nabegakh*), the national heritage of Daghestan, as "a sanguinary work about feudal robbers, intended to arouse the hatred of Moslems against the *Kâfir* and to glorify banditry." In 1954, following the death of Stalin, most national epics were restored to favor and recognized as "popular" and "worthy of survival," with the exception, however, of *Dédé-Korkut* and *The Song of the Incursions*. As for Shâmil, his misadventures began once more in 1957. He is again regarded as nothing more than an agent for the blackest kind of reaction. It is true that during the summer of 1956, after the execution of Baghirov, the press in Baku had exaggerated and openly attacked "Czarist colonialism."

It is noteworthy that the most important historical work on the Soviet Union appeared in France, and in French, in 1960. We refer to *Mouvements nationaux chez les musulmans de Russie* ("National Movements among the Moslems of Russia"), by Alexandre Bennigsen and Chantal Quelquejay. This completely objective study is based on an impressive number of Russian and Tartar sources systematically analyzed for the first time. Without it there can be no understanding of the history of the first ten years of the Soviet regime—ten years that were decisive. The reader becomes acquainted with Sultan-Galiev (*Ali-ev*), a Moslem Tartar of Kazan, who was a close collaborator with Stalin in 1918, then condemned as a counter-revolutionary in 1929. Well ahead of his time, he wrote in March 1918: "All colonial Moslem peoples are proletarian peoples, and since almost all classes in Moslem society were formerly oppressed by colonialists, all of them have the right to the title of proletarians. . . . The national movement in Moslem countries has the character of a socialist revolution." On the other hand, Europe seemed to him to have extinguished any flames of revolutionary ardor. The problem, therefore, he declared in 1923, was to establish "the dictatorship of the colonial and semi-colonial countries over the industrial metropoles" and, to this end, create a communist "Colonial Internationale" composed of "oppressed peoples"—from which the U.S.S.R. would be excluded. These ideas, along with their author, were condemned in 1929. Today, the rehabilitation of certain Tartar "bourgeois nationalists" does not mean that "the bourgeois national ideology is to be regarded as something relatively progressive before the October Revolution" (*Kommunist*, Moscow, August 1958).

The case of black Africa illustrates rather well perhaps what may be expected from a third type of solution—one that appeals to a spirit and methods that are purely and simply scientific. Obviously, we are not speaking of ambitious *surveys* or of views that are a bit too . . . too cavalier. We will reject premature syntheses, especially when their author —like George Peter Murdock (*Africa, Its Peoples and Their Culture History*, New York, 1959), a specialist in Amerindians and the Pacific—admits in his preface that his direct contact with Africa was limited to a week in Egypt (1921), four days in the Cape (1945), and two weeks in Kenya and Tanganyika (1957). We prefer to follow the suggestions appearing in two recent articles [3] and to review the proceedings of the Fourth International African Seminar (Dakar, December, 1961).

On this latter occasion some very important papers were read. Certain ones were rather theoretical but rich in information. One such was by Jan Vansina on the use of diachronic models in the history of Africa. According to his definition, a *model* is "the abstract representation of a concrete structure—in this case, the global structure of society and its culture. A diachronic model represents the changes from one synchronic model to another and later synchronic model and indicates the causes and directions of the changes." Everyone was in agreement on recognizing the need for combining written and oral sources, archeology and epigraphy, ethnology and linguistics. In this area the methods called "glottochronology" were criticized by those (including the writer) who strongly doubt the "reality" of Hattori's equation ($t = \log C/1 - 4 \log r$), which suggests that languages showing a common relationship in basic vocabulary to the extent of 23%, are separated from each other by at least six thousand years (?) Fortunately, other contributions were of a more practical nature. The problem of historical *dates* was frankly discussed.

Indeed, a certain number of very important dates in African history are commonly accepted by the specialists without further questioning, and these dates appear as established certainties in all text books. Now two examples, offered at the Seminar in Dakar, deserve thoughtful consideration. The first one concerns the dominant ethnic group of the present-day Upper Volta, the Mossi. Until now no one has challenged the view that the Mossi empires were originally formed in the 11th century. Still, there is no more basis for this assumption than a simple opinion by Delafosse, subsequently adopted by Dim Delobsom. As an historical certainty, we know that 33 Mossi rulers (Moro-Naba) have reigned down to the present time, each for an average of 14 years. This adds up to a total of 462 years, bringing us to the end of the 15th century. According to tradition, the first king of Dagomba reigned about 1450. And J. D. Fage, who "started the whole business," drew this conclusion: "Originally, horsemen arriving from the East, most probably towards the end of the 13th century, split up and established the Mossi States (in the 14th century) and the Maprussi-Dagomba (in the 15th)." For my part, I wanted to object to the universal credence so readily given to an event and a date based on pure speculation and not on history. The question at issue was the capture and destruction of Ghana by Sundiata in 1240. Now it is Delafosse, and only Delafosse, who affirms all this (in 1912, in his *Haut-Sénégal et Niger*, II, 180), whereas the griots of Kéyla, interviewed by Vidal in 1922, appear on the contrary to believe that the Mali hegemony in Ghana did not expand until a century later. And these griots are regarded as the qualified "archivists" of the Keita family. Delafosse gives no details of his oral sources which he himself admits he rectified and "amalgamated." He rejects out of hand the evidence—including that of Ibn Khaldun—testifying to the fact that, at least until the end of the 14th century, there was no doubt about the existence of a Ghana, a country from which Ibn Khaldun had met a mufti in Cairo in 1393. And this mufti was the very one who provided Ibn Khaldun with most of the information we possess on the rulers of Mali. All these facts were brought to light and published, beginning in 1929, by Charles Monteil in his *Empires du Mali* (which J. D. Fage considered in 1959 as "the best source for Mali"). In the light of these circumstances, why then, and how did it happen that Djibril Tamsir Niane, in his *Recherches sur l'empire du Mali* (Conakry, *Etudes guinéennes*, 1 April 1959) merely adopted the speculations of Delafosse and lamented the fact that the griots were "reluctant to speak"?

This question of oral sources is often badly formulated. G. P. Murdock (1959) denied their having any value other than that of an informant's personal reminiscences. And we must admit that criticisms are justified which fail to find any solid basis for certain works such as those of Leo Frobenius who, before ever having set foot in Africa, published *eighteen* books on the dark continent including one on *Die Weltan-*

schauung der Naturvölker (1898). From 1904 until his death in 1938, he made about ten expeditions to Africa. But Frobenius does not appear to have had the slightest acquaintance with any Negro-African language. He never offers a single original *text* and gives only very vague information about his informants. It is quite obvious that it is no easy matter to gather and utilize oral traditions. It was all of fifty years (1948) before Charles Monteil conceived the publication of the famous *Légende du Ouagadou* after having noted the Soninké text of the work in the French Sudan in June, 1898, so difficult did he regard the interpretation of the language of its chronicler. The caste of certain traditionalist griots—the Soninké *gesere* and the Mandé *dyali*—acquired their information from their most reputable elders. Naturally, one finds a number of confusing statements, falsifications, garbled texts, and legends interwoven with historical facts. These accounts have to be revised, carefully pruned of extraneous material, and critically evaluated. But all the more reason for not rejecting them *in toto* since they constitute the *only* existing sources of information. Yves Person pointed out (at the Seminar in Dakar) the futility of archeological excavations in a damp tropical milieu. In the Ivory Coast metallic objects are totally lost from rust in less than a century. And written sources (except for René Caillé) are nonexistent for the southern part of the western Sudan until the end of the 19th century! Must we therefore resign ourselves to a complete ignorance of its history? Surely not. Already a widespread use of the traditional system of "age classes" has permitted the establishment of a rough sort of chronology. In other places figures reached by computing "generations" of 25 years each will help the historian "go back" as far as the 16th century. Moreover, Yves Person has practiced what he preaches. He speaks Malinké fluently and has assiduously collected the oral recollections of former companions of Samory (1835–1900). A few are still alive, like his barber and confidant, Mamadou Touré, who is a centenarian. . . . The historic figure of Samory will thus assume its true dimensions, equally removed from colonial injustice and from legendary hero-worship.

Wherever practicable, much is of course anticipated from archeological findings. The excavations by Thomassey and Mauny in Koumbi Saleh perhaps gave rise to premature hopes and expectations. They uncovered the remains of a city one square kilometer in size, built of dry stones without mortar (like other cities of the Sahara), containing the site of a single mosque and two cemeteries without tombstones. Was this perhaps *one* of the historic capitals of Ghana? How can we date from the 12th century what remains of its houses? Do the houses of Tagdaost in the eastern part of Mauritania, uncovered in 1961 beneath ruins from the 17th century, perhaps date further back than the 16th century? Have we located the Aoudaghost described by Arabian geographers? It is of course still too soon to know for sure. Surprises are in store from the study of epigraphy. Inscriptions from Gao (on the Niger), dated in the 12th century (1100 to 1150), bear the names of unknown sovereigns on leaves of chloritoschist. . . . The field is vast, and the task is immense.

One of the countries of black Africa that is apparently the best known is also one with surprises in store. The history of Senegal remains to be written. In order to "decolonize" it, it will not suffice simply to transform Lat Dior, the last *dâmel* of Cayor, who was judged a despicable plunderer by Faidherbe, into a great hero of the national resistance movement. It will be far more important to show how and why his conversion to Mohammedanism brought about the conversion of the great majority of Wolofs at the end of the 19th century. The task of simply making an inventory of ancient sources is yet to be done. Happily, such sources do exist. First of all there are the Arab sources. Unfortunately, the identification of place names and individual names is purely hypothetical because of the absence of diacritical markings missing in most manuscripts, notably in those of one of the oldest and most interesting chronicles, Al-Bakri (late 11th century). The latter, however, gives only second-hand reports gathered from merchants and travelers in Cordova. There is need for a patient effort to examine, analyze, re-translate, and compare the different writings of Arab authors in order to begin "dusting off" their works. There is also a need for knowledge in depth of West Africa, its languages, and its customs. In any event, the researcher will discover the recorded cases of early conversions to Islam—at least among the princes. He will also discover ties of every description with the Maghreb and the presence, during the Middle Ages, of Judaized black Africans. The first Europeans to write about the west coast of Africa were the Portuguese, or foreigners in the pay of Portugal, beginning in the 15th century (the age of "Discovery" dating from 1434). Alongside skillful compilations—like those of Morave Valentin Fernandes (1506)—an investigator will find eye witness accounts like those of the young Venetian Alvise da Ca' da Mosto (1455–56) or of Captain André Alvares d'Almada (1594), and he will come to appreciate the critical and already scientific attitude of Duarte Pacheco Pereira (1506–08). Also it will be necessary to examine the texts themselves, the originals, and not simply truncated editions and unreliable translations. In this connection, the publications of Lisbon and Bissao are indispensable. Of the Wolofs, whom he calls *Ziloffi*, we can always say, like Ca' da Mosto: *sono homini de molte parole* ("They are men of many words"). All such evidence is precious, in particular for the history of the Islamization of Senegal.

But the most amazing contribution, perhaps the decisive one, comes from the oral traditions collected by the griots. After the appearance of studies by Gaden (1912) and Rousseau (1929–33), followed by those of Joire (1942) and Robin (1946) on the former "amphibious" kingdom of Wâlo, Amadou Wade, a scholar of Dagana, on the River, collected about the year 1942 a chronological list of 52 "kings" (*Brak*) in which each of the latter appears with his name and the number of years he reigned. Wade acquired his data from information transmitted from father to son in the griot families. Since the list concludes with Faidherbe (1854), by subtracting the total of additional reigns, it is easy to deduce the fact that the kingdom of Wâlo dates back to the early years of the 13th century, as does the origin of the Wolof ethnic group. It is noteworthy that Amadou Wade's notes are in Arabic, a language still used in West Africa by writers and chroniclers.

Clearly, it is indispensable, desirable, and possible to rid colonial history of the prejudices of colonialists. It is not always an easy thing to do, as witness the case of the U.S.S.R. It should be somewhat easier to do so in Africa where so many independent states can now say and write what they please. But that is not the fundamental problem.

To decolonize the writing of history, is it not the first task to stop regarding one's object of study as a "colony," that is to say, as a second-class research terrain which need not be studied with the same care and standards as are applied to European history? Are not the histories of Africa and Asia deserving of just as much effort and attention? Is there not a need to abandon, for the time being, those vast syntheses which are premature for the most part, and to return to first-hand *sources,* whether written or oral? Is not the first necessity, for African researchers in particular, to begin work at once "on location" by interrogating and listening to the "traditionalists"—as long as there are still some to be found—to probe deeply into their own Negro-African languages and seek earnestly for their own roots and origins?

Then, and only then, will the basic requirement have been met, whatever its shortcomings, and history will have finally become "decolonized."

(Translated from the French by Robert A. Wagoner, State University of New York Maritime College.)

NOTES

1. "Hérodotage" = Hérodote (Herodotus) + "dotage" (drivel, twaddle) (Trans. note).

2. Bernanos said of the Roman: "We know that he is a pig." (*Nous autres, Français,* 1939, p. 19.)

3. Hubert Deschamps: *"Pour une histoire de l'Afrique"* (*Diogène,* no. 37, Jan.–Mar. 1962) and Henri Moniot: *"Pour une histoire de l'Afrique noire"* (*Annales,* no. 1, Jan.–Feb. 1962).

J. F. A. Ajayi

THE PLACE OF AFRICAN HISTORY AND CULTURE IN THE PROCESS OF NATION-BUILDING IN AFRICA SOUTH OF THE SAHARA (1960)

In contrast to nineteenth century Europe where the basic aim of nationalism was to fit people who shared the same culture and language into a nation state, the fundamental yearning of African nationalism has been to weld peoples speaking different languages and having different traditional cultures into one nation state. Whereas it was the Romantic Movement that characterised European nationalism, running through African nationalism are the iconoclastic spirit of the French Revolution and the universal values of the *philosophes*. While European nationalism began with cultural renaissance, many critics have pointed to the African nationalist's disregard of tradition, "African nationalism's disregard of what actually gives meaning to most African lives." [1]

THE FEAR OF LOCALISM

The roots of this disregard of tradition go back to the middle of the nineteenth century when the call to create new nations along the European pattern first began to be heard in West Africa and at a few centres in South and East Africa. It was a call for men to emancipate themselves from the local and the particular and to seek a universal fatherland. The call came largely through European Christian missionaries who believed that Christianity could flourish in Africa only if a new social and political order similar to that of Europe was established. They believed that European civilisation was the culmination of all human progress and that the new African nations could have no better pattern and should aim at nothing different. This development was most important in West Africa

SOURCE. J. F. A. Ajayi, "The Place of African History and Culture in the Process of Nation-Building in Africa South of the Sahara," reprinted from *Journal of Negro Education*, XXX, 3, 1960, pp. 206–213.

where the call came first to people who had already been forcibly emancipated by the slave trade from their villages and the ancestral gods and had found their way as freed men into mission schools in Sierra Leone. They in turn became teachers and catechists spreading down the West African coast and at many points pushing into the interior, building schools, preaching disbelief in the old gods, and gathering new converts together in little enclaves around the Mission House where traditional stories and fables and graven images and heathenish drums and dances were tabooed. In place of the old songs and drums and festivals were the new hymns and the harmonica and the magic lantern shows. In place of local history and legend was substituted the history of man as summed up in the Old and the New Testaments.[2]

These men viewed the traditional cultures as obstacles to full participation in the new life not only because they were sinful, but also because they weakened one's attachment to those "universal Christian values that were the common heritage of all civilised men." The old society and culture were not just to be reformed; they were to be destroyed, not by force but by attrition: they were crumbling away and they were doomed to die an easy, painless death in the face of the new dynamic Christian civilisation. It is true that evidence was not lacking that the traditional cultures were not so decadent; that they survived in Cuba and Brazil and were surviving in Freetown next door to the chapels and the churches. But such unfortunate survivals were viewed as a challenge to the preachers and the teachers to redouble their efforts, not to change their tactics. It is also true that at least for one reason the traditional cultures could not be wholly disregarded. It was obvious that the new doctrine could not be made to reach the masses except through the indigenous languages. But that was only a temporary concession to traditional culture. It was believed that as this doctrine reached the masses and converted them, it would by its own force emancipate them from their traditional cultures to the "universal Christian values."

Thus, all along the coast, there were rising up a cosmopolitan group of people, conscious of themselves as members of a new generation of the "African Race." They dreamt of a new nation "which shall render incalculable benefits to Africa," "hold a position among the states of Europe," "rank among the civilised nations of the earth." They championed the missions and courted European ways and attitudes because it was to Christianity, European commerce and technological civilisation that they looked for bringing about the nation of their dreams. In their anxiety to achieve the larger polities where the African can take advantage of the new technological civilisation of Europe, they lost sight of their self-respect and their right to self-determination. They were so anxious to win recognition and esteem abroad that they disdained their

cultural heritage. And they were increasingly to be despised by the Europeans who had created them.

Side by side with these men, there grew up a smaller, rebellious
group. This began with men like Bishop Crowther whose work on the
indigenous languages had been thorough and deep enough to appreciate
at least some aspects of the traditional cultures. Then there were a few
others who slipped from the apron strings of the missionaries and took
some interest in local politics and therefore began to discover unsuspected
vitality in the indigenous social and political institutions. Above all, there
was Edward Blyden who, because of his knowledge of Arabic, opened
up communications with learned men and rulers of Muslim states in the
West African interior, the Imamate of Futa Jallon, the sprawling empire
of Al Hajj Umar, and later, the empire of Samory Ture, new and developing polities of undoubted vitality. While the Christian leaders on the
coast were dreaming of the new nation that would bring prestige to
Africans, Blyden found the Muslim leaders actually creating and governing empires of which Africans could be proud:

> They read constantly the same books, and from this they derive that
> community of ideas and that understanding of each other . . . which gives
> them the power of ready organisation and effective action. . . . Without the
> aid or hindrance of foreigners, then, they are growing up gradually and nor-
> mally to take their place in the great family of nations, a distinct but integral
> part of the great human body, who will neither be spurious Europeans, bastard
> Americans, nor savage Africans, but men developed upon the basis of their
> own idiosyncracies and according to the exigencies of the climate and country.[8]

Blyden urged Africans to emancipate themselves from the mental slavery
imposed by European culture and to rediscover themselves. He urged
them to establish their own independent churches and a West African
university where African studies would be welcomed and respected.

From such views resulted the experiment at Abeokuta and in the
Fante Confederacy to graft European ideas of government on to the
existing political institutions. A few people began to discard their European names and dresses, and to take interest in traditional religious
liturgies, and traditional art forms, and dancing. Others began to collect
traditions of origin, and a few notable works appeared on traditional history and laws and customs. Perhaps of the greatest lasting influence of all
the new changes was the rise of the African Church movement. There
were schisms in a number of the established mission churches. African
churches were set up, taking various attitudes to polygamy and seeking
their identities by experimenting with new liturgies, vestments and ceremonies.

Thus quite early in the history of nationalism in Africa was posed
the question of the relevance of African history and culture in the reconstruction of Africa. Most educated Africans in the nineteenth century, so

conscious of the evils of the slave trade and the rising tide of racialism in Europe, proclaimed the universality of man and a common stake in all that is best in the cultural heritage of the human race, and this included the technological culture of Europe. In celebrating the national independence of Liberia in 1855, Dr. Alexander Crummel declared:

> All the preceding generations of mankind and all the various nations, have lived for every successive generation. . . . The Hebrew polity, . . . was not local in its bearing and intents; but that in its ultimate ends and aims, it was *our* polity, and the polity of all Christendom, ay, of all the world.[4]

A favourite quotation of the educated Africans in this period was from Niehbuhr, the German historian:

> There is not in history the record of a single indigenous civilisation; there is no where, in any reliable document, the report of any people lifting themselves out of barbarism. The historic civilisations are all exotic.[5]

To this Blyden opposed the view that "Every race . . . has a soul, and the soul of the race finds expression in its institutions, and to kill those institutions is to kill the soul. . . . No people can profit by or be helped under institutions which are not the outcome of their own character." [6] He was not advocating isolation: the African was a "distinct but integral part of the great human body." What he protested against was the imperialism of those who denied the African the right of self-determination, the interference of those who "imagined that the African had in his native home no social organisation of his own, that he was destitute of any religious ideas and entirely without any foundation of morality," [7] and wished to supply the deficiency in their own way.

But Blyden did not really resolve the question posed. When asked how soon traditional African states developing "gradually and normally" without outside interference would catch up with the technological civilisation of Europe and win recognition abroad, his answer was "God's time is the best." [8] Besides, he knew something of traditional African culture from his travels and from the works of Mary Kingsley. But he did not know enough of it to be able to show what aspects of it were relevant for the work of reconstruction, and what had to be rejected if the danger of "localism" was to be avoided. Indeed, he said little about traditional African culture. It was not the "universal values" of Christianity that he opposed so much as the lack of choice the Christian missionaries and European imperialists imposed on the African. His real answer to Christianity was not traditional culture but Islam, again with its universal values, but without racial discrimination and without imperialism and loss of self-government. Thus, the experiments of the African Church movement to discover what was relevant for the new age and what was not came to very little. Even the African Church shied away from localism. They entered into communion with American Negroes and began to talk, rather vaguely at first, of Ethiopianism and Pan-Africanism.

In any case, not all the protests of Blyden could stem the tide of European imperialism. In the last quarter of the nineteenth century, Africa was partitioned into spheres of European influence and units of European administration. And that altered the situation considerably.

THE NECESSITY OF SELF-GOVERNMENT

In many ways, the aims and objectives which the various colonial powers declared in justifying their action in Africa were similar to the goals that the African nationalists set themselves—the creation of larger, economically and technologically developed nations able to take their places on a basis of equality with other nations in the world. The colonial powers created the framework of the larger units. They built the first railways and highways. They established cosmopolitan administrative and commercial capitals, civil services and trade unions, where new unities were being forged. Gradually, as the European administrations became more and more effective, the colonial boundaries, arbitrary as many of them were, began to acquire some significance for the African. Each territorial unit was becoming the focus of some national loyalty of its own.

That is to say, the colonial regimes were providing the framework of the future nations. And this explains the large measure of cooperation which they received initially from the educated Africans as distinct from the traditional rulers. So great has been the yearning of African nationalism for larger polities that the later demand for self-government seems almost an afterthought. If it were true, as it is often argued, that economic development, roads and railways and similar infrastructure, could by themselves weld African peoples into nations, then the argument for self-government is considerably weakened. As a French Colonial officer said eloquently in 1946 when the first demands for self-government began to be heard:

A new African world exists which we have called into being and which our native policy has brought to birth. . . . Our methods have justified themselves; we have powerfully renewed Africa. . . . On what ideological grounds is it proposed to put a stop to this experiment. What so-called realism can ignore our actual achievement.[9]

The increasing demand for self-government is itself the answer that the policy of the colonial governments have not been so successful in calling into being the new Africa.

There was, of course, no hope of the colonial powers advancing very far the economic and technological development of Africa, not to talk of the creation of nation states. The prediction of Blyden has been more than justified, that:

> It is not the business of Imperialism to make *men* but to create subjects, not to save souls, but to rule bodies. It must have a certain repulsiveness. On its moral side, it must be imperious, with pronounced self-confidence, a certain unsympathising straightness, a pride of itself and an inevitable ignorance of others.[10]

The very presence of the white man in a position of rigid superiority over the black man undermined the confidence of the black man in himself. The colonial regimes were based on the prestige of the white man; official policy, tacitly or explicitly, was calculated to maintain this prestige. As Lugard put it:

> The white man's prestige must stand high when a few score are responsible for the control and guidance of millions. His courage must be undoubted, his word and pledge absolutely inviolate, his sincerity transparent. There is no room for "mean whites" in tropical Africa. Nor is there room for those who, however high their motives, are content to place themselves on the same level as the uncivilised races. They lower the prestige by which alone the white races can hope to govern and to guide.[11]

It was to maintain this prestige of the white man that the education of the black man had to be controlled, not only through the prejudices of the white teacher and the white text-book author, but also sometimes by actual directives of the administrations in laws said to be designed for the best interests of the black man. Within this philosophy of education, the white man had a glorious and heroic history, the black man had none at all. The white man was always brave and courageous, the black man, if not lying and sneaking and lazing around, was only fierce and savage. White men fought wars and levied indemnities, black men only raided their neighbours and extorted tributes. Whatever cultural traits the white man had and the black man did not have, like writing, the wheel, the plough, and even eating forks, were essentials of civilisation, but what the black man prided himself on, like rhythm, courtesy, respect of elders, and a stable philosophy of an ordered world, did not really count. Europe was the centre of the world, and all worthwhile achievements have been by white men. One witty geography book still in use in the 1930's proclaimed that Africa was the land of man-like apes and ape-like men. Others confirmed that the climate of Europe was the best in the world, temperate, equable; Africa was too hot and too humid for constructive work.

The point here is that in the process, not only did the white man come to believe that as a white man he was inherently superior to the black man, but that the black man also began generally to accept this point of view. And this happened most where the African was closest to the European settler in Africa. The colonial regimes could not accept the African and his culture. Where they made a show of accepting him, it was because they wished to destroy his culture. And where they made a pretence of tolerating his culture, it was because they could not accept him as an equal. They could not practise the "universal Christian values" of brotherhood and equality, and yet, by their nature, they undermined the African's belief in his cultural heritage and destroyed his self-respect. In this, they de-humanised the African; they devalued Africa's human resources, the greatest assets they had to develop. That is why the colonial regimes failed. They could maintain law and order, and exploit some material resources, but they could not bring the new Africa into being. They could produce isolated individual Africans capable of outstanding achievements, but they could never hope to inspire such confidence or generate such enthusiasm among the masses as would combine individual energies and loyalties into the common pool of a great national effort. And if the African nationalist is to succeed any better than the European imperialist, he must recognise that a nation is not built by material resources alone.

To some extent, every African political leader engaged in the nationalist struggle for self-government realises this. To engage in the struggle at all, he must have emancipated himself from the feeling of inferiority imposed on him by the colonial regime. He needs an ideological answer to imperialism. He must believe in the future of Africa, and to do so convincingly, he must base his belief on a confident assessment of the achievements of the African in the past. For, "if the African has no past heritage, and no future except by imitation of European ways at a pace which the European thinks safe," [12] the experiment in self-government is bound to fail. If the past fills the nationalist leader with fear, he would say like the un-emancipated Northern Rhodesian, that "If the European were to go, then we would all have to go back to the grass huts, to the ancestral ways of living, and I don't want to do that." [13] If he has any gnawing feelings of doubt about the future, he would demand less than self-government. Apart from his own personal emancipation, in order to succeed in the nationalist struggle, he would also need to restore the self-confidence of his followers and to rehabilitate them as men. He cannot do this without reference to the history and the culture of his people. Like the missionary seeking mass conversion, the nationalist leader realises that he cannot reach the people effectively except in the language, the symbols, the culture, they understand. That is why the nationalist struggle and the organisation of the nationalist party becomes an important exercise in national education and a major step in the building up of national unity and a common political loyalty.

RESOLVING THE DILEMMA

So much is obvious. The colonial period has proved Blyden right. Self-respect, self-determination, is a necessity of genuine social and political reconstruction. "The only healthy form of imitation is based on self-knowledge; any other form can never be discriminating." [14] If there is to be progress, the African must develop confidence in himself, and this he can do only if he understands his own cultural development and respects his own cultural heritage. The real question is how does he go about it, how does he distinguish in his cultural heritage what is relevant to his present predicament and what is not? The old dilemma remains, only the colonial period has made it much more difficult to resolve. Blyden's view of the traditional states developing "without the aid or hindrance of foreigners . . . growing up gradually and normally," borrowing what they like from where they choose, is a thing of the past. Self-government today means the rise of new political leaders basing their rights not on traditional sanctions but on mass support. Economic and technological development to raise the standard of living of the people cannot wait indefinitely until "God's time." And yet the nationalist leader attempting to rally the masses and reestablish their self-confidence by appealing to their cultural heritage soon realises that the more each cultural group takes pride in its own heritage, the more difficult it is to achieve the common loyalty to a large political unit which is necessary for development and is the fundamental goal of African nationalism. With increasing self-government the old fear of "localism" reappears under the name of "tribalism."

The problem is very real. It explains why in areas where the already complex ethnic composition of the territorial units has been complicated by the importation of Europeans as a separate and privileged community, and of Indians and Arabs also as separate if not so privileged communities, the nationalist leaders usually refrain from references to the African's cultural heritage. In East and Central Africa, with the exception of Jomo Kenyatta,[15] it is not the nationalists but the traditional rulers opposing national integration who appeal to history and culture. In South Africa, it is the white minority government believing not in national integration but in apartheid who appeal constantly to history and culture. In West Africa where the nationalists and the traditional rulers have come closest together, and the nationalist movement is most conscious of the African's cultural heritage, the danger of "tribalism" remains—the danger that a cultural group might in the name of national integration colonise the others and deny them their self-government, or that the self-consciousness of the different cultural groups might tear the nation asunder.

To some extent, Pan-Africanism to which Blyden's group turned will provide the answer. This is the answer of the East African leaders, Julius Nyerere, Tom Mboya; the South African National Congress; as well as some notable leaders in West Africa like Kwame Nkrumah and Nnamdi Azikiwe. Apart from encouraging greater African unity and correcting some of the anomalies of the old colonial boundaries, Pan-Africanism will save the African from localism. It will save him from trying to live in the past as in a museum. He will only concentrate on such values of the past as the common Pan-African experience shows to be valid and relevant to development today. Instead of being parochial, he will be encouraged to develop loyalties both at the local, the national, the Pan-African and the inter-national levels.

But is this an adequate answer? The ideal of Pan-Africanism is more real today than it was sixty years ago, but it is still a dream and a hope of the intellectual élite. It has little meaning for the masses. For the peasant in the village, the idea of culture on a Pan-African level implies a great measure of abstraction, and, to quote the words of Leopold Senghor used in other connections, abstraction implies impoverishment.[16] Such abstraction enables any politician to think up anything to his immediate advantage and pass it off as an essential value in the African cultural heritage.

This degree of abstraction, however, is a measure of our own ignorance of the actual history and culture of the different African peoples, and only increased knowledge can save the situation. Our cultural heritage is what we carry with us in our bones. Its values that are valid for us are those of which we are conscious. Only education and increased knowledge can deepen and widen that consciousness. It is largely through education and increased knowledge of the past that individuals are resolving for themselves on the personal level the dilemma we have posed. Mphahelele, for example, claims to be "the personification of the African paradox, detribalised, Westernised, but still African—minus the conflicts." [17] On the national and the Pan-African level, it is increased research into African history, and a dissemination of knowledge of the history and culture of different African peoples throughout the continent, that will resolve the dilemma. Increased knowledge of the actual state and development of the cultures of different African peoples in the past will not foretell the future, but it will provide understanding. Understanding on the part of artists and writers will reactivate old cultures and establish the values from the past that are relevant today and are of general Pan-African validity.

That the African past must play an important part in the process of nation-building in Africa today is no longer in doubt. Research and more understanding are still needed to determine what aspects of the past will be most relevant and in what way. The increasing measure of self-government, and the important decisions that are now being made for the future makes the necessity for this research more pressing. The old dilemma must now be resolved. We may sum up in the words of Karl W. Deutsch:

> Autonomy requires both intake from the present and recall from memory . . . a continuous balancing of a limited past within a limited system making its own decisions affecting the future. . . .
>
> A person blind and deaf or insensible to further impressions; an organisation or people effectively isolated to all messages or experiences from its larger physical or social environment . . . —all tend to lose more or less of their power of self-steering. . . . On the other hand, a person without memory, an organisation without values or policy, a people without effective tradition, a ship or a missile without set goal—all these no longer steer, but drift.[18]

NOTES

1. Peregrine Worsthorne: "Defying History," in *The Twentieth Century,* Vol. 165, No. 980, April 1959. Special Issue entitled *The New Africa,* p. 401.

2. For a fuller discussion of this period, see J. F. A. Ajayi: "Nineteenth Century Origins of Nigerian Nationalism" in the forthcoming issue of the *Journal of the Historical Society of Nigeria.*

3. Edward Blyden: *The Prospects of the African,* an Address delivered at the celebration of the Anniversary of the Independence of Liberia, at Willesden, July 1874. (London 1874).

4. Alexander Crummell: "The duty of a Rising Christian State to Contribute to the World's Well-Being and Civilisation," in a collection of the author's papers entitled *The Future of Africa* (New York, 1862), pp. 63–4.

5. *Ibid.,* p. 107.

6. Edward Blyden: "West Africa before Europe," and "West African Problems," two Addresses delivered in England in 1903, in *West Africa before Europe and Other Addresses,* p. 140, p. 101.

7. *Ibid.,* p. 131.

8. Edward Blyden: "Islam in the Western Sudan," in *West Africa before Europe and Other Addresses,* p. 6.

9. R. Delavignette: *Freedom and Authority in French West Africa* (O.U.P. 1950), p. 146. (A translation of *Service Africain,* Paris, 1946.)

10. Edward Blyden: "Islam in the Western Sudan," *loc. cit.,* p. 73.

11. F. D. Lugard: *The Dual Mandate.* (London, 1923, p. 59.)

12. K. O. Dike: "History and Self-Government," in *West Africa,* a London Weekly, February–March 1953.

13. Edward G. Olsen: "Crisis in Central Africa," in *Journal of Human Relations,* Vol. VIII, Nos. 3 and 4, 1960. Special Issue entitled *Dawn in the Dark Continent: Polities, Problems, Promises,* p. 501.

14. K. O. Dike: *op. cit.*

15. Jomo Kenyatta: *Facing Mount Kenya* (London 1953). "It is the culture which he inherits that gives a man his dignity as well as his material prosperity," p. 317.

16. L. S. Senghor, talking of the oral quality of African music said:

"Codification, fixing in writing, while it offers certain advantages, does not make those advantages certain. Writing is synonymous with abstraction, and therefore with impoverishment," in "Constructive Elements of a Civilisation of African-Negro Inspiration," in *The Unity of Negro Cultures*, Report of the Second Congress of Negro Writers and Artists, Presence Africaine, nos. 24 and 25, February–May 1959.

17. E. Mphahlele: "The Dilemma of the Elite" in *The New Africa, op. cit.*, p. 325.

18. Karl W. Deutsch: *Nationalism and Social Communication* (M.I.T. 1953), p. 142.

R. C. Majumdar

NATIONALIST HISTORIANS (1961)

Historiography was practically unknown to the Hindus at the beginning of the nineteenth century. With the spread of English education in the second quarter of that century, the Indians began to learn, along with many other modern ideas, the value of historical knowledge, and also gained a great deal of information about the history not only of India but also of the whole world. A deep interest in the study of history and cultivation of the art of writing history may thus be said to have grown in India about the middle of the last century. Historiography in modern India, at least among the Hindus, is thus barely a century old.

Unfortunately the Hindus gained their first knowledge of the history of their own country from treatises which gave unmistakable evidence of deep-seated prejudices against the Hindu culture and civilization, both of the past and of the present times. The natural resentment against this had a twofold effect. It whetted their appetite to learn more of the historical facts which would enable them to refute the charges or calumnies in books written by the foreigners. At the same time it laid an undue emphasis on the duty of Indian students to study history with a view to vindicating their past culture against unfounded charges of the European writers. This considerably narrowed down the scope of history, and added an element of acerbity in historical judgement. It was partially responsible for occasional lapses of that detached attitude, balanced judgement, and proper perspective which form the basis of true history. It is only against this background that we can understand the real significance of the phrase "nationalist historians," when applied to India. It is a comparative term to be used by way of contrast with the foreign histori-

SOURCE. R. C. Majumdar, "Nationalist Historians," from C. H. Philips (editor), *Historians of India, Pakistan and Ceylon,* London: Oxford University Press under the auspices of the School of Oriental and African Studies, 1961, pp. 416–428.

ans, mainly British. It does not necessarily connote a body of men whose sole object was to glorify their country's past at any cost, though, as will be shown later, such a feeling was not always or altogether absent. Nor need the term be confined to Indians, for even Europeans, including Englishmen, indulged in theories and criticisms which distinguish the so-called nationalist historians of India. As a matter of fact, not unoften we find that even the most extreme views of nationalist historians of India were based on, or derived from, those propounded by European scholars.

For the purpose of present discussion, the designation "nationalist historians" is confined to Indians. It is, however, difficult to draw a line between nationalist and other Indian historians. In a sense, it may be argued that some sort of nationalist bias may be traced among all Indian historians. But the same thing may be said, more or less, of historians of all nationalities, when writing the history of their own country. We therefore restrict the use of the term to those Indians who are not purely or merely actuated by a scientific spirit to make a critical study of an historical problem concerning India, like any other country, but whose primary or even secondary objects include an examination or re-examination of some points of national interest or importance, particularly those on which full or accurate information is not available or which have been misunderstood, misconceived or wrongly represented. Such an object is not necessarily in conflict with a scientific and critical study, and a nationalist historian is not, therefore, necessarily a propagandist or a charlatan.

Subject to these preliminary remarks, we may proceed to analyse the various forces that were at work in creating nationalist histories in India and giving them the shape, form or direction in which they have developed.

Broadly speaking, nationalist history of India was originally a reaction against the British histories of India, and later gathered its strength and inspiration from the awakening of national consciousness among the Indians. Still later, it received further impetus from the countrywide agitation for securing political rights which slowly merged itself into the movement to free India from the yoke of the British. In order to understand its origin and nature we must begin with an account of some typical text-books on Indian history, written by British authors, *which had a wide currency in India.*

The first in point of time was the *History of British India* by James Mill, published in 1818. He begins with an elaborate account of the Hindus and seeks to prove that the abject condition in which the English found them in the eighteenth century represents their normal condition throughout their history. He ridicules the "hypothesis of a high state of civilisation" propounded by Sir William Jones in regard to the ancient Hindus and observes: [1]

Their laws and institutions are adapted to the very state of society which those who visit them now behold, such as could neither begin, nor exist, under any other than one of the rudest and weakest states of the human mind. As the manners, the arts and sciences of the ancient Hindus are entirely correspondent with the state of their laws and institutions, everything we *know* of the ancient state of Hindustan conspires to prove that it was rude.[2]

In forming a comparative estimate, Mill declares that the people of Europe, even during the feudal ages, were greatly superior to the Hindus.[3] Proceeding further he observes: "In truth, the Hindu like the Eunuch, excels in the qualities of a slave."[4] A few lines further on he remarks: "In the still more important qualities, which constitute what we call the moral character, the Hindu ranks very low."[5] After all this, it scarcely surprises us to be told that "it will not admit of any long dispute, that human nature in India gained, and gained very considerably, by passing from a Hindu to a Mohammadan government."[6]

There is no doubt that Mill's view was primarily due to ignorance. But it is impossible to absolve him altogether of a deep-rooted prejudice against the Hindus. Speaking from the historical point of view, he committed the great blunder of reading the present into the past. Unfortunately, this sort of prejudice or blunder marked the average Englishman in India and, more or less, clouded the visions of subsequent English historians of India also, the difference being one of degree, not of kind. Elphinstone, for example, whose *History of India* was published in 1841, was very sympathetic to the Hindus. Yet it seemed to him extraordinary that the Arabs "should not have overrun India as easily as they did Persia."[7] He suggested all possible and impossible reasons for this, but never even hinted at the only rational explanation that would have occurred to any unprejudiced mind, viz. that the Hindu rulers had strength enough to resist the Arabs. Again, in the face of the clear testimony of the *Periplus of the Erythraean Sea,* regarding the maritime activities of the Indians, Elphinstone tacitly assumed that the trade was "conducted by Greeks and Arabs."[8] Though he admits the trade intercourse between India and western countries by land or sea at an even earlier date, he regarded it as "uncertain whether the natives of India took a share in it beyond their own limits."[9] Elphinstone's *History of India* was a standard text-book in the examinations of the Indian Civil Service in England and the Universities in India as far back as 1866, or perhaps even earlier. The young Englishmen formed their notion of the Hindus, over whom they ruled with iron hand, from a book which contains such passages as: "The most prominent vice of the Hindus is want of veracity, in which they outdo most nations even of the East."[10]

The third great English historian of India, V. A. Smith, writing at the beginning of this century, emphasized, in his account of ancient India, "the inherent weakness of the greatest Asiatic armies when confronted

with European skill and discipline," [11] and prophesied the inevitable re-
lapse of India into political chaos, which has been her normal condition,
except for rare intervals, "if the hands of the benevolent despotism which
now holds her in its iron grasp should be withdrawn." [12]

I have mentioned these three historians because they were the leading authorities on the subject so far as an average Indian was concerned;
for even in the first decade of this century, when I was a college student,
all the three books were prescribed as text-books for Indian history.
To an Indian mind, therefore, these three books, to which others may be
easily added, represent the general trend of Englishmen's views from the
beginning to the end of British rule.

Several other tendencies among European writers may be clearly
noted throughout the nineteenth century. Even when positive evidence
was being brought to light about the past greatness of the Hindus, there
was a conscious and deliberate effort to minimize its importance. This
was sought to be done by various ways. One was to deny the antiquity
of Indian culture by suggesting the lowest possible (or even impossible)
date for her literary works like the Vedas and Epics. Another method
was to belittle this culture by suggesting that Indians borrowed most,
if not the whole, of their culture from the Greeks [13] and where that
appeared to have no basis, from the Assyrians, Persians, Babylonians, etc.
Wherever there was the least similarity between Indian and foreign ideas,
Indians were taken to be the borrowers. The Epics were supposed to be
indebted to Homer's works, Indian drama, mathematics, philosophy, and
astronomy were derived from the Greeks, and even Krishnacult was derived from Christ. The very poor evidence on which such theses were
boldly enunciated, even by learned scholars, demonstrated a prejudiced
mind rather than bad logical deduction or inference.

The third method was to belittle the value of Indian culture by
selecting or stressing only its weak points and ignoring its better aspects.

A class of writers, more particularly the Christian missionaries, took
special care to bring into prominent relief the social abuses, religious
superstitions, and those actions of the Hindu gods and goddesses, and
corrupt practices sanctioned by Hinduism which were grossly immoral or
highly obnoxious to modern minds. But their righteous indignation was
not provoked by similar abuses in their own society and religion.

Thus while the burning of widows was regarded as a barbarous trait
in Hindu culture, no thought was given to the burning of heretics in
Europe. While caste system was condemned, no reference was made,
even for the sake of comparison, to the slavery and serfdom in ancient
and medieval Europe, and the treatment of the "blacks" by the "whites"
in modern times.

Generally speaking, the European writers, with a few honourable
exceptions, were guilty of this kind of partisan national spirit, and often

indulged in the habit of comparing the Hindu with the European culture by contrasting the worst features of the former with the best aspects of the latter.

The inevitable reaction was not long in coming. The Hindus, particularly the English-educated class, were provoked beyond measure by the general tone of English writers and were eager to accept the challenge. The response to the arrogant claims of superiority by the British writers and their belittling of the Hindu culture took various forms and covered a wide range. It would be a laborious task to trace in detail the growth of Indian reaction to various points at issue in chronological stages of development, and it must suffice to take a broad view and analyse the main trends of thought.

As could be easily anticipated, the cause of Hindu religion and its sacred literature was taken up first. The attitude was both defensive and aggressive. Minds influenced by the rationalist spirit made an attempt to prove that Hindu religion and society mean only the purer forms as enunciated in the Vedas, and that the later growths do not deserve that appellation. Thus the worship of images, degraded forms of caste-system, and many abuses that crept into Hindu religion and society in later times —things which formed the targets of European criticism—were all sought to be swept away as so many accretions of degenerate times. The extreme form of this view is represented by Dayananda Saraswati, who put a new interpretation upon the Vedas, differing radically both from the traditional as well as western, in order to prove that they contain the most rational ideas on every subject and even anticipated the scientific discoveries of the nineteenth century.

Another school sought to prove that Hinduism, taken in all its aspects of development, formed a highly spiritual force, and justified the social evils and religious superstitions by giving them a new interpretation and a spiritual significance. This school is represented at its best by Rajnarain Bhose, Bhudev Mukherji, Chandra Nath Basu, Bankim Chandra Chatterji and others, while one of its extreme and extravagant exponents was Sasadhar Tarkachudamani. This school not only defended Hinduism against all criticism by foreigners, but asserted the superiority of Hinduism to all other religions, particularly Christianity.

The material side of Hindu culture was also defended with equal zeal against European criticism, and this task was facilitated by the Europeans themselves. The archaeological discoveries and researches in ancient Indian history, carried on mostly by them, revealed a number of valuable and interesting data which were utilized by Indians to disprove the inferiority of Hindu culture, *vis-à-vis* the western, so long asserted by the Europeans. The writings of Rajendralal Mitra and Ramkrishna Gopal Bhandarkar and a few others show Indian scholarship at its best. The results of the researches of these Indian scholars and a galaxy of distin-

guished oriental scholars of Europe were brought together in three com-
pendious volumes entitled *Civilization in Ancient India* by R. C. Dutt,
in the closing years of the eighties of the last century. This may be
regarded as the first nationalist history in the best sense of the term. It is
"nationalist" more in a negative than in a positive sense. In other words,
it is free from the prejudiced outlook of European writers which had
hitherto dominated the works of Indian history. But it is equally free from
the extravagant nationalist sentiments of the Indians which were provoked by it. This does not mean that Mr. Dutt's book is free from errors.
But the errors are mostly those of judgement and ignorance of facts, and
very rarely, if at all, the outcome of a preconceived national bias. This
is best evidenced by the fact that the book did not fully satisfy either
the Hindus or the Europeans. The orthodox Hindus held that life in the
Vedic age was more spiritual, more pious, and contemplative in its tone
and character, than that depicted in the book, and they refused to accept
its account of the rude self-assertion and boisterous greed for conquests
of the Vedic warriors. On the other hand, the Europeans took the opposite
view. Dr. Kern observed, while reviewing the book, that "some scholars
delight in describing all that was robust and manly and straightforward
in the character of the Vedic Hindus, while others portray their coarse-
ness and imperfections." He was of opinion that Dutt adhered to the first
school, but that the truth lies midway.

Whatever we may think of Kern's criticism, it has to be admitted that
the rationalist outlook of Mr. Dutt is sadly lacking in much that was
written by Indians in later times. This will be best understood from a
reference to extreme views on certain points.

As regards the antiquity of Hindu civilization Dutt followed more
or less the views of Max Müller, but later Indian writers have carried it
much further back. B. G. Tilak referred the Vedas to third millennium B.C.
while A. C. Das placed the composition of at least some hymns of the
Rigveda to ancient geological epochs, probably before the end of the
Tertiary epoch.

While stressing the infinite superiority of Hinduism in the spiritual
field, attempt was made to show that ancient India was not much behind
modern Europe even in scientific achievements. It was claimed that not
only firearms of bigger size, but even aeroplanes were known in the age
represented by the Epics. Dr. R. K. Mookerji's book, *A History of Indian
Shipping and Maritime Activity* was a rejoinder to Elphinstone's assumption mentioned above.

While a class of Europeans was anxious to prove that Indian culture
was mostly derived from foreign sources, some Indian scholars declared
with equal vehemence that India was almost immune from any outside
influence. Actuated by the same spirit, it has been strongly held by a

section of Indian scholars that India was the original home of the Aryans and they spread from this country to Europe.

The criticism of social abuses was met in two different ways. Some denied, for example, that the caste system was an ancient system, while others justified it by specious arguments about division of labour, and the analogy of similar institutions in European countries.

The same procedure was followed in regard to the position of women. It was pointed out by some that the status of women in the Vedic period was very high and that they also occupied an honourable position in later times. On the other hand, their secluded life and position of inferiority were justified by others on social, economic, religious, and spiritual grounds, and the low or degraded position of women in many respects, even in Europe, was sought to be proved as an indirect justification.

So far, we have dealt with the effect of reaction provoked by European writers on Indian history. A further impetus to the nationalist historians was given by the growth of national consciousness among the Indians, mainly caused by the spread of English education, and through it, of western ideas. Its first effect was a demand for higher political status mainly by the institution of popular Government on the western model. All the objections which the British Government advanced against such concessions were sought to be met by arguments based on Indian history.

The British were never tired of repeating that India was not a country but a congeries of smaller States, and the Indians were not a nation but a conglomeration of peoples of diverse creeds and sects. The nationalist arguments against this view were summed up in a scholarly treatise entitled *The Fundamental Unity of India,* by Dr. R. K. Mookerji. The religious unity and spiritual fellowship among the Hindus all over India was held to be the basis of nationalism which overrode barriers of language and distance; the ideals of an all-India Empire and full or partial realization of it in the past, were stressed in justification of its demands for the present.

In order to prove the fitness of the Indians for democratic type of Government prevailing in the West, the history of the republican tribes in India, to which attention was drawn by Rhys Davids, formed the subject of a good deal of study and research. But sober attempts in this direction were marred by extravagant claims made by writers of the type of K. P. Jayaswal. He sought to prove that not only a constitutional form of Government, but the entire parliamentary system, including Address to the Throne and Voting of Grants, was prevalent in ancient India. He also gave a new interpretation to many words and passages in inscriptions and literary texts in order to prove that responsible Government, with all that it implies in the West, existed in ancient India with its full paraphernalia.

With the growth of nationalist sentiment, the Hindus began to lay great stress on their heroic fights against Muslims. Tod's *Annals and Antiquities of Rajasthan* served as a model and a store-house of materials. Inspiring historical accounts were written of the long-drawn-out struggles between the Rājputs and the Muslims, in which the Rājputs almost always came out with flying colours. Similarly in delineating the history of the Marāthās, great stress was laid on their successful campaigns against the Muslims, inspired by the ideal of founding a Hindu Empire (*Hindu Pad Padshahi*). Their treatment of the Rājputs and plundering raids against the Hindus were either forgotten or ignored. Similarly the alleged faults of Shivaji were either exonerated or minimized, and sometimes even explained away. The Sikhs also appeared as fighters for freedom against both the British and the Muslims. Ranjit Singh became the ideal states-man and the battle of Chilianwala counted as a victory of the Sikhs. The heroic activities of the Rājputs, Marāthās, and Sikhs were cast into a new mould to suit the spirit of the time. So modified, they became popular themes and formed the subject-matter of novels, stories and poems written by such eminent men as Bankim Chandra, Rabindranath and R. C. Dutt.

There was also a psychology behind all this. Hindus wanted to remove the stigma of their easy defeat at the hands of the British, and refute the view of the British Government that they were unable to protect India without their help. As all this implied deficiency in military skill and lack of bravery and heroism, the historic examples of the Rājputs, Marāthās, and Sikhs were enlisted in support of their claim for military greatness.

Urged by the same motive, the Hindu historians sought to belittle the military achievements of the British. The Battle of Plassey, which laid the foundation of the British rule, was held to be the result of treachery, but no great importance was attached to the successive British victories against Mir Kasim and Shah Alam. English victories in the Sikh wars were set down to bribery of the Sikh leaders, but Chilianwala was quoted as an evidence of the superiority of Sikh military skill. Above all, they were never tired of pointing out that it was mainly with the help of Indian soldiers that the British had won India. Not much notice was taken of the numerous battles, like those at Kirkee or Sitabaldi, in which a handful of troops commanded by the British defeated Indian soldiers more than ten times their number.

With the development of nationalism and political consciousness, the nationalist history was also marked by an intense hatred against the British. The activities of the British Government, as well as of individual Britishers, were painted in the blackest colours. The economic exploita-tion of India, involving ruin of trade and industry, and impoverishment of India almost to the level of starvation, formed the theme of laborious works of men like Dadābhai Naoroji and R. C. Dutt, who followed in the footsteps of Digby. Their moderate tone offers a striking contrast to the writings of Major B. D. Basu who made a long catalogue of the evil deeds, errors of omission and commission, of the British in both economic and political spheres. His books are profusely documented, and his charges, supported by facts and figures, are not easy to refute. But his scathing comments leave no doubt that his main object was to draw a lurid picture of the British in India and to arraign them before the bar of public opinion of the world. Historical criticism of various measures of the Indian Government, both in regard to internal administration and in respect of Native States, was definitely marred by a nationalist bias. The most glaring example of the former is furnished by the almost unanimous condemnation of the policy of promoting English education which was represented as a deliberate move only to prepare a set of clerks. As to the latter, Dalhousie's policy of annexing Native States was strongly condemned, though a hundred years later highest praises were reserved for the man who followed it in a more thoroughgoing way and by far more dictatorial methods.

Individuals, especially those who distinguished themselves in founding the British Empire, like Clive, Warren Hastings, and Wellesley, came in for a good deal of criticism. It comprised both well-deserved condemnation and unmerited censure, but there was an unmistakable animus in these writings inspired by nationalist feelings. As an instance, a reference may be made to a book entitled *Clive, the Forger*. A lack of balanced judgement, accompanied by a truculent mood, was also in evidence in criticisms of frankly reactionary Viceroys like Lytton and Curzon. Correspondingly, those who opposed the British were regarded with sympathy, sometimes much more than they deserved. Siraj-ud-Daula and Mir Kasim were represented as great heroes and patriots, fighting to the last for the sake of their country. The Black-hole tragedy was repudiated as a myth, and the massacres of Monghyr were lightly passed over. Even Nandakumar was hailed as a great martyr.

The aversion towards the English also found good scope in severe denunciation of the colonial imperialism of the British, and, in particular, their attitude towards the Boers and the Irish. The hypocrisy of the British and their unlimited greed for power and pelf were taken for granted. Napoleon's description of the British as a nation of shopkeepers struck the right chord in the heart of the Indians, and formed the basis of their judgement of English character.

The struggle for freedom against the British, which took a definite shape early in this century, intensified some of these anti-British feelings, and introduced new ones. Besides, it ushered in a new type of nationalist movement in Indian historiography. This may be generalized as a deliberate re-interpretation of Indian history in order to infuse enthusiasm in the fight for freedom and sustain or strengthen the cherished creeds and slogans of the Indian political leaders. An instance of the former is afforded by the re-naming of the Sepoy Mutiny of 1857 as the Indian War of Independence. V. D. Savarkar's book with this title is a typical specimen of the representation of history from an extremely nationalist point of view.

Hindu-Muslim unity was believed by the political leaders to be a *sine qua non* for ultimate success in the fight for freedom, particularly as the British Government held out the differences between the two communities as the chief obstacle to the grant of Dominion Status to India. The entire history of India during the Muslim period was accordingly re-interpreted in order to prove that the Hindus and Muslims always behaved towards each other like good brothers and formed one nation; that the Hindus were not a subject people during the so-called Muslim period, and that it is the British who for the first time imposed foreign rule upon India. Even a man like Lala Lajpat Rai supported all this with elaborate arguments in his *Young India,* and a committee set up by the Congress published a voluminous treatise in support of this thesis. Dr. Tarachand's book, *Influence of Islam on Indian Culture,* is another attempt in the same direction, though more divorced from historical facts, and less justified on grounds of national exigency.

The growth of party politics had full repercussion on history. The history of the political struggle during the first half of this century has been deeply coloured by the political views of the party to which the author belonged. The two books, *Indian National Evolution* and *Indian Politics since the Mutiny,* written respectively by A. C. Majumdar and C. Y. Chintamani, two veteran members of the Moderate party, and *A Nation in the Making,* an autobiographical memoir of Surendranath Banerji, one of the great leaders of the party, are more or less party pamphlets rather than sober history. The two books written by Hiren Mukherji [14] and R. Palme Dutt [15] plainly betray the influence of communist ideals. It is hardly necessary to refer to numerous other historical writings of the period which are frankly propagandist and are deeply coloured by the ideologies of the Revolutionary, Socialist, Communist, and other parties.

In conclusion, it must be pointed out that the nationalist school of history has not vanished from India with the achievement of independence. Ideas and notions, once acquired, die hard, and many historical conceptions or slogans which were clearly the outcome of political exigencies during the period of struggle for freedom, have come to stay, even though the necessity of the same has disappeared. In addition, fresh tendencies are gathering force, which, if unchecked, would again pervert the history of India. The non-violent method of struggle against the British, initiated by Mahatma Gandhi, has now become a regular creed with an influential section of people, and they are re-interpreting Indian history in order to prove that "non-violence" has been the eternal creed in Indian politics. Whether such a view, opposed to all known facts of Indian history, except the isolated case of Asoka, would ultimately succeed in re-shaping or modifying the history of India, it is difficult to say. But the signs are not very propitious.

Another ominous tendency is a sharp turn towards orthodoxy in interpreting the religious institutions and social ideas of the past. It seems to be due to the psychological tendency to connect the political bondage to the West with the ideological changes brought about by western influence. So the freedom from one naturally cries for freedom from the other. The desire to remodel India according to the genius of Indian culture is natural enough, and welcome within certain limits. But it involves a clear conception of what Indian culture is, and this gives a tempting opportunity to re-shape Indian history. In a democratic age, everyone seems to assume that a knowledge of Indian history is a birthright of every Indian, and requires no patient study or research. So different images of Indian culture are being formed by different interpretations of Indian history according to individual idea, taste, or fancy.

Orthodoxy being a more potent force in Indian society, there lies the danger of nationalist Indian history taking a sharp turn towards the right. But the opposite tendency of a sharp turn towards the left is also not altogether lacking. The newly acquired ideal of a "secular State" is opposed to all known facts of Indian history. But it is sought to be buttressed by a new conception of Indian history and culture, which recognizes no distinct Hindu or Muslim culture in modern India, and looks upon these, along with European or western culture, as so many streams meeting together only to mingle and lose their separate entities in the sea of Indian culture. The Muslims, however, repudiate any such idea, and Islamic culture is not only recognized as a distinct entity, but has been formally adopted as the basis of the new State of Pakistan. In India, however, a small but gradually increasing class of influential persons now fight shy of the term "Hindu" as a designation of a cultural unit, and only think in terms of an Indian culture. Whatever may be the value of such an idea in shaping India's culture, it becomes positively dangerous when it encroaches upon the domain of Indian history and seeks to ignore the existence of Hindu culture as one of the most potent and patent facts of Indian history even today.

Having thus discussed some of the main trends of the nationalist history in India, it is necessary to say a few words about its merits and defects. As regards the latter, broad hints have been given above how nationalist historians not unoften deviated from the true principles of historical study in order to support a particular point of view. In extreme cases and due to political exigencies, they ignored patent facts of history or deliberately misrepresented them, or drew important conclusions from extremely insufficient data. In many cases, the judgement was warped by strong political or party feelings, and history was made a handmaid of current political agitation, or party propaganda. In short, the nationalist history of India exhibits more or less the same defects as are inherent in national histories of any other country.

On the credit side, it must be remembered that the study of history in India received its first impetus from nationalist sentiment and was largely sustained by it throughout the British period. A good many historical works, belonging to the "nationalist" class, in spite of their professed or implied nationalist tendency, deservedly occupy a very high place. A great deal of patient and industrious study has been devoted by Indian scholars in various branches of history, particularly the economic condition of India during the British period, and the progress of the ancient Hindus in such fields as political thought, administrative organization, trade, and maritime activity, fine arts, and positive sciences, where they were least expected to achieve any distinction at all. The share of the Indians in the reconstruction of their political and social history is also not negligible. Above all, they have made a new approach to the study of Indian history. They have stressed the point that the political or dynastic history, the materials for which India lacks, is not necessarily the only or even the main aspect of "history," but have rightly drawn our attention to the cultural history for which India has abundant materials. Therein also lies, according to them, the true history of India. This idea was adumbrated by Rabindranath in his inimitable language, and has now caught the imagination of India. The importance of the part of India lying to the south of the Vindhyas has been fully realized from this point of view, and due importance had been attached to the synthesis of Aryan and Dravidian culture. A great change has come in their outlook of modern times. "The true history of India during the British period does not consist of the activities of the East India Company or of its successor, the British Crown, but of the upheaval which led to the transformation of Indian society, through the activities of India's own sons." K. M. Panikkar's book, A Survey of Indian History, published in 1947, from which the above sentence is quoted, may be looked upon as one of the most recent nationalist histories, and the following passage from it throws an interesting light on the nationalist historians of today:

Ever since India became conscious of her nationhood . . . there was a growing demand for a history of India which would try and reconstruct the past in a way that would give us an idea of our heritage. Brought up on text books written by foreigners whose one object would seem to have been to prove that there was no such thing as "India," we had each to "discover India for ourselves." I do not think it is an exaggeration to say that it was a spiritual adventure for most of us to gain in some measure an understanding of the historical processes which have made us what we are and to evaluate the heritage that has come down to us through five thousand years of development.

Much of their efforts in all the various directions noted above may be traced to nationalist sentiment, but the result shows that such sentiments are not incompatible with a high standard of achievement.

Time is perhaps not yet ripe for a proper valuation of the nationalist history of India. It would be an interesting study to institute a comparison between the deviation from the correct historical standard to which Indian history has been subjected by the nationalist sentiments of Indians on the one hand and the nationalist-cum-imperialistic ideas of Englishmen on the other. The consequences of the withdrawal of British power from India and the benefits of British rule formed the subjects of keen and acrimonious dispute between Indian and English nationalist schools. The truth of the assertions and assumptions, so confidently made on both sides in this connection on the basis of historical study, may now be partially tested in the light of actual events in India, since she attained her independence. Nine years' time is no doubt a very short period in the history of a nation, and no final judgement is possible on the results of such a short experiment. Still many predictions on both sides have proved to be false, and many defects in both the points of view already strike a discerning eye. It is difficult for an Indian or an Englishman of the present generation to pass a correct judgement on the relative merits or demerits of the history of India which was influenced by the nationalist sentiment either of Indians or of Englishmen. But there is no doubt that there were nationalist histories of India of both these types, and both seriously erred, though in opposite directions. The extent of their errors must be left to the verdict of history.

NOTES

1. James Mill, *The History of British India*, fifth edition (London, 1858), ii, 109.

2. *Ibid.*, p. 115.

3. *Ibid.*, p. 148.

4. *Ibid.*, p. 365.

5. *Ibid.*, p. 366.

6. *Ibid.*, p. 342.

7. Mountstuart Elphinstone, *The History of India*, ninth edition (London, 1916), p. 305.

8. *Ibid.*, p. 183.

9. *Ibid.*, p. 182.

10. *Ibid.*, p. 213.

11. V. A. Smith, *The Early History of India*, second edition (Oxford, 1908), p. 109. For comments on this, cf. R. C. Majumdar, *Ancient India* (Banaras, 1952), p. 109.

12. *Ibid.*, p. 331.

13. The following passage may be read with interest in this connection: "We know that the trigonometric sine is not mentioned by Greek mathematicians and astronomers, that it was used in India from the Gupta period onwards (third century). . . . The only conclusion possible is that the use of sines was an Indian development and not a Greek one. But Tannery, persuaded that the Indians could not have made any mathematical inventions, preferred to assume that the sine was a Greek idea not adopted by Hipparchus, who gave only a table of chords. For Tannery, the fact that the Indians knew of sines was sufficient proof that they must have heard about them from the Greeks." J. Needham, "History of Science and Technology in India and South-east Asia," *Proceedings of the National Institute of Sciences of India,* xviii, No. 4 (1952), p. 360 (reprinted from *Nature,* Vol. 168, 14 July 1951, pp. 64 ff.). "Paul Tannery, so famous for his studies on ancient mathematics" (*ibid.*), represents a type, not an individual.

14. *India Struggles for Freedom* (Bombay, 1946).

15. *India Today* (Bombay, 1947).

B. Oetomo

SOME REMARKS
ON MODERN INDONESIAN HISTORIOGRAPHY (1961)

As with those of many Asian peoples today, we can divide the Indonesian historical writings into a traditional and a modern section. The traditional section is made up of writings produced by Indonesians who were still living in a cultural milieu which was completely untouched by modern western ideas and values. On the other hand modern Indonesian historiography consists of historical writings of Indonesians who graduated from some kind of a modern western educational institution and who were thus influenced in some important respects by modern western ideas and values.

The traditional section of Indonesian historical writings will be treated by Professor Berg, Dr. Hooykaas, and Dr. Noorduyn. And we shall confine ourselves to the subject mentioned in the title of this paper.

Among Indonesian writers we find a few who have usually published their books or articles in the Dutch language, for example authors like Husein Djajadiningrat, Purbotjaroko, Priyono and Pryohutomo. Their writings will not be discussed in this paper, not only because those authors can be considered as belonging to the Dutch School, but also because their main interest is often merely directed to the literary aspects of traditional Indonesian culture.

Thus, our remarks will mainly concern the modern historical writings in the Indonesian language.

Modern historiography was practically unknown in Indonesian society before the nineteen-twenties. Its coming into existence was closely related to the rise of modern nationalist movement in Indonesia. Since

SOURCE. B. Oetomo, "Some Remarks on Modern Indonesian Historiography," from D. C. E. Hall (editor), *Historians of South East Asia*, London: Oxford University Press under the auspices of the School of Oriental and African Studies, 1961, pp. 73–84.

this movement can be considered partly a result of modern education for Indonesians, we shall begin with a very brief review of the development of its institutions during the colonial period. Thereafter follows an outline of the nationalistic notion of Indonesian history.

Although the Dutch primary schools in Java were open to Indonesians since about 1820, until the last ten years of the nineteenth century their numbers at these schools remained very small. In 1847 there were for instance only thirty-seven Indonesian pupils at all Dutch primary schools on the island.[1] It was actually only after 1914 that thousands of Indonesians received a primary education along western lines.[2]

The first nationalist leaders, the promoters in 1908 of the first national association of Indonesians, the *Budi Utomo*, were graduates of the "Java Medical School"[3] which was founded in 1851. Later on nationalist leaders were recruited from graduates of educational institutions on academic level such as the Bandung Higher Technical School (founded in 1920) and the Batavia Law School (founded in 1924). Between the years 1920 and 1940 about one hundred Indonesians went to Holland in order to get their degrees at the Dutch universities.

A remarkable fact in this development is that not one Indonesian completed courses in the science of history. We think this absolute lack of scientifically trained Indonesian historians has to a large extent determined the present condition of modern Indonesian historiography.

During the first years after its birth the nationalist movement formulated its aim as a "respectable existence of the people" and "a more harmonious development of country and peoples of the Netherlands Indies."[4] In order to achieve this aim the early Indonesian nationalists followed "quiet" methods such as founding national schools or stimulating native science, arts, and industry.

But when Sukarno's Partai Nasional Indonesia (PNI) came into existence in 1927 those quiet methods were abandoned. This party was based on the principle of self-determination and its leaders stated explicitly their determination to strive for a form of government responsible only to the Indonesian people itself. Thus they proclaimed a national struggle for independence to be achieved by their own powers and without the help from foreigners, against imperialism and capitalism, which were held responsible for the oppression of the Indonesian people. Moreover, it was believed by the PNI that such a struggle for freedom could only succeed by means of a nationalistic mass-action. Accordingly the quiet methods no longer sufficed and consequently mass-meetings were introduced in Indonesian life. The speeches and addresses at such meetings were calculated to stimulate national consciousness among the masses and to infuse them with enthusiasm for the fight for freedom.

It was in relation to this last point that the image of the past and ideas on Indonesian history took shape and played a role in the nationalist movement.

Ir. Sukarno, who incidentally graduated from the Bandung Higher Technical School, was one of the first modern Indonesians to formulate ideas on their people's history. He explained those ideas in his defence (2 December 1930) when he was tried for "subversive" action against the Dutch government.[5]

There are three ways to promote nationalism, Sukarno said, "first we point out to the people that they have a glorious past, secondly we intensify the notion among our people that the present time is dark, and the third way is to show them the promising, pure and luminous future and how to get there." Stated briefly his scheme consisted of a "glorious past," a "dark present," and a "promising future."[6]

The image of a glorious past is built up from stories about the "greatness" of the empires and kingdoms of Sriwijaya, Malayu, Kediri, Singosari, Mojopait, and Mataram, and from the notion that during those glorious days the Indonesian colours were seen in Madagascar, Persia, and China. While reading or learning the history of those times every Indonesian, Sukarno believed, would feel a new spirit and new forces arising within himself; in this way the knowledge of a glorious past might revive the hope and national feelings of the people who would consequently obtain a new spirit and new powers.

Sukarno's conception of the dark present refers to conditions during the colonial period, from the days of the Dutch East Indies Company (founded in 1602) till his own times. Indeed, those conditions were painted by the PNI leader in the blackest colours.

The stern ferocious and greedy Company has sacrificed thousands of Indonesian lives while destroying whole kingdoms. Its policy was based on the principle of "divide and rule," and even decent Dutch writers hold the opinion that the Company's ends and means were horrible. After the end of the Company's rule (1799) the "Culture System" (introduced in 1830) in its turn took over the exploitation of the Indonesian people. This system, kept up by whippings and beatings, caused poverty, pauperism and famine, and brought the Indonesian masses into slavery. Lastly, modern imperialism (from 1870 onwards) made of the Indonesians a nation of wage-earners and a wage-earner among the nations. Imperialism checked the progress of Indonesian society, disorganized social life and left the individuals without civil rights to defend themselves against its detrimental forces.[7]

Reading those words in 1956 one might easily be led to ask what need there was of such a representation of the colonial period. The leader himself has provided the answer: "The wretched lot of the people during the present colonial period will keep most strongly alive the nationalist sentiments amongst them."[8] And the history of Indonesian nationalism thus far has clearly demonstrated how successful Sukarno has been in inciting the imagination of the masses and thus infusing them with enthusiasm for the fight against colonialism.

No doubt this enthusiasm as a result of Sukarno's words has formed one of the most powerful forces which had brought Indonesian nationalism to its victory after a battle of relatively short duration. Future historians will certainly ascribe much credit to Sukarno for his great contribution to the achievement of Indonesian independence.

It is comprehensible that, against this background of the nationalist struggle, no other Indonesian has yet tried to criticize or to correct intentionally and explicitly these concepts of Indonesian history. Only in a book by Pringgodigdo entitled *Sedjarah Pergerakan Rakjat Indonesia* (*History of the Indonesian People's Movement*) (Djakarta, 1949), we find an opinion on the causes of nationalism which is different from that expressed by Sukarno in his above-mentioned defence. While the latter saw the Indonesian movement caused exclusively by the deplorable condition of the people,[9] Pringgodigdo mentioned—in addition to the "always present desire of the people for a better life"—other factors connected with its birth and growth. The author pointed to the Japanese victory over Russia in 1905, the Young-Turkish movement and the Chinese Revolution of 1911 as factors outside the country. The internal factors among others consist of the intellectual capacity of the Indonesians due to the growth of educational opportunities, the recognition by the Dutch government of the right of public meeting, the introduction of political institutions such as the Volksraad (People's Council) and the improved means of communication.[10]

But apart from Pringgodigdo the above-mentioned conception has exercised great influence upon every Indonesian historical writing even when it was written ten or more years after 1930, the year in which it was formulated for the first time.

For example, the glorious past was narrated by Muhammad Yamin in his book on Gadjah Mada (third printing, Djakarta, 1948), the prime minister of the kingdom of Mojopait between the years 1331 and 1364. It is a popular notion in Indonesia that Gadjah Mada was the first Indonesian politician who succeeded in unifying the archipelago. The importance of his position in present-day thinking is well illustrated by the fact that the University of Jogjakarta (founded in 1947) was named after him. When they speak of the "Golden Age" of their history the Indonesians are referring to the days of Gadjah Mada.

A few quotations from Yamin's book will show the kind of images the Indonesians have of those days.

Since the kingdom of Mojopait was a well-organized state, its social and political atmosphere provided a fruitful condition for the development of arts and literature. In general, cultural life was flourishing and the life of the people was profoundly affected by religion. Between the beginning of the fourteenth and the middle of the fifteenth century many books were composed, while the number of monuments in Eastern Java increased very much during the same period.

In Gadjah Mada's time many inscriptions on stone or copper were published in order to commemorate important events or to be used as pieces of evidence. All recent as well as obsolete documents were kept and great care was taken that they would not just disappear.

Justice was arranged in such a way that it satisfied the people's sense of justice. Sentences were passed in harmony of common and statute law. The Judges occupied a high position in society, they were inferior only to the king and his family.

To promote the welfare of the country several central services were called into existence, for instance for taking care of the taxes, duties and condition of the roads. There were also special services for health, irrigation, traffic, agriculture and public security. Much   attention was paid to the Departments of War and Commerce.[11]

Moreover Mr. Yamin imparted to his readers the existence of some kind of a representative government at that time. He wrote about a State's Council consisting of representatives from the islands outside Java and from other parts of the empire.[12]

Apart from that, in a textbook on Indonesian History by Sanusi Pané (*Sedjarah Indonesia,* fourth printing, Djakarta, 1950) which is being used in secondary schools, we find this evaluation of Mojopait:

Its Golden Age during the days of Rajasanegara (the king) and Gadjah Mada can be compared with the time during which Europe was beginning to free herself from feudalism. At that time cities were formed, while trade and handicraft grew in importance.[13]

Here, too, the nationalistic perspective on Indonesian history is evident.

Another salient feature of modern Indonesian historical writing is the emphasis on the struggle against the Dutch government. In fact, all recent publications contain stories about leaders or personalities who played an important part in the several revolts against Dutch colonial government or in the early days of the national movement. To mention a few examples:

Diponegoro by Muhammad Yamin (1945) is a book on the hero of the Java War (1825–30). *Tuanku Imam Bondjol* by Dawis Datuk Madjolelo and Ahmad Marzuki (1951) is a story about the leader during the Padri (west coast of Sumatra) War from 1821–32. *Teku Umar dan* and *Tjut Nja Din* (written by Hazil in 1952) were leading personalities in the Acheh War (1873–1904). *Kartini* (by Mrs. Hurustiati Subandrio) was a prominent young woman living from 1879 till 1904 who is considered in Indonesia as the forerunner of the women's movement. A biography of Dr. Sutomo (who died in 1936), one of the promoters of *Budi Utomo,* was produced by Imam Supardi. And a life-history of Tjipto Mangunkusumo (who died in 1943), another prominent personality in the early days of national movement, was published by M. Balfas.

In these books the heroes are represented as brave, noble, energetic, steadfast, loyal, well-read, sacrificing, patriotic, poetical, and so on. There is no doubt that the production of this kind of literature is still functionally related to the nationalistic idea, and that they are intended to rouse their readers to the fight for freedom. Obviously, their moral lesson amounts to this: we have a glorious past, the present time is dark, let us fight for a promising future just like the sample set by our heroes.

We would like to stress the importance and necessity of such efforts to increase the numbers of Indonesians supporting the nationalist idea. Because, only with the greatest possible numbers of Indonesians on the side of nationalism can its fight against colonialism and for a better future be quickly brought to a successful end.

Since the functional character of modern Indonesian historiography has now been shown, one may not expect from its authors that they are solely directed by the search for the truth. In fact, we can observe that the desire to produce nationalistic literature is almost always much stronger than the desire to conform to scientific standards. Consequently, the value of those writings for the scientific study of Indonesian history is not evident. And this constitutes the other side of the medal with a functional historiography.

Up to this day modern Indonesian historiography has not yet produced new contributions to the science of history. No Indonesian has yet reported discoveries of new facts or unknown documents. Findings by Indonesians of new inter-relationships between already known facts or events still fail to appear. All the knowledge of the above-mentioned authors is based on Dutch literature or traditional literature which has been made accessible by Dutch scholars. Nevertheless, with the exception of Sukarno, not one writer made notes referring to the sources used, although two of the writers published a list of consulted works on the last page of their books.

A few words about the way Sukarno made use of the Dutch works written by Snouck Hurgronje, Colenbrander, Veth, Kielstra, Stokvis, Gonggrijp, and van Gelderen. Sukarno quoted only those parts of these works which supported his point of view. No sincere effort was made by him to arrive at an understanding of what had really happened during the colonial period. His sole object was to present a picture of a deplorable time. Thus he did not critically evaluate the facts and information derived from the consulted literature, nor did he strive for a well-balanced judgement on the period.

And although with later Indonesian writers their intention to present a preconceived picture was perhaps less prominent than with Sukarno, no essential change for the better has taken place, because scientific training has still been lacking. It is self-evident that accordingly, historical works which have been the fruits of real scholarship or of careful, critical, accurate and painstaking studies are non-existent. There is as yet no sign of a renaissance in Indonesian historiography. Of course, in considering this fact it should be borne in mind that the Indonesians achieved their independence only a few years ago.

Although the relative absence of scientific historiography will certainly not cause disaster to Indonesian society, we believe that such a state of affairs is rather unfortunate. In order to clarify this point we shall briefly outline the most important changes which have been taking place in the Indonesian society during the last century, with special reference to Java.

Before the appearance of Europeans in the archipelago social and cultural life was largely centred around the sacred position of the king. In such a context, religion, literature, sculpture, and political organization were not only intertwined and interrelated to each other, but they often also had the magical function of enforcing or legitimating the sacred power of the king. Society was mainly agrarian in character and its members considered the king as the origin of fertility of the soil, thus as a source of prosperity of his subjects. Moreover, to these subjects the king was also the guardian of the security of the whole community.[14]

Though at the end of the sixteenth century a spirit for trade and commerce was certainly present, it was not as prominent as among Europeans of the same days. Economically Indonesian culture remained on a peasant-village basis.

During the Dutch control of power Indonesian society on Java experienced profound changes. It began when the Dutch East Indies Company controlled the Indonesian waters necessary for the establishment of her trade monopoly.[15] This put an end to all Javanese shipping and overseas trade, thus, the economic development in this respect was checked for a long time.[16]

Afterwards, with the political control of the island well in Dutch hands, the Indonesian king was made subordinate to the Dutch Governor General, thus putting an end to the king's central function in his society, because, directives for administrative and other measures no longer originated from the Indonesian king, but from the Company's offices or from The Hague and Amsterdam. And often the measures introduced were based on reasons unknown or foreign to the king and his subjects. Consequently, sacred kingship, which for ages has formed the central basis of traditional Indonesian society and culture, was seriously undermined, and gradually the social order connected with it broke down.

Of course we have much oversimplified the picture of processes covering such a long period of time. We are fully aware that historical reality was far more complicated than outlined above. For example, although they have ruled out the political and social influence of the Indonesian king the Dutch maintained his bupati's (the king's governors for important cities) who continued living as much as possible according to their traditional way of life till the outbreak of the Pacific War. Thus, although cut off from their original context, many parts or elements of the traditional order remained in existence as survivals long after the actual breakdown of that order.

Besides the tendency towards social disintegration during Dutch rule we can also observe signs, however weak, pointing towards a process of social integration.

One of the most salient facts during this period was that the Dutch succeeded in bringing the most important parts of the Indonesian islands into one political and administrative unity. This development imparted to the Indonesians—peoples with a great diversity of cultures—the notion that they belong together. On such a basis an awareness of a common lot could grow and accordingly the formulation of a common will was made possible.

Another very important and interesting side of the history of Dutch rule is the process by which the Indonesians got acquainted with ideas, techniques, modes of thinking and values originating from the western world, through the introduction of modern educational institutions. In fact, all social and political weapons or instruments used by the Indonesian nationalists in fighting the Dutch were learned from or made possible by the modern education created in Indonesia by the Dutch themselves.

At the same time we know very well that it was not the explicit intention of colonial government to emancipate the Indonesians in the shortest possible time. The dominant motivation for maintaining their rule over Indonesia was in fact the desire for material profit to the homecountry. Nevertheless, viewed historically, the existence of integrating factors in Dutch rule cannot be denied.

As demonstrated, Dutch measures caused a dissolution of the traditional order on one hand, and on the other they opened possibilities of modern development. However, the latter has been carried out unintentionally and unexplicitly, while many elements of the traditional order still received some support from the Dutch colonial government.

These circumstances conditioned a great deal the mental development of educated Indonesians. While today their behaviour is no longer motivated exclusively by traditional values, often statements such as "We have our own 'eastern' way of solving things" or "We should save our own traditional eastern culture by guarding ourselves against western influences" can still be heard amongst them.

It is evident that such a state of mind has something to do with their attitude towards modern culture. Since the Dutch only quite recently introduced higher learning in Indonesia, the process of its transference to Indonesians could not have yielded many results by the end of colonial rule. And in comparison with other Asian peoples such as the Indians and Filipinos, the minds of educated Indonesians have generally not yet been seized by modern science or scientific attitude. We cannot yet observe amongst them an eager acceptance of the intrinsic essence of modern culture.

Seemingly the Indonesians have not yet made up their minds as to which direction they will move in social and cultural respects. It is clear how transitional is the character of present-day society and culture in Indonesia.

After the recognition of independence gradually more Indonesians expressed the view that they should live according to conditions also found with modern nations. If we are to take such statements seriously, it means that the Indonesians should promote social development in the direction of a society and culture in which first, the recognition of the ultimate value of human personality, second, modern science and achievements based on it, and lastly, elements from the Indonesian heritage, will be integrated successfully. In fact, it is our personal opinion that such is the only one direction in which the Indonesians should go, if they want to maintain themselves as an independent nation in this modern world.

In other words we think that history has called upon the Indonesians to modernize their society to a condition in which the best sides and highest achievements of modern culture can flourish unobstructedly. However, the starting point for this desired development can only be constituted by the present social and historical reality. And here we have touched the point where the science of history—apart from being a source for intellectual delight—can perform an important role in Indonesian efforts at social reconstruction.

In the first place history is of importance for the knowledge of present-day social reality. Because the present situation can only be adequately understood and comprehended if we have sufficient knowledge of past events and processes leading to it. Secondly, European and American history can provide a wealth of information on modern societies. The Indonesian may learn from it which are the best sides and highest achievements of modern culture, and, which events, processes, values, attitudes, and techniques have led to those sides and achievements. In general, the history of modern and western peoples may also produce lessons from their mistakes, giving opportunities to learners to take precautions in order to avoid the same mistakes.

It is understandable, however, that at this moment there can be little or no interest among Indonesians in studies in history. The market for such books is negligible and no one can find time for performing historical research. Actually, every branch of intellectual life is suffering from this lack of time for activity in it. This may be caused by the country's general condition, which still necessitates the consumption of all psychic energies in the daily struggle for the strengthening of the recently established social and political order, and for earning a living. It is self-evident then that there can be little opportunity for the sublimation of energies not fully exhausted into more cultural and intellectual achievements.

But apart from this there are of course other factors determining the present lack of interest in scientific historiography. First of all there was no living tradition of historiography. In this respect, modern educated Indonesians are completely cut off from traditional culture.

Moreover, since the Indonesian notions about their past were conditioned by their education at Dutch schools, their school-knowledge of Indonesian history consists largely of the Dutch perspective on it. Under these circumstances the Indonesians have learned at school that the heroes of revolts against the Dutch were usually cruel and unreliable terrorists. And the Indonesian defeats were always evaluated according to the Dutch colonial point of view. Every Indonesian educated at a Dutch school can still recount unpleasant memories of history lessons during his primary and secondary school years. Thus the subject of history was not only made unattractive to Indonesians but it also became unpopular amongst them.

Furthermore, higher learning was—as already stated—only recently introduced in Indonesia. Besides, it did not teach history in any of its curricula and as a consequence it could not encourage historical research among Indonesians, nor could it correct their historical notions, which were much influenced in one or another way, in a negative or positive sense, by the Dutch colonial perspective. Consequently the Indonesian understanding of the nature of the present transitional phase of their development remained scanty, while there is on the other hand no great interest in reliable knowledge concerning the present time, knowledge which might be useful for further social development.

Another explanatory factor can be found in the image the Indonesians cherished concerning Europeans or western peoples in general. Seen through Indonesian eyes Westerners in pre-war colonial society seemed only concerned with materialistic life. And, since relations between white and colonized people based on social equality were almost unknown in colonial Indonesia,[17] no real personal contacts took place between Dutch and Indonesian intellectuals. As a result of this, cultural exchange between them was impossible and accordingly the more valuable sides of modern Western and European culture remained unnoticed by most educated Indonesians. Thus, in their minds, western peoples live mainly for materialism and colonialism, both of which are sharply contrasted with Indonesian ideals of the "spiritual East." Along these lines the notion of the "undesirable West" became prevalent among Indonesians, causing them to become uninterested in the backgrounds and history of western peoples.

For our last remark we shall turn again to the nationalists' scheme of history. According to this scheme Indonesian history should be divided into three stages, i.e., a glorious past, a colonial era full of troubles, difficulties and humiliations, and as a third stage a promising future. The implication of such a conception is clearly that all troubles, difficulties, and humiliations will be over as soon as the second stage passes into the third.

Now, in 1930 Sukarno's representation of the future was as follows:

No millions of guilders will flow any more to other countries. There will be a people's community with a social organization in harmony to its needs. The political structure will be as democratic as possible, arts and science flourishing, culture unobstructed. A Federated Republic of Indonesia will live in peace and friendship with other nations and the Indonesian colours will constitute an ornament at the firmament of the East. A powerful, outwardly and inwardly sound nation will be ours.[18]

We have already stated how powerfully and successfully this ideal functioned during the decades before the Indonesian Republic became reality. At the moment, however, the question arises whether such an expectation of the future formulated in 1930 can still serve as an inspiration for social action. Will it not be necessary to redirect or adjust the scheme to the present needs until it can again become an inspiration for social action as powerful as it was before the international recognition of the Indonesian government? And will such a new inspiration be able to rouse more citizens to do their utmost in order to secure the moral, social, and political integrity of their Nation?

Only the future can disclose the answer to those questions.

NOTES

1. I. J. Brugmans, *De geschiedenis van het Onderwijs in Nederlands Indië* (*The History of Education in the Netherlands Indies*). (Groningen, 1938), p. 139.

2. Cf. I. J. Brugmans, *De verbreiding van de Nederlandse taal in Indië* (*The Spread of the Dutch Language in the Indies*). (Koloniale Studieén, 1937), p. 58.

3. B. H. M. Vlekke, *Geschiedenis van de Indische Archipel* (*History of Indian Archipelago*). (Roermond, 1947), p. 412.

4. More information on Indonesian national movement can be found a.o. in: A. Vandenbosch, *The Dutch East Indies* (Berkeley, Los Angeles, 1944); G. M. Kahin, *Nationalism and Revolution in Indonesia* (New York, 1953); J. M. Pluvier, *Overzicht van de ontwikkeling der Nationale Beweging in Indonesië* (*Review of the Development of National Movement in Indonesia*). (The Hague, 1953).

5. Ir. Sukarno's defence was translated in Dutch and published under the title: *Indonesië klaagt aan* (*Indonesia Accuses*) (Amsterdam, 1931).

6. *Indonesië klaagt aan*, p. 64.

7. Chapter II of the same publication, pp. 18–36.

8. *Ibid.*, p. 65.

9. *Ibid.*, p. 41.

10. *Pringgodigdo*, pp. 7–9.

11. M. Yamin, *Gadjah Mada*, pp. 28–31.

12. *Ibid.*, p. 29.

13. S. Pané, Book I, p. 116.

14. Cf. W. F. Wertheim, *Nederlandse cultuurinvloeden in Indonesië* (*Dutch Cultural Influences in Indonesia*). (Amsterdam, 1948), pp. 3–4.

15. Cf. B. Schrieke, *Indonesian Sociological Studies,* pt. I (The Hague, 1955), pp. 72–73.

16. Or, in the words of Van Leur: "The conquest of the spice islands by the Dutch East India Company put a stop to a complete branch of traditional trade and thus disorganized the whole of it." *Indonesian Trade and Society* (The Hague, 1955, p. 122).

17. This was indicated in the "Verslag van de Commissie Visman" (Report of the Visman Commission), pt. II (New York, 1944), pp. 85 and 89.

18. *Indonesië klaagt aan*, p. 67.

F. J. West

THE STUDY
OF COLONIAL HISTORY (1961)

Charles Kingsley, a popular novelist,—he had written *Westward Ho*
among other books and was yet to write *The Water Babies,*—was appointed to the Regius Chair of Modern History in Cambridge in May
1860. His lectures, it was said, were those of "a poet and a moralist, a
politician and a theologian, and, above all, a friend and counsellor of
young men." They were, his critics agreed, certainly not those of an historian and a scholar. Such attacks upon him as an historical novelist rather
than an historian, combined with the strain of coming up to Cambridge
from his rectory twice a year to deliver his lectures, caused him to resign
his chair in 1869, to be succeeded by John Robert Seeley. Seeley was a
classicist, who had also published a religious work, *Ecce Homo,* the centre
of one of those ferocious Victorian doctrinal controversies. He had published nothing historical but historical speculation had always interested
him, and thus qualified, he became Regius Professor, holding the Chair
until 1895. After his Inaugural Lecture, W. H. Thompson, the witty and
acid Master of Trinity, observed, "Well, well. I did not think we should
so soon have occasion to regret poor Kingsley." Such were the beginnings
of the serious study of imperial and colonial History in English universities.

In 1883 Seeley published *The Expansion of England,* a book which
was composed of lectures which he had delivered in Cambridge. Seeley
had always, even in his Inaugural Lecture, insisted that history was political history, and primarily useful for the practice of politics. Indeed,
when the History Tripos was established in 1873, he had tried to insist
that it be the Political Tripos, and failing this, infused a strong political
element into the syllabus. In the preface to *The Expansion of England*

SOURCE. F. J. West, "The Study of Colonial History," reprinted from *Journal of
Southeast Asian History,* II, 3, 1961, pp. 70–82, by permission of the author.

he had asserted that "the ultimate object of all my teaching here is to establish this fundamental connexion, to show that politics and history are only different aspects of the same study"[1] and when he came to examine imperial history, he did so in terms of the relations between European powers, and for a strong practical purpose. As he says in his first lecture:[2]

Some countries, such as Holland and Sweden, might pardonably regard their history as in a manner wound up. They were once great, but the conditions of this greatness have passed away, and they now hold a secondary place. Their interest in their own past is therefore either sentimental or purely scientific; the only practical lesson of their history is a lesson of resignation. But England has grown steadily greater and greater, absolutely at least if not always relatively. It is far greater now than it was in the 18th century; it was far greater in the 18th century than in the 17th, far greater in the 17th than in the 16th. The prodigious greatness to which it has attained makes the question of its future infinitely important, and at the same time most anxious, because it is evident that the great colonial extension of our state exposes it to new dangers, from which in its ancient, insular insignificance it was free.

The consequences of this view are worked out in the rest of the book. The first half is concerned with the history of the First British Empire: the expansion of England up to the loss of the American colonies. What Seeley concerned himself with were the wars and rivalries of the European powers which possessed colonies: Spain, Holland, France, England. He traced the events by which England subdued her rivals and established her greatness. The second half is concerned with India, "the brightest jewel of the Crown." Once again, his analysis was wholly political: how we conquered India, how we govern India.

No doubt this political interest in the Empire was a natural attitude to Seeley and his contemporaries (Macaulay was, after all, a practising politician), and it is an attitude which has coloured a great deal of subsequent historical writing. Applied to imperial history, it has meant the study of the areas coloured red on the map. Forty years or more after Seeley had lectured in Cambridge, the echoes of his theme still lingered in the preface to the first volume of the *Cambridge History of the British Empire* published in 1929. The editors stated in their preface that,[3]

Out of the ambitions of that adventurous age (i.e. the Tudor) when men dreamed great dreams for England and set out to realise them, grew the maritime state which, shaped amid the successive conflicts of modern history, has developed in the twentieth century into the British Commonwealth of Nations. A long study of colonisation and imperial policy, of the rise and growth of new nations and the assumption of vast responsibilities, a story varied in its scene but finding its unity in the activities of a maritime and commercial people, runs through the intervening centuries. The time has not yet come when that story can fully be written. The British Empire is still in the long period of its growth.

There was, of course, in the monumental volumes that followed, an advance on Seeley. Historians began to look at imperial history not merely from the centre of Empire, but from the outskirts too. Thus the general plan of the work was a number of volumes dealing with the Empire seen from England, and others which dealt with individual dominions and colonies, India being treated separately although two of the Indian books fitted into the scheme of the history of the Empire. Nevertheless, both the general history and the Indian volumes were built on a political framework. They equated Empire with political sovereignty, and within each dominion or colony, they dealt primarily with political history. In the Indian volumes, the writers were concerned with war and rivalries, European competition and struggles, the organisation of the East India Company, and the legal, administrative, and financial, institutions required to run the Indian Empire.

The tradition of Seeley in which these volumes stand was modified when the second of them was published, very much out of its chronological order, in 1940, because some of the contributors had begun to discard the old pre-occupation with political empire and to treat the expansion of England as something more than the extension of political sovereignty. C. R. Fay coined the phrase "informal empire," [4] and began to look at regions not under political control but which saw the economic activity of Englishmen. The investment of British capital in the dominions had, of course, attracted some notice earlier, but its significance could only begin to be explained when it was compared with British investment in South America or China which were outside the political bonds of empire. By discarding the political connexion as the chief *criterion* for the study of imperial history, it was possible to treat the expansion of England much more adequately.

In 1953 John Gallagher and Ronald Robinson carried Fay's approach a stage further, and denied that the traditional political interpretation which had distinguished between an "imperialist" phase and an "anti-imperialist" one, and connected both with the rise or decline of the doctrines of "Free trade" (by taking the statements of political economists at their face value), could be maintained at all.[5] They quoted a diverse collection of economists and political philosophers; Lenin, for example, who said that

When free competition was at its height, i.e. between 1840 and 1860 the leading British bourgeois politicians were . . . of the opinion that the liberation of colonies and their complete separation from Great Britain was inevitable and desirable;

Professor Langer who wrote that in the last quarter of the 19th century

There was an obvious danger that the British [export] market would be steadily restricted. Hence the emergence and sudden flowering of the movement for expansion. . . . Manchester doctrine had been belied by the facts. It was an outworn theory to be thrown into the discard.[6]

In fact, of course, even in terms of the orthodox political view of empire, this anti and pro imperialist distinction was dubious, but in the regions of "informal empire" the distinction was absolute nonsense. Gallagher and Robinson maintain that a steady policy of imperial interest was consistently maintained; even when it was accompanied, as it was in the case of the Transvaal, by political withdrawal. British paramountcy, they say, was steadily upheld. As Lord Aberdeen said in 1845,

it is unnecessary to add that Her Majesty's government will not view with indifference the assumption by another power of a Protectorate which they, with due regard for the true interests of those [Pacific] islands, have refused.[7]

The inadequacies of "political empire" as an approach to the study of colonial history have become obvious although this does not prevent historians writing books which still rest on what the Governor said to the Colonial Office and *vice versa*. The view has steadily gained ground that the history of the expansion of England must be seen as part of the general expansion of Europe, and as the activity of some Englishmen or some Frenchmen rather than *the* English or *the* French.[8] With sad lapses, the idea of "informal empire" as a vital part of the process of expansion has come to be fairly generally accepted. What is not yet generally acknowledged is that even this change of attitude, which is primarily that of the economic historian, does not go far enough. The emphasis is still on European activity, and although this is more adequately studied than ever before, a large sector of imperial or colonial history is still ignored in the majority of writings on colonial policy and practice by failure to give due importance to non-European activity. There are, of course, exceptions, notably among those historians who have had to face the task of writing African or Asian history, but it is still possible for a scholar to write, for example, about the policy of Sir Stamford Raffles in Java without discussing, almost without mentioning, the Javanese.[9] It may seem a commonplace that in many colonial areas European activity is only one part of a situation which includes the activity of the indigenous people and perhaps other races, and that any account which leaves out their existence and their inter-actions with Europeans is defective,[10] but such an obvious truth, if it is acknowledged at all, is often given a propitiatory nod before the writer settles down to the dynamic factor of the European presence.

An explanation of this ignorance or half hearted recognition is not difficult. Preoccupation with the "white" dominions of settlement, concentration on the study of policy rather than practice, both play their part in diverting attention from the existence and the importance of indigenous people. But the major difficulties have probably been technical.

Many of the indigenous societies with which Europeans have come into contact in their colonies have been pre-literate; they have had none of the documents with which an historian normally works. Some recognition of the difficulty is revealed in the attempt which scholars have made to commit to paper tribal traditions or genealogies, but this is only to deal with one aspect of the problem. The real need is to know the social structure of indigenous peoples, the ways in which it changes in contact with Europeans, and the ways in which European activity is affected by indigenous culture and the changes which occur within it. Such knowledge is the field of social anthropology into which historians have seldom had the courage to trespass. Even if they had, the further difficulty arises that social anthropology generally deals with the contemporary situation not with past ones, and such information as it can provide may not be directly relevant to the study of the past. Faced with a pre-literate society in the colonial situation, it is all too easy to conclude that it is outside the scope of historical knowledge, to concentrate on what can be adequately known from the records of European activity, and to rest content with only a partial description of the reality of much imperial or colonial history.

II

Any one of the small number of recent books in the Pacific could be used to illustrate both the difficulties and the dangers of trying to write colonial history of the kind which will adequately describe the realities of the colonial situation,[11] but it seems more profitable, certainly less invidious, to take an example from a recent piece of research of my own on comparative colonial administration in the South Pacific.[12]

One of the colonies used in the comparison was Tahiti or, more formally, French Polynesia. There is an enormous literature about Tahiti, but very little of it is historiography.[13] The legendary affection of Tahitian women, the romance of the South Seas, the lives of Gaugin and Loti, the missionaries, travellers, traders, and beach combers, all have contributed to it, but the history of Tahiti has yet to be well written. French scholars have generally ignored the Pacific colonies, and British ones have contented themselves with incidental references or summary dismissal. S. H. Roberts, for example, who wrote the standard English book on French colonial policy, devoted five pages to Tahiti, regarded the French annexation as the destruction of a well organised native kingdom which was abandoned by Britain in its hour of need.[14] Of the French administration he observes that

it kept the group stagnant, destroyed native life almost entirely. The lantana spreads, the hibiscus grows: the natives decline, but those who remain are luscious tawny morsels for the French. . . . Tahiti represents the spirit of

colonisation drugged and confused by the gentle and ever so desirable lasciv-
iousness of those tropical lands where existence is easy and the natives com-
plaisant. "Ari'ana there is tomorrow": but so far, not for Tahiti.

To other scholars, like J. M. Ward, Tahiti is merely a place which
was the scene of law and disorder in the early 19th century and which
was the occasion of Anglo-French imperial rivalry.[15] Both accounts do
Tahiti less than justice, because it has an interest in its own right as the
first missionary kingdom in the Pacific,[16] because what happened on a
small scale in Tahiti under missionary influence and French colonial practice, illustrates some of the processes involved in colonial rule in other
larger and less easily studied areas, because Tahiti offers an opportunity
of writing much more than conventional colonial history.

The starting point for a history of colonial rule in Tahiti is the nature
of Tahitian society before the Europeans came, for the customs and social
organisation of the Society Islanders are factors of major importance
in the course of events, and they vitally affected the way in which the
institutions of colonial rule operated. A number of European accounts
survive from the days of first contact between white men and the Polyne-
sians, of which the outstanding one is that of Captain Cook, a careful and
exact observer.[17] Writing in his journal on 21 June 1769, Cook described
an incident which will serve to illustrate both the value and the limitations of his account.[18]

> This morning a Chief whose name is Oamo, and one we had not seen
> before, came to the Fort, there came with him a Boy about 7 years of Age
> and a young Woman of about 18 or 20; at the time of their Coming Obarea
> and several others were in the Fort, they went out to meet them, having first
> uncover'd their heads and bodies as low as their waists and the same thing
> was done by all those that were on the outside of the Fort; as we looked upon
> this as a ceremonial Respect and had not seen it paid to anyone before we
> thought that this Oamo must be some extraordinary person, and wonder'd to
> see so little notice taken of him after the ceremony was over. The young
> Woman that came along with him Could not be prevail'd upon to come into
> the Fort and the Boy was carried upon a Mans Back, altho' he was as able to
> walk as the Man who carried him. This lead us to inquire who they were and
> we was inform'd that the Boy was Heir apparent to the Sovereignty of the
> Island and the young woman was his sister and as such the respect was paid
> them, which was due to no one else except the *Areedehi* which was not Tootaha
> from what we could learn, but some other person we had not seen, or like
> to do, for they say he is no friend of ours and therefore will not come near us.
> The young Boy above-mention'd is Son to Oamo by Obarea, but Oamo and
> Obarea did not at this time live together as man and wife he not being able to
> endure with her troublesome disposission. I mention this because it shews that
> separation in the Marrige state is not unknown to this people.

Cook carefully noted details which other European visitors did not, and
this entry is an invaluable account of certain characteristics of the Tahitians, but the significance of what he saw could not be known to Cook,

partly because he knew nothing of Tahitian society other than his own observation, partly because his attitude was that of a European explaining what he saw in terms of concepts taken, naturally enough, from his own society. Thus he mentions the idea of Sovereignty and the idea of Divorce, and he interprets what he saw in terms of them. This is a general characteristic of most European records of contact with the Tahitians, and even missionaries who, a little later, lived and worked among the people, could not escape this natural tendency to explain what they saw in terms of attitude and values of their own European society.[19] Orsmond, a missionary who was described by his contemporary Moerenhout as being "the European most deeply versed in Polynesian tradition" (he spoke Tahitian fluently and knew many old chiefs and priests whose words he recorded), still used concepts like "royalty" and "kingship" to describe Tahitian society, words like "idleness" to describe Tahitian personal qualities, and, being a missionary, refused to use any words at all to describe certain features of society over which, he said, "a curtain must forever be dropped." [20] We must be grateful for the facts which such Europeans collected, but look elsewhere for their significance before they can be used to help the writing of colonial history; look, in fact, to the social anthropologist who, using these records and studying the social structure of Tahiti and other Polynesian islands, can provide what he would call a "conceptual framework" by which the historian may begin to interpret the significance of what observers like Cook saw.[21]

The incident which he described in June 1769 becomes significant only when Tahitian witness is heard. Cook became aware of a change in the power of his friends Oamo, Obarea, and their son, and he and Bligh of the *Bounty* who visited Tahiti in 1788, discovered that the powerful chief of the Matavai Bay region was the man whom Cook described in the entry quoted as someone he had not seen, the man whom he called the *Areedehi,* and whom he discovered in his next voyage to be called Otoo. Both he and later European visitors, having decided that Obarea, whom they treated as "queen" of Tahiti, had lost her power, transferred the sovereignty to Otoo whom they treated as "king." By the time the missionaries had realised the error of this belief, it was too late; having been treated as "king" Otoo had behaved like one and European fortunes in Tahiti were bound up with his. The reality behind these appearances (or disappearances) of powerful chiefs was much more complicated than Europeans realised, and it could certainly not be adequately described in terms of "sovereignty" and "kingship." The complications were difficult enough even for the Tahitian born within the chiefly class.

When Henry Adams, seeking relief from personal sorrows and relaxation after his professional exhaustion with the *History of the United States,* landed in Tahiti in 1891, he made friends with an old lady who had been born in 1824 or thereabouts, and who united in her person two of the lines of descent of famous Tahitian chiefly families. Lying on her mat, she related to Adams her genealogy, the traditions she had heard in her youth, and the Tahitian politics which lay behind the appearances presented to Europeans.[22] The people whom Cook met in June 1769, whose Tahitian names were Amo, Purea, and Tuteha, had recently figured in a change in the balance of power inside Tahitian society. Amo and Purea belonged to the ruling family in one of the three districts which were traditionally pre-eminent, although they had family connections which gave them status in the Matavai Bay district. A little while before Cook's arrival but after Captain Wallis' discovery of Tahiti in 1767, this family had been over-thrown by an attack led by Tuteha (whose social status was not so high as theirs) and Vehiatua (head of a famous but less distinguished family), because of the ambitions of Purea for her son, the boy Cook had seen.[23] The reverence with which Amo was greeted at the Fort was intended in fact for this boy who, in Tahitian custom, assumed his father's rank and authority at birth, the latter becoming guardian. Purea's ambitions were resented and finally forcibly resisted because they represented breaches of Tahitian custom, and when Cook met the family they were refugees; indeed when Cook and Banks visited the family district the bones of their supporters were still scattered along the beach.[24] Because of their traditional rank and family connections Amo, Purea, and the boy especially, were received with marks of respect at Matavai Bay, but politically their power was weak. Tuteha was more politically important and Otoo, whose Tahitian name was Tu or later Pomare, although of higher traditional rank than Tuteha, was also politically overshadowed by him. Purea's son never recovered political eminence, and when Tuteha was killed in the defeat of his attack on the ally who had helped him achieve his victory, Tu or Pomare emerged into prominence. On Cook's later visits and during Bligh's period of five months on the island, Pomare ventured to come to Matavai Bay to meet them, which he had not dared to do earlier, and with the support of European muskets began to lay the foundations of his power which eventually led to a Tahitian kingdom de facto under his control as well as, in European beliefs, de jure.

The Tahitian side of the story begins to lend some depth to an account of what their society was like when the Europeans came, and what was happening from their point of view, but, valuable as it is, it is still preserved by Europeans whose perception was controlled by their own assumptions, and it is a story told by Tahitians of chiefly rank. Henry Adams' "chiefess," or Orsmond's informants, introduced some of the complexities which are missing from purely European records, but they too fail to exhaust the realities of the situation. A good deal of Adams' Tahiti is expressed in European concepts which his informant could scarcely have held; he had in part interpreted his story in terms intelligible and familiar to his European readers.[25] And no doubt the replies Orsmond received to his enquiries were coloured by the concepts in terms of which he framed his questions. An illustration of this is Adams' statement, which may very well have been the chiefess' belief in 1891, that Tahitian society was an aristocratic society,[26] and his story of the downfall of Purea and the rise of Pomare is a story of quarrelling chiefs in which other people move dimly and insignificantly in the background. Orsmond's account, too, is dominated by the principle of aristocracy. Both records are aware that "kingship" is not really a concept which was known in Tahitian society, but they have replaced it with a class structure which is essentially European. Tahitian society was something more than this again.

How much more is revealed, not by written records, whether of European or Tahitian bias, but by knowledge of how Tahitian society worked derived from a social anthropologist's general belief about the working of society of the Polynesian type, of which there are surviving, functioning, examples. Now it is undoubtedly true that there was an organised and graded system of rank in Tahiti.[27] There was a broad division between titled people, the *arii*, and untitled ones, and there were further distinctions of status within each of these two groups. Thus an *arii* might be a small local chief, of which there were many, or one to whom Cook's description *areedehi*, correctly *arii rahi* or *arii nui*, might be applied: a great chief of whom there were relatively few (perhaps only five) of whom three had specially high social status. Many early European visitors stressed the arbitrary power of these high chiefs, symbolised by the respect paid to Amo and Purea's son, the fact that he was carried to avoid the ground becoming charged with his *mana* which would prevent its use by lesser people, the power to lay a ban on certain economic consumption, the right to order human sacrifices, the death which overtook those who walked behind him or stood higher than he did. In fact, this chiefly power was neither so absolute nor so arbitrary as it appeared; it had very definite limits. These were in part geographical. An *arii nui's* authority did not extend generally over Tahiti, and Amo's presence at Matavai Bay and the respect the son received were due to a family connection with the district; they would probably not have ventured into the district beyond, nor received their ceremonial respect if they did.[28] Stricter limitations still were imposed by the nature of Tahitian society. The lesser chiefs who were heads of extended families or the landed gentry who thought not of the *arii* class controlled their own family lands, were to a large extent autonomous, paid their reverence to the great chief but by their direct control over their people could grant or withhold the co-operation upon which his actual power depended.[29] At this lesser chiefly level, the relationship between a chief, a landed gentleman, and his people, was much more patriarchal than aristocratic; it was a reciprocal relationship, as indeed, although overlaid by *tabu,* was that with the high chiefs. The reciprocity was expressed in the open councils which advised the high chief, in the economic services which were rendered to him and which he returned in the form of feasts or by organising ceremonial activity, and in the religious services he rendered: by focussing in his person the *mana* or mystical power of Polynesian cosmology, representing the first line of descent from an ancestor or a god, he adjusted the relations between gods and men, sometimes himself, sometimes through a class of priests who upheld his authority. And a chief's authority rested ultimately on his religious function, on supernatural sanctions, for his physical power had no necessary relationship to his social or religious pre-eminence; [30] and in political and economic activity, in the last resort he responded to the needs of his people or he perished. He was bound in a web of custom which regulated his behaviour and that of his people, custom which operated to define and control relationships all the way down the social scale; and which, when broken, brought about physical and supernatural penalties. Thus, for example, Purea was overthrown when she flouted Tahitian custom,[31] and thus was her son's high chiefly rank recognised even when his physical power was broken: to his people he was still a necessary part of their life. If he, and not Purea, had violated custom he might have been overthrown or deprived of his title, but his place as a focus of *mana,* as a symbol of the unity of his people, would have been filled by another in the same, or as close a line of descent as possible. Such a "functional" hypothesis is essential to an historian's understanding of what really happened in Tahitian society, and to any explanation of the effects of European contact; especially is it necessary to explain the history and the operation of European institutions in such a Polynesian setting.

The "kingship" is an example. From the European point of view, deriving from a monarchical society, a king was a natural thing to find, and a convenient one: for the purposes of European commerce and mission activity, it was useful to have one ruler who could be deemed to be sovereign, who could be held responsible for his people's acts, who could order or influence them in suitable directions. It was a short step from this belief to actually helping him to establish and maintain his "kingship." The "monarchy" was an alien concept which depended, on the surface, upon European sanctions, but had this been the whole story, it would have collapsed much sooner than it did. For some of the roots of "King" Pomare's strength tapped the deeper levels of Tahitian custom. His family may traditionally have been insignificant, but it was rising in prestige before the Europeans came. By marriage and descent, by the sacred stone from the ancient and fabulous home of chiefs in the island of Raiatea, by the right to wear the sacred red-feather girdle, Pomare had become a high chief, and when he began his conquest of his "kingdom," it was a victory consolidated by Polynesian custom.[32] Thus through an ancestor he claimed and took for his son the title Vehiatua, he arranged that the first children of the famous Papara family of Amo and Purea should be married to his own children, and he established his own rights in defeated districts by assuming their titles of rank and a seat in their marae.[33]

Pomare was concerned to acquire the traditional qualifications and symbols of rank throughout the island, and whether or not his "monarchy" was supported or resisted depended quite as much upon his satisfying these Tahitian *criteria* as upon his European support. In default of other claimants, Pomare satisfied the need for a high chief in those districts in which he assumed the titles of rank, until other changes within Tahiti caused the needs themselves to disappear; changes such as the conversion to Christianity wrought in destroying the concept of *mana*, or the French attempt to create an individual system of land tenure, or the creation of courts of justice to supplement and eventually to replace Tahitian custom. As these changes worked themselves out, the Polynesian bases of the kingship vanished, as did the challenge to them from the districts, like Papara, in which they had never been firmly established. When the "kingship" was finally dispensed with by the French government in 1880, its Polynesian functions had largely vanished, but in the first third of the 19th century any historical account which leaves out its traditional aspects to concentrate upon its European relationships is ignoring the realities of this colonial situation.

III

There is no difference in principle between this analysis of a small section of Tahitian history and the analysis which might be offered to explain most African and Asian situations; indeed Tahiti is in some respects more difficult because the old society has largely vanished and the possibility of examining, as a guide to an historical account, a current situation in which the old idea of rank and authority still operate, has gone.[34] Hence the social anthropologist, as well as the historian, must rely rather more on informed guesswork than would normally be the case, but guesswork guided, not merely by the recorded historical facts but by a considerable body of knowledge about the workings of Polynesian society in Samoa, Tonga, New Zealand, and other Pacific areas. In much of Africa, and Asia, this element of informed guesswork could be very much reduced because in many of the areas of European activity, the social structure of the indigenous people exposed to it still functions, albeit in modified ways, incorporating the old order or having a living tradition of it.

An objection may well be made that guesswork, however well-informed, has no place in historical scholarship; to which answer may be made on two grounds. The first is that even the most orthodox historians use it. Sentences which include the words "it must have . . . ," or "it is very likely that . . ." are example of nothing else, and as such they are received with the respect due to an opinion of a scholar well versed in his period. He (or she) is using a general theory or set of assumptions about how men and women in institutions behave in their own society. The second is that "informed guesswork" or "well based assumptions" in this context can be stated as hypotheses which are part of the logical structure of any historical explanation, as Carl Hempel has shown: [35] to explain a particular situation it is always necessary to assume certain general laws or hypotheses. Very often, when these are made explicit, they turn out to be almost common place beliefs about human nature or the nature of society, beliefs which the theoretical framework of social anthropology can only help to refine and make more precise. And when the historian is dealing with societies different from his own tradition, he *must* use the findings of social anthropology to provide those assumptions about human behaviour which in his own he assumes (sometimes erroneously) that he knows by reason of his upbringing or instinctively.

Every major advance in English historical writing has been due to the recognition that the assumptions on which the men of a different time acted are different from our own. Thus Spelman and Dugdale reacted against the 17th century common law lawyers' view that the feudal age could be interpreted in terms of the contemporary conflict between Crown and Parliament, thus Sir Lewis Namier exposed the real character of 18th century politics against the Whig view of history that the 18th century could be interpreted in terms of Mr. Gladstone. It would now be generally accepted that the first step in historical understanding of a particular period is to look at the world as the men of the time saw it, not as it seems to us.[36] Whatever else one may do afterwards—build patterns after the manner of Toynbee or write historical novels—, an age must be understood in its own terms first of all before it can be used to illustrate the present or predict the future. The recognition of this truth is in one sense easier, and in another harder, for the colonial historian. Obviously he cannot easily assume that he knows how a primitive people will behave, how their institutions work, what their values are from his own experience or from interpreting their documents because they have none in any usual historical sense. Nor is it too difficult to recognise that the European records which survive are written in terms of European concepts: sovereignty, for example, in Tahiti; and therefore are of limited value as a straightforward record of what the indigenous people were really like. But the conclusion that colonial history written from these records is only half the story is much more difficult to recognise, and it is avoided by asserting that, after all, the colonial power was the dynamic factor, European activity what really mattered. Recognition is harder primarily because it involves embracing another discipline, entering into a world of often repellent jargon and unfamiliar conceptual frameworks. Still, it is all that can be done. If the historian wishes to write, for example, the history of the sandal-wood trade in Fiji or European settlement in Kenya, he must know what Fijian society and Kikuyu society were and how they reacted before he can begin to approach the truth of a complicated colonial situation. He may console himself with the thought that this necessity is only a variant of the advice once offered by Professor Tawney: that what the historian needs is not more documents but stronger boots.

NOTES

1. J. R. Seeley, *The Expansion of England* (London 1883).
2. J. R. Seeley, pp. 1–2.
3. *Cambridge History of the British Empire* (Cambridge, 1929), i, v.
4. *C.H.B.E.,* ii (Cambridge, 1940), 399.
5. John Gallagher and Ronald Robinson, "The Imperialism of Free Trade," *Economic History Review,* vol. vi, no. i, pp. 1–15.
6. Gallagher and Robinson, p. 2.
7. Gallagher and Robinson, pp. 3–4.
8. J. W. Davidson, *The Study of Pacific History* (Australian National University, Canberra, 1955), pp. 8–9 is one of the most recent statements of the view.
9. For example, M. Perham, *Native Administration in Nigeria* (Oxford 1937); J. S. Furnivall, *Colonial Policy and Practice* (Cambridge, 1949); L. H. Gann, *The Birth of a Plural Society* (Manchester 1958), have all begun to come to grips with the existence and the importance of indigenous peoples but, unfortunately, J. S. Bastin, *The Native Policies of Sir Stamford Raffles in Java and Sumatra* (Oxford 1957), has not.
10. *C.H.B.E.* III. (1959) in its references to Africa or Malaya hardly touches upon the indigenous peoples.
11. For example J. D. Legge, *Britain in Fiji 1858–1880* (London 1958), who makes an attempt to explain Fijian society; W. P. Morrell, *Britain in the Pacific Islands* (Oxford 1960), who is aware of the problem but principally concerned with Europeans; C. D. Rowley, *The Australians in German New Guinea* (Melbourne 1959) who fails to grapple with it; J. C. Beaglehole, *The Journals of Captain James Cook* (Cambridge for the Hakluyt Society 1955) vol. i. clxxii, whose discussion is admirable but doubted by some anthropologists.
12. Part of a comparative study of native administration in Fiji, American Samoa, and French Polynesia, published under the title *Political Advancement in the South Pacific,* Oxford University Press, 1961.
13. See C. R. H. Taylor, *A Pacific Bibliography* (Wellington 1951).
14. S. H. Roberts, *History of French Colonial Policy* (London 1929) vol. ii, pp. 1786–1893.

15. J. M. Ward, *British Policy in the South Pacific* (Sydney 1948); or J. T. Brookes, *International Rivalry in the Pacific Islands 1800–1875* (California 1941).

16. A fact adequately recognized by mission histories and, in a more scholarly way by A. A. Koskinen, *Missionary Influence as a Political Factor in the Pacific Islands* (Helsinki 1953).

17. Others were Sir Joseph Banks, Bougainville, George Foster, J. R. Foster, J. A. Moerenhout, George Vancouver, S. Wallis, W. Bligh, and J. Wilson, all of whose journals or records are in print; see Taylor, *op. cit.*

18. Beaglehole, pp. 103–4.

19. W. Ellis, *Polynesian Researches* (London 1831); Teuira Henry, *Ancient Tahiti* (Honolulu 1928).

20. Orsmond's papers are incorporated into Teuira Henry's book, the original manuscript having disappeared. Teuira was his grand-daughter who taught in Tahiti: Ellis, p. 240.

21. The principal anthropological works are R. W. Williamson, *The Social and Political Systems of Central Polynesia* (Cambridge 1924), 3 vols.; E. S. C. Handy, *History and Culture in the Society Islands* (Honolulu 1930); and a more modern interpretation, M. D. Sahlins, *Social Stratification in Polynesia* (Seattle 1958). I am also indebted to Professor Douglas Oliver of Harvard University who is presently engaged in anthropological research in the Society Islands.

22. H. Adams, *Tahiti: Memoirs of Arii Taimai* (New York 1947).

23. By name Teriirere i Tooarai, *arii nui* of Papara.

24. *Journal of Sir Joseph Banks* (London 1896), p. 104.

25. One statement will suffice. "In the absence of sons, daughters inherited chieferies and property in the lands that went with the chief's names or titles, and these chiefesses in their own right were much the same sort of personages as female sovereigns in European history; they figured as prominently in island politics as Catherine of Russia, or Maria Theresa of Austria, or Marie Antoinette of France, or Marie Louise of Parma, in the politics of Europe." Adams, p. 10.

26. Adams, p. 15.

27. Sahlins, pp. 38–41; Handy, p. 42 ff.

28. Adams, p. 7, quoting Arii Taimai in the first person.

29. Handy, pp. 48, 75–76.

30. Adams, p. 8.

31. Adams, pp. 42–6. Purea, having imposed a *rahui* (ban on certain economic consumption) to prepare a feast for Teriirere at which he would wear the sacred feather girdle for the first time, refused to entertain her female relatives, as by custom she should, when they visited her for the express purpose of breaking the *rahui* in this way. The war against Papara avenged the insult.

32. Such victories had been known in pre-European Tahiti. The Papara chiefs had themselves overthrown the power of the more ancient family of Vaiari. What distinguished Pomare's victory was not really his new weapons, but the fact that European support made it permanent.

33. The *marae* of which there were a great many to be seen in Tahiti by the early visitors, was a stone meeting place in which each member of the

family had a seat or leaning stone. It was a social, ceremonial, and religious meeting place, with which went the family title and lands. A seat in the *marae* established rights in both of these. The *marae* also helped to preserve the family genealogy, and the socially superior families had ancient and famous *marae*. Thus Vaiari, the most distinguished, had two, the *marae* Farepua and the *marae* Tahiti from which the head of the family took his titles, Maheanu of Farepua, Teriinui of Tahiti, the last of which was borne by Adams' friend Arii Taimai. Without a seat in the *marae* of district or family a man or woman had no standing.

34. Unlike Samoa, where the *matai* system of rank and titles still functions and is an essential part of the machinery of modern government, see F. M. Keesing, *Modern Samoa* (London 1934).

35. C. G. Hempel, "The Function of General Laws in History," *Journal of Philosophy*, Vol. 39.

36. V. H. Galbraith, *Studies in the Public Records* (London 1948), p. 6 ff.

G. E. von Grunebaum

PROBLEMS

OF MUSLIM NATIONALISM (1954)

I

"A nationality," in the words of Louis Wirth, "may be conceived of as a people who, because of the belief in their common descent and their mission in the world, by virtue of their common cultural heritage and historical career aspire to sovereignty over a territory or seek to maintain or enlarge their political or cultural influence in the face of opposition. Nationalism refers to the social movements, attitudes and ideologies which characterise the behavior of nationalities engaged in the struggle to achieve, maintain, or enhance their position in the world." [1]

To assess potentialities and function of nationalism in the contemporary Muslim world these fundamental facts must be taken into consideration:

(1) The unity of the Muslim world such as it is has long ceased to be political; it is based on the reality of a religious, and the conviction of a cultural tie among the "believing" nations or groups.

(2) In essence, this unity has always consisted in the successful superimposition by aristocracies of fighters and scholars (often at loggerheads) of certain standards of belief and (especially) conduct over a considerable number of highly divers local traditions.

(3) By modifying or broadening Wirth's definition of a nationality to include "a community who because of the belief in their common descent or their common faith . . ." the community of Islam, the *umma Muhammadiyya*, could be subsumed under it—in counterdistinction to Christianity but in analogy to Judaism.

(4) Nationalistic movements have, in the past, at various times

SOURCE. G. E. von Grunebaum, "Problems of Muslim Nationalism," from R. N. Frye (editor), *Islam and the West*, The Hague: Mouton & Company, 1959, pp. 7–29.

threatened or disrupted the political unity of Islam while leaving intact, in the minds of the Muslims, its religious and cultural oneness.

(5) At other times, movements of a typically cultural nationalism have tried to pry loose large areas of the *dār al-Islām* from the supremacy of Arab culture that acted, as it were, as the representative of the Prophetic tradition, or else to insert their ideas and their spokesmen into the framework of this culture and its bearers while leaving intact both its continuity and its sense of identity. In many instances the compromise of the local "nationalistic" with the universal "Islamic" tradition or movement was attained through the rebels seeking leadership in a multinational state or a culturally pluralistic *umma* rather than political independence or cultural *apartheid*.

(6) Finally, it needs to be remembered that the consensus of the pious of the last three or four generations seems agreed to consider nationalism within Islam a scourge not known prior to Western expansion into and interference with the *dār al-Islām*—an idea which while in conflict with historical fact is significant as a self-view which involves a program.

National states have been in existence within the domain of Islam for many a century; yet the Canon Law recognises only the one and indivisible *umma Muḥammadiyya*. Intent upon maintaining the unity of the faith which was seen to be contingent on the oneness of the religious community and made visible in the oneness of the Law the spiritual leadership of the believers have always been passionately interested in the integrity (and expansion) of the Muslim territory as a whole while exhibiting scant concern with its distribution among the competing princes of the day.

The problem of present-day nationalisms in Muslim-dominated countries differs therefore from that of nationalisms in the West essentially in three ways:

(1) The Muslim nationalisms operate within a religious and cultural organism which itself shows certain characteristics of a nationality and with whose "super-nationalism" it stands in competition;

(2) in virtue of this situation, but also because of their immediate origin as hostile children of the West and their consequent current ideology they are apt to be or appear as anti-Islamic and in any event as secularising movements; and

(3) due to the derivation from Western sources of much of their intellectual and emotional inspiration they are in the ambiguous position of nativistic movements of foreign kindling, of apostles of the future greatness of their community that can be realised only by a curtailment of that community's most cherished institutional and intellectual and even religious achievements—these very achievements appearing now at the same time as warranty and obstacle of glory to come.

II

Much of ancient philosophy is imbued with scepticism regarding the ultimate value of (political) power; Christianity has added the sentiment that it will be more wholesome for the salvation-bent soul to avoid any contact with it; many a strict Muslim especially if his piety showed an ascetic or mystic hue would view power and its responsibilities as a foremost spiritual risk. It is these circles who circulated dicta like the answer allegedly given by 'Umar, the second caliph, when asked why he did not spread administrative responsibilities among the most outstanding companions of the Prophet: They are too eminent, *ajall*, to be soiled by administration, *al-'amal*.[2]

This attitude is not, however, that of the consensus of the doctors. The Muslim theologian was not weighted down by that typically Christian feeling that power is sinful in itself and that its exercise calls for an explanation not only but an apology. On the contrary, the community and their spokesmen realised from the very beginning that Islam could not be perfected unless within an Islamic political organisation whose maintenance and advancement were, to say the least, a prerequisite to the service of God, if they did not in themselves constitute such service. Ibn Taimiyya (d. 1328), the great Hanbalite theologian whose influence has been growing for the last two hundred years, declares it a duty to consider the exercise of power as a form of religion, as one of the acts by which man draws nearer to God.[3] And in our own time Muḥammad Rašīd Ridà (d. 1935) has reaffirmed the inseparability of Islam as a religion and Islam as a political entity by stating that Islam is not fully in being as long as there does not exist a strong and independent Muslim state that is able to put into operation the laws of Islam.[4] The Muslim as nationalist is thus not impeded (as the Christian is) by an uneasy conscience when it comes to that glorification and potentially ruthless utilisation of power which is, after all, one of the chief characteristics of a nationalistic movement.

To quote Wirth once more: "The personal feeling of expansion with which nationalism infuses a citizenry, and the collective force which such a movement generates, is not likely to halt abruptly after the formal goals of the movement have been attained. After a nationality has achieved political autonomy, it sometimes redefines its aims in terms of empire or degenerates into a state of national chauvinism."[5] The Islamic tradition as such will not impede a government to make itself the tool and promoter of that development which is best described in the words of Aldous Huxley. "Within five years of achieving its liberty every oppressed nationality takes to militarism, and within two or three generations, sometimes within a single generation, it becomes, if circumstances are propitious, an imperialist aggressor, eager to inflict upon its neighbors the oppression of which itself it was so recently the victim." [6]

National socialism in Germany had to hamstring the opposition of the Churches; but the conflict we observe in Egypt between the nationalistic government and the conservative Muslims is of a different order. It does not turn on the aversion of the religious to the consolidation of a power felt to be basically evil but on the divergent aims of two rivaling totalitarianisms opposed not in their attitude to power and its utilisation as such but to the ideology to which this power should be made serviceable; it is the conflict of an internationalist pan-Islamic and a nationalist Egyptian (Pan-Arab or the like) expansionism. The advocacy by the Indian Muslim, 'Alī al-Hasanī an-Nadwī (1913–), of the transfer of political leadership to the Muslim world is couched in the customary nationalistic terms not excluding the readiness to use force against the West to make Islam prevail.[7]

While thus the traditional Muslim will agree with the Muslim nationalist as regards his power concept he will find himself in intense disagreement when it comes to the allocation of loyalties and in intellectual as well as emotional difficulties when he is confronted with the nationalist's dynamic or operational (or pragmatic) ideas of law and the state.

Few culture areas have been subjected to as much and as violent change as that of Islam; none perhaps has as consistently refused to accept the ontological reality of change. The truth of Islam as it has come to be held in some contrast to the more flexible outlook of its origins is not only one and indivisible, it is also immutable; it is neither growing nor shrinking; its understanding may vary in adequacy but it has been changelessly available since it was vouchsafed to mankind through the Seal of the Prophets. This goes for doctrine and conduct as well as for their institutionalisation. Where the social reality fails to come up to the ideal human heedlessness is at fault; but the ideal needs no revision. Even though the consensus of the learned has in fact been developed into an instrument of legislative adjustment and even though there exists a rather keen sense of the cleavage separating the Islamic origins from the reality of contemporary Islam, development is still acceptable only either as decline, i.e. as the abandonment of divine precept, or as the remedying of some misunderstanding, as the uncovery of some implication of the revealed truth that had hitherto been missed.

It need scarcely be said that this outlook makes it none too easy to come to terms with historical development as such, with the particular phase one happens to find oneself in, and above all, to arrive at a comprehensive over-view of one's cultural milieu. It also tends to discourage the idea of legislation, and especially of short-term legislation as a suitable means of improving the state of society, which is rather to be ameliorated by the energy of a just and God-fearing executive. At this point the

Muslim outlook comes very close to that of the Christian Middle Ages of which it has been said that "Where a modern democrat is prepared to respect the law in so far as he can regard himself as its author, medieval obedience was founded on the opposite sentiment, that laws were respectable in so far as they were not made by man." While modern thought (to quote another author) regards legislation as the highest activity of the state, to which judicial enforcement is logically subordinate, medieval (and Muslim) thought typically admitted legislation only as "a part of the judicial procedure—a more or less surreptitious incident of 'jus dicere.'" [8] One need only think of the *mazālim* jurisdiction and the court of the *muhtasib* to admit the applicability of this observation to the Islamic world.

The traditional Muslim's first loyalty is to his faith and the community of the true believers; attachment to family or local group would usually follow, with dedication to his prince (rather than his state) relegated to the third place. In accordance with this attitude the law considered any Muslim a full-fledged "citizen" of the Muslim-ruled state in which he happened to find himself. Hence the possibility of taking employment in distant countries under different princes; in one sense no Muslim could be an alien in any Muslim land. European control of Muslim countries caused the first break in this practice,[9] local nationalism has by now almost abolished it. So nationalism with its limited notion of citizenship has undercut Muslim political mobility; and the modern nationality concept together with the nationalism that developed it has been under severe attack by conservative opinion as the very worst of the many fateful gifts which the West has induced the East to accept. That nationalism, even within the accidental limits of existing states, such as Iraq or Lebanon, will represent a unifying element counteracting the separatism or at least the indifference to the larger unit of the local religious, tribal, ethnic communities which outside the protective shell of a territorial state would be neither economically nor politically viable entities, this positive aspect of an Arab or Pakistani feeling the traditional orthodox is apt to overlook. The (relative) social isolation of the various subcommunities makes it possible for such unawareness to persist in comparatively wide circles while at the same time the adjusting of parochialism to nationalism remains the most irksome problem of domestic politics.

It must be remembered in this connection that "secular" nationalism in the Arabic-speaking areas is of two (not always neatly separated) kinds. It may be focussed on the individual state or it may tend to include the *'arabiyya* as a whole. As a rough generalisation the intelligentsia (and the non-Muslim intelligentsia even more than the Muslim) may be said to incline toward a pan-Arab, governmental circles toward a local nationalism, which is not to suggest that the pan-Arab feeling is not being played for all it is worth whenever expedient (at present for instance in relation to the problem of North Africa).

The creed of pan-Arab nationalism, genetically but not inherently connected with democratic aspirations, can be sketched somewhat as follows. The community of the Arabs, i.e., the Arabic-speaking peoples, stretching from the Persian Gulf to the Atlantic inhabits regions that present considerable geographical similarities and that possess great economic potentialities. Their population represents "a young race that has its origin in the harmonious fusion of various human strains which Islam has brought together in one crucible." Within this community there is no distinction of color or race. The blood mixture has resulted in a great similarity of intellectual and moral aptitudes even though the variety of physical types has been maintained. This Arab "race" is extremely "prolific, courageous, enthusiastic, enduring, patient, and guided by the spirit of fairness." The absolute superiority of Arabic over all other languages allows it a great civilisational role.[10] The influence of Islam confers on "Arabism" a sense of spiritual values which sets it off against the materialism of the West. What internal divisions exist, such as sects or tribes, are but the result of ignorance or foreign interference.[11] Add to this the claim offered in varying degrees of conviction that the most outstanding features of modern civilisation in the West have their origin in the Arab-Muslim tradition and the peculiar feeling of being a chosen people derived from their central position within Islam and you have all the elements from which historical constructs are constantly being devised and revised, all designed to justify aspiration and hope for the future in terms of past achievement.

More important than to point out the factual and even the psychological weaknesses in the soi-disant historical ideology of Arab nationalism is the realisation that this kind of defensive pseudo-learning has been paralleled in other areas under comparable circumstances. Thus the rise of France and French civilisation in the Renaissance of the sixteenth century was accompanied by the "*légende gauloise.*" No less a thinker than Jean Bodin (d. 1596) has had his hand in the development of the myth, according to which there existed at a very early date in France a highly advanced civilisation from which the Greeks were to borrow the secret of their arts and sciences. Reviling the Greeks and Romans as liars and charlatans because of their claim to cultural innovation the French nationalist historians of the time try to see the rise of their country prefigured, as it were, in the perfection of Gaulish civilisation of which classical civilisation was but an ungrateful beneficiary.[12] Measured by this cobweb of legends the pan-Arab myth surprises by its sanity and realism.

Myth or reality—the Arab finds himself entangled in a number of circles or life-cycles which he has to arrange and value in some orderly sequence. There is his nation (in the narrower sense), there is the *'arabiyya,* there is the world of Islam; there may be geopolitical units which invite identification; there is the relationship to the West which needs to be clarified for to a certain extent the interpretation the Arab puts upon it provides the key to his self-interpretation.

Last year the prime minister of Egypt, Col. Gamal Abdel Nasser, published a series of three magazine articles under the title *The Philosophy of the Revolution.*[13] In this highly informative booklet, written with the forthright superficiality of the practical politician, the concept of the life-circles within which Egypt or any Egyptian has to move is set forth poignantly and in a manner to make it immediately evident how a different shade of nationalistic orientation would have to express itself.

After first observing that "the era of isolation is now gone," Gamal Abdel Nasser states:

I survey our conditions and find out we are in a group of circles which should be the theatre of our activity and in which we try to move as much as we can. . . .
We cannot look stupidly at a map of the world not realising our place therein and the role determined to us (*sic*) by that place. Neither can we ignore that there is an Arab circle surrounding us and that this circle is as much a part of us as we are part of it, that our history has been mixed with it and that its interests are linked with ours. These are actual facts and not mere words.
Can we ignore that there is a continent of Africa in which fate has placed us and which is destined today to witness a terrible struggle on its future? This struggle will affect us whether we want it or not.
Can we ignore that there is a Moslem world with which we are tied by bonds which are not only forged by religious faith but also tightened by the facts of history. I said once that fate plays no jokes. It is not in vain that our country lies to the Southwest of Asia close to the Arab world, whose life is intermingled with ours. It is not in vain that our country lies in the North East of Africa, a position from which it gives upon the dark continent wherein rages today the most violent struggle between white colonisers and black natives for the possession of its inexhaustible resources. It is not in vain that Islamic civilisation and Islamic heritage, which the Mongols ravaged in their conquest of the old Islamic capitals, retreated and sought refuge in Egypt where they found shelter and safety as a result of the counterattack with which Egypt repelled the invasion of these Tartars at Ein Galout.[14]

As if the ranking of the circles had not been made sufficiently explicit Gamal Abdel Nasser continues:

There is no doubt that the Arab circle is the most important and the most closely connected with us. Its history merges with ours. We have suffered the same hardships, lived the same crises and when we fell prostrate under the spikes of the horses of conquerors they lay with us. . . .[15] If we direct our attention after that to the second circle, the circle of the continent of Africa, I would say, without exaggeration, that we cannot, in any way, stand aside, even if we wish to, away from the sanguinary and dreadful struggle now raging in the heart of Africa between five million whites and two hundred million Africans. . . . The third circle now remains; the circle that goes beyond continents and oceans and to which I referred, as the circle of our brethren in faith who turn with us, whatever part of the world they are in, towards the same Kibla in Mecca, and whose pious lips whisper reverently the same prayers.[16]

Touching upon the feelings which a visit to the Ka'ba in Mecca had aroused in him Gamal Abdel Nasser concludes:

When my mind travelled to the eighty million Moslems in Indonesia, the fifty in China and the several other million in Malaya, Siam, and Burma, and the hundred million in Pakistan, the hundred million or more in the Middle East, and the forty in Russia, as well as the other millions in the distant parts of the world, when I visualise these millions united in one faith I have the great consciousness of the tremendous potentialities that cooperation amongst them all can achieve: a cooperation that does not deprive them of their loyalty to their countries but which guarantees for them and their brethren a limitless power.[17]

In this passage the intoxication with the (generously exaggerated) number of Muslims is less significant than the anxiousness to forestall the accusation of wishing to weaken their "patriotic" loyalty in favor of their Islamic loyalty and the hierarchic sequencing of the circles themselves. Leaving aside the play given to the African circle which at this moment at least reflects government policy rather than popular sentiment, it is Gamal Abdel Nasser's rating of: Egypt—the Arab World—the Muslim World, faithful reflection of political realities though it is, which the Muslim Brotherhood would wish to reverse and the pan-Arab intellectual to modify.

While the facts of life are likely to sustain for the time being at least Gamal Abdel Nasser's outlook on the Arab nation-state within the Islamic world as a whole, conservative Islam has in every single Arabic state (apart from Lebanon) won an ideological battle turning on the designation in its constitution of Islam as the official religion of the particular state. Perhaps I should have said that almost everywhere this intrusion of denominationalism into what was intended as the supreme evidence of modernisation occurred without audible demurrers on the part of the more secular-minded; but in Syria the question whether she was to be called an Islamic state (which in many a sense she obviously is) became a hotly debated issue. It has been indicated that the conservatives carried the day by obtaining the insertion in the Constitutions of 1950 and 1953 of a compromise formulation of their viewpoint by means of the statements that: "1. The religion of the President of the Republic is Islam. 2. Muslim Law, fiqh, is the principal source of legislation." (The second statement is of great programmatic significance but outside of the area of personal status of scant accuracy.)

The Muslim conservative has never ceased to argue that in Islam political conduct and religion, *siyāsa* and *dīn,* are inseparable and that the decline of the Islamic state, often reckoned from the death of 'Alī, the last of the *rāshidūn* caliphs, in 661, was primarily due to the breaking asunder of the life of the *umma* in a religious and a worldly segment. Western democracy has lent the conservative spokesmen an additional argument.

The principle followed in the constitutions of the world, in the organization of parties, and in the procedures of representative assemblies, as acknowledged by the entire world, is that the opinion of the majority is to be followed and acted upon. If, therefore, we say that the religion of the state is Islam, it being the religion of nine-tenths of the Syrians and of ninety-eight per cent of the Arabs, will we have exceeded the truth or deviated from democracy? (Note in this connection that) the states which have specified a particular religion in their constitution have not only taken the religion of the majority as the official religion, but in many cases have even taken the sect of the majority as the official religious sect.[18]

Let me remind you in passing that it will be the application of that very principle of democratic vote-counting of which they have been the fervent advocates that will in a perfectly legitimate way continue the non-Muslim communities in their precarious position of semi-outsiders—as long as the citizen's place in society in even the most modernistically structured Near Eastern state will remain primarily determined by his religious affiliation. By indirection, Shaykh as-Sibā'ī's next paragraphs illuminate this situation.

We, the Syrians, advocates of Arab unity, consider ourselves to be a part of the Arab nation and consider our Syrian fatherland to be part of the greater Arab fatherland. Our republic is today a member of the Arab League and will tomorrow, by the grace of God, be part of a single Arab state. According to the lowest estimate the Arabs number seventy million, of whom sixty-eight are Muslims and two are Christians, and all the states of the Arab League (except for Lebanon which has a special position) either specify that the religion of the state is Islam in their constitutions, as is the case with Egypt, Iraq and Jordan; or else their existence is implicitly based on that fact, as is the case with Saudi Arabia and Yemen.

Thus the establishment of Islam as the state religion will be a strong factor for unity between ourselves and our Arab brethren and a formal symbol of the *rapprochement* between the states of the Arab League. Why, therefore, should we neglect the strongest factor—popular and official—for Arab unity? Why should we refuse to face reality?[19]

You will have noticed that the Shaykh while, not unlike Gamal Abdel Nasser, he seems to ascend from Syria via the Arab nation to the unity of Islam, sees in Islam the true bond that holds together the individual states and almost their principal raison d'être, and besides, you will not have missed the fact that his pan-Arab feeling is considerably warmer than that of the Egyptian premier.

But the significance of Shaykh as-Sibā'ī's plea goes even further when at a later point he deals with the difference between Western (and

Turkish) and Arab nationalism and by implication touches upon the current key problem of the Near East (and other large areas of the world), its cultural relationship to the West.

National unity among the Arabs will not be achieved by throwing away the sympathies of sixty millions and by neglecting the national religious tie between them. Although it is understood that the nationalism of Europe decrees as a fundamental tenet the expulsion of religion, that step is not incumbent on us, the Arabs. Nazi Germany may have found in Christianity a religion which was foreign to it. Turanian Turkey may find in Islam a religion foreign to it. But the Arabs will never find in Islam a religion foreign to them. In fact they believe that Arab nationalism was born only when they embraced Islam and that this nationalism would not be so vital as it obviously is were it not for Islam. Therefore, let the advocates of nationalism distinguish between Europe and the East, between the Christianity of the West and the Islam of the Arabs.[20]

III

Islam's cultural and religious affinities as recognised by Revelation itself are with Christianity and Judaism, or in modern terms, with the Western rather than the Asiatic world. Modernism has, if anything, emphasised this fact. It is the spectacle of Western scientific and social progress, brought home to the Muslim world through its political superiority, which in the last analysis constitutes the foremost inducement to Westernize. Westernisation develops what secularising tendencies there are in the Islamic heritage, it relegates the Canon Law, in a sense the greatest achievement of traditional Islam, to the background and it assails the social basis of traditional society by changing the status of women, introducing democratic procedures, and a new kind of education.

The radicalism of the change and perhaps even more so its inevitability have aroused a wide-spread emotional resistance which finds expression on different levels. A conservative paper like *Al-Islam, An Independent Exponent of Orthodox Islam* (Karachi, Pakistan), may write editorially:

Our intelligentsia, utterly ignorant of the scientific implications of the progress made by the West, sing the praises of Western culture only because it gives them opportunities of indulging in frivolous and vulgar pursuits. They hate Religion because it bans all such harmful activities. They want the separation of Religion from political life because by doing so they have no moral scruples. Bribery and nepotism, blackmarketing and smuggling, prostitution and games of chance can only be tolerated in an irreligious society and that is what the Intelligentsia want. The only attribute the Intelligentsia have ingrained out of their contact with Western life is HYPOCRISY which leads them to attain power by appealing to the democratic and religious sentiments of the people and then to condemn both Democracy and Religion.[21]

But within the ranks of the Modernisers themselves the resistance can be felt as well; there it takes the form of an intense uneasiness about the derivative character of much of the cultural (and political) advance achieved (or aimed at). This uneasiness leads in turn to a tendency to interpret the borrowing as indigenous growth, to let, in other words, heterogenetic change be experienced as orthogenetic—we have, in another cultural context, seen an outgrowth of this same psychological need in the short-lived fashion of the *légende gauloise*. A general observation will be in order at this point.

Seen from the standpoint of the receiving community the most important variable in the transmission of influence (leaving aside its concrete content) is the power relationship between itself and the community from which it borrows. The psychological difficulties accompanying the urge to adapt will be the stronger, the more obvious the power differential between the two culture areas. The intelligentsia of the early Abbasid period steeped itself in Hellenistic ways of thinking, took over Indian methods of medicine, adopted Iranian principles of administration, and in general delighted in widening its horizon and gratifying its curiosity about the world without feeling any (but occasional religious) hesitations about taking over elements of non-Arab and non-Muslim origin. The traditions from which influence would emanate were either politically dead like Hellenism or subjugated like Iran or irrelevant for the destiny of the empire like India. The sense of the Muslims of being masters in their own house was in no way weakened by the knowledge that they were taking over the best the others had to offer, on the contrary, it merely strengthened their belief in the potentialities of their aspirations. Under those circumstances when borrowing would sap neither their freedom of action nor their self-assurance the heterogenetic character of much of the advance did not cause any emotional hardship.

The complexion of Westernisation during the last hundred and fifty years is totally different. It was the inadequacy of their power which first induced in some of the Muslim élites a readiness to reform. Not the perfecting of potential or heritage was the objective of the admission of Western influence but the removal of what was felt to be an inferiority; and this inferiority was most smarting in the political area. The question was not what to adopt, whence to select, but rather, what to retain or perhaps even, was there, in the traditional culture, anything worth retaining? This question could be asked from a more or less pragmatic viewpoint: Can we ever become the political equals of the West unless we Westernise completely? or from a more or less theoretical viewpoint: What is there in our tradition that is worth keeping in the light of the Western cultural experience? In any possible answer a radical heterogenetic transformation was implied.

To be effective, the transformation had to be total or nearly so. It was not a matter of allowing Western technology or natural science or military art to be grafted on the traditional intellectual structure. New content would not be enough nor would new methods. The change had to be admitted down to the very roots, the vantage point of the civilisation that is, and its objective. One may say, incidentally, that the greatest difficulty encountered by the Muslim world in their struggle with Westernisation is the contradiction between their success in adopting the foreign aspiration and their failure (or unwillingness) to let go of their traditional vantage point. In practical terms, the transformation which the mere existence of occidental civilisation as the spiritual equipment of a supreme power organisation imposed affected mores as well as institutions, economic and social structure as well as the reading of Holy Writ. The Western concept of the nation state did away with the traditional concept of the Muslim as a citizen of the Muslim world; Western ideas of literature and art effected a transvaluation of traditional forms and norms of self-expression—the despised folk art came to be prized, the age-old canons of poetry to be discarded; foreign patterns supplanted rather than supplemented the inherited kinds; the representational arts long felt to be in opposition to religious injunctions were taken up. Even as parliamentary institutions had to be introduced as much to suit a novel situation as to prove oneself to the West and to himself, even so in every sphere of life a new kind of completeness had to be reached to match the accomplishments of Western precedent and to allow for self-respect through a substantiation of equality of achievement, however rudimentary. The individual found himself playing to two galleries at the same time. The world of tradition was as real as ever although submerged and out of fashion; its emotional hold had been broken only in relatively rare cases; the Westernised world held the stage; the future of the nation depended on progressive assimilation and so again did for countless hearts their self-respect. But the community, too, had to become (and continues to be) double-faced, tending to overplay Westernisation achieved before the comity of nations and tending to draw strength from underplaying it before the more backward or the more traditional-minded in their own ranks.

Westernisation made uncertain not only the present but the past as well. Muslim history needed to be rewritten. In part, occidental methods had to be applied to the unearthing and sifting of objective facts. In the main, however, it had to be decided where the guilt for the predicament of the present was to be placed. Was it the theologians of the Middle Ages whose distortion of the Prophetic message caused the drying up of the Islamic inspiration? Was it the Mamluks whose ruthless rule sapped the strength of Egypt beyond recovery? Or was it Muḥammad 'Alī whose precipitate steps toward Europeanisation did more harm than good by creating that psychological confusion that still lies at the bottom of the incessant political unrest of the country? There is no end of questions of this order and they are becoming more burning as it is less possible to brush them aside by pointing to colonialism as the root of all evil. And even if colonialism is impugned the problem is only pushed back one step, for it would be difficult not to ask further: What was it that weakened the Muslim world to such an extent that it no longer could or would resist the intruder? But history has to be consulted not only to ascertain the villain. It needs to be consulted even more closely to yield the glories of the Muslim past that may be taken as a warranty of a glorious future. As has happened typically if perhaps less obviously in European national-istic movements the past is made into the supreme metaphysical justifica-tion of the aspirations for the future. The Muslim world has been revising its history for the last hundred years; but a satisfactory integration of adequate self-interpretation, Western methodological technique, and the psychological demands of the times has not yet been achieved. With all this, the lack of certainty about one's place in the universal development is painful as well as politically unsettling.[22]

The all too obvious heterogenetic character of Western influence and the major borrowings that are due to it mars to a large extent the satisfaction that would otherwise be inherent in the very substantial and very real progress accomplished in the path of the newly adopted aspira-tion. The tendency followed both consciously and unconsciously is to let the heterogenetic appear as orthogenetic wherever possible. The bor-rowed element is envisaged as something bestowed on the West many a century ago and now come home, as it were, modified perhaps yet of Muslim origin. Or it is found adumbrated or even enjoined in the Holy Book. Or it is accounted for as a legitimate, a logical development from Muslim presuppositions correctly interpreted. Parliament and monogamy are intimated in the Qur'ān; equality was practised during the early period of the empire; the devotion to pure science is characteristic of the Muslim legacy; so is tolerance to minorities; and concern with social ills. The tendency to appropriate as many of the results of Westernisation as possible by making them into orthogenetic developments will, of course, at times conflict with that scholarly conscience that has been made more delicate in consequence of contact with Western ideas of scientific effort. But in the long run there can be no doubt where popular consciousness will seek its orientation.

With all these psychological impediments Westernisation continues to proceed apace—fundamentally the power relation between Europe and the Near East has not been altered; it may be, though, that more of a semblance of autonomous choice has been restored to the countries concerned. Theirs is now the belief that they are catching up with the West and they overlook not only the distance which still separates them from that technological status that marks the first stage of equality at-tained but also the undeniable fact that the West is still moving ahead at a very considerable speed especially on that technological level where

Westernisation can be measured by the public most easily. The international political organisation which the West has imposed on the world fosters the illusion of Westernisation attained and thus, by indirection, renders the gains of Westernisation more secure. On the other hand, the idealistic or fictitious assumptions under which the international bodies are apt to operate may in the long run endanger Westernisation by whittling away at the political prestige of the West. The impulse to Westernisation through an increased belief in its being achieved represents an orthogenetic development which is counteracted by the decrease in the psychological impulse to allow oneself to be influenced.[23]

Where does all this leave Near Eastern, Arab, Muslim nationalism? It will doubtless be compelled to continue Westernisation; its self-realisation, not to say its self-preservation, is depending on increased admission of Western ideas and techniques—organisational, economic, cultural.[24] At the same time conservative pressure will force the concealment of the borrowing wherever possible behind the veil of the orthogenetic legend. Political stability, the most urgent short-range problem, is contingent on the stabilisation of self-respect, and self-esteem in turn depends on an amalgamation of prides—pride in the Muslim past and its assimilative powers, pride in the moral and intellectual courage to undertake an all but complete rebuilding of one's life-structure and to embark on the most hazardous adventure open to man, the rethinking and redefining of his universe in range and kind, and of his own identity in it.

NOTES

1. *American Journal of Sociology*, XLI (1935–36), p. 723.

2. Tartūšī (d. 1126 or 1131), *Sirāj al-mulūk* (Cairo, 1306/1888), p. 116.[11–13]

3. *As-Siyāsa 'š-šar'iyya fī islāh ar-rā'ī wa'r-ra'iyya*, edd. 'Alī Sāmī an-Naššār & Ahmad Zakī 'Atiyya (2nd.; Cairo, 1951;? the foreword is dated: May 24, 1952), p. 174: [7–8] fa'l-wājib ittihād al-imāra dīnan wa-qurbatan yataqarrabu bihā ilà 'llāh; fa-inna 't-taqarrub ilaihi fī-hā bi-tā'ati-hi wa-tā'at rasūli-hi min afdal al-qarabāt. Trans. H. Laoust, *Le traité de droit public d'Ibn Tainnya* (Beirut, 1948), pp. 173–74; the translation is quoted in part by L. Gardet, *La cité musulmane* (Paris, 1954), p. 107.

4. *Al-Hilāfa au al-imāma 'l-'uzmà* (Cairo, 1922/1341), p. 114; [21–23] trans. H. Laoust, *Le califat dans la doctrine de Rašīd Ridā* (Beirut, 1938), p. 194; cf. also Gardet, *op. cit.*, p. 22. In his Commentary of the Qur'ān (*Tafsīr al-Manār* [Cairo, 1927–34], I, 11) Muhammad Rašīd Ridà reports that perusal of *al-'Urwa 'l-wuthqà*, the short-lived journal which, in 1884, Muhammad 'Abduh (d. 1905) and Jamāl ad-Dīn al-Afghānī (d. 1897) published in Paris, impressed him above all in three respects. (1) He found there an exposition of the way in which God deals customarily with man and the societal order.

(2) He obtained confirmation of the fact that Islam is a religion of political dominance and power uniting the happiness of both worlds. It is a religion at the same time spiritual, social, and military; its military strength being destined to protect the Law as well as the vitality of the religious community but not to compel the conversion of the outsider. (3) He found it asserted that the Muslims had no nationality proper apart from their affiliation with their religious community; they are brothers who are not permitted to split for reasons of birth, language or government. Rashīd Ridà became acquainted with *al-ʿUrwa* as late as 1892/93; cf. J. Jomier, *Le commentaire coranique du Manār* (Paris, 1954), pp. 28–31.

5. *Loc. cit.*, p. 726.

6. *Themes and Variations* (London, 1950), p. 45. One feels reminded of G. Bachelard's observation: "En fait, penser à une puissance, c'est déjà, non seulement s'en servir, c'est surtout en abuser. Sans cette volonté d'abuser, la conscience de la puissance ne serait pas claire." (*La psychanalyse du feu* [9th ed.; Paris, 1949], pp. 157–58). The progress of science, first of geography, later of social psychology, and besides, the lesson of immediate historical experience, has deprived mankind of both stage and actors in the tragicomedy of its self-idealisation. The mythical lands of the North and the West had to be abandoned, the noble savage has disappeared and behind him in rapid succession the noble proletarian and the noble victim of imperialist oppression. The innocence of a human collective never outlasts its bondage. One wonders where a future utopianism will be able to locate its dreams to impregnate them with an illusion of reality; all considered it is the imperial powers at their stage of saturation and incipient decline that show collective mankind at its best, that is in this context, at its politically most tolerant.

7. Mā dā hasara 'l-ʿālam bi'nhitāt al-muslimīn? (2nd. ed.: Cairo, 1370/-1951), pp. 241–42; 247–48.

8. Ewart Lewis, *Medieval Political Ideas* (New York, 1954), I, 2, quoting (in part) H. M. V. Reade, *Cambridge Mediaeval History*, VI, p. 616, and John Dickinson, *The Statesman's Book of John of Salisbury* (New York, 1927), Introduction, p. LIV, n. 164.

9. Cf. Gardet, *op. cit.*, p. 29, n. 1, on the case of ʿAbdalhakīm, a Tunisian and therefore *protégé français*, who, in 1905, was denied by a French court that Moroccan citizenship which on the basis of traditional Muslim law he had claimed as a resident of Morocco.

10. The position of their language in the cultural self-view of the French comes to mind. It characterises the different mentalities of the two areas of civilisation that what to the Arabs is a signal reason of pride in their tongue, its wealth in synonyms, is considered by the French a dangerous weakness— the ideal language is to have one word for each object and each concept; synonyms are but a complicating factor in the vocabulary endangering that clarity which is its true aim and glory; cf. H. Gillot, *La querelle des anciens et des modernes en France* (Paris, 1914), p. 445, and the discussions extending throughout the 17th and 18th century on French as the *langue universelle*. The Arabic point of view is defended, as it were, by Théophile Gautier (1811– 1872) who prefaces his appreciation of Balzac's style with this observation. "La langue française, épurée par les classiques du dix-septième siècle, n'est

propre lorsqu'on veut s'y conformer qu'à rendre des idées générales, et qu'à peindre des figures conventionnelles dans un milieu vague." (Quoted by E. R. Curtius, *Balzac* [Bonn, 1923], p. 435.)

11. R. Montagne, "La crise politique de l'Arabisme (Juin 1937–Juin 1938)," *La France méditerranéenne et africaine,* I (1938), p. 19—a summary of an article by 'Abdarrahmān 'Azzām, published in *al-'Arab* (Jerusalem) of August 27, 1932 (not accessible to the writer). Cf. the position taken by al-Kawākibī (1849–1902) in his *Umm al-Qurà*, as summarised by S. G. Haim, *Oriente Moderno,* XXX (1955), 133–34.

12. Cf. Gillot, *op. cit.,* pp. 125–30. The devaluation of the Roman element in the Byzantine heritage by Theodoros Metochites (d. 1332) is another instance of a nationalistic movement striving for self-understanding at the expense of historical insight; cf. H.-G. Beck, *Theodoros Metochites. Die Krise des byzantinischen Weltbildes in vierzehnten Jahrhundert* (Munich, 1952), pp. 80–81.

13. Cairo: Dar al-Maaref, 1954; 73 pp.; published also in Arabic and in French.

14. Pp. 53–55. The battle was fought in 1260.

15. P. 56.

16. Pp. 70–71.

17. P. 73.

18. Shaykh Mustafà as-Sibā'ī (1910–   ), writing in the Syrian newspaper *al Manār,* February, 1950; trans. R. B. Winder, *The Muslim World,* XLIV (1954), pp. 217–226. The above passage is from p. 219.

19. *Ibid.,* p. 220. In this connection the observations of A. J. Toynbee on "The Ineffectiveness of Panislamism," *A Study of History* (London, New York, Toronto, 1934–54), VIII, pp. 692–95, make interesting reading.

20. *Ibid.,* p. 223; cf. Nadwī's dictum, *op. cit.,* p. 247: [9] fa'l-islām huwa qaumiyyat al-'ālam al-'arabī. Similar the integration of Arab nationalism and Islamic universalism attempted by the 'Irāqī 'Abdarrahmān al-Bazzāz who sees Islam as the expression of "Arabism"; he, too, contrasts Arab nationalism which does not find itself in conflict with Islam with Turkish nationalism which does; cf. his *al-Islām wa'l-qaumiyya 'l-'arabiyya* (Baghdād, 1952), translated by S. G. Haim, *Die Welt des Islams,* N.S., III (1954), 201–218. Here we meet with a "secularisation," as it were, of that line of thought which inspired the observation of Muhammad Rashīd Ridā (in 1900) that countries conquered by the Arabs were lasting conquests of Islam whereas the better part of the countries conquered by the Turks turned out to be a burden for Islam. The relevant passage from *al-Manār* was translated by Miss Haīm in *Oriente Moderno,* XXXVI (1956), 415–16. It is worth recalling that from its very inception the theory of Arab nationalism was moulded by the necessity to establish its compatibility with an Islamic outlook. The Christian treatment of the problem presented by a division of loyalties between religious and political affiliation provides an illuminating contrast. Cf., e.g., Fr. Anselm Stolz O.B., *Benediktinische Monatsschrift,* XVII (1935), 132: ". . . (The Christian) würde das Wesen der Kirche als beginnendes Gottesreich verkennen . . . , wollte er Werte des Volkstums denen der Kirche ebenbürtig an die Seite stellen oder gar ihnen überordnen." Stolz goes on to quote from the *Letter to Diognetus* a

passage to the effect that the Christians live as strangers in their own father-land. In this context it may be pertinent to recall P. K. Hitti's observation that the Shī'a authorities in Karbalā' and Najaf "still consider Islam supranational demanding loyalty that is transcendent and providing laws as good for the twentieth as for the seventh century"; *Cahiers d'histoire mondiale*, II (1955), pp. 630–31.

21. Issue of January 1, 1955 (Vol. III, no. 1), p. 1.

22. Among the "Modernists" Muhammad Rashīd Ridà, *Tafsīr al-Manār* (Cairo, 1927–34), I, pp. 309–13, esp. p. 311, shows his awareness of the educational importance of history. Cf. also Jomier, *op. cit.*, p. 110.

23. Cf. the present writer's (unpublished) study, *The Problem of Cultural Influence*, section IV.

24. Cf. Nadwī, *op. cit.*, pp. 229–231, on the acceptance of European aims by Europe's Asiatic opponents.